SAXON MATH™
Course 1

Teacher's Manual
Volume 2

Stephen Hake

SAXON™
A Harcourt Achieve Imprint

www.SaxonPublishers.com
1-800-284-7019

Acknowledgements

This book was made possible by the significant contributions of many individuals and the dedicated efforts of a talented team at Harcourt Achieve.

Special thanks to:

- Melody Simmons and Chris Braun for suggestions and explanations for problem solving in Courses 1-3,

- Elizabeth Rivas and Bryon Hake for their extensive contributions to lessons and practice in Course 3,

- Sue Ellen Fealko for suggested application problems in Course 3.

The long hours and technical assistance of John and James Hake on Courses 1-3, Robert Hake on Course 3, Tom Curtis on Course 3, and Roger Phan on Course 3 were invaluable in meeting publishing deadlines. The saintly patience and unwavering support of Mary is most appreciated.

– Stephen Hake

Staff Credits

Editorial: Jean Armstrong, Shelley Farrar-Coleman, Marc Connolly, Hirva Raj, Brooke Butner, Robin Adams, Roxanne Picou, Cecilia Colome, Michael Ota

Design: Alison Klassen, Joan Cunningham, Deborah Diver, Alan Klemp, Andy Hendrix, Rhonda Holcomb

Production: Mychael Ferris-Pacheco, Heather Jernt, Greg Gaspard, Donna Brawley, John-Paxton Gremillion

Manufacturing: Cathy Voltaggio

Marketing: Marilyn Trow, Kimberly Sadler

E-Learning: Layne Hedrick, Karen Stitt

ISBN 978-1-5914-1786-6
ISBN 1-5914-1786-4

SAXON MATH™

Course 1
Content Overview

ABOUT THE AUTHOR

Stephen Hake has authored five books in the Saxon Math series. He writes from 17 years of classroom experience as a teacher in grades 5 through 12 and as a math specialist in El Monte, California. As a math coach, his students won honors and recognition in local, regional, and statewide competitions.

Stephen has been writing math curriculum since 1975 and for Saxon since 1985. He has also authored several math contests including Los Angeles County's first Math Field Day contest. Stephen contributed to the 1999 National Academy of Science publication on the Nature and Teaching of Algebra in the Middle Grades.

Stephen is a member of the National Council of Teachers of Mathematics and the California Mathematics Council. He earned his BA from United States International University and his MA from Chapman College.

EDUCATIONAL CONSULTANTS

Nicole Hamilton
Consultant Manager
Richardson, TX

Joquita McKibben
Consultant Manager
Pensacola, FL

John Anderson
Lowell, IN

Beckie Fulcher
Gulf Breeze, FL

Heidi Graviette
Stockton, CA

Brenda Halulka
Atlanta, GA

Marilyn Lance
East Greenbush, NY

Ann Norris
Wichita Falls, TX

Melody Simmons
Nogales, AZ

Benjamin Swagerty
Moore, OK

Kristyn Warren
Macedonia, OH

Mary Warrington
East Wenatchee, WA

Table of Contents

Integrated and Distributed Units of Instruction

Section 1 *Lessons 1–10, Investigation 1*

Math Focus:
Number and Operations • Algebra

Distributed Strands:
Number and Operations • Algebra • Geometry • Measurement • Data Analysis and Probability

Maintaining & Extending

Power Up
Facts pp. 7, 12, 18, 23, 28, 32, 36, 42, 46, 50

Mental Math Strategies pp. 7, 12, 18, 23, 28, 32, 36, 42, 46, 50

Problem Solving Strategies pp. 7, 12, 18, 23, 28, 32, 36, 42, 46, 50

Enrichment
Early Finishers pp. 17, 22, 31, 41

Extensions p. 57

Standards Benchmark Check Point

Math Focus:
Number and Operations • Problem Solving

Distributed Strands:
Number and Operations • Algebra • Measurement • Data Analysis and Probability • Problem Solving

---

Maintaining & Extending

Power Up
Facts pp. 58, 63, 68, 73, 78, 82, 87, 93, 99, 105

Mental Math Strategies
pp. 58, 63, 68, 73, 78, 82, 87, 93, 99, 105

Problem Solving Strategies
pp. 58, 63, 68, 73, 78, 82, 87, 93, 99, 105

Enrichment
Early Finishers pp. 77, 81, 92, 98, 104, 108

Extensions p. 111

Standards Benchmark Check Point

Section 3 — Lessons 21–30, Investigation 3

Math Focus:
Number and Operations • Geometry

Distributed Strands:
Number and Operations • Geometry • Measurement • Problem Solving

Maintaining & Extending

Power Up
Facts pp. 112, 117, 122, 127, 132, 136, 141, 145, 150, 156

Mental Math Strategies
pp. 112, 117, 122, 127, 132, 136, 141, 145, 150, 156

Problem Solving Strategies
pp. 112, 117, 122, 127, 132, 136, 141, 145, 150, 156

Enrichment
Early Finishers pp. 116, 126, 131, 144, 155, 160

Extensions p. 163

Standards Benchmark Check Point

Math Focus:
Number and Operations • Measurement

Distributed Strands:
Number and Operations • Geometry • Measurement • Data Analysis and Probability • Problem Solving

Maintaining & Extending

Power Up
Facts pp. 164, 169, 174, 178, 182, 187, 191, 195, 200, 205

Mental Math Strategies
pp. 164, 169, 174, 178, 182, 187, 191, 195, 200, 205

Problem Solving Strategies
pp. 164, 169, 174, 178, 182, 187, 191, 195, 200, 205

Enrichment
Early Finishers pp. 177, 194, 204

Extensions p. 214

Standards Benchmark Check Point

Standards Benchmark Check Point

Math Focus:
Number and Operations • Geometry

Distributed Strands:
Number and Operations • Geometry • Measurement • Data Analysis and Probability • Problem Solving

Maintaining & Extending

Power Up
Facts pp. 268, 272, 276, 280, 285, 289, 295, 299, 306, 310

Mental Math Strategies
pp. 268, 272, 276, 280, 285, 289, 295, 299, 306, 310

Problem Solving Strategies
pp. 268, 272, 276, 280, 285, 289, 295, 299, 306, 310

Enrichment
Early Finishers pp. 279, 284, 294, 298, 305, 309

Extensions p. 318

Standards Benchmark
Check Point

Section 7 — Lessons 61–70, Investigation 7

Math Focus:
Number and Operations • Geometry

Distributed Strands:
Number and Operations • Algebra • Geometry • Measurement • Problem Solving

Maintaining & Extending

Power Up
Facts pp. 320, 324, 329, 333, 337, 342, 346, 349, 353, 358

Mental Math Strategies pp. 320, 324, 329, 333, 337, 342, 346, 349, 353, 358

Problem Solving Strategies pp. 320, 324, 329, 333, 337, 342, 346, 349, 353, 358

Enrichment
Early Finishers pp. 323, 332, 352, 357, 362

Extensions p. 367

Standards Benchmark Check Point

Math Focus:
   Number and Operations • Geometry

Distributed Strands:
   Number and Operations • Geometry • Measurement • Problem Solving

Maintaining & Extending

Power Up
Facts pp. 368, 375, 380, 385, 390, 395, 399, 404, 408, 413

Mental Math Strategies
pp. 368, 375, 380, 385, 390, 395, 399, 404, 408, 413

Problem Solving Strategies
pp. 368, 375, 380, 385, 390, 395, 399, 404, 408, 413

Enrichment
Early Finishers pp. 379, 384, 394, 403, 412

Extensions p. 420

Standards Benchmark Check Point

TABLE OF CONTENTS

Section 9 *Lessons 81–90, Investigation 9*

Math Focus:
Algebra • Measurement

Distributed Strands:
Number and Operations • Algebra • Geometry • Measurement • Data Analysis and Probability
• Problem Solving

Maintaining & Extending

Power Up
Facts pp. 421, 426, 431, 436, 441, 447, 452, 456, 460, 465
Mental Math Strategies pp. 421, 426, 431, 436, 441, 447, 452, 456, 460, 465
Problem Solving Strategies pp. 421, 426, 431, 436, 441, 447, 452, 456, 460, 465
Enrichment
Early Finishers pp. 435, 440, 446, 451, 455, 469
Extensions p. 472

Standards Benchmark Check Point

Section 10 | Lessons 91–100, Investigation 10

Math Focus:
Number and Operations • Geometry

Distributed Strands:
Number and Operations • Algebra • Geometry • Measurement • Data Analysis and Probability

Maintaining & Extending

Power Up
Facts pp. 474, 479, 484, 488, 493, 497, 503, 508, 513, 517

Mental Math Strategies pp. 474, 479, 484, 488, 493, 497, 503, 508, 513, 517

Problem Solving Strategies pp. 474, 479, 484, 488, 493, 497, 503, 508, 513, 517

Enrichment
Early Finishers pp. 478, 483, 487, 496, 516, 523

Extensions p. 527

Standards Benchmark Check Point

Section 11   *Lessons 101–110, Investigation 11*

Math Focus:
  Algebra • Geometry

Distributed Strands:
  Number and Operations • Algebra • Geometry • Measurement • Problem Solving

Maintaining & Extending

Power Up
Facts pp. 528, 533, 538, 548, 553, 557, 561, 566, 573

Mental Math Strategies
pp. 528, 533, 538, 548, 553, 557, 561, 566, 573

Problem Solving Strategies
pp. 528, 533, 538, 543, 548, 553, 557, 561, 566, 573

Enrichment
Early Finishers pp. 532, 572

Extensions p. 581

Standards Benchmark Check Point

Math Focus:
Measurement • Problem Solving

Distributed Strands:
Number and Operations • Algebra • Geometry • Measurement • Problem Solving

Maintaining & Extending

Power Up
Facts pp. 582, 587, 592, 597, 602, 606, 612, 617, 621, 626

Mental Math Strategies
pp. 582, 587, 592, 597, 602, 606, 612, 617, 621, 626

Problem Solving Strategies
pp. 582, 587, 592, 597, 602, 606, 612, 617, 621, 626

Enrichment
Early Finishers pp. 591, 601, 605, 611, 616, 629

Extensions p. 635

Standards Benchmark Check Point

Contents by Strand

This chart gives you an overview of the instruction of math concepts by strand in *Saxon Math* Course 1. The chart shows where in the textbook each topic is taught and references the New Concepts section of a lesson or the instructional part of an Investigation.

	LESSONS
NUMBERS AND OPERATIONS	
Numeration	
digits	12, 21
read and write whole numbers and decimals	35, 46
place value to trillions	12, 32, 92
number line (integers, fractions)	9, 14, 17
expanded notation	32, 46, 92
comparison symbols ($=, <, >$)	9
compare and order rational numbers	9, 14, 44, 76
Basic operations	
add, subtract, multiply, and divide integers	2, 3, 5, 10, 100, 104, 112
add, subtract, multiply, and divide decimal numbers	1, 37, 45, 53
add, subtract, multiply, and divide fractions and mixed numbers	24, 25, 26, 29, 36, 50, 54, 57, 59, 61, 62, 66, 68, 70, 72
mental math strategies	1-120
regrouping in addition, subtraction, and multiplication	36, 48, 63
multiplication notations: $a \times b, a \cdot b, a(b)$	2
division notations: division box, division sign, and division bar	2
division with remainders	2, 111
Properties of numbers and operations	
even and odd integers	10, 19
factors, multiples, and divisibility	2, 19, 21, 25
prime and composite numbers	19
greatest common factor (GCF)	20
least common multiple (LCM)	30
divisibility tests (2, 3, 5, 9, 10)	21
prime factorization of whole numbers	65, 73
positive exponents of whole numbers, decimals, fractions	73, 92
square roots	38, 39
order of operations	5, 84, 92
inverse operations	1, 2, 4, 87, 106

	LESSONS
Estimation	
round whole numbers, decimals, mixed numbers	**16, 51**
estimate sums, differences, products, quotients	**16**
estimate squares and square roots	**89**
ALGEBRA	
Ratio and proportional reasoning	
fractional part of a whole, group, set, or number	**6, 22, 77, 117**
equivalent fractions	**26, 29, 55, 56**
convert between fractions, terminating decimals, and percents	**33, 35, 73, 74, 75, 99**
reciprocals of numbers	**30, 50**
identify/find percent of a whole, group, set, or number	**94, 105, 119**
percents greater than 100%	**94**
solve proportions with unknown in one term	**83, 85, 101**
find unit rates and ratios in proportional relationships	**88**
apply proportional relationships such as similarity, scaling, and rates	**23, 80; Investigation 11**
estimate and solve applications problems involving percent	**105, 119**
Patterns, relations, and functions	
use, describe, extend arithmetic sequence (with a constant rate of change)	**10**
input-output tables	**10, 82, 96**
analyze a pattern to verbalize a rule	**10, 82, 96**
Variables, expressions, and equations	
solve equations using concrete and pictorial models	**114, 116**
formulate an equation with one unknown variable given a problem situation	**11, 15, 42, 82, 87, 91, 105, 114**
solve one-step equations with whole numbers	**87**
solve two-step equations with whole numbers	**106, 116**
GEOMETRY	
Describe basic terms	
point	**7**
segment	**7**
ray	**7**
line	**7**
angle	**28, 69**
plane	**28, 69**

	LESSONS
Describe properties and relationships of lines	
parallel, perpendicular, and intersecting	**28, 71, 97**
horizontal, vertical, and oblique	**18; Investigation 7**
Describe properties and relationships of angles	
acute, obtuse, right	**28; Investigation 3**
complementary and supplementary	**69, 71, 97**
angles formed by transversals	**97**
angle bisector	**Investigation 8**
calculate to find unknown angle measures	**71, 97, 98**
Describe properties and relationships of polygons	
regular	**2, 60**
interior and exterior angles	**97, 98**
sum of angle measures	**98**
similarity and congruence	**68, 79, 108, 109**
classify triangles	**93**
classify quadrilaterals	**60, 64; Investigation 6**
3-Dimensional figures	
represent in 2-dimensional world using nets	**Investigations 6, 12**
draw 3-dimensional figures	**Investigation 6**
Coordinate geometry	
name and graph ordered pairs	**Investigation 7**
identify reflections, translations, rotations, and symmetry	**108**
graph reflections across the horizontal or vertical axes	**108**
MEASUREMENT	
Measuring physical attributes	
use customary units of length, area, volume, weight, capacity	**7, 31, 78, 82, 102**
use metric units of length, area, volume, weight, capacity	**7, 8, 82**
use temperature scales: Fahrenheit, Celsius	**10, 32**
use units of time	**13, 32**

	LESSONS
Systems of measurement	
convert in the U.S. Customary System	**78, 81, 114**
convert in the metric system	**7, 114**
convert between systems	**7**
unit multipliers	**95, 114**
Solving measurement problems	
perimeter of polygons, circles, complex figures	**8, 47, 60, 71, 103**
area of triangles, rectangles, and parallelograms	**31, 71, 79**
area of circles	**86**
area of complex figures	**107**
surface area of right prisms and cylinders	**Investigation 12**
estimate area	**86, 118**
volume of right prisms, cylinders, pyramids, and cones	**120; Investigation 12**
estimate volume	**78**
Solving problems of similarity	
scale factor	**83; Investigation 11**
scale drawings: two-dimensional	**Investigation 11**
Use appropriate measurement instruments	
ruler (U.S. customary and metric)	**7, 17**
compass	**27; Investigation 8**
protractor	**Investigation 3**
thermometer	**10, 100**
DATA ANALYSIS AND PROBABILITY	
Data collection and representation	
collect data	**Investigation 4**
display data	**Investigations 1, 4, 5**
tables and charts	**Investigation 5**
frequency tables	**Investigations 1, 9**
pictographs	**Investigation 5**
line graphs	**18**
histograms	**Investigation 1**

	LESSONS
bar graphs	Investigation 4
circle graphs	40, Investigation 5
line plots	Investigations 4, 5
stem-and-leaf plots	Investigation 5
choose an appropriate graph	Investigation 5
draw and compare different representations	40; Investigation 5
Data set characteristics	
mean, median, mode, and range	18; Investigation 5
Probability	
experimental probability	Investigations 9, 10
make predictions based on experiments	Investigations 9, 10
accuracy of predictions in experiments	Investigation 9
theoretical probability	Investigation 9
sample spaces	58
simple probability	58, 77: Investigation 9
probability of compound events	Investigation 10
probability of the complement of an event	77; Investigation 10
probability of independent events	Investigations 9, 10
PROBLEM SOLVING	
Four-step problem-solving process	1-120
Problem-solving strategies	1-120

Lesson Planner

LESSON	NEW CONCEPTS	MATERIALS	RESOURCES
61	• Adding Three or More Fractions		**Power Up H**
62	• Writing Mixed Numbers as Improper Fractions	Manipulative Kit: Overhead fraction circles Fraction manipulatives from Investigation 2	**Power Up G**
63	• Subtracting Mixed Numbers with Regrouping, Part 2		**Power Up D**
64	• Classifying Quadrilaterals	Dot paper or grid paper	**Power Up J**
65	• Prime Factorization • Division by Primes • Factor Trees		**Power Up H** **Primes and Composites poster**
66	• Multiplying Mixed Numbers	Grid paper	**Power Up J**
67	• Using Prime Factorization to Reduce Fractions		**Power Up J**
68	• Dividing Mixed Numbers	Manipulative Kit: inch rulers; color tiles; grid paper	**Power Up I**
69	• Lengths of Segments • Complementary and Supplementary Angles	Manipulative Kit: inch rulers Dot or grid paper	**Power Up J**
70	• Reducing Fractions Before Multiplying		**Power Up G**
Inv. 7	• The Coordinate Plane	Masking tape	**Investigation Transparency 14** **Investigation Activity 15** or graph paper, 7 per student

Problem Solving

Strategies

- **Write an Equation**   Lessons 62, 63, 66, 69
- **Make a Table**   Lesson 61, 64
- **Make It Simpler**   Lesson 63
- **Use Logical Reasoning**   Lessons 64, 65, 67, 68, 69, 70
- **Draw a Diagram**   Lesson 70
- **Work Backwards**   Lesson 66

Real-World Applications

pp. 322, 323, 327, 330, 332, 334, 335, 336, 340–342, 344, 345, 347, 351, 355, 357, 360–362

4-Step Process

Teacher Edition   Lessons 61–70
(Power-Up Discussions)

Connections

Math and Other Subjects

- **Math and History**   pp. 334, 360
- **Math and Geography**   p. 330
- **Math and Science**   p. 361
- **Math and Architecture**   p. 323
- **Math and Art**   pp. 332, 347
- **Math and Sports**   pp. 323, 351
- **Math and Music**   pp. 327, 360

Math to Math

- **Problem Solving and Measurement**   Lessons 62, 63, 64, 65, 66, 67, 68, 69, 70
- **Algebra and Problem Solving**   Lessons 65, 68, 70
- **Fractions, Decimals, Percents and Problem Solving**   Lessons 61, 62, 63, 64, 65, 66, 67, 68, 69, 70
- **Fractions and Measurement**   Lessons 62, 63, 66, 67, 68, 69, 70
- **Measurement and Geometry**   Lessons 62, 63, 64, 65, 66, 67, 68, 69, 70, Inv. 7
- **Algebra, Measurement, and Geometry**   Lesson 67
- **Probability and Statistics**   Lessons 62, 63, 64, 65, 66, 67, 68

Communications

Discuss

pp. 346, 359

Explain

pp. 323, 328, 330, 335, 340, 346, 356, 363

Formulate a Problem

pp. 330, 344, 345, 361

Representation

Manipulatives/Hands On

pp. 352, 364–366

Model

pp. 324, 334, 355, 367

Represent

pp. 323, 325, 339, 344, 348, 356, 357, 365–367

Student Resources

- **eBook**   Anytime
- **Online Resources** at
  www.SaxonPublishers.com/ActivitiesC1
    Graphing Calculator Activity   Inv. 7
    Real-World Investigation 4   after Lesson 64
    Online Activities
    Math Enrichment Problems
    Math Stumpers

Teacher Resources

- **Resources and Planner CD**
- **Adaptations CD**   Lessons 61–70
- **Test & Practice Generator CD**
- **eGradebook**
- **Answer Key CD**

This set of lessons concentrates on developing arithmetic skills with mixed numbers, among the most challenging aspects of working with rational numbers.

Fractions and Operations

Computation with fractions is emphasized throughout the school year.

Students add three or more mixed numbers in Lesson 61, subtract mixed numbers with regrouping in Lesson 63, and multiply and divide mixed numbers in Lessons 66 and 68.

Equivalence

Students continue to represent numbers in a variety of forms.

Students learn to write mixed numbers as improper fractions in Lesson 62. After students learn to write prime factorization in Lesson 65, they learn to reduce fractions with large terms by using prime factorization in Lesson 67 and they learn to reduce fractions before multiplying, commonly called canceling, in Lesson 70.

Spatial Thinking

These lessons build upon the concepts involving angles and polygons introduced earlier in the year.

Students classify quadrilaterals by attending to distinctive attributes in Lesson 64. Students identify pairs of complementary and supplementary angles in Lesson 69.

Algebraic Thinking

A foundational concept of algebra, geometry, and the rest of secondary mathematics is the coordinate plane.

Investigation 7 introduces the coordinate plane and provides students the opportunity to practice locating and graphing points in the plane.

Assessment

A variety of weekly assessment tools are provided.

After Lesson 65:	After Lesson 70:
• Power-Up Test 12	• Power-Up Test 13
• Cumulative Test 12	• Cumulative Test 13
• Performance Activity 12	• Customized Benchmark Test
	• Performance Task 13

LESSON	NEW CONCEPTS	PRACTICED	ASSESSED
61	• Adding Three or More Fractions	Lessons 61, 62, 64, 65, 66, 69, 73, 74, 76, 77, 78, 82, 94, 96, 102, 105, 110, 114, 120	Tests 13, 14, 15
62	• Writing Mixed Numbers as Improper Fractions	Lessons 62, 63, 64, 65, 66, 67, 68, 69, 70, 72, 73, 74, 75, 89, 91	Test 13
63	• Subtracting Mixed Numbers with Regrouping, Part 2	Lessons 63, 64, 66, 67, 68, 70, 71, 73, 74, 77, 81, 86, 87, 91, 93, 95, 97, 106, 108, 112, 113, 117, 118, 119	Tests 13, 14, 15, 16, 17, 18, 16, 22
64	• Classifying Quadrilaterals	Lessons 64, 67, 69, 70, 72, 73, 74, 75, 76, 77, 78, 79, 80, 81, 82, 84, 87, 90, 93, 96, 98, 119	Tests 13, 14
65	• Prime Factorization	Lessons 65, 66, 68, 69, 74, 75, 77, 78, 79, 81, 83, 84, 85, 88, 91, 93, 104, 105, 106, 110, 111, 112, 113	Tests 12, 13, 14, 15, 23
65	• Division by Primes	Lessons 65, 66, 68, 69, 71, 73, 74, 75, 77, 79, 81, 83, 91, 97, 99, 104, 105, 106, 110, 111, 113, 117, 120	Test 13
65	• Factor Trees	Lessons 65, 66, 69, 73, 75, 77, 78, 79, 82, 91, 93, 99, 104, 105, 106, 110, 111, 113, 117, 120	Test 13
66	• Multiplying Mixed Numbers	Lessons 66, 67, 68, 69, 74, 77, 78, 81, 82, 83, 86, 87, 89, 101, 113, 115	Tests 14, 15, 16, 17, 18, 19, 21
67	• Using Prime Factorization to Reduce Fractions	Lessons 67, 68, 69, 70, 71, 72, 74, 75, 77, 79, 81, 83	Tests 14, 15
68	• Dividing Mixed Numbers	Lessons 68, 69, 71, 72, 76, 77, 78, 79, 80, 81, 82, 83, 84, 85, 86,87, 88, 89, 91, 94, 95, 96, 97, 98, 99, 100, 101, 102, 103, 106, 108, 109, 110, 111, 117, 118	Tests 14, 15, 16, 17, 18, 19, 21, 22
69	• Lengths of Segments	Lessons 69, 73, 88, 91, 94, 95, 96, 99, 101, 110	Test & Practice Generator
69	• Complementary and Supplementary Angles	Lessons 71, 72, 73, 76, 80, 84, 85, 86, 88, 89, 98, 99, 102	Test & Practice Generator
70	• Reducing Fractions Before Multiplying	Lessons 70, 71, 72, 73, 74, 75, 76, 79, 80, 81, 84, 88, 92, 96, 99, 102, 105, 107	Tests 14, 15, 16, 17, 18, 21
Inv. 7	• The Coordinate Plane	Investigation 7, Lessons 71, 72, 73, 74, 75, 76, 77, 78, 79, 80, 81, 84, 86, 87, 88, 90, 91, 92, 93, 94, 96, 101, 102, 103, 104, 108, 110, 112, 113, 114, 115, 116, 119, 120	Tests 15, 16, 17, 18, 19, 21, 22

• Adding Three or More Fractions

Objectives
• Add three or more fractions or mixed numbers.

Lesson Preparation

Materials
• **Power Up H** (in *Instructional Masters*)

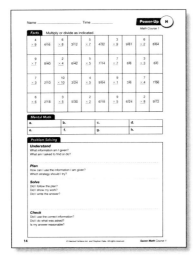

Power Up H

Math Language

Maintain	English Learners (ESL)
least common denominator	compass

Technology Resources

Student eBook Complete student textbook in electronic format.

Resources and Planner CD Assessment, reteaching, and instructional masters, plus a pacing calendar with standards.

Test and Practice Generator CD Create additional practice sheets and custom-made tests.

www.SaxonPublishers.com Visit for more student activities and planning materials.

Inclusion

Adaptations CD Adapted lessons, investigations, practice and assessments.

Meeting Standards

National Council of Teachers of Mathematics (NCTM)

Numbers and Operations

NO.1a Work flexibly with fractions, decimals, and percents to solve problems

NO.2a Understand the meaning and effects of arithmetic operations with fractions, decimals, and integers

NO.3c Develop and use strategies to estimate the results of rational-number computations and judge the reasonableness of the results

Connections

CN.4b Understand how mathematical ideas interconnect and build on one another to produce a coherent whole

Problem-Solving Strategy: Make a Table

A large piece of cardstock is 1 mm thick. If we fold it in half, and then fold it in half again, we find we have a stack of 4 layers of cardstock that is 4 mm high. If it were possible to continue folding the cardstock in half, how thick would the stack of layers be after 10 folds? Is that closest in height to a book, a table, a man, or a bus?

Understand *Understand the problem.*

"What information are we given?"

A piece of cardstock is 1 mm thick. We are going to repeatedly fold the cardstock in half.

"What are we asked to do?"

We are asked to determine how high the stack of paper is that has been folded in half 10 times.

Plan *Make a plan.*

"What problem-solving strategy will we use?"

We will *make a table.*

Solve *Carry out the plan.*

"How do we begin?"

First, we need to make a table to find the thickness of the layers after ten folds.

"What information needs to be included in our table?"

The number of folds, the number of the layers of paper that results, and the height of the resulting stack.

Number of Folds	0	1	2	3	4	5	6	7	8	9	10
Layers of Paper	1	2	4	8	16	32	64	128	256	512	1024
Height of Stack	1 mm	2	4	8	16	32	64	128	256	512	1024 mm

Teacher Note: Ask students to identify any patterns they see in the table. Ask if they can predict the number of layers for 11, 12, and 13 folds.

"How high is 1024 mm?"

There are 1000 millimeters in 1 meter, so the stack of paper is more than a meter high, higher than a table.

Check *Look back.*

"Did we answer the question that was asked?"

Yes. We found the height of the folded stack and used our knowledge that 1000 millimeters = 1 meter to know that the height of the stack would be more than the height of a table because a table is about 1 meter high.

Teacher Note: Ask students if they think that it is possible to fold a piece of paper ten times. Have them try it. Some students will think that if they start with a large enough piece of paper, they will be able to do it; however, it is impossible to fold it that number of times. Ask them how many times they were able to fold whatever size paper they started with.

Facts
Distribute **Power Up H** to students. See answers below.

Mental Math
Before students begin the Mental Math exercise, do this counting exercise as a class.

Count up and down by $\frac{1}{4}$s between $\frac{1}{4}$ and 4.

Encourage students to share different ways to mentally compute these exercises. Strategies for exercises **c** and **d** are listed below.

c. Subtract 200, then Add 1
$750 - 200 = 550; 550 + 1 = 551$
Add 1 to 750 and Add 1 to 199
$750 + 1 = 751$ and $199 + 1 = 200$;
$751 - 200 = 551$

d. Subtract \$2.00, then Subtract \$0.50
$\$8.25 - \$2.00 = \$6.25$;
$\$6.25 - \$0.50 = \$5.75$
Subtract \$3.00, then Add \$0.50
$\$8.25 - \$3.00 = \$5.25$;
$\$5.25 + \$0.50 = \$5.75$

Problem Solving
Refer to **Power-Up Discussion**, p. 320F.

2 New Concepts

Instruction
"When you added two fractions whose denominators were different, you usually renamed the fractions using the least common denominator. In this problem, there are three fractions. How can you find the least common denominator of three fractions?" Sample: List several multiples of each denominator, circle the common multiples, then choose the least common multiple.

Students should generalize that a method used to find the LCM of two numbers can also be used to find the LCM of more than two numbers.

Example 1
Instruction
Remind students of the three steps used to add fractions: Shape, Operate, and Simplify (SOS).

(continued)

• Adding Three or More Fractions

Power Up   *Building Power*

facts   Power Up H

mental math

a. **Number Sense:** 4×750 3000

b. **Number Sense:** $283 + 250$ 533

c. **Number Sense:** $750 - 199$ 551

d. **Calculation:** $\$8.25 - \$2.50$ \$5.75

e. **Number Sense:** Double $12\frac{1}{2}$.   25

f. **Number Sense:** $\frac{900}{30}$ 30

g. **Probability:** What is the probability of rolling a 3 on a number cube? $\frac{1}{6}$

h. **Calculation:** $6 \times 10, \div 3, \times 2, \div 4, \times 5, \div 2, \times 4$ 100

problem solving   A large piece of cardstock is 1 mm thick. If we fold it in half, and then fold it in half again, we have a stack of 4 layers of cardstock that is 4 mm high. If it were possible to continue folding the cardstock in half, how thick would the stack of layers be after 10 folds? Is that closest in height to a book, a table, a man, or a bus?   1024 mm; a table

New Concept   *Increasing Knowledge*

Pedro, Leticia, and Quan shared a pizza. Pedro ate half the pizza, Leticia ate $\frac{1}{4}$ of the pizza, and Quan ate $\frac{1}{8}$ of the pizza. Together the three friends ate what fraction of the pizza?

To add three or more fractions, we find a common denominator for all the fractions being added. Once we determine a common denominator, we can rename the fractions and add. We usually use the **least common denominator**, which is the least common multiple of all the denominators.

Example 1

Add $\frac{1}{2} + \frac{1}{4} + \frac{1}{8}$ and draw a diagram illustrating the addition.

Solution

To add, we first we find a common denominator. The LCM of 2, 4, and 8 is 8, so we rename all fractions as eighths. Then we add and simplify if possible.

Facts   Multiply or divide as indicated.

$\begin{array}{r}4\\ \times 9\\ \hline 36\end{array}$	$4\overline{)16}$	$\begin{array}{r}6\\ \times 8\\ \hline 48\end{array}$	$3\overline{)12}$	$\begin{array}{r}5\\ \times 7\\ \hline 35\end{array}$	$4\overline{)32}$	$\begin{array}{r}3\\ \times 9\\ \hline 27\end{array}$	$9\overline{)81}$	$\begin{array}{r}6\\ \times 2\\ \hline 12\end{array}$	$8\overline{)64}$
$\begin{array}{r}9\\ \times 7\\ \hline 63\end{array}$	$8\overline{)40}$	$\begin{array}{r}2\\ \times 4\\ \hline 8\end{array}$	$6\overline{)42}$	$\begin{array}{r}5\\ \times 5\\ \hline 25\end{array}$	$7\overline{)14}$	$\begin{array}{r}7\\ \times 7\\ \hline 49\end{array}$	$8\overline{)8}$	$\begin{array}{r}3\\ \times 3\\ \hline 9\end{array}$	$6\overline{)0}$
$\begin{array}{r}7\\ \times 3\\ \hline 21\end{array}$	$2\overline{)10}$	$\begin{array}{r}10\\ \times 10\\ \hline 100\end{array}$	$3\overline{)24}$	$\begin{array}{r}4\\ \times 5\\ \hline 20\end{array}$	$9\overline{)54}$	$\begin{array}{r}9\\ \times 1\\ \hline 9\end{array}$	$3\overline{)6}$	$\begin{array}{r}7\\ \times 4\\ \hline 28\end{array}$	$7\overline{)56}$
$\begin{array}{r}6\\ \times 6\\ \hline 36\end{array}$	$2\overline{)18}$	$\begin{array}{r}3\\ \times 5\\ \hline 15\end{array}$	$5\overline{)30}$	$\begin{array}{r}2\\ \times 2\\ \hline 4\end{array}$	$6\overline{)18}$	$\begin{array}{r}9\\ \times 5\\ \hline 45\end{array}$	$6\overline{)24}$	$\begin{array}{r}2\\ \times 8\\ \hline 16\end{array}$	$9\overline{)72}$

We illustrate the addition with fractions of a circle.

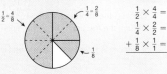

$\frac{1}{2} = \frac{4}{8}$ $\frac{1}{4} = \frac{2}{8}$

$\frac{1}{2} \times \frac{4}{4} = \frac{4}{8}$
$\frac{1}{4} \times \frac{2}{2} = \frac{2}{8}$
$+ \frac{1}{8} \times \frac{1}{1} = \frac{1}{8}$
$\overline{\qquad \frac{7}{8}}$

Verify Why don't we need to simplify $\frac{7}{8}$? $\frac{7}{8}$ is not an improper fraction; it is in lowest terms.

Example 2

Add: $1\frac{1}{2} + 2\frac{1}{3} + 3\frac{1}{6}$

Solution

Thinking Skill

Predict

If we rename $\frac{1}{2}$, $\frac{1}{3}$, and $\frac{1}{6}$ as fractions with a common denominator that is not the LCM, will the sum be the same?   Yes, because the fractions will still have the same values.

A common denominator is 6. We rename all fractions. Then we add the whole numbers, and we add the fractions. We simplify the result if possible.

$$1\frac{1}{2} \times \frac{3}{3} = 1\frac{3}{6}$$
$$2\frac{1}{3} \times \frac{2}{2} = 2\frac{2}{6}$$
$$+ 3\frac{1}{6} \times \frac{1}{1} = 3\frac{1}{6}$$
$$\overline{\qquad 6\frac{6}{6} = 7}$$

Justify What steps do you use to simplify $6\frac{6}{6}$?   Sample: $\frac{6}{6}$ is equal to 1.
$6 + 1 = 7$

▶ Add:

a. $\frac{1}{2} + \frac{3}{4} + \frac{1}{8}$ $1\frac{3}{8}$ **b.** $\frac{1}{2} + \frac{1}{3} + \frac{1}{6}$ 1   **c.** $1\frac{1}{2} + 1\frac{1}{3} + 1\frac{1}{4}$ $4\frac{1}{12}$

d. $\frac{1}{2} + \frac{2}{3} + \frac{5}{6}$ 2   **e.** $\frac{1}{2} + \frac{3}{4} + \frac{7}{8}$ $2\frac{1}{8}$ **f.** $1\frac{1}{4} + 1\frac{1}{8} + 1\frac{1}{2}$ $3\frac{7}{8}$

g. Find the perimeter of the triangle. $1\frac{1}{2}$ in.

$\frac{5}{8}$ in.

$\frac{3}{8}$ in.

$\frac{1}{2}$ in.

h. Select one of the exercises **a–f** and write a word problem that involves adding the fractions.   See student work.

▶ See Math Conversations in the sidebar.

Example 2

Instruction

Explain that one way to check the sum of mixed numbers for reasonableness is to round each addend to the nearest whole number.

Since $1\frac{1}{2}$ rounds to 2, $2\frac{1}{3}$ rounds to 2, and $3\frac{1}{6}$ rounds to 3, the sum of $2 + 2 + 3$ or 7 represents a reasonable estimate of the exact answer.

Practice Set

Problems a–f (Error Alert)

Generally speaking, the lengthier the computation, the greater the likelihood that a student will make an error completing that computation. When students rename fractions, remind them that choosing the least common multiple can reduce the amount of arithmetic that needs to be completed.

Math Conversations

Discussion opportunities are provided below.

Problem 3 *Analyze*

Extend the Problem

"How can we use a divisibility rule to check the exact answer?" Sample: The divisor is 3, so use the divisibility rule for 3. Since the sum of the digits in 2769 is 24, and 24 is divisible by 3, 2769 is divisible by 3. So we should expect an exact answer that does not have a remainder.

Problem 17 *Predict*

Before completing the problem, ask students to discuss the pattern and identify its rule. To find the next term in the sequence, divide the previous term by 10 (or multiply the previous term by $\frac{1}{10}$).

Errors and Misconceptions

Problems 4 and 5

The fraction part of each subtrahend is greater than the fraction part of each minuend. Watch for students who give an incorrect answer because they converted the mixed numbers to improper fractions incorrectly.

Problem 9

Watch for students who want to write a decimal equivalent for $\frac{5}{6}$ because a fraction bar represents division and the Order of Operations state that multiplication and division is to be completed from left to right. Point out that $\frac{5}{6}$ is a repeating decimal and in this case, lead students to see that it is better to not change the form. Students will understand why when they simplify 6^2 to 36.

(continued)

---

1. Convert the improper fraction $\frac{20}{6}$ to a mixed number. Remember to reduce the fraction part of the mixed number. $3\frac{1}{3}$
(25)

2. A fathom is 6 feet. How many feet deep is water that is $2\frac{1}{2}$ fathoms deep?   15 feet
(29)

▶ **3.** In 3 hours 2769 cars passed through a tollbooth. What is the average number of cars that pass through the tollbooth per hour?   923 cars
(18)

▶ *** 4.** $5\frac{1}{2} - 1\frac{2}{3}$ $3\frac{5}{6}$ ▶ *** 5.** $5\frac{1}{3} - 2\frac{1}{2}$ $2\frac{5}{6}$
(57)   (57)

* 6. $1\frac{1}{2} + 2\frac{1}{3} + 3\frac{1}{4}$ $7\frac{1}{12}$ *** 7.** $3\frac{3}{4} + 3\frac{1}{3}$ $7\frac{1}{12}$
(61)   (59)

8. Compare:
(38, 56)
   a. $\frac{2}{3} \ominus \frac{3}{5}$ **b.** $4^2 \ominus \sqrt{144}$

▶ **9.** $\frac{5}{6} \times 6^2$ 30   **10.** $\frac{3}{8} \cdot \frac{2}{3}$ $\frac{1}{4}$
(29, 38)   (29)

11. How many $\frac{2}{3}$s are in $\frac{3}{8}$? ($\frac{3}{8} \div \frac{2}{3}$) $\frac{9}{16}$
(54)

12. $(4 - 0.4) \div 4$ 0.9   **13.** $4 - (0.4 \div 4)$ 3.9
(53)   (53)

14. Which digit in 49.63 has the same place value as the 7 in 8.7?   6
(34)

15. $1500.00; Round $642.23 to $600 and $861.17 to $900. Then add $600 and $900.

15. *Estimate*   Find the sum of $642.23 and $861.17 to the nearest hundred dollars. Explain how you arrived at your answer.
(16)

16. Elizabeth used a compass to draw a circle with a radius of 4 cm.
(47)
   a. What was the diameter of the circle? Describe how the radius and diameter are related.   8 cm; The diameter is twice the radius.

   b. What was the circumference of the circle? (Use 3.14 for π.)   25.12 cm

▶ *** 17.** *Predict*   What is the next number in this sequence?   0.1 (or $\frac{1}{10}$)
(10)
         ..., 100, 10, 1, ...

18. The perimeter of a square is 1 foot. How many square inches cover its area?   9 square inches
(38)

19. *Connect*   What is the ratio of the value of a dime to the value of a quarter? $\frac{2}{5}$
(23)

Find each unknown number:

20. $15m = 3 \cdot 10^2$ 20   **21.** $\frac{1}{10} = \frac{n}{100}$ 10
(4, 38)   (42)

22. By what fraction name for 1 must $\frac{2}{3}$ be multiplied to form a fraction with a denominator of 15? $\frac{5}{5}$
(42)

23. What time is 5 hours 15 minutes after 9:50 a.m.?   3:05 p.m.
(32)

▶ See Math Conversations in the sidebar.

English Learners

For problem 16, remind students that a **compass** is a tool used to draw a circle. If possible, show the students an actual compass. Say,

"A compass is a tool that is used to create a perfect circle. All points on the circle will be exactly the same distance from the center point."

Have students give examples of things they might draw using a compass.

24. *Analyze* The area of a square is 16 square inches. What is its
perimeter? 16 inches
₍₃₈₎

25. This figure shows the shape of home plate
on a baseball field. What kind of a polygon is
shown? pentagon
₍₆₀₎

26. $8.28; Round
$4.95 to $5 and
round $2.79 to $3.
Add $5 and $3
and get $8.
Mentally multiply
7% and $8 and
get 56¢. Add
56¢ to $8 and
get $8.56. Since
we rounded
the prices up
to estimate, the
answer of $8.28 is
reasonable.

26. *Explain* The sales-tax rate was 7%. Dexter bought two items, one for
$4.95 and the other for $2.79. What was the total cost of the two items
including sales tax? Describe how to use estimation to check whether
your answer is reasonable.
₍₄₁₎

27. Ramla bought a sheet of 100 stamps from the post office for $39. What
was the price of each stamp? $0.39
₍₅₂₎

28. *Represent* Draw a rectangular prism. A rectangular prism has how
many
_(Inv. 6)

    a. faces?   **b.** edges?   **c.** vertices?
       6 faces   12 edges   8 vertices

Refer to the cube shown below to answer problems **29** and **30**.

28. Sample:

* 29. Each face of a cube is a square. What is the
area of each face of this cube? 9 cm²
_(Inv. 6)

3 cm

* 30. Find the total surface area of the cube by
adding up the area of all of the faces of the
cube. 54 cm²
_(Inv. 6)

Early Finishers
*Math and
Architecture*

The Pentagon in Washington, D.C. is the world's largest office building. Each
of the five sides of the Pentagon is 921 feet long. What is the perimeter of the
Pentagon in yards? 921 ft × 5 sides = 4605 feet long ÷ 3 = 1535 yards

Lesson 61   323

▶ See Math Conversations in the sidebar.

Looking Forward

Adding three or more fractions
prepares students for:

• **Lesson 63,** subtracting mixed
numbers with regrouping.

• **Lesson 72,** using a fractions
chart to review the addition and
subtraction of fractions.

---

3 **Written Practice** *(Continued)*

Math Conversations
Discussion opportunities are provided below.

Problem 25 *Analyze*
Extend the Problem
*"What relationship is shared by the sides
and the vertices of a pentagon?"* Sample:
Two sides meet at a vertex; a pentagon has
the same number of sides and vertices.

Problem 28 *Represent*
*"For the prism you drew, how many pairs of
opposite faces are congruent?"* three

*"What is the name of a rectangular prism
that has six congruent faces?"* a cube

Errors and Misconceptions
Problem 26
An answer of $8.28 represents finding the
sales tax of each item individually. Remind
students that sales tax is applied to the sum
of the costs of the items, and not to each item
individually.

Writing Mixed Numbers as Improper Fractions

Objectives

- Change a mixed number to an improper fraction.
- Find the product of two mixed numbers by changing each number to an improper fraction and then multiplying.

Lesson Preparation

Materials

- **Power Up G** (in *Instructional Masters*)
- **Manipulative kit: overhead fraction circles**
- **Teacher-provided material: fraction manipulatives** from Investigation 2

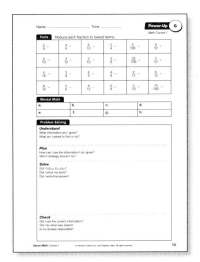

Power Up G

Math Language

English Learners (ESL)

describe

Technology Resources

Student eBook Complete student textbook in electronic format.

Resources and Planner CD Assessment, reteaching, and instructional masters, plus a pacing calendar with standards.

Test and Practice Generator CD Create additional practice sheets and custom-made tests.

www.SaxonPublishers.com Visit for more student activities and planning materials.

Inclusion

Adaptations CD Adapted lessons, investigations, practice and assessments.

Meeting Standards

National Council of Teachers of Mathematics (NCTM)

Numbers and Operations

NO.1a Work flexibly with fractions, decimals, and percents to solve problems

NO.2a Understand the meaning and effects of arithmetic operations with fractions, decimals, and integers

Connections

CN.4a Recognize and use connections among mathematical ideas

Representation

RE.5b Select, apply, and translate among mathematical representations to solve problems

Problem-Solving Strategy: Write an Equation

There are approximately 520 nine-inch long noodles in a 1-pound package of spaghetti. Placed end-to-end, how many feet of noodles are in a pound of uncooked spaghetti?

(Understand) **Understand the problem.**

"What information are we given?"

There are 520 nine-inch-long noodles in a 1-pound package of spaghetti.

"What are we asked to do?"

We are asked to find how many feet the noodles would reach if placed end-to-end.

(Plan) **Make a plan.**

"How can we use the information we know to do what we are asked to do?"

We will *write an equation* to determine the combined length of the noodles. Then we will convert the length from inches to feet.

(Solve) **Carry out the plan.**

"What is the combined length of 520 spaghetti noodles?"

Placed end-to-end, 520 spaghetti noodles would reach 520 × 9 in. = 4680 in.

"What is this length in feet?"

There are 12 inches in 1 foot. To change units from inches to feet, we divide by 12. Placed end-to-end, the noodles would reach 4680 ÷ 12 = 390 feet.

(Check) **Look back.**

"Did we find the answer to the question that was asked?"

Yes. We found how far (in feet) 520 nine-inch noodles would reach if the noodles were placed end-to-end.

Teacher Note: Ask students to relate the 390 feet to an actual distance. For example, if they started at one end of the school, would the spaghetti lined up end to end reach the other end of the school? They could relate the distance to a football field, which is 360 ft from goal post to goal post.

• **Writing Mixed Numbers as Improper Fractions**

1 Power Up

Facts
Distribute **Power Up G** to students. See answers below.

Mental Math
Before students begin the Mental Math exercise, do this counting exercise as a class.

Count by 12s from 12 to 144.

Encourage students to share different ways to mentally compute these exercises. Strategies for exercises **a** and **f** are listed below.

a. Use a Fact
$5 \times 4 = 20$, so $5 \times 40 = 200$
Multiply Tens
$5 \times 40 = 5 \times 4$ tens = 20 tens = 200
f. Shift the Decimal Points
$\frac{\$25}{10} = \frac{\$2.5}{1} = \$2.50$
Use a Division Pattern
$\$30 \div 10 = \$3$ and $\$20 \div 10 = \$2$,
so $\$25 \div 10 = \$2.50$

Problem Solving
Refer to **Power-Up Discussion**, p. 324B.

2 New Concepts

Instruction
Ask students to count the total number of sixths and the number of shaded sixths in the illustration at the bottom of the page. 24 total; 23 shaded

(continued)

Manipulative Use

You can model the illustrations in this lesson using the **Overhead Fraction Circles** from the Manipulative Kit.

---

facts   Power Up G

mental math

   a. Number Sense: 5×40 200

   b. Number Sense: $475 + 1200$ 1675

   c. Calculation: 3×84 252

   d. Calculation: $\$8.50 + \$2.50$ $\$11.00$

   e. Fractional Parts: $\frac{1}{3}$ of $\$36.00$ $\$12.00$

   f. Number Sense: $\frac{\$25}{10}$ $\$2.50$

   g. Measurement: Convert 240 seconds into minutes.   4 minutes

   h. Calculation: $6 \times 8, - 4, \div 4, \times 2, + 2, \div 6, \div 2$ 2

problem solving

There are approximately 520 nine-inch long noodles in a 1-pound package of spaghetti. Placed end to end, how many feet of noodles are in a pound of uncooked spaghetti?   390 ft

New Concept   *Increasing Knowledge*

Here is another word problem about pies. In this problem we will change a mixed number to an improper fraction.

There were $3\frac{5}{6}$ pies on the shelf. The restaurant manager asked the server to cut the whole pies into sixths. Altogether, how many slices of pie were there after the server cut the pies?

Thinking Skill

Model

Use your fraction manipulatives to represent $3\frac{5}{6}$.

We illustrate this problem with circles. There were $3\frac{5}{6}$ pies on the shelf.

The server cut the whole pies into sixths. Each whole pie then had six slices.

Facts   Reduce each fraction to lowest terms.

$\frac{2}{8} = \frac{1}{4}$	$\frac{4}{6} = \frac{2}{3}$	$\frac{6}{10} = \frac{3}{5}$	$\frac{2}{4} = \frac{1}{2}$	$\frac{5}{100} = \frac{1}{20}$	$\frac{9}{12} = \frac{3}{4}$
$\frac{4}{10} = \frac{2}{5}$	$\frac{4}{12} = \frac{1}{3}$	$\frac{2}{10} = \frac{1}{5}$	$\frac{3}{6} = \frac{1}{2}$	$\frac{25}{100} = \frac{1}{4}$	$\frac{3}{12} = \frac{1}{4}$
$\frac{4}{16} = \frac{1}{4}$	$\frac{3}{9} = \frac{1}{3}$	$\frac{6}{9} = \frac{2}{3}$	$\frac{4}{8} = \frac{1}{2}$	$\frac{2}{12} = \frac{1}{6}$	$\frac{6}{12} = \frac{1}{2}$
$\frac{8}{16} = \frac{1}{2}$	$\frac{2}{6} = \frac{1}{3}$	$\frac{8}{12} = \frac{2}{3}$	$\frac{6}{8} = \frac{3}{4}$	$\frac{5}{10} = \frac{1}{2}$	$\frac{75}{100} = \frac{3}{4}$

The three whole pies contain 18 slices (3 × 6 = 18). The 5 additional slices from the $\frac{5}{6}$ of a pie bring the total to 23 slices (23 sixths). This problem illustrates that $3\frac{5}{6}$ is equivalent to $\frac{23}{6}$.

Now we describe the arithmetic for changing a mixed number such as $3\frac{5}{6}$ to an improper fraction. Recall that a mixed number has a whole-number part and a fraction part.

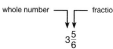

whole number   fraction

$$3\frac{5}{6}$$

The denominator of the mixed number will also be the denominator of the improper fraction.

$$3\frac{5}{6} = \frac{\ }{6}$$

same denominator

The denominator indicates the size of the fraction "pieces." In this case the fraction pieces are sixths, so we change the whole number 3 into sixths. We know that one whole is $\frac{6}{6}$, so three wholes is $3 \times \frac{6}{6}$, which is $\frac{18}{6}$. Therefore, we add $\frac{18}{6}$ and $\frac{5}{6}$ to get $\frac{23}{6}$.

$$3\frac{5}{6}$$
$$\frac{6}{6} + \frac{6}{6} + \frac{6}{6} + \frac{5}{6} = \frac{23}{6}$$
$$\frac{18}{6} + \frac{5}{6} = \frac{23}{6}$$

Example 1

Write $2\frac{3}{4}$ as an improper fraction.

Solution

The denominator of the fraction part of the mixed number is fourths, so the denominator of the improper fraction will also be fourths.

$$2\frac{3}{4} = \frac{\ }{4}$$

We change the whole number 2 into fourths. Since 1 equals $\frac{4}{4}$, the whole number 2 equals $2 \times \frac{4}{4}$, which is $\frac{8}{4}$. We add $\frac{8}{4}$ and $\frac{3}{4}$ to get $\frac{11}{4}$.

$$2\frac{3}{4}$$
$$\frac{8}{4} + \frac{3}{4} = \frac{11}{4}$$

Represent   Draw a model to show that $2\frac{3}{4} = \frac{11}{4}$.

English Learners

Refer to the instruction at the top of the page. Explain what it means to **describe** the arithmetic. Say,

"When we 'describe' the arithmetic, we explain the steps we use. To change a mixed number to an improper fraction, we:

1. Write the whole number as a fraction.

2. Add the fraction part of the mixed number."

Demonstrate changing $3\frac{5}{6}$ to an improper fraction as shown on the student page. Ask for a volunteer to describe the arithmetic for changing $4\frac{2}{3}$ to an improper fraction.

2 New Concepts (Continued)

Instruction

Suggest that students check this answer by converting the improper fraction to a mixed number.

"How can we change $\frac{23}{6}$ to a mixed number?" A fraction bar represents division, so divide 23 by 6.

Invite a volunteer to complete the division at the board or overhead. Then ask students to compare answers, and conclude that since $\frac{23}{6} = 3\frac{5}{6}$, the answer is correct.

Example 1

Instruction

If students are having difficulty writing mixed numbers as improper fractions, demonstrate that $2\frac{3}{4} = \frac{11}{4}$ by drawing the following illustration on the board.

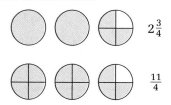

(continued)

Example 2

Instruction

If students are having difficulty writing mixed numbers as improper fractions, demonstrate that $5\frac{2}{3} = \frac{17}{3}$ by drawing the following illustration on the board.

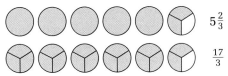

$5\frac{2}{3}$

$\frac{17}{3}$

Example 3

Instruction

The Math Background has additional information about this example.

Practice Set

Problems a–i ⌈Error Alert⌉

Whenever necessary, review with students the different ways to change a mixed number to an improper fraction. For additional practice, students can complete the problems shown below.

$2\frac{1}{6}$ $\frac{13}{6}$ $5\frac{1}{2}$ $\frac{11}{2}$ $4\frac{5}{6}$ $\frac{29}{6}$ $10\frac{2}{3}$ $\frac{32}{3}$

Example 2

Write $5\frac{2}{3}$ as an improper fraction.

Solution

Thinking Skill

Evaluate

Which method of changing a mixed number to an improper fraction do you prefer, the method in example 1 or example 2? Why? See student work.

We see that the denominator of the improper fraction will be thirds.

$$5\frac{2}{3} = \frac{}{3}$$

Some people use a quick, mechanical method to find the numerator of the improper fraction. Looking at the mixed number, they multiply the denominator by the whole number and then add the numerator. The result is the numerator of the improper fraction.

$$5\frac{2}{3} = \frac{17}{3}$$

Example 3

Write $1\frac{2}{3}$ and $2\frac{2}{5}$ as improper fractions. Then multiply the improper fractions. What is the product?

Solution

First we write $1\frac{2}{3}$ and $2\frac{2}{5}$ as improper fractions.

$$\lceil 1\frac{2}{3} \rceil \qquad \lceil 2\frac{2}{5} \rceil$$

$$\frac{3}{3} + \frac{2}{3} = \frac{5}{3} \qquad \frac{10}{5} + \frac{2}{5} = \frac{12}{5}$$

Next we multiply $\frac{5}{3}$ by $\frac{12}{5}$.

$$\frac{5}{3} \cdot \frac{12}{5} = \frac{60}{15}$$

The result is an improper fraction, which we simplify.

$$\frac{60}{15} = 4$$

So $1\frac{2}{3} \times 2\frac{2}{5}$ equals **4**.

Practice Set ▸ Write each mixed number as an improper fraction:

a. $2\frac{4}{5}$ $\frac{14}{5}$ **b.** $3\frac{1}{2}$ $\frac{7}{2}$ **c.** $1\frac{3}{4}$ $\frac{7}{4}$

d. $6\frac{1}{4}$ $\frac{25}{4}$ **e.** $1\frac{5}{6}$ $\frac{11}{6}$ **f.** $3\frac{3}{10}$ $\frac{33}{10}$

g. $2\frac{1}{3}$ $\frac{7}{3}$ **h.** $12\frac{1}{2}$ $\frac{25}{2}$ **i.** $3\frac{1}{6}$ $\frac{19}{6}$

j. Write $1\frac{1}{2}$ and $3\frac{1}{3}$ as improper fractions. Then multiply the improper fractions. What is the product? $\frac{3}{2} \cdot \frac{10}{3} = \frac{30}{6} = 5$

▸ See Math Conversations in the sidebar.

Math Background

In example 3, students are asked to find the product of two mixed numbers. The first step in finding such a product is to change each mixed number to an improper fraction.

After that step has been completed and before multiplying the improper fractions, students can look for factor pairs that are equal to 1. Drawing loops around these factor pairs, or canceling them, will simplify the arithmetic that needs to be completed.

$$1\frac{2}{3} \times 2\frac{2}{5} = \frac{\cancel{5}}{3} \times \frac{12}{\cancel{5}} = \frac{12}{3} = 4$$

▶ **1.** In music there are whole notes, half notes, quarter notes, and eighth
(54)   notes.

   a. How many quarter notes equal a whole note?   4 quarter notes

   b. How many eighth notes equal a quarter note?   2 eighth notes

* **2.** Don is 5 feet $2\frac{1}{2}$ inches tall. How many inches tall is that? $62\frac{1}{2}$ inches
(62)

3. *Classify*   Which of these numbers is not a prime number?   **B**
(19)

    A 11   **B** 21   **C** 31   **D** 41

▶ * **4.** *Analyze*   Write $1\frac{1}{3}$ and $1\frac{1}{2}$ as improper fractions, and multiply the
(62)   improper fractions. What is the product? $\frac{4}{3} \cdot \frac{3}{2} = \frac{12}{6} = 2$

5. If the chance of rain is 20%, what is the chance that it will not rain?
(58)   80%

6. The prices for three pairs of skates were $36.25, $41.50, and $43.75.
(18)   What was the average price for a pair of skates? Estimate to show that
   your answer is reasonable. $40.50; Each amount is close to $40, so $40
   is about the average price.

7. *Evaluate*   Instead of dividing 15 by $2\frac{1}{2}$, Solomon doubled both numbers
(43)   and then divided mentally. What was Solomon's mental division problem
   and its quotient? $30 \div 5 = 6$

Find each unknown number:

* **8.** $m - 4\frac{3}{8} = 3\frac{1}{4}$ $7\frac{5}{8}$ **9.** $n + \frac{3}{10} = \frac{3}{5}$ $\frac{3}{10}$
(43, 59)   (43, 56)

10. $6d = 0.456$ 0.076   **11.** $0.04w = 1.5$ 37.5
(43, 45)   (43, 49)

* **12.** $\frac{1}{2} + \frac{3}{4} + \frac{5}{8}$ $1\frac{7}{8}$ * **13.** $\frac{5}{6} - \frac{1}{2}$ $\frac{1}{3}$
(61)   (57)

14. $\frac{1}{2} \cdot \frac{4}{5}$ $\frac{2}{5}$ **15.** $\frac{2}{3} \div \frac{1}{2}$ $1\frac{1}{3}$
(29)   (54)

16. $1 - (0.2 - 0.03)$ 0.83   **17.** $(0.14)(0.16)$ 0.0224
(40)   (39)

18. One centimeter equals 10 millimeters. How many millimeters does
(49)   2.5 centimeters equal?   25 millimeters

19. List all of the common factors of 18 and 24. Then circle the greatest
(19)   common factor.   1, 2, 3, ⑥

▶* **20.** *Analyze*   Ten marbles are in a bag. Four of the marbles are red.
(58)

   a. If one marble is drawn from the bag, what is the probability that it will
   be red? $\frac{2}{5}$

   b. Write the complement of the event in **a** and state its probability.
   The probability of drawing not red is $\frac{3}{5}$.

   c. Describe the relationship between the event and its complement.
   The sum of the probability of an event and its complement is 1: $\frac{2}{5} + \frac{3}{5} = 1$.

21. *Analyze*   If the perimeter of a square is 40 mm, what is the area of the
(38)   square? 100 mm^2

▶ See Math Conversations in the sidebar.

Math Conversations

Discussion opportunities are provided below.

Problem 4   Analyze

After students write the improper fractions
and before they find the product of those
fractions, give them an opportunity to look for
factor pairs that are equal to 1.

> *"Look at the improper fractions that you
> wrote. Is there a factor pair that is equal
> to 1 in your fractions? Explain your
> answer."* Yes; the 3 in the denominator of
> $\frac{4}{3}$ and the 3 in the numerator of $\frac{3}{2}$ is a factor
> pair that is equal to 1.

> *"Why is the factor pair equal to 1?"*
> A fraction bar represents division, and three
> divided by three is one.

> *"Before we multiply the improper fractions,
> what can we do with the factor pair?"*
> Sample: We can cross out each 3.

> *"Will crossing out each 3 before we multiply
> change the product?"* no

Ask students to complete the arithmetic by
reducing $\frac{4}{2}$ to lowest terms.

Problem 20   Analyze

> *"Probability is a ratio that is often written
> as a fraction. What must you remember to
> do each time you write a fraction for an
> answer to a problem?"* Reduce the fraction
> to lowest terms whenever possible.

Errors and Misconceptions
Problem 1

If students have difficulty understanding
the part of a whole each note represents, ask
them to write the relationship of the notes as
fractions.

eighth note $= \frac{1}{8}$
quarter note $= \frac{1}{4}$
half note $= \frac{1}{2}$
whole note $= 1$

Repeated addition can then be used to find,
for example, the number of eighth notes in a
half note.

$$\frac{1}{8} + \frac{1}{8} + \frac{1}{8} + \frac{1}{8} = \frac{4}{8} = \frac{1}{2}$$

(continued)

Math Conversations

Discussion opportunities are provided below.

Problem 28 *Analyze*

Extend the Problem

"Describe three different ways to find 40% of 200. At least one of the ways you describe must involve mental math."

Sample: Use multiplication to find $\frac{2}{5}$ of 200; find the product of 0.4 and 200; find 10% of 200 mentally by shifting the decimal point one place to the left, then multiply 20 by 4 or count on by 20 four times.

Problem 30 *Analyze*

"To find the median of a set of data, how does the data need to be arranged?"

ordered from least to greatest or from greatest to least

---

22. At 6 a.m. the temperature was −6°F. At noon the temperature was 14°F.
(14) From 6 a.m. to noon the temperature rose how many degrees? 20°F

23. Lisa used a compass to draw a circle with a radius of $1\frac{1}{2}$ inches.
(47)
　　a. What was the diameter of the circle? 3 inches

　　b. What was the circumference of the circle? (Use 3.14 for π.)
　　　9.42 inches

The circle graph below shows the favorite sport of 100 people. Refer to the graph to answer problems **24–27.**

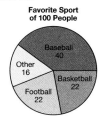

Favorite Sport of 100 People

24. How many more people favored baseball than favored football?
(40) 18 more people

25. What fraction of the people surveyed favored baseball? $\frac{2}{5}$
(40)

26. No. Sample: A majority of 100 people is at least 51 people. No sport was the favorite sport of 51 or more people.

26. *Explain* Was any sport the favorite sport of the majority of the people
(40) surveyed? Write one or two sentences to explain your answer.

27. *Connect* Since baseball was the favorite sport of 40 out of 100 people,
(40) it was the favorite sport of 40% of the people surveyed. What percent of the people answered that football was their favorite sport? 22%

▶ **28.** What number is 40% of 200? 80
(41)

29. Here we show 18 written as a product of prime numbers:
(19)
$$2 \cdot 3 \cdot 3$$

Write 20 as a product of prime numbers. $2 \cdot 2 \cdot 5$

▶ **30.** *Analyze* Judges awarded Sandra these scores for her performance on
(Inv. 5) the vault:
$$9.1, \ 8.9, \ 9.0, \ 9.2, \ 9.2$$

What is the median score? 9.1

▶ See Math Conversations in the sidebar.

Looking Forward

Writing mixed numbers as improper fractions prepares students for:

- **Lesson 66,** multiplying a mixed number and a whole number or two mixed numbers.
- **Lesson 68,** dividing a mixed number by a whole number or a mixed number.
- **Lesson 72,** using a fractions chart to recall steps for multiplying or dividing fractions and multiplying three fractions.
- **Lesson 92,** simplifying powers of fractions.
- **Lesson 115,** writing percents as fractions.

Subtracting Mixed Numbers with Regrouping, Part 2

Objectives
- Rename fractions so that they have common denominators and then regroup to subtract mixed numbers.

Materials
- **Power Up D** (in *Instructional Masters*)

Power Up D

Math Language

English Learners (ESL)

sea level

Technology Resources

Student eBook Complete student textbook in electronic format.

Resources and Planner CD Assessment, reteaching, and instructional masters, plus a pacing calendar with standards.

Test and Practice Generator CD Create additional practice sheets and custom-made tests.

www.SaxonPublishers.com Visit for more student activities and planning materials.

Inclusion

Adaptations CD Adapted lessons, investigations, practice and assessments.

Meeting Standards

National Council of Teachers of Mathematics (NCTM)

Numbers and Operations

NO.1a Work flexibly with fractions, decimals, and percents to solve problems

NO.2a Understand the meaning and effects of arithmetic operations with fractions, decimals, and integers

NO.3a Select appropriate methods and tools for computing with fractions and decimals from among mental computation, estimation, calculators or computers, and paper and pencil, depending on the situation, and apply the selected methods

Problem Solving

PS.1c Apply and adapt a variety of appropriate strategies to solve problems

Problem-Solving Strategy: Make It Simpler/
Write an Equation

Rhett chooses a marble at random from each of the four boxes below. From which box is he *most* likely to choose a blue marble?

A 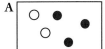 B 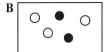 C 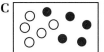 D

(Understand) **Understand the problem.**

"What information are we given?"

Four boxes each have a different proportion of blue and white marbles.

"What are we asked to do?"

Determine from which box Rhett is most likely to select a blue marble at random.

(Plan) **Make a plan.**

"What problem-solving strategy will we use?"

We will use logical thinking to *make the problem simpler*. We will then need to *write an equation* to find the probability.

(Solve) **Carry out the plan.**

"Will he be most likely to choose a blue marble from a box that has more blue than white, an equal number of blue and white, or more white than blue marbles?"

More blue than white.

"Which boxes have more blue than white marbles?"

The first and fourth boxes each have one more blue marble than white marbles.

"What is the probability of selecting a blue marble from the first box?"

$\frac{3}{5}$

"From the fourth box?"

$\frac{4}{7}$

"How can we find which fraction represents the box with the greater probability of selecting a blue marble?"

We can convert both fractions to either fractions with common denominators or to decimals.

"What is the probability of Rhett selecting a blue marble from each box?"

Box 1 has a probability of $\frac{3}{5} = \frac{21}{35} = 0.60$. Box 4 has a probability of $\frac{4}{7} = \frac{20}{35} \approx 0.57$.

"From which box will he most likely select a blue marble?"

box 1

(Check) **Look back.**

"Did we answer the question that was asked?"

Yes. We found the probability of selecting a blue marble from the two boxes that contained more blue marbles than white marbles, and then concluded that Rhett had the greater likelihood of selecting blue from box 1, because the probability was greater than the probability for selecting blue from box 4.

Teacher Note: Ask students to explain how we made the problem simpler. Ask them if we had to make it simpler in order to solve the problem. Help students understand that it saves time and is a more efficient way to solve problems.

• Subtracting Mixed Numbers with Regrouping, Part 2

facts | Power Up D

mental math |
a. **Number Sense:** 5×140 700

b. **Number Sense:** $420 - 50$ 370

c. **Calculation:** 4×63 252

d. **Calculation:** $\$8.50 - \$2.50$ $6.00

e. **Number Sense:** Double $7\frac{1}{2}$.   15

f. **Number Sense:** $\frac{\$25}{100}$ $0.25

g. **Measurement:** How many inches are in 6 feet?   72 in.

h. **Calculation:** $5 \times 10, - 20, + 2, \div 4, + 1, \div 3, - 3$ 0

problem solving | Rhett chooses a marble at random from each of the four boxes below. From which box is he *most* likely to choose a blue marble?   A

New Concept   *Increasing Knowledge*

Since Lesson 48 we have practiced subtracting mixed numbers with regrouping. In this lesson we will rename the fractions with common denominators before subtracting.

To subtract $1\frac{1}{2}$ from $3\frac{2}{3}$, we first rewrite the fractions with common denominators. Then we subtract the whole numbers and the fractions. If possible, we simplify.

$$
\begin{array}{r}
3\frac{2}{3} \times \frac{2}{2} = 3\frac{4}{6} \\
- 1\frac{1}{2} \times \frac{3}{3} = 1\frac{3}{6} \\
\hline
2\frac{1}{6}
\end{array}
$$

When subtracting, it is sometimes necessary to regroup. We rewrite the fractions with common denominators before regrouping.

Lesson 63   329

Facts
Distribute **Power Up D** to students. See answers below.

Mental Math
Before students begin the Mental Math exercise, do this counting exercise as a class.

Count up and down by $\frac{1}{8}$s between $\frac{1}{8}$ and 2.

Encourage students to share different ways to mentally compute these exercises. Strategies for exercises **b** and **e** are listed below.

b. Subtract 20, then Add 20
$400 - 50 = 350; 350 + 20 = 370$
Count Back by Tens
Start with 420. Count: 410, 400, 390, 380, 370

e. Double 7 and Double $\frac{1}{2}$
Double 7 is 14 and double $\frac{1}{2}$ is 1; $14 + 1 = 15$
Use a Pattern
Since double 7 is 14 and double 8 is 16, double $7\frac{1}{2}$ is 15.

Problem Solving
Refer to **Power-Up Discussion,** p. 329B.

Instruction
"Look at the $\frac{2}{3}$ in $3\frac{2}{3}$ and at the $\frac{1}{2}$ in $1\frac{1}{2}$. Why is $\frac{2}{3}$ multiplied by two halves and $\frac{1}{2}$ multiplied by three thirds?" Two halves and three thirds were used because 6 is the least common multiple of the denominators.

After reviewing the subtraction, ask,

"When is it necessary to regroup?"
Whenever the fraction in the subtrahend is greater than the fraction in the minuend.

(continued)

Facts   Multiply.

$\begin{array}{r}7\\ \times 7\\ \hline 49\end{array}$	$\begin{array}{r}4\\ \times 6\\ \hline 24\end{array}$	$\begin{array}{r}8\\ \times 1\\ \hline 8\end{array}$	$\begin{array}{r}2\\ \times 2\\ \hline 4\end{array}$	$\begin{array}{r}0\\ \times 5\\ \hline 0\end{array}$	$\begin{array}{r}6\\ \times 3\\ \hline 18\end{array}$	$\begin{array}{r}8\\ \times 9\\ \hline 72\end{array}$	$\begin{array}{r}5\\ \times 8\\ \hline 40\end{array}$	$\begin{array}{r}6\\ \times 2\\ \hline 12\end{array}$	$\begin{array}{r}10\\ \times 10\\ \hline 100\end{array}$
$\begin{array}{r}9\\ \times 4\\ \hline 36\end{array}$	$\begin{array}{r}2\\ \times 5\\ \hline 10\end{array}$	$\begin{array}{r}9\\ \times 6\\ \hline 54\end{array}$	$\begin{array}{r}7\\ \times 3\\ \hline 21\end{array}$	$\begin{array}{r}5\\ \times 5\\ \hline 25\end{array}$	$\begin{array}{r}7\\ \times 2\\ \hline 14\end{array}$	$\begin{array}{r}6\\ \times 8\\ \hline 48\end{array}$	$\begin{array}{r}3\\ \times 5\\ \hline 15\end{array}$	$\begin{array}{r}9\\ \times 9\\ \hline 81\end{array}$	$\begin{array}{r}5\\ \times 4\\ \hline 20\end{array}$
$\begin{array}{r}3\\ \times 4\\ \hline 12\end{array}$	$\begin{array}{r}6\\ \times 5\\ \hline 30\end{array}$	$\begin{array}{r}8\\ \times 2\\ \hline 16\end{array}$	$\begin{array}{r}4\\ \times 4\\ \hline 16\end{array}$	$\begin{array}{r}6\\ \times 7\\ \hline 42\end{array}$	$\begin{array}{r}8\\ \times 8\\ \hline 64\end{array}$	$\begin{array}{r}2\\ \times 3\\ \hline 6\end{array}$	$\begin{array}{r}7\\ \times 4\\ \hline 28\end{array}$	$\begin{array}{r}5\\ \times 9\\ \hline 45\end{array}$	$\begin{array}{r}3\\ \times 8\\ \hline 24\end{array}$
$\begin{array}{r}3\\ \times 9\\ \hline 27\end{array}$	$\begin{array}{r}7\\ \times 8\\ \hline 56\end{array}$	$\begin{array}{r}2\\ \times 4\\ \hline 8\end{array}$	$\begin{array}{r}5\\ \times 7\\ \hline 35\end{array}$	$\begin{array}{r}3\\ \times 3\\ \hline 9\end{array}$	$\begin{array}{r}9\\ \times 7\\ \hline 63\end{array}$	$\begin{array}{r}4\\ \times 8\\ \hline 32\end{array}$	$\begin{array}{r}0\\ \times 0\\ \hline 0\end{array}$	$\begin{array}{r}9\\ \times 2\\ \hline 18\end{array}$	$\begin{array}{r}6\\ \times 6\\ \hline 36\end{array}$

2 New Concepts (Continued)

Example
Instruction

"In this subtraction example, we used addition to check our answer. We also could have used subtraction to check our answer. Explain how." Subtract the exact answer from the minuend and compare the result to the subtrahend. If the numbers are the same, the problem checks.

Invite a volunteer to show the arithmetic for such a check on the board or overhead.

Practice Set
Problems a–i [Error Alert]

To successfully complete each problem, students must choose a common denominator and rename one or both fractions. Also, all of the nine problems require regrouping except for **a** and **g**.

Because several steps must be completed to find each answer, remind students of the importance of checking their work, and encourage them to choose addition or subtraction to check each answer.

Problem j [Formulate]

Invite students to exchange the word problems they write, then solve the problems and compare answers.

3 Written Practice

Math Conversations
Discussion opportunities are provided below.

Problem 1 [Connect]

Invite several students to each write on the board or overhead a single expression to represent the information. Then discuss with students why the expressions are correct and/or identify the changes that must be made to make them correct.
Sample: $(0.6 + 0.4) - (0.6 \times 0.4)$

Errors and Misconceptions
Problem 2 [Analyze]

If students need help recognizing that addition is used to solve the problem, ask them to create a simple sketch of the situation.

For example, after drawing a horizontal line to represent sea level, students should sketch the mountain above the line and label the elevation of its peak, and sketch the valley below the line and label the elevation of its floor.

(continued)

[Example]

Thinking Skill
[Explain]

Why did we regroup in this example but not in the previous problem? In this example we could not subtract the renamed fractions, but in the previous problem we could.

Subtract: $5\frac{1}{2} - 1\frac{2}{3}$

[Solution]

We rewrite the fractions with common denominators. Before we can subtract, we must regroup. After we subtract, we simplify if possible.

$$5\frac{1}{2} \times \frac{3}{3} = \overset{4}{\cancel{5}}\overset{9}{\frac{\cancel{3}}{6}}$$
$$- 1\frac{2}{3} \times \frac{2}{2} = 1\frac{4}{6}$$
$$\overline{3\frac{5}{6}}$$

[Justify] Why can we use addition to check the answer?   Sample: Addition and subtraction are inverse operations. The three numbers that form a subtraction fact also form an addition fact.

Practice Set ▶ Subtract:

a. $5\frac{1}{2} - 3\frac{1}{3}$ $2\frac{1}{6}$ **b.** $4\frac{1}{4} - 2\frac{1}{3}$ $1\frac{11}{12}$ **c.** $6\frac{1}{2} - 1\frac{3}{4}$ $4\frac{3}{4}$

d. $7\frac{2}{3} - 3\frac{5}{6}$ $3\frac{5}{6}$ **e.** $6\frac{1}{6} - 1\frac{1}{2}$ $4\frac{2}{3}$ **f.** $4\frac{1}{3} - 1\frac{1}{2}$ $2\frac{5}{6}$

g. $4\frac{5}{6} - 1\frac{1}{3}$ $3\frac{1}{2}$ **h.** $6\frac{1}{2} - 3\frac{5}{6}$ $2\frac{2}{3}$ **i.** $8\frac{2}{3} - 5\frac{3}{4}$ $2\frac{11}{12}$

j. [Formulate] Write a word problem that involves subtracting mixed numbers.   See student work.

[Written Practice]   *Strengthening Concepts*

▶ *** 1.** [Connect] What is the difference between the sum of 0.6 and 0.4 and the product of 0.6 and 0.4?   0.76
   (12, 53)

▶ *** 2.** [Analyze] Mt. Whitney, the highest point in California, has an elevation of 14,494 feet *above* sea level. From there one can see Death Valley, which contains the lowest point in California, 282 feet *below* sea level. The floor of Death Valley is how many feet below the peak of Mt. Whitney?   14,776 feet
   (14)

5. $680; $678.25 is more than $670 but less than $680. It is closer to $680 because it is more than $675, which is halfway between $670 and $680.

6. 12:45 p.m.; Sample: I added 2 hours to 10:15 a.m. and got 12:15 p.m. Then I added half an hour to 12:15 p.m. and got 12:45 p.m.

* 3. [Conclude] It was 39° outside at 1 p.m. By 7 p.m. the temperature had dropped 11° and was below freezing. What was the temperature at 7 p.m.? On what scale is the temperature being measured?   28°; Fahrenheit
   (10)

* 4. Write the mixed number $4\frac{2}{3}$ as an improper fraction. $\frac{14}{3}$
   (62)

* 5. [Explain] Round $678.25 to the nearest ten dollars. Describe how you decided upon your answer.
   (62)

6. [Explain] What time is $2\frac{1}{2}$ hours after 10:15 a.m.? How did you find your answer?
   (32)

7. $(30 \times 15) \div (30 - 15)$ 30   **8.** Compare: $\frac{5}{8} \bigcirc \frac{2}{3}$
   (5)   (56)

9. $w - 3\frac{2}{3} = 1\frac{1}{2}$ $5\frac{1}{6}$ **10.** $\frac{6}{8} - \frac{3}{4}$ 0
   (43)   (55)

330   *Saxon Math Course 1*

▶ See Math Conversations in the sidebar.

English Learners

Refer students to problem 2. Draw the following diagram on the board.

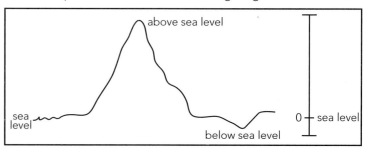

"Sea level is used to measure how far above or below the ocean a place is located."

Explain how the number line is used to show the distance from sea level. Invite volunteers to mark the height of Mt. Whitney and the depth of Death Valley on the number line.

11. $6\frac{1}{4} - 5\frac{5}{8}$ $\frac{5}{8}$ **12.** $\frac{3}{4} \times \frac{2}{5}$ $\frac{3}{10}$
(63)   (29)

13. $\frac{3}{4} \div \frac{2}{5}$ $1\frac{7}{8}$ **14.** $(1 - 0.4)(1 + 0.4)$ 0.84
(54)   (53)

15. How much money is 60% of $45? $27
(41)

16. $0.4 \div 8$ 0.05   **17.** $8 \div 0.4$ 20
(45)   (49)

▶ **18.** *Predict* What is the next number in this sequence?   1 (or 1.0)
(10)

0.2, 0.4, 0.6, 0.8, …

19. What is the tenth prime number?   29
(19)

* **20.** What is the perimeter of this rectangle? $3\frac{3}{4}$ in.
(8, 59)

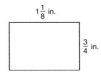
$1\frac{1}{8}$ in.

$\frac{3}{4}$ in.

* **21.** A triangular prism has how many
(Inv. 6)
    a. faces?   5 faces

    b. edges?   9 edges

    c. vertices?   6 vertices

▶ **22.** Write $2\frac{1}{2}$ and $1\frac{1}{5}$ as improper fractions. Then multiply the improper
(16) fractions and simplify the product. $\frac{5}{2} \cdot \frac{6}{5} = \frac{30}{10} = 3$

23. This rectangle is divided into two congruent
(31) regions. What is the area of the shaded
region?   150 sq. cm

30 cm

10 cm

* **24.** A ton is 2000 pounds. How many pounds is $2\frac{1}{2}$ tons?   5000 pounds
(15, 62)

25. *Connect* Which arrow could be pointing to 0.2 on this number line?   C
(50)

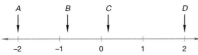
A   B   C   D

–2   –1   0   1   2

26. *Evaluate* The paper cup would not roll
(47) straight. One end was 7 cm in diameter, and
the other end was 5 cm in diameter. In one
roll of the cup,

    a. how far would the larger end roll?   22 cm

    b. how far would the smaller end roll?   16 cm

    (Round each answer to the nearest centimeter. Use 3.14 for π.)

Lesson 63   331

▶ See Math Conversations in the sidebar.

Math Conversations

Discussion opportunities are provided below.

Problem 18   Predict

Before completing the problem, ask students
to discuss the pattern and identify its rule.
Sample: To find the next term in the sequence,
add 0.2 to the previous term.

After students name the next term, ask,

> *"Does this sequence have a one hundredth
> term?"* yes

> *"Describe how mental math can be used
> to name the one hundredth term of
> this sequence."* To find any term in the
> sequence, multiply the number of the term
> by 0.2. So the one hundredth term is
> 100×0.2. I know that 100×2 is 200, so
> 100×0.2 is 20.0 or 20.

Problem 22   Analyze

Some students may not recognize that the
improper fractions contain a factor pair that is
equal to 1.

Although students do not need to recognize
the factor pair to complete the problem
successfully, such a recognition can, generally
speaking, make a computation easier to
complete. Also, looking for and recognizing
factors of this nature now is a skill students
will often use in more advanced mathematics
courses in the future.

(continued)

Math Conversations

Discussion opportunities are provided below.

Problem 27 [Analyze]

Extend the Problem

Challenge students who have an interest in baseball or who play baseball to answer the following question.

"How many outs did Jefferson make in those 240 at-bats?" Not enough information is given; we are only told the number of hits. In the remainder of the 168 at-bats ($240 - 72$), Jefferson likely made many outs, but he may have also earned, for example, a number of walks.

Problem 30 [Analyze]

Extend the Problem

"In the mixture, what is the ratio of yellow paint to red paint? Give your answer as a fraction, and explain how you found the answer." $\frac{2}{3}$; Sample explanation: Change each fraction to a whole number by multiplying each fraction by the same whole number; $\frac{1}{2} \times 4 = 2$ and $\frac{3}{4} \times 4 = 3$.

▶ **27.** Jefferson got a hit 30% of the 240 times he went to bat during the
(29, 33) season. Write 30% as a reduced fraction. Then find the number of hits Jefferson got during the season. $\frac{3}{10}$; 72 hits

28. Jena has run 11.5 miles of a 26.2-mile race. Find the remaining distance
(43) Jena has to run by solving this equation: 14.7 mi

$$11.5 \text{ mi} + d = 26.2 \text{ mi}$$

29. The sales-tax rate was 7%. The two CDs cost $15.49 each. What was
(41) the total cost of the two CDs including tax? $33.15

▶* **30.** Rosa is mixing paint in ceramics class. She mixes $\frac{1}{2}$ teaspoon of yellow
(57) paint with $\frac{3}{4}$ teaspoon of red paint to make orange paint. How much orange paint does Rosa make? $1\frac{1}{4}$ teaspoons

---

Early Finishers
Real-World Application

The drama club had their first annual meeting this afternoon. The officers had decided to order pizza for all the new members this year. They ordered one cheese, one mushroom, and one tomato pizza. Due to the rain, the turnout for the meeting was small and there was a lot of pizza left. They had $\frac{1}{4}$ of the cheese pizza, $\frac{1}{2}$ of the mushroom pizza and $\frac{5}{12}$ of the tomato pizza left. How much leftover pizza did the drama club have?   LCM is 12; $\frac{1}{4} + \frac{1}{2} + \frac{5}{12} = \frac{3}{12} + \frac{6}{12} + \frac{5}{12} = \frac{14}{12} = 1\frac{2}{12} = 1\frac{1}{6}$ leftover pizza.

▶ See Math Conversations in the sidebar.

Looking Forward

Renaming and regrouping to subtract mixed numbers with different denominators prepares students for:

• **Lesson 72,** using a fractions chart to review steps for subtracting fractions.

• Classifying Quadrilaterals

Objectives

- Identify, classify, and draw quadrilaterals according to the characteristics of their sides and angles.

Lesson Preparation

Materials

- **Power Up J** (in *Instructional Masters*)
- **Teacher-provided material:** dot paper or grid paper

Power Up Test J

Math Language

New

parallelogram	square
rectangle	trapezium
rhombus	trapezoid

Technology Resources

Student eBook Complete student textbook in electronic format.

Resources and Planner CD Assessment, reteaching, and instructional masters, plus a pacing calendar with standards.

Test and Practice Generator CD Create additional practice sheets and custom-made tests.

www.SaxonPublishers.com Visit for more student activities and planning materials.

Inclusion

Adaptations CD Adapted lessons, investigations, practice and assessments.

Meeting Standards

National Council of Teachers of Mathematics (NCTM)

Geometry

GM.1a Precisely describe, classify, and understand relationships among types of two- and three-dimensional objects using their defining properties

Communication

CM.3a Organize and consolidate their mathematical thinking through communication

CM.3b Communicate their mathematical thinking coherently and clearly to peers, teachers, and others

Problem-Solving Strategy: Make a Table/
Use Logical Reasoning

Emily has a blue folder, a green folder, and a red folder. She uses one folder each for her math, science, and history classes. She does not use her blue folder for math. Her green folder is not used for science. She does not use her red folder for history. If her red folder is not used for math, what folder does Emily use for each subject? Make a table to show your work.

(Understand) **Understand the problem.**

"What information are we given?"

Emily has blue, green, and red folders; one each for math, science, and history.
    Fact 1: The blue folder is not used for math.
    Fact 2: The green folder is not used for science.
    Fact 3: The red folder is not used for history.
    Fact 4: The red folder is not used for math.

"What are we asked to do?"

Make a table that relates the colors of the folders to the school subjects and find the color folder Emily uses for each subject.

(Plan) **Make a plan.**

"What problem-solving strategy will we use?"

We have been asked to *make a table,* and we will *use logical reasoning* to help us fill it in.

(Solve) **Carry out the plan.**

"How do we begin?"

We will set up our table and fill in the information that we already know.

	Blue	Green	Red
History	Yes	No	No Fact 3
Math	No Fact 1	Yes	No Fact 4
Science	No	No Fact 2	Yes

"What do we know about the colors of folders for math?"

The blue and red folders are not used for math.

"What else do we know?"

We know that Emily did not use a green folder for science or a red folder for history.

"How do we complete the table?"

Use logical reasoning. If Emily did not use a red or blue folder for math, she must have used a green folder for math. That means that she did not use the green folder for history and since we also know that she did not use the red folder for history, the only possible folder for history is blue. The only remaining folder color is red. Therefore, she must use the red folder for science.

"What folder did Emily use for each subject?"

A blue folder for history, a green for math, and a red for science.

(Check) **Look back.**

"Did we answer the question that was asked?"

Yes. We made a table that showed what colors of folders Emily used for each subject.

•Classifying Quadrilaterals

Building Power

facts | Power Up J

mental math
a. **Number Sense:** 5×240 1200

b. **Number Sense:** $4500 + 450$ 4950

c. **Calculation:** 7×34 238

d. **Calculation:** $7.50 + 7.50 $15.00

e. **Fractional Parts:** $\frac{1}{4}$ of $20.00 $5.00

f. **Number Sense:** $\frac{$75}{10}$ $7.50

g. **Measurement:** How many meters are in 200 centimeters?   2 m

h. **Calculation:** $6 \times 8, \div 2, + 1, \div 5, - 1, \times 4, \div 2$ 8

problem solving
Emily has a blue folder, a green folder, and a red folder. She uses one folder each for her math, science, and history classes. She does not use her blue folder for math. Her green folder is not used for science. She does not use her red folder for history. If her red folder is not used for math, what folder does Emily use for each subject? Make a table to show your work.   History: blue folder; Math: green folder; Science: red folder.

	blue	green	red
H			No
M	No		No
S		No	

Increasing Knowledge

Math Language
The prefix *quadri-* means four. A quadrilateral is a polygon with four sides.

We learned in Lesson 60 that quadrilaterals are polygons with four sides. We can classify (sort) quadrilaterals by the characteristics of their sides and angles. The following table describes the various classifications of quadrilaterals:

Classifications of Quadrilaterals

Shape	Characteristic	Name
	No sides parallel	Trapezium
	One pair of parallel sides	Trapezoid
	Two pairs of parallel sides	Parallelogram
	Parallelogram with equal sides	Rhombus
	Parallelogram with right angles	Rectangle
	Rectangle with equal sides	Square

---

1 Power Up

Facts
Distribute **Power Up J** to students. See answers below.

Mental Math
Before students begin the Mental Math exercise, do this counting exercise as a class.

Count up and down by 25s between 25 and 300.

Encourage students to share different ways to mentally compute these exercises. Strategies for exercises **b** and **e** are listed below.

b. **Add 400, then Add 50**
   $4500 + 400 = 4900; 4900 + 50 = 4950$
   Add 500, then Subtract 50
   $4500 + 500 = 5000; 5000 - 50 = 4950$
e. **Divide by 4**
   $20 \div 4 = 5
   Find $\frac{1}{2}$ of $\frac{1}{2}$ of $20
   $\frac{1}{2}$ of $20 = $10; \frac{1}{2}$ of $10 = 5

Problem Solving
Refer to **Power-Up Discussion,** p. 333B.

2 New Concepts

Instruction
Draw and label the different quadrilaterals on the board or overhead, and encourage students to use the drawings as a reference during this lesson. Use several colors to highlight the parallel sides of the quadrilaterals. Then discuss the characteristics of each quadrilateral with students.

(continued)

Facts   Write each mixed number as an improper fraction.

$2\frac{1}{2} = \frac{5}{2}$	$2\frac{2}{5} = \frac{12}{5}$	$1\frac{3}{4} = \frac{7}{4}$	$2\frac{3}{4} = \frac{11}{4}$	$2\frac{1}{8} = \frac{17}{8}$
$1\frac{2}{3} = \frac{5}{3}$	$3\frac{1}{2} = \frac{7}{2}$	$1\frac{5}{6} = \frac{11}{6}$	$2\frac{1}{4} = \frac{9}{4}$	$1\frac{1}{8} = \frac{9}{8}$
$5\frac{1}{2} = \frac{11}{2}$	$1\frac{3}{8} = \frac{11}{8}$	$5\frac{1}{3} = \frac{16}{3}$	$3\frac{1}{4} = \frac{13}{4}$	$4\frac{1}{2} = \frac{9}{2}$
$1\frac{7}{8} = \frac{15}{8}$	$2\frac{2}{3} = \frac{8}{3}$	$1\frac{5}{8} = \frac{13}{8}$	$3\frac{3}{4} = \frac{15}{4}$	$7\frac{1}{2} = \frac{15}{2}$

2 New Concepts (Continued)

Clarify the classification of a square—and the other quadrilaterals—by drawing the following diagram on the board or overhead.

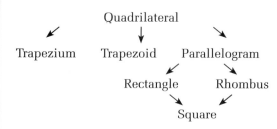

Quadrilateral

Trapezium   Trapezoid   Parallelogram

Rectangle   Rhombus

Square

Discuss each level of the diagram with students.

"The diagram shows that a trapezium, a trapezoid, and a parallelogram are all quadrilaterals, and shows that a rectangle is a parallelogram and a quadrilateral. What is a square?" A square is a rectangle, a rhombus, a parallelogram, and a quadrilateral.

Example 2
Instruction

Demonstrate how to draw a parallelogram on the board or overhead. Then give each student a sheet of dot or grid paper and ask them to draw and label examples of each kind of quadrilateral.

Practice Set

Problem e Verify

Ask students to use an example to support, or a non-example to disprove, the statement. The statement is true; ask students to share and discuss their examples.

Problem f Verify

Ask students to use an example to support, or a non-example to disprove, the statement. The statement is true; ask students to share and discuss their examples.

Notice that squares, rectangles, and rhombuses are all parallelograms. Also notice that a square is a special kind of rectangle, which is a special kind of parallelogram, which is a special kind of quadrilateral, which is a special kind of polygon. A square is also a special kind of rhombus.

Example 1

Thinking Skill

Justify

How can we rewrite the statement in example 1 so that it is true? All rectangles are parallelograms, or some parallelograms are rectangles.

Is the following statement true or false?

All parallelograms are rectangles.

Solution

We are asked to decide whether every parallelogram is a rectangle. Since a rectangle is a special kind of parallelogram, some parallelograms are rectangles. However, some parallelograms are not rectangles. Since not all parallelograms are rectangles, the statement is **false.**

Example 2

Draw a pair of parallel lines. Then draw another pair of parallel lines. These lines should intersect the first pair but not be perpendicular to the first pair. What is the name for the quadrilateral that is formed by the intersecting lines?

Solution

We draw the first pair of parallel lines.

We draw the second pair of lines so that the lines are not perpendicular to the first pair.

At right we have colored the segments that form the quadrilateral. The quadrilateral formed is a **parallelogram.**

Practice Set

b. A parallelogram has two pairs of parallel sides; a trapezoid has only one pair of parallel sides.

a. What is a quadrilateral?   A quadrilateral is a four-sided polygon.

b. Describe the difference between a parallelogram and a trapezoid.

c. Model Draw a rhombus that is a square. ☐

d. Model Draw a rhombus that is not a square. ▱

▶ e. Verify True or false: Some rectangles are squares.   true

▶ f. Verify True or false: All squares are rectangles.   true

Written Practice   *Strengthening Concepts*

* **1.** When the sum of 1.3 and 1.2 is divided by the difference of 1.3 and 1.2,
(12, 53)   what is the quotient?   25

2. William Shakespeare was born in 1564 and died in 1616. How many
(13)   years did he live?   52 years

▶ See Math Conversations in the sidebar.

Inclusion

Refer students to the "Quadrilaterals" chart in the Student Reference Guide. Review the qualities of each quadrilateral with students. Ask questions such as,

"Is every square a rectangle?" yes; *"Is every rectangle a square?"* no; *"What name describes every trapezoid and every parallelogram?"* quadrilateral

Draw different quadrilaterals on the board. Ask students to give as many names as possible to each figure.

Math Background

Can a parallelogram be both a rectangle and a rhombus?

Yes, a square is a parallelogram that is both a rectangle and a rhombus. A square is a rectangle because it has all of the characteristics of a rectangle (four right angles). In addition, it has four equal-length sides. A square is also a rhombus because it has all of the characteristics of a rhombus (four equal-length sides). A square is the only parallelogram that is both a rectangle and a rhombus.

4. A square is a four-sided polygon, so it is a quadrilateral. The four sides of a square have the same length, and the four angles have the same measure, so a square is "regular."

3. Duane kicked a 45-yard field goal. How many feet is 45 yards?
(15)   135 feet

▶ *** 4.** **Explain** Why is a square a regular quadrilateral?
(60)

* 5. A regular hexagon has a perimeter of 36 inches. How long is each
(60)   side?   6 inches

6. $\dfrac{1}{4} = \dfrac{?}{100}$ 25
(42)

7. $\dfrac{8 \times 8}{8 + 8}$ 4
(5)

* 8. $5\dfrac{2}{3} + 3\dfrac{3}{4}$ $9\dfrac{5}{12}$
(59)

* 9. $\dfrac{1}{2} + \dfrac{2}{3} + \dfrac{1}{4}$ $1\dfrac{5}{12}$
(61)

10. $\dfrac{9}{10} - \dfrac{1}{2}$ $\dfrac{2}{5}$
(57)

* 11. $6\dfrac{1}{2} - 2\dfrac{7}{8}$ $3\dfrac{5}{8}$
(63)

12. Compare: $2 \times 0.4 \; \textcircled{<} \; 2 + 0.4$
(44)

13. 4.8×0.35 1.68
(39)

14. $1 \div 0.4$ 2.5
(49)

15. How many $0.12 pencils can Mr. Velazquez buy for $4.80?   40 pencils
(15)

16. **Estimate** Round the product of 0.33 and 0.38 to the nearest
(51)   hundredth.   0.13

17. Multiply the length by the width to find the
(31)   area of this rectangle. $\dfrac{3}{8}$ sq. in.

$\dfrac{1}{2}$ in.

$\dfrac{3}{4}$ in.

▶ *** 18.** **Conclude** Is every rectangle a parallelogram?   yes
(64)

19. **Analyze** What is the twelfth prime number?   37
(19)

20. The area of a square is 9 cm².
(38)
    a. How long is each side of the square?   3 cm

    b. What is the perimeter of the square?   12 cm

Refer to the box shown below to answer problems **21** and **22**.

* 21. This box has how many faces? Draw a net
(Inv. 6)   to show how the box would look if you cut it
apart and flattened it.   6 faces; See student
work.

▶ *** 22.** If this box is a cube and each edge is
(Inv. 6)   10 inches long, then

    a. what is the area of each face?   100 in.²

    b. what is the total surface area of the cube?   600 in.²

23. There are 100 centimeters in a meter. How many centimeters equal
(15)   2.5 meters?   250 centimeters

* 24. Write the mixed numbers $1\dfrac{1}{2}$ and $2\dfrac{1}{2}$ as improper fractions. Then multiply
(62)   the improper fractions and simplify the product. $\dfrac{3}{2} \cdot \dfrac{5}{2} = \dfrac{15}{4} = 3\dfrac{3}{4}$

Lesson 64   335

▶ See Math Conversations in the sidebar.

Math Conversations
Discussion opportunities are provided below.

Problem 4   Explain
Extend the Problem
"Is every rhombus a regular quadrilateral? Explain why or why not." No; regular polygons are equilateral and equiangular. A rhombus is equilateral but not necessarily equiangular. A square is the only rhombus that is regular.

Problem 18   Conclude
"What are the characteristics of a parallelogram?" a quadrilateral with opposite sides that are both congruent and parallel, opposite angles are congruent and adjacent angles are supplementary

"What are the characteristics of a rectangle?" a quadrilateral with opposite sides that are both congruent and parallel, and four right angles

"Is every rectangle a parallelogram?" yes

Problem 22   Analyze
Extend the Problem
"How would the total surface area of the cube change if the length of each edge was doubled?" The total surface area would become 4 times greater than it was.

"How would the total surface area of the cube change if the length of each edge was halved?" The total surface area would become $\dfrac{1}{4}$ of what it was.

(continued)

Math Conversations

Discussion opportunities are provided below.

Problem 25 *Verify*

"How is a number that is prime different from a number that is not prime?" Sample: A prime number is a counting number greater than 1 whose only two factors are the number 1 and itself; a number that is greater than 1 and not prime has more than two factors.

Problem 30 *Predict*

A variety of predictions are possible; accept reasonable answers.

Errors and Misconceptions
Problem 29a and 29b

Students are asked to find temperature differences, and because "differences" imply subtraction, students may have difficulty recognizing that addition is used to find the differences.

To help students understand why addition is used, draw and label a number line from −10 to 10 by ones on the board or overhead. After plotting each pair of temperatures, help students recognize that the difference of those temperatures is the sum of each temperature's distance from zero.

▶* **25.** *Verify* The numbers 2, 3, 5, 7, and 11 are prime numbers. The
  (19) numbers 4, 6, 8, 9, 10, and 12 are not prime numbers, but they can be formed by multiplying prime numbers.

$$4 = 2 \cdot 2$$
$$6 = 2 \cdot 3$$
$$8 = 2 \cdot 2 \cdot 2$$

Show how to form 9, 10, and 12 by multiplying prime numbers.
$9 = 3 \cdot 3$; $10 = 2 \cdot 5$; $12 = 2 \cdot 2 \cdot 3$

26. Write 75% as an unreduced fraction. Then write the fraction as a
(33, 35) decimal number. $\frac{75}{100}$; 0.75

27. Reduce: $\dfrac{2 \cdot 2 \cdot 2 \cdot 3 \cdot 3}{2 \cdot 2 \cdot 3 \cdot 5 \cdot 5}$ $\frac{6}{25}$
(54)

28. *Analyze* Find the missing distance d in the equation below. 9.6 mi
(43)

$$16.6 \text{ mi} + d = 26.2 \text{ mi}$$

Refer to the double-line graph below to answer problems **29** and **30**.

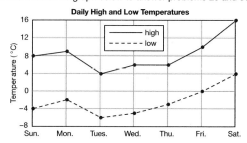

Daily High and Low Temperatures

▶* **29.** **a.** The difference between Tuesday's high and low temperatures was
  (18) how many degrees? 10°C

  b. The difference between the lowest temperature of the week and the highest temperature of the week was how many degrees? 22°C

▶* **30.** *Predict* If the daily high temperature dropped 5 degrees the day after
  (18) this graph was completed, what probably happened to the daily low temperature? Explain. It probably dropped about 5 degrees. The graph's lines seem to be following each other closely, about 10–12 degrees apart.

▶ See Math Conversations in the sidebar.

Looking Forward

Identifying, classifying, and drawing quadrilaterals according to the characteristics of their sides and angles prepare students for:

- **Investigation 7,** graphing and connecting points on a coordinate plane to create rectangles and other shapes.
- **Lesson 71,** identifying and finding measures of opposite and adjacent angles in parallelograms and finding the area of a parallelogram.
- **Lesson 91,** identifying and using geometric formulas for the perimeter and area of squares, rectangles, parallelograms, and triangles.
- **Lesson 93,** identifying and classifying triangles.
- **Lesson 110,** determining lines of symmetry.

- ## Prime Factorization
- ## Division by Primes
- ## Factor Trees

Objectives
- Identify a composite number as a number with more than two factors.
- Write the prime factorization of a given composite number.
- Use division by primes to find the prime factorization of a given number.
- Make a factor tree to find the prime factorization of a given number.

Lesson Preparation

Materials
- **Power Up H** (in *Instructional Masters*)

Optional
- **Primes and Composites poster**

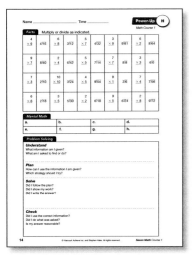

Power Up H

Math Language

New	English Learners (ESL)
composite number	stack
prime factorization	
factor tree	

Technology Resources

Student eBook Complete student textbook in electronic format.

Resources and Planner CD Assessment, reteaching, and instructional masters, plus a pacing calendar with standards.

Test and Practice Generator CD Create additional practice sheets and custom-made tests.

www.SaxonPublishers.com Visit for more student activities and planning materials.

Inclusion

Adaptations CD Adapted lessons, investigations, practice and assessments.

Meeting Standards

National Council of Teachers of Mathematics (NCTM)

Numbers and Operations

NO.1f Use factors, multiples, prime factorization, and relatively prime numbers to solve problems

Problem Solving

PS.1c Apply and adapt a variety of appropriate strategies to solve problems

Representation

RE.5b Select, apply, and translate among mathematical representations to solve problems

Problem-Solving Strategy: Use Logical Reasoning

Use the digits 6, 7, and 8 to complete this multiplication problem.

$$
\begin{array}{r}
23\_ \\
\times \underline{\quad\_} \\
\hline
166\_
\end{array}
$$

(Understand) **Understand the problem.**

"What information are we given?"

We are shown a multiplication problem that has the digits 6, 7, and 8 missing.

"What are we asked to do?"

We are asked to fill in the missing digits.

(Plan) **Make a plan.**

"How can we use the information we know to do what we are asked to do?"

We will *use number sense and logical reasoning* to find where each digit goes.

(Solve) **Carry out the plan.**

"Can we eliminate 6, 7, or 8 as a choice for the missing digit in the product?"

We know that when we multiply the last digits of the factors, the product must end in the third missing digit. We list the possible factor pairs to see which pair gives us the third digit in the ones place of the product. $6 \times 7 = 42$, $6 \times 8 = 48$, $7 \times 8 = 56$. Since 56 ends with 6 we know that the ones digits of the factors must be 7 and 8 and the product must end in 6.

"With 6 as the digit in the product, how do we determine the placement of the 7 and 8?"

We can use estimation to help us decide where to place the 7 and 8. If we estimate 8 times a number in the 230s, we get a product that is too big. Therefore, the 8 must be in the top factor and the 7 must be the bottom factor.

"What do we write for our answer?"

$$
\begin{array}{r}
23\underline{8} \\
\times \quad \underline{7} \\
\hline
166\underline{6}
\end{array}
$$

Teacher Note: Encourage students to estimate 8×230. If they are unsure, suggest that they begin by mentally multiplying 8×200 to get 1600 and then multiplying 8×3 to get 240, giving a total that is 1840.

(Check) **Look back.**

"Did we find the answer to the question that was asked?"

Yes. We placed the digits 6, 7, and 8 to create a valid multiplication problem. When we multiply 238×7, we do get 1666.

- Prime Factorization
- Division by Primes
- Factor Trees

611
613
633

facts | Power Up H

mental math
a. **Number Sense:** 5×60 300
b. **Number Sense:** $586 - 50$ 536
c. **Calculation:** 3×65 195
d. **Calculation:** $\$20.00 - \$2.50$ $17.50
e. **Number Sense:** Double 75¢. $1.50
f. **Number Sense:** $\frac{\$75}{100}$ $0.75
g. **Primes and Composites:** Name the prime numbers between 10 and 20.   11, 13, 17, and 19
h. **Calculation:** $9 \times 9, - 1, \div 2, + 2, \div 6, + 3, \div 10$ 1

problem solving
Use the digits 6, 7, and 8 to complete this multiplication problem:

$$\begin{array}{r} 23\_ \\ \times \underline{} \\ \hline 166\_ \end{array} \qquad \begin{array}{r} 238 \\ \times 7 \\ \hline 1666 \end{array}$$

New Concepts   Increasing Knowledge

prime factorization

Every whole number greater than 1 is either a prime number or a **composite number.** A prime number has *only two* factors (1 and itself), while a composite number has *more than two* factors. As we studied in Lesson 19, the numbers 2, 3, 5, and 7 are prime numbers. The numbers 4, 6, 8, and 9 are composite numbers. All composite numbers can be formed by multiplying prime numbers together.

Thinking Skill

List

What are all the factors of 4, 6, 8, and 9?
4: 1, 2, 4;
6: 1, 2, 3, 6;
8: 1, 2, 4, 8;
9: 1, 3, 9

$$4 = 2 \cdot 2$$
$$6 = 2 \cdot 3$$
$$8 = 2 \cdot 2 \cdot 2$$
$$9 = 3 \cdot 3$$

When we write a composite number as a product of its prime factors, we have written the **prime factorization** of the number. The prime factorizations of 4, 6, 8, and 9 are shown above. Notice that if we had written 8 as $2 \cdot 4$ instead of $2 \cdot 2 \cdot 2$, we would not have completed the prime factorization of 8. Since the number 4 is not prime, we would complete prime factorization by "breaking" 4 into its prime factors of 2 and 2.

Lesson 65   337

1 Power Up

Facts
Distribute **Power Up H** to students. See answers below.

Mental Math
Before students begin the Mental Math exercise, do this counting exercise as a class.

Count by 9s from 9 to 108.

Encourage students to share different ways to mentally compute these exercises. Strategies for exercises **a** and **e** are listed below.

a. **Use a Multiplication Fact**
$5 \times 6 = 30$, so $5 \times 60 = 300$
Count on by 50
$5 \times 60 = 6 \times 50$, so start with 50. Count: 100, 150, 200, 250, 300

e. **Double the Place Values**
Double 70¢ = 140¢ and double 5¢ = 10¢;
140¢ + 10¢ = 150¢ or $1.50
Change 75¢ to Quarters
3 quarters $\times$ 2 = 6 quarters;
6 quarters = $1.50

Problem Solving
Refer to **Power-Up Discussion,** p. 337B.

2 New Concepts

Instruction
You may wish to display the **Primes and Composites** concept poster as you discuss this topic with students.

Ask students to name all of the factors of 4, 6, 8, and 9. As students name the factors, write them in order from least to greatest on the board or overhead:

Number	Factors
4	1, 2, 4
6	1, 2, 3, 6
8	1, 2, 4, 8
9	1, 3, 9

"What kind of number has more than two factors?" a composite number

(continued)

Facts   Multiply or divide as indicated.

$\begin{array}{r}4\\\times 9\\\hline 36\end{array}$	$4\overline{)16}$	$\begin{array}{r}6\\\times 8\\\hline 48\end{array}$	$3\overline{)12}$	$\begin{array}{r}5\\\times 7\\\hline 35\end{array}$	$4\overline{)32}$	$\begin{array}{r}3\\\times 9\\\hline 27\end{array}$	$9\overline{)81}$	$\begin{array}{r}6\\\times 2\\\hline 12\end{array}$	$8\overline{)64}$
$\begin{array}{r}9\\\times 7\\\hline 63\end{array}$	$8\overline{)40}$	$\begin{array}{r}2\\\times 4\\\hline 8\end{array}$	$6\overline{)42}$	$\begin{array}{r}5\\\times 5\\\hline 25\end{array}$	$7\overline{)14}$	$\begin{array}{r}7\\\times 7\\\hline 49\end{array}$	$8\overline{)8}$	$\begin{array}{r}3\\\times 3\\\hline 9\end{array}$	$6\overline{)0}$
$\begin{array}{r}7\\\times 3\\\hline 21\end{array}$	$2\overline{)10}$	$\begin{array}{r}10\\\times 10\\\hline 100\end{array}$	$3\overline{)24}$	$\begin{array}{r}4\\\times 5\\\hline 20\end{array}$	$9\overline{)54}$	$\begin{array}{r}9\\\times 1\\\hline 9\end{array}$	$3\overline{)6}$	$\begin{array}{r}7\\\times 4\\\hline 28\end{array}$	$7\overline{)56}$
$\begin{array}{r}6\\\times 6\\\hline 36\end{array}$	$2\overline{)18}$	$\begin{array}{r}3\\\times 5\\\hline 15\end{array}$	$5\overline{)30}$	$\begin{array}{r}2\\\times 2\\\hline 4\end{array}$	$6\overline{)18}$	$\begin{array}{r}9\\\times 5\\\hline 45\end{array}$	$6\overline{)24}$	$\begin{array}{r}2\\\times 8\\\hline 16\end{array}$	$9\overline{)72}$

Instruction

To help students identify the smallest prime number, the next-smallest prime number, and so on when they divide by primes, list the first four prime numbers 2, 3, 5, and 7 on the board or overhead.

Make sure students recognize that in any prime factorization,
- the prime factors are listed in order from least to greatest, and
- a prime factor can appear more than once.

Example 1
Instruction

Some students may not immediately understand the change from dividing by 2 to dividing by 3. To clarify ask,

"Why does the division by primes change from dividing by 2 to dividing by 3?" Both 36 and 18 are divisible by 2. Since 9 is not prime, we go to the next prime number, 3.

(continued)

---

division by primes

In this lesson we will show two methods for factoring a composite number, **division by primes** and **factor trees.** We will use both methods to factor the number 60.

To factor a number using division by primes, we write the number in a division box and begin dividing by the smallest prime number that is a factor. The smallest prime number is 2. Since 60 is divisible by 2, we divide 60 by 2 to get 30.

$$2\overline{)60} \atop 30$$

Since 30 is also divisible by 2, we divide 30 by 2. The quotient is 15. Notice how we "stack" the divisions.

$$\begin{array}{r} 15 \\ 2\overline{)30} \\ 2\overline{)60} \end{array}$$

Although 15 is not divisible by 2, it is divisible by the next-smallest prime number, which is 3. Fifteen divided by 3 produces the quotient 5.

$$\begin{array}{r} 5 \\ 3\overline{)15} \\ 2\overline{)30} \\ 2\overline{)60} \end{array}$$

Five is a prime number. The only prime number that divides 5 is 5.

$$\begin{array}{r} 1 \\ 5\overline{)5} \\ 3\overline{)15} \\ 2\overline{)30} \\ 2\overline{)60} \end{array}$$

By dividing by prime numbers, we have found the prime factorization of 60.

$$60 = 2 \cdot 2 \cdot 3 \cdot 5$$

Example 1

Use division by primes to find the prime factorization of 36.

Solution

We begin by dividing 36 by its smallest prime-number factor, which is 2. We continue dividing by prime numbers until the quotient is 1.[1]

$$\begin{array}{r} 1 \\ 3\overline{)3} \\ 3\overline{)9} \\ 2\overline{)18} \\ 2\overline{)36} \end{array}$$

$$36 = 2 \cdot 2 \cdot 3 \cdot 3$$

---

[1] Some people prefer to divide only until the quotient is a prime number. When using that procedure, the final quotient is included in the prime factorization of the number.

338　*Saxon Math Course 1*

Math Background

When numbers are expressed as the product of factors, the result is a factorization.

Each composite number has more than one factorization. For example, 3 × 8 and 2 × 3 × 4 are each factorizations of 24.

However, each composite number has one and only one prime factorization.

English Learners

Recreate the prime factorization for 60 using division by primes on the board. Explain what it means to **stack** the divisions. Say,

"When we use division by primes to find the prime factorization of a number, we stack the divisions or place them one on top of the other."

Ask a volunteer to give another example of something you might stack. (books, chairs, papers)

factor trees | To make a factor tree for 60, we simply think of any two whole numbers whose product is 60. Since 6 × 10 equals 60, we can use 6 and 10 as the first two "branches" of the factor tree.

The numbers 6 and 10 are not prime numbers, so we continue the process by factoring 6 into 2 · 3 and by factoring 10 into 2 · 5.

The circled numbers at the ends of the branches are all prime numbers. We have completed the factor tree. We will arrange the factors in order from least to greatest and write the prime factorization of 60.

$$60 = 2 \cdot 2 \cdot 3 \cdot 5$$

Example 2

Use a factor tree to find the prime factorization of 60. Use 4 and 15 as the first branches.

Solution

Thinking Skill

Connect

What other whole number pairs could we use as the first two branches of a factor tree for 60?
2 and 30; 3 and 20; 5 and 12; 6 and 10

Some composite numbers can be divided into many different factor trees. However, when the factor tree is completed, the same prime numbers appear at the ends of the branches.

$$60 = 2 \cdot 2 \cdot 3 \cdot 5$$

Practice Set

c. Sample:

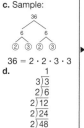

$36 = 2 \cdot 2 \cdot 3 \cdot 3$

d.
$$\begin{array}{r} 1 \\ 3\overline{)3} \\ 2\overline{)6} \\ 2\overline{)12} \\ 2\overline{)24} \\ 2\overline{)48} \end{array}$$
$48 = 2 \cdot 2 \cdot 2 \cdot 2 \cdot 3$

a. **Classify** Which of these numbers are composite numbers? 20, 21, 22
19, 20, 21, 22, 23

b. Write the prime factorization of each composite number in problem a. $20 = 2 \cdot 2 \cdot 5$; $21 = 3 \cdot 7$; $22 = 2 \cdot 11$

c. **Represent** Use a factor tree to find the prime factorization of 36.

d. Use division by primes to find the prime factorization of 48.

e. Write 125 as a product of prime factors. $125 = 5 \cdot 5 \cdot 5$

▶ See Math Conversations in the sidebar.

---

2 New Concepts (Continued)

Instruction

Point out that the order of the factors in a factor tree is not important because the factors will be written in order from least to greatest after the prime factorization of the tree is complete.

Have students note that in the factor tree for 60, the order of any of the factors could be reversed and the prime factorization would remain the same.

Example 2

Instruction

On the board or overhead, have students help you demonstrate how other factors of 60, such as 2 and 30, and 3 and 20, can be used as the first branches of a factor tree.

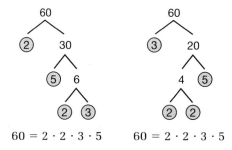

$$60 = 2 \cdot 2 \cdot 3 \cdot 5 \qquad 60 = 2 \cdot 2 \cdot 3 \cdot 5$$

Practice Set

Problem a **Classify**

"How many factors does a composite number have?" more than two

Problem c **Represent**

"Once your factor tree is complete, and you write the prime factorization of 36, how should you arrange the prime factors?" from least to greatest

(continued)

Inclusion

To factor a number using division by primes, write the number in a division box, and begin dividing by the smallest prime number that is a factor. Teach students to try dividing by the prime numbers 2, 3, or 5 first. Continue dividing until the quotient is 1. The divisors are the prime factors of the number.

Example: Factor 420 into prime factors using division by primes.

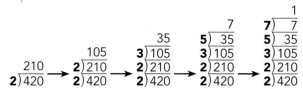

The divisors are the prime factors.

$$420 = 2 \cdot 2 \cdot 3 \cdot 5 \cdot 7$$

2 New Concepts (Continued)

Practice Set
Problem f *Generalize*
"After you write the prime factorization of any number, how can you check your answer?" Sample: Find the product of the prime factors and compare it to the number that was factored.

3 Written Practice

Math Conversations
Discussion opportunities are provided below.

Problem 4 *Represent*
"When you write a prime factorization of a number, what kind of factors do you write?" only prime factors

"In a prime factorization, can the same prime factor appear more than once?" yes

Problem 5 *Classify*
"How is a composite number different from a prime number?" Sample: A composite number has more than two factors. A prime number has exactly two factors.

Problem 17 *Connect*
Extend the Problem
Encourage students to describe a variety of ways to find the number of quarters in $20 using mental math. Sample: Multiply the number of quarters in one dollar by 20; $4 \times 20 = 80$

Errors and Misconceptions
Problem 7
Answers of $\frac{4}{10}$ or $\frac{2}{5}$ represent finding the probability of a red outcome. Review the concept of the complement of a probability event with students who answer $\frac{4}{10}$ or $\frac{2}{5}$, then ask those students to read and solve the problem again.

If necessary, remind students that the sum of the probability of an event, and the probability of the complement of that event, is 1.

(continued)

---

f. *Generalize* Write the prime factorization of 10, 100, 1000, and 10,000. What patterns do you see in the prime factorizations of these numbers? The number of 2s and 5s in the prime factorization increase by one as the powers of 10 increase.

Written Practice   *Strengthening Concepts*

1. The total land area of the world is about fifty-seven million, five hundred
   (12) six thousand square miles. Use digits to write that number of square miles. 57,506,000 square miles

2. The African white rhinoceros can reach a height of about $5\frac{1}{2}$ feet. How
   (15) many inches is $5\frac{1}{2}$ feet? 66 inches

3. Jenny shot 10 free throws and made 6. What fraction of her shots did
   (29, 42) she make? What percent of her shots did she make? $\frac{3}{5}$; 60%

4. Sample:

   $40 = 2 \cdot 2 \cdot 2 \cdot 5$

* 4. *Represent* Make a factor tree for 40. Then write the prime factorization
   (65) of 40.

* 5. *Classify* Which of these numbers is a composite number? A
   (65)
   A 21   **B** 31   **C** 41

* 6. Write $2\frac{2}{3}$ as an improper fraction. Then multiply the improper fraction
   (62) by $\frac{3}{8}$. What is the product? $\frac{8}{3} \cdot \frac{3}{8} = 1$

7. Four of the ten marbles in the bag are red. If one marble is drawn from
   (58) the bag, what ratio expresses the probability that the marble will not be red? $\frac{3}{5}$

* 8. $8\frac{1}{2} + 1\frac{1}{3} + 2\frac{1}{6}$ 12   * 9. $\frac{1}{12} + \frac{1}{6} + \frac{1}{2}$ $\frac{3}{4}$
   (61)   (61)

Find each unknown number:

10. $15\frac{3}{4} - m = 2\frac{1}{8}$ $13\frac{5}{8}$ 11. $\frac{4}{25} = \frac{n}{100}$ 16
   (43)   (42)

12. $12w = 0.0144$ 0.0012   13. $\frac{3}{8} \times \frac{1}{3} = y$ $\frac{1}{8}$
   (45)   (29)

14. Compare: $\frac{1}{2} - \frac{1}{3} \ominus \frac{2}{3} - \frac{1}{2}$
   (56)

15. $1 - (0.2 + 0.48)$ 0.32
   (38)

16. $12.96; Two dozen is 24. The price is 50¢ each, which is half a dollar each. So 24 erasers cost $12. 12 times 8¢ is 96¢. Add $12 and 96¢ and get $12.96.

16. *Explain* What is the total cost of two dozen erasers that are priced
   (15, 41) at 50¢ each if 8% sales tax is added? Describe a way to perform the calculation mentally.

17. *Connect* The store manager put $20.00 worth of quarters in the
   (15) change drawer. How many quarters are in $20.00? 80 quarters

* 18. A pyramid with a square base has how many
   (Inv. 6)
   a. faces? 5 faces
   b. edges? 8 edges
   c. vertices? 5 vertices

▶ See Math Conversations in the sidebar.

19.

$$
\begin{array}{r}
1 \\
5\overline{)5} \\
5\overline{)25} \\
2\overline{)50}
\end{array}
$$

$$50 = 2 \cdot 5 \cdot 5$$

* 19. Use division by primes to find the prime factorization of 50.
(65)

➤* 20. **Connect** What is the name of a six-sided polygon? How many vertices
(60) does it have? hexagon; 6 vertices

* 21. Write $3\frac{4}{7}$ as an improper fraction. $\frac{25}{7}$
(62)

22. The area of a square is 36 square inches.
(38)
   a. What is the length of each side? 6 inches

   b. What is the perimeter of the square? 24 inches

23. Write 16% as a reduced fraction. $\frac{4}{25}$
(33)

24. How many millimeters long is the line segment below? 50 mm
(7)

25. **Estimate** A meter is about $1\frac{1}{10}$ yards. About how many meters long is
(7) an automobile? about 4 meters or 3 m

* 26. Write the prime factorization of 375 and of 1000. What method did
(65) you use? $375 = 3 \cdot 5 \cdot 5 \cdot 5$; $1000 = 2 \cdot 2 \cdot 2 \cdot 5 \cdot 5 \cdot 5$; See student work.

27. Reduce: $\dfrac{3 \cdot 5 \cdot 5 \cdot 5}{2 \cdot 2 \cdot 2 \cdot 5 \cdot 5 \cdot 5}$ $\frac{3}{8}$
(54)

28. 94 feet; The radius is 15 ft, so the diameter is 30 ft. π is a little more than 3, and 3 times 30 ft is 90 ft, so 94 ft is reasonable.

➤ 28. **Estimate** The radius of the carousel is 15 feet. If the carousel turns
(47) around once, a person riding on the outer edge will travel how far?
Round the answer to the nearest foot. (Use 3.14 for π.) Describe how to
mentally check whether the answer is reasonable.

29. Eighty percent of the 20 answers were correct. How many answers were
(29, 33) correct? 16 answers

30. **Verify** The prefix "rect-" in rectangle means "right." A rectangle is a
(54) "right-angle" shape. Why is every square also a rectangle? Sample: A
rectangle is a four-sided polygon with four right angles. Since every square
is four-sided with four right angles, every square is a rectangle. (A rectangle
need not be longer than it is wide.)

➤ See Math Conversations in the sidebar.

---

3 **Written Practice** *(Continued)*

Math Conversations
Discussion opportunities are provided below.

Problem 20 **Connect**
"What are vertices of polygons?" points
where two sides of the polygon meet, or
intersect

Problem 28 **Estimate**
Extend the Problem
Challenge students to solve the following
related problem, and then explain how they
found the answer.

***"How far from the center of the carousel is
a person who travels about 50 feet in one
turn?"*** about 8 feet

Looking Forward
Expressing a composite number
as the product of prime factors
prepares students for:

- **Lesson 67,** using prime
factorization to reduce fractions.

- **Lesson 73,** writing the prime
factorization of composite
numbers with exponents.

Assessment   30–40 minutes   *For use after Lesson 65*

Distribute **Cumulative Test 12** to each student. Two versions of the test are available in *Saxon Math Course 1 Course Assessments Book*. Have students complete the **Power-Up Test** first. Allow 10 minutes. Then have students work the 20 numbered items on the **Cumulative Test.** Students may use copies of the answer sheet to record their work. Track individual and class progress with the **Test Analysis** forms.

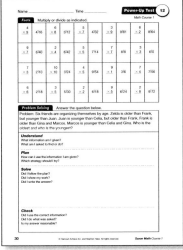

Power-Up Test 12

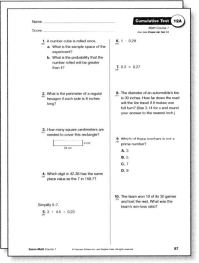

Cumulative Test 12A

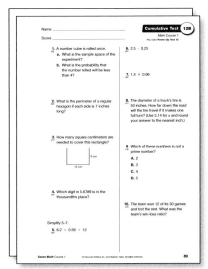

Alternative Cumulative Test 12B

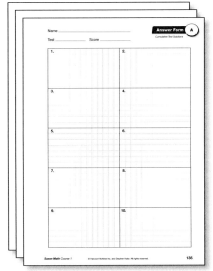

Optional Answer Forms

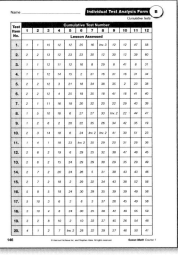

Individual Test Analysis Form

Class Test Analysis Form

Reteaching

Students who score below 80% on the assessment may be in need of reteaching. Look for the causes of student mistakes. If errors are conceptual, refer to the *Reteaching Masters* for reteaching.

Representing Fractions, Decimals and Percents
Assign after Lesson 65 and Test 12

Objectives
- Represent 10 equal parts of a whole.
- Label parts of wholes with fractions, decimals, and percents.
- Use fractions, decimals, and percents to describe a part of a whole.
- Communicate ideas through writing.

Materials
Performance Activity 12
Blank paper that is at least 5" long (One each per student.)

Preparation
Make copies of **Performance Activity 12.** (One each per student.)

Time Requirement
15–30 minutes; Begin in class and complete at home.

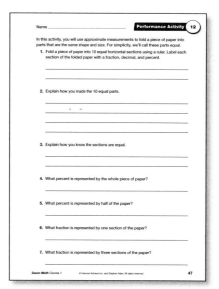

Performance Activity 12

Activity
Explain to students that for this activity they will fold pieces of paper into ten equal parts using a ruler. They will label each section with a fraction, decimal, and percent. They will use fractions, decimals, and percents to describe different parts of the whole pieces of paper. They will be required to explain how they folded the pieces of paper into ten equal parts and how they know the parts are equal. Explain that all of the information students need is on **Performance Activity 12.**

Criteria for Evidence of Learning
- Folds a piece of paper into ten equal parts accurately and labels each part correctly with a fraction, decimal, and percent.
- Uses fractions, decimals, and percents to accurately describe a part of the whole piece of paper.
- Communicates ideas clearly through writing.

Meeting Standards

National Council of Teachers of Mathematics (NCTM)

Numbers and Operations

NO.1a Work flexibly with fractions, decimals, and percents to solve problems

Geometry

GM.4c Use visual tools such as networks to represent and solve problems

Connections

CN.4b Understand how mathematical ideas interconnect and build on one another to produce a coherent whole

● Multiplying Mixed Numbers

Objectives

- Multiply a mixed number by a whole number.
- Multiply a mixed number by a mixed number.

Lesson Preparation

Materials

- **Power Up J** (in *Instructional Masters*)
- **Teacher-provided material:** grid paper

Power Up Test J

Math Language

Maintain	English Learners (ESL)
terms	fabric

Technology Resources

Student eBook Complete student textbook in electronic format.

Resources and Planner CD Assessment, reteaching, and instructional masters, plus a pacing calendar with standards.

Test and Practice Generator CD Create additional practice sheets and custom-made tests.

www.SaxonPublishers.com Visit for more student activities and planning materials.

Inclusion

Adaptations CD Adapted lessons, investigations, practice and assessments.

Meeting Standards

National Council of Teachers of Mathematics (NCTM)

Numbers and Operations

NO.1a Work flexibly with fractions, decimals, and percents to solve problems

NO.3a Select appropriate methods and tools for computing with fractions and decimals from among mental computation, estimation, calculators or computers, and paper and pencil, depending on the situation, and apply the selected methods

Problem Solving

PS.1b Solve problems that arise in mathematics and in other contexts

Representation

RE.5b Select, apply, and translate among mathematical representations to solve problems

Problem-Solving Strategy: Work Backwards/ Write an Equation

In this figure a square and a regular pentagon share a common side. The area of the square is 25 square centimeters. What is the perimeter of the pentagon?

Understand **Understand the problem.**

"What information are we given?"

We are shown a picture of a square and a regular pentagon that share a side in common. We are told the area of the square is 25 square centimeters.

"What are we asked to do?"

Find the perimeter of the pentagon.

Plan **Make a plan.**

"What problem solving-strategy will we use?"

We will *work backwards* from the information we have about the square, and then *write an equation* to solve for the perimeter of the pentagon.

Solve **Carry out the plan.**

"How do we begin?"

To find the side length we use the formula for area of a square, $A = s^2$, where s is the side length. If the area of the square in the picture is 25 square centimeters, then each side of the square is 5 centimeters long.

"How do we find the perimeter of the pentagon?"

One side of the square is also one side of the pentagon. We are told the pentagon is a regular pentagon, so we know its 5 sides are equal lengths. We multiply 5 centimeters by the number of sides and get 25 centimeters.

$$5 \times 5 \text{ cm} = 25 \text{ cm}$$

Check **Look back.**

"Did we answer the question that was asked?"

Yes. We found the perimeter of the pentagon in the diagram.

• Multiplying Mixed Numbers

Facts
Distribute **Power Up J** to students. See answers below.

Mental Math
Before students begin the Mental Math exercise, do this counting exercise as a class.

Count up and down by $\frac{1}{8}$s between $\frac{1}{8}$ and 2.

Encourage students to share different ways to mentally compute these exercises. Strategies for exercises **c** and **d** are listed below.

c. Multiply Tens and Multiply Ones
$(8 \times 20) + (8 \times 3) = 160 + 24 = 184$
Multiply by 25, then Subtract 8 × 2
$8 \times 25 = 200; 200 - 16 = 184$

d. Add 25¢ and Subtract 25¢
$1.75 + \$0.25 = \$2.00$ and
$1.75 - \$0.25 = \$1.50;$
$2.00 + \$1.50 = \$3.50$
Add 25¢ and Add 25¢, then Subtract 50¢
$2.00 + \$2.00 = \$4.00;$
$4.00 - \$0.50 = \$3.50$

Problem Solving
Refer to **Power-Up Discussion,** p. 342B.

Instruction
Remind students that the acronym SOS can be used to represent the three steps. Then review Step 1 with them.

"To write a whole number as an improper fraction, we write the number as the numerator of a fraction that has a denominator of 1. Such as $10 = \frac{10}{1}$. Can this method be used to change any whole number to an improper fraction?" yes

"How can we change a mixed number such as $5\frac{2}{3}$ to an improper fraction?"
Sample: Write 3 as the denominator, then add 2 to the product of 5 and 3 and write the result as the numerator.

"What improper fraction is equivalent to $5\frac{2}{3}$?" $\frac{17}{3}$

(continued)

---

facts	Power Up J
mental math	**a. Number Sense:** 5×160 800
	b. Number Sense: $376 + 99$ 475
	c. Calculation: 8×23 184
	d. Calculation: $\$1.75 + \$1.75$ \$3.50
	e. Fractional Parts: $\frac{1}{3}$ of \$60.00 \$20.00
	f. Number Sense: $\frac{\$30}{10}$ \$3.00
	g. Measurement: Which is greater, 5 years or a decade? a decade
	h. Calculation: $8 \times 8, -4, \div 2, +3, \div 3, +1, \div 6, \div 2$ 1

problem solving	In this figure a square and a regular pentagon share a common side. The area of the square is 25 square centimeters. What is the perimeter of the pentagon? 25 cm

Recall from Lesson 57 the three steps to solving an arithmetic problem with fractions.

Thinking Skill

Verify

How do we write a mixed number as a fraction? We multiply the denominator by the whole number and add the numerator. We write that sum as the numerator over the denominator.

Step 1: Put the problem into the correct shape (if it is not already).

Step 2: Perform the operation indicated.

Step 3: Simplify the answer if possible.

Remember that putting fractions into the correct shape for adding and subtracting means writing the fractions with common denominators. To multiply or divide fractions, we do not need to use common denominators. However, we must write the fractions in **fraction form.** This means we will write mixed numbers and whole numbers as improper fractions. We write a whole number as an improper fraction by making the whole number the numerator of a fraction with a denominator of 1.

Example 1

A length of fabric was cut into 4 equal sections. Each of 4 students received $2\frac{2}{3}$ yd of fabric. How much fabric was there before it was cut?

Facts	Write each mixed number as an improper fraction.

$2\frac{1}{2} = \frac{5}{2}$	$2\frac{2}{5} = \frac{12}{5}$	$1\frac{3}{4} = \frac{7}{4}$	$2\frac{3}{4} = \frac{11}{4}$	$2\frac{1}{8} = \frac{17}{8}$
$1\frac{2}{3} = \frac{5}{3}$	$3\frac{1}{2} = \frac{7}{2}$	$1\frac{5}{6} = \frac{11}{6}$	$2\frac{1}{4} = \frac{9}{4}$	$1\frac{1}{8} = \frac{9}{8}$
$5\frac{1}{2} = \frac{11}{2}$	$1\frac{3}{8} = \frac{11}{8}$	$5\frac{1}{3} = \frac{16}{3}$	$3\frac{1}{4} = \frac{13}{4}$	$4\frac{1}{2} = \frac{9}{2}$
$1\frac{7}{8} = \frac{15}{8}$	$2\frac{2}{3} = \frac{8}{3}$	$1\frac{5}{8} = \frac{13}{8}$	$3\frac{3}{4} = \frac{15}{4}$	$7\frac{1}{2} = \frac{15}{2}$

Solution

This is an equal groups problem. To find the original length of the fabric we multiply $2\frac{2}{3}$ yd by 4. First, we write $2\frac{2}{3}$ and 4 in fraction form.

$$\frac{8}{3} \times \frac{4}{1}$$

Second, we multiply the numerators to find the numerator of the product, and we multiply the denominators to find the denominator of the product.

$$\frac{8}{3} \times \frac{4}{1} = \frac{32}{3}$$

Third, we simplify the product by converting the improper fraction to a mixed number.

$$\frac{32}{3} = 10\frac{2}{3}$$

Before the fabric was cut it was $\mathbf{10\frac{2}{3}}$ **yd** long.

Evaluate How can we use estimation to check whether our answer is reasonable?   Round $2\frac{2}{3}$ to 3 and multiply by 4. $3 \times 4 = 12$. $10\frac{2}{3}$ is close to 12, so it is a reasonable answer.

Example 2

Multiply: $2\frac{1}{2} \times 1\frac{1}{3}$

Solution

First, we write the numbers in fraction form.

$$\frac{5}{2} \times \frac{4}{3}$$

Reading Math
Recall that the **terms** of a fraction are the numerator and the denominator.

Second, we multiply the terms of the fractions.

$$\frac{5}{2} \times \frac{4}{3} = \frac{20}{6}$$

Third, we simplify the product.

$$\frac{20}{6} = 3\frac{2}{6} = \mathbf{3\frac{1}{3}}$$

Sketching a rectangle on a grid is a way to check the reasonableness of a product of mixed numbers. To illustrate the product of $2\frac{1}{2}$ and $3\frac{1}{2}$, we use a grid that is at least 3 by 4 so that a $2\frac{1}{2}$ by $3\frac{1}{2}$ rectangle fits on the grid.

We sketch the rectangle and estimate the area. There are 6 full squares, 5 half squares, and a quarter square. Since 2 half squares equal a whole square, the area is about $8\frac{3}{4}$ square units.

Instruction

Remind students of the importance of checking their work, and explain that estimation is a good way to check the products of factors that are mixed numbers. Then demonstrate the three methods described below on the board or overhead.

One way to use estimation is to round one or both factors to the nearest whole number. Then multiply and compare the estimate to the exact answer. For example, an estimate of the answer in example 1 is 12, because $2\frac{2}{3}$ rounds to 3 and $3 \times 4 = 12$.

A second way to use estimation is to round each factor down and multiply, then round each factor up and multiply, to find the range in which the exact answer must be found. For example, an estimate of the exact answer in example 2 is between 2 and 6, because $2 \times 1 = 2$ and $3 \times 2 = 6$.

A third way to use estimation to check an exact answer is to let the mixed numbers represent the length and width of a rectangle. Then use a grid to estimate the area of that rectangle as shown in the grid below example 2 in the student book.

Ask students to use the third method to check the reasonableness of the products in examples 1 and 2.

Example 1   Example 2

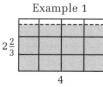

Area is a little more than 10. Answer is reasonable.

Area is about 3. Answer is reasonable.

(continued)

English Learners

Refer students to example 1 and explain the meaning of the word **fabric.** Say,

> *"Fabric is another word for material or cloth. Fabric is cut and sewn to make many items we use daily."*

Ask volunteers to give an example of something made from fabric.

Practice Set
Problems a–i [Error Alert]
Ask students to check each exact product using one of the estimation methods described below.
- Round one or both factors to the nearest whole number.
- Round each factor down and round each factor up and use multiplication to find a range of correct answers.
- Use a grid.

For each problem, students should use the estimate to decide the reasonableness of the answer.

Problem k [Formulate]
Invite students to exchange word problems, then solve the problems and compare answers.

Math Conversations
Discussion opportunities are provided below.

Problem 17 [Represent]
"When we find the prime factors of a composite number, are we finding numbers that are bigger than the composite number, or smaller?" smaller

"We must find the prime factorization of 30. Will the prime number 2 be a part of that factorization? Explain why or why not."
Yes; 2 is a factor of 30 (or 30 is a multiple of 2) and 2 is a prime number.

Errors and Misconceptions
Problem 2b
To find the probability that a girl's name will be chosen, students must first find the number of girls in the class. The number of girls is found using subtraction, and the numbers to subtract are found elsewhere in the problem.

When expressing the probability of any event as a fraction, remind students to always express the fraction in lowest terms.

Problems 8–12
To complete problems **8–10**, students must use common denominators. Watch for students who mistakenly use common denominators to complete problems **11** and **12**.

(continued)

Practice Set ▶ Multiply:

j. e.

$2\frac{2}{3}$

$2\frac{1}{2}$

Area is more than 0 and near 7.

h.

2

$2\frac{3}{4}$

Area is more than 5 but less than 6.

a. $1\frac{1}{2} \times \frac{2}{3}$ 1

b. $1\frac{2}{3} \times \frac{3}{4}$ $1\frac{1}{4}$

c. $1\frac{1}{2} \times 1\frac{2}{3}$ $2\frac{1}{2}$

d. $1\frac{2}{3} \times 3$ 5

e. $2\frac{1}{2} \times 2\frac{2}{3}$ $6\frac{2}{3}$

f. $3 \times 1\frac{3}{4}$ $5\frac{1}{4}$

g. $3\frac{1}{3} \times 1\frac{2}{3}$ $5\frac{5}{9}$

h. $2\frac{3}{4} \times 2$ $5\frac{1}{2}$

i. $2 \times 3\frac{1}{2}$ 7

j. Check the reasonableness of the products in **e** and **h** by sketching rectangles on a grid.

k. [Formulate] Write and solve a word problem about multiplying a whole number and a mixed number. See student work.

Written Practice   Strengthening Concepts

1. Fifty percent of the 60 questions on the test are multiple choice. Find the number of multiple-choice questions on the test. 30 questions
(29, 33)

2. [Analyze] Twelve of the 30 students in the class are boys.
(58)
   a. What is the ratio of boys to girls in the class? $\frac{2}{3}$

   ▶ **b.** If each student's name is placed in a hat and one name is drawn, what is the probability that it will be the name of a girl? $\frac{3}{5}$

3. [Analyze] Some railroad rails weigh 155 pounds per yard. How much would a 33-foot-long rail weigh? 1705 pounds
(15)

* 4. $1\frac{1}{2} \times 2\frac{2}{3}$ 4   *** 5.** $2\frac{2}{3} \times 2$ $5\frac{1}{3}$
(66)   (66)

6. The sum of five numbers is 200. What is the average of the numbers? 40
(18)

7. $\frac{100 + 75}{100 - 75}$ 7   ▶ **8.** $1\frac{1}{5} + 3\frac{1}{2}$ $4\frac{7}{10}$ ▶ *** 9.** $\frac{1}{3} + \frac{1}{6} + \frac{1}{12}$ $\frac{7}{12}$
(5)   (59)   (61)

▶*** 10.** $35\frac{1}{4} - 12\frac{1}{2}$ $22\frac{3}{4}$ ▶ **11.** $\frac{4}{5} \times \frac{1}{2}$ $\frac{2}{5}$ ▶ **12.** $\frac{4}{5} \div \frac{1}{2}$ $1\frac{3}{5}$
(63)   (29)   (54)

13. $0.25 \div 5$ 0.05   **14.** $5 \div 0.25$ 20
(45)   (49)

15. What is the product of the answers to problems 13 and 14? 1
(39)

16. [Verify] Which of the following is equal to $\frac{1}{2} + \frac{1}{2}$? C
(54)
   A $\frac{1}{2} - \frac{1}{2}$ **B** $\left(\frac{1}{2}\right)^2$ **C** $\frac{1}{2} \div \frac{1}{2}$

17. See student work. Sample:

$30 = 2 \cdot 3 \cdot 5$

▶*** 17.** [Represent] Use a factor tree to find the prime factorization of 30.
(65)

18. If three pencils cost a total of 75¢, how much would six pencils cost? $1.50
(15)

▶ See Math Conversations in the sidebar.

19. Seven and one half percent is equivalent to the decimal number
(41) 0.075. If the sales-tax rate is $7\frac{1}{2}$%, what is the sales tax on a $10.00 purchase? $0.75

▶* **20.** **Analyze** One side of a regular pentagon measures 0.8 meter. What is
(60) the perimeter of the regular pentagon?   4 meters

21. Twenty minutes is what fraction of an hour? $\frac{1}{3}$
(29)

22. The temperature dropped from 12°C to −8°C. This was a drop of how
(14) many degrees?   20°C

The bar graph below shows the weights of different types of cereals packaged in the same size boxes. Refer to the graph to answer problems 23–25.

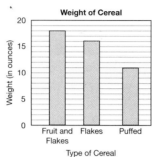

23. What is the range of the weights?   7 ounces
(Inv. 5)

24. What is the mean weight of the three types of cereal?   15 ounces
(Inv. 5)

* **25.** **Formulate** Write a comparison word problem that relates to the graph,
(13) and then answer the problem.   Sample: The flakes cereal weighs how much more than the puffed cereal?; 5 ounces

▶* **26.** **Connect** Use division by primes to find the prime factorization of 400.
(65)

27. **Analyze** Simon covered the floor of a square room with 144 square
(38) floor tiles. How many floor tiles were along each wall of the room?
12 tiles

28. **Estimate** The weight of a 1-kilogram object is about 2.2 pounds.
(46) A large man may weigh 100 kilograms. About how many pounds is that?   about 220 pounds

29. Reduce: $\frac{5 \cdot 5 \cdot 5 \cdot 7}{2 \cdot 2 \cdot 2 \cdot 5 \cdot 5 \cdot 5}$ $\frac{7}{8}$
(54)

* **30.** **Classify** Which of these polygons is not a regular polygon?   B
(60)

A   B ▭   C ⬠   D ⬡

26.
$$\begin{array}{r} 1 \\ 5\overline{)5} \\ 5\overline{)25} \\ 2\overline{)50} \\ 2\overline{)100} \\ 2\overline{)200} \\ 2\overline{)400} \end{array}$$
$400 =$
$2 \cdot 2 \cdot 2 \cdot 2 \cdot 5 \cdot 5$

▶ See Math Conversations in the sidebar.

Math Conversations
Discussion opportunities are provided below.

Problem 20   Analyze
"How many sides does a pentagon have?" 5

"What does it mean if a pentagon is regular?" All of its sides are the same length and all of its angles are the same measure.

Problem 26   Connect
With the student's help, create a list on the board or overhead of factor pairs that can be used to create the first branch of the tree. Possible factor pairs include 2 × 200, 4 × 100, 5 × 80, 8 × 50, 10 × 40, 16 × 25, and 20 × 20.

Lead students to generalize that choosing a factor pair such as 20 × 20 will create a more "balanced" tree than choosing a factor pair such as 2 × 200.

Looking Forward

Multiplying a mixed number and a whole number or two mixed numbers prepares students for:

- **Lesson 68,** dividing mixed numbers by a whole number or a mixed number.
- **Lesson 70,** reducing fractions before multiplying.
- **Lesson 72,** using a fractions chart to recall the steps for multiplying or dividing fractions and multiplying three fractions.
- **Lesson 92,** simplifying powers of fractions.
- **Lesson 94,** writing fractions and decimals as percents.

• Using Prime Factorization to Reduce Fractions

Objectives
• Use prime factorization to reduce fractions.

Lesson Preparation

Materials
• **Power Up J** (in *Instructional Masters*)

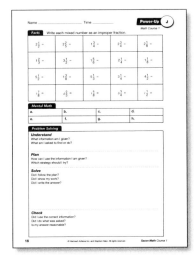

Power Up Test J

Math Language

Maintain	English Learners (ESL)
reduce	collage

Technology Resources

Student eBook Complete student textbook in electronic format.

Resources and Planner CD Assessment, reteaching, and instructional masters, plus a pacing calendar with standards.

Test and Practice Generator CD Create additional practice sheets and custom-made tests.

www.SaxonPublishers.com Visit for more student activities and planning materials.

Inclusion

Adaptations CD Adapted lessons, investigations, practice and assessments.

Meeting Standards

National Council of Teachers of Mathematics (NCTM)

Numbers and Operations

NO.1a Work flexibly with fractions, decimals, and percents to solve problems

NO.1f Use factors, multiples, prime factorization, and relatively prime numbers to solve problems

Problem Solving

PS.1c Apply and adapt a variety of appropriate strategies to solve problems

Representation

RE.5b Select, apply, and translate among mathematical representations to solve problems

Problem-Solving Strategies: Use Logical Reasoning

Copy this problem and fill in the missing digits.

$$\begin{array}{r} \underline{}\,\underline{} \\ \times \qquad 7 \\ \hline 999{,}999 \end{array}$$

(Understand) *Understand the problem.*

"What information are we given?"

We are shown a multiplication problem with six missing digits in the multiplicand.

"What are we asked to do?"

Fill in the missing digits.

(Plan) *Make a plan.*

"What problem-solving strategy will we use?"

We could *use logical reasoning* and number sense to find the missing digits.

"Is there anything we know about missing factors that can make the task easier?"

If we know the product and one factor, we can find the missing factor by dividing.

(Solve) *Carry out the plan.*

"What numbers do we divide?"

We divide 999,999 by 7.

$$\begin{array}{r} 142{,}857 \\ 7\overline{)999{,}999} \end{array}$$

"How do we show the solution to the problem?"

$$\begin{array}{r} 142{,}857 \\ \times \qquad 7 \\ \hline 999{,}999 \end{array}$$

(Check) *Look back.*

"Did we complete the task?"

yes

"How can we check our answer?"

We can perform the multiplication to be sure the product is 999,999.

• Using Prime Factorization to Reduce Fractions

Facts

Distribute **Power Up J** to students. See answers below.

Mental Math

Before students begin the Mental Math exercise, do this counting exercise as a class.

Count down by 2s from 10 to negative 10.

Encourage students to share different ways to mentally compute these exercises. Strategies for exercises **b** and **d** are listed below.

  b. Change 341 to 340, then Add 1
     340 − 50 = 290; 290 + 1 = 291
  Change 341 to 350, then Subtract 9
     350 − 50 = 300; 300 − 9 = 291
  d. Subtract $1, then Add 25¢
     $9.25 − $1 = $8.25; $8.25 + 25¢ = $8.50
  Subtract 25¢ from Each Number
     $9.00 − 50¢ = $8.50

Problem Solving

Refer to **Power-Up Discussion,** p. 346B.

Instruction

A generalization students should make about factoring the terms of fractions is that a goal of the factoring is to identify common factors that are equivalent to 1.

Explain that the first step to complete when reducing fractions with large terms is to factor the numerator and factor the denominator. The factoring can be accomplished by making a factor tree or division by primes.

> **"Why is a 5 in the numerator and a 5 in the denominator changed to a 1 in the numerator and a 1 in the denominator?"**
> The factor pairs are equivalent to 1 over 1.

Example

Instruction

Ask students to describe how a calculator can be used to check the answer $\frac{3}{8}$. Divide 375 by 1000 and divide 3 by 8 to learn the decimal equivalent of each fraction, then compare. If the decimal equivalents are the same, the assumption can be made that the answer is correct.

(continued)

---

facts | Power Up J

mental math

  a. Number Sense: 5×260 1300
  b. Number Sense: $341 - 50$ 291
  c. Calculation: 3×48 144
  d. Calculation: $9.25 - 75¢$ $8.50
  e. Number Sense: Double $1.25. $2.50
  f. Number Sense: $\frac{\$30}{100}$ $0.30
  g. Measurement: Which is greater, 3 yards or 5 feet? 3 yd
  h. Calculation: $6 \times 6, -1, \div 5, \times 2, +1, \div 3, \div 2$ $2\frac{1}{2}$

problem solving

Copy this problem and fill in the missing digits:

$$\begin{array}{r} \text{\_\_\_,\_\_\_} \\ \times \quad\quad 7 \\ \hline 999,999 \end{array} \qquad \begin{array}{r} 142,857 \\ \times \quad\quad 7 \\ \hline 999,999 \end{array}$$

New Concept *Increasing Knowledge*

Thinking Skill

Explain

What are two strategies for finding the prime factorization of a number?
division by primes, factor trees

One way to **reduce** fractions with large terms is to factor the terms and then reduce the common factors. To reduce $\frac{125}{1000}$, we could begin by writing the prime factorizations of 125 and 1000.

$$\frac{125}{1000} = \frac{5 \cdot 5 \cdot 5}{2 \cdot 2 \cdot 2 \cdot 5 \cdot 5 \cdot 5}$$

We see three pairs of 5s that can be reduced. Each $\frac{5}{5}$ reduces to $\frac{1}{1}$.

$$\frac{\overset{1}{\cancel{5}} \cdot \overset{1}{\cancel{5}} \cdot \overset{1}{\cancel{5}}}{2 \cdot 2 \cdot 2 \cdot \underset{1}{\cancel{5}} \cdot \underset{1}{\cancel{5}} \cdot \underset{1}{\cancel{5}}} = \frac{1}{8}$$

We multiply the remaining factors and find that $\frac{125}{1000}$ reduces to $\frac{1}{8}$.

Example

Reduce: $\dfrac{375}{1000}$

Thinking Skill

Discuss

When is it helpful to use prime factorization to reduce a fraction? If the terms are large or if the GCF is not obvious.

Solution

We write the prime factorization of both the numerator and the denominator.

$$\frac{375}{1000} = \frac{3 \cdot 5 \cdot 5 \cdot 5}{2 \cdot 2 \cdot 2 \cdot 5 \cdot 5 \cdot 5} = \frac{3 \cdot \overset{1}{\cancel{5}} \cdot \overset{1}{\cancel{5}} \cdot \overset{1}{\cancel{5}}}{2 \cdot 2 \cdot 2 \cdot \underset{1}{\cancel{5}} \cdot \underset{1}{\cancel{5}} \cdot \underset{1}{\cancel{5}}} = \frac{3}{8}$$

Then we reduce the common factors and multiply the remaining factors.

Facts Write each mixed number as an improper fraction.

$2\frac{1}{2} = \frac{5}{2}$	$2\frac{2}{5} = \frac{12}{5}$	$1\frac{3}{4} = \frac{7}{4}$	$2\frac{3}{4} = \frac{11}{4}$	$2\frac{1}{8} = \frac{17}{8}$
$1\frac{2}{3} = \frac{5}{3}$	$3\frac{1}{2} = \frac{7}{2}$	$1\frac{5}{6} = \frac{11}{6}$	$2\frac{1}{4} = \frac{9}{4}$	$1\frac{1}{8} = \frac{9}{8}$
$5\frac{1}{2} = \frac{11}{2}$	$1\frac{3}{8} = \frac{11}{8}$	$5\frac{1}{3} = \frac{16}{3}$	$3\frac{1}{4} = \frac{13}{4}$	$4\frac{1}{2} = \frac{9}{2}$
$1\frac{7}{8} = \frac{15}{8}$	$2\frac{2}{3} = \frac{8}{3}$	$1\frac{5}{8} = \frac{13}{8}$	$3\frac{3}{4} = \frac{15}{4}$	$7\frac{1}{2} = \frac{15}{2}$

Practice Set ▸ Write the prime factorization of both the numerator and the denominator of each fraction. Then reduce each fraction.

a. $\dfrac{875}{1000}$ $\dfrac{5 \cdot 5 \cdot 5 \cdot 7}{2 \cdot 2 \cdot 2 \cdot 5 \cdot 5 \cdot 5} = \dfrac{7}{8}$ b. $\dfrac{48}{400}$ $\dfrac{2 \cdot 2 \cdot 2 \cdot 2 \cdot 3}{2 \cdot 2 \cdot 2 \cdot 2 \cdot 5 \cdot 5} = \dfrac{3}{25}$

c. $\dfrac{125}{500}$ $\dfrac{5 \cdot 5 \cdot 5}{2 \cdot 2 \cdot 5 \cdot 5 \cdot 5} = \dfrac{1}{4}$ d. $\dfrac{36}{81}$ $\dfrac{2 \cdot 2 \cdot 3 \cdot 3}{3 \cdot 3 \cdot 3 \cdot 3} = \dfrac{4}{9}$

Written Practice   *Strengthening Concepts*

* 1. Allison is making a large collage of a beach scene. She needs 2 yards of
(66) blue ribbon for the ocean, $\frac{1}{2}$ yard of yellow ribbon for the sun, and $\frac{3}{4}$ yard of green ribbon for the grass. Ribbon costs $2 a yard. How much money will Allison need for ribbon? $6.50

2. **Estimate** A mile is 5280 feet. A nautical mile is about 6080 feet. A
(13) nautical mile is about how much longer than a mile? about 800 feet

3. **Verify** Instead of dividing $1.50 by $0.05, Marcus formed an
(43) equivalent division problem by mentally multiplying both the dividend and the divisor by 100. Then he performed the equivalent division problem. What is the equivalent division problem Marcus formed, and what is the quotient? $150 ÷ $5 = 30 (not $30.00 or 30¢)

Find each unknown number:

4. 6 cm + k = 11 cm 5 cm   **5.** 8g = 9.6 1.2
(3)   (43)

6. $\dfrac{7}{10} - w = \dfrac{1}{2}$ $\frac{1}{5}$ **7.** $\dfrac{3}{5} = \dfrac{n}{100}$ 60
(43)   (42)

* 8. The perimeter of a quadrilateral is 172 inches. What is the average
(60, 64) length of each side? Can we know for certain what type of quadrilateral this is? Why or why not?

8. 43 inches; No; There is not enough given information to know the type of quadrilateral. Many combinations of four side lengths total 172 inches and can form a quadrilateral.

9. $100.00 − ($46.75 + $9.68)   **10.** (2 × 0.3) − (0.2 × 0.3) 0.54
(5) $43.57   (53)

▸*** 11.** **Analyze** $4\dfrac{1}{4} - 2\dfrac{7}{8}$ $1\frac{3}{8}$ ▸*** 12.** **Analyze** $2\dfrac{2}{3} \times \sqrt{9}$ 8
(63)   (38, 66)

13. $3\dfrac{1}{3} + 2\dfrac{3}{4}$ $6\frac{1}{12}$ *** 14.** $1\dfrac{1}{3} \times 2\dfrac{1}{4}$ 3
(59)   (66)

15. 1.44 ÷ 60 0.024   **16.** $6.00 ÷ $0.15 40
(45)   (49)

17. Five dollars was divided evenly among 4 people. How much money did
(15) each receive? $1.25

▸ See Math Conversations in the sidebar.

---

2 New Concepts (Continued)

Practice Set
Problems a–d [Error Alert]
To give students practice finding prime factorizations using different methods, have them divide by primes for problems a and c and make factor trees for problems b and d.

3 Written Practice

Math Conversations
Discussion opportunities are provided below.

Problem 11 [Analyze]
"Before you can subtract mixed numbers whose fraction parts have unlike denominators, what must you do?" Choose a common denominator and rename one or both fractions using that denominator.

"What is the least common denominator of 4 and 8?" 8

Problem 12 [Analyze]
"How is the Order of Operations used to simplify this expression?" The Order of Operations states that the square root of 9 must be simplified before the factors are multiplied.

(continued)

Math Background

Factoring the terms of a fraction, then identifying common factors that are equivalent to 1, produces the same reduced fraction as dividing the numerator and the denominator of a fraction by their greatest common factor (GCF).

For example, students are shown in this lesson how factoring is used to reduce $\frac{125}{1000}$ to its simplest form of $\frac{1}{8}$. The same result can be achieved by dividing $\frac{125}{1000}$ by $\frac{125}{125}$, because 125 is the GCF of 125 and 1000.

In their future studies of polynomials and other algebraic expressions, students will frequently factor out the GCF of a variety of terms.

Math Conversations

Discussion opportunities are provided below.

Problem 23 Analyze

"What is the product of any number and its reciprocal?" 1

"If the missing number is the reciprocal of $1\frac{1}{2}$, will the product of the factors be 1?" yes

"What should we do to the mixed number $1\frac{1}{2}$ to help find its reciprocal?" change it to an improper fraction

Problem 26 Estimate

Extend the Problem

"Explain how to estimate the number of hours it would take the minute hand to travel one mile." Sample: 38 inches is about 1 yard, and there are 1760 yards in 1 mile, so it takes the minute hand about 1760 hours to travel a mile.

Point out that 1760 hours is about 73 days.

Problem 29 Represent

"How many faces does a number cube have?" six

"How many dots are on the faces of the cube that you cannot see?" two, four, and six

Errors and Misconceptions

Problem 18 Conclude

If the word "regular" is overlooked, there is not enough information remaining in the problem to solve it successfully.

The following questions can be used to help students identify the figure as a square.

"Some polygons are regular, and some are not. What is a regular polygon?" All of the sides of the polygon have the same length and all of the angles of the polygon have the same measure.

"A quadrilateral has 4 sides. What kind of quadrilateral is a regular quadrilateral?" a square

---

▶ **18.** Conclude The area of a regular quadrilateral is 100 square inches. What
(60) is its perimeter? What is the name of the quadrilateral? 40 inches; square

* **19.** Write the prime factorizations of 625 and of 1000. Then
(67) reduce $\frac{625}{1000}$. $\frac{5 \cdot 5 \cdot 5 \cdot 5}{2 \cdot 2 \cdot 2 \cdot 5 \cdot 5 \cdot 5} = \frac{5}{8}$

* **20.** What is the area of the rectangle shown below? $1\frac{1}{8}$ in.²
(31, 66)

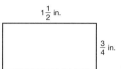

21. Thirty-six of the 88 piano keys are black. What fraction of the piano
(29) keys are black? $\frac{9}{22}$

22. Sample:

* **22.** Represent Draw a rectangular prism. Begin by drawing two congruent
(Inv. 6) rectangles.

▶* **23.** Analyze $1\frac{1}{2} \times \square = 1\frac{2}{3}$
(30, 62)

24. There are 1000 meters in a kilometer. How many meters are in
(15) 2.5 kilometers? 2500 meters

25. Connect Which arrow could be pointing to 0.1 on the number line? C
(50)

▶ **26.** Estimate If the tip of the minute hand is 6 inches from the center of the
(47) clock, how far does the tip travel in one hour? Round the answer to the nearest inch. (Use 3.14 for π.) 38 inches

27. Connect A basketball is an example of what geometric solid? sphere
(Inv. 6)

28. Write 51% as a fraction. Then write the fraction as a decimal
(33, 35) number. $\frac{51}{100}$; 0.51

▶* **29.** Represent What is the probability of rolling
(19, 58) a prime number with one toss of a number cube? The probability of rolling a 2, 3, or 5 is $\frac{1}{2}$.

* **30.** Conclude This quadrilateral has one pair
(64) of parallel sides. What kind of quadrilateral is it? trapezoid

▶ See Math Conversations in the sidebar.

English Learners

Refer students to problem 1. Write the word *collage* on the board. Say,

"A collage is a collection of things such as paper, ribbon, and pictures glued to a flat surface."

Ask a student to list items they might include in a collage of a beach scene.

Looking Forward

Using prime factorization to reduce fractions prepares students for:

• **Lesson 68,** dividing mixed numbers.

• **Lesson 70,** dividing fractions by reducing fraction terms before multiplying.

• **Lesson 72,** using a fractions chart to recall operations with fractions and reducing fractions.

• **Lesson 75,** reducing fractions when writing fractions as percents.

• Dividing Mixed Numbers

Objectives

- Divide a mixed number by a whole number.
- Divide a mixed number by a mixed number.

Lesson Preparation

Materials

- **Power Up I** (in *Instructional Masters*)
- **Manipulative kit: inch rulers, color tiles**

Optional
- **grid paper**

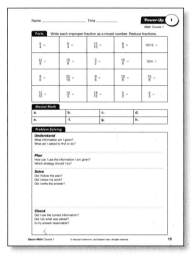

Power Up Test I

Math Language

Maintain

reciprocals

Technology Resources

Student eBook Complete student textbook in electronic format.

Resources and Planner CD Assessment, reteaching, and instructional masters, plus a pacing calendar with standards.

Test and Practice Generator CD Create additional practice sheets and custom-made tests.

www.SaxonPublishers.com Visit for more student activities and planning materials.

Inclusion

Adaptations CD Adapted lessons, investigations, practice and assessments.

Meeting Standards

National Council of Teachers of Mathematics (NCTM)

Numbers and Operations

NO.1a Work flexibly with fractions, decimals, and percents to solve problems

NO.2a Understand the meaning and effects of arithmetic operations with fractions, decimals, and integers

NO.3a Select appropriate methods and tools for computing with fractions and decimals from among mental computation, estimation, calculators or computers, and paper and pencil, depending on the situation, and apply the selected methods

Representation

RE.5b Select, apply, and translate among mathematical representations to solve problems

Problem-Solving Strategies: Use Logical Reasoning

Megan has many gray socks, white socks, and black socks in a drawer. In the dark she pulled out two socks that did not match. How many more socks does Megan need to pull from the drawer to be certain to have a matching pair?

(Understand) **Understand the problem.**

"What information are we given?"

Megan pulled out two socks that do not match from a drawer that holds gray, white, and black socks in a drawer.

"What are we asked to do?"

Determine the number of socks Megan must pull from the drawer to be certain to have a matching pair.

(Plan) **Make a plan.**

"What problem-solving strategy will we use?"

We will *use logical reasoning* to solve the problem.

(Solve) **Carry out the plan.**

"If Megan pulls one more sock, will she have a matching pair?"

It is possible that Megan will pull a matching sock, but it is not certain. Megan's drawer contains three different colors of socks. So when she pulls a third sock, she might end up with one sock of each color.

"If Megan pulls a fourth sock, will she have a matching pair?"

Yes. When Megan pulls a fourth sock, she will have four socks of at most three different colors, so at least two socks are certain to match.

"How many more socks must Megan pull from the drawer?"

Megan has already pulled two socks, so she only needs to pull two more socks.

(Check) **Look back.**

"Did we find the answer to the question that was asked?"

Yes. We found how many more socks Megan needed to pull to be certain she has a matching pair.

• **Dividing Mixed Numbers**

612
613
633

Power Up   *Building Power*

facts	Power Up I
mental math	**a. Number Sense:** 5×80 400
	b. Number Sense: $275 + 1500$ 1775
	c. Calculation: 7×42 294
	d. Calculation: \$5.75 + 50¢ \$6.25
	e. Fractional Parts: $\frac{1}{4}$ of \$48.00 \$12.00
	f. Number Sense: $\frac{\$120}{10}$ \$12.00
	g. Measurement: Which is greater, 1 meter or 100 millimeters? 1 m
	h. Calculation: $7 \times 8, -1, \div 5, \times 2, -1, \div 3, -8$ −1

problem solving	Megan has many gray socks, white socks, and black socks in a drawer. In the dark she pulled out two socks that did not match. How many more socks does Megan need to pull from the drawer to be certain to have a matching pair? 2 socks

New Concept   *Increasing Knowledge*

Recall the three steps to solving an arithmetic problem with fractions.

Step 1: Put the problem into the correct shape (if it is not already).

Step 2: Perform the operation indicated.

Step 3: Simplify the answer if possible.

In this lesson we will practice dividing mixed numbers. Recall from Lesson 66 that the correct shape for multiplying and dividing fractions is fraction form. So when dividing, we first write any mixed numbers or whole numbers as improper fractions.

Example 1

Shawna is pouring $2\frac{2}{3}$ cups of plant food into equal amounts to feed 4 plants. How much plant food is there for each plant?

Lesson 68   349

Facts   Write each improper fraction as a mixed number. Reduce fractions.

$\frac{5}{4} = 1\frac{1}{4}$	$\frac{6}{4} = 1\frac{1}{2}$	$\frac{15}{10} = 1\frac{1}{2}$	$\frac{8}{3} = 2\frac{2}{3}$	$\frac{15}{12} = 1\frac{1}{4}$
$\frac{12}{8} = 1\frac{1}{2}$	$\frac{10}{8} = 1\frac{1}{4}$	$\frac{3}{2} = 1\frac{1}{2}$	$\frac{15}{6} = 2\frac{1}{2}$	$\frac{10}{4} = 2\frac{1}{2}$
$\frac{8}{6} = 1\frac{1}{3}$	$\frac{25}{10} = 2\frac{1}{2}$	$\frac{9}{6} = 1\frac{1}{2}$	$\frac{10}{6} = 1\frac{2}{3}$	$\frac{15}{8} = 1\frac{7}{8}$
$\frac{12}{10} = 1\frac{1}{5}$	$\frac{10}{3} = 3\frac{1}{3}$	$\frac{18}{12} = 1\frac{1}{2}$	$\frac{5}{2} = 2\frac{1}{2}$	$\frac{4}{3} = 1\frac{1}{3}$

---

1 Power Up

Facts
Distribute **Power Up I** to students. See answers below.

Mental Math
Before students begin the Mental Math exercise, do this counting exercise as a class.

Count down by 5s from 25 to negative 25.

Encourage students to share different ways to mentally compute these exercises. Strategies for exercises **a** and **e** are listed below.

a. Use a Multiplication Fact
   $5 \times 8 = 40$, so $5 \times 80 = 400$
Count on by 50
   $5 \times 80 = 8 \times 50$: Start with 50.
   Count: 100, 150, 200, 250, 300, 350, 400
e. Divide Place Values by 4
   $\$40 \div 4 = \$10$ and $\$8 \div 4 = \$2$;
   $\$10 + \$2 = \$12$
Find $\frac{1}{2}$ of $\frac{1}{2}$
   $\frac{1}{2}$ of \$48 = \$24 and $\frac{1}{2}$ of \$24 = \$12

Problem Solving
Refer to **Power-Up Discussion**, p. 349B.

2 New Concepts

Instruction
Using reciprocals is an important part of dividing mixed numbers. Before discussing example 1, write the terms shown below on the board or overhead and ask students to name the reciprocal of each term.

$$8 \quad \frac{1}{8} \quad \frac{2}{5} \quad \frac{5}{2} \quad \frac{a}{b} \quad \frac{b}{a}$$

"What is the product of a number and its reciprocal?" 1

(continued)

Example 1
Instruction
Have students multiply to find $\frac{1}{4}$ of $2\frac{2}{3}$. Point out that the answer, $\frac{2}{3}$, is the same as the answer to $2\frac{2}{3} \div 4$.

Example 2
Instruction
Point out that the division $2\frac{2}{3} \div 1\frac{1}{2}$ represents finding the number of $1\frac{1}{2}$s in $2\frac{2}{3}$.

After completing the solution, discuss different ways that estimation may be able to be used to check the exact answer for reasonableness. For example, since $2\frac{2}{3} \div 1\frac{1}{2}$ represents finding the number of $1\frac{1}{2}$s in $2\frac{2}{3}$, lead students to infer that the exact answer should be greater than 1 because the number of $1\frac{1}{2}$s in $2\frac{2}{3}$ is more than 1. Also, the exact answer should be less than 2 because two $1\frac{1}{2}$s make 3, and 3 is greater than $2\frac{2}{3}$.

Practice Set
Problems b and d [Error Alert]
Students must recognize that the word "of" implies multiplication, and each problem should be rewritten as the product of two factors.

Point out that $\frac{1}{4} \times 1\frac{3}{5}$ is the same as $1\frac{3}{5} \div 4$ and $\frac{1}{3} \times 2\frac{2}{5}$ is the same as $2\frac{2}{5} \div 3$.

Solution

Shawna is dividing $2\frac{2}{3}$ cups of plant food into four equal groups. We divide $2\frac{2}{3}$ by 4. We write the numbers as improper fractions.

$$\frac{8}{3} \div \frac{4}{1}$$

Math Language
Reciprocals are two numbers whose product is 1.

To divide, we find the number of 4s in 1. (That is, we find the reciprocal of 4.) Then we use the reciprocal of 4 to find the number of 4s in $\frac{8}{3}$.

$$1 \div \frac{4}{1} = \frac{1}{4}$$

$$\frac{8}{3} \times \frac{1}{4} = \frac{8}{12}$$

We simplify the answer.

$$\frac{8}{12} = \frac{2}{3}$$

There is $\frac{2}{3}$ cup of plant food for each plant. Notice that dividing a number by 4 is equivalent to finding $\frac{1}{4}$ of the number. Instead of dividing $2\frac{2}{3}$ by 4, we could have directly found $\frac{1}{4}$ of $2\frac{2}{3}$.

Example 2

Divide: $2\frac{2}{3} \div 1\frac{1}{2}$

Solution

Thinking Skill
Justify
Describe in your own words how to divide mixed numbers.
Sample:
Change the mixed numbers to improper fractions. Replace the second fraction with its reciprocal and multiply.

We write the mixed numbers as improper fractions.

$$\frac{8}{3} \div \frac{3}{2}$$

To divide, we find the number of $\frac{3}{2}$s in 1. (That is, we find the reciprocal of $\frac{3}{2}$.) Then we use the reciprocal of $\frac{3}{2}$ to find the number of $\frac{3}{2}$s in $\frac{8}{3}$.

$$1 \div \frac{3}{2} = \frac{2}{3}$$

$$\frac{8}{3} \times \frac{2}{3} = \frac{16}{9}$$

We simplify the improper fraction $\frac{16}{9}$ as shown below.

$$\frac{16}{9} = 1\frac{7}{9}$$

Practice Set

Find each product or quotient:

a. $1\frac{3}{5} \div 4$ $\frac{2}{5}$

▶ **b.** $\frac{1}{4}$ of $1\frac{3}{5}$ $\frac{2}{5}$

c. $2\frac{2}{5} \div 3$ $\frac{4}{5}$

▶ **d.** $\frac{1}{3}$ of $2\frac{2}{5}$ $\frac{4}{5}$

e. *Generalize* Why is dividing by 4 the same as multiplying by $\frac{1}{4}$?   Sample: Both operations divide the whole amount into fourths.

▶ See Math Conversations in the sidebar.

Math Background

When dividing fractions, a common misconception is that dividing by $\frac{1}{2}$ is the same as dividing by 2.

A simple way to show that dividing by $\frac{1}{2}$ is different than dividing by 2 is to apply those operations to a counting number greater than 1. For example:

- Dividing 6 by 2 is the same as finding the number of 2s in 6, and the answer is 3.

- Dividing 6 by $\frac{1}{2}$ is the same as finding the number of $\frac{1}{2}$s in 6, and the answer is 12.

Fraction manipulatives can also be used to show that $6 \div 2$ is different than $6 \div \frac{1}{2}$.

f. $1\frac{2}{3} \div 2\frac{1}{2}$ $\frac{2}{3}$

g. $2\frac{1}{2} \div 1\frac{2}{3}$ $1\frac{1}{2}$

h. $1\frac{1}{2} \div 1\frac{1}{2}$ 1

i. $7 \div 1\frac{3}{4}$ 4

j. Gabriel has $2\frac{1}{4}$ hours to finish three projects. If he divides his time equally, what fraction of an hour can he spend on each project? $\frac{3}{4}$ hour

Written Practice   *Strengthening Concepts*

1. What is the difference between the sum of $\frac{1}{2}$ and $\frac{1}{4}$ and the product of $\frac{1}{2}$
(12, 55) and $\frac{1}{4}$? $\frac{5}{8}$

2. Bill ran a half mile in two minutes fifty-five seconds. How many seconds
(15) is that?   175 seconds

3. The gauge of a railroad—the distance between the two tracks—is
(15) usually 4 feet $8\frac{1}{2}$ inches. How many inches is that? $56\frac{1}{2}$ inches

▶ *** 4.** $1\frac{1}{2} \div 2\frac{2}{3}$ $\frac{9}{16}$
(68)

▶ *** 5.** $1\frac{1}{3} \div 4$ $\frac{1}{3}$
(68)

6. In six games Yvonne scored a total of 108 points. How many points
(18) per game did she average?   18 points per game

7.
$\frac{2 \cdot 2 \cdot 2 \cdot 3}{2 \cdot 2 \cdot 2 \cdot 5 \cdot 5} = \frac{3}{25}$

* 7. Write the prime factorizations of 24 and 200. Then reduce $\frac{24}{200}$.
(67)

Find each unknown number:

* 8. $m - 5\frac{3}{8} = 1\frac{3}{16}$ $6\frac{9}{16}$
(59)

9. $3\frac{3}{5} + 2\frac{7}{10} = n$ $6\frac{3}{10}$
(59)

10. $25d = 0.375$ 0.015
(45)

11. $\frac{3}{4} = \frac{w}{100}$ 75
(42)

* 12. $5\frac{1}{8} - 1\frac{1}{2}$ $3\frac{5}{8}$
(63)

* 13. $3\frac{1}{3} \times 1\frac{1}{2}$ 5
(66)

* 14. $3\frac{1}{3} \div 1\frac{1}{2}$ $2\frac{2}{9}$
(68)

15. What is the area of a rectangle that is 4 inches long and $1\frac{3}{4}$ inches
(31, 66) wide?   7 square inches

16. $(3.2 + 1) - (0.6 \times 7)$ 0
(53)

17. $12.5 \div 0.4$ 31.25
(49)

▶ *** 18.** *Analyze*   The product 3.2×10 equals which of the following?   **B**
(52)
   A $32 \div 10$ **B** $320 \div 10$ **C** $0.32 \div 10$

19. *Estimate*   Find the sum of 6416, 5734, and 4912 to the nearest
(16) thousand.   17,000

20. *Verify*   Instead of dividing 800 by 24, Arturo formed an equivalent
(43) division problem by dividing both the dividend and the divisor by 8.
   Then he quickly found the quotient of the equivalent problem. What is
   the equivalent problem Arturo formed, and what is the quotient? Write
   the quotient as a mixed number. $100 \div 3 = 33\frac{1}{3}$

Lesson 68   351

▶ See Math Conversations in the sidebar.

Math Conversations

Discussion opportunities are provided below.

Problem 23 [Analyze]

Extend the Problem

"Does one chance in a million mean that for every million tickets sold, there will be one winner? Explain why or why not." No; a one in a million chance means there are one million possible outcomes. For the number of tickets sold, there may be zero winners, one winner, or more than one winner.

Problem 25 [Analyze]

Write $6 \div 3$ and $\frac{6}{1} \times \frac{1}{3}$ on the board or overhead.

"How does the quotient of 6 ÷ 3 compare to the product of 6 × $\frac{1}{3}$? Use mental math to decide." The quotients are the same.

Write $6 \div 3 = 2$ and $6 \times \frac{1}{3} = 2$. Lead students to generalize that dividing a number by 3 produces the same result as multiplying that number by $\frac{1}{3}$. Then challenge students to use mental math to complete problem 25.

Early Finishers

Students may choose to use tiles or grid paper. Explain that the congruent sections must be different shapes for a new configuration to be acceptable. A vertical line dividing the grid into four 1 by 4 sections is considered to be the same as a horizontal line dividing the grid into four 4 by 1 sections.

---

21. The perimeter of a square is 2.4 meters.
(38)
    a. How long is each side of the square? 0.6 meter

    b. What is the area of the square? 0.36 square meter

22. What is the tax on an $18,000 car if the tax rate is 8%? $1440
(41)

▶ **23.** [Analyze] If the probability of an event occurring is 1 chance in a million,
(58) then what is the probability of the event not occurring? $\frac{999,999}{1,000,000}$

24. [Classify] Why is a circle not a polygon? Polygons have straight sides.
(60) Since a circle is curved, it is not a polygon.

▶* **25.** [Analyze] Compare: $\frac{1}{3} \times 4\frac{1}{2}$  $4\frac{1}{2} \div 3$
(66, 68)

26. [Estimate] Use a ruler to find the length of this line segment to the
(17) nearest eighth of an inch. $1\frac{7}{8}$ in.
_____

27. [Conclude] Which angle in this figure is an obtuse angle? ∠WMX or
(28) ∠XMW

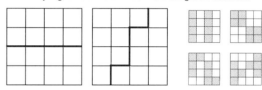

28. Write 3% as a fraction. Then write the fraction as a decimal
(33, 35) number. $\frac{3}{100}$; 0.03

29. [Connect] A shoe box is an example of what geometric solid?
(Inv. 6) rectangular prism

30. Sunrise occurred at 6:20 a.m., and sunset occurred at 5:45 p.m.
(32) How many hours and minutes were there from sunrise to sunset?
11 hr 25 min

Early Finishers
Choose A Strategy

Each 4 by 4 grid below is divided into 2 congruent sections.

Find four ways to divide a 4 by 4 grid into 4 congruent sections.
Act It Out or Draw a Picture
Accept any answer that meets the criteria.

▶ See Math Conversations in the sidebar.

Looking Forward

Dividing a mixed number by a whole number or a mixed number prepares students for:

- **Lesson 70,** dividing fractions by reducing fraction terms before multiplying.

- **Lesson 72,** using a fractions chart to recall the steps for dividing fractions.

- **Lesson 115,** converting mixed number percents to fractions.

• Lengths of Segments
• Complementary and Supplementary Angles

Objectives

- Write an equation showing that the length of a segment is equal to the sum of the lengths of its parts and solve the equation for the missing length.
- Identify complementary and supplementary angles.
- Name and find the measure of the complement of an angle.
- Name and find the measure of the supplement of an angle.

Lesson Preparation

Materials

- **Power Up J** (in *Instructional Masters*)

Optional
- **Manipulative kit:** inch rulers
- **Teacher-provided material:** dot or grid paper

Power Up Test J

Math Language

New	English Learners (ESL)
complementary angles	appear
supplementary angles	

Technology Resources

Student eBook Complete student textbook in electronic format.

Resources and Planner CD Assessment, reteaching, and instructional masters, plus a pacing calendar with standards.

Test and Practice Generator CD Create additional practice sheets and custom-made tests.

www.SaxonPublishers.com Visit for more student activities and planning materials.

Inclusion

Adaptations CD Adapted lessons, investigations, practice and assessments.

Meeting Standards

National Council of Teachers of Mathematics (NCTM)

Geometry

GM.1a Precisely describe, classify, and understand relationships among types of two- and three-dimensional objects using their defining properties

GM.4d Use geometric models to represent and explain numerical and algebraic relationships

Measurement

ME.2b Select and apply techniques and tools to accurately find length, area, volume, and angle measures to appropriate levels of precision

Connections

CN.4a Recognize and use connections among mathematical ideas

Problem-Solving Strategies: Use Logical Reasoning/ Write an Equation

Nathan used a one-yard length of string to form a rectangle that was twice as long as it was wide. What was the area that was enclosed by the string?

(Understand) **Understand the problem.**

"What information are we given?"

Nathan formed a rectangle from one yard of string. The length of the rectangle was twice the width of the rectangle.

"What are we asked to do?"

Determine the area of the rectangle formed by the string.

(Plan) **Make a plan.**

"What problem-solving strategy will we use?"

We will use *logical reasoning* to help us determine the length and the width, and then *write an equation* to find the area.

(Solve) **Carry out the plan.**

"What do we need to know to find the area of a rectangle?"

We will need to know the length and width of the rectangle in order to find its area. In order to do that we can convert the yard to inches.

"If the perimeter is 36 inches, then what do we know about the sum of the length and width of the rectangle?"

The length plus the width will be half of 36 or 18 inches.

"If the length plus the width is 18 inches, how can we determine each dimension?"

We are told that the length is twice the width. We can use logical reasoning to figure out that for every three units of measurement, one unit will be width and two units will be length. 18 can be divided into three groups of 6, so the width is one group of 6 inches, and the length is two groups of 6, or 12 inches.

"What is the area of the rectangle enclosed by Nathan's string?"

12 inches $\times$ 6 inches = 72 square inches

(Check) **Look back.**

"Did we complete the task?"

Yes. We found the area of the rectangle enclosed by Nathan's string (72 square inches).

"Does the answer make sense?"

Yes. We said that the length of the rectangle is 12 inches and the width is 6 inches. We know that the perimeter is $2l + 2w$. So, $2 \times 12 + 2 \times 6 = 24 + 12 = 36$. The perimeter is 36 in. or 1 yard and that is the length of string that Nathan used.

- **Lengths of Segments**
- **Complementary and Supplementary Angles**

621
624
625

Building Power

facts	Power Up J
mental math	**a. Number Sense:** 5×180 900
	b. Number Sense: $530 - 50$ 480
	c. Calculation: 6×44 264
	d. Calculation: $\$6.00 - \$1.75$ 4.25
	e. Number Sense: Double $1.75. 3.50
	f. Number Sense: $\frac{\$120}{100}$ 1.20
	g. Measurement: Which is greater, 36 inches or 1 yard? equal
	h. Calculation: $6 \times 5, + 2, \div 4, \times 3, \div 4, - 2, \div 2, \div 2$ 1

problem solving	Nathan used a one-yard length of string to form a rectangle that was twice as long as it was wide. What was the area that was enclosed by the string? 72 in.^{2} or $\frac{1}{2}$ ft^2

New Concepts Increasing Knowledge

lengths of segments

Reading Math
We can use symbols to designate lines, rays, and segments:
$\overleftrightarrow{AB}$ = line AB
$\overrightarrow{AB}$ = ray AB
$\overline{AB}$ = segment AB

Letters are often used to designate points. Recall that we may use two points to identify a line, a ray, or a segment. Below we show a line that passes through points A and B. This line may be referred to as line AB or line BA. We may abbreviate line AB as $\overleftrightarrow{AB}$.

The ray that begins at point A and passes through point B is ray AB, which may be abbreviated $\overrightarrow{AB}$. The portion of line AB between and including points A and B is segment AB (or segment BA), which can be abbreviated $\overline{AB}$ (or $\overline{BA}$).

In the figure below we can identify three segments: $\overline{WX}$, $\overline{XY}$, and $\overline{WY}$. The length of $\overline{WX}$ plus the length of $\overline{XY}$ equals the length of $\overline{WY}$.

Lesson 69   353

---

1 Power Up

Facts
Distribute **Power Up J** to students. See answers below.

Mental Math
Before students begin the Mental Math exercise, do this counting exercise as a class.

Count up and down by $\frac{1}{4}$s between $\frac{1}{4}$ and 4.

Encourage students to share different ways to mentally compute these exercises. Strategies for exercises **c** and **e** are listed below.

c. Multiply Place Values
$6 \times 40 = 240$ and $6 \times 4 = 24$;
$240 + 24 = 264$
Multiply 6 × 50, then Subtract 6 × 6
$6(50) = 300, 300 - 36 = 264$
e. Double Place Values
Double $1 is $2 and double 75¢ is $1.50;
$2 + \$1.50 = \$3.50$
Double $2, then Subtract Double 25¢
Double $2 is $4 and double 25¢ is 50¢;
$4 - \$0.50 = \$3.50$

Problem Solving
Refer to **Power-Up Discussion,** p. 353B.

2 New Concepts

Instruction
Copy line *AB* on the board or overhead exactly as shown in the text.

"This is line AB." Write $\overleftrightarrow{AB}$.

Erase everything to the left of point *A*.

"This is ray AB." Write $\overrightarrow{AB}$.

Erase everything to the right of Point *B*.

"This is line segment AB." Write $\overline{AB}$.

(continued)

Facts   Write each mixed number as an improper fraction.

$2\frac{1}{2} = \frac{5}{2}$	$2\frac{2}{5} = \frac{12}{5}$	$1\frac{3}{4} = \frac{7}{4}$	$2\frac{3}{4} = \frac{11}{4}$	$2\frac{1}{8} = \frac{17}{8}$
$1\frac{2}{3} = \frac{5}{3}$	$3\frac{1}{2} = \frac{7}{2}$	$1\frac{5}{6} = \frac{11}{6}$	$2\frac{1}{4} = \frac{9}{4}$	$1\frac{1}{8} = \frac{9}{8}$
$5\frac{1}{2} = \frac{11}{2}$	$1\frac{3}{8} = \frac{11}{8}$	$5\frac{1}{3} = \frac{16}{3}$	$3\frac{1}{4} = \frac{13}{4}$	$4\frac{1}{2} = \frac{9}{2}$
$1\frac{7}{8} = \frac{15}{8}$	$2\frac{2}{3} = \frac{8}{3}$	$1\frac{5}{8} = \frac{13}{8}$	$3\frac{3}{4} = \frac{15}{4}$	$7\frac{1}{2} = \frac{15}{2}$

Example 1

Instruction

Throughout this lesson, make sure that students can correctly read and interpret the various symbols that are included in a figure's name. For example,

$\overline{LN}$ is read "line segment LN" and L and N each represent a different point on that line segment.

Instruction

Students will learn in Lesson 98 that the sum of the interior angles of any triangle is 180°. Since the largest angle of a right triangle is 90°, the two other angles of a right triangle are always acute angles and are always complementary angles.

Example 2

Instruction

It may be easier for students to recognize the supplement and the complement of $\angle RWS$ if you first draw the figure on the board or overhead, then shade $\angle RWS$.

When finding the supplement of $\angle RWS$, students should remember that a straight line can be formed by two angles that are supplementary.

When finding the complement of $\angle RWS$, students should remember that a right or 90° angle can be formed by two angles that are complementary.

(continued)

In this figure the length of $\overline{LM}$ is 4 cm, and the length of $\overline{LN}$ is 9 cm. What is the length of $\overline{MN}$?

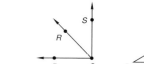

Solution

The length of $\overline{LM}$ plus the length of $\overline{MN}$ equals the length of $\overline{LN}$. With the information in the problem, we can write the equation shown below, where the letter *l* stands for the unknown length:

$$4\text{ cm} + l = 9\text{ cm}$$

Since 4 cm plus 5 cm equals 9 cm, we find that the length of $\overline{MN}$ is **5 cm**.

complementary and supplementary angles

Complementary angles are two angles whose measures total 90°. In the figure on the left below, $\angle PQR$ and $\angle RQS$ are complementary angles. In the figure on the right, $\angle A$ and $\angle B$ are complementary angles.

Thinking Skill

Verify

Can an angle that is complementary be an obtuse angle? Explain. No. The measure of an obtuse angle is between 90° and 180°. The sum of complementary angles is exactly 90°.

We say that $\angle A$ is the complement of $\angle B$ and that $\angle B$ is the complement of $\angle A$.

Supplementary angles are two angles whose measures total 180°. Below, $\angle 1$ and $\angle 2$ are supplementary, and $\angle A$ and $\angle B$ are supplementary. So $\angle A$ is the supplement of $\angle B$, and $\angle B$ is the supplement of $\angle A$.

Example 2

In the figure at right, $\angle RWT$ is a right angle.

  a. Which angle is the supplement of $\angle RWS$?

  b. Which angle is the complement of $\angle RWS$?

Solution

  a. Supplementary angles total 180°. Angle *QWS* is 180° because it forms a line. So the angle that is the supplement of $\angle RWS$ is $\angle QWR$ (or $\angle RWQ$).

  b. Complementary angles total 90°. Angle *RWT* is 90° because it is a right angle. So the complement of $\angle RWS$ is $\angle SWT$ (or $\angle TWS$).

Math Background

A number of different pairs of angles can be supplementary angles. For example, since the sum of the measures of two supplementary angles is 180°, an acute angle and an obtuse angle may be supplementary angles, or two right angles may be supplementary angles.

However, two acute angles cannot be supplementary angles because the sum of their measures is less than 180°, and two obtuse angles cannot be supplementary angles because the sum of their measures is greater than 180°.

Practice Set

a. In this figure the length of $\overline{AC}$ is 60 mm and the length of $\overline{BC}$ is 26 mm. Find the length of $\overline{AB}$. **34 mm**

b. The complement of a 60° angle is an angle that measures how many degrees? **30°**

c. The supplement of a 60° angle is an angle that measures how many degrees? **120°**

d. No. Supplementary angles total 180°, but acute angles have measures less than 90°. Two angles with measures less than 90° cannot total 180°.

d. **Conclude** If two angles are supplementary, can they both be acute? Why or why not?

e. Name two angles in the figure at right that appear to be supplementary. $\angle 1$ and $\angle 2$

f. Name two angles that appear to be complementary. $\angle 2$ and $\angle 3$

► See Math Conversations in the sidebar.

Written Practice   *Strengthening Concepts*

1.

► *1. **Model** Draw a pair of parallel lines. Then draw a second pair of parallel
(28, 64) lines that are perpendicular to the first pair. Trace the quadrilateral that is formed by the intersecting pairs of lines. What kind of quadrilateral did you trace? **rectangle**

► 2. **Connect** What is the quotient if the dividend is $\frac{1}{2}$ and the divisor is $\frac{1}{8}$? **4**
(54)

3. The highest weather temperature recorded was 136°F in Africa. The
(14) lowest was −129°F in Antarctica. How many degrees difference is there between these temperatures? **265°F**

► 4. **Estimate** A dollar bill is about 6 inches long. Placed end to end, about
(15) how many **feet** would 1000 dollar bills reach? **about 500 feet**

*5. Write the prime factorization of both the numerator and the denominator
(67) of this fraction. Then reduce the fraction. $\frac{3 \cdot 3 \cdot 5}{2 \cdot 2 \cdot 2 \cdot 3 \cdot 3} = \frac{5}{8}$

$$\frac{45}{72}$$

► *6. **Conclude** In quadrilateral *QRST*, which segment appears to be
(64) parallel to $\overline{RS}$? $\overline{QT}$ or $\overline{TQ}$

7. In 10 days Juana saved $27.50. On average, how much did she save
(13) per day? **$2.75 per day**

Lesson 69   355

Lesson 69   **355**

Math Conversations

Discussion opportunities are provided below.

Problem 18 [Explain]

"What is a counting number?" Sample: Any whole number greater than zero.

"What is a composite number?" Sample: Any counting number that has more than two factors.

Problem 19 [Represent]

With the student's help, create a list on the board or overhead of factors pairs that can be used to create the first branch of the tree. Possible factor pairs include 2×125, 5×50, and 10×25.

"After our factor tree is complete, how do we arrange the factors when we write the prime factorization of 250?" The factors are written in order from least to greatest.

"In a prime factorization, can a factor appear more than once?" yes

Problem 26 [Connect]

"What equation can we use to solve for the length of line segment WY? Use l for length. Explain your answer." Sample: $l = 53 \text{ mm} + 35 \text{ mm}$; the whole is divided into two parts, and because both parts are given, addition is used to find the whole.

Errors and Misconceptions
Problem 16

Remind students that mixed numbers need to be put in the correct "shape" for multiplying by writing each mixed number as an improper fraction. Also remind students to convert the product to a mixed number and simplify if possible.

(continued)

---

* **8.** $\frac{1 \times 2 \times 3 \times 4 \times 5}{1 + 2 + 3 + 4 + 5}$ 8
(5)

9. $3\frac{1}{2} + 2\frac{3}{4} + 1\frac{5}{8}$ $7\frac{7}{8}$
(61)

Find each unknown number:

10. $m + 1\frac{3}{4} = 5\frac{3}{8}$ $3\frac{5}{8}$
(63)

11. $\frac{3}{4} - f = \frac{1}{3}$ $\frac{5}{12}$
(56)

12. $\frac{2}{5}w = 1$ $\frac{5}{2}$
(30)

13. $\frac{8}{25} = \frac{n}{100}$ 32
(42)

* **14.** $1\frac{2}{3} \div 2$ $\frac{5}{6}$
(68)

* **15.** $2\frac{2}{3} \times 1\frac{1}{5}$ $3\frac{1}{5}$
(66)

▶ **16.** $\frac{2.4}{0.08}$ 30
(49)

17. **a.** What is the perimeter of this square?   10 m
(38)   **b.** What is the area of this square?   6.25 sq. m

2.5 m

▶ * **18.** [Explain] How can you determine whether a counting number is a composite number?   If a counting number is divisible by a counting number other than itself or 1, then the number is composite.
(65)

19. Sample:

250

25   10

5   5   2   5

$250 = 2 \cdot 5 \cdot 5 \cdot 5$

▶ * **19.** [Represent] Make a factor tree to find the prime factorization of 250.
(65)

20. A stop sign has the shape of an eight-sided polygon. What is the name of an eight-sided polygon?   octagon
(60)

21. There were 15 boys and 12 girls in the class.
(29)   **a.** What fraction of the class was made up of girls? $\frac{4}{9}$

   b. What was the ratio of boys to girls in the class? $\frac{5}{4}$

22. [Verify] Instead of dividing $4\frac{1}{2}$ by $1\frac{1}{2}$, Carla doubled both numbers before dividing mentally. What was Carla's mental division problem and its quotient? $9 \div 3 = 3$
(43)

23. What is the reciprocal of $2\frac{1}{2}$? $\frac{2}{5}$
(30, 62)

24. There are 1000 grams in 1 kilogram. How many grams are in 2.25 kilograms?   2250 grams
(15)

25. How many **millimeters** long is the line below?   35 mm
(7)

▶ * **26.** [Connect] The length of $\overline{WX}$ is 53 mm. The length of $\overline{XY}$ is 35 mm. What is the length of $\overline{WY}$?   88 mm
(69)

W   X   Y

▶ See Math Conversations in the sidebar.

Teacher Tip

A **tagboard model of a flexible parallelogram** is suggested for use in Lesson 71. You may want to began preparing the model now.

27. Sample:

27. *(Inv. 6)* **Represent** Draw a cylinder.

28. *(50)* Arrange these numbers in order from least to greatest: −1, 0, 0.1, 1

0.1, 1, −1, 0

▶ **29.** *(33)* **Represent** Draw a circle and shade $\frac{1}{4}$ of it. What percent of the circle is shaded? ⊕; 25%

30. *(Inv. 6)* How many smaller cubes are in the large cube shown below? 8 cubes

Early Finishers
Real-World Application

Taylor and her friends at school decided to make ribbons for their classmates to wear for spirit week. Taylor's mother offered to buy two rolls of ribbon. If each roll of ribbon is 25 yards in length and each ribbon is cut to $7\frac{1}{2}$ inches long, how many ribbons can Taylor and her friends make to give away at school? Show your work. Hint: 1 yard = 36 inches. 25 yds × 36 inches = 900 inches; $900 \div 7\frac{1}{2} = 900 \div \frac{15}{2} = 900 \times \frac{2}{15} = 120$ ribbons per roll; 2 rolls × 120 ribbons = 240 ribbons

▶ See Math Conversations in the sidebar.

---

3 Written Practice *(Continued)*

Math Conversations

Discussion opportunities are provided below.

Problem 29 **Represent**

"Suppose the whole circle is shaded. What percent of the circle would be shaded?" 100%

"Describe two different ways to find $\frac{1}{4}$ of 100%." Multiply 100% by $\frac{1}{4}$ or divide 100% by 4.

"Why can you multiply or divide to find this answer?" Multiplying a number by $\frac{1}{4}$ is the same as dividing that number by 4 or dividing a number by 4 is the same as multiplying that number by $\frac{1}{4}$.

Looking Forward

Identifying complementary and supplementary angles and naming and finding the measure of an angle's complement or supplement prepare students for:

- **Lesson 71,** finding the measures of opposite and adjacent angles in parallelograms.
- **Lesson 97,** understanding relationships between angles formed by a transversal line intersecting two parallel lines.
- **Lesson 98,** finding the sum of the angle measures of triangles and quadrilaterals and understanding that an interior and exterior angle of a polygon are supplementary.

• Reducing Fractions Before Multiplying

Objectives

• Reduce fraction terms before multiplying.

Lesson Preparation

Materials

• **Power Up G** (*in Instructional Masters*)

Power Up G

Math Language

	English Learners (ESL)
	pair

Technology Resources

Student eBook Complete student textbook in electronic format.

Resources and Planner CD Assessment, reteaching, and instructional masters, plus a pacing calendar with standards.

Test and Practice Generator CD Create additional practice sheets and custom-made tests.

www.SaxonPublishers.com Visit for more student activities and planning materials.

Inclusion

Adaptations CD Adapted lessons, investigations, practice and assessments.

Meeting Standards

National Council of Teachers of Mathematics (NCTM)

Numbers and Operations

NO.1a Work flexibly with fractions, decimals, and percents to solve problems

NO.1f Use factors, multiples, prime factorization, and relatively prime numbers to solve problems

NO.2a Understand the meaning and effects of arithmetic operations with fractions, decimals, and integers

Problem Solving

PS.1c Apply and adapt a variety of appropriate strategies to solve problems

Problem-Solving Strategy: Draw a Diagram;
Use Logical Reasoning

The Crunch-O's cereal company makes two different cereal boxes. One is family size (12 in. high, 9 in. long, 2 in. wide) and the other is single-serving size (5 in. high, 3 in. long, 1 in. wide). Each of their boxes is made out of one piece of cardboard. Below is a net of the family size box. Use this diagram to draw a net for the single-serving box.

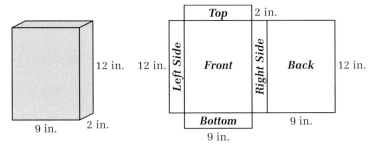

Understand **Understand the problem.**

"What information are we given?"

We have been given a rectangular prism, its measurements, and its net.

"What are we asked to do?"

Create a net for a rectangular prism with a height of 5 in., length of 3 in., and a width of 1 in.

Plan **Make a plan.**

"What problem-solving strategy will we use?"

We have been asked to *draw a diagram* and *use logical reasoning*.

"What do we know about the faces of rectangular prisms?"

They have 6 faces, and opposite faces are congruent.

Solve **Carry out the plan.**

"What is the first step to drawing a net?"

Draw one face, and then think of where each face is connected in relation to the one we drew.

"Draw the front of the prism and connect all the other pieces. Label each piece as you go. If you have trouble it may help to make a sketch of the rectangular prism."

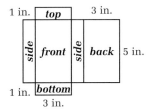

Check **Look back.**

"Is our solution reasonable?"

Yes. We can see that if we cut out the net and fold it together, it would form a rectangular prism.

• Reducing Fractions
   Before Multiplying

6ll
6l2
6l3
l33

1 Power Up

Facts
Distribute **Power Up G** to students. See answers below.

Mental Math
Before students begin the Mental Math exercise, do this counting exercise as a class.

Count up and down by 2s between negative 10 and 10.

Encourage students to share different ways to mentally compute these exercises. Strategies for exercises **b** and **f** are listed below.

b. Add 100, then Subtract 1
   $476 + 100 = 576$; $576 - 1 = 575$
   Subtract 1 and Add 1
   $476 - 1 = 475$ and $99 + 1 = 100$;
   $475 + 100 = 575$
f. Shift the Decimal Points
   $\frac{\$250}{10} = \frac{\$25.0}{1.0} = \frac{\$25}{1} = \$25$
   Break Apart $250
   $\$200 \div 10 = \$20$ and $\$50 \div 10 = \$5$;
   $\$20 + \$5 = \$25$

Problem Solving
Refer to **Power-Up Discussion**, p. 358B.

facts | Power Up G

mental math

a. **Number Sense:** 5×280 1400

b. **Number Sense:** $476 + 99$ 575

c. **Calculation:** 3×54 162

d. **Calculation:** $\$4.50 + \$1.75$ $6.25

e. **Fractional Parts:** $\frac{1}{3}$ of $90.00 $30.00

f. **Number Sense:** $\frac{\$250}{10}$ $25.00

g. **Geometry:** A square has a perimeter of 24 cm. What is the length of the sides of the square?   6 cm

h. **Calculation:** $5 \times 10, \div 2, + 5, \div 2, - 5, \div 10, - 1$ 0

problem solving | The Crunch-O's cereal company makes two different cereal boxes. One is family size (12 in. high, 9 in. long, 2 in. wide) and the other is single-serving size (5 in. high, 3 in. long, 1 in. wide). Each of their boxes is made out of one piece of cardboard. To the right is a net of the family size box. Use this diagram to draw a net for the single-serving box.

2 New Concepts

Instruction
Help students generalize that reducing the terms of fractions before multiplying helps produce products that are simpler to reduce, or products that are already in simplest form.

Caution students that when canceling, a numerator must be paired with a denominator, and not with another numerator.

(continued)

Thinking Skill

Connect

Sometimes we can reduce the numerators and the denominators of both fractions. Reduce the following:

$\frac{4}{9} \times \frac{3}{8}$

$\frac{\overset{1}{\cancel{4}}}{\underset{3}{\cancel{9}}} \times \frac{\overset{1}{\cancel{3}}}{\underset{2}{\cancel{8}}}$

Before two or more fractions are multiplied, we might be able to reduce the fraction terms, even if the reducing involves different fractions. For example, in the multiplication below we see that the number 3 appears as a numerator and as a denominator in different fractions.

$$\frac{3}{5} \times \frac{2}{3} = \frac{6}{15} \qquad \frac{6}{15} \text{ reduces to } \frac{2}{5}$$

We may reduce the common terms (the 3s) before multiplying. We reduce $\frac{3}{3}$ to $\frac{1}{1}$ by dividing both 3s by 3. Then we multiply the remaining terms.

$$\frac{\overset{1}{\cancel{3}}}{5} \times \frac{2}{\underset{1}{\cancel{3}}} = \frac{2}{5}$$

By reducing before we multiply, we avoid the need to reduce after we multiply. Reducing before multiplying is also known as **canceling.**

Facts   Reduce each fraction to lowest terms.

$\frac{2}{8} = \frac{1}{4}$	$\frac{4}{6} = \frac{2}{3}$	$\frac{6}{10} = \frac{3}{5}$	$\frac{2}{4} = \frac{1}{2}$	$\frac{5}{100} = \frac{1}{20}$	$\frac{9}{12} = \frac{3}{4}$
$\frac{4}{10} = \frac{2}{5}$	$\frac{4}{12} = \frac{1}{3}$	$\frac{2}{10} = \frac{1}{5}$	$\frac{3}{6} = \frac{1}{2}$	$\frac{25}{100} = \frac{1}{4}$	$\frac{3}{12} = \frac{1}{4}$
$\frac{4}{16} = \frac{1}{4}$	$\frac{3}{9} = \frac{1}{3}$	$\frac{6}{9} = \frac{2}{3}$	$\frac{4}{8} = \frac{1}{2}$	$\frac{2}{12} = \frac{1}{6}$	$\frac{6}{12} = \frac{1}{2}$
$\frac{8}{16} = \frac{1}{2}$	$\frac{2}{6} = \frac{1}{3}$	$\frac{8}{12} = \frac{2}{3}$	$\frac{6}{8} = \frac{3}{4}$	$\frac{5}{10} = \frac{1}{2}$	$\frac{75}{100} = \frac{3}{4}$

Example 1

Simplify: $\frac{5}{6} \times \frac{1}{5}$

Solution

We reduce before we multiply. Since 5 appears as a numerator and as a denominator, we reduce $\frac{5}{5}$ to $\frac{1}{1}$ by dividing both 5s by 5. Then we multiply the remaining terms.

$$\frac{\overset{1}{\cancel{5}}}{6} \times \frac{1}{\underset{1}{\cancel{5}}} = \frac{1}{6}$$

Example 2

Simplify: $1\frac{1}{9} \times 1\frac{1}{5}$

Solution

First we write the numbers in fraction form.

$$\frac{10}{9} \times \frac{6}{5}$$

We mentally pair 10 with 5 and 6 with 9.

We reduce $\frac{10}{5}$ to $\frac{2}{1}$ by dividing both 10 and 5 by 5. We reduce $\frac{6}{9}$ to $\frac{2}{3}$ by dividing both 6 and 9 by 3.

$$\frac{\overset{2}{\cancel{10}}}{\underset{3}{\cancel{9}}} \times \frac{\overset{2}{\cancel{6}}}{\underset{1}{\cancel{5}}} = \frac{4}{3}$$

We multiply the remaining terms. Then we simplify the product.

$$\frac{4}{3} = 1\frac{1}{3}$$

Thinking Skill

Discuss

Why might you want to reduce before you multiply? Sample: It is easier to see common factors when the numbers are small.

Example 3

Simplify: $\frac{5}{6} \div \frac{5}{2}$

Solution

Thinking Skill

Justify

Explain how to divide any two fractions. Sample: Replace the fraction after the division sign with its reciprocal and multiply.

This is a division problem. We first find the number of $\frac{5}{2}$s in 1. The answer is the reciprocal of $\frac{5}{2}$. We then use the reciprocal of $\frac{5}{2}$ to find the number of $\frac{5}{2}$s in $\frac{5}{6}$.

$$1 \div \frac{5}{2} = \frac{2}{5}$$

$$\downarrow$$

$$\frac{5}{6} \times \frac{2}{5}$$

Example 1

Instruction

Remind students that $\frac{5}{5}$ and $\frac{1}{1}$ are equivalent fractions.

Example 2

Instruction

In the improper fractions, students should recognize that 6 is paired with 9, and 10 is paired with 5, because each pair of numbers have at least one common factor that is greater than 1.

> *"What factor that is greater than 1 is common to both 6 and 9?"* 3

> *"What factor that is greater than 1 is common to both 10 and 5?"* 5

Help students generalize that each pair of numbers should be divided by the greatest common factor of those numbers.

Example 3

Instruction

It is essential for students to understand that canceling can only occur within factors. In other words, canceling applies to multiplication only.

> *"What operation must be present for you to cancel a numerator in an expression and a denominator elsewhere in that expression?"* multiplication

(continued)

English Learners

Explain what it means to **pair** numbers. Say,

> *"When we pair numbers, we put them together in twos. In Example 2, you are asked to pair 10 with 5. In this case, the numbers are paired because they have a common factor."*

Ask volunteers to give an example of a pair of numbers with a common factor.

Math Background

Fraction terms can be reduced before multiplying because reducing the terms produces the same product as reducing the terms after multiplying.

However, reducing the terms before multiplying makes it easier to simplify the product. For some factors, reducing the terms before multiplying will produce a product that is already in simplest form.

Practice Set
Problems a–f [Error Alert]
One way for students to check each problem is to find the product of the factors, then reduce the product and compare it to the product of the reduced factors.

Problems g–i [Error Alert]
Watch for students who cancel two terms in the numerators or two terms in the denominators.

3 Written Practice

Math Conversations
Discussion opportunities are provided below.

Problem 2 [Connect]
To help students write an equation that can be used to represent the problem, ask them to give an example of a simpler problem. Sample: How many 2s in 8?

"**What operation is used to solve our simpler problem?**" division

"**What equation could we use to represent the number of $\frac{1}{8}$s in $\frac{1}{2}$?**" Sample: $\frac{1}{2} \div \frac{1}{8} = n$

Ask students to write and solve the equation, then compare answers. $\frac{1}{2} \div \frac{1}{8} = 4$

Problem 3 [Verify]
"**To form an equivalent division problem, it is better to multiply both mixed numbers by an even number instead of an odd number. Why?**" The fraction parts of the mixed numbers have a denominator of 2. Multiplying by any even number will eliminate the fractions. Multiplying by an odd number will always result in a fraction.

Encourage volunteers to write examples on the board or overhead to support their explanations.

Errors and Misconceptions
Problem 14
A common error when finding the average of three numbers is to assume the middle number represents the average. Although the mean and the median of a data set are occasionally the same, the assumption is generally not correct. Work with students who report the average of the numbers as 5 to compare and contrast mean, median, and mode.

(continued)

Now we have a multiplication problem. We cancel before we multiply.

$$\frac{\overset{1}{\cancel{5}}}{\underset{3}{\cancel{6}}} \times \frac{\overset{1}{\cancel{2}}}{\underset{1}{\cancel{5}}} = \frac{1}{3}$$

Note: We may cancel the terms of fractions only when multiplying. A division problem must be rewritten as a multiplication problem before we may cancel the terms of the fractions. We do not cancel the terms of fractions in addition or subtraction problems.

Practice Set ▸ Reduce before multiplying:

 a. $\frac{3}{4} \cdot \frac{4}{5}$ $\frac{3}{5}$ **b.** $\frac{2}{3} \cdot \frac{3}{4}$ $\frac{1}{2}$ **c.** $\frac{8}{9} \cdot \frac{9}{10}$ $\frac{4}{5}$

▸ Write in fraction form. Then reduce before multiplying.

 d. $2\frac{1}{4} \times 4$ 9 **e.** $1\frac{1}{2} \times 2\frac{2}{3}$ 4 **f.** $3\frac{1}{3} \times 2\frac{1}{4}$ $7\frac{1}{2}$

▸ Rewrite each division problem as a multiplication problem. Then reduce before multiplying.

 g. $\frac{2}{5} \div \frac{2}{3}$ $\frac{3}{5}$ **h.** $\frac{8}{9} \div \frac{2}{3}$ $1\frac{1}{3}$ **i.** $\frac{9}{10} \div 1\frac{1}{5}$ $\frac{3}{4}$

Written Practice *Strengthening Concepts*

1. Alaska was purchased from Russia in 1867 for seven million, two
(12) hundred thousand dollars. Use digits to write that amount. $7,200,000

▸ **2.** **Connect** How many eighth notes equal a half note?   4 eighth notes
(54)

▸ **3.** **Verify** Instead of dividing $12\frac{1}{2}$ by $2\frac{1}{2}$, Shannon doubled both numbers
(43) and then divided. Write the division problem Shannon formed, as well as its quotient. $25 \div 5 = 5$

Reduce before multiplying:

* 4. $\frac{5}{6} \cdot \frac{4}{5}$ $\frac{2}{3}$ *** 5.** $\frac{5}{6} \div \frac{5}{2}$ $\frac{1}{3}$ *** 6.** $\frac{9}{10} \cdot \frac{5}{6}$ $\frac{3}{4}$
(70)   (70)   (70)

7. What number is halfway between $\frac{1}{2}$ and 1 on the number line? $\frac{3}{4}$
(17)

8. $\sqrt{100} + 10^2$ 110   **9.** $3\frac{2}{3} + 4\frac{5}{6}$ $8\frac{1}{2}$
(38)   (59)

10. $7\frac{1}{8} - 2\frac{1}{2}$ $4\frac{5}{8}$ **11.** $4.37 + 12.8 + 6$ 23.17
(63)   (38)

12. $0.46 \div 5$ 0.092   **13.** $60 \div 0.8$ 75
(45)   (49)

▸ **14.** **Evaluate** What is the average of the three numbers marked by the
(18) arrows on this decimal number line? (First estimate whether the average will be more than 5 or less than 5.)   5.1

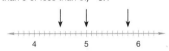

360 *Saxon* Math Course 1

▸ See Math Conversations in the sidebar.

15. **Verify** The division problem 1.5 ÷ 0.06 is equivalent to which of the
(49) following? **B**

   A 15 ÷ 6   **B** 150 ÷ 6   **C** 150 ÷ 60

16. There are 1000 milliliters in 1 liter. How many milliliters are in 3.8 liters?
(39) 3800 milliliters

Find each unknown number:

17. $\frac{2}{3} + n = 1$ $\frac{1}{3}$ **18.** $\frac{2}{3}m = 1$ $\frac{3}{2}$ **19.** $f - \frac{3}{4} = \frac{5}{6}$ $1\frac{7}{12}$
(43)   (30)   (56)

20. A pyramid with a triangular base has how many
(60,
Inv. 6)   **a.** faces?   4 faces

   b. edges?   6 edges

   c. vertices?   4 vertices

Write the numbers in fraction form. Then reduce before multiplying.

* 21. $1\frac{2}{3} \times 1\frac{1}{5}$ 2   *** 22.** $\frac{8}{9} \div 2\frac{2}{3}$ $\frac{1}{3}$
(70)   (70)

Refer to the line graph below to answer problems **23–25.**

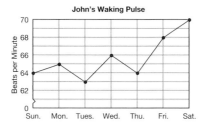

John's Waking Pulse

23. When John woke on Saturday, his pulse was how many beats per
(18) minute more than it was on Tuesday?   7 beats per minute more

24. On Monday John took his pulse for 3 minutes before marking the graph.
(18) How many times did his heart beat in those 3 minutes?   195 times

▶ **25.** **Formulate** Write a question that relates to the graph and answer the
(18) question.   See student work.

▶* **26.** **Analyze** Write the prime factorization of both the numerator and the
(67) denominator of this fraction. Then reduce the fraction.
 $\frac{2 \cdot 2 \cdot 2 \cdot 3 \cdot 3}{2 \cdot 2 \cdot 3 \cdot 5 \cdot 5} = \frac{6}{25}$ $\frac{72}{300}$

▶ See Math Conversations in the sidebar.

Math Conversations

Discussion opportunities are provided below.

Problem 15 Verify

Ask students to solve the problem using only mental math.

"How many places does the decimal point move, and in which direction does it move, when you multiply a number by 10, 100, or 1000?" 10: one place to the right; 100: two places to the right; 1000: three places to the right.

"How many places does the decimal point move, and in which direction does it move, when you divide a number by 10, 100, or 1000?" 10: one place to the left; 100: two places to the left; 1000: three places to the left.

"Which answer choice is equivalent to 1.5 ÷ 0.06? Why?" b; multiplying both 1.5 and 0.06 by 100 results in the equivalent division problem 150 ÷ 6.

Problem 25 Formulate

Extend the Problem

Invite students to exchange questions, then answer the questions and compare answers.

Problem 26 Analyze

"Describe when you can, and when you cannot, cancel terms of a fraction." Sample: When a number in the numerator and a number in the denominator share a common factor greater than 1, the common factor can be used to divide the terms and change them to smaller numbers.

Errors and Misconceptions
Problems 21 and 22

After the mixed numbers in each problem are rewritten as improper fractions, students must recognize that problem **22** is unlike problem **21**. In problem **21**, students can reduce the terms of the fractions before multiplying. However, in problem **22**, students cannot reduce the terms until the division is rewritten as $\frac{8}{9} \times \frac{3}{8}$.

(continued)

Math Conversations

Discussion opportunities are provided below.

Problem 29 Analyze

Extend the Problem

"Line segments AD and BC are parallel. Explain how we know this to be true."

Each line segment creates a 90° angle with line segment CD.

Analyze In rectangle $ABCD$ the length of $\overline{AB}$ is 2.5 cm, and the length of $\overline{BC}$ is 1.5 cm. Use this information and the figure below to answer problems **27–30**.

27. What is the perimeter of this rectangle?   8 cm
(8)

28. What is the area of this rectangle?   3.75 cm²
(31)

▶* **29.** Name two segments perpendicular to $\overline{DC}$. $\overline{AD}$ (or $\overline{DA}$) and $\overline{BC}$ (or $\overline{CB}$)
(64)

* **30.** If $\overline{BD}$ were drawn on the figure to divide the rectangle into two equal parts, what would be the area of each part?   1.875 cm²
(31)

Early Finishers
Real-World Application

Roland went to the local Super Store yesterday. He bought a new paint roller and roller pan for $8.97, a gallon of milk for $2.89, a magazine for $1.59, and two identical gallons of paint without marked prices. He paid a total of $47.83 before tax. Find the price for each gallon of paint. $8.97 + $2.89 + $1.59 = $13.45, $47.83 − $13.45 = $34.38, $34.38 ÷ 2 = $17.19 for each gallon of paint

▶ See Math Conversations in the sidebar.

Looking Forward

Reducing, or canceling, terms before multiplying fractions prepares students for:

- **Lesson 72,** using a fractions chart to recall the steps for multiplying or dividing fractions and multiplying three fractions.
- **Lesson 94,** writing fractions and decimals as percents.
- **Lesson 95,** reducing units before multiplying.
- **Lesson 114,** using unit multipliers to convert from one unit of measurement to another.
- **Lesson 115,** converting mixed number percents to fractions.

Assessment   30–40 minutes   For use after Lesson 70

Distribute **Cumulative Test 13** to each student. Two versions of the test are available in *Saxon Math Course 1 Course Assessments Book*. Have students complete the **Power-Up Test** first. Allow 10 minutes. Then have students work the 20 numbered items on the **Cumulative Test.** Students may use copies of the answer sheet to record their work. Track individual and class progress with the **Test Analysis** forms.

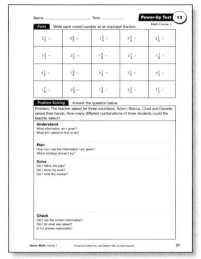

Power-Up Test 13

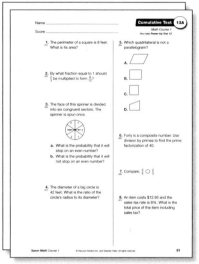

Cumulative Test 13A

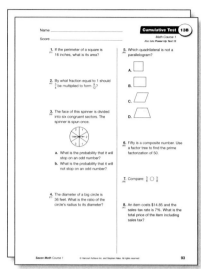

Alternative Cumulative Test 13B

Optional Answer Forms

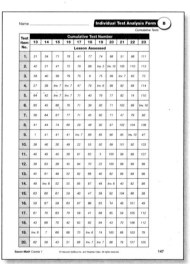

Individual Test Analysis Form

Class Test Analysis Form

Reteaching

Students who score below 80% on the assessment may be in need of reteaching. Look for the causes of student mistakes. If errors are conceptual, refer to the *Reteaching Masters* for reteaching.

Customized Benchmark Assessment

You can develop customized benchmark tests using the Test Generator located on the *Test & Practice Generator CD.*

This chart shows the lesson, the standard, and the test item question that can be found on the *Test & Practice Generator CD.*

LESSON	NEW CONCEPTS	LOCAL STANDARD	TEST ITEM ON CD
61	• Adding Three or More Fractions		7.61.1
62	• Writing Mixed Numbers as Improper Fractions		7.62.1
63	• Subtracting Mixed Numbers with Regrouping, Part 2		7.63.1
64	• Classifying Quadrilaterals		7.64.1
65	• Prime Factorization		7.65.1
	• Division by Primes		7.65.2
	• Factor Trees		7.65.3
66	• Multiplying Mixed Numbers		7.66.1
67	• Using Prime Factorization to Reduce Fractions		7.67.1
68	• Dividing Mixed Numbers		7.68.1
69	• Lengths of Segments		7.69.1
	• Complementary and Supplementary Angles		7.69.2
70	• Reducing Fractions Before Multiplying		7.70.1

Using the Test Generator CD

- Develop tests in both English and Spanish.
- Choose from multiple-choice and free-response test items.
- Clone test items to create multiple versions of the same test.
- View and edit test items to make and save your own questions.
- Administer assessments through paper tests or over a school LAN.
- Monitor student progress through a variety of individual and class reports —for both diagnosing and assessing standards mastery.

Drawing and Comparing Three-dimensional Shapes

Assign after Lesson 70 and Test 13

Objectives
- Draw different views of three-dimensional shapes.
- Compare three-dimensional shapes.
- Communicate ideas through writing.

Materials
Performance Tasks 13A and **13B**

Preparation
Make copies of **Performance Tasks 13A** and **13B**. (One each per student.)

Time Requirement
30–60 minutes; Begin in class and complete at home.

Task
Explain to students that that will be drawing different views of different geometrical shapes. They will also be required to compare a right prism to a square pyramid and a cylinder to a cone. Point out that all of the information students need is on **Performance Tasks 13A** and **13B.**

Criteria for Evidence of Learning
- Draws different views of three-dimensional figures accurately.
- Makes accurate statements about the similarities and differences between a right prism and a square pyramid and between a cylinder and a cone.
- Communicates ideas clearly through writing.

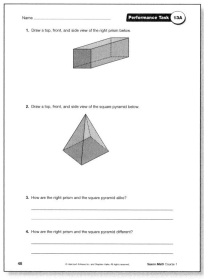

Performance Task 13A

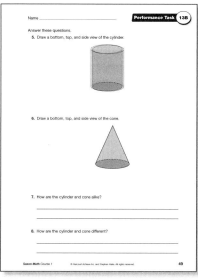

Performance Task 13B

National Council of Teachers of Mathematics (NCTM)

Geometry
GM.1a Precisely describe, classify, and understand relationships among types of two- and three-dimensional objects using their defining properties

GM.4a Draw geometric objects with specified properties, such as side lengths or angle measures

GM.4c Use visual tools such as networks to represent and solve problems

Communication
CM.3d Use the language of mathematics to express mathematical ideas precisely

Representation
RE.5a Create and use representations to organize, record, and communicate mathematical ideas

Focus on
● The Coordinate Plane

Objectives
- Identify the coordinates of a point on a coordinate plane.
- Graph points on a coordinate plane.
- Locate the vertices of a shape on a coordinate plane, then draw segments between the points to draw the shape.

Lesson Preparation

Materials
- **Investigation Activity 15** (in *Instructional Masters*) or **graph paper,** 7 per student
- **Investigation Activity 14 Transparency** (in *Instructional Masters*)

Optional
- **Teacher-provided material:** masking tape

Math Language

New		English Learners (ESL)
coordinate plane	x-axis	unique
coordinates	y-axis	
graph		
ordered pair		
origin		

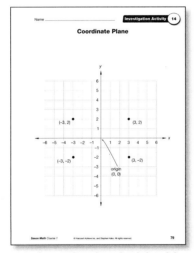

Investigation Activity 14

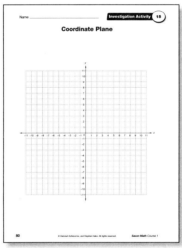

Investigation Activity 15

Technology Resources

Student eBook Complete student textbook in electronic format.

Resources and Planner CD Assessment, reteaching, and instructional masters, plus a pacing calendar with standards.

Test and Practice Generator CD Create additional practice sheets and custom-made tests.

www.SaxonPublishers.com Visit for more student activities and planning materials.

Inclusion

Adaptations CD Adapted lessons, investigations, practice and assessments.

Meeting Standards

National Council of Teachers of Mathematics (NCTM)

Geometry

GM.2a Use coordinate geometry to represent and examine the properties of geometric shapes

GM.2b Use coordinate geometry to examine special geometric shapes, such as regular polygons or those with pairs of parallel or perpendicular sides

GM.4c Use visual tools such as networks to represent and solve problems

GM.4d Use geometric models to represent and explain numerical and algebraic relationships

Focus on

622

• The Coordinate Plane

By drawing two number lines perpendicular to each other and by extending the unit marks, we can create a grid called a **coordinate plane**.

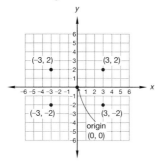

The point at which the number lines intersect is called the **origin**. The horizontal number line is called the **x-axis**, and the vertical number line is called the **y-axis**. We **graph** a point by marking a dot at the location of the point. We can name the location of any point on this coordinate plane with two numbers. The numbers that tell the location of a point are called the **coordinates** of the point.

Thinking Skill

Explain

On the coordinate plane, where will a point whose ordered pair contains two negative numbers be located? This point will be located in the lower left portion of the coordinate plane.

The coordinates of a point are written as an **ordered pair** of numbers in parentheses; for example, (3, −2). The first number is the x-coordinate. It shows the horizontal (↔) direction and distance from the origin. The second number, the y-coordinate, shows the vertical (↕) direction and distance from the origin. The sign of the coordinate shows the direction. Positive coordinates are to the right or up, and negative coordinates are to the left or down.

Look at the coordinate plane above. To graph (3, −2), we begin at the origin and move three units to the right along the x-axis. From there we move down two units and mark a dot. We may label the point we graphed (3, −2).

On the coordinate plane, we also have graphed three other points and identified their coordinates. Notice that each pair of coordinates is different and designates a unique point:

$$(3, -2)$$
$$(3, 2)$$
$$(-3, 2)$$
$$(-3, -2)$$

Math Background

The axes of a coordinate plane divide the plane into four quadrants.

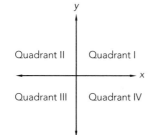

All points in Quadrant I are ordered pairs of the form (+x, +y).

All points in Quadrant II are ordered pairs of the form (−x, +y).

All points in Quadrant III are ordered pairs of the form (−x, −y).

All points in Quadrant IV are ordered pairs of the form (+x, −y).

In this investigation, students will locate and plot points in all four quadrants of the coordinate plane.

Instruction

Place the transparency of **Lesson Activity 14** Coordinate Plane on an overhead projector. Point out the x-axis, the y-axis, and the coordinates (0, 0) of the origin.

Using a pointer, show students how to locate each point shown on the transparency. For example:

"To locate (−3, −2), we begin at the origin and move three units to the left along the x-axis. From there, we move down two units."

The following questions will help students form generalizations about points in the coordinate plane.

"Suppose the x-coordinate of an ordered pair is positive. Which direction will that point be from the origin?" to the right

"Suppose the x-coordinate of an ordered pair is negative. Which direction will that point be from the origin?" to the left

"Suppose the y-coordinate of an ordered pair is positive. Which direction will that point be from the origin?" above

"Suppose the y-coordinate of an ordered pair is negative. Which direction will that point be from the origin?" below

---

English Learners

Refer students to the last paragraph. Write the word **unique** on the board. Say,

"Unique has a similar meaning as 'one of a kind'. Each of your math books is unique because each one has different markings, tears, or book covers on it."

Ask the students to give examples of other classroom items that are unique.

Math Conversations

Discussion opportunities are provided below.

Before completing problems **1–6,** ask students the general questions shown below. The questions will help reinforce the concept that every point in the coordinate plane represents a unique location that has a direction and exact distance from the origin.

"Which points will have a positive x-coordinate? Explain why." *A, B, G,* and *H;* all of the points are to the right of the origin.

"Which points will have a negative x-coordinate? Explain why." *C, D, E,* and *F;* all of the points are to the left of the origin.

"Which points will have a positive y-coordinate? Explain why." *A, B, C,* and *D;* all of the points are above the origin.

"Which points will have a negative y-coordinate? Explain why." *E, F, G,* and *H;* all of the points are below the origin.

▶ Refer to the coordinate plane below to answer problems **1–6.**

Thinking Skill

Conclude

If you connected the points in alphabetical order (start with *AB* and end with *HA*), what type of polygon would you make? octagon

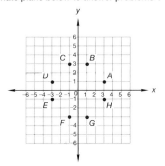

1. What are the coordinates of point *A*? (3, 1)

2. Which point has the coordinates (−1, 3)? point *C*

3. What are the coordinates of point *E*? (−3, −1)

4. Which point has the coordinates (1, −3)? point *G*

5. What are the coordinates of point *D*? (−3, 1)

6. Which point has the coordinates (3, −1)? point *H*

The coordinate plane is useful in many fields of mathematics, including algebra and geometry.

In the next section of this investigation we will designate points on the plane as vertices of rectangles. Then we will calculate the perimeter and area of each rectangle.

Suppose we are told that the vertices of a rectangle are located at (3, 2), (−1, 2), (−1, −1), and (3, −1). We graph the points and then draw segments between the points to draw the rectangle.

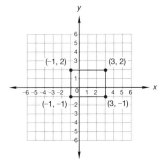

Visit www.SaxonPublishers.com/ActivitiesC1 *for a graphing calculator activity.*

▶ See Math Conversations in the sidebar.

We see that the rectangle is four units long and three units wide. Adding the lengths of the four sides, we find that the perimeter is **14 units.** To find the area, we can count the unit squares within the rectangle. There are three rows of four squares, so the area of the rectangle is 3×4, which is **12 square units.**

Use graph paper or **Investigation Activity 15** to create a coordinate plane. Use the coordinate plane for the exercises that follow.

▶ **7.** _Represent_ The vertices of a rectangle are located at $(-2, -1)$, $(2, -1)$, $(2, 3)$, and $(-2, 3)$.

7. a.

    a. Graph the rectangle. What do we call this special type of rectangle?   square

    b. What is the perimeter of the rectangle?   16 units

    c. What is the area of the rectangle?   16 sq. units

▶ **8.** _Represent_ The vertices of a rectangle are located at $(-4, 2)$, $(0, 2)$, $(0, 0)$, and $(-4, 0)$.

8. a.

    a. Graph the rectangle. Notice that one vertex is located at $(0, 0)$. What is the name for this point on the coordinate plane?   origin

    b. What is the perimeter of the rectangle?   12 units

    c. What is the area of the rectangle?   8 sq. units

    9. Three vertices of a rectangle are located at $(3, 1)$, $(-2, 1)$, and $(-2, -3)$.

9. a.

    a. Graph the rectangle. What are the coordinates of the fourth vertex? $(3, -3)$

    b. What is the perimeter of the rectangle?   18 units

    c. What is the area of the rectangle?   20 sq. units

As the following activity illustrates, we can use coordinates to give directions for making a drawing.

Activity

Drawing on the Coordinate Plane

Materials needed:

- 4 copies of **Investigation Activity 15**

▶ **10.** _Verify_ Christy made a drawing on a coordinate plane as shown on the next page. Then she wrote directions for making the drawing. Follow Christy's directions to make a similar drawing on your coordinate plane. The coordinates of the vertices are listed in order, as in a "dot-to-dot" drawing.   See student work.

Investigation 7   **365**

▶ See Math Conversations in the sidebar.

Instruction

Write the formula $A = lw$ on the board or overhead and remind students that the formula is used to find the area of a rectangle.

Explain that one way for students to think of the area of the rectangle is the amount of the plane that is enclosed by its boundaries.

Math Conversations

Discussion opportunities are provided below.

Problem 7 _Represent_

Before students plot the points, ask them to describe, in a general way, how to plot any point in the coordinate plane. Begin at the origin. Move the distance and the direction (to the left or to the right) indicated by the x-coordinate. Then move the distance and the direction (up or down) indicated by the y-coordinate.

Problem 8 _Represent_

Students will discover that points can be located on either axis of the coordinate plane.

  "Where is a point located if its x-coordinate is zero and its y-coordinate is not zero?" on the y-axis

  "Where is a point located if its x-coordinate is not zero and its y-coordinate is zero?" on the x-axis

Activity

Instruction

It will be helpful for students to have a ruler to complete this activity.

Math Conversations

Discussion opportunities are provided below.

Problem 10 _Verify_

Before completing the problem, ask students to look at the points that need to be plotted.

  "Are all of the x- and y-coordinates of the points integers?" no

  "Some x- and y-coordinates represent halves, such as $-1\frac{1}{2}$ and $1\frac{1}{2}$. Explain how we can graph points that are at intervals of halves instead of wholes." Sample: Plot a point halfway between two grid lines.

(continued)

Math Conversations

Discussion opportunities are provided below.

Problem 11 Represent

Give students an opportunity to recall that points may be located on either axis of the coordinate plane.

"It is possible for a point to be on the x-axis, and not above it or below it. For any point on the x-axis, which of its coordinates will be zero? Why?" The *y*-coordinate will be zero because the *y*-coordinate indicates distance above or below the origin. For any point on the *x*-axis, the distance above or below the origin is zero.

"It is also possible for a point to be on the y-axis, and not to the left or right of it. For any point on the y-axis, which of its coordinates will be zero? Why?" The *x*-coordinate will be zero because the *x*-coordinate indicates distance to the left or to the right of the origin. For any point on the *y*-axis, the distance to the left or to the right of the origin is zero.

(continued)

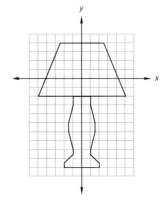

Christy's Directions

On your coordinate plane, draw segments to connect the following points in order:

a. $(-1, -2)$ **b.** $(-1, -3)$ **c.** $(-1\frac{1}{2}, -5)$ **d.** $(-1\frac{1}{2}, -6)$

e. $(-1, -8)$ **f.** $(-1, -8\frac{1}{2})$ **g.** $(-2, -9\frac{1}{2})$ **h.** $(2, 10)$

i. $(2, -10)$ **j.** $(2, -9\frac{1}{2})$ **k.** $(1, -8\frac{1}{2})$ **l.** $(1, -8)$

m. $(1\frac{1}{2}, -6)$ **n.** $(1\frac{1}{2}, -5)$ **o.** $(1, -3)$ **p.** $(1, -2)$

Lift your pencil and restart:

a. $(-2\frac{1}{2}, 4)$ **b.** $(2\frac{1}{2}, 4)$ **c.** $(5, -2)$

d. $(-5, -2)$ **e.** $(-2\frac{1}{2}, 4)$

▶ **11.** *Conclude* Carlos wrote the following directions for a drawing. Follow his directions to make the drawing on your own paper. Draw segments to connect the following points in order: See student work. The figure should look like a space shuttle.

a. $(-9, 0)$ **b.** $(6, -1)$ **c.** $(8, 0)$

d. $(7, 1)$ **e.** $(6, \frac{1}{2})$ **f.** $(6, -1)$

g. $(9, -2\frac{1}{2})$ **h.** $(10, -2)$ **i.** $(7, 1)$

j. $(6, 1\frac{1}{2})$ **k.** $(-10\frac{1}{2}, 3)$ **l.** $(-11, 2)$

m. $(-10\frac{1}{2}, 0)$ **n.** $(-10, -1\frac{1}{2})$ **o.** $(9, -2\frac{1}{2})$

p. $(-3, -3\frac{1}{2})$ **q.** $(-7, -8)$ **r.** $(-10, -8)$

s. $(-9, -1\frac{1}{2})$

▶ See Math Conversations in the sidebar.

Lift your pencil and restart:

a. $(-10\frac{1}{2}, 0)$ **b.** $(-11, -\frac{1}{2})$ **c.** $(-12, \frac{1}{2})$

d. $(-11\frac{1}{2}, 1)$ **e.** $(-12, 1\frac{1}{2})$ **f.** $(-11\frac{1}{2}, 2)$

g. $(-12, 2\frac{1}{2})$ **h.** $(-11, 3\frac{1}{2})$ **i.** $(-10\frac{1}{2}, 3)$

j. $(-11\frac{1}{2}, 8)$ **k.** $(-9\frac{1}{2}, 8)$ **l.** $(-7, 3)$

m. $(-6, 2\frac{1}{2})$ **n.** $(-7, 3)$ **o.** $(-6, 5)$

p. $(-4, 5)$ **q.** $(-1, 2)$

▶ **12.** *Model* On a coordinate plane, make a straight-segment drawing. Then write directions for making the drawing by listing the coordinates of the vertices in "dot-to-dot" order. Trade directions with another student, and try to make each other's drawings.   See student work.

---

extensions ▶ **a.** *Represent* Use whole numbers, fractions, and mixed numbers to write the coordinates for each point.
$A (\frac{1}{3}, \frac{1}{3})$ $B (3, 2)$ $C (1\frac{2}{3}, 4)$
$D (3\frac{2}{3}, 3\frac{2}{3})$ $E (2, 3)$ $F (4, \frac{1}{3})$

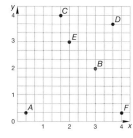

▶ **b.** *Represent* Use the given coordinates to identify the point at each location. Express the coordinates as whole numbers or decimal numbers.
$(6, 6)$ D $(4.5, 3)$ E $(2.5, 1.5)$ B
$(3.5, 0)$ F $(3, 4.5)$ A $(0.5, 5.5)$ C

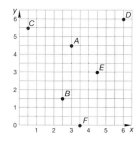

▶ **c.** *Generalize* Graph these points on a coordinate graph. Then connect the points.

$(4, 2), (6, 2), (2, 4), (8, 4), (4, 6), (6, 6)$

• What polygon did you form?   hexagon
• Name a set of points that when connected would form a hexagon inside the hexagon you drew.
Sample: $(4, 3), (6, 3), (3, 4), (7, 4), (4, 5), (6, 5)$

Investigation 7   **367**

▶ See Math Conversations in the sidebar.

Activity (Continued)

Math Conversations
Discussion opportunities are provided below.

Problem 12 *Model*
Encourage students to make creative designs if they wish, such as a star or geometric pattern. After the drawings have been completed, invite students to title their drawing.

You might choose to encourage students to display their completed drawings in the classroom.

Extensions
a. *Represent* Before completing the activity, have students note the scale of the axes.

"What does each grid line of the axes represent? Explain how you know."
Thirds; the distance between any two consecutive whole numbers is divided into three equal parts.

b. *Represent* Before completing the activity, have students note the scale of the axes.

"What does each grid line of the axes represent? Explain how you know."
Halves; the distance between any two consecutive whole numbers is divided into two equal parts.

c. *Generalize* After students connect the first set of points on the graph, they can form any hexagon as long as it fits totally inside the original hexagon.

Looking Forward
Identifying coordinates of points, graphing points, and connecting points to create rectangles and other shapes on the coordinate plane prepares students for:

• **Lesson 96,** graphing functions in the coordinate plane.

Lesson Planner

LESSON	NEW CONCEPTS	MATERIALS	RESOURCES
71	• Parallelograms	Manipulative Kit: metric rulers Two yardsticks or metersticks, straightedges, graph paper, pencils, scissors, tagboard or card stock, brads	**Power Up D** **Geometric Formulas poster**
72	• Fractions Chart • Multiplying Three Fractions	Manipulative Kit: inch rulers, grid or dot paper, 3 × 5 cards	**Power Up H**
73	• Exponents • Writing Decimal Numbers as Fractions, Part 2		**Power Up J** **Place Value poster**
74	• Writing Fractions as Decimal Numbers • Writing Ratios as Decimal Numbers	Calculators	**Power Up I**
75	• Writing Fractions and Decimals as Percents, Part 1	Graph paper	**Power Up K**
76	• Comparing Fractions by Converting to Decimal Form	Manipulative Kit: inch rulers Graph paper	**Power Up G**
77	• Finding Unstated Information in Fraction Problems	Graph paper	**Power Up K**
78	• Capacity	Containers of differing capacity, 1-gallon container of water, index cards, dry beans, rice	**Power Up J**
79	• Area of a Triangle	Manipulative Kit: inch rulers Pencil, paper, scissors	**Power Up K** **Geometric Formulas poster**
80	• Using a Constant Factor to Solve Ratio Problems	Graph paper	**Power Up I**
Inv. 8	• Geometric Construction of Bisectors	Manipulative Kit: compasses, rulers, protractors Pencils, unlined paper	**Investigation Activity 16 and 17 Transparencies** **Investigation Activity 17**

Problem Solving

Strategies

- **Find a Pattern** Lessons 71, 80
- **Make an Organized List** Lesson 73
- **Make It Simpler** Lesson 80
- **Use Logical Reasoning** Lessons 72, 74, 75, 76, 78, 79, 80
- **Draw a Diagram** Lessons 74, 78, 79
- **Work Backwards** Lesson 77
- **Guess and Check** Lessons 75, 76

Real-World Applications

pp. 372, 374, 377–378, 382–383, 387–389, 391–393, 395–397, 399, 401–403, 404, 406–408, 410, 413–414, 416

4-Step Process

Teacher Edition Lessons 71–80 (Power-Up Discussions)

Communications

Discuss

pp. 369, 404

Explain

pp. 373, 381, 384, 391–392, 402, 405, 410

Formulate a Problem

p. 378

Connections

Math and Other Subjects

- **Math and Science** pp. 374, 377, 382, 401, 402, 403, 414
- **Math and Sports** pp. 395, 401, 415
- **Math and Geography** p. 372

Math to Math

- **Problem Solving and Measurement** Lessons 71, 72, 73, 74, 75, 76, 77, 78, 79
- **Algebra and Problem Solving** Lessons 73, 74, 76, 77
- **Fractions, Percents, Decimals and Problem Solving** Lessons 71, 72, 73, 74, 75, 76, 77, 78, 79, 80

Representation

Manipulatives/Hands On

pp. 369–371, 379, 394, 398, 405, 408, 415

Model

pp. 369, 370, 379, 394, 398, 401, 402, 406, 408, 414, 416

Represent

pp. 370, 373, 388, 398, 403, 407, 415

Formulate an Equation

pp. 382, 387, 388, 396, 415, 416

Technology

Student Resources

- **eBook**
- **Calculator** Lesson 74
- **Online Resources** at www.SaxonPublishers.com/ActivitiesC1
  Online Activities
  Math Enrichment Problems
  Math Stumpers

Teacher Resources

- **Resources and Planner CD**
- **Adaptations CD** Lessons 71–80
- **Test & Practice Generator CD**
- **eGradebook**
- **Answer Key CD**

A major focus of study in the middle-grade program is proportional relationships. This set of lessons helps students summarize operations with fractions and apply the ideas to ratio situations.

Fractions and Operations

Students generalize the similarities and differences for different algorithms.

Lesson 72 summarizes arithmetic with fractions and mixed numbers and introduces a chart to help students recall the necessary steps for each operation.

Equivalence

Representing fraction, decimals, and percents in equivalent forms is emphasized in these lessons.

In Lessons 73–76 students convert between fraction, decimal, and percent forms of rational numbers, and students learn another way to compare fractions by first converting to decimal form.

Problem Solving

Word problems involving fractions are a trouble spot for most students.

Word problems involving fractions may contain implied information, and in Lesson 77 students practice finding unstated information in these problems.

Spatial Thinking

Spatial reasoning is applied to parallelograms.

After classifying quadrilaterals in Lesson 64, students focus on attributes of parallelograms in Lesson 71.

Perimeter and Area

Concepts of perimeter and area are applied to parallelograms and triangles.

Students perform an activity that illustrates the method for calculating the area of a parallelogram. In Lesson 79 students learn that every triangle is half of a parallelogram, which leads to the formula for finding the area of a triangle.

Equivalent Measurements

Students convert measurements within the same measurement system.

Lesson 78 is a measurement lesson on capacity. Students identify and convert between measures in the U.S. Customary and metric systems.

Proportional Thinking

Students use a graphic organizer to translate ratio and solve ratio problems.

A key feature of a proportional relationship is that the ratio between two variables is constant. Students learn that this constant is called a scale factor. In Lesson 80 students solve ratio problems by finding equivalent ratios.

Constructions

The classical tools of geometry are the compass and the straightedge.

In Investigation 8 students learn to construct bisectors of segments and angles.

Assessment

A variety of weekly assessment tools are provided.

After Lesson 75:
- Power-Up Test 14
- Cumulative Test 14
- Performance Activity 14

After Lesson 80:
- Power-Up Test 15
- Cumulative Test 15
- Customized Benchmark Test
- Performance Task 15

LESSON	NEW CONCEPTS	PRACTICED	ASSESSED
71	• Parallelograms	Lessons 71, 73, 75, 76, 80, 81, 82, 86, 84, 85, 86, 87, 89, 91, 94, 96, 100, 102, 104, 113, 115, 118	Tests 15, 17, 20
72	• Fractions Chart	Lessons 72, 73, 74, 75, 76, 77, 78, 79, 80, 81, 82, 83, 84, 86, 87, 88, 89, 90, 91, 92, 94, 95, 96, 98, 99, 102, 105, 107, 110	Tests 15, 16, 17, 18, 19, 20, 21, 22, 23
	• Multiplying Three Fractions	Lessons 72, 73, 74, 75, 76, 79, 80, 81, 83, 84, 89, 90, 91, 94, 95, 96, 99, 102, 105, 107, 120	Test & Practice Generator
73	• Exponents	Lessons 73, 74, 75, 76, 77, 78, 79, 82, 83, 84, 88, 91, 93, 95, 96, 97, 99, 104, 105, 106, 110, 111, 116, 117, 120	Tests 19, 20, 22, 23
	• Writing Decimal Numbers as Fractions, Part 2	Lessons 73, 74, 76, 77, 78, 80, 81, 83, 85, 87, 89, 90, 94, 95, 97, 98, 99, 103, 106, 114	Tests 20, 21, 22, 23
74	• Writing Fractions as Decimal Numbers	Lessons 74, 76, 77, 78, 80, 81, 83, 84, 85, 87, 88, 89, 91, 92, 93, 94, 95, 96, 97, 98, 99, 102, 109, 116, 118	Tests 15, 19, 20, 22
	• Writing Ratios as Decimal Numbers	Lessons 74, 76, 77, 78, 80, 81, 83, 84, 85, 87, 88, 89, 91, 92, 93, 94, 95, 96, 97, 98, 99, 102, 109, 116, 118	Tests 15, 19, 20, 22
75	• Writing Fractions and Decimals as Percents, Part 1	Lessons 75, 76, 77, 78, 79, 80, 81, 82, 83, 84, 85, 86, 87, 88, 90, 91, 92, 93, 95, 96, 97, 98, 99, 106, 116, 119	Tests 16, 17, 19
76	• Comparing Fractions by Converting to Decimal Form	Lessons 76, 77, 78, 80, 81, 85, 95, 96, 97, 113	Test 16
77	• Finding Unstated Information in Fraction Problems	Lessons 77, 78, 79, 80, 83, 85, 90, 91, 92, 93, 95, 98, 99, 104, 108, 114, 116, 117, 118	Tests 16, 18, 20
78	• Capacity	Lessons 78, 79, 80, 81, 82, 84, 85, 87, 88, 89, 90, 92, 93, 94, 95, 96, 99, 100, 101, 103, 105, 106, 107, 108, 120	Test 16
79	• Area of a Triangle	Lessons 79, 80, 83, 84, 86, 88, 89, 90, 91, 92, 93, 94, 97, 99, 100, 102, 103, 105, 106, 113, 116, 117, 119, 120	Tests 16, 17, 18, 19, 21, 22, 23
80	• Using a Constant Factor to Solve Ratio Problems	Lessons 80, 81, 85, 86, 88, 89, 91, 98, 101, 103, 104, 105, 111, 112, 113, 118, 119	Tests 18, 20
Inv. 8	• Geometric Construction of Bisectors	Lesson 110	Test & Practice Generator

• Parallelograms

Objectives

- Identify opposite and adjacent angles in a parallelogram.
- Find the measure of an angle in a parallelogram when the measure of its opposite angle or adjacent angle is known.
- Create and use a model to show that parallelograms with sides the same length may have different areas.
- Find the area of a parallelogram.

Lesson Preparation

Materials

- **Power Up D** (in *Instructional Masters*)
- **Manipulative kit: metric rulers**
- **Teacher-provided: demonstration parallelogram** assembled using two 8-in. and two 10-in. strips of tagboard or cardboard, 4 brads, **graph paper, pencils, scissors**

Optional
- **Geometric Formulas poster**
- **Teacher-provided material: two yard or metersticks**

Math Language

New	Maintain	English Learners (ESL)
base	perpendicular	flexible
height	supplementary angles	

Technology Resources

Student eBook Complete student textbook in electronic format.

Resources and Planner CD Assessment, reteaching, and instructional masters, plus a pacing calendar with standards.

Test and Practice Generator CD Create additional practice sheets and custom-made tests.

www.SaxonPublishers.com Visit for more student activities and planning materials.

Inclusion

Adaptations CD Adapted lessons, investigations, practice and assessments.

Power Up D

Meeting Standards

National Council of Teachers of Mathematics (NCTM)

Geometry

GM.1a Precisely describe, classify, and understand relationships among types of two- and three-dimensional objects using their defining properties

GM.4a Draw geometric objects with specified properties, such as side lengths or angle measures

Measurement

ME.2b Select and apply techniques and tools to accurately find length, area, volume, and angle measures to appropriate levels of precision

Problem-Solving Strategy: Find a Pattern

Griffin used 14 blocks to build this three-layer pyramid. How many blocks would he need to build a six-layer pyramid? How many blocks would he need for the bottom layer of a nine-layer pyramid?

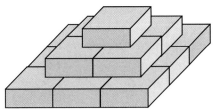

(Understand) **Understand the problem.**

"What information are we given?"

Griffin used 14 blocks to build a 3-layer pyramid.

"What are we asked to do?"

Determine how many blocks are needed to build a six-layer pyramid, and then determine how many blocks are needed for the bottom layer of a nine-layer pyramid.

(Plan) **Make a plan.**

"What problem-solving strategies will we use?"

We will *find a pattern*.

"How will we see a pattern?"

We will list the number of blocks in each layer and look for the pattern in the numbers.

(Solve) **Carry out the plan.**

"How many blocks are in each of the three layers in the picture?"

1×1, 2×2, and 3×3 for totals of 1, 4, and 9

"What is the pattern?"

Continuing from the top layer down, each layer has as many block as the number of the layer squared.

"What is the pattern extended to nine terms?"

1, 4, 9, 16, 25, 36, 49, 64, 81

"How many blocks are in the bottom layer of a nine-layer pyramid?"

81

"How many blocks are needed to build a six-layer pyramid?"

$1 + 4 + 9 + 16 + 25 + 36 = 91$ blocks.

(Check) **Look back.**

"Did we find the answers to the questions that were asked?"

Yes. We found that there are 91 blocks in a six-layer pyramid and 81 blocks on the bottom layer of a nine-layer pyramid.

1 Power Up

Facts

Distribute **Power Up D** to students. See answers below.

Mental Math

Before students begin the Mental Math exercise, do this counting exercise as a class.

Count by 12s from 12 to 144.

Encourage students to share different ways to mentally compute these exercises. Strategies for exercises **a** and **d** are listed below.

  a. Multiply Place Values, then Add
     $(5 \times 400) + (5 \times 80) = 2000 + 400 = 2400$
     Find 5 × 500, then Subtract 5 × 20
     $(5 \times 500) - (5 \times 20) = 2500 - 100 = 2400$
  d. Subtract $9, then Add 25¢
     $\$10 - \$9 = \$1; \$1 + 25¢ = \$1.25$
     Subtract $8, then Subtract 75¢
     $\$10 - \$8 = \$2; \$2 - 75¢ = \$1.25$

Problem Solving

Refer to **Power-Up Discussion**, p. 368F.

2 New Concepts

Instruction

Display the **Geometric Formulas** concept poster as you discuss parallelograms with students.

  "What kind of angle is angle C?" an acute angle

  "What is the measure of an acute angle?" less than 90°

  "What kind of angle is angle B?" an obtuse angle

  "What is the measure of an obtuse angle?" greater than 90° and less than 180°

(continued)

• Parallelograms

Power Up   *Building Power*
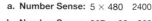

facts   Power Up D

mental math

  a. Number Sense: 5×480 2400
  b. Number Sense: $367 - 99$ 268
  c. Calculation: 8×43 344
  d. Calculation: $\$10.00 - \$8.75$ $1.25
  e. Number Sense: Double $2.25. $4.50
  f. Number Sense: $\frac{\$250}{100}$ $2.50
  g. Geometry: A square has an area of 25 in.². What is the length of the sides of the square?   5 in.
  h. Calculation: $8 \times 9, + 3, \div 3, \times 2, - 10, \div 5, + 3, \div 11$ 1

problem solving

Griffin used 14 blocks to build this three-layer pyramid. How many blocks would he need to build a six-layer pyramid? How many blocks would he need for the bottom layer of a nine-layer pyramid?   91 blocks; 81 blocks

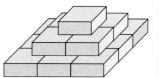

New Concept   *Increasing Knowledge*

In this lesson we will learn about various properties of parallelograms. The following example describes some angle properties of parallelograms.

Example 1

In parallelogram *ABCD*, the measure of angle *A* is 60°.

Reading Math
Give two other ways to name ∠*C*. ∠*BCD* and ∠*DCB*

  a. What is the measure of ∠*C*?
  b. What is the measure of ∠*B*?

Solution

  a. Angles *A* and *C* are opposite angles in that they are opposite to each other in the parallelogram. The opposite angles of a parallelogram have equal measures. So the measure of angle *C* equals the measure of angle *A*. Thus the measure of ∠*C* is **60°**.

Facts   Multiply.

7 × 7 = 49	4 × 6 = 24	8 × 1 = 8	2 × 2 = 4	0 × 5 = 0	6 × 3 = 18	8 × 9 = 72	5 × 8 = 40	6 × 2 = 12	10 × 10 = 100
9 × 4 = 36	2 × 5 = 10	9 × 6 = 54	7 × 3 = 21	5 × 5 = 25	7 × 2 = 14	6 × 8 = 48	3 × 5 = 15	9 × 9 = 81	5 × 4 = 20
3 × 4 = 12	6 × 5 = 30	8 × 2 = 16	4 × 4 = 16	6 × 7 = 42	8 × 8 = 64	2 × 3 = 6	7 × 4 = 28	5 × 9 = 45	3 × 8 = 24
3 × 9 = 27	7 × 8 = 56	2 × 4 = 8	5 × 7 = 35	3 × 3 = 9	9 × 7 = 63	4 × 8 = 32	0 × 0 = 0	9 × 2 = 18	6 × 6 = 36

b. Angles *A* and *B* are adjacent angles in that they share a side. (Side *AB* is a side of ∠*A* and a side of ∠*B*.) The adjacent angles of a parallelogram are supplementary. So ∠*A* and ∠*B* are supplementary, which means their measures total 180°. Since ∠*A* measures 60°, ∠*B* must measure **120°** for their sum to be 180°.

Model A flexible model of a parallelogram is useful for illustrating some properties of a parallelogram. A model can be constructed of brads and stiff tagboard or cardboard.

Lay two 8-in. strips of tagboard or cardboard over two parallel 10-in. strips as shown. Punch a hole at the center of the overlapping ends. Then fasten the corners with brads to hold the strips together.

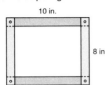

If we move the sides of the parallelogram back and forth, we see that opposite sides always remain parallel and equal in length. Though the angles change size, opposite angles remain equal and adjacent angles remain supplementary.

With this model we also can observe how the area of a parallelogram changes as the angles change. We hold the model with two hands and slide opposite sides in opposite directions. The maximum area occurs when the angles are 90°. The area reduces to zero as opposite sides come together.

  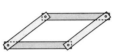

Discuss The area of a parallelogram changes as the angles change. Does the perimeter change?

The flexible model shows that parallelograms may have sides that are equal in length but areas that are different. To find the area of a parallelogram, we multiply two **perpendicular** measurements. We multiply the **base** by the **height** of the parallelogram.

No, the perimeter does not change because the lengths of the sides do not change.

Example 1
Instruction

To help students recognize angle measures, draw parallelogram *ABCD* on the board or overhead.

Label the measures of the angles given in the problem and found in the solution: ∠*A* = 60°, ∠*B* = 120°, and ∠*C* = 60°.

Then ask students to describe two different ways to find the measure of angle *D*. Sample: Angles *B* and *D* are opposite angles, so the measure of angle *D* equals the measure of angle *B*. Since angle *B* is 120°, angle *D* is 120°. Or, angles *C* and *D* are adjacent angles, and adjacent angles of a parallelogram are supplementary. The measures of angles *C* and *D* must total 180°. Since angle *C* is 60°, angle *D* is 120°.

Encourage students to find the sum of the four angle measures to learn that the sum of the angle measures of a quadrilateral is 360°.

Instruction

"Our model of the parallelogram is made from two 8-inch strips and two 10-inch strips. What is the perimeter of our model?" about 36 in.

"If the shape of our model changes, does the perimeter of the model change?" no

(continued)

English Learners

Refer to the drawing of the model of the parallelogram. Say,

"Flexible means that something is easily bent or changed. In this drawing the shape of the model is flexible."

Ask a volunteer to explain the word flexible in relation to everyday situations.

Manipulative Use

Demonstrate **how to construct the flexible model of a parallelogram** that is described above. Move the sides of the model to form several different parallelograms. For each parallelogram you form, help students recognize that the area of the parallelogram changes, but its perimeter remains constant.

Instruction

Distribute the materials to each student, then ask students to draw a parallelogram by following the steps of the activity.

Explain that the steps should be used as a guide, and students should draw a parallelogram that has a different base and a different height than the parallelogram described in the activity.

After the students complete drawing the parallelogram, ask,

> **"How can you check if the segments you drew are parallel?"** Sample: For each segment, count the number of units the top endpoint is to the right and up from the bottom endpoint. If the distance and the direction are the same for each segment, the segments are parallel.

Before cutting the parallelogram into two pieces, have students note that although one cut line is shown, two other cut lines are possible—one is to the right of the given cut line and the other is to the left.

(continued)

The base of a parallelogram is the length of one of the sides. The height of a parallelogram is the perpendicular distance from the base to the opposite side. The following activity will illustrate why the area of a parallelogram equals the base times the height.

Activity

Area of a Parallelogram

Materials needed:

- graph paper
- ruler
- pencil
- scissors

Represent Tracing over the lines on the graph paper, draw two parallel segments the same number of units long but shifted slightly as shown.

Then draw segments between the endpoints of the pair of parallel segments to complete the parallelogram.

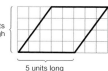

4 units high

5 units long

The base of the parallelogram we drew has a length of 5 units. The height of the parallelogram is 4 units. Your parallelogram might be different. How many units long and high is your parallelogram? Can you easily count the number of square units in the area of your parallelogram?

Model Use scissors to cut out your parallelogram.

Then select a line on the graph paper that is perpendicular to the first pair of parallel sides that you drew. Cut the parallelogram into two pieces along this line.

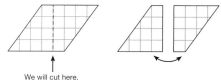

We will cut here.

Rearrange the two pieces of the parallelogram to form a rectangle. What is the length and width of the rectangle? How many square units is the area of the rectangle?

Our rectangle is 5 units long and 4 units wide. The area of the rectangle is 20 square units. So the area of the parallelogram is also 20 square units.

By making a perpendicular cut across the parallelogram and rearranging the pieces, we formed a rectangle having the same area as the parallelogram. The length and width of the rectangle equaled the base and height of the parallelogram. Therefore, by multiplying the base and height of a parallelogram, we can find its area.

Example 2

Find the area of this parallelogram:

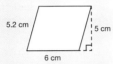

Solution

We multiply two perpendicular measurements, the base and the height. The height is often shown as a dashed line segment. The base is 6 cm. The height is 5 cm.

$$6 \text{ cm} \times 5 \text{ cm} = 30 \text{ sq. cm}$$

The area of the parallelogram is **30 sq. cm.**

Practice Set

Conclude Refer to parallelogram *QRST* to answer problems **a–d.**

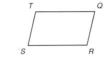

a. Which angle is opposite ∠Q? ∠S

b. Which angle is opposite ∠T? ∠R

▸ **c.** Name two angles that are supplements of ∠T. ∠S and ∠Q

d. If the measure of ∠R is 100°, what is the measure of ∠Q? 80°

▸ Calculate the perimeter and area of each parallelogram:

e.

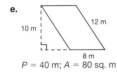

P = 40 m; *A* = 80 sq. m

f.

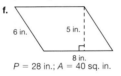

P = 28 in.; *A* = 40 sq. in.

Lesson 71   371

▸ See Math Conversations in the sidebar.

---

2 New Concepts (Continued)

Instruction

If students count unit squares to determine the area of the rectangle, remind them that the multiplications 5 × 4 or 4 × 5 can also be used.

Example 2

Instruction

Make sure students recognize that the height (5 cm) of the parallelogram is different than the length of the slanted side (5.2 cm).

"Which measurements of the parallelogram are used to find its area?" 6 cm and 5 cm, or its side length

"Which measurements of the parallelogram are used to find its perimeter?" 6 cm and 5.2 cm, or its side lengths

Practice Set

Problem c [Error Alert]

When one angle is a supplement of another angle, students must recognize that the sum of the measures of the angles is 180°.

Problems e and f [Error Alert]

To calculate the perimeter, students must use the side lengths, and not the height, of the parallelogram. To calculate the area, students must use the height, not the slanted side, of the parallelogram.

(continued)

Practice Set
Problem g [Analyze]

Help students understand that this is a two-step problem. Ask students to identify what they can find with the information given. the area of the parallelogram on the left

Ask:

"What is the area of the parallelogram on the left?" Area = base × height = 12 × 6 = 72 cm²

"How can we use this answer to find the height of the parallelogram on the right?" We can substitute the values we know into the formula for the area of a parallelogram and solve for h:

$$A = b \times h$$
$$72 = 9 \times h$$
$$\frac{72}{9} = \frac{9h}{9}$$
$$8 = h$$

3 Written Practice

Math Conversations
Discussion opportunities are provided below.

Problem 4 [Analyze]
"Which terms of these fractions can we cancel before we multiply? Explain why." $\frac{3}{3}$ and $\frac{2}{8}$ can be canceled because $\frac{2}{3}$ and $\frac{3}{8}$ are factors of a multiplication; $\frac{3}{3}$ cancels to $\frac{1}{1}$ and $\frac{2}{8}$ cancels to $\frac{1}{4}$.

Problem 5 [Analyze]
"What is the fraction form of each mixed number?" $\frac{5}{4}$ and $\frac{8}{3}$

Problem 6 [Analyze]
"When can you cancel the two 3s?" After the division is rewritten as the product of $\frac{3}{4}$ and the reciprocal of $\frac{3}{8}$, which is $\frac{8}{3}$.

Problem 7 [Analyze]
"Explain how to write a whole number in fraction form." Write the whole number as the numerator of a fraction having 1 as its denominator.

(continued)

> **g.** [Analyze] A formula for finding the area of a parallelogram is $A = bh$. This formula means

Area = base × height

The base is the length of one side. The height is the perpendicular distance to the opposite side. Here we show the same parallelogram in two different positions, so the area of the parallelogram is the same in both drawings. What is the height in the figure on the right?   8 cm

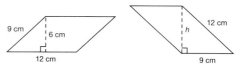

1. What is the least common multiple of 6 and 10?   30
(30)

2. [Analyze] The highest point on land is Mt. Everest, whose peak is 29,035 feet above sea level. The lowest point on land is the Dead Sea, which dips to 1371 feet below sea level. What is the difference in elevation between these two points?   30,406 feet
(14)

3. The movie lasted 105 minutes. If the movie started at 1:15 p.m., at what time did it end?   3:00 p.m.
(32)

[Analyze] In problems **4–7**, reduce the fractions, if possible, before multiplying.

▸ * 4. $\frac{2}{3} \cdot \frac{3}{8}$ $\frac{1}{4}$
(70)

▸ * 5. $1\frac{1}{4} \cdot 2\frac{2}{3}$ $3\frac{1}{3}$
(70)

▸ * 6. $\frac{3}{4} \div \frac{3}{8}$ 2
(70)

▸ * 7. $4\frac{1}{2} \div 6$ $\frac{3}{4}$
(70)

8. $6 + 3\frac{3}{4} + 2\frac{1}{2}$ $12\frac{1}{4}$ **9.** $5 - 3\frac{1}{8}$ $1\frac{7}{8}$ **10.** $5\frac{1}{4} - 1\frac{7}{8}$ $3\frac{3}{8}$
(59)   (63)   (63)

11. $(3.5)^2$ 12.25
(39)

12. $15\overline{)\$75.00}$ $5.00
(2)

13. $(1 + 0.6) \div (1 - 0.6)$ 4
(53)

14. Quan ordered a \$4.50 bowl of soup. The tax rate was $7\frac{1}{2}$% (which equals 0.075). He paid for the soup with a \$20 bill.
(41)

  a. What was the tax on the bowl of soup?   34¢

  b. What was the total price including tax?   \$4.84

  c. How much money should Quan get back from his payment?   \$15.16

* 15. What is the name for the point on the coordinate plane that has the coordinates (0, 0)?   origin
(Inv. 7)

▸ See Math Conversations in the sidebar.

▶* 16. **Represent** Refer to the coordinate plane below to locate the points
(Inv. 7) indicated.

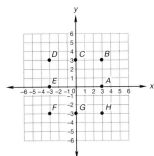

Name the points that have the following coordinates:

a. $(-3, 3)$ point D   **b.** $(0, -3)$ point G

Identify the coordinates of the following points:

c. H $(3, -3)$ **d.** E $(-3, 0)$

Find each unknown number:

17. $1.2f = 120$ 100   **18.** $\frac{120}{f} = 1.2$ 100
(49)   (49)

▶* 19. Write the prime factorization of both the numerator and the denominator
(67) of this fraction. Then reduce the fraction. $\frac{2 \cdot 2 \cdot 2 \cdot 2 \cdot 2 \cdot 2}{2 \cdot 2 \cdot 2 \cdot 2 \cdot 2 \cdot 7} = \frac{2}{7}$

$$\frac{64}{224}$$

20. The perimeter of a square is 6.4 meters. What is its area?
(38) 2.56 square meters

21. **Analyze** What fraction of this circle is not
(Inv. 2) shaded? $\frac{3}{4}$

22. **Explain** If the radius of this circle is 1 cm,
(47) what is the circumference of the circle? (Use
3.14 for π.) How did you find your answer? 6.28 cm; Sample: I multiplied
the radius by 2 to find the diameter. Then I multiplied the diameter by 3.14.

23. **Estimate** A centimeter is about as long as this segment:
(7)

⎯⎯⎯

About how many centimeters long is your little finger? Answers will
vary but should be near 5 cm.

Lesson 71   373

▶ See Math Conversations in the sidebar.

---

3 **Written Practice** *(Continued)*

Math Conversations

Discussion opportunities are provided below.

Problem 16 **Represent**

**"A point lies to the left of the origin. Is
the sign of its x-coordinate positive or
negative?"** negative

**"A point lies above the origin. Is the sign
of its y-coordinate positive or negative?"**
positive

**"A point lies to the right of the origin. Is
the sign of its x-coordinate positive or
negative?"** positive

**"A point lies below the origin. Is the sign
of its y-coordinate positive or negative?"**
negative

As students plot and locate points, help them
generalize that the sign of a x-coordinate
describes distance to the left or to the right
of the y-axis and the sign of a y-coordinate
describes distance above or below the x-axis.

Problem 19 **Analyze**

Extend the Problem

**"We reduced the given fraction to $\frac{2}{7}$.
Describe two ways we could check
our answer."** Sample: Reduce $\frac{64}{224}$ by
division and compare the quotient to $\frac{2}{7}$;
use multiplication to decide if the prime
factorization of the numerator is equal
to 64 and the prime factorization of the
denominator is equal to 224.

Errors and Misconceptions
Problem 16

When working in the coordinate plane,
students should develop the following
general ideas.

• Coordinates are ordered pairs of the form
(x, y), where the x-coordinate represents
horizontal direction and distance from the
origin, and the y-coordinate represents
vertical direction and distance from
the origin.

One way to offer additional practice is to
write the four sign-only coordinates shown
below on the board or overhead.

$$(+, +) (+, -) (-, +) (-, -)$$

Then ask students to generalize where in the
coordinate plane each point can be found. For
example, a point whose x-coordinate and
y-coordinate are positive $(+, +)$ can be found
to the right of the y-axis and above the x-axis,
that is, in the first quadrant.

(continued)

Math Conversations

Discussion opportunities are provided below.

Problem 27 Analyze

"What do you know to be true about the lengths of the sides of a square?" all of the sides are the same length

"Is a square a regular polygon?" yes

"Problem 27 tells us about a regular triangle. What is true about the lengths of the sides of a regular triangle?" all of the sides are the same length

---

24. **Connect** Water freezes at 32°
(10) Fahrenheit. The temperature shown on the thermometer is how many degrees Fahrenheit above the freezing point of water? 4°F

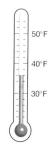

25. Ray watched TV for one hour. He determined that commercials were
(29, 33) shown 20% of that hour. Write 20% as a reduced fraction. Then find the number of minutes that commercials were shown during the hour. $\frac{1}{5}$; 12 minutes

26. Name the geometric solid shown
(Inv. 6) at right. cone

▶* **27.** **Analyze** This square and regular triangle
(60) share a common side. The perimeter of the square is 24 cm. What is the perimeter of the triangle? 18 cm

28. Choose the appropriate unit for the area of your state. C
(31) **A** square inches   **B** square yards   **C** square miles

* **29.** **a.** What is the perimeter of this
(71)   parallelogram? 36 cm

   b. What is the area of this
      parallelogram? 70 cm²

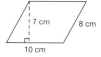

* **30.** **Conclude** In this figure ∠BMD is a right angle.
(69) Name two angles that are
   a. supplementary.

   b. complementary.
   a. ∠AMB (or ∠BMA) and ∠BMC (or ∠CMB);
      or ∠CMD (or ∠DMC) and ∠DMA (or ∠AMD)
   b. ∠BMC (or ∠CMB) and ∠CMD (or ∠DMC)

▶ See Math Conversations in the sidebar.

Looking Forward

Identifying and finding the measure of opposite and adjacent angles in a parallelogram and finding and exploring the area of a parallelogram prepare students for:

• **Lesson 79,** finding the area of triangles.

• **Lesson 91,** identifying and using geometric formulas to find the perimeter and area of squares, rectangles, parallelograms, and triangles.

• **Lesson 98,** finding the sum of the angle measures of triangles and quadrilaterals.

• Fractions Chart
• Multiplying Three Fractions

Objectives

- Recognize the rules for adding, subtracting, multiplying, and dividing fractions.
- Follow three steps to multiply three or more fractions or mixed numbers.

Lesson Preparation

Materials

- **Power Up H** (in *Instructional Masters*)
- **Manipulative kit:** inch rulers
- **Teacher-provided material:** dot or grid paper, 3 × 5 cards

Power Up H

Math Language

	English Learners (ESL)
	remaining terms

Technology Resources

Student eBook Complete student textbook in electronic format.

Resources and Planner CD Assessment, reteaching, and instructional masters, plus a pacing calendar with standards.

Test and Practice Generator CD Create additional practice sheets and custom-made tests.

www.SaxonPublishers.com Visit for more student activities and planning materials.

Inclusion

Adaptations CD Adapted lessons, investigations, practice and assessments.

Meeting Standards

National Council of Teachers of Mathematics (NCTM)

Numbers and Operations

NO.1a Work flexibly with fractions, decimals, and percents to solve problems

NO.1f Use factors, multiples, prime factorization, and relatively prime numbers to solve problems

NO.2a Understand the meaning and effects of arithmetic operations with fractions, decimals, and integers

NO.3a Select appropriate methods and tools for computing with fractions and decimals from among mental computation, estimation, calculators or computers, and paper and pencil, depending on the situation, and apply the selected methods

Problem-Solving Strategy: Use Logical Reasoning

Kioko was thinking of two numbers whose average was 24. If one of the numbers was half of 24, what was the other number?

(Understand) **Understand the problem.**

"What information are we given?"

Two numbers have an average of 24. One of the numbers is half of 24.

"What are we asked to do?"

We are asked to find the second number Kioko was thinking of.

(Plan) **Make a plan.**

"What problem-solving strategy will we use?"

We will *use logical reasoning* and basic number sense.

"What do we know about the average of two numbers that can help us solve the problem?"

The average of two numbers is halfway between the two numbers.

(Solve) **Carry out the plan.**

"From the given information, what is one of Kioko's numbers?"

One of Kioko's numbers is half of 24, which is 12.

"Twenty-four is halfway between 12 and what number?"

Twelve is 12 less than 24. So the unknown number is 12 more than 24, which is 36.

(Check) **Look back.**

"Did we complete the task?"

Yes. We found Kioko's other number.

"How can we show that our answer is correct?"

We will find the average of 12 and 36 to see if it is 24, as stated in the problem. $12 + 36 = 48$; $48 \div 2 = 24$. We are correct. The average is 24.

- Fractions Chart
- Multiplying Three Fractions

36 pts

Power Up | *Building Power*

facts | Power Up H

mental math
a. **Number Sense:** 3×125 375
b. **Number Sense:** $275 + 50$ 325
c. **Number Sense:** $3 \times \$0.99$ $2.97
d. **Calculation:** $\$20.00 - \$9.99$ $10.01
e. **Fractional Parts:** $\frac{1}{3}$ of $6.60 $2.20
f. **Decimals:** $\$2.50 \times 10$ $25.00
g. **Statistics:** Find the average 45, 33, and 60.   46
h. **Calculation:** $2 \times 2, \times 2, \times 2, \times 2, - 2, \div 2$ 15

problem solving | Kioko was thinking of two numbers whose average was 24. If one of the numbers was half of 24, what was the other number?   36

New Concepts | *Increasing Knowledge*

fractions chart

We have learned three steps to take when performing pencil-and-paper arithmetic with fractions and mixed numbers:

Step 1: Write the problem in the correct **shape**.

Step 2: Perform the **operation**.

Step 3: **Simplify** the answer.

The letters S.O.S. can help us remember the steps as "shape," "operate," and "simplify." We summarize the S.O.S. rules we have learned in the following fractions chart.

Fractions Chart

	+ −	× ÷	
1. Shape	Write fractions with common denominators.	Write numbers in fraction form.	
2. Operate	Add or subtract the numerators.	**×** Cancel.	**÷** Find reciprocal of divisor, then cancel.
		Multiply numerators. Multiply denominators.	
3. Simplify	Reduce fractions. Convert improper fractions.		

Lesson 72   375

---

1 Power Up

Facts
Distribute **Power Up H** to students. See answers below.

Mental Math
Before students begin the Mental Math exercise, do this counting exercise as a class.

Count up and down by $\frac{1}{8}$s between $\frac{1}{8}$ and 2.

Encourage students to share different ways to mentally compute these exercises. Strategies for exercises **d** and **e** are listed below.

d. **Subtract $10, then Add 1¢**
$\$20 - \$10 = \$10; \$10 + 1¢ = \$10.01$
Add 1¢ to Each Amount
$\$20.00 + 1¢ = \$20.01$ and
$\$9.99 + 1¢ = \$10; \$20.01 - \$10 = \$10.01$

e. **Divide Place Values**
$\$6 \div 3 = \$2$ and $60¢ \div 3 = 20¢;$
$\$2 + 20¢ = \$2.20$
Use Repeated Addition
Since $\$2 + \$2 + \$2 = \$6$ and $20¢ + 20¢ + 20¢ = 60¢$, $\frac{1}{3}$ of $6.60 = $2.20.

Problem Solving
Refer to **Power-Up Discussion**, p. 375B.

2 New Concepts

If students need to review their work with fractions, refer to Lessons 57, 66, and 68.

(continued)

Facts | Multiply or divide as indicated.

4 ×9 ── 36	4 4)16	6 ×8 ── 48	4 3)12	5 ×7 ── 35	8 4)32	3 ×9 ── 27	9 9)81	6 ×2 ── 12	8 8)64
9 ×7 ── 63	5 8)40	2 ×4 ── 8	7 6)42	5 ×5 ── 25	2 7)14	7 ×7 ── 49	1 8)8	3 ×3 ── 9	0 6)0
7 ×3 ── 21	5 2)10	10 ×10 ── 100	8 3)24	4 ×5 ── 20	6 9)54	9 ×1 ── 9	2 3)6	7 ×4 ── 28	8 7)56
6 ×6 ── 36	9 2)18	3 ×5 ── 15	6 5)30	2 ×2 ── 4	3 6)18	9 ×5 ── 45	4 6)24	2 ×8 ── 16	8 9)72

Instruction

Explain to students that the fractions chart summarizes what they have learned about operations with fractions and mixed numbers. After students examine the chart, ask them to
- describe the steps for addition or subtraction with fractions or mixed numbers.
- describe the steps for multiplication.
- describe the steps for division.

Example

Instruction

Remind students that reducing a term in a numerator and in a denominator of the fractions means that both terms are divisible by a common factor greater than 1.

"After the mixed numbers are written as improper fractions, why can we reduce a 3 in the numerator and a 3 in the denominator?" The greatest common factor of the numbers is 3, and $3 \div 3 = 1$.

"Why can we reduce an 8 in the numerator and a 4 in the denominator?" The greatest common factor of 8 and 4 is 4; $8 \div 4 = 2$ and $4 \div 4 = 1$.

Practice Set

Problem a [Error Alert]

Drawing the chart and using it for reference can help students minimize the number of errors they may make. You might choose to ask students to draw the chart in the front of their math notebooks or on 3 by 5 cards.

(continued)

- Below the $+$ and $-$ symbols we list the steps for adding or subtracting fractions.
- Below the $\times$ and $\div$ symbols, we list the steps for multiplying or dividing fractions.

The "shape" step for addition and subtraction is the same; we write the fractions with common denominators. Likewise, the "shape" step for multiplication and division is the same; we write both numbers in fraction form.

Math Language
Recall that **canceling** means reducing before multiplying.

At the "operate" step, however, we separate multiplication and division. When multiplying fractions, we may reduce (cancel) before we multiply. Then we multiply the numerators to find the numerator of the product, and we multiply the denominators to find the denominator of the product. When dividing fractions, we first replace the divisor of the division problem with its reciprocal and change the division problem to a multiplication problem. We cancel terms, if possible, and then multiply.

The "simplify" step is the same for all four operations. We reduce answers when possible and convert answers that are improper fractions to mixed numbers.

multiplying three fractions

To multiply three or more fractions, we follow the same steps we take when multiplying two fractions:

Step 1: We write the numbers in fraction form.

Step 2: We cancel terms by reducing numerator-denominator pairs that have common factors. Then we multiply the remaining terms.

Step 3: We simplify if possible.

Example

Multiply: $\frac{2}{3} \times 1\frac{3}{5} \times \frac{3}{4}$

Solution

First we write $1\frac{3}{5}$ as the improper fraction $\frac{8}{5}$. Then we reduce where possible before multiplying. Multiplying the remaining terms, we find the product.

$$\frac{2}{\underset{1}{\cancel{3}}} \times \frac{\overset{2}{\cancel{8}}}{5} \times \frac{\overset{1}{\cancel{3}}}{\underset{1}{\cancel{4}}} = \frac{4}{5}$$

Practice Set ▶

b. Step 1: Write the fractions so that the denominators are the same. Step 2: Add the numerators but not the denominators. Step 3: Simplify the answer if possible.

a. Draw the fractions chart from this lesson.   See student work.

b. Describe the three steps for adding fractions.

c. Describe the steps for dividing fractions.   (See below.)

▶ Multiply:

d. $\frac{2}{3} \cdot \frac{4}{5} \cdot \frac{3}{8}$ $\frac{1}{5}$

e. $2\frac{1}{2} \times 1\frac{1}{10} \times 4$ 11

c. Step 1: Write any mixed numbers in fraction form. Step 2: Rewrite the division problem as a multiplication problem by changing the divisor to its reciprocal. Cancel terms; then multiply the fractions. Step 3: Simplify the answer if possible.

▶ See Math Conversations in the sidebar.

Teacher Tip

To complete the example, students will need to **recall how to change a mixed number to an improper fraction.** If necessary, invite volunteers to demonstrate on the board or overhead different ways to make such a change.

English Learners

Explain the meaning of **remaining** terms. Say,

"When we cancel terms, we cross them out. The remaining terms are the ones that are not crossed out. They are the terms that are left after canceling is complete."

Refer students to example 2. Ask a volunteer to reduce by canceling and then name the remaining terms.

Written Practice
Strengthening Concepts

1. What is the average of 4.2, 2.61, and 3.6?   3.47
(18)

2. *Connect* Four tablespoons equals $\frac{1}{4}$ cup. How many tablespoons
(54) would equal one full cup?   16 tablespoons

3. The temperature on the moon ranges from a high of about 130°C
(14) to a low of about −110°C. This is a difference of how many
degrees?   240°C

4. Four of the 12 marbles in the bag are blue. If one marble is taken from
(58) the bag, what is the probability that the marble is
a. blue? $\frac{1}{3}$ **b.** not blue? $\frac{2}{3}$

c. What word names the relationship between the events in **a** and **b**?
complementary

5. The diameter of a circle is 1 meter. The circumference is how many
(7, 47) centimeters? (Use 3.14 for π.)   314 centimeters

6. *Connect* What fraction of a dollar is a nickel? $\frac{1}{20}$
(29)

Find each unknown number:

7. $n - \frac{1}{2} = \frac{3}{5}$ $1\frac{1}{10}$ **8.** $1 - w = \frac{7}{12}$ $\frac{5}{12}$
(56)   (43)

9. $w + 2\frac{1}{2} = 3\frac{1}{3}$ $\frac{5}{6}$ **10.** $1 - w = 0.23$ 0.77
(59)   (43)

11. Write the standard decimal number for the following: 60.43
(46)

$$(6 \times 10) + \left(4 \times \frac{1}{10}\right) + \left(3 \times \frac{1}{100}\right)$$

12. *Estimate* Which of these numbers is closest to 1?   **B**
(50) **A** −1   **B** 0.1   **C** 10

13. What is the largest prime number that is less than 100?   97
(19)

▶* **14** *Classify* Which of these figures is not a parallelogram?   **C**
(64) **A**   **C**

   B   **D**

▶ **15.** *Connect* A loop of string two feet around is formed to make a square.
(38) **a.** How many inches long is each side of the square?   6 inches

b. What is the area of the square in square inches?   36 square inches

▶ See Math Conversations in the sidebar.

Practice Set
Problems d and e [Error Alert]
To help students find the correct products,
encourage them to use the three steps—Shape,
Operate, and Simplify—to solve the problems,
or invite volunteers to describe each step in
problem d and in problem e to the class.

3 Written Practice

Math Conversations
Discussion opportunities are provided below.

Problem 1 [Analyze]
Extend the Problem
*"How can we use rounding and estimation
to help decide the reasonableness of our
answer?"* Sample: Make an estimate by
rounding each addend to the nearest whole
number, then divide the sum of the addends
by 3 and compare. Since the sum of the
rounded addends is 11 and 12 ÷ 4 = 3, the
exact answer should be less than 3.

Problem 14 [Classify]
*"How many pairs of parallel sides does a
parallelogram have?"* two pairs

Problem 15 [Connect]
Suggest that students draw and label the sides
of a square to help solve this problem.

(continued)

3 Written Practice (Continued)

Math Conversations

Discussion opportunities are provided below.

Problem 16 [Conclude]

"Because Figure ABCD is a rectangle, what kind of angles are angles A, B, C, and D?"
right or 90° angles

"If two angles are complementary, what is the sum of their measures?" 90°

"What is the sum of the measures of two angles that are supplementary?" 180°

Problem 21 [Analyze]

Extend the Problem

"Describe a way we could check our exact answer of $\frac{3}{5}$ for reasonableness."
Sample: Use divisibility rules to reduce $\frac{72}{120}$ to simplest form.

Invite volunteers to demonstrate the different ways on the board or overhead.

(continued)

▶* **16.** [Conclude] Figure *ABCD* is a rectangle.
(69)
   a. Name an angle complementary to ∠*DCM*.
   ∠*MCB* or ∠*BCM*
   b. Name an angle supplementary to ∠*AMC*.
   ∠*CMB* (or ∠*BMC*) or ∠*DCM* (or ∠*MCD*)

Refer to this menu and the information that follows to answer problems **17–19.**

Menu

		Juice:	
Grilled Chicken Sandwich	$3.49	Small	$0.89
Green Salad	$3.29	Medium	$1.09
Pasta Salad	$2.89	Large	$1.29

From this menu the Johnsons ordered two grilled chicken sandwiches, one green salad, one small juice, and two medium juices.

17. What was the total price of the Johnsons' order? $13.34
(1)

18. If 7% tax is added to the bill, and if the Johnsons pay for the food with a
(41) $20 bill, how much money should they get back? $5.73

19. [Formulate] Make up an order from the menu. Then calculate the bill,
(1) not including tax. See student work.

20. If *A = lw*, and if *l* equals 2.5 and *w* equals 0.4, what does *A* equal? 1
(47)

▶* **21.** Write the prime factorization of both the numerator and the denominator
(66) of this fraction. Then reduce the fraction. $\frac{2 \cdot 2 \cdot 2 \cdot 3 \cdot 3}{2 \cdot 2 \cdot 2 \cdot 3 \cdot 5} = \frac{3}{5}$

$$\frac{72}{120}$$

Refer to the coordinate plane below to answer problems **22** and **23.**

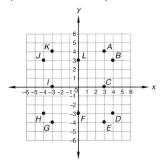

* **22.** Identify the coordinates of the following points:
(Inv. 7)
   a. *K* (−3, 4)   **b.** *F* (0, −3)

* **23.** Name the points that have the following coordinates:
(Inv. 7)
   a. (3, −4) point *E*   **b.** (−3, 0) point *I*

▶ See Math Conversations in the sidebar.

24. Sample:

▶ **24.** *(Model)* Draw a pair of parallel lines. Then draw a second pair of parallel lines perpendicular to the first pair of lines and about the same distance apart. Trace the quadrilateral that is formed by the intersecting lines. Is the quadrilateral a rectangle?   yes
(64)

▶ **25.** $\dfrac{1}{2} \cdot \dfrac{5}{6} \cdot \dfrac{3}{5}$ $\dfrac{1}{4}$
(72)

▶ **26.** $3 \times 1\dfrac{1}{2} \times 2\dfrac{2}{3}$ 12
(72)

▶ **27.** $\dfrac{3}{4} \div 2$ $\dfrac{3}{8}$
(54)

▶ **28.** $1\dfrac{1}{2} \div 1\dfrac{2}{3}$ $\dfrac{9}{10}$
(68)

29. (0.12)(0.24)   0.0288
(39)

30. 0.6 ÷ 0.25   2.4
(49)

Early Finishers
Real-World Application

LaDonna had errands to run and decided to park her car in front of a parking meter rather than drive from store to store. She calculated that she would spend about 20 minutes in the post office and 10 minutes at the hardware store. Then she would spend 5 minutes picking up her clothes from the cleaner's and another 30 minutes eating lunch.

The sign on the meter read

$0.25 = 15 minutes

$0.10 = 6 minutes

$0.05 = 3 minutes

a. How much time will LaDonna spend to finish doing her errands?   65 minutes

b. If the meter has ten minutes left, how much money will she need to put into the meter?   At least $0.95

Lesson 72   379

▶ See Math Conversations in the sidebar.

Looking Forward

Multiplying three or more fractions or mixed numbers prepares students for:

• **Lesson 92,** simplifying powers of fractions.

Math Conversations

Discussion opportunities are provided below.

Problem 24 Model

If students have difficulty recognizing that a rectangle is formed by the pairs of intersecting lines, have them use a ruler and draw the lines on grid or dot paper.

You may need to point out that a square is also classified as a rectangle.

Problem 25 Analyze

"Which terms of these fractions can you reduce before multiplying?" 3 and 6; 5 and 5

"Why can you reduce those terms?" Sample: 3 and 6 can be reduced because each can be divided by 3; 5 and 5 can be reduced because 5 ÷ 5 = 1.

Problem 28 Analyze

"Can you cancel the denominator 2 in $1\dfrac{1}{2}$ and the numerator 2 in $1\dfrac{2}{3}$? Explain why or why not." No; terms of fractions can only be canceled when multiplying and when the numbers are in fraction form.

Errors and Misconceptions
Problem 26

Students who cancel the denominator 2 in the mixed number $1\dfrac{1}{2}$ and the numerator 2 in the mixed number $2\dfrac{2}{3}$ are likely to name 14 as the answer.

Invite a volunteer to solve the problem on the board or overhead, and demonstrate that terms of fractions in a multiplication can only be canceled after whole numbers and mixed numbers have been rewritten as improper fractions.

Problem 27

An answer of $1\dfrac{1}{2}$ represents canceling the denominator 4 and the numerator 2 before the division is rewritten as a multiplication.

Remind students that canceling can only occur in multiplication. Then ask students to complete the following division.

$$\dfrac{2}{3} \div \dfrac{3}{2} \quad \dfrac{4}{9}$$

• Exponents
• Writing Decimal Numbers as Fractions, Part 2

Objectives

- Read expressions with exponents.
- Find the value of expressions with exponents.
- Write the prime factorization of a number using exponents.
- Write a decimal number as a fraction or mixed number.

Lesson Preparation

Materials

- Power Up J (in *Instructional Masters*)

Optional

- Place Value poster

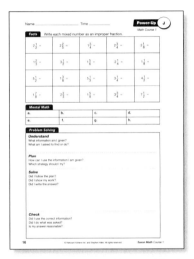

Power Up J

Math Language

New	Maintain
power	exponent

Technology Resources

Student eBook Complete student textbook in electronic format.

Resources and Planner CD Assessment, reteaching, and instructional masters, plus a pacing calendar with standards.

Test and Practice Generator CD Create additional practice sheets and custom-made tests.

www.SaxonPublishers.com Visit for more student activities and planning materials.

Inclusion

Adaptations CD Adapted lessons, investigations, practice and assessments.

Meeting Standards

National Council of Teachers of Mathematics (NCTM)

Numbers and Operations

NO.1a Work flexibly with fractions, decimals, and percents to solve problems

NO.1e Develop an understanding of large numbers and recognize and appropriately use exponential, scientific, and calculator notation

NO.2a Understand the meaning and effects of arithmetic operations with fractions, decimals, and integers

Problem-Solving Strategy: Make an Organized List

How many different ways can Gunther spin a total of 6 if he spins each spinner once?

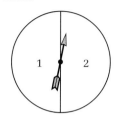  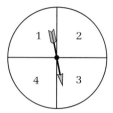

(Understand) **Understand the problem.**

"What information are we given?"

Gunther spins each of three spinners once.

"What are we asked to do?"

List the possible combinations of the three spinners resulting in a total of 6 points.

(Plan) **Make a plan.**

"What problem-solving strategy will we use?"

We will *make an organized list.*

(Solve) **Carry out the plan.**

"How do we begin?"

We will list the combinations that Gunther can spin with all three spinners that total 6.

"If Gunther spins a 1 on the first spinner, how can 6 be achieved?"

1, 1, 4   1, 2, 3   1, 3, 2

"If Gunther spins a 2 on the first spinner, how can 6 be achieved?"

2, 1, 3   2, 2, 2   2, 3, 1

"Are there any other ways for the total to be 6?"

There are other ways to total 6 with only two spinners, but not with all three spinners.

(Check) **Look back.**

"Did we find the answer to the question that was asked?"

Yes. Gunther can achieve a 6 in six different ways:
1, 1, 4   1, 2, 3   1, 3, 2   2, 1, 3   2, 2, 2   2, 3, 1.

Teacher Note: Encourage students to explore other questions related to the spinners such as, What is the greatest number of points that Gunther could get in one spin of each spinner? What is the least number of points Gunther could get? If Gunther spins a 1 on the first spinner and a 1 on the second spinner, what are the possible totals he could get?

1 Power Up

Facts
Distribute **Power Up J** to students. See answers below.

Mental Math
Before students begin the Mental Math exercise, do this counting exercise as a class.

Count up and down by 25s between 25 and 300.

Encourage students to share different ways to mentally compute these exercises. Strategies for exercises **a** and **e** are listed below.

a. **Multiply Hundreds, Tens, and Ones**
   $4 \times 100 = 400$; $4 \times 10 = 40$; $4 \times 2 = 8$;
   $400 + 40 + 8 = 448$
   Count On by 110, then Add 4×2
   Start with 110. Count: 220, 330, 440.
   $440 + (4 \times 2) = 440 + 8 = 448$

e. **Double Each Place Value**
   Double $3 is $6 and double 50¢ is $1;
   $6 + $1 = $7
   Use a Pattern
   Since double $3 is $6 and double $4 is $8, double $3.50 is $7.00.

Problem Solving
Refer to **Power-Up Discussion**, p. 380B.

2 New Concepts

Instruction
Read each expression aloud with the class. Then reinforce the concept that an exponent indicates the number of times that the base is used as a factor by having students write each expression as repeated multiplication on the board or overhead.

$$5^2 = 5 \cdot 5$$
$$10^3 = 10 \cdot 10 \cdot 10$$
$$3^4 = 3 \cdot 3 \cdot 3 \cdot 3$$
$$2^5 = 2 \cdot 2 \cdot 2 \cdot 2 \cdot 2$$

(continued)

---

facts   Power Up J

mental math
   a. **Calculation:** 4×112 448
   b. **Number Sense:** $475 - 150$ 325
   c. **Calculation:** $4 \times \$0.99$ $3.96
   d. **Calculation:** $2.99 + \$1.99$ $4.98
   e. **Number Sense:** Double $3.50. $7.00
   f. **Decimals:** $3.50 \div 10$ $0.35
   g. **Statistics:** Find the median of the set of numbers: 30, 61, 22, 46, 13   30
   h. **Calculation:** $3 \times 3, \times 3, + 3, \div 3, - 3, \times 3$ 21

problem solving
How many different ways can Gunther spin a total of 6 if he spins each spinner once?   6 ways

New Concepts   *Increasing Knowledge*

exponents

Math Language
Recall that an **exponent** is written as a small number on the upper right-hand side of the base number.

Since Lesson 38 we have used the exponent 2 to indicate that a number is multiplied by itself.

$$5^2 \text{ means } 5 \cdot 5$$

Exponents indicate repeated multiplication, so

$$5^3 \text{ means } 5 \cdot 5 \cdot 5$$
$$5^4 \text{ means } 5 \cdot 5 \cdot 5 \cdot 5$$

The exponent indicates how many times the base is used as a factor.

We read numbers with exponents as **powers.** Note that when the exponent is 2, we usually say "squared," and when the exponent is 3, we usually say "cubed." The following examples show how we read expressions with exponents:

Facts   Write each mixed number as an improper fraction.

$2\frac{1}{2} = \frac{5}{2}$	$2\frac{2}{5} = \frac{12}{5}$	$1\frac{3}{4} = \frac{7}{4}$	$2\frac{3}{4} = \frac{11}{4}$	$2\frac{1}{8} = \frac{17}{8}$
$1\frac{2}{3} = \frac{5}{3}$	$3\frac{1}{2} = \frac{7}{2}$	$1\frac{5}{6} = \frac{11}{6}$	$2\frac{1}{4} = \frac{9}{4}$	$1\frac{1}{8} = \frac{9}{8}$
$5\frac{1}{2} = \frac{11}{2}$	$1\frac{3}{8} = \frac{11}{8}$	$5\frac{1}{3} = \frac{16}{3}$	$3\frac{1}{4} = \frac{13}{4}$	$4\frac{1}{2} = \frac{9}{2}$
$1\frac{7}{8} = \frac{15}{8}$	$2\frac{2}{3} = \frac{8}{3}$	$1\frac{5}{8} = \frac{13}{8}$	$3\frac{3}{4} = \frac{15}{4}$	$7\frac{1}{2} = \frac{15}{2}$

Thinking Skill

Explain

How does the quantity *two to the third power* differ from the quantity *three to the second power?* Two to the third power, or 2^3, is the base, 2, multiplied three times: $2 \times 2 \times 2 = 8$. Three to the second power, or 3^2, is the base, 3, multiplied twice: $3 \times 3 = 9$.

5^2	"five to the second power" or "five squared"
10^3	"ten to the third power" or "ten cubed"
3^4	"three to the fourth power"
2^5	"two to the fifth power"

Example 1

Compare: $3^4 \bigcirc 4^3$

Solution

We find the value of each expression.

3^4 means $3 \cdot 3 \cdot 3 \cdot 3$, which equals 81.

4^3 means $4 \cdot 4 \cdot 4$, which equals 64.

Since 81 is greater than 64, we find that 3^4 is greater than 4^3.

$$3^4 > 4^3$$

Example 2

Write the prime factorization of 1000, using exponents to group factors.

Solution

Using a factor tree or division by primes, we find the prime factorization of 1000.

$$1000 = 2 \cdot 2 \cdot 2 \cdot 5 \cdot 5 \cdot 5$$

We group the three 2s and the three 5s with exponents.

$$1000 = 2^3 \cdot 5^3$$

Example 3

Simplify: $100 - 10^2$

Solution

We perform operations with exponents before we add, subtract, multiply, or divide. Ten squared is 100. So when we subtract 10^2 from 100, the difference is zero.

$$100 - 10^2$$
$$100 - 100 = 0$$

writing decimal numbers as fractions, part 2

We will review changing a decimal number to a fraction or mixed number. Recall from Lesson 35 that the number of places after the decimal point indicates the denominator of the decimal fraction (10 or 100 or 1000, etc.). The digits to the right of the decimal point make up the numerator of the fraction.

Lesson 73   381

Example 1

Instruction

"What inequality symbols do we often use when we compare?" the greater than symbol (>) and the less than symbol (<)

"What symbol of equality is sometimes used when we compare?" the equals sign (=)

Example 2

Instruction

Invite two volunteers to the board or overhead. Ask one volunteer to find the prime factorization of 1000 using a factor tree. Ask the other volunteer to find the prime factorization of 1000 using division by primes.

Example 3

Instruction

"Think about the Order of Operations. When an expression or an equation contains more than one operation, which operation is performed first?" the operation or operations in parentheses or other grouping symbols

Make sure students understand that operations with exponents represent the second step in the Order of Operations.

Students should conclude from the example that because there are no parentheses or other grouping symbols present, the first step to be completed is to simplify 10^2.

(continued)

Math Background

When working with powers of 10, the exponent represents the number of zeros in the standard form of each number.

$10^0 = 1$ (no zero) $10^5 = 100,000$ (five zeros)

$10^1 = 10$ (one zero) $10^6 = 1,000,000$ (six zeros)

$10^2 = 100$ (two zeros) $10^7 = 10,000,000$ (seven zeros)

$10^3 = 1000$ (three zeros) $10^8 = 100,000,000$ (eight zeros)

$10^4 = 10,000$ (four zeros) $10^9 = 1,000,000,000$ (nine zeros)

Example 4

Instruction

To help students recall decimal place value, you may want to display the **Place Value** concept poster as students complete examples 4 and 5.

Example 5

Instruction

When reducing fractions, remind students to divide both terms of the fraction by the greatest common factor of those terms.

Practice Set

Problems a–c [Error Alert]

Watch for students who write the product of the base and the exponent to simplify each expression. For example, a student simplifies 10^4 to 40 because $10 \cdot 4 = 40$. Ask those students to circle the exponent in each expression. Then have them write the base as a factor the circled number of times: $10^4 = 10 \cdot 10 \cdot 10 \cdot 10$.

Problems e–j [Error Alert]

Explain that one way for students to check their work is to compare each decimal number to 1. If a decimal number is less than 1, its equivalent will be a proper fraction. If a decimal number is greater than or equal to 1, its equivalent will be a whole or mixed number.

---

3 Written Practice

Math Conversations

Discussion opportunities are provided below.

Problem 1 [Formulate]

Extend the Problem

Ask students to write a related equation that can also be used to solve the problem. Sample: A related equation for $102 - 98.6 = d$ is $98.6 + d = 102$.

Students may be interested to learn that the degrees Celsius equivalent for 98.6 degrees Fahrenheit is 37°C.

(continued)

Example 4

Thinking Skill

Connect

What is the denominator of each of these decimal fractions: 0.2, 0.43, 0.658? 10, 100, 1000

Write 0.5 as a common fraction.

Solution

We read 0.5 as "five tenths," which also names the fraction $\frac{5}{10}$. We reduce the fraction.

$$\frac{5}{10} = \frac{1}{2}$$

Example 5

Write 3.75 as a mixed number.

Solution

Thinking Skill

Verify

How do you reduce $\frac{75}{100}$ to $\frac{3}{4}$? Divide the numerator and denominator by 25.

The whole-number part of 3.75 is 3, and the fraction part is 0.75. Since 0.75 has two decimal places, the denominator is 100.

$$3.75 = 3\frac{75}{100}$$

We reduce the fraction.

$$3\frac{75}{100} = 3\frac{3}{4}$$

Practice Set   Find the value of each expression:

▶ **a.** 10^4 10,000   ▶ **b.** $2^3 + 2^4$ 24   ▶ **c.** $2^2 \cdot 5^2$ 100

d. Write the prime factorization of 72 using exponents. $72 = 2^3 \cdot 3^2$

▶ Write each decimal number as a fraction or mixed number:

e. 12.5 $12\frac{1}{2}$ **f.** 1.25 $1\frac{1}{4}$ **g.** 0.125 $\frac{1}{8}$

h. 0.05 $\frac{1}{20}$ **i.** 0.24 $\frac{6}{25}$ **j.** 10.2 $10\frac{1}{5}$

Written Practice   *Strengthening Concepts*

▶ **1.** *(38)* **Formulate**   Tomas's temperature was 102°F. Normal body temperature is 98.6°F. How many degrees above normal was Tomas's temperature? Write an equation and solve the problem. $102 - 98.6 = d$; 3.4°F

2. *(11)* **Formulate**   Jill has read 42 pages of a 180-page book. How many pages are left for her to read? Write an equation and solve the problem. $180 - 42 = d$; 138 pages

3. *(18)* **Formulate**   If Jill wants to finish the book in the next three days, then she should read an average of how many pages per day? Write an equation and solve the problem. $3p = 138$; 46 pages per day

* 4. *(73)* Write 2.5 as a reduced mixed number. $2\frac{1}{2}$

* 5. *(73)* Write 0.35 as a reduced fraction. $\frac{7}{20}$

▶ See Math Conversations in the sidebar.

6. What is the total cost of a $12.60 item when $7\frac{1}{2}$% (0.075) sales tax
(41) is added? $13.55

* 7. $\frac{3}{4} \times 2 \times 1\frac{1}{3}$ 2
(72)

▶ *** 8.** *Analyze* $(100 - 10^2) \div 5^2$ 0
(73)

9. $3 + 2\frac{1}{3} + 1\frac{3}{4}$ $7\frac{1}{12}$
(61)

10. $5\frac{1}{6} - 3\frac{1}{2}$ $1\frac{2}{3}$
(63)

* 11. $\frac{3}{4} \div 1\frac{1}{2}$ $\frac{1}{2}$
(68)

12. $7 \div 0.4$ 17.5
(49)

* 13. Compare:
(44, 73)
   a. $5^2 \overset{<}{\bigcirc} 2^5$

   b. $0.3 \overset{>}{\bigcirc} 0.125$

14. The diameter of a quarter is about 2.4 cm.
(47)
   a. What is the circumference of a quarter? (Use 3.14 for π.)   7.536 cm

   b. What is the ratio of the radius of the quarter to the diameter of the
   quarter? $\frac{1}{2}$

Find each unknown number:

15. $25m = 0.175$ 0.007
(45)

16. $1.2 + y + 4.25 = 7$ 1.55
(43)

17. Which digit is in the ten-thousands place in 123,456.78?   2
(34)

▶ **18.** Arrange these numbers in order from least to greatest: $0, \frac{1}{10}, \frac{1}{4}, \frac{1}{2}, 1$
(56)
$$1, \frac{1}{2}, \frac{1}{10}, \frac{1}{4}, 0$$

* 19. Write the prime factorization of 200 using exponents. $2^3 \cdot 5^2$
(73)

20. The store offered a 20% discount on all tools. The regular price of a
(41) hammer was $18.00.
   a. How much money is 20% of $18.00? $3.60

   b. What was the price of the hammer after the discount? $14.40

▶ *** 21.** *Connect* The length of $\overline{AB}$ is 16 mm. The length of $\overline{AC}$ is 50 mm. What
(69) is the length of $\overline{BC}$?   34 mm

22. One half of the area of this square is shaded.
(31) What is the area of the shaded region?
   18 sq. in.

6 in.

23. *Verify* Is every square a rectangle?   yes
(64)

▶ *** 24.** *Analyze* $\dfrac{2^2 + 2^3}{2}$ 6
(73)

Lesson 73   383

▶ See Math Conversations in the sidebar.

Students may need help **factoring numbers that are powers of 10.** Teach
them to begin by factoring 10 into prime factors. Then have them count the
number of zeros in the given number to write the exponents of each factor.
Use the following examples to demonstrate the pattern:

$10 = 2^1 \cdot 5^1$ 10 has one zero, so the exponents of 2 and 5 are 1.

$100 = 2^2 \cdot 5^2$ 100 has two zeros, so the exponents of 2 and 5 are 2.

$1000 = 2^3 \cdot 5^3$ 1000 has three zeros, so the exponents of 2 and 5 are 3.

$10{,}000 = 2^4 \cdot 5^4$ 10,000 has four zeros, so the exponents of 2 and 5 are 4.

Students can also use this strategy to write the prime factorization of a
multiple of a power of 10. Demonstrate using the following examples:

$200 = 2 \cdot 100$

$200 = 2 \cdot 2^2 \cdot 5^2 = 2^3 \cdot 5^2$

$6000 = 2 \cdot 3 \cdot 1000$

$6000 = 2 \cdot 3 \cdot 2^3 \cdot 5^3 = 2^4 \cdot 3 \cdot 5^3$

Math Conversations
Discussion opportunities are provided below.

Problem 8   *Analyze*
*"The Order of Operations state that
operations in parentheses must be
completed first. In these parentheses there
are two operations. Which operation do
we complete first? Explain why."* Simplify
10^2; the Order of Operations state that
operations with exponents are to be
completed before subtracting.

Problem 21   *Connect*
To help solve the problem, encourage students
to sketch the figure on another sheet of paper
and label the given distances.

*"Name the operation that is used to
solve this problem, and explain why that
operation is used."* Subtraction; the whole,
and one part of the whole, is given. To find
the unknown part, subtract the known part
from the whole.

Problem 24   *Analyze*
*"What operations are present in this
expression?"* exponents (twice), addition,
and division

*"Which operation or operations are
completed first? Tell why."* Both operations
with exponents; if an expression does not
contain parentheses or other grouping
symbols, operations with exponents are
completed before adding, subtracting,
multiplying, or dividing.

Errors and Misconceptions
Problem 18
A common misconception when comparing
unit fractions is that the unit fractions must be
rewritten as equivalent fractions that share a
common denominator.

Point out that unit fractions can be compared
simply by comparing the denominators of
the fractions. Help students generalize that
the greater the denominator, the lesser the
fraction, and the lesser the denominator, the
greater the fraction.

(continued)

3 Written Practice (Continued)

Math Conversations

Discussion opportunities are provided below.

Problem 25 [Explain]

Ask students to support their explanations by writing a variety of fraction forms on the board or overhead.

Problem 30 [Conclude]

"How are the angles of a parallelogram related?" Opposite pairs of angles in a parallelogram have the same measure.

Errors and Misconceptions

Problem 28

Watch for students who simplify 9^2 to 18.

---

25. Before we multiply fractions, we write any mixed numbers and any whole numbers as improper fractions.

▶* **25.** [Explain] The fractions chart from Lesson 72 says that the proper
(72) "shape" for multiplying fractions is "fraction form." What does that mean?

Refer to this coordinate plane to answer problems **26** and **27**.

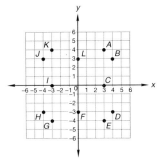

* **26.** Identify the coordinates of the following points:
(Inv. 7)
    a. H $(-4, -3)$ **b.** L $(0, 3)$

* **27.** Name the points that have the following coordinates:
(Inv. 7)
    a. $(-4, 3)$ point J   **b.** $(3, 0)$ point C

▶* **28.** If s equals 9, what does s^2 equal? 81
(73)

29. Name an every day object that has the same shape as each of these
(Inv. 6) geometric solids:
    a. cylinder   **c.** sphere

    b. rectangular prism   **d.** cube Answers will vary.

▶* **30.** [Conclude] The measure of $\angle W$ in
(71) parallelogram WXYZ is 75°.
    a. What is the measure of $\angle X$? 105°

    b. What is the measure of $\angle Y$? 75°

Early Finishers
Real-World Application

A teacher asked 23 students to close their eyes, then raise the hand up when they thought 60 seconds had elapsed. The results, in seconds, are shown below.

    61 65 73 80 35 56 57 71 52 86 39 58
    55 67 63 66 83 70 51 54 66 64 41

Which type of display—a stem-and-leaf plot or a line graph—is the most appropriate way to display this data? Draw your display and justify your choice. stem-and-leaf plot; Sample: A stem-and-leaf plot is the most appropriate display because it can be used to display individual data points. A line graph usually displays a change over time. See student graphs.

▶ See Math Conversations in the sidebar.

Looking Forward

Changing decimal numbers to reduced fractions or mixed numbers prepares students for:

- **Lesson 74,** using division to convert fractions to decimal numbers.

- **Lessons 75 and 94,** writing fractions and decimals as percents.

- **Lesson 76,** comparing fractions by converting them from fractional to decimal form.

- **Lesson 99,** expressing fraction-decimal-percent equivalents in table form.

• Writing Fractions as Decimal Numbers
• Writing Ratios as Decimal Numbers

Objectives
- Convert fractions and mixed numbers to decimal numbers.
- Use a calculator to convert a fraction to a decimal number.
- Convert ratios to decimal numbers.

Lesson Preparation

Materials
- **Power Up I** (in *Instructional Masters*)
- **Teacher-provided material:** calculators

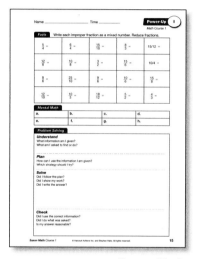

Power Up I

Math Language

	English Learners (ESL)
	cubed

Technology Resources

Student eBook Complete student textbook in electronic format.

Resources and Planner CD Assessment, reteaching, and instructional masters, plus a pacing calendar with standards.

Test and Practice Generator CD Create additional practice sheets and custom-made tests.

www.SaxonPublishers.com Visit for more student activities and planning materials.

Inclusion

Adaptations CD Adapted lessons, investigations, practice and assessments.

Meeting Standards

National Council of Teachers of Mathematics (NCTM)

Numbers and Operations

NO.1a Work flexibly with fractions, decimals, and percents to solve problems

NO.1d Understand and use ratios and proportions to represent quantitative relationships

NO.2a Understand the meaning and effects of arithmetic operations with fractions, decimals, and integers

Representation

RE.5a Create and use representations to organize, record, and communicate mathematical ideas

Problem-Solving Strategies: Draw a Diagram/ Use Logical Reasoning

A 60-inch × 104-inch rectangular tablecloth was draped over a rectangular table. Eight inches of cloth hung over the 60 inch, left edge of the table, 3 inches over the back, 4 inches over the right edge, and 7 inches over the front. In which directions (left, back, right, and/or forward) and by how many inches should the tablecloth be shifted so that equal amounts of cloth hang over opposite edges of the table? What are the dimensions of the table?

(Understand) Understand the problem.

"What information are we given?"

A rectangular tablecloth was draped over a rectangular table. Eight inches of cloth hung over the left edge of the table, 3 inches over the back, 4 inches over the right edge, and 7 inches over the front.

"What are we asked to do?"

Determine in which directions (L, B, R, and F) and by how many inches the tablecloth should be shifted so that equal amounts of cloth hang over opposite edges of the table. Determine the size of the table.

(Plan) Make a plan.

"What problem-solving strategy will we use?"

We will *draw a diagram* and *use logical reasoning.*

(Solve) Carry out the plan.

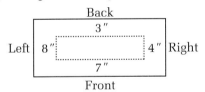 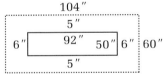

"How do we begin?"

We draw a diagram that shows the tablecloth measurements and table.

"How can we balance the front and back?"

Because $7 + 3 = 10$ and $10 \div 2 = 5$, we would slide the tablecloth 2 inches toward the back.

"How can we balance the left and right?"

Because $8 + 4 = 12$ and $12 \div 2 = 6$, we would slide the tablecloth 2 inches to the right.

"What are the dimensions of the table?"

The length of the table cloth minus the overlap will give us the length of the table: 60 in. − 10 in. = 50 in. The width of the table cloth minus the overlap will give us the width of the table: 104 in. − 12 in. = 92 in. Therefore, the table is 50 inches by 92 inches.

(Check) Look back.

"Did we answer the questions that were asked?"

Yes. We were asked to determine by how many inches we should shift the tablecloth so that equal amounts hung over opposite edges of the table. We found that sliding the tablecloth back 2 inches and to the right 2 inches, the overhang on opposite sides would be equal.

- Writing Fractions as Decimal Numbers
- Writing Ratios as Decimal Numbers

611
613
633

Power Up | Building Power

facts | Power Up I

mental math

a. **Number Sense:** 3×230 690

b. **Number Sense:** $430 + 270$ 700

c. **Calculation:** $5 \times \$0.99$ $4.95

d. **Calculation:** $\$5.00 - \$1.98$ $3.02

e. **Fractional Parts:** $\frac{1}{4}$ of $2.40 $0.60

f. **Decimals:** $\$1.25 \times 10$ $12.50

g. **Statistics:** Find the median of the set of numbers:

101, 26, 125, 84, 152   101

h. **Calculation:** $5 \times 5, -5, \times 5, \div 2, +5, \div 5$ 11

problem solving

A 60 in.-by-104 in. rectangular tablecloth was draped over a rectangular table. Eight inches of the 104-inch length of cloth hung over the left edge of the table, 3 inches over the back, 4 inches over the right edge, and 7 inches over the front.

In which directions (left, back, right, and/or forward) and by how many inches should the tablecloth be shifted so that equal amounts of cloth hang over opposite edges of the table? What are the dimensions of the table?   The tablecloth should be shifted 2 in. to the right and 2 in. back.; 50 in.-by-92 in.

New Concepts | Increasing Knowledge

writing fractions as decimal numbers

We learned earlier that a fraction bar indicates division. So the fraction $\frac{1}{2}$ also means "1 divided by 2," which we can write as $2\overline{)1}$. By attaching a decimal point and zero, we can perform the division and write the quotient as a decimal number.

$$\frac{1}{2} \longrightarrow \begin{array}{r} 0.5 \\ 2\overline{)1.0} \\ \underline{1\ 0} \\ 0 \end{array}$$

We find that $\frac{1}{2}$ equals the decimal number 0.5. To convert a fraction to a decimal number, we divide the numerator by the denominator.

Lesson 74   385

---

1 Power Up

Facts
Distribute **Power Up I** to students. See answers below.

Mental Math
Before students begin the Mental Math exercise, do this counting exercise as a class.

Count up and down by 5s between negative 25 and 25.

Encourage students to share different ways to mentally compute these exercises. Strategies for exercises **b** and **e** are listed below.

b. **Subtract 30 and Add 30**
$430 - 30 = 400$ and $270 + 30 = 300$;
$400 + 300 = 700$
Add Hundreds, then Add Tens
$400 + 200 = 600$ and $30 + 70 = 100$;
$600 + 100 = 700$

e. **Divide Place Values**
$\$2 \div 4 = 50¢$ and $40¢ \div 4 = 10¢$;
$50¢ + 10¢ = 60¢$
Use a Division Pattern
Since $24 \div 4 = 6$ and $2.4 \div 4 = 0.6$,
$\$2.40 \div 4 = \$0.60$.

Problem Solving
Refer to **Power-Up Discussion,** p. 385B.

2 New Concepts

Instruction
Remind students that $\frac{1}{2}$ and 0.5 are equivalent because they are different names for the same number.

(continued)

Facts   Write each improper fraction as a mixed number. Reduce fractions.

$\frac{5}{4} = 1\frac{1}{4}$	$\frac{6}{4} = 1\frac{1}{2}$	$\frac{15}{10} = 1\frac{1}{2}$	$\frac{8}{3} = 2\frac{2}{3}$	$\frac{15}{12} = 1\frac{1}{4}$
$\frac{12}{8} = 1\frac{1}{2}$	$\frac{10}{8} = 1\frac{1}{4}$	$\frac{3}{2} = 1\frac{1}{2}$	$\frac{15}{6} = 2\frac{1}{2}$	$\frac{10}{4} = 2\frac{1}{2}$
$\frac{8}{6} = 1\frac{1}{3}$	$\frac{25}{10} = 2\frac{1}{2}$	$\frac{9}{6} = 1\frac{1}{2}$	$\frac{10}{6} = 1\frac{2}{3}$	$\frac{15}{8} = 1\frac{7}{8}$
$\frac{12}{10} = 1\frac{1}{5}$	$\frac{10}{3} = 3\frac{1}{3}$	$\frac{18}{12} = 1\frac{1}{2}$	$\frac{5}{2} = 2\frac{1}{2}$	$\frac{4}{3} = 1\frac{1}{3}$

2 New Concepts (Continued)

Example 1
Instruction
"What part of the fraction $\frac{1}{4}$ represents division?" the fraction bar

Example 2
Instruction
Have students use their calculators to act out the steps of the solution.

Example 3
Instruction
After discussing the solution, challenge volunteers to explain, and then demonstrate, how to use a calculator to check the answer.

(continued)

Example 1

Convert $\frac{1}{4}$ to a decimal number.

Solution

The fraction $\frac{1}{4}$ means "1 divided by 4," which is $4\overline{)1}$. By attaching a decimal point and zeros, we can complete the division.

$$\begin{array}{r} 0.25 \\ 4\overline{)1.00} \\ \underline{8} \\ 20 \\ \underline{20} \\ 0 \end{array}$$

Example 2

Use a calculator to convert $\frac{15}{16}$ to a decimal number.

Solution

Begin by clearing the calculator. Then enter the fraction with these keystrokes.

$$\boxed{1}\ \boxed{5}\ \boxed{\div}\ \boxed{1}\ \boxed{6}\ \boxed{=}$$

After pressing the equal sign, the display shows the decimal equivalent of $\frac{15}{16}$:

0.9375

The answer is reasonable because both $\frac{15}{16}$ and 0.9375 are less than but close to 1.

Example 3

Write $7\frac{2}{5}$ as a decimal number.

Solution

The whole number part of $7\frac{2}{5}$ is 7, which we write to the left of the decimal point. We convert $\frac{2}{5}$ to a decimal by dividing 2 by 5.

$$\frac{2}{5} \longrightarrow 5\overline{)2.0}^{\,0.4}$$

Since $\frac{2}{5}$ equals 0.4, the mixed number $7\frac{2}{5}$ equals **7.4**.

Model Use a calculator to check the answer.

writing ratios as decimal numbers Converting ratios to decimal numbers is similar to converting fractions to decimal numbers.

Example 4

A number cube is rolled once. Express the probability of rolling an even number as a decimal number.

386   **Saxon** Math Course 1

Math Background

A special symbol is sometimes needed to write the decimal equivalents for some fractions.

For example, the quotient when $\frac{1}{3}$ is written as a decimal is 0.3333… with the three dots indicating that the digit 3 continues to repeat without end. To represent this repeating pattern, a bar is written over the digit (or digits) that repeat. So $0.\overline{3}$ is used to represent the decimal equivalent for $\frac{1}{3}$.

Another example of a repeating decimal is $0.\overline{18}$, which is the decimal equivalent for $\frac{2}{11}$.

Left Page

Solution

Probabilities are often expressed as decimal numbers between 0 and 1. Since three of the six numbers on a number cube are even, the probability of rolling an even number is $\frac{3}{6}$, which equals $\frac{1}{2}$.

We convert $\frac{1}{2}$ to a decimal by dividing 1 by 2.

$$2\overline{)1.0} \quad \frac{0.5}{}$$

Thus the probability of rolling an even number with one roll of a number cube is **0.5**.

Practice Set ▸ Convert each fraction or mixed number to a decimal number:

a. $\frac{3}{4}$ 0.75   **b.** $4\frac{1}{5}$ 4.2   **c.** $\frac{1}{8}$ 0.125

d. $\frac{7}{20}$ 0.35   **e.** $3\frac{3}{10}$ 3.3   **f.** $\frac{7}{25}$ 0.28

You may use a calculator to convert these numbers to decimal numbers:

g. $\frac{11}{16}$ 0.6875   **h.** $\frac{31}{32}$ 0.96875   ▸ **i.** $3\frac{24}{64}$ 3.375

j. In a bag are three red marbles and two blue marbles. If Chad pulls one marble from the bag, what is the probability that the marble will be blue? Express the probability ratio as a fraction and as a decimal number. $\frac{2}{5}$; 0.4

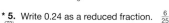

Written Practice *Strengthening Concepts*

▸ *** 1.** *(73)* **Analyze** What is the difference when five squared is subtracted from four cubed? 39

* 2. *(15)* On LeAnne's map, 1 inch represents a distance of 10 miles. If Dallas, TX and Fort Worth, TX are 3 inches apart on the map, approximately how many miles apart are they? 30 miles

* 3. *(74)* Convert $2\frac{3}{4}$ to a decimal number. 2.75

* 4. *(58, 74)* Tito spins the spinner once.

    a. What is the sample space of the experiment? sample space = {1, 2, 3, 4, 5}

    b. What is the probability that he spins a number greater than 1? Express the probability ratio as a fraction and as a decimal. $\frac{4}{5}$; 0.8

* 5. *(73)* Write 0.24 as a reduced fraction. $\frac{6}{25}$

Lesson 74   387

▸ See Math Conversations in the sidebar.

English Learners

Write the word **cubed** on the board. Say,

"To cube a number means to multiply it by itself three times ($n^3 = n \times n \times n$)."

Ask a volunteer to show how to cube the number 2.

$$(2^3 = 2 \times 2 \times 2 = 8)$$

Right Page

2 New Concepts (Continued)

Example 4
Instruction

After completing the problem, ask

"The probability of an even outcome can also be expressed as a percent. Explain how to find the percent equivalent for 0.5, then name the percent equivalent."

To change a decimal number to a percent, multiply by 100% which is the same as shifting the decimal point two places to the right; 0.5 = 50%.

Practice Set
Problems a–f [Error Alert]

Remind students to place a decimal point in each quotient before beginning each division.

Problem i [Error Alert]

To find the decimal equivalent, students do not need to first use paper and pencil to rename the mixed number as an improper fraction. Instead, they can input the same paper and pencil steps they would follow into the calculator.

The input $64 \times 3 + 24 =$ will produce the numerator of the mixed number.

Then the input $\div\ 64 =$ will produce the decimal equivalent.

$$64 \times 3 + 24 = \boxed{216} \div 64 = \boxed{3.375}$$

3 Written Practice

Math Conversations
Discussion opportunities are provided below.

Problem 1 [Analyze]

Ask students to write a symbolic expression to represent the expression. Write the expression on the board or overhead. $4^3 - 5^2$

"This expression contains subtraction and operations with exponents. To simplify the expression, which operation or operations do we complete first? Why?" Operations with exponents; in the Order of Operations, powers and roots are completed before other operations.

"Does four cubed simplify to 12? Why or why not?" No; 4^3 is the same as $4 \cdot 4 \cdot 4$ or 64.

"What number does five squared simplify to?" 25

(continued)

Lesson 74   **387**

3 Written Practice (Continued)

Math Conversations

Discussion opportunities are provided below.

Problem 24 `Classify`

"What characteristics do rectangles and squares share?" Both figures are quadrilaterals having four right angles and congruent and parallel opposite sides.

Errors and Misconceptions

Problem 15

Encourage students to include perspective lines in their drawings. Explain that perspective lines are dashed lines that outline the perimeter of the non-visible faces of the prism.

(continued)

---

6. `Formulate` Steve hit the baseball 400 feet. Lesley hit the golf ball
(13) 300 yards. How many feet farther did the golf ball travel than the baseball? After converting yards to feet, write an equation and solve the problem. $900 - 400 = d$; 500 feet

7. If $A = bh$, and if b equals 12 and h equals 8, then what does A
(2) equal? 96

* 8. Compare: $3^2 \bigcirc 3 + 3$
(73)

9. $\dfrac{1}{2} + \dfrac{2}{3} + \dfrac{1}{6}$ $1\frac{1}{3}$ **10.** $3\frac{1}{4} - 1\frac{7}{8}$ $1\frac{3}{8}$
(61)   (63)

11. $\dfrac{5}{8} \cdot \dfrac{3}{5} \cdot \dfrac{4}{5}$ $\frac{3}{10}$ **12.** $3\frac{1}{3} \times 3$ 10
(72)   (66)

13. $\dfrac{3}{4} \div 1\frac{1}{2}$ $\frac{1}{2}$ **14.** $(4 + 3.2) - 0.01$ 7.19
(68)   (38)

▶ **15.** `Represent` Draw a triangular prism. Sample:
(Inv. 6)

16. `Formulate` LaFonda bought a dozen golf balls for $10.44. What
(15) was the cost of each golf ball? Write an equation and solve the problem. $12g = 10.44$; $0.87

17. Estimate the product of 81 and 38. 3200
(16)

18. In tour days Jamar read 42 pages, 46 pages, 35 pages, and 57 pages.
(18) What was the average number of pages he read per day? 45 pages per day

19. What is the least common multiple of 6, 8, and 12? 24
(30)

20. $24 + c + 96 = 150$ 30
(3)

21. Write the prime factorization of both the numerator and the denominator
(67) of this fraction. Then reduce the fraction. $\dfrac{2 \cdot 2 \cdot 2 \cdot 5}{2 \cdot 2 \cdot 2 \cdot 2 \cdot 3} = \frac{5}{12}$
$$\frac{40}{96}$$

* 22. `Analyze` If the perimeter of this square is
(47) 40 centimeters, then

   a. what is the diameter of the circle?
   10 centimeters
   b. what is the circumference of the circle?
   (Use 3.14 for π.) 31.4 centimeters

24. All four sides of a square are the same length. Some rectangles are longer than they are wide, so not all the sides are the same length.

23. Twenty-four of the three dozen cyclists rode mountain bikes. What
(29) fraction of the cyclists rode mountain bikes? $\frac{2}{3}$

▶*** 24.** `Classify` Why are some rectangles not squares?
(64)

▶ See Math Conversations in the sidebar.

25. **Connect** Which arrow could be pointing to $\frac{3}{4}$?   B
(17)

26. **Conclude** In quadrilateral *PQRS*, which
(64) segment appears to be
   a. parallel to $\overline{PQ}$? $\overline{SR}$ or $\overline{RS}$

   b. perpendicular to $\overline{PQ}$? $\overline{PS}$ or $\overline{SP}$

27. **Analyze** The figure at right shows a cube
(Inv. 6) with edges 3 feet long.

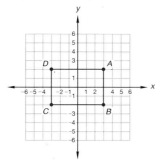

   a. What is the area of each face of the
   cube?   9 ft^2

   b. What is the total surface area of the
   cube?   54 ft^2

Refer to this coordinate plane to answer problems 28 and 29.

* 28. Identify the coordinates of the following points:
(Inv. 7)
   a. *C*   (–3, –2)   **b.** origin   (0, 0)

29. **Connect** One pair of parallel segments in rectangle *ABCD* is $\overline{AB}$ and
(64) $\overline{DC}$. Name a second pair of parallel segments. $\overline{DA}$ (or $\overline{AD}$) and $\overline{CB}$ (or
$\overline{BC}$)

30. Farmer Ruiz planted corn on 60% of his 300 acres. Find the number of
(41) acres planted with corn.   180 acres

▶ See Math Conversations in the sidebar.

Math Conversations

Discussion opportunities are provided below.

Problem 25 **Connect**

Students must recognize that the tick marks
divide the number line into halves, then infer
that arrow *B* represents $\frac{3}{4}$ because it is located
halfway between $\frac{1}{2}$ and 1.

Problem 27 **Analyze**

*"How many faces of the cube are not
visible?"* three

*"How do all of the faces of a cube
compare?"* All of the faces of a cube are
congruent (same size and shape).

*"Explain how multiplication can be used
to find the total surface area of the
cube."* Multiply the surface area of one face
by six.

Looking Forward

Using division to convert fractions to decimal numbers prepares students for:

• **Lessons 75 and 94,** writing fractions and decimals as percents.

• **Lesson 76,** comparing fractions by converting them to decimal form.

• **Lesson 99,** expressing fraction-decimal-percent equivalents in table form.

• **Lesson 113,** multiplying by powers of ten.

•Writing Fractions and Decimals as Percents, Part 1

Objectives

- Write a fraction as a percent.
- Write a decimal as a percent.

Lesson Preparation

Materials

- **Power Up K** (in *Instructional Masters*)
- **Teacher-provided material:** graph paper

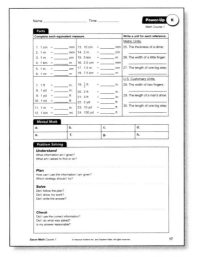

Power Up K

Math Language

English Learners (ESL)

shift

Technology Resources

Student eBook Complete student textbook in electronic format.

Resources and Planner CD Assessment, reteaching, and instructional masters, plus a pacing calendar with standards.

Test and Practice Generator CD Create additional practice sheets and custom-made tests.

www.SaxonPublishers.com Visit for more student activities and planning materials.

Inclusion

Adaptations CD Adapted lessons, investigations, practice and assessments.

Meeting Standards

National Council of Teachers of Mathematics (NCTM)

Numbers and Operations

NO.1a Work flexibly with fractions, decimals, and percents to solve problems

Problem Solving

PS.1c Apply and adapt a variety of appropriate strategies to solve problems

Problem-Solving Strategies: Use Logical Reasoning/ Guess and Check

The sum of the digits of a five-digit number is 25. What is the five-digit number if the last digit is two less than the fourth, the fourth digit is two less than the third, the third digit is two less than the second, and the second digit is two less than the first digit?

(Understand) **Understand the problem.**

"What information are we given?"

We know that the sum of the digits of a five-digit number is 25 and we know the following facts.

> Fact 1: The fifth digit (in ten thousands' place) is two less than the fourth digit.
> Fact 2: The fourth digit is two less than the third digit.
> Fact 3: The third digit is two less than the second digit.
> Fact 4: The second digit is two less than the first digit.

"What are we asked to do?"

Find the five-digit number whose digits add up to 25 and that fit the criteria stated in the four facts.

(Plan) **Make a plan.**

"What problem-solving strategy will we use?"

We will *use logical reasoning* and *guess and check* to find the digits.

"Besides the four facts, what else do we know about the number?"

From the four facts, we also know that all of the digits of the five-digit number are different. We can also conclude that the first digit (in ones' place) must be the greatest and that the fifth digit is the least.

(Solve) **Carry out the plan.**

"What is the pattern in the digits of the number we are looking for?"

Each digit is 2 less than the previous digit.

"What digit can we eliminate as a possibility for the first digit?"

We can eliminate 0 as a digit in ten thousands' place because if it were 0, the number would be a four-digit number instead of a five-digit number.

"If the digit in the one's place is 1, what would the other digits be?"

Each digit would be 2 greater than the previous digit (moving from right to left). Starting with 1 would give us the number 97,531.

"What is the sum of the digits in 97,531?"

$1 + 3 + 5 + 7 + 9 = 25$. Using *guess and check*, we found the number. It is 97,531.

(Check) **Look back.**

"Did we complete the task?"

Yes. The sum of the five digits of 97,531 is 25. The fifth digit is 2 less than the fourth; the fourth is 2 less than the third; the third is 2 less than the second; and the second is 2 less than the first. The number 97,531 meets all of the criteria stated in the problem.

"Is it necessary to know that the sum of the digits is 25 to solve the problem?"

No, there is no other number that satisfies the other conditions of the problem.

Teacher Note: This solution shows one strategy. Students may have other strategies such as writing all of the five-digit numbers whose digit sums are 25 and then arranging them to fit the criteria.

Facts

Distribute **Power Up K** to students. See answers below.

Mental Math

Before students begin the Mental Math exercise, do this counting exercise as a class.

Count by 12s from 12 to 144.

Encourage students to share different ways to mentally compute these exercises. Strategies for exercises **b** and **d** are listed below.

b. **Subtract 300, then Add 50**
   $625 - 300 = 325; 325 + 50 = 375$
   Subtract 200, then Subtract 50
   $625 - 200 = 425; 425 - 50 = 375$

d. **Add $2, then Count Back 1¢**
   $2.50 + 2.00 = 4.50$; Count: $4.49
   Add 1¢ and Subtract 1¢
   $2.50 - 1¢ = 2.49$ and $1.99 + 1¢ = 2$;
   $2.49 + 2 = 4.49$

Problem Solving

Refer to **Power-Up Discussion**, p. 390B.

2 **New Concepts**

Instruction

Remind students that a percent is a ratio of a number to 100, and percent means "per hundred."

(continued)

• Writing Fractions and Decimals as Percents, Part 1

3483

Power Up | *Building Power*

facts | Power Up K

mental math
a. **Calculation:** 504×6 3024
b. **Number Sense:** $625 - 250$ 375
c. **Calculation:** $3 \times \$1.99$ $5.97
d. **Calculation:** $\$2.50 + \$1.99$ $4.49
e. **Number Sense:** Double $1.60. $3.20
f. **Decimals:** $\$12.50 \div 10$ $1.25
g. **Statistics:** Find the median of the set of numbers:
   28, 32, 44, 17, 15, 26   27
h. **Calculation:** $6 \times 6, -6, \div 6, -5, \times 2, +1$ 1

problem solving | The sum of the digits of a five-digit number is 25. What is the five digit number if the last digit is two less than the fourth, the fourth digit is two less than the third, the third is two less than the second, and the second digit is two less than the first digit?   97531

New Concept | *Increasing Knowledge*

A percent is actually a fraction with a denominator of 100. Instead of writing the denominator 100, we can use a percent sign (%). So $\frac{25}{100}$ equals 25%.

Example 1

Write $\frac{3}{100}$ as a percent.

Solution

A percent is a fraction with a denominator of 100. Instead of writing the denominator, we write a percent sign. We write $\frac{3}{100}$ as **3%**.

Example 2

Write $\frac{3}{10}$ as a percent.

Facts

Complete each equivalent measure.				Write a unit for each reference.
				Metric Units:
1. 1 cm	= 10 mm	13. 10 cm	= 100 mm	25. The thickness of a dime:
2. 1 m	= 1000 mm	14. 2 m	= 200 cm	millimeter
3. 1 m	= 100 cm	15. 5 km	= 5000 m	26. The width of a little finger:
4. 1 km	= 1000 m	16. 2.5 cm	= 25 mm	centimeter
5. 1 in.	= 2.54 cm	17. 1.5 m	= 150 cm	27. The length of one big step:
6. 1 mi	≈ 1610 m	18. 7.5 km	= 7500 m	meter
7. 1 ft	= 12 in.	19. $\frac{1}{2}$ ft	= 6 in.	U.S. Customary Units:
8. 1 yd	= 36 in.	20. 2 ft	= 24 in.	28. The width of two fingers:
9. 1 yd	= 3 ft	21. 3 ft	= 36 in.	inch
10. 1 mi	= 5280 ft	22. 2 yd	= 6 ft	29. The length of a man's shoe:
		23. 10 yd	= 30 ft	foot
11. 1 m	≈ 39 in.	24. 100 yd	= 300 ft	30. The length of one big step:
12. 1 km	≈ 0.62 mi			yard

Solution

First we will write an equivalent fraction that has a denominator of 100.

$$\frac{3}{10} = \frac{?}{100}$$

We multiply $\frac{3}{10}$ by $\frac{10}{10}$.

$$\frac{3}{10} \cdot \frac{10}{10} = \frac{30}{100}$$

We write the fraction $\frac{30}{100}$ as **30%**.

Example 3

Of the 30 students who took the test, 15 earned an A. What percent of the students earned an A?

Solution

Fifteen of the 30 students earned an A. We write this as a fraction and reduce.

$$\frac{15}{30} = \frac{1}{2}$$

To write $\frac{1}{2}$ as a fraction with a denominator of 100, we multiply $\frac{1}{2}$ by $\frac{50}{50}$.

$$\frac{1}{2} \cdot \frac{50}{50} = \frac{50}{100}$$

The fraction $\frac{50}{100}$ equals **50%**.

Example 4

Write 0.12 as a percent.

Solution

The decimal number 0.12 is twelve hundredths.

$$0.12 = \frac{12}{100}$$

Twelve hundredths is equivalent to **12%**.

Example 5

Write 0.08 as a percent.

Solution

The decimal 0.08 is eight hundredths.

$$0.08 = \frac{8}{100}$$

Eight hundredths is equivalent to **8%**.

Lesson 75   391

Example 6
Instruction
Write various decimal numbers on the board, and ask volunteers to each choose a decimal number and change it to a percent by shifting the decimal point two places to the right and adding the percent sign (%).

Practice Set
Problem g [Error Alert]
If students need additional help, tell them to reduce the fraction $\frac{12}{30}$ so the denominator of the reduced fraction is a factor of 100. Demonstrate that either $\frac{4}{10}$ or $\frac{2}{5}$ will work, but $\frac{12}{30}$ to $\frac{6}{15}$ will not work because 15 is not a factor of 100.

Problems i–n [Error Alert]
If students complete these problems by shifting the decimal points, make sure that they shift the decimal points two places to the right and add a percent symbol.

---

3 Written Practice

Math Conversations
Discussion opportunities are provided below.

Problem 2 [Analyze]
"Describe a way you can solve this problem or check the answer using only mental math." Sample: Add 1 hour to 2:30 p.m., add $\frac{1}{2}$ hour to 3:30 p.m., then add 5 minutes to 4:00 p.m.

Encourage students to describe and share a variety of ways.

Errors and Misconceptions
Problem 1
If students find the reciprocal of $\frac{3}{5}$ ($\frac{5}{3}$) instead of the reciprocal of $2\frac{3}{5}$, remind them to change the mixed number $2\frac{3}{5}$ to an improper fraction before finding the reciprocal.

For additional practice with this skill, ask students to find the reciprocal of each of the following mixed numbers.

$$1\frac{2}{3} \quad \frac{3}{5} \qquad 6\frac{3}{4} \quad \frac{4}{27} \qquad 10\frac{5}{8} \quad \frac{8}{85}$$

Problem 2
Remind students that the number of minutes is renamed as 1 hour and 5 minutes.

$$\begin{array}{r} 2 \text{ hr } 30 \text{ min} \\ + 1 \text{ hr } 35 \text{ min} \\ \hline 3 \text{ hr } 65 \text{ min} = 4 \text{ hr } 5 \text{ min or } 4{:}05 \text{ p.m.} \end{array}$$

(continued)

Example 6

Write 0.8 as a percent.

Solution

The decimal number 0.8 is eight tenths. If we place a zero in the hundredths place, the decimal is eighty hundredths.

$$0.8 = 0.80 = \frac{80}{100}$$

Eighty hundredths equals **80%**.

Notice that when a decimal number is converted to a percent, the decimal point is shifted two places to the right. In fact, shifting the decimal point two places to the right is a quick and useful way to write decimal numbers as percents.

Practice Set — Write each fraction as a percent:

a. $\frac{31}{100}$ 31% **b.** $\frac{1}{100}$ 1% **c.** $\frac{1}{10}$ 10%

d. $\frac{3}{50}$ 6% **e.** $\frac{7}{25}$ 28% **f.** $\frac{2}{5}$ 40%

▶ **g.** Twelve of the 30 students earned a B on the test. What percent of the students earned a B? 40%

h. Jorge correctly answered 18 of the 20 questions on the test. What percent of the questions did he answer correctly? 90%

▶ Write each decimal number as a percent:

i. 0.25 25% **j.** 0.3 30% **k.** 0.05 5%

l. 1.0 100% **m.** 0.7 70% **n.** 0.15 15%

Written Practice — *Strengthening Concepts*

▶ **1.** [Connect] What is the reciprocal of two and three fifths? $\frac{5}{13}$
(30, 62)

2. What time is one hour thirty-five minutes after 2:30 p.m.? 4:05 p.m.
(32)

3. A 1-pound box of candy cost $4.00. What was the cost per ounce (1 pound = 16 ounces)? $0.25 per ounce
(15)

4. [Estimate] Freda bought a sandwich for $4.00 and a drink for 94¢. Her grandson ordered a meal for $6.35. What was the total price of all three items when 8% sales tax was added? Explain how to use estimation to check whether your answer is reasonable.
(41)

5. If the chance of rain is 50%, then what is the chance it will not rain? 50%
(58)

4. $12.19; Round 94¢ to $1 and round $6.35 to $6. Add $4, $1, and $6 and get $11. Tax is 8¢ per dollar, which comes to about 88¢ for the meal. So the estimated total is $11.88. Since $6.35 was rounded down more than 94¢ was rounded up, the answer $12.19 is reasonable.

▶ See Math Conversations in the sidebar.

English Learners

Write the word **shift** on the board. Say,

"To shift something means to move it. When we shift decimal points, the value of the number changes."

Ask a volunteer to write 0.80 on the board and shift the decimal point to the right one place. How does the shift of the decimal point change the value of the number? (It is increased by ten times or becomes 8.)

---

6. Sample:

12 edges

6. *(Inv. 6)* **Represent** Draw a cube. How many edges does a cube have?

* 7. *(74, 75)* **a.** Write $\frac{3}{4}$ as a decimal number.   0.75

    b. Write the answer to part **a** as a percent.   75%

* 8. *(75)* **a.** Write $\frac{3}{20}$ as a fraction with a denominator of 100. $\frac{15}{100}$

    b. Write $\frac{3}{20}$ as a percent.   15%

* 9. *(33, 74)* Write 12% as a reduced fraction. Then write the fraction as a decimal number. $\frac{3}{25}$; 0.12

Find each unknown number:

10. *(42)* $\frac{7}{10} = \frac{n}{100}$ 70

11. *(43)* $5 - m = 3\frac{1}{8}$ $1\frac{7}{8}$

12. *(38, 43)* $1 - w = 0.95$ 0.05

13. *(59)* $m + 1\frac{2}{3} = 3\frac{1}{6}$ $1\frac{1}{2}$

14. *(57)* $\left(\frac{1}{2} + \frac{1}{3}\right) - \frac{1}{6}$ $\frac{2}{3}$

* 15. *(72)* $3\frac{1}{2} \times 1\frac{1}{3} \times 1\frac{1}{2}$ 7

16. *(39)* $(0.43)(2.6)$ 1.118

17. *(45)* $0.26 \div 5$ 0.052

▶* 18. *(75)* Nathan correctly answered 17 of the 20 questions on the test. What percent of the questions did Nathan answer correctly?   85%

19. *(47)* **Estimate** The diameter of the big tractor tire was about 5 feet. As the tire rolled one full turn, the tire rolled about how many feet? Round the answer to the nearest foot. (Use 3.14 for π.)   about 16 feet

20. *(34)* **Connect** Which digit in 4.87 has the same place value as the 9 in 0.195?   7

21. *(67)* Write the prime factorization of both the numerator and denominator of $\frac{18}{30}$. Then reduce the fraction. $\frac{2 \cdot 3 \cdot 3}{2 \cdot 3 \cdot 5} = \frac{3}{5}$

22. *(20)* What is the greatest common factor of 18 and 30?   6

23. *(30)* If the product of two numbers is 1, then the two numbers are which of the following?   **B**

    A equal   **B** reciprocals   **C** opposites   **D** prime

24. *(64)* **Verify** Why is every rectangle a quadrilateral?   A quadrilateral is a four-sided polygon, and every rectangle has four sides.

25. *(47)* If b equals 8 and h equals 6, what does $\frac{bh}{2}$ equal?   24

26. Sample:

▶* 26. *(65, 73)* **Represent** Find the prime factorization of 400 using a factor tree. Then write the prime factorization of 400 using exponents. $2^4 \cdot 5^2$

▶ See Math Conversations in the sidebar.

Math Conversations

Discussion opportunities are provided below.

Problem 18   Analyze

Extend the Problem

"What is the ratio of the number of questions Nathan answered correctly to the number of questions altogether?" $\frac{17}{20}$

"What is the ratio of the number of questions Nathan answered incorrectly to the number of questions altogether?" $\frac{3}{20}$

"Are the ratios $\frac{17}{20}$ and $\frac{3}{20}$ in simplest form? Explain why or why not." Yes; for each fraction, the only common factor of the numerator and the denominator is 1.

Problem 26   Represent

Extend the Problem

Invite seven students to the board and ask each student to make a factor tree for 400 using a different factor pair to begin the tree. The factor pairs students should choose from include 2 × 200, 4 × 100, 5 × 80, 8 × 50, 10 × 40, 16 × 25, and 20 × 20.

As students work at the board, have the remainder of the students choose a factor pair and complete a factor tree using pencil and paper.

After the factor trees have been completed, ask all of the students to write and then compare the prime factorization of 400. Students should conclude that the variety of factor trees all produced the same prime factorization with exponents of 400.

(continued)

Math Conversations

Discussion opportunities are provided below.

Problem 27 Represent

"The ordered pair (3, 1) represents a point. Describe the exact location of that point."

From the origin, the point is located 3 units to the right of the *y*-axis and 1 unit up from the *x*-axis.

Ask the question again for each of the three other vertices of the rectangle.

▶* **27.** (Inv. 7) **Represent** Draw a coordinate plane on graph paper. Then draw a rectangle with vertices located at (3, 1), (3, −1), (−1, 1), and (−1, −1). (See below.)

28. (8, 31) Refer to the rectangle drawn in problem **27** to answer parts **a** and **b** below.

   a. What is the perimeter of the rectangle? 12 units

   b. What is the area of the rectangle? 8 square units

* **29.** (71) **a.** What is the perimeter of this parallelogram? 70 cm

   b. What is the area of this parallelogram? 240 cm²

12 cm 15 cm 20 cm

30. (64) **Model** Draw two parallel segments of different lengths. Then form a quadrilateral by drawing two segments that connect the endpoints of the parallel segments. Is the quadrilateral a rectangle?
Sample: ; no

Early Finishers
Math and Science

The Moon is Earth's only natural satellite. The average distance from Earth to the Moon is approximately 620² kilometers. This distance is about 30 times the diameter of Earth.

   a. Simplify 620² kilometers. 620 × 620 = 384,400 kilometers.

   b. Find the diameter of Earth. Round your answer to the nearest kilometer.
384,400 ÷ 30 = 12,813 kilometers

27.

▶ See Math Conversations in the sidebar.

Looking Forward

Writing fractions and decimals as percents prepares students for:

• **Lesson 94,** writing fractions and decimals as percents by multiplying by 100%.

• **Lesson 99,** expressing fraction-decimal-percent equivalents in table form.

• **Lesson 115,** writing percents as fractions.

Assessment   30–40 minutes

For use after Lesson 75

Distribute **Cumulative Test 14** to each student. Two versions of the test are available in *Saxon Math Course 1 Course Assessments Book*. Have students complete the **Power-Up Test** first. Allow 10 minutes. Then have students work the 20 numbered items on the **Cumulative Test.** Students may use copies of the answer sheet to record their work. Track individual and class progress with the **Test Analysis** forms.

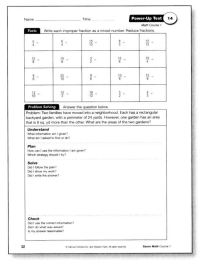

Power-Up Test 14

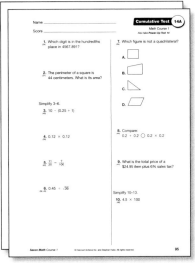

Cumulative Test 14A

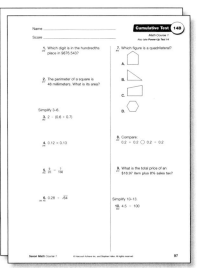

Alternative Cumulative Test 14B

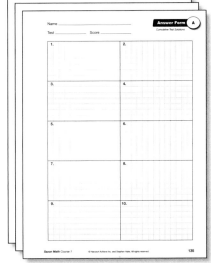

Optional Answer Forms

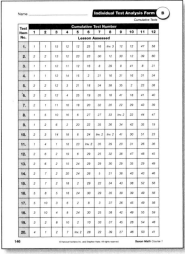

Individual Test Analysis Form

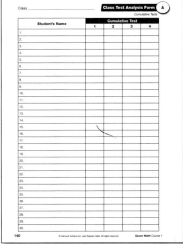

Class Test Analysis Form

Reteaching

Students who score below 80% on the assessment may be in need of reteaching. Look for the causes of student mistakes. If errors are conceptual, refer to the *Reteaching Masters* for reteaching.

Examples and Non-Examples in Geometry

Assign after Lesson 75 and Test 14

Objectives

- Use examples and non-examples to support or disprove mathematical statements relating to geometry.
- Communicate ideas through writing.

Materials

Performance Activity 14

Preparation

Make copies of **Performance Activity 14.** (One each per student.)

Time Requirement

15–30 minutes; Begin in class and complete at home.

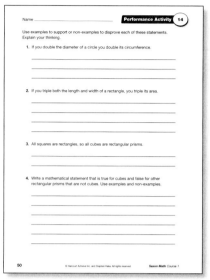

Performance Activity 14

Activity

Explain to students that for this activity they will use examples and non-examples to support or disprove mathematical statements. They will also write mathematical statements that are true for cubes and false for other rectangular prisms that are not cubes. They will be required to explain their thinking. Explain that all of the information students need is on **Performance Activity 14.**

Criteria for Evidence of Learning

- Uses examples and non-examples correctly to support or disprove a mathematical statement.
- Communicates ideas clearly through writing.

National Council of Teachers of Mathematics (NCTM)

Geometry

GM.1a Precisely describe, classify, and understand relationships among types of two- and three-dimensional objects using their defining properties

Reasoning and Proof

RP.2b Make and investigate mathematical conjectures

RP.2c Develop and evaluate mathematical arguments and proofs

Communication

CM.3a Organize and consolidate their mathematical thinking through communication

• Comparing Fractions by Converting to Decimal Form

Objectives
- Compare fractions by converting each fraction to decimal form.

Materials
- **Power Up G** (in *Instructional Masters*)
- **Manipulative kit: inch rulers**
- **Teacher-provided material: graph paper**

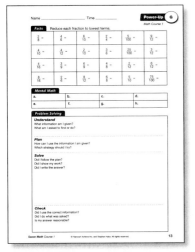

Power Up G

Math Language

English Learners (ESL)
halfway

Technology Resources

Student eBook Complete student textbook in electronic format.

Resources and Planner CD Assessment, reteaching, and instructional masters, plus a pacing calendar with standards.

Test and Practice Generator CD Create additional practice sheets and custom-made tests.

www.SaxonPublishers.com Visit for more student activities and planning materials.

Inclusion

Adaptations CD Adapted lessons, investigations, practice and assessments.

Meeting Standards

National Council of Teachers of Mathematics (NCTM)

Numbers and Operations

NO.1a Work flexibly with fractions, decimals, and percents to solve problems

NO.1b Compare and order fractions, decimals, and percents efficiently and find their approximate locations on a number line

Problem Solving

PS.1c Apply and adapt a variety of appropriate strategies to solve problems

Problem-Solving Strategy: Use Logical Reasoning/ Guess and Check

In the 4 × 200 m relay, Sarang ran first, then Gemmie, then Joyce, and finally Karla. Each girl ran her 200 meters 2 seconds faster than the previous runner. The team finished the race in exactly 1 minute and 50 seconds. How fast did each runner run her 200 meters?

(Understand) **Understand the problem.**

"What information are we given?"

Four girls ran the 4 × 200 meter relay in 1 minute 50 seconds. Each girl ran 2 seconds faster than the runner who ran before her.

"What are we asked to do?"

Determine the length of time each girl ran her leg (her part of the race).

(Plan) **Make a plan.**

"What problem-solving strategy will we use?"

We will *use logical reasoning* and *guess and check.*

(Solve) **Carry out the plan.**

"How many seconds is 1 minute 50 seconds?"

1 minute = 60 seconds; 60 + 50 = 110 seconds

"What is the average time of the four girls?"

110 ÷ 4 = 27.5 seconds.

"What will be our guess (and check) for the four running times?"

We will guess 25 seconds, 27 seconds, 29 seconds, and 31 seconds. The total is 112 seconds, which is 2 seconds too slow. We will then guess 24 seconds, 26 seconds, 28 seconds, and 30 seconds. The total is 108 seconds, which is too fast.

"What do we know from our guesses?"

That the numbers are between the two sets of numbers we guessed.

"What is between 24 and 25?... 26 and 27?... 28 and 29?... 30 and 31?"

24.5, 26.5, 28.5, and 30.5

"What are the girls' running times?"

24.5 + 26.5 + 28.5 + 30.5 = 110 seconds. Sarang ran her leg in 30.5 seconds, Gemmie in 28.5 seconds, Joyce in 26.5 seconds, and Karla in 24.5 seconds.

(Check) **Look back.**

"Did we find the answer to the question that was asked?"

Yes. We found times for the four girls that each increased by 2 seconds and totaled 110 seconds (1 minute 50 seconds).

•Comparing Fractions by Converting to Decimal Form

6ll
6l3
633
(26,43)

Power Up | Building Power

facts	Power Up G

mental math

a. **Calculation:** 4×208 832

b. **Calculation:** $380 + 155$ 535

c. **Calculation:** $4 \times \$1.99$ $7.96

d. **Calculation:** $\$10.00 - \$4.99$ $5.01

e. **Fractional Parts:** $\frac{1}{5}$ of $4.50 $0.90

f. **Decimals:** $\$0.95 \times 100$ $95.00

g. **Probability:** How many different four digit numbers can be made with the digits 6, 4, 2, 9 using each digit exactly once?   24

h. **Calculation:** $8 \times 8, -4, \div 2, +2, \div 4, \times 3, +1, \div 5$ 5

problem solving

In the 4×200 m relay, Sarang ran first, then Gemmie, then Joyce, and finally Karla. Each girl ran her 200 meters 2 seconds faster than the previous runner. The team finished the race in exactly 1 minute and 50 seconds. How fast did each runner run her 200 meters?   Sarang 30.5 seconds, Gemmie 28.5 seconds, Joyce 26.5 seconds, Karla 24.5 seconds

New Concept | *Increasing Knowledge*

We have compared fractions by drawing pictures of fractions and by writing fractions with common denominators. Another way to compare fractions is to convert the fractions to decimal form.

Example 1

Compare these fractions. First convert each fraction to decimal form.

$$\frac{3}{5} \bigcirc \frac{5}{8}$$

Solution

We convert each fraction to a decimal number by dividing the numerator by the denominator.

$$\frac{3}{5} \longrightarrow 5\overline{)3.0}^{\,0.6} \qquad \frac{5}{8} \longrightarrow 8\overline{)5.000}^{\,0.625}$$

Lesson 76   395

---

1 Power Up

Facts
Distribute **Power Up G** to students. See answers below.

Mental Math
Before students begin the Mental Math exercise, do this counting exercise as a class.

Count up and down by 2s between negative 12 and 12.

Encourage students to share different ways to mentally compute these exercises. Strategies for exercises **b** and **c** are listed below.

b. Add 20 and Subtract 20
$380 + 20 = 400$ and $155 - 20 = 135$; $400 + 135 = 535$
Break Apart 155
$380 + (120 + 35) = 500 + 35 = 535$

c. Change $1.99 to $2, then Subtract $4 \times$ 1¢
$(4 \times \$2) - (4 \times 1¢) = \$8 - 4¢ = \$7.96$
Count On by $2, then Count Back by 1¢
Start with $2. Count $4, $6, $8; Start with $8. Count: $7.99, $7.98, $7.97, $7.96

Problem Solving
Refer to **Power-Up Discussion**, p. 395B.

2 New Concepts

Instruction
In Lesson 56, students learned to compare fractions such as $\frac{3}{5}$ and $\frac{5}{8}$ by rewriting the fractions as $\frac{24}{40}$ and $\frac{25}{40}$. Remind students of their work in that lesson, and invite them to use the idea of common denominators to check their answers in today's lesson.

(continued)

Facts | Reduce each fraction to lowest terms.

$\frac{2}{8} = \frac{1}{4}$	$\frac{4}{6} = \frac{2}{3}$	$\frac{6}{10} = \frac{3}{5}$	$\frac{2}{4} = \frac{1}{2}$	$\frac{5}{100} = \frac{1}{20}$	$\frac{9}{12} = \frac{3}{4}$
$\frac{4}{10} = \frac{2}{5}$	$\frac{4}{12} = \frac{1}{3}$	$\frac{2}{10} = \frac{1}{5}$	$\frac{3}{6} = \frac{1}{2}$	$\frac{25}{100} = \frac{1}{4}$	$\frac{3}{12} = \frac{1}{4}$
$\frac{4}{16} = \frac{1}{4}$	$\frac{3}{9} = \frac{1}{3}$	$\frac{6}{9} = \frac{2}{3}$	$\frac{4}{8} = \frac{1}{2}$	$\frac{2}{12} = \frac{1}{6}$	$\frac{6}{12} = \frac{1}{2}$
$\frac{8}{16} = \frac{1}{2}$	$\frac{2}{6} = \frac{1}{3}$	$\frac{8}{12} = \frac{2}{3}$	$\frac{6}{8} = \frac{3}{4}$	$\frac{5}{10} = \frac{1}{2}$	$\frac{75}{100} = \frac{3}{4}$

2 New Concepts (Continued)

Example 1
Instruction
It may be necessary to help some students recall how to compare decimal numbers. Remind them to begin comparing the digits in the tenths place, and if they find the digits are equal, point out that the comparison moves to the digits in the hundredths place, then to the digits in the thousandths place, and so on.

Example 2
Instruction
Have students notice that the decimal dividend results in a decimal point in the quotient.

Practice Set
Problems a–f [Error Alert]
Encourage students to place a decimal point in the quotient immediately after writing each dividend.

Problem c [Error Alert]
When comparing two numbers, students sometimes expect that either a > symbol or a < symbol will be the answer to a comparison problem. Since other answers and symbols can be possible, watch for students who do not recognize that $\frac{15}{25}$ and $\frac{3}{5}$ are equivalent fractions.

3 Written Practice

Math Conversations
Discussion opportunities are provided below.

Problem 1 [Connect]
"What operation does the word 'product' represent?" multiplication

"What exponent does the term 'squared' represent?" 2

"What exponent does the term 'cubed' represent?" 3

(continued)

We write both numbers with the same number of decimal places. Then we compare the two numbers.

$$0.600 < 0.625$$

Since 0.6 is less than 0.625, we know that $\frac{3}{5}$ is less than $\frac{5}{8}$.

$$\frac{3}{5} < \frac{5}{8}$$

Thinking Skill

Explain

How do we compare decimal numbers? If the whole number parts are equal, we start by comparing the digits in the tenths place. If the tenths digits are equal, we compare the digits in the hundredths place, and so on.

Example 2

Compare: $\frac{3}{4} \bigcirc 0.7$

Solution

First we write the fraction as a decimal.

$$\frac{3}{4} \longrightarrow 4\overline{)3.00}^{\,0.75}$$

Then we compare the decimal numbers.

$$0.75 > 0.70$$

Since 0.75 is greater than 0.7, we know that $\frac{3}{4}$ is greater than 0.7.

$$\frac{3}{4} > 0.7$$

Practice Set ▶ Change the fractions to decimals to compare these numbers:

a. $\frac{3}{20} \ominus \frac{1}{8}$ **b.** $\frac{3}{8} \ominus \frac{2}{5}$ **c.** $\frac{15}{25} \ominus \frac{3}{5}$

d. $0.7 \ominus \frac{4}{5}$ **e.** $\frac{2}{5} \ominus 0.5$ **f.** $\frac{3}{8} \ominus 0.325$

Written Practice   *Strengthening Concepts*

▶ *** 1.** *(73)* [Connect] What is the product of ten squared and two cubed?   800

2. *(50)* [Connect] What number is halfway between 4.5 and 6.7?   5.6

3. *(15)* [Formulate] It is said that one year of a dog's life is the same as 7 years of a human's life. Using that thinking, a dog that is 13 years old is how many "human" years old? Write an equation and solve the problem. $13 \cdot 7 = y$; 91 years old

▶ *** 4.** *(76)* Compare. First convert each fraction to decimal form.

$$\frac{2}{5} \ominus \frac{1}{4}$$

* 5. *(74, 75)* **a.** What fraction of this circle is shaded? $\frac{3}{4}$

   b. Convert the answer from part **a** to a decimal number.   0.75

   c. What percent of this circle is shaded?   75%

▶ See Math Conversations in the sidebar.

English Learners

Write the word **halfway** on the board and draw a number line. Say,

"Halfway refers to a middle or central point. A number that is halfway between two numbers is an equal distance on the number line from each of the numbers."

Ask a volunteer to find the number that is halfway between 4 and 8. (6)

6. Choose the appropriate units for measuring the circumference of a
(7, 27) juice glass.   **A**

    A centimeters   **B** meters   **C** kilometers

* 7. **a.** Convert $2\frac{1}{2}$ to a decimal number.   2.5
(73, 74)

    b. Write 3.75 as a reduced mixed number. $3\frac{3}{4}$

* 8. **a.** Write 0.04 as a reduced fraction. $\frac{1}{25}$
(73, 75)

    b. Write 0.04 as a percent.   4%

9. **Verify** Instead of dividing 200 by 18, Sam found half of each number
(43) and then divided. Show Sam's division problem and write the quotient
as a mixed number. $100 \div 9 = 11\frac{1}{9}$

10. $6\frac{1}{3} + 3\frac{1}{4} + 2\frac{1}{2}$ $12\frac{1}{12}$ **11.** $\frac{4}{5} = \frac{?}{100}$ 80
(61)   (42)

➤* 12. **Analyze** $\left(2\frac{1}{2}\right)\left(3\frac{1}{3}\right)\left(1\frac{1}{5}\right)$ 10 *** 13.** $5 \div 2\frac{1}{2}$ 2
(72)   (68)

Find each unknown number:

➤ 14. $6.7 + 0.48 + n = 8$ 0.82   **➤ 15.** $12 - d = 4.75$ 7.25
(43)   (43)

16. 0.35×0.45 0.1575   **17.** $4.3 \div 10^2$ 0.043
(39)   (38, 52)

18. Find the median of these numbers: 0.27
(Inv. 5)
                      0.3, 0.25, 0.313, 0.2, 0.27

19. **Estimate** Find the sum of 3926 and 5184 to the nearest
(16) thousand.   9000

➤ 20. **List** Name all the prime numbers between 40 and 50.   41, 43, 47
(19)

* 21. Twelve of the 25 students in the class earned As on the test. What
(75) percent of the students earned As?   48%

Refer to the triangle to answer problems **22** and **23**.

22. What is the perimeter of this triangle?
(8) 48 mm

➤ 23. **Analyze** Angles *T* and *R* are complementary.
(69) If the measure of ∠*R* is 53°, then what is the
measure of ∠*T*?   37°

20 mm   12 mm
    T 16 mm *S*

➤ 24. **Estimate** About how many **millimeters** long is this line segment?
(7) about 45 mm

cm 1   2   3   4   5

Lesson 76   397

➤ See Math Conversations in the sidebar.

---

3 **Written Practice** (Continued)

Math Conversations

Discussion opportunities are provided below.

Problem 12   Analyze

**"To solve this problem, describe one way
you can reduce the amount of arithmetic
you need to complete."** Sample: After
rewriting the mixed numbers as improper
fractions, cancel the terms that are
equivalent to 1, and reduce those terms that
can be divided by a common factor.

Problem 23   Analyze

**"What is the measure of angle RST? Explain
how you know."** 90°; The symbol at the
vertex of the angle represents a right angle
and the degree measure of a right angle
is 90.

**"How are two angles that are
complementary different from two angles
that are supplementary?"** The sum of the
measures of two complementary angles
is 90°; the sum of the measures of two
supplementary angles is 180°.

Problem 24   Estimate

Extend the Problem

**"Is the segment closer to 1 inch long or
2 inches long? Explain how you know."**
Sample: 1 in. is about $2\frac{1}{2}$ cm, so 2 in. is
about 5 cm. The length of the segment is
closer to 5 cm than to $2\frac{1}{2}$ cm, so the length
of the segment is closer to 2 inches than to
1 inch.

Errors and Misconceptions
Problems 4, 14, and 15

When comparing, adding, or subtracting
decimal numbers, some students may choose
to write the numbers on unlined paper in
vertical columns aligned by place value.
To help increase the likelihood of correct
answers, recommend to these students that
they work on grid paper or lined paper turned
sideways.

Problem 20

Some students may use a guess-and-check or
trial-and-error strategy to identify the prime
numbers. Remind these students of their
previous study of divisibility, and suggest
that they use the tests for divisibility by 2, 3,
and 5, to eliminate the composite numbers
between 40 and 50. (All composite numbers
less than 49 have 2, 3, or 5 as factors.) After
they check for divisibility by 7, their work
will be completed.

(continued)

Math Conversations

Discussion opportunities are provided below.

Problem 27 [Represent]

Extend the Problem

"Name three points on the coordinate plane that form a right isosceles triangle." Check student's answers; one possibility is (0, 0), (0, 5), and (5, 0).

Problem 30 [Model]

It is possible that some of the figures that are formed can be classified as something more than a quadrilateral. For example, some figures may be right trapezoids.

Encourage students to work in small groups to discuss the figures and name them in as many different ways as possible.

---

* **25.** This parallelogram is divided into two congruent triangles.
(71)

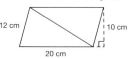

   12 cm   10 cm

20 cm

   a. What is the area of the parallelogram?   200 cm²

   b. What is the area of one of the triangles?   100 cm²

26. How many small cubes were used to form
(Inv. 6) this rectangular prism?
12 cubes

▶* **27.** [Represent] Sketch a coordinate plane on graph paper. Graph point *A*
(Inv. 7) (1, 2), point *B* (−3, −2), and point *C* (1, −2). Then draw segments to connect the three points. What type of polygon is figure *ABC*?   triangle; (See below.)

28. [Conclude] In the figure drawn in problem 27,
(28)
   a. which segment is perpendicular to $\overline{AC}$? $\overline{BC}$ or $\overline{CB}$

   b. which angle is a right angle?   ∠*C*

29. If *b* equals 12 and *h* equals 9, what does $\frac{bh}{2}$ equal?   54
(47)

▶* **30.** [Model] Draw a pair of parallel lines. Draw a third line perpendicular to
(64) the parallel lines. Complete a quadrilateral by drawing a fourth line that intersects but is not perpendicular to the pair of parallel lines. Trace the quadrilateral that is formed. Is the quadrilateral a rectangle?
Sample: 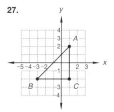 ; no

27.

▶ See Math Conversations in the sidebar.

Looking Forward

Comparing fractions by converting them to decimal form prepares students for:

- **Lesson 99,** expressing fraction-decimal-percent equivalents in table form.

- **Lesson 113,** multiplying by powers of ten.

• Finding Unstated Information in Fraction Problems

Objectives

- Diagram fractional-parts statements.
- Find unstated information from fractional-parts statements.

Lesson Preparation

Materials

- **Power Up K** (in *Instructional Masters*)
- **Teacher-provided material:** graph paper

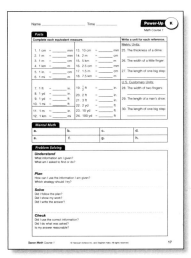

Power Up K

Math Language

	English Learners (ESL)
	category

Technology Resources

Student eBook Complete student textbook in electronic format.

Resources and Planner CD Assessment, reteaching, and instructional masters, plus a pacing calendar with standards.

Test and Practice Generator CD Create additional practice sheets and custom-made tests.

www.SaxonPublishers.com Visit for more student activities and planning materials.

Inclusion

Adaptations CD Adapted lessons, investigations, practice and assessments.

Meeting Standards

National Council of Teachers of Mathematics (NCTM)

Numbers and Operations

NO.1a Work flexibly with fractions, decimals, and percents to solve problems

NO.1d Understand and use ratios and proportions to represent quantitative relationships

Problem Solving

PS.1c Apply and adapt a variety of appropriate strategies to solve problems

Problem-Solving Strategy: Work Backwards

Kathleen read an average of 45 pages per day for four days. If she read a total of 123 pages during the first three days, how many pages did she read on the fourth day?

(Understand) **Understand the problem.**

"What information are we given?"

Kathleen read 123 pages over three days, and an average of 45 pages per day over four days.

"What are we asked to do?"

Find the number of pages Kathleen read on the fourth day.

(Plan) **Make a plan.**

"How can we use the information we know to do what we are asked to do?"

We will use our number sense about averages to *work backwards* from the average to the specific numbers of pages.

(Solve) **Carry out the plan.**

"How can we determine the total number of pages Kathleen read over four days?"

The average was obtained by dividing the total number of pages by 4, so 45 pages × 4 days is 180 pages. Kathleen read 180 pages over four days.

"How will we find the number of pages Kathleen read on the fourth day?"

We know Kathleen read 123 pages during the first three days and we know the total number of pages she read, so we can subtract to find the number of pages she read on the fourth day. 180 pages − 123 pages = 57 pages.

(Check) **Look back.**

"Did we answer the question that was asked?"

Yes. We found the number of pages Kathleen read on the fourth day.

"How can we check to make sure that our answer is correct?"

We will add up the pages she read and find the average. 123 + 57 = 180 and 180 ÷ 4 = 45. The average is 45 and therefore our answer of 57 pages must be correct.

• Finding Unstated Information in Fraction Problems

612
613

Power Up   *Building Power*

facts | Power Up K

mental math |
   a. Calculation: 311 × 5   1555
   b. Number Sense: 565 − 250   315
   c. Calculation: 5 × $1.99 $9.95
   d. Calculation: $7.50 + $1.99 $9.49
   e. Number Sense: Double 80¢. $1.60
   f. Decimals: 6.5 ÷ 100   0.065
   g. Statistics: Find the median of the set of numbers: 134, 147, 125, 149, 158, 185.   148
   h. Calculation: 10 × 10, × 10, − 1, ÷ 9, − 11, ÷ 10   10

problem solving | Kathleen read an average of 45 pages per day for four days. If she read a total of 123 pages during the first three days, how many pages did she read on the fourth day?   57 pages

New Concept   *Increasing Knowledge*

Often fractional-parts statements contain more information than what is directly stated. Consider this fractional-parts statement:

   Three fourths of the 28 students in the class are boys.

This sentence directly states information about the number of boys in the class. It also *indirectly* states information about the number of girls in the class. In this lesson we will practice finding several pieces of information from fractional-parts statements.

Example 1

Diagram this statement. Then answer the questions that follow.

   Three fourths of the 28 students in the class are boys.

   a. Into how many parts is the class divided?
   b. How many students are in each part?
   c. How many parts are boys?
   d. How many boys are in the class?

Lesson 77   **399**

Facts

Complete each equivalent measure.

						Write a unit for each reference.
						Metric Units:
1. 1 cm	=	10 mm	13. 10 cm	=	100 mm	25. The thickness of a dime:
2. 1 m	=	1000 mm	14. 2 m	=	200 cm	millimeter
3. 1 m	=	100 cm	15. 5 km	=	5000 m	26. The width of a little finger:
4. 1 km	=	1000 m	16. 2.5 cm	=	25 mm	centimeter
5. 1 in.	=	2.54 cm	17. 1.5 m	=	150 cm	27. The length of one big step:
6. 1 mi	≈	1610 m	18. 7.5 km	=	7500 m	meter
						U.S. Customary Units:
7. 1 ft	=	12 in.	19. $\frac{1}{2}$ ft	=	6 in.	28. The width of two fingers:
8. 1 yd	=	36 in.	20. 2 ft	=	24 in.	inch
9. 1 yd	=	3 ft	21. 3 ft	=	36 in.	29. The length of a man's shoe:
10. 1 mi	=	5280 ft	22. 2 yd	=	6 ft	foot
11. 1 m	≈	39 in.	23. 10 yd	=	30 ft	30. The length of one big step:
12. 1 km	≈	0.62 mi	24. 100 yd	=	300 ft	yard

---

1 Power Up

Facts
Distribute **Power Up K** to students. See answer below.

Mental Math
Before students begin the Mental Math exercise, do this counting exercise as a class.

Count up and down by $\frac{1}{8}$s between $\frac{1}{8}$ and 2.

Encourage students to share different ways to mentally compute these exercises. Strategies for exercises **b** and **e** are listed below.

  b. Subtract Hundreds First
    (500 − 200) + (65 − 50) = 300 + 15 = 315
    Subtract 15 from 565, then Add 15
    550 − 250 = 300; 300 + 15 = 315
  e. Double Dimes
    Double 8 dimes is 16 dimes or $1.60.
    Use an Addition Pattern
    Double 8 is 16, so double 80¢ is 160¢.

Problem Solving
Refer to **Power-Up Discussion,** p. 399B.

2 New Concepts

The statement below is another example of a fractional-parts statement that contains unstated information.

   Two thirds of fifteen students earned an A.

Write the statement on the board or overhead. Explain that it contains indirect information about the number of students who did not earn an A, then ask students to explain how to identify that number. Sample: $1 - \frac{2}{3} = \frac{1}{3}$, and $\frac{1}{3}$ of 15 = 5.

Encourage students to think of other examples of fractional-parts statements that contain unstated information, and share those statements with the class. Challenge classmates to describe or identify the unstated information in each statement.

(continued)

Example 1
Instruction

Provide an opportunity for students to make a diagram and find unstated information in a fraction problem about your class. Give them a fractional-parts statement that describes some part of the class. For example, "Three fifths of the students in our class today are girls or one third of the students in our class are wearing jeans today." Invite a group of students to diagram your statement on the board. Then ask all of your students a series of questions similar to the questions from the example.

Example 2
Instruction

"If we draw a rectangle to represent the marbles in the bag, into how many equal parts should we divide the rectangle? Explain why." Since the problem uses fifths to describe the probability of an outcome, we divide the rectangle into five equal parts.

"How many marbles would each part of the rectangle represent? Explain why." Each part would represent 6 marbles because there are 30 marbles altogether and $30 \div 5 = 6$.

(continued)

---

e. How many parts are girls?

f. How many girls are in the class?

Solution

We draw a rectangle to represent the whole class. Since the statement uses fourths to describe a part of the class, we divide the rectangle into four parts. Dividing the total number of students by four, we find there are seven students in each part. We identify three of the four parts as boys and one of the four parts as girls. Now we answer the questions.

$$\frac{1}{4} \text{ are girls.} \begin{cases} \end{cases}$$
$$\frac{3}{4} \text{ are boys.} \begin{cases} \end{cases}$$

28 students

7 students

7 students

7 students

7 students

a. The denominator of the fraction indicates that the class is divided into **four parts** for the purpose of this statement. It is important to distinguish between the number of *parts* (as indicated by the denominator) and the number of *categories*. There are two categories of students implied by the statement—boys and girls.

b. In each of the four parts there are **seven students**.

c. The numerator of the fraction indicates that **three parts** are boys.

d. Since three parts are boys and since there are seven students in each part, we find that there are **21 boys** in the class.

e. Three of the four parts are boys, so only **one part** is girls.

f. There are seven students in each part. One part is girls, so there are **seven girls**.

Example 2

There are thirty marbles in a bag. If one marble is drawn from the bag, the probability of drawing red is $\frac{2}{5}$.

a. How many marbles are red?

b. How many marbles are not red?

c. The complement of drawing a red marble is drawing a not red marble. What is the probability of drawing a not red marble?

d. What is the sum of the probabilities of drawing red and drawing not red?

Solution

a. The probability of drawing red is $\frac{2}{5}$, so $\frac{2}{5}$ of the 30 marbles are red.

$$\frac{2}{5} \cdot 30 = 12$$

There are **12 red marbles**.

English Learners

Write the words "boys" and "girls" on the board. Say:

"Categories allow us to divide a group into smaller groups with similar characteristics. For instance, we can divide the class into categories such as boys and girls."

Ask the students to think of categories of things in the classroom. (books, supplies, maps, etc.)

Math Background

When working with unstated information in fraction problems, the idea that 1 represents the whole can help students solve or check a variety of problems.

If one sector of a circle graph represents $\frac{4}{9}$ of the graph, the remaining sectors represent $1 - \frac{4}{9}$ or $\frac{5}{9}$ of the graph.

Encourage students to consider the idea that 1 represents the whole as they search for unstated information in fraction problems.

b. Twelve of the 30 marbles are red, so **18 marbles are not red.**

c. The probability of drawing a not red marble is $\frac{18}{30} = \frac{3}{5}$.

d. The sum of the probabilities of an event and its complement is **1.**

$$\frac{2}{5} + \frac{3}{5} = 1$$

Practice Set

Model Diagram this statement. Then answer the questions that follow.

Three eighths of the 40 little engines could climb the hill.

40 engines
5 engines
5 engines
5 engines
5 engines
5 engines
5 engines
5 engines
5 engines

$\frac{3}{8}$ could climb the hill.

$\frac{5}{8}$ could not climb the hill.

▶ **a.** Into how many parts was the group divided?   8 parts

▶ **b.** How many engines were in each part?   5 engines

c. How many parts could climb the hill?   3 parts

d. How many engines could climb the hill?   15 engines

e. How many parts could not climb the hill?   5 parts

f. How many engines could not climb the hill?   25 engines

Read the statement and then answer the questions that follow.

The face of a spinner is divided into 12 equal sectors. The probability of spinning red on one spin is $\frac{1}{4}$.

g. How many sectors are red?   3

h. How many sectors are not red?   9

▶ **i.** What is the probability of spinning not red in one spin? $\frac{3}{4}$

j. What is the sum of the probabilities of spinning red and not red?   1
How are the events related?   The events are complementary.

Written Practice *Strengthening Concepts*

1. The weight of an object on the Moon is about $\frac{1}{6}$ of its weight on Earth.
(29)   A person weighing 114 pounds on Earth would weigh about how much on the Moon?   about 19 pounds

▶ *** 2.** *Estimate* Estimate the weight of an object in your classroom such as
(22)   a table or desk. Use the information in problem 1 to calculate what the approximate weight of the object would be on the moon. Round your answer to the nearest pound.   See student work.

* 3. Mekhi was at bat 24 times and got 6 hits.
(29, 75)   **a.** What fraction of the times at bat did Mekhi get a hit? $\frac{1}{4}$

b. What percent of the times at bat did Mekhi get a hit?   25%

Lesson 77   401

▶ See Math Conversations in the sidebar.

Example 2
Instruction
As students discuss answers to the questions, ask a volunteer to work at the board or overhead and show the arithmetic for each answer.

Practice Set
Problems a and b [Error Alert]
The answers for problems **a** and **b** are the most important answers in the sequence of questions because incorrect answers will likely result in incorrect answers for the remainder of the questions.

Problem i [Error Alert]
Students should recognize that the probability of not red is the complement of the probability of red. Since the sum of a probability and its complement is 1, the probability of not red is $1 - \frac{1}{4}$ or $\frac{3}{4}$.

3 Written Practice

Math Conversations
Discussion opportunities are provided below.

Problem 2 [Estimate]
"Finding $\frac{1}{6}$ of a number is the same as dividing by what number?" 6

(continued)

Math Conversations

Discussion opportunities are provided below.

Problem 4 [Model]

a. *"What operation is used to find the number of parts?"* division

b. *"Why does each part represent 6 students?"* There are 30 students divided into 5 equal parts; $30 \div 5 = 6$.

c. *"What arithmetic must we complete to find the number of boys?"* $\frac{3}{5} \times 30$

d. *"Explain how subtraction can be used to find the answer and multiplication can be used to check the answer."* Subtract the number of boys from 30 to find the number of girls. Since $\frac{3}{5}$ of the class are boys, $\frac{2}{5}$ are girls, and to check the number of girls found by subtracting, find $\frac{2}{5}$ of 30.

Problem 21 [Analyze]

Extend the Problem

Write the three prime factorizations shown below on the board.

$$2^3 \cdot 3 \cdot 7 \qquad 2 \cdot 3^2 \cdot 11 \qquad 2^3 \cdot 3 \cdot 5$$

Explain that one of the prime factorizations represents the prime factorization of 120.

"Using only mental math, name the prime factorization that represents 120."

Students should infer that 7 and 11 are not factors of 120, so any prime factorization containing those factors cannot be a prime factorization of 120.

Ask students to simplify $2^3 \cdot 3 \cdot 5$ and to check their answer.

Errors and Misconceptions
Problem 6

When writing a mixed number for a decimal number, students sometimes write exactly what they read and do not recognize the need to reduce. For example, 3.6 is read as "three and six tenths" and written as $3\frac{6}{10}$. Remind students to reduce fractions to simplest form whenever possible.

(continued)

4.

30 students	
$\frac{3}{5}$ are boys.	6 students
	6 students
	6 students
$\frac{2}{5}$ are girls.	6 students
	6 students

▶ *** 4.** [Model] Diagram this statement. Then answer the questions that follow.
(77) *There are 30 students in the class. Three fifths of them are boys.*

   a. Into how many parts is the class divided?   5 parts

   b. How many students are in each part?   6 students

   c. How many boys are in the class?   18 boys

   d. How many girls are in the class?   12 girls

* 5. a. In the figure below, what fraction of the group is shaded? $\frac{2}{5}$
(74, 75)

   b. Convert the fraction in part **a** to a decimal number.   0.4

   c. What percent of the group is shaded?   40%

▶ *** 6.** Write the decimal number 3.6 as a mixed number. $3\frac{3}{5}$
(73)

Find each unknown number:

  7. $3.6 + a = 4.15$ 0.55   **8.** $\frac{2}{5}x = 1$ $\frac{5}{2}$
  (43)   (30)

9. If the chance of rain is 60%, then the chance that it will not rain is 40%. It is more likely to rain, because 60% is greater than 40%.

  9. [Explain] If the chance of rain is 60%, is it more likely to rain or not to
  (58) rain? Why?

* 10. Three fifths of a circle is what percent of a circle?   60%
(75)

11. A temperature of $-3°F$ is how many degrees below the freezing
(10, 14) temperature of water?   35°F

* 12. Compare:
(73, 76)
   a. $0.35 \;\ominus\; \dfrac{7}{20}$ b. $3^2 \;\ominus\; 2^3$

13. $\frac{1}{2} + \frac{2}{3}$ $1\frac{1}{6}$ **14.** $3\frac{1}{5} - 1\frac{3}{5}$ $1\frac{3}{5}$
(57)   (63)

15. $\frac{1}{2} + \frac{3}{4} + \frac{7}{8}$ $2\frac{1}{8}$ **16.** $3 \times 1\frac{1}{3}$ 4
(61)   (66)

17. $3 \div 1\frac{1}{3}$ $2\frac{1}{4}$ **18.** $1\frac{1}{3} \div 3$ $\frac{4}{9}$
(68)   (68)

19. What is the perimeter of this rectangle?
(8) 4.8 cm

20. What is the area of this rectangle?
(31) 1.35 sq.cm

1.5 cm

0.9 cm

▶*** 21.** Write the prime factorization of 1000 using exponents. $2^3 \cdot 5^3$
(65)

22. Coats were on sale for 40% off. One coat was regularly priced at $80.
(41)
   a. How much money would be taken off the regular price of the coat during the sale? $32

   b. What would be the sale price of the coat? $48

▶ See Math Conversations in the sidebar.

23. Patricia bought a coat that cost $38.80. The sales-tax rate was 7%.
(41)
  a. What was the tax on the purchase? $2.72

  b. What was the total purchase price including tax? $41.52

24. **Classify** Is every quadrilateral a polygon? yes
(64)

25. What time is one hour fourteen minutes before noon? 10:46 a.m
(32)

26. **Estimate** What percent of this rectangle appears to be shaded? **B**
(Inv. 2)
  A 20%   **C** 60%
  B 40%   **D** 80%

27.
y

* 27. **Represent** Sketch a coordinate plane on graph paper. Graph point
(Inv. 7) W (2, 3), point X (1, 0), point Y (−3, 0), and point Z (−2, 3). Then draw $\overline{WX}$, $\overline{XY}$, $\overline{YZ}$, and $\overline{ZW}$.

* 28. **a.** **Conclude** Which segment in problem 27 is parallel to $\overline{WX}$? $\overline{ZY}$ or $\overline{YZ}$
(71)
  b. Which segment in problem 27 is parallel to $\overline{XY}$? $\overline{WZ}$ or $\overline{ZW}$

29. Write the prime factorization of both the numerator and the denominator
(67) of this fraction. Then reduce the fraction. $\frac{2 \cdot 3 \cdot 5 \cdot 7}{2 \cdot 5 \cdot 5 \cdot 7} = \frac{3}{5}$

$$\frac{210}{350}$$

30. **a.** **Connect** The moon has the shape of what geometric solid? sphere
(47,
Inv. 6)
  b. **Estimate** The diameter of the moon is about 2160 miles. Calculate the approximate circumference of the moon using 3.14 for π. Round the answer to the nearest ten miles. 6780 miles

---

Early Finishers
Choose A Strategy

Simplify each prime factorization below. Then identify which prime factorization does not belong in the group. Explain your reasoning.

$3^2 \times 2^3$ $2^2 \times 3^3 \times 5$ $2^2 \times 3^2 \times 5^2$ 3^5 $2^4 \times 7^2$
  72   540   900   243   784

Samples: Use Logical Reasoning; All of the prime factorizations except $2^4 \times 7^2$ represent numbers that are divisible by 3, so $2^4 \times 7^2$ does not belong in the group; all the prime factorizations except 3^5 represent even numbers, so 3^5 does not belong in the group.

▶ See Math Conversations in the sidebar.

Math Conversations
Discussion opportunities are provided below.

Problem 30b Estimate
Extend the Problem

Write "24,900 miles" on the board or overhead. Explain that 24,900 miles is the approximate circumference of the Earth at its equator. Then challenge students to estimate the fraction of the Earth's circumference that the moon's circumference represents. Sample: $\frac{1}{4}$ because $\frac{6000}{24,000}$ is $\frac{1}{4}$.

Early Finishers

Students may observe that the first three prime factorizations represent numbers that are divisible by 6. You may need to help students recall that a number divisible by 6 is also divisible by 2 and by 3. The fourth prime factorization represents a number that is divisible by 3 but not by 2. The last prime factorization represents a number that is divisible by 2 but not 3.

Others answers are possible. For example, it is correct to say that 3^5 does not belong because it represents a number that is not divisible by 2.

Looking Forward

Diagramming and finding unstated information in fractional-parts problems prepares students for:

- **Lesson 117,** finding a whole when a fraction is known using a diagram.

• Capacity

Objectives

- Identify and convert between units of capacity within the U.S. Customary System.
- Identify and convert between units of capacity within the metric system.

Lesson Preparation

Materials

- **Power Up J** (in *Instructional Masters*)
- **Teacher-provided material: empty containers** representing different units of capacity; **1-gallon container of water, index cards**

Optional
- **Teacher-provided material: dry beans, rice**

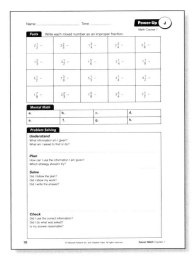

Power Up J

Math Language

New	English Learners (ESL)
capacity	overflow

Technology Resources

Student eBook Complete student textbook in electronic format.

Resources and Planner CD Assessment, reteaching, and instructional masters, plus a pacing calendar with standards.

Test and Practice Generator CD Create additional practice sheets and custom-made tests.

www.SaxonPublishers.com Visit for more student activities and planning materials.

Inclusion

Adaptations CD Adapted lessons, investigations, practice and assessments.

Meeting Standards

National Council of Teachers of Mathematics (NCTM)

Measurement

ME.1a Understand both metric and customary systems of measurement

ME.1b Understand relationships among units and convert from one unit to another within the same system

ME.1c Understand, select, and use units of appropriate size and type to measure angles, perimeter, area, surface area, and volume

Connections

CN.4b Understand how mathematical ideas interconnect and build on one another to produce a coherent whole

Problem-Solving Strategies: Draw a Diagram/ Use Logical Reasoning

Raul's PE class built a training circuit on a circular path behind their school. There are six light poles spaced evenly around the circuit, and it takes Raul 64 seconds to mow the path from the first pole to the third pole. At this rate, how long will it take Raul to mow once completely around the path?

(Understand) **Understand the problem.**

"What information are we given?"

The training circuit is circular and there are six light poles evenly spaced around the circuit. We also know that it took Raul 64 seconds to mow from the first pole to the third pole.

"What are we asked to do?"

Determine how long it would take Raul to mow around the entire path.

(Plan) **Make a plan.**

"What problem-solving strategy will we use?"

We will *draw a diagram* and then *use logical reasoning* to solve the problem.

"What do we know about the shape of the training circuit?"

It is circular and there are light poles spaced evenly around the circumference.

(Solve) **Carry out the plan.**

Teacher Note: As you carry out the plan, draw the diagram on the board.

"How do we begin?"

We will draw a circle and figure out where to place the light poles.

"What do we know about circles that will help us space the light poles?"

Circles measure $360°$. Since there are 6 poles, we can divide 360 by 6 to find that they must be $60°$ apart. If we start at the 12 o'clock position, we can draw dots to represent poles at 2 o'clock, 4 o'clock, 6 o'clock, 8 o'clock, and 10 o'clock.

"What fraction of the circle did Raul mow in 64 seconds?"

The poles divide the circumference into six equal parts. From the first pole to the third pole is 2 of the 6 parts. Since $\frac{2}{6}$ equals $\frac{1}{3}$, Raul mowed $\frac{1}{3}$ of the circuit in 64 seconds. He could mow $\frac{3}{3}$ in 3×64 seconds if he mows at the same rate.

"How long would it take Raul to mow?"

192 seconds or 3 minutes and 12 seconds

(Check) **Look back.**

"Did we find the answer to the question that was asked?"

Yes. We found the length of time it would take Raul to mow the circular training path.

Facts

Distribute **Power Up J** to students. See answers below.

Mental Math

Before students begin the Mental Math exercise, do this counting exercise as a class.

Count up and down by 3s between negative 15 and 15.

Encourage students to share different ways to mentally compute these exercises. Strategies for exercises **a** and **b** are listed below.

  a. **Break Apart 325**
   $(4 \times 300) + (4 \times 25) = 1200 + 100$
   $= 1300$
  Count On by 325
   Start with 325. Count: 650, 975, 1300
  b. **Add Hundreds First**
   $1500 + (200 + 75) = 1700 + 75 = 1775$
  Change 275 to 300, then Subtract 25
   $1500 + 300 = 1800; 1800 - 25 = 1775$

Problem Solving

Refer to **Power-Up Discussion,** p. 404B.

2 **New Concepts**

Instruction

Discuss the arithmetic that would be needed to change from one unit of liquid measure to another. For example, to change quarts to gallons, divide the number of quarts by 4, and to change gallons to quarts, multiply the number of gallons by 4.

(continued)

LESSON
78   • Capacity

facts | Power Up J

mental math

  a. Calculation: 4×325 1300
  b. Number Sense: $1500 + 275$ 1775
  c. Calculation: $3 \times \$2.99$ $8.97
  d. Calculation: $\$20.00 - \$2.99$ $17.01
  e. Fractional Parts: $\frac{1}{3}$ of $2.40 $0.80
  f. Decimals: 1.75×100 175
  g. Statistics: Find the median of the set of numbers: 384, 127, 388, 484, 488, 120.   386
  h. Calculation: $9 \times 11, + 1, \div 2, - 1, \div 7, - 2, \times 5$ 25

problem solving

Raul's PE class built a training circuit on a circular path behind their school. There are six light poles spaced evenly around the circuit, and it takes Raul 64 seconds to mow the path from the first pole to the third pole. At this rate, how long will it take Raul to mow once completely around the path?
192 seconds (or 3 minutes, 12 seconds)

New Concept   *Increasing Knowledge*

To measure quantities of liquid in the U.S. Customary System, we use the units gallons (gal), quarts (qt), pints (pt), cups (c), and ounces (oz). In the metric system we use liters (L) and milliliters (mL). The relationships between units within each system are shown in the following table:

Thinking Skill

Discuss

Name some real world situations where we use the word *quarter*.
quarter (of a dollar), quarter mile, quarter pound, quarter after (hour)

Equivalence Table for Units of Liquid Measure

U.S. Customary System	Metric System
1 gallon = 4 quarts	
1 quart = 2 pints	
1 pint = 2 cups	1 liter = 1000 milliliters
1 cup = 8 ounces	

Facts   Write each mixed number as an improper fraction.

$2\frac{1}{2} = \frac{5}{2}$	$2\frac{2}{5} = \frac{12}{5}$	$1\frac{3}{4} = \frac{7}{4}$	$2\frac{3}{4} = \frac{11}{4}$	$2\frac{1}{8} = \frac{17}{8}$
$1\frac{2}{3} = \frac{5}{3}$	$3\frac{1}{2} = \frac{7}{2}$	$1\frac{5}{6} = \frac{11}{6}$	$2\frac{1}{4} = \frac{9}{4}$	$1\frac{1}{8} = \frac{9}{8}$
$5\frac{1}{2} = \frac{11}{2}$	$1\frac{3}{8} = \frac{11}{8}$	$5\frac{1}{3} = \frac{16}{3}$	$3\frac{1}{4} = \frac{13}{4}$	$4\frac{1}{2} = \frac{9}{2}$
$1\frac{7}{8} = \frac{15}{8}$	$2\frac{2}{3} = \frac{8}{3}$	$1\frac{5}{8} = \frac{13}{8}$	$3\frac{3}{4} = \frac{15}{4}$	$7\frac{1}{2} = \frac{15}{2}$

Math Language

Note that we use *ounces* to measure capacity and weight. However, these are two different units of measurement. When we measure capacity we often refer to *fluid ounces.*

Common container sizes based on the U.S. Customary System are illustrated below. These containers are named by their **capacity,** that is, by the amount of liquid they can contain. Notice that each container size has half the capacity of the next-largest container. Also, notice that a quart is one "quarter" of a gallon.

1 gallon $\frac{1}{2}$ gallon   1 quart   1 pint   1 cup

Food and beverage containers often have both U.S. Customary and metric capacities printed on the containers. Using the information found on 2-liter seltzer bottles and $\frac{1}{2}$-gallon milk cartons, we find that one liter is a little more than one quart. So the capacity of a 2-liter bottle is a little more than the capacity of a $\frac{1}{2}$-gallon container.

2-liter bottle $\frac{1}{2}$-gallon container

Example 1

A half gallon of milk is how many pints of milk?

Solution

Two pints equals a quart, and two quarts equals a half gallon. So a half gallon of milk is **4 pints.**

Example 2

Which has the greater capacity, a 12-ounce can or a 1-pint container?

Solution

A pint equals 16 ounces. **So a 1-pint container has more capacity than a 12-ounce can.**

Practice Set

a. What fraction of a gallon is a quart? $\frac{1}{4}$

b. A 2-liter bottle has a capacity of how many milliliters?   2000 mL

c. A half gallon of orange juice will fill how many 8-ounce cups?
8 8-ounce cups

d. **Explain** The entire contents of a full 2-liter bottle are poured into an empty half-gallon carton. Will the half-gallon container overflow? Why or why not?   The half-gallon carton will overflow because 2 liters is a little more than half of a gallon.

Lesson 78   405

▶ See Math Conversations in the sidebar.

2 New Concepts (Continued)

Instruction

Ask students to give examples of liquids that are often measured in gallons, quarts, pints, ounces, liters, and milliliters. Sample: gallons, milk; quarts, juice; pints, cream; cups, water; liters, sports drinks; milliliters, drops of medicine.

To help students gain a sense of different units of capacity, bring a wide variety of clean, empty plastic containers such as milk cartons and water bottles to class. Give students an opportunity to examine and compare the containers.

Point out that a 2-liter bottle is slightly larger than a $\frac{1}{2}$-gallon container and that a liter is slightly more than a quart.

Then use a 1-gallon container of water to demonstrate how two cups fill the empty pint container, two pints fill the quart container, and two quarts fill a $\frac{1}{2}$-gallon container.

Practice Set

Problems a–c [Error Alert]

To complete these problems, students need to know the capacity benchmarks that are shown in the equivalence table on the first page of this lesson.

If students are not familiar with the benchmarks, invite them to copy the chart on an index card or in their math notebooks and use it for reference.

Math Background

The diagram at the right shows the relationships shared by U.S. Customary units of capacity. It shows that a gallon (G) contains 4 quarts (Q), that each contain two pints (P), that each contain two cups (C).

Liquids

English Learners

Refer students to **d** in the Practice Set. Explain the meaning of **overflow.** Say,

"When you try to put more into a container than it will hold, it will overflow or spill over."

Demonstrate the meaning of overflow. Fill a container with beans or rice. Pour the contents into a smaller container to show how the beans or rice overflow.

3 Written Practice

Math Conversations
Discussion opportunities are provided below.

Problem 3 Analyze
"Explain how you can use a divisibility rule to find the numbers that are multiples of 3." If the sum of the digits of the number is divisible by 3, the number is divisible by 3. The sum of the digits in 40 is 4, so 40 is not divisible by 3. The sum of the digits in 41 is 5, so 41 is not divisible by 3. And so on.

Problems 4b–4d Model
Demonstrate on the board or overhead, or invite a volunteer to demonstrate, the arithmetic that is used to find the answer to each question.
Problem 4b: $60 \div 5$
Problem 4c: $60 - 12$
Problem 4d: $60 - 48$

Problem 10 Analyze
Extend the Problem
"Suppose that the number of shaded squares in the rectangle was tripled. What percent of the rectangle would be shaded? Use mental math to name the answer." 75%

Errors and Misconceptions
Problems 2 and 28b
When making conversions, some students may not recognize the operation that must be used.
- To change a larger unit to a smaller unit, multiply.
- To change a smaller unit to a larger unit, divide.

Encourage students to use and remember these generalizations.

Problem 5 Classify
Some students may incorrectly name zero as the answer. Although zero is not a prime number and is not a composite number, zero is also not a counting number.

"What numbers belong to the set of counting numbers?" 1, 2, 3, 4, 5, and so on

(continued)

---

1. What is the difference when the product of $\frac{1}{2}$ and $\frac{1}{2}$ is subtracted from the sum of $\frac{1}{2}$ and $\frac{1}{2}$? $\frac{3}{4}$
(12, 55)

2. The claws of a Siberian tiger are 10 centimeters long. How many millimeters is that?   100 millimeters
(7)

3. Analyze   Sue was thinking of a number between 40 and 50 that is a multiple of 3 and 4. Of what number was she thinking?   48
(25)

4. 60 lights
- 12 lights
- 12 lights
- 12 lights
- 12 lights
$\frac{4}{5}$ were on.
- 12 lights
$\frac{1}{5}$ were off.

* 4. Model   Diagram this statement. Then answer the questions that follow.
(77)
Four fifths of the 60 lights were on.

  a. Into how many parts have the 60 lights been divided?   5 parts

  b. How many lights are in each part?   12 lights

  c. How many lights were on?   48 lights

  d. How many lights were off?   12 lights

5. Classify   Which counting number is neither a prime number nor a composite number?   1
(65)

Find each unknown number:

6. $\frac{4}{5}m = 1$ $\frac{5}{4}$
(30)

7. $\frac{4}{5} + w = 1$ $1\frac{1}{5}$
(43)

8. $\frac{4}{5} \div x = 1$ $\frac{4}{5}$
(43)

9. $\frac{3}{4} = \frac{n}{100}$ 75
(42, 43)

* 10. a. What fraction of the rectangle below is shaded? $\frac{1}{4}$
(74, 75)

  b. Write the answer to part **a** as a decimal number.   0.25

  c. What percent of the rectangle is shaded?   25%

* 11. Convert the decimal number 1.15 to a mixed number. $1\frac{3}{20}$
(73)

* 12. Compare:
(73, 76)
  a. $\frac{3}{5} \ominus 0.35$

  b. $\sqrt{100} \oslash 1^4 + 2^3$

13. $\frac{5}{6} - \frac{1}{2}$ $\frac{1}{3}$
(57)

14. $4\frac{1}{4} - 3\frac{1}{3}$ $\frac{11}{12}$
(63)

15. $\frac{1}{2} + \frac{2}{3} + \frac{5}{6}$ 2
(51)

16. $1\frac{1}{2} \times 2\frac{2}{3}$ 4
(66)

17. $1\frac{1}{2} \div 2\frac{2}{3}$ $\frac{9}{16}$
(68)

18. $2\frac{2}{3} \div 1\frac{1}{2}$ $1\frac{7}{9}$
(68)

19. a. What is the perimeter of this square?   2 in.
(38)

  b. What is the area of this square? $\frac{1}{4}$ in.^{2}

$\frac{1}{2}$ in.

▶ See Math Conversations in the sidebar.

Inclusion

Materials: dry beans, empty liter, gallon, quart, pint, and cup containers

Students with special needs will benefit from hands-on experience with equivalent liquid measures. Use dry beans in place of liquids.

Have students transfer beans from one container to another and ask,

"How many pints are needed to fill 3 quarts?" 6

"Which is greater, 2 quarts or 8 cups?" Both are equal.

As students become more comfortable with the customary units ask,

"How many pints does it take to fill a half gallon?" 4

"How many cups can half a quart fill?" 2

To help students relate metric and customary measures, demonstrate that a liter and a quart are almost equivalent. Then ask,

"How many liters does it take to fill a half-gallon container?" about 2

20. **Verify** "The opposite sides of a rectangle are parallel." True or false? **true**
(64)

* 21. What is the average of 3^3 and 5^2? **26**
(73)

* 22. The diameter of the small wheel was 7 inches. The circumference was about 22 inches. Write the ratio of the circumference to the diameter of the circle as a decimal number rounded to the nearest hundredth. **3.14**
(51, 74)

23. How many inches is $2\frac{1}{2}$ feet? **30 inches**
(66)

24. **Connect** Which arrow below could be pointing to 0.1? **C**
(50)

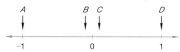

A   B C   D

-1 0   1

25. **Represent** Draw a quadrilateral that is not a rectangle. **See student work. Figure should have four sides and no more than two right angles.**
(64)

26. Sample:

900

9   100

③ ③ 10   10

② ⑤ ② ⑤

▶ **26.** **Represent** Find the prime factorization of 900 by using a factor tree. Then write the prime factorization using exponents. $2^2 \cdot 3^2 \cdot 5^2$
(65, 73)

27. Three vertices of a rectangle have the coordinates (5, 3), (5, −1), and (−1, −1). What are the coordinates of the fourth vertex of the rectangle? **(−1, 3)**
(Inv. 7)

* 28. Refer to this table to answer **a** and **b**.
(78)

3 teaspoons = 1 tablespoon
16 tablespoons = 1 cup
2 cups = 1 pint
2 pints = 1 quart
4 quarts = 1 gallon

    a. A teaspoon of soup is what fraction of a tablespoon of soup? $\frac{1}{3}$

▶   **b.** How many cups of milk is a gallon of milk? **16 cups**

* 29. **Estimate** A liter is closest in size to which of the following? **B**
(78)
    A pint   **B** quart   **C** $\frac{1}{2}$ gallon   **D** gallon

* 30. In 1881 Clara Barton founded the American Red Cross, an organization that helps people during emergencies. The Red Cross organizes "blood drives" in which people can donate a pint of blood to help hospital patients who will undergo surgery. How many ounces is a pint? **16 ounces**
(78)

▶ See Math Conversations in the sidebar.

Math Conversations

Discussion opportunities are provided below.

Problem 26   Represent

Extend the Problem

At the board or overhead, write the two prime factorizations shown below.

$$2^2 \cdot 3 \cdot 5 \qquad 2 \cdot 3^2 \cdot 5$$

Ask students to compare the factorizations, then invite a volunteer to the board or overhead and ask the volunteer to write >, <, or = to complete the comparison. **<**

Repeat the activity several times using these factorizations or others of your own design.

$2^2 \cdot 5^2$	<	$2 \cdot 5 \cdot 11$
$2 \cdot 7 \cdot 11$	>	$3 \cdot 5 \cdot 7$
$2^3 \cdot 3^2 \cdot 7$	<	$2 \cdot 3^3 \cdot 13$

Each time a comparison has been completed, ask

"Did you use mental math or paper and pencil to complete the comparison? Explain why you chose that method."

Looking Forward

Identifying and converting between units of capacity within the U.S. Customary System and within the metric system prepares students for:

- **Lesson 81,** converting one or more measurements to the same unit and performing arithmetic operations with units of measurement.

- **Lesson 102,** converting units of mass and weight and performing operations of addition and subtraction with units of measurement.

- **Investigation 11,** using scale drawings and models to determine actual or scale dimensions.

- **Lesson 114,** using unit multipliers to convert one unit of measure to another unit of measure.

Area of a Triangle

Objectives

- Demonstrate that a triangle's area is half the area of a parallelogram with the same base and height.
- Use the formulas $A = \frac{1}{2}bh$ and $A = \frac{bh}{2}$ to calculate the area of a triangle.

Lesson Preparation

Materials

- **Power Up K** (in *Instructional Masters*)
- **Manipulative kit: inch rulers**
- **Teacher-provided material: pencil and paper, scissors**
- **Geometric Formulas poster**
Optional
- **Investigation Activity 15** (in *Instructional Masters*)

Power Up K

Math Language

Maintain	English Learners (ESL)
congruent	formula

Technology Resources

Student eBook Complete student textbook in electronic format.

Resources and Planner CD Assessment, reteaching, and instructional masters, plus a pacing calendar with standards.

Test and Practice Generator CD Create additional practice sheets and custom-made tests.

www.SaxonPublishers.com Visit for more student activities and planning materials.

Inclusion

Adaptations CD Adapted lessons, investigations, practice and assessments.

Meeting Standards

National Council of Teachers of Mathematics (NCTM)

Geometry

GM.4d Use geometric models to represent and explain numerical and algebraic relationships

Measurement

ME.1c Understand, select, and use units of appropriate size and type to measure angles, perimeter, area, surface area, and volume

ME.2b Select and apply techniques and tools to accurately find length, area, volume, and angle measures to appropriate levels of precision

Problem-Solving Strategy: Use Logical Reasoning/ Draw a Diagram

The restaurant serves four different soups and three different salads. How many different soup-and-salad combinations can diners order? Draw a diagram to support your answer.

(Understand) **Understand the problem.**

"What information are we given?"

We are told that a restaurant serves four different soups and three different salads.

"What are we asked to do?"

We are asked to find how many different combinations of soup and salad diners could order.

(Plan) **Make a plan.**

"What problem-solving strategies could we use?"

We will *use logical reasoning* and *draw a diagram*.

(Solve) **Carry out the plan.**

"How do we begin?"

We will see how many combinations of soup and salad we can make with one type of soup.

"How will we use that information to answer the question?"

If we know how many combinations with one type of soup, we can use logical reasoning to figure out how many combinations with four types of soup.

"How many combinations are there for one type of soup?"

If we call the first soup A and the three salads 1, 2, and 3, we would have three combinations: A1, A2, and A3.

"How many combinations would there be for soups B, C, and D?"

There would be 3 for each soup, so there would be a total of 4 × 3 or 12 combinations of soups and salads.

"How could we draw a diagram to support the answer?"

We will draw a tree diagram with branches from each of the four soups.

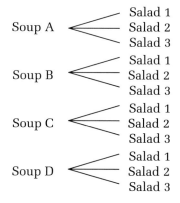

Soup A — Salad 1, Salad 2, Salad 3
Soup B — Salad 1, Salad 2, Salad 3
Soup C — Salad 1, Salad 2, Salad 3
Soup D — Salad 1, Salad 2, Salad 3

(Check) **Look back.**

"Did we find the answer to the questions that were asked?"

Yes. We found the number of soup-and-salad combinations and we supported our answer with a diagram.

① Power Up

Facts

Distribute **Power Up K** to students. See answers below.

Mental Math

Before students begin the Mental Math exercise, do this counting exercise as a class.

Count up and down by 12s between 12 and 144.

Encourage students to share different ways to mentally compute these exercises. Strategies for exercises **b** and **e** are listed below.

b. Subtract Hundreds, then Tens
$1000 - 400 = 600; 600 - 20 = 580$
Subtract 20 from 1000, then Subtract 400
$1000 - 20 = 980; 980 - 400 = 580$
e. Double Tens, then Double Ones
$\$20 \times 2 = \$40$ and $\$4 \times 2 = \$8;$
$\$40 + \$8 = \$48$
Double \$25, then Subtract \$2
Double \$25 is \$50; $\$50 - \$2 = \$48$

Problem Solving

Refer to **Power-Up Discussion,** p. 408B.

② New Concepts

Instruction

Display the **Geometric Formulas** poster as you discuss the area of a triangle with students.

(continued)

Activity

Distribute pencil, paper, scissors, and a ruler to each student. You may want to have students fold, cut, and arrange their own triangles as you demonstrate the steps, or you may want students to read the directions carefully and complete the activity independently.

408   *Saxon Math Course 1*

LESSON
79
• Area of a Triangle

Power Up   *Building Power*

facts	Power Up K
mental math	**a. Calculation:** 307×6 1842
	b. Number Sense: $1000 - 420$ 580
	c. Calculation: $4 \times \$2.99$ \$11.96
	d. Calculation: $\$5.75 + \$2.99$ \$8.74
	e. Number Sense: Double \$24. \$48.00
	f. Decimals: 0.125×100 12.5
	g. Measurement: How many liters are in a kiloliter? 1000 liters
	h. Calculation: $2 \times 2, \times 2, \times 2, - 1, \times 2, + 2, \div 2, \div 2$ 8

problem solving	The restaurant serves four different soups and three different salads. How many different soup-and-salad combinations can diners order? Draw a diagram to support your answer. 12 combinations; see script for diagram

New Concept   *Increasing Knowledge*

In this lesson we will demonstrate that the area of a triangle is half the area of a parallelogram with the same base and height.

Activity

Area of a Triangle

Materials needed:

- pencil and paper
- ruler
- scissors

Model Fold the paper in half, and draw a triangle on the folded paper.

Math Language
Recall that **congruent** polygons have the same size and shape.

While the paper is folded, use your scissors to cut out the triangle so that you have two congruent triangles.

408   *Saxon Math Course 1*

Facts

Complete each equivalent measure.

1. 1 cm	= 10 mm	13. 10 cm	= 100 mm		
2. 1 m	= 1000 mm	14. 2 m	= 200 cm		
3. 1 m	= 100 cm	15. 5 km	= 5000 m		
4. 1 km	= 1000 m	16. 2.5 cm	= 25 mm		
5. 1 in.	= 2.54 cm	17. 1.5 m	= 150 cm		
6. 1 mi	≈ 1610 m	18. 7.5 km	= 7500 m		

Write a unit for each reference.

Metric Units:

25. The thickness of a dime: millimeter

26. The width of a little finger: centimeter

27. The length of one big step: meter

7. 1 ft	= 12 in.	19. $\frac{1}{2}$ ft	= 6 in.
8. 1 yd	= 36 in.	20. 2 ft	= 24 in.
9. 1 yd	= 3 ft	21. 3 ft	= 36 in.
10. 1 mi	= 5280 ft	22. 2 yd	= 6 ft
11. 1 m	≈ 39 in.	23. 10 yd	= 30 ft
12. 1 km	≈ 0.62 mi	24. 100 yd	= 300 ft

U.S. Customary Units:

28. The width of two fingers: inch

29. The length of a man's shoe: foot

30. The length of one big step: yard

---

408   *Saxon Math Course 1*

Arrange the two triangles to form a parallelogram. What fraction of the area of the parallelogram is the area of one of the triangles? $\frac{1}{2}$

We find that whatever the shape of a triangle, its area is half the area of the parallelogram with the same base and height.

Recall that the area of a parallelogram can be found by multiplying its base by its height ($A = bh$). So the area of a triangle can be determined by finding half of the product of its base and height.

parallelogram   triangle
$A = bh$ $A = \frac{1}{2}bh$

Thinking Skill

Analyze

Why are multiplying by $\frac{1}{2}$ and dividing by 2 equivalent operations? Because multiplying by $\frac{1}{2}$ and dividing by 2 are both halving operations.

Since multiplying by $\frac{1}{2}$ and dividing by 2 are equivalent operations, the formula may also be written as

$$A = \frac{bh}{2}$$

In the following examples we will use both formulas stated above. From our calculations of the areas of rectangles and parallelograms, we remember that the base and the height are *perpendicular* measurements.

Example 1

Find the area of the triangle at right.

Solution

Reading Math

The area of a figure is expressed in square units. Read the abbreviation "cm²" as *square centimeters.*

The area of the triangle is half the product of the base and height. The height must be *perpendicular* to the base. The height in this case is 4 cm. Half the product of 8 cm × 4 cm is 16 cm².

$$A = \frac{1}{2}(8 \text{ cm})(4 \text{ cm})$$

$$A = 16 \text{ cm}^2$$

English Learners

Write "Area of a Triangle = $\frac{1}{2}bh$" on the board. Say,

"A formula shows us the steps needed to calculate a value. This formula tells us that the way to find the area of a triangle is to multiply $\frac{1}{2}$ times the product of the base and height of the triangle."

Ask a volunteer to choose a number value for the base and height of the triangle and then find the area.

Math Background

The triangle that is pictured in the Area of a Triangle activity is a right triangle. However, students may use other triangles, such as acute triangles or obtuse triangles, to complete the activity.

If students choose to use a variety of triangles, invite them to compare their results to those of their classmates after the activity has been completed.

---

2 New Concepts *(Continued)*

Instruction

In Lesson 71, an activity was used to explore why the area of a parallelogram equals the base times the height. If necessary, review this activity with students.

Example 1

Instruction

Make sure students notice that the base and the height of a triangle intersect at right angles. Remind them that a right angle has a measure of 90° and is indicated by a square corner symbol.

"*What is the measure of the base and the height of this triangle?*" The base is 8 cm and the height is 4 cm.

(continued)

2 New Concepts *(Continued)*

Example 2
Instruction

"Which measure, 3 meters or 5 meters, represents the height of the triangle? Explain why." 3 meters; the height must be perpendicular to a base. The 5 meter side of the triangle is not perpendicular to either of the other sides.

Make sure students notice the exponent 2 in the answer. Point out that measurements of area must be labeled in square units.

Practice Set
Problem a [Error Alert]

If students mistakenly identify the height of the triangle as 7 ft and give an answer of 35 ft^2, remind them that the height of the triangle is perpendicular to its base. In other words, the height forms a right angle with the base.

Problem d [Error Alert]

Some students may be confused by a height that is located outside the triangle. Explain that a triangle having an obtuse angle at its base has a height that is outside the triangle.

Point out that the area of this obtuse triangle is found by using the same formulas ($A = \frac{1}{2}bh$ or $A = \frac{bh}{2}$) that are used to find the areas of other triangles.

Make sure students notice that the base is the length of the side of the triangle, and does not include the extension of the side.

3 Written Practice

Math Conversations
Discussion opportunities are provided below.

Problem 2 [Analyze]
Extend the Problem

"Assume that the 2-liter bottle is full. How many ounces are the same as 2 liters?"
67.6 oz

(continued)

Find the area of this right triangle:

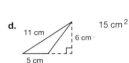

Solution

We find the area by multiplying the base by the height and then dividing by 2. All right triangles have two sides that are perpendicular, so we use the perpendicular sides as the base and height.

$$A = \frac{(4\text{ m})(3\text{ m})}{2}$$

$$A = \mathbf{6\ m^2}$$

Practice Set   Find the area of each triangle:

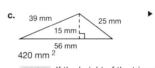

a. 30 ft^2

b. 24 in.^{2}

c. 420 mm^2

d. 15 cm^2

e. [Predict] If the height of the triangle in **c** is doubled to 30 mm, would the area double? Calculate to check your prediction.   Yes. 15 × 2 = 30, $\frac{1}{2}$(56)(30) = 840, and 840 ÷ 2 = 420.

Written Practice   *Strengthening Concepts*

1. [Explain] If you know both the perimeter and the length of a rectangle, how can you determine the width of the rectangle?   Sample: Divide the perimeter by 2 and subtract the length from the quotient.
(8)

* 2. A 2-liter bottle contained 2 qt 3.6 oz of beverage. Use this information to compare a liter and a quart:
(78)

$$1 \text{ liter} \ominus 1 \text{ quart}$$

3. Mr. Johnson was 38 years old when he started his job. He worked for 33 years. How old was he when he retired?   71 years old
(11)

4. [Verify] Answer "true" or "false" for each statement:
(64)
   a. "Every rectangle is a square."   false
   b. "Every rectangle is a parallelogram."   true

▸ See Math Conversations in the sidebar.

5. Ninety percent of 30 trees are birch trees.
(23, 41)
    a. How many trees are birch trees?   27 trees

    b. What is the ratio of birch trees to all other trees? $\frac{9}{1}$

* 6. Eighteen of the twenty-four runners finished the race.
(75, 77)
    a. What fraction of the runners finished the race? $\frac{3}{4}$

    b. What fraction of the runners did not finish the race? $\frac{1}{4}$

    c. What percent of the runners did not finish the race?   25%

▶ *** 7.** _Analyze_   This parallelogram is divided into two congruent triangles.
(79)   What is the area of each triangle?   120 mm²

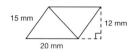
15 mm   12 mm
20 mm

▶ *** 8.** $10^3 \div 10^2$ 10   **9.** 6.42 + 12.7 + 8   27.12
(73)   (38)

10. 1.2(0.12)   0.144   **11.** 64 ÷ 0.08   800
(39)   (49)

12. $3\frac{1}{3} \times \frac{1}{5} \times \frac{3}{4}$ $\frac{1}{2}$ **13.** $2\frac{1}{2} \div 3$ $\frac{5}{6}$
(72)   (68)

Find each unknown number:

14. 10 − q = 9.87   0.13   **15.** 24m = 0.288   0.012
(43)   (45)

16. $n - 2\frac{3}{4} = 3\frac{1}{3}$ $6\frac{1}{12}$ **17.** $w + \frac{1}{4} = \frac{5}{6}$ $\frac{7}{12}$
(63)   (57)

18. The perimeter of a square is 80 cm. What is its area?   400 sq. cm
(38)

19. Write the decimal number for the following: 96.03
(46)

$$(9 \times 10) + (6 \times 1) + \left(3 \times \frac{1}{100}\right)$$

▶*** 20.** _Connect_   Juana set the radius on the compass to 10 cm and drew a
(47)   circle. What was the circumference of the circle? (Use 3.14 for π.)
     62.8 cm

21. Which of these numbers is closest to zero?   B
(50)
    A −2   **B** 0.2   **C** 1   **D** $\frac{1}{2}$

22. _Estimate_   Find the product of 6.7 and 7.3 by rounding each number to
(51)   the nearest whole number before multiplying. Explain how you arrived at
  your answer.   49; Round 6.7 to 7 and round 7.3 to 7. Then multiply 7 by 7.

▶*** 23.** _Analyze_   The expression 2^4 (two to the fourth power) is the prime
(73)   factorization of 16. The expression 3^4 is the prime factorization of what
  number?   81

24. What number is halfway between 0.2 and 0.3?   0.25
(18, 45)

▶ See Math Conversations in the sidebar.

Math Conversations
Discussion opportunities are provided below.

Problem 7   Analyze
"What measure represents the base of each triangle?" 20 millimeters

"Why isn't the side of the triangle labeled 15 millimeters the base of the triangle?" The side is not perpendicular to either of the other two sides of the triangle.

Problem 20   Connect
"What part of a circle is a radius?" A radius is a line segment that has one endpoint at the center of the circle and its other endpoint on the circle.

"What two formulas can be used to find the circumference of a circle?" $C = 2\pi r$ and $C = \pi d$

Problem 23   Analyze
"In the expression 'three to the fourth power,' which number represents the base?" 3

"Which number represents the exponent?" 4

"What does the exponent tell us about the base?" The exponent tells the number of times the base is used as a factor.

"What repeated multiplication represents the expression 'three to the fourth power'?" $3 \cdot 3 \cdot 3 \cdot 3$

Errors and Misconceptions
Problem 7
If students find the area of the parallelogram (by finding the sum of the areas of both triangles) instead of the area of each triangle, encourage them to reread the problem carefully and note that the question asks for the area of each triangle.

Problem 8
Students must remember to complete the operations with exponents before dividing.

Remind students to always follow the Order of Operations whenever they simplify expressions that contain more than one operation.

(continued)

Math Conversations

Discussion opportunities are provided below.

Problem 27 [Analyze]

"What are vertices?" Sample: the point where two sides of a polygon meet

Problem 28b [Analyze]

"What is perimeter a measure of?" Sample: distance around a figure

25. [Connect] To what decimal number is the arrow pointing on the number
(50) line below?   10.2

```
        ↓
  ├──┼──┼──┼──┼──┼──┼──┼──┼──┼──┤
  10                            11
```

26. Which quadrilateral has only one pair of parallel sides?   trapezoid
(64)

▶* **27.** [Analyze] The coordinates of the vertices of a quadrilateral are (–5, 5),
(64, (1, 5), (3, 1), and (–3, 1). What is the name for this kind of quadrilateral?
Inv. 7) parallelogram

[Analyze] In the figure below, a square and a regular hexagon share a
common side. The area of the square is 100 sq. cm. Use this information to
answer problems **28** and **29**.

* **28. a.** [Analyze] What is the length of each side
(38)   of the square?   10 cm

▶   **b.** What is the perimeter of the square?
          40 cm

29. a. What is the length of each side of the hexagon?   10 cm
(8)
    b. What is the perimeter of the hexagon?   60 cm

30. Write the prime factorization of both the numerator and the denominator
(67) of this fraction. Then reduce the fraction. $\frac{2 \cdot 2 \cdot 2 \cdot 2 \cdot 2}{2 \cdot 2 \cdot 2 \cdot 2 \cdot 3} = \frac{2}{3}$

$$\frac{32}{48}$$

Early Finishers
Real-World
Application

Mrs. Singh takes care of eight children. Half of the children drink four cups
of milk a day. The other half drink two cups of milk a day. How many gallons
of milk would Mrs. Singh have to purchase to have enough milk for the
children for four days?   One gallon = 16 cups; Each day the children drank
16 + 8 = 24 cups of milk. 24 cups × 4 days = 96 cups. 96 cups ÷ 16 cups in
each gallon = 6 gallons of milk

▶ See Math Conversations in the sidebar.

Looking Forward

Finding the area of triangles
prepares students for:

- **Lesson 91,** using geometric
  formulas to find perimeter and
  area.
- **Lesson 107,** finding the area of
  complex shapes.
- **Investigation 12,** finding the
  surface area of a triangular prism.

Teacher Tip

For problem **27,** some students
may need graph paper or a copy
of **Investigation Activity 15**
Coordinate Plane to graph the
quadrilateral.

Continue to encourage sketching
graphs without graph paper.

Using a Constant Factor to Solve Ratio Problems

Objectives

- Draw and use a ratio box to sort ratio numbers and actual counts.
- Find the constant factor when the ratio and one actual count is known.
- Multiply a ratio term by the constant factor to find the actual count.

Lesson Preparation

Materials

- **Power Up I** (in *Instructional Masters*)

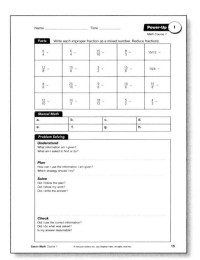

Power Up I

Math Language

English Learners (ESL)

determine

Technology Resources

Student eBook Complete student textbook in electronic format.

Resources and Planner CD Assessment, reteaching, and instructional masters, plus a pacing calendar with standards.

Test and Practice Generator CD Create additional practice sheets and custom-made tests.

www.SaxonPublishers.com Visit for more student activities and planning materials.

Inclusion

Adaptations CD Adapted lessons, investigations, practice and assessments.

Meeting Standards

National Council of Teachers of Mathematics (NCTM)

Numbers and Operations

NO.1d Understand and use ratios and proportions to represent quantitative relationships

NO.3d Develop, analyze, and explain methods for solving problems involving proportions, such as scaling and finding equivalent ratios

Problem Solving

PS.1c Apply and adapt a variety of appropriate strategies to solve problems

Problem-Solving Strategy: Use Logical Reasoning/ Make it Simpler/Find a Pattern

A seven-digit phone number consists of a three-digit prefix followed by four digits. How many different phone numbers are possible for a particular prefix?

(Understand) **Understand the problem.**

"What information are we given?"

Seven-digit phone numbers consist of one particular three-digit prefix followed by four random digits.

"What are we asked to do?"

Determine how many different phone numbers are possible for a particular prefix.

(Plan) **Make a plan.**

"What problem-solving strategy will we use?"

We will *use logical reasoning* and *make it simpler* to see if we can *find a pattern*.

(Solve) **Carry out the plan.**

"If a phone number had only one digit, how many different phone numbers would be possible?"

There would be 10 possible phone numbers: 1, 2, 3, 4, 5, 6, 7, 8, 9, and 0.

"Using only two digits, how many different phone numbers would be possible?"

There are 100 different two-digit combinations: 01 through 99, plus 00.

"Using only three digits, how many different phone numbers would be possible?"

There are 1000 different three-digit combinations: 001 through 999, plus 000.

"How many combinations can be formed with the four digits following the prefix?"

We can form the combinations 0001 through 9999, plus the combination 0000. That is 10,000 different phone numbers.

(Check) **Look back.**

"Did we complete the task?"

Yes. We found there are 10,000 different phone numbers that can be formed for a particular three-digit prefix.

• Using a Constant Factor to
Solve Ratio Problems

6 11
6 13
6 33

(3 depts)

facts | Power Up I

mental math

a. **Calculation:** 4 × 315   1260

b. **Number Sense:** 380 + 170   550

c. **Calculation:** 5 × $2.99 $14.95

d. **Calculation:** $10.00 − $7.99 $2.01

e. **Fractional Parts:** $\frac{1}{4}$ of $4.80 $1.20

f. **Decimals:** 37.5 ÷ 100   0.375

g. **Measurement:** How many quarts are in a gallon?   4 qt

h. **Calculation:** 5 × 5, × 5, − 25, ÷ 4, ÷ 5, − 5   0

problem solving | A seven digit phone number consists of a three-digit prefix followed by four digits. How many different phone numbers are possible for a particular prefix?   10,000 phone numbers

New Concept · Increasing Knowledge

Consider the following ratio problem:

To make green paint, the ratio of blue paint to yellow paint is 3 to 2. For 6 ounces of yellow paint, how much blue paint is needed?

We see two uses for numbers in ratio problems. One use is to express a ratio. The other use is to express an actual count. A ratio box can help us sort the two uses by placing the ratio numbers in one column and the actual counts in another column. We write the items being compared along the left side of the rows.

	Ratio	Actual Count
Blue Paint	3	
Yellow Paint	2	6

We are told that the ratio of blue to yellow was 3 to 2. We place these numbers in the ratio column, assigning 3 to the blue paint row and 2 to the yellow paint row. We are given an actual count of 6 ounces of yellow paint, which we record in the box. We are asked to find the actual count of blue paint, so that portion of the ratio box is empty.

Lesson 80   413

Facts
Distribute **Power Up I** to students. See answers below.

Mental Math
Before students begin the Mental Math exercise, do this counting exercise as a class.

Count up and down by 7s between negative 35 and 35.

Encourage students to share different ways to mentally compute these exercises. Strategies for exercises **d** and **e** are listed below.

 d. **Subtract $8, then Add 1¢**
   $10 − $8 = $2; $2 + 1¢ = $2.01
 Subtract $7, then Subtract 99¢
   $10 − $7 = $3; $3 − 99¢ = $2.01
 e. **Divide Dollars, then Divide Cents**
   $4 ÷ 4 = $1; 80¢ ÷ 4 = 20¢;
   $1 + 20¢ = $1.20
 Find $\frac{1}{2}$ of $\frac{1}{2}$
   $\frac{1}{2}$ of $4.80 is $2.40; $\frac{1}{2}$ of $2.40 is $1.20

Problem Solving
Refer to **Power-Up Discussion**, p. 413B.

Instruction
Draw the ratio box on the board or overhead and complete the box as you complete the example.

Ask each student to draw the same ratio box on a sheet of paper, and then duplicate your actions to complete the box.

"What information are we given in this problem?" The ratio of blue paint to yellow paint is 3 to 2, and there are 6 ounces of yellow paint.

"What information are we asked to find?" the number of ounces of blue paint

(continued)

Facts | Write each improper fraction as a mixed number. Reduce fractions.

$\frac{5}{4} = 1\frac{1}{4}$	$\frac{6}{4} = 1\frac{1}{2}$	$\frac{15}{10} = 1\frac{1}{2}$	$\frac{8}{3} = 2\frac{2}{3}$	$\frac{15}{12} = 1\frac{1}{4}$
$\frac{12}{8} = 1\frac{1}{2}$	$\frac{10}{8} = 1\frac{1}{4}$	$\frac{3}{2} = 1\frac{1}{2}$	$\frac{15}{6} = 2\frac{1}{2}$	$\frac{10}{4} = 2\frac{1}{2}$
$\frac{8}{6} = 1\frac{1}{3}$	$\frac{25}{10} = 2\frac{1}{2}$	$\frac{9}{6} = 1\frac{1}{2}$	$\frac{10}{6} = 1\frac{2}{3}$	$\frac{15}{8} = 1\frac{7}{8}$
$\frac{12}{10} = 1\frac{1}{5}$	$\frac{10}{3} = 3\frac{1}{3}$	$\frac{18}{12} = 1\frac{1}{2}$	$\frac{5}{2} = 2\frac{1}{2}$	$\frac{4}{3} = 1\frac{1}{3}$

Instruction

It may be helpful for students to connect the concept of multiplying both terms of a ratio by the constant factor to a concept they have worked with many times before—multiplying a fraction by 1 to make an equivalent fraction. To help students make the connection, write the following equation on the board or overhead.

$$\frac{3}{2} = \frac{?}{6}$$

"The ratio and the actual count are equivalent fractions. To make an equivalent fraction for $\frac{3}{2}$ that has a denominator of 6, what do we multiply $\frac{3}{2}$ by?" $\frac{3}{3}$

Write $\frac{3}{2} \times \frac{3}{3} = \frac{9}{6}$. Point out that since each term of the fraction $\frac{3}{2}$ is multiplied by 3, 3 is the constant factor.

Example

Instruction

Another way to solve the problem is to find an equivalent fraction for $\frac{2}{5}$ that has a numerator of 30. (The constant factor 15 would be used.)

Practice Set

Problem a Model

"The constant factor for this problem is 12. Why is 12 the constant factor?" The actual number of girls is 60, and the ratio number of girls is 5; $60 \div 5 = 12$

"How is the constant factor 12 used to solve this problem?" Multiply the ratio number of boys by 12 to find the actual number of boys.

Ratio numbers and actual counts are related by **a constant factor.** If we multiply the terms of a ratio by the constant factor, we can find the actual count. Recall that a ratio is a reduced form of an actual count. If we can determine the factor by which the actual count was reduced to form the ratio, then we can recreate the actual count.

	Ratio	Actual Count
Blue Paint	3 × constant factor	?
Yellow Paint	2 × constant factor	6

We see that 2 can be multiplied by 3 to get 6. So 3 is the constant factor in this problem. That means we can multiply each ratio term by 3. Multiplying the ratio term 3 by the factor 3 gives us an actual count of 9 ounces of blue paint.

Example

Sadly, the ratio of flowers to weeds in the garden is 2 to 5. There are 30 flowers in the garden, about how many weeds are there?

Solution

We will begin by drawing a ratio box.

	Ratio	Actual Count
Flowers	2	30
Weeds	5	

To determine the constant factor, we study the row that has two numbers. In the "flowers" row we see the ratio number 2 and the actual count 30. If we divide 30 by 2, we find the factor, which is 15. Now we will use the factor to find the prediction of weeds in the garden.

$$\text{Ratio} \times \text{constant factor} = \text{actual count}$$
$$5 \times 15 = 75$$

There are about **75 weeds** in the garden.

Practice Set

Model Draw a ratio box and use a constant factor to solve each ratio problem:

a.

	Ratio	A.C.
Boys	6	b
Girls	5	60

a. The ratio of boys to girls in the cafeteria was 6 to 5. If there were 60 girls, how many boys were there? Factor is 12; 72 boys

b. The ratio of ants to flies at the picnic was 8 to 3. If there were 24 flies, predict how many ants were there? Factor is 8; 64 ants

Written Practice

Strengthening Concepts

b.

	Ratio	A.C.
Ants	8	a
Flies	3	24

1. What is the mean of 96, 49, 68, and 75? What is the range? 72; 47
(Inv. 5)

2. The average depth of the ocean beyond the edges of the continents is $2\frac{1}{2}$ miles. How many feet is that? (1 mile = 5280 ft) 13,200 ft
(66)

▶ See Math Conversations in the sidebar.

English Learners

Write the term **determine** on the board. Say,

"When you determine an answer, you decide on or select an answer. You determine what the answer will be."

Ask a volunteer to determine the factors of 24. (1, 2, 3, 4, 6, 8, 12, 24)

3. *Formulate* The 168 girls who signed up for soccer were divided
(15) equally into 12 teams. How many players were on each team? Write an
equation and solve the problem. $12p = 168$; 14 players

Analyze Parallelogram *ABCD* is divided into two congruent triangles.
Segments *BA* and *CD* measure 3 in. Segments *AD* and *BC* measure 5 in.
Segment *BD* measures 4 in. Refer to this figure to answer problems **4** and **5.**

4. a. What is the perimeter of the parallelogram?   16 in.
(71)
b. What is the area of the parallelogram?   12 in.²

* 5. a. What is the perimeter of each triangle?   12 in.
(79)
b. What is the area of each triangle?   6 in.²

6. *Conclude* This quadrilateral has one pair of
(64) parallel sides. What is the name of this kind
of quadrilateral?   trapezoid

7. *Verify* "All squares are rectangles." True or false?   true
(64)

* 8. *Represent* If four fifths of the 30 students in the class were present,
(77) then how many students were absent?   6 students

* 9. The ratio of dogs to cats in the neighborhood was 2 to 5. If there were
(80) 10 dogs, predict how many cats were there.   25 cats

* 10. Write as a percent:
(75)
a. $\frac{19}{20}$ 95%   **b.** 0.6   60%

* 11. *Connect* **a.** What percent of the perimeter of a square is the length of
(74, 75) one side?   25%

b. What is the ratio of the side length of a square to its perimeter?
Express the ratio as a fraction and as a decimal. $\frac{1}{4}$, 0.25

* 12. Compare: **a.** 0.5 $\bigcirc$ $\frac{3}{4}$ **b.** 3 qts $\bigcirc$ 1 gal
(76)

* 13. Write 4.4 as a reduced mixed number. $4\frac{2}{5}$
(73)

14. Write $\frac{1}{8}$ as a decimal number.   0.125
(74)

15. $\frac{5}{6} + \frac{1}{2}$ $1\frac{1}{3}$ **16.** $\frac{5}{8} - \frac{1}{4}$ $\frac{3}{8}$ **17.** $2\frac{1}{2} \times 1\frac{1}{3} \times \frac{3}{5}$ 2
(57)   (57)   (72)

Find each unknown number:

18. $4 - a = 2.6$ 1.4   **19.** $3n = 1\frac{1}{2}$ $\frac{1}{2}$
(43)   (68)

20. $5x = 0.36$ 0.072   **21.** $0.9y = 63$ 70
(45)   (49)

Lesson 80   415

▶ See Math Conversations in the sidebar.

3 **Written Practice**

Math Conversations
Discussion opportunities are provided below.

Problem 3 *Formulate*
Extend the Problem
"**Name a related equation that can be used
to solve the problem.**" Sample: A related
equation for $12p = 168$ is $p = \frac{168}{12}$.

Problem 8 *Represent*
Before solving this problem, encourage
students to diagram the statement.

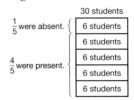

Problem 11 *Connect*
If students are unsure of the answer, ask,

"**How many sides does a square have?**" 4

"**How do the lengths of the four sides of a
square compare?**" all of the sides are the
same length

"**What fraction of the distance around a
square is the length of one side of the
square?**" $\frac{1}{4}$

"**Our answer must be expressed as a
percent. How can we change a fraction to
a percent?**" Find the decimal equivalent,
then shift the decimal point two places to
the right and write a percent sign.

(continued)

Math Conversations

Discussion opportunities are provided below.

Problem 25 **Formulate**

Extend the Problem

Invite students to exchange word problems, then solve the problems and compare answers.

Problem 27 **Evaluate**

Some students may need graph paper or a copy of **Investigation Activity 15** (in *Instructional Masters*) to graph the quadrilateral.

Continue to encourage sketching graphs without graph paper.

Errors and Misconceptions

Problem 26

Students sometimes make mistakes naming equivalent measures because they are not familiar with the relationships shared by those measures.

Encourage those students to memorize the relationships shared by equivalent measures. For problem **26,** students can refer to Lesson 78 to review the relationships.

Also point out that finding equivalent measures is a very practical skill many people use in their everyday lives.

---

22. Round 0.4287 to the hundredths place.   0.43
(51)

Refer to the bar graph below to answer problems **23–25.**

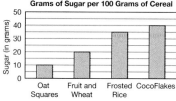
Grams of Sugar per 100 Grams of Cereal

23. **Estimate**   Frosted Rice contains about how many grams of sugar per
(Inv. 5)   100 grams of cereal?   about 35 grams

24. **Estimate**   Fifty grams of CocoFlakes would contain about how many
(Inv. 5)   grams of sugar?   about 20 grams

▶ **25.** **Formulate**   Write a problem about comparing that refers to the bar
(Inv. 5)   graph, and then answer the problem.   See student work.

▶* **26.** There was one quart of milk in the carton. Oscar poured one cup of milk
(78)   on his cereal. How many cups of milk were left in the carton?   3 cups

▶ **27.** **Evaluate**   Three vertices of a square are (3, 0), (3, 3), and (0, 3).
(Inv. 7)   **a.** What are the coordinates of the fourth vertex of the square?   (0, 0)

   b. What is the area of the square?   9 units^2

28. **Conclude**   Which of these angles could be the complement of a 30°
(69)   angle?   A

29. If $A = \frac{1}{2}bh$, and if $b = 6$ and $h = 8$, then what does A equal?   24
(47)

30. **Model**   Draw a pair of parallel segments that are the same length.
(64)   Form a quadrilateral by drawing two segments between the endpoints of the parallel segments. Is the quadrilateral a parallelogram?   Samples:

   ▭ , ▱ , and ▯ ; yes

▶ See Math Conversations in the sidebar.

Looking Forward

Drawing ratio boxes and finding scale factors to solve ratio problems prepare students for:

- **Lesson 88,** using proportions and ratio boxes to solve ratio problems.

- **Lesson 101,** using proportions and ratio boxes to solve ratio problems involving totals.

- **Lesson 105,** using proportions and ratio boxes to solve percent problems.

- **Investigation 11,** using scale drawings and models to find actual and scale dimensions and to find the scale and the scale factor.

Assessment   *30–40 minutes*   *For use after Lesson 80*

Distribute **Cumulative Test 15** to each student. Two versions of the test are available in *Saxon Math Course 1 Course Assessments Book*. Have students complete the **Power-Up Test** first. Allow 10 minutes. Then have students work the 20 numbered items on the **Cumulative Test.** Students may use copies of the answer sheet to record their work. Track individual and class progress with the **Test Analysis** forms.

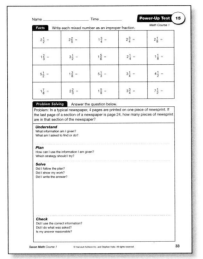

Power-Up Test 15

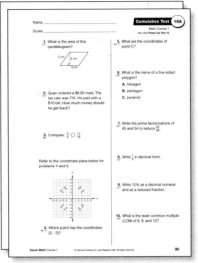

Cumulative Test 15A

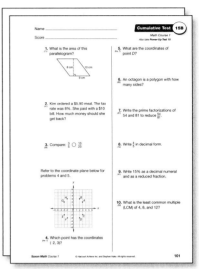

Alternative Cumulative Test 15B

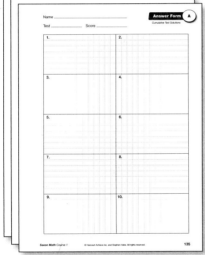

Optional Answer Forms

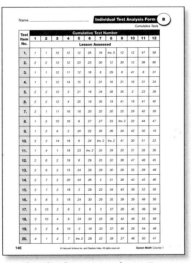

Individual Test Analysis Form

Class Test Analysis Form

Reteaching

Students who score below 80% on the assessment may be in need of reteaching. Look for the causes of student mistakes. If errors are conceptual, refer to the *Reteaching Masters* for reteaching.

You can develop customized benchmark tests using the Test Generator located on the *Test & Practice Generator CD*.

This chart shows the lesson, the standard, and the test item question that can be found on the *Test & Practice Generator CD*.

LESSON	NEW CONCEPTS	LOCAL STANDARD	TEST ITEM ON CD
71	• Parallelograms		8.71.1
72	• Fractions Chart		8.72.1
	• Multiplying Three Fractions		8.72.2
73	• Exponents		8.73.1
	• Writing Decimal Numbers as Fractions, Part 2		8.73.2
74	• Writing Fractions as Decimal Numbers		8.74.1
	• Writing Ratios as Decimal Numbers		8.74.2
75	• Writing Fractions and Decimals as Percents, Part 1		8.75.1
76	• Comparing Fractions by Converting to Decimal Form		8.76.1
77	• Finding Unstated Information in Fraction Problems		8.77.1
78	• Capacity		8.78.1
79	• Area of a Triangle		8.79.1
80	• Using a Constant Factor to Solve Ratio Problems		8.80.1

Using the Test Generator CD
• Develop tests in both English and Spanish.
• Choose from multiple-choice and free-response test items.
• Clone test items to create multiple versions of the same test.
• View and edit test items to make and save your own questions.
• Administer assessments through paper tests or over a school LAN.
• Monitor student progress through a variety of individual and class reports —for both diagnosing and assessing standards mastery.

Polygons on the Coordinate Plane

Assign after Lesson 80 and Test 15

Objectives
- Plot vertices of polygons on the coordinate plane.
- Draw a polygon on the coordinate plane and label the vertices as ordered pairs.
- Communicate ideas through writing.

Materials
Performance Tasks 15A and **15B**

Preparation
Make copies of **Performance Tasks 15A** and **15B**. (One each per student.)

Time Requirement
30–60 minutes; Begin in class and complete at home.

Task
Explain to students that for this task they will plot the vertices of polygons on a coordinate plane and identify the polygons. They will also draw polygons on the coordinate plane and label the vertices as ordered pairs. They will be required to explain how they know their drawings of parallelograms are parallelograms. Point out that all of the information students need is on **Performance Tasks 15A** and **15B**.

Criteria for Evidence of Learning
- Plots vertices of polygons accurately on the coordinate plane and identifies the polygons correctly.
- Draws a polygon accurately on the coordinate plane and names the vertices correctly as ordered pairs.
- Communicates ideas clearly through writing.

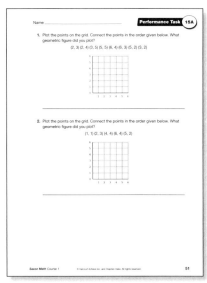

Performance Task 15A

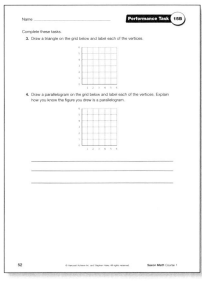

Performance Task 15B

National Council of Teachers of Mathematics (NCTM)

Geometry

GM.1a Precisely describe, classify, and understand relationships among types of two- and three-dimensional objects using their defining properties

GM.2a Use coordinate geometry to represent and examine the properties of geometric shapes

GM.2b Use coordinate geometry to examine special geometric shapes, such as regular polygons or those with pairs of parallel or perpendicular sides

GM.4a Draw geometric objects with specified properties, such as side lengths or angle measures

Communication

CM.3d Use the language of mathematics to express mathematical ideas precisely

Representation

RE.5a Create and use representations to organize, record, and communicate mathematical ideas

Focus on
• Geometric Construction of Bisectors

Objectives
- Use a compass and straightedge to construct the perpendicular bisector of a given line segment.
- Use a compass and straightedge to construct the bisector of a given angle.

Lesson Preparation

Materials
- **Investigation Activity 16 Transparency** (in *Instructional Masters*)
- **Investigation Activity 17** (in *Instructional Masters*)
- **Manipulative kit: compasses, rulers, protractors**
- **Teacher-provided material: pencils, several sheets of unlined paper**

Optional
- **Investigation Activity 17 Transparency** (in *Instructional Masters*)

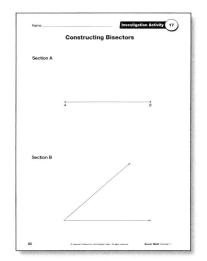

Investigation Activity 17

Math Language

New	English Learners (ESL)
angle bisector	bisects
bisect	
construction	
perpendicular bisector	

Technology Resources

Student eBook Complete student textbook in electronic format.

Resources and Planner CD Assessment, reteaching, and instructional masters, plus a pacing calendar with standards.

Test and Practice Generator CD Create additional practice sheets and custom-made tests.

www.SaxonPublishers.com Visit for more student activities and planning materials.

Inclusion

Adaptations CD Adapted lessons, investigations, practice and assessments.

Meeting Standards

National Council of Teachers of Mathematics (NCTM)

Geometry

GM.4a Draw geometric objects with specified properties, such as side lengths or angle measures

Measurement

ME.2b Select and apply techniques and tools to accurately find length, area, volume, and angle measures to appropriate levels of precision

Focus on
• Geometric Construction of Bisectors

Since Lesson 27 we have used a compass to draw circles of various sizes. We can also use a compass together with a straightedge and a pencil to construct and divide various geometric figures.

Materials needed:

- Compass
- Ruler
- Pencil
- Several sheets of unlined paper
- Investigation Activity 17

Perpendicular Bisectors

Represent The first activity in this investigation is to **bisect** a segment. The word *bisect* means "to cut into two equal parts." We bisect a line segment when we draw a line (or segment) through the midpoint of the line segment. Below, segment *AB* is bisected by line *r* into two parts of equal length.

> **Math Language**
> A **line** extends in opposite directions without end. A line cannot be bisected because it has no midpoint. A **segment** is a part of a line with two distinct endpoints.

In section A of **Investigation Activity 17,** you will see segment *AB*. Follow these directions to bisect the segment.

Step 1: Set your compass so that the distance between the pivot point of the compass and the pencil point is more than half the length of the segment. Then place the pivot point of the compass on an endpoint of the segment and "swing an arc" on both sides of the segment, as illustrated.

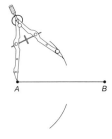

Investigation 8 **417**

Math Background

There is a difference between drawing, sketching, and constructing a geometric figure.

- Drawing a figure usually involves using a ruler and a protractor to measure lengths of sides and angles.

- Sketching a figure usually involves only paper and pencil or pen. A straightedge is not required to ensure lines and segments are straight, and a ruler or protractor is not required to ensure sides and angles are properly measured.

- Constructing a figure always requires exactness. Straightedges and compasses are the only tools that are permitted. Constructions do not involve rulers or protractors to measure the figure as it is being constructed.

In this investigation, students will use a compass and a ruler to construct an angle bisector and a perpendicular bisector of a line segment.

Activity 1

Instruction
Place the transparency of **Investigation Activity 16** Perpendicular Bisectors on an overhead projector. Explain that the midpoint of segment *AB* is the point at which line *r* intersects segment *AB*. Also point out that line *r* is perpendicular to segment *AB*.

> **"Describe the kind of angles formed at the intersection of line r and segment AB."**
> right or 90° angles

Instruction
Demonstrate each step of Activity 1 for students before they perform the steps on their own.

Place the transparency of **Investigation Activity 17** Constructing Bisectors on the overhead projector. Use a compass to swing an arc on both sides of segment *AB,* as described in the text.

(continued)

Activity 1 (Continued)

Instruction

Using the transparency of **Investigation Activity 17** Constructing Bisectors and a compass, show students how to construct intersecting arcs.

For this step of the activity, it is important for students to not change the radius of their compass from step 1. As you construct the intersecting arcs, emphasize to students that the radius of your compass has not changed from the previous step.

Complete the demonstration for students by drawing the perpendicular bisector of segment *AB* on Section B of the transparency of **Investigation Activity 17.**

After students draw the perpendicular bisector, ask

"How can we use a ruler to check that segment AB is divided into two smaller segments of equal length?" Measure each smaller segment; if the lengths are identical, segment *AB* is bisected.

Give students time to check their work.

Activity 2

Instruction

"In the previous activity, we bisected a line segment. What happens to a line segment that is bisected?" The segment is divided into two equal segments or halves.

"In this activity, we will bisect an angle. What will happen to an angle that is bisected?" The angle will be divided into two equal angles or halves.

(continued)

Step 2: Without resetting the radius of the compass, move the pivot point of the compass to the other endpoint of the segment. Swing an arc on both sides of the segment so that the arcs intersect as shown. (It may be necessary to return to the first endpoint to extend the first set of arcs until the arcs intersect on both sides of the segment.)

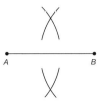

Thinking Skill

Explain

Why do we set our compass so that the distance from the pivot point to the pencil point is more than half the length of the segment?
If we set the distance shorter than half the length of the segment, the arcs would not intersect.

Step 3: Draw a line through the two points where the arcs intersect.

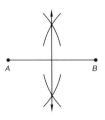

The line bisects the segment and is perpendicular to it. Thus the line is called a **perpendicular bisector** of the segment.

Check your work with a ruler. You should find that the perpendicular bisector has divided segment *AB* into two smaller segments of equal length.

Practice the procedure again by drawing your own line segment on a blank sheet of paper. Position the segment on the page so that there is enough area above and below the segment to draw the arcs you need to bisect the segment. Refer to the directions above if you need to refresh your memory.

Activity 2

Angle Bisectors

Represent In Section B of **Activity 17** an angle is shown. You will bisect the angle by drawing a ray halfway between the two sides of the angle.

Math Language
A **ray** is part of a line with one endpoint. The **vertex** of an angle is the common endpoint of two rays that form the sides of the angle.

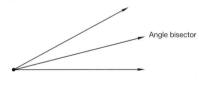

Angle bisector

English Learners

Refer to the bisector drawn in step 3. Say,

"This diagram shows line segment AB with a vertical line crossing it. The vertical line divides the line into two equal parts. We say that the line bisects line segment AB."

On the board, draw three line segments labeled *MN*, each crossed by a perpendicular line. Only one of the lines should bisect one of the line segments. Ask,

"Which line bisects line segment MN?"

Mark the parts of the bisected line as equal and say,

"The line bisects MN, or divides it into two equal parts."

Tell students that the prefix, **bi-**, means two.

Follow these directions to bisect the angle.

Step 1: Place the pivot point of the compass on the vertex of the angle, and sweep an arc across both sides of the angle.

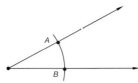

The arc intersects the sides of the angle at two points, which we have labeled A and B. Point A and point B are both the same distance from the vertex.

Step 2: Set the compass so that the distance between the pivot point of the compass and the pencil point is more than half the distance from point A to point B. Place the pivot point of the compass on point A, and sweep an arc as shown.

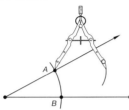

Step 3: Without resetting the radius of the compass, move the pivot point of the compass to point B and sweep an arc that intersects the arc drawn in step 2.

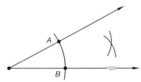

Step 4: Draw a ray from the vertex of the angle through the intersection of the arcs.

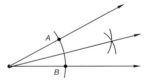

The ray is the **angle bisector** of the angle.

Activity 2 (Continued)

Instruction
Remind students that it is again important for them to not change the radius of their compass from the previous step of the activity.

After students draw the angle bisector, ask

"How can we use a protractor to check that the ray we constructed divides the angle into two smaller angles of equal measure?"
Measure each smaller angle; if the degree measures are identical, the angle is bisected.

Give students time to check their work.

Activity 3

Instruction
During the activity, circulate among students and check to make sure all of the construction marks are present for each construction.

Use a protractor to check your work. You should find that the angle bisector has divided the angle into two smaller angles of equal measure.

Practice the procedure again by drawing an angle on a blank sheet of paper. Make the angle a different size from the one on the investigation activity. Then bisect the angle using the method presented in this activity.

Activity 3

Constructing Bisectors

In this activity you will make a page similar to **Investigation Activity 17** to give to another student. On an unlined sheet of paper, draw a line segment and draw an angle. The sizes of the segment and the angle should be different from the sizes of the line segment and angle on the activity page.

As your teacher directs, exchange papers. Using a compass and straightedge, construct the perpendicular bisector of the segment and the angle bisector of the angle on the sheet you are given. The arcs you draw in the construction should be visible so that your work can be checked.

extensions   Use the figure below and your protractor to answer questions **a–c**. Support each answer with angle measurements.

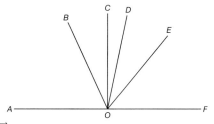

a. Does $\overrightarrow{OB}$ bisect ∠AOE?   Yes. Sample: Angle AOE measures 130°. Both angles formed by ray OB measure 65°.

b. Does $\overrightarrow{OD}$ bisect ∠BOE?   No. Sample: Angle BOE measures 65°. Ray OD forms ∠BOD, which measures 37°, and ∠DOE, which measures 28°.

c. Use angle measures to classify these angles in the figure as acute, obtuse, or right.

∠AOE 130°, obtuse   ∠AOB 65°, acute   ∠BOD 37°, acute

∠AOC 90°, right   ∠EOF 50°, acute   ∠BOF 115°, obtuse

Looking Forward
Using a compass and straightedge to bisect line segments and angles prepares students for:

• **Lesson 110,** understanding and finding lines of symmetry.

Lesson Planner

LESSON	NEW CONCEPTS	MATERIALS	RESOURCES
81	• Arithmetic with Units of Measure	Manipulative Kit: inch rulers	Power Up K Investigation Activity 15
82	• Volume of a Rectangular Prism	Manipulative Kit: wooden color cubes	Power Up L Investigation Activity 15
83	• Proportions	Manipulative Kit: inch rulers Tape and scissors	Power Up I
84	• Order of Operations, Part 2	Calculators	Power Up K Investigation Activity 15
85	• Using Cross Products to Solve Proportions		Power Up L Investigation Activity 15
86	• Area of a Circle		Power Up G Investigation Activity 15 Lesson Activity 18 Transparency Geometric Formulas poster
87	• Finding Unknown Factors		Power Up D Investigation Activity 15
88	• Using Proportions to Solve Ratio Word Problems	Manipulative Kit: inch rulers	Power Up L Investigation Activity 15
89	• Estimating Square Roots	Calculators	Power Up K
90	• Measuring Turns	Construction paper Spinner marked North, South, East, West	Power Up J Investigation Activity 15
Inv. 9	• Experimental Probability	Manipulative Kit: number cubes Marbles or any other differently-colored identical objects, opaque bag, pencil and paper	

Problem Solving

Strategies

- **Make an Organized List**   Lesson 86
- **Make a Chart**   Lesson 81
- **Make It Simpler**   Lessons 83, 88, 90
- **Use Logical Reasoning**   Lessons 83, 85, 87, 88, 89, 90
- **Draw a Diagram**   Lessons 82, 89
- **Write an Equation**   Lesson 87
- **Guess and Check**   Lesson 85
- **Work Backwards**   Lesson 84

Real-World Applications

pp. 421, 424–425, 428–429, 431, 433–435, 438–440, 444–445, 449–451, 453–454, 456–459, 462, 466–469

4-Step Process

Teacher Edition   Lessons 81–90 (Power-Up Discussions)

Communications

Discuss

pp. 427, 448, 457, 467, 471

Explain

pp. 433, 439, 444, 458, 459, 467

Formulate a Problem

pp. 459, 464

Connections

Math and Other Subjects

Math and History   p. 452

Math and Science   pp. 444, 453

Math and Sports   pp. 444, 445

Math and Other Cultures   p. 433

Math to Math

Measurement and Problem Solving
  Lessons 81, 84, 86, 87, 88, 89, 90

Algebra and Problem Solving   Lessons 87, 88

Fractions, Percents, Decimals and
  Problem Solving   Lessons 81, 82, 83, 84, 85, 86, 87, 88, 89, 90

Fractions and Measurement   Lessons 81, 82, 83, 84, 85, 86, 87, 88, 89, 90

Measurement and Geometry   Lessons 81, 82, 83, 84, 85, 86, 87, 88, 89, 90

Probability and Statistics   Lessons 82, 85, 86, 89

Representation

Manipulatives/Hands On

pp. 425, 427, 429, 435, 459, 469

Model

pp. 425, 430, 440, 458–459, 462, 467, 469

Represent

p. 435

Technology

Student Resources

- eBook
- Calculator   Lessons 84, 89
- Online Resources at
  www.SaxonPublishers.com/ActivitiesC1
    Graphing Calculator Activity   Lesson 83
    Real-World Investigation 5   after Lesson 88
    Online Activities
    Math Enrichment Problems
    Math Stumpers

Teacher Resources

- Resources and Planner CD
- Adaptations CD   Lessons 81–90
- Test & Practice Generator CD
- eGradebook
- Answer Key CD

Proportional relationships take center stage in this section of lessons. Students learn to use ratios to describe proportional situations. Algebraic thinking is extended with additional problems involving the order of operations.

Proportional Thinking

Students use a "ratio box" to write and set up proportions for ratio problems.

Students write and solve proportions in Lesson 83 and learn to solve proportions using cross products in Lesson 85. These skills are applied in Lesson 88 as students use proportions to solve ratio problems.

Area and Volume

The concept of volume is introduced.

Students calculate the volume of rectangular prisms in Lesson 82 and find the areas of circles in Lesson 86. Geometric calculations usually involve measures, and students learn to deal with units in calculations in Lesson 81.

Spatial Thinking

Students identify relationships between polygons and angles.

The interior angle measures of a geometric figure are related to the measures of its exterior angles, and in Lesson 90 students use the concept of a turn to find the exterior angles of polygons.

Algebraic Thinking

The order of operations is crucial for evaluating expressions and solving equations.

If a calculation involves more than one operation, it is necessary to follow the agreed upon order of operations. Order of Operations was introduced in Lesson 5. Students learn more about it in Lesson 84. Students solve equations with unknown factors in Lesson 87. Students also learn to estimate square roots in Lesson 89.

Probability and Statistics

Students learn the difference between theoretical and experimental probability.

Many games of chance involve probabilities that can be calculated theoretically. However, in the real world decision makers often need to make choices based on probabilities that are not easily calculated theoretically but are best determined through statistical studies or experimentation. In Investigation 9 students explore the topic of experimental probability.

Assessment

A variety of weekly assessment tools are provided.

After Lesson 85:
• Power-Up Test 16
• Cumulative Test 16
• Performance Activity 16

After Lesson 90:
• Power-Up Test 17
• Cumulative Test 17
• Customized Benchmark Test
• Performance Task 17

LESSON	NEW CONCEPTS	PRACTICED	ASSESSED
81	• Arithmetic with Units of Measure	Lessons 81, 82, 83, 84, 85, 87, 89, 90, 92, 95, 96, 98, 99, 101, 102, 103, 104, 105, 106, 107, 109	Test 17
82	• Volume of a Rectangular Prism	Lessons 82, 83, 84, 85, 86, 87, 88, 89, 90, 93, 95, 98, 99, 100, 101, 102, 103, 104, 105, 106, 107, 108, 109, 110, 111, 113, 114, 115, 116, 117, 118, 119, 120	Tests 17, 18, 20, 21, 22
83	• Proportions	Lessons 83, 84, 87, 88, 89, 90, 91, 92, 93, 95, 96, 98, 99, 100, 102, 104, 109	Tests 17, 18, 19, 20, 21, 22
84	• Order of Operations, Part 2	Lessons 84, 85, 86, 87, 88, 89, 90, 92, 93, 96, 97, 98, 99, 100, 101, 102, 104, 106, 107, 112, 117	Test 17
85	• Using Cross Products to Solve Proportions	Lessons 85, 86, 87, 88, 89, 90, 91, 92, 93, 95, 96, 97, 99, 100, 102, 103, 104, 105, 107, 108, 111, 112, 114, 115, 116, 117, 118, 120	Tests 17, 19, 20, 21, 22
86	• Area of a Circle	Lessons 86, 88, 89, 90, 92, 94, 95, 98, 100, 102, 104, 108, 110, 114, 116, 117, 119	Tests 18, 20, 21, 22
87	• Finding Unknown Factors	Lessons 87, 88, 89, 90, 91, 93, 96, 97, 98, 99, 100, 101, 102, 104, 105, 106, 107, 108, 109, 110	Tests 17, 18
88	• Using Proportions to Solve Ratio Word Problems	Lessons 88, 89, 91, 93, 98, 101, 103, 104, 105, 106, 108, 109, 110, 112, 113, 117, 119, 120	Tests 18, 20
89	• Estimating Square Roots	Lessons 89, 90, 91, 92, 93, 95, 96, 99, 104, 115, 118, 120	Tests 18, 20
90	• Measuring Turns	Lessons 90, 91, 92, 95, 96, 97, 99, 103, 110	Test 20
Inv. 9	• Experimental Probability	Lessons 91, 93, 98	Test & Practice Generator

Arithmetic with Units of Measure

Objectives

- Add, subtract, multiply, and divide units of measure.

Materials

- **Power Up K** (in *Instructional Masters*)
- **Manipulative kit: inch rulers**
Optional
- **Investigation Activity 15** (in *Instructional Masters*) or **graph paper**

Power Up K

Math Language

English Learners (ESL)

measurements

Technology Resources

Student eBook Complete student textbook in electronic format.

Resources and Planner CD Assessment, reteaching, and instructional masters, plus a pacing calendar with standards.

Test and Practice Generator CD Create additional practice sheets and custom-made tests.

www.SaxonPublishers.com/ Visit for more student activities and planning materials.

Inclusion

Adaptations CD Adapted lessons, investigations, practice and assessments.

National Council of Teachers of Mathematics (NCTM)

Numbers and Operations

NO.2a Understand the meaning and effects of arithmetic operations with fractions, decimals, and integers

Measurement

ME.1a Understand both metric and customary systems of measurement

ME.1b Understand relationships among units and convert from one unit to another within the same system

Connections

CN.4a Recognize and use connections among mathematical ideas

Problem-Solving Strategy: Make a Chart

Alexis has 6 coins that total exactly $1.00. Name one coin she must have and one coin she cannot have.

(Understand) **Understand the problem.**

"What information are we given?"

Alexis has 6 coins that total exactly $1.00.

"What are we asked to do?"

Figure out what one coin must be among the six coins she has and what one coin cannot be among the coins she has.

(Plan) **Make a plan.**

"What problem-solving strategy will we use?"

We will *make a chart* of the various coin combinations that Alexis could have.

(Solve) **Carry out the plan.**

"What are all of the different possible coins we must consider?"

half-dollar, quarter, dime, nickel, penny

"How can we keep track of the possible combinations?"

We will *make a table* to make sure that we have all of the combinations.

"Is it possible that she has some pennies?"

No, because it would have to be 5 pennies leaving one coin to equal 95¢. Since this is impossible, we have found that Alexis cannot have a penny.

"If she has a half-dollar, how many ways can we make 50¢ with 5 coins?"

One way is 5 dimes. Another is one quarter, one dime, and three nickels. There are no other ways to make 50¢ with 5 coins.

"Can the combination be made without half-dollars?"

Yes, she could have 3 quarters. Three quarters have a value of 75¢. The remaining three coins, 2 dimes and 1 nickel, equal 25¢ for a total of $1.00.

"Are there other combinations that could equal $1.00?"

No, we have exhausted all of the possible combinations.

"Can we name the one coin she must have?"

Yes, we will look at the chart and see that every combination includes dimes. Alexis must have at least one dime.

Half-dollars	Quarters	Dimes	Nickels	Pennies	Total Value
1		5		x	$1.00
1	1	1	3	x	$1.00
	3	2	1	x	$1.00

(Check) **Look back.**

"Did we answer the question?"

Yes. Although we do not know all the coins Alexis has, we found that Alexis must have at least one dime and she cannot have a penny.

• Arithmetic with Units of Measure

28 pts

facts | Power Up K

625
613
633

mental math
a. **Calculation:** 311 × 7   2177
b. **Number Sense:** 2000 − 1250   750
c. **Calculation:** 4 × $9.99 $39.96
d. **Calculation:** $2.50 + $9.99 $12.49
e. **Number Sense:** Double $5.50. $11.00
f. **Decimals:** 0.075 × 100   7.5
g. **Measurement:** How many milliliters are in 2 liters?   2000 mL
h. **Calculation:** 8 × 8, + 6, ÷ 2, + 1, ÷ 6, × 3, ÷ 2   9

problem solving
Alexis has 6 coins that total exactly $1.00. Name one coin she **must** have and one coin she cannot have.   dime; penny

New Concept | Increasing Knowledge

Recall that the operations of arithmetic are addition, subtraction, multiplication, and division. In this lesson we will practice adding, subtracting, multiplying, and dividing units of measure.

We may add or subtract measurements that have the same units. If the units are not the same, we first convert one or more measurements so that the units are the same. Then we add or subtract.

Example 1

Add: **2 ft + 12 in.**

Solution

The units are not the same. Before we add, we either convert 2 feet to 24 inches or we convert 12 inches to 1 foot.

Convert to Inches	Convert to Feet
2 ft + 12 in.	2 ft + 12 in.
↓	↓
24 in. + 12 in. = **36 in.**	2 ft + 1 ft = **3 ft**

Either answer is correct, because 3 feet equals 36 inches.

Facts

Complete each equivalent measure.			Write a unit for each reference.
			Metric Units:
1. 1 cm = __10__ mm	13. 10 cm = __100__ mm		25. The thickness of a dime: __millimeter__
2. 1 m = __1000__ mm	14. 2 m = __200__ cm		
3. 1 m = __100__ cm	15. 5 km = __5000__ m		26. The width of a little finger: __centimeter__
4. 1 km = __1000__ m	16. 2.5 cm = __25__ mm		
5. 1 in. = __2.54__ cm	17. 1.5 m = __150__ cm		27. The length of one big step: __meter__
6. 1 mi ≈ __1610__ m	18. 7.5 km = __7500__ m		
			U.S. Customary Units:
7. 1 ft = __12__ in.	19. ½ ft = __6__ in.		28. The width of two fingers: __inch__
8. 1 yd = __36__ in.	20. 2 ft = __24__ in.		
9. 1 yd = __3__ ft	21. 3 ft = __36__ in.		29. The length of a man's shoe: __foot__
10. 1 mi = __5280__ ft	22. 2 yd = __6__ ft		
11. 1 m ≈ __39__ in.	23. 10 yd = __30__ ft		30. The length of one big step: __yard__
12. 1 km ≈ __0.62__ mi	24. 100 yd = __300__ ft		

---

1 Power Up

Facts
Distribute **Power Up K** to students. See answers below.

Mental Math
Before students begin the Mental Math exercise, do this counting exercise as a class.

Count up and down by 25s between negative 150 and 150.

Encourage students to share different ways to mentally compute these exercises. Strategies for exercises **a** and **b** are listed below.

  a. **Break Apart 311**
     (7 × 300) + (7 × 11) = 2100 + 77 = 2177
     Multiply Place Values
     (300 × 7) + (10 × 7) + (1 × 7) =
     2100 + 70 + 7 = 2177
  b. **Subtract 1200, then Subtract 50**
     2000 − 1200 = 800; 800 − 50 = 750
     Subtract 1300, then Add 50
     2000 − 1300 = 700; 700 + 50 = 750

Problem Solving
Refer to **Power-Up Discussion**, p. 421F.

2 New Concepts

Instruction
Invite students to name or describe situations in the everyday world that involve adding, subtracting, multiplying, or dividing units of measure.

You might choose to have students list the situations on the board. Allow the list to remain displayed throughout the remainder of the lesson.

Example 1
Instruction
Make sure students recognize that the addition cannot be completed until the measurement units are the same.

(continued)

Lesson 81   421

Instruction

Important generalizations for students to make in this lesson are:

- Units of measurement *will not* change if those units are added or subtracted.
- Units of measurement *must* change if those units are multiplied or divided.

Write the generalizations on the board or overhead. As students complete the examples in this lesson, remind them of the generalization that applies to each example.

You may choose to invite students to refer to the generalizations as they complete the Practice Set exercises.

Write this equation on the board or overhead:

$$cm \cdot cm = cm^2$$

To help students understand why the product $cm \cdot cm = cm^2$, write 5^2 below the cm^2. Then ask students to name the repeated multiplication used to simplify 5^2 to 25.

$$5 \cdot 5 = 5^2$$

Point out that in the same way, $cm \cdot cm$ is a repeated multiplication that produces the product cm^2.

(continued)

Notice that in each equation in example 1, the units of the sum are the same as the units of the addends. The units do not change when we add or subtract measurements. However, the units *do* change when we multiply or divide measurements.

When we find the area of a figure, we multiply the lengths. Notice how the units change when we multiply.

To find the area of this rectangle, we multiply 2 cm by 3 cm. The product has a different unit of measure than the factors.

$$2 \text{ cm} \cdot 3 \text{ cm} = 6 \text{ sq. cm}$$

Reading Math

Remember that the dot (·) indicates multiplication.

A centimeter and a square centimeter are two different kinds of units. A centimeter is used to measure length. It can be represented by a line segment.

_____
1 cm

A square centimeter is used to measure area. It can be represented by a square that is 1 centimeter on each side.

1 sq. cm

The unit of the product is a different unit because we multiplied the units of the factors. When we multiply 2 cm by 3 cm, we multiply both the numbers and the units.

$$2 \text{ cm} \cdot 3 \text{ cm} = \underline{2 \cdot 3} \ \underline{\text{cm} \cdot \text{cm}}$$
$$\qquad\qquad\quad 6 \qquad \text{sq. cm}$$

Instead of writing "sq. cm," we may use exponents to write "cm · cm" as "cm²." Recall that we read cm² as "square centimeters."

$$2 \text{ cm} \cdot 3 \text{ cm} = \underline{2 \cdot 3} \ \underline{\text{cm} \cdot \text{cm}}$$
$$\qquad\qquad\quad 6 \qquad \text{cm}^2$$

Example 2

Multiply: 6 ft · 4 ft

Solution

We multiply the numbers. We also multiply the units.

$$6 \text{ ft} \cdot 4 \text{ ft} = \underline{6 \cdot 4} \ \underline{\text{ft} \cdot \text{ft}}$$
$$\qquad\qquad\quad 24 \qquad \text{ft}^2$$

The product is **24 ft²**, which can also be written as "24 sq. ft."

Math Background

Units of measure are often expressed as ratios. For example, miles per gallon is a ratio used to measure motor vehicle fuel efficiency in the United States.

Other commonly used ratios include miles per hour (mph), which is used to measure speed, and pounds per square inch (PSI), which is used to measure pressure.

English Learners

Write **measurements** on the board. Ask students to tell you the meaning of the word. Say,

"When you determine the length, width, height, volume, capacity, weight, time, etc., you are finding measurements. Measurements tell us the size, amount, or capacity of something."

Ask a volunteer to give you the approximate measurements of classroom items. (book, paper, pencil)

Units also change when we divide measurements. For example, if we know both the area and the length of a rectangle, we can find the width of the rectangle by dividing.

$$\text{Area} = 21 \text{ cm}^2$$
7 cm

To find the width of this rectangle, we divide 21 cm² by 7 cm.

$$\frac{21 \text{ cm}^2}{7 \text{ cm}} = \frac{\overset{3}{\cancel{21}} \text{ cm} \cdot \text{cm}}{\underset{1}{\cancel{7}} \text{ cm}}$$

We divide the numbers and write "cm²" as "cm · cm" in order to reduce the units. The quotient is 3 cm, which is the width of the rectangle.

Example 3

Divide: $\dfrac{25 \text{ mi}^2}{5 \text{ mi}}$

Solution

To divide the units, we write "mi²" as "mi · mi" and reduce.

$$\frac{\overset{5}{\cancel{25}} \text{ mi} \cdot \text{mi}}{\underset{1}{\cancel{5}} \text{ mi}}$$

The quotient is **5 mi.**

Sometimes when we divide measurements, the units will not reduce. When units will not reduce, we leave the units in fraction form. For example, if a car travels 300 miles in 6 hours, we can find the average speed of the car by dividing.

Reading Math

The word *per* means "for each" and is used in place of the division bar.

$$\frac{300 \text{ mi}}{6 \text{ hr}} = \frac{\overset{50}{\cancel{300}} \text{ mi}}{\underset{1}{\cancel{6}} \text{ hr}}$$

The quotient is $50\frac{\text{mi}}{\text{hr}}$, which is 50 miles per hour (50 mph).

Notice that speed is a quotient of distance divided by time.

Example 4

Divide: $\dfrac{300 \text{ mi}}{10 \text{ gal}}$

Solution

We divide the numbers. The units do not reduce.

$$\frac{300 \text{ mi}}{10 \text{ gal}} = \frac{\overset{30}{\cancel{300}} \text{ mi}}{\underset{1}{\cancel{10}} \text{ gal}}$$

The quotient is $30\frac{\text{mi}}{\text{gal}}$, which is 30 miles per gallon.

Lesson 81   423

Instruction

Remind students of the formula for finding the area of a rectangle.

$$\text{Area} = \text{length} \times \text{width}$$

Write the formula on the board or overhead and substitute the given values from the instruction into the formula:

$$A = l \times w$$
$$21 \text{ cm}^2 = 7 \text{ cm} \times w$$

"We can find the width of the rectangle by dividing the area by the length."

Then write:

$$w = \frac{21 \text{ cm}^2}{7 \text{ cm}} = \frac{\overset{3}{\cancel{21}} \text{ cm} \cdot \text{cm}}{\underset{1}{\cancel{7}} \text{ cm}}$$
$$= 3 \text{ cm}$$

Example 3

Instruction

"Explain how 25 in the numerator and 5 in the denominator were canceled." The greatest common factor of the numbers is 5, and each number was divided by 5.

Instruction

"The greatest common factor of 300 and 6 was used to reduce $\frac{300}{6}$. What is the greatest common factor of 300 and 6?" 6

Example 4

Instruction

Point out that although the numbers 300 and 10 reduce by dividing both by a common factor, the units miles and gallons do not reduce because they are two different measurement units.

"We have studied units of length, units of capacity, and units of time. In Example 4, we divide 300 miles by 10 gallons. Since miles are a unit of linear measure and gallons are a unit of capacity, the units do not reduce, so the quotient contains both units."

(continued)

Practice Set

Problem a [Error Alert]
Before the subtraction can be completed, students must recognize that one or both units must be changed so that the units are the same.

Problems b–d [Error Alert]
Check to make sure that the answers are labeled correctly. Students should recognize that multiplication and division will cause the units to change.

3 **Written Practice**

Math Conversations
Discussion opportunities are provided below.

Problem 2 [Connect]
"Describe two different methods that could be used to solve this problem." Change 945 milliliters to liters or change 1 liter to milliliters.

Problem 10 [Predict]
Suggest that students draw a ratio box to help solve this problem.

	Ratio	Actual Count
Red	3	
Blue	4	24

(continued)

Practice Set ▸ Simplify:

a. 2 ft − 12 in. (Write the difference in inches.)   12 in.

b. 2 ft × 4 ft   8 ft²   **c.** $\frac{12\ cm^2}{3\ cm}$ 4 cm   **d.** $\frac{300\ mi}{5\ hr}$ 60 $\frac{mi}{hr}$

Written Practice   *Strengthening Concepts*

* 1. The Jones family had two gallons of milk before they ate breakfast. The
(78) family used two quarts of milk during breakfast. How many quarts of milk did the Jones family have after breakfast?   6 quarts

▸ *** 2.** [Connect] One quart of milk is about 945 milliliters of milk. Use this
(78) information to compare a quart and a liter:

1 gallon ⊖ 4 liters

3. [Analyze] Carol cut $2\frac{1}{2}$ inches off her hair three times last year. How
(66) much longer would her hair have been at the end of the year if she had not cut it? $7\frac{1}{2}$ inches

* 4. The plane flew 1200 miles in 3 hours. Divide the distance by the time to
(81) find the average speed of the plane.   400 $\frac{miles}{hour}$

5. Write the prime factorization of both the numerator and the denominator
(67) of this fraction. Then reduce the fraction. $\frac{2\cdot3\cdot3\cdot3}{3\cdot3\cdot3\cdot5}=\frac{2}{5}$

$$\frac{54}{135}$$

6. The basketball team scored 60% of its 80 points in the second half.
(29, 33) Write 60% as a reduced fraction. Then find the number of points the team scored in the second half. $\frac{3}{5}$; 48 points

7. What is the area of this parallelogram?
(71)   600 m²

8. What is the perimeter of this
(71) parallelogram?   100 m

26 m   25 m   24 m

9. False. All
trapezoids have
one pair of
parallel sides,
but all rectangles
have two pairs of
parallel sides.

9. [Verify] "Some rectangles are trapezoids." True or false? Why?
(64)

▸*** 10.** [Predict] The ratio of red marbles to blue marbles in the bag was 3 to 4.
(80) If 24 marbles were blue, how many were red?   18 marbles

* 11. Arrange these numbers in order from least to greatest: $\frac{1}{5}$, 0.4, $\frac{1}{2}$
(76)

$$\frac{1}{2}, \frac{1}{5}, 0.4$$

* 12. a. What decimal number is equivalent to $\frac{4}{25}$?   0.16
(74, 75)

   b. What percent is equivalent to $\frac{4}{25}$?   16%

13. (10 − 0.1) × 0.1   0.99   **14.** (0.4 + 3) ÷ 2   1.7
(53)   (53)

15. $\frac{5}{8} + \frac{3}{4}$ $1\frac{3}{8}$ **16.** $3 - 1\frac{1}{8}$ $1\frac{7}{8}$ **17.** $4\frac{1}{2} - 1\frac{3}{4}$ $2\frac{3}{4}$
(57)   (63)   (63)

▸ See Math Conversations in the sidebar.

18. $\frac{5}{6} \cdot \frac{4}{5} \cdot \frac{3}{8}$ $\frac{1}{4}$ (72)   **19.** $4\frac{1}{2} \times 1\frac{1}{3}$ 6 (66)   **20.** $3\frac{1}{3} \div 1\frac{2}{3}$ 2 (68)

Analyze The perimeter of this square is two meters. Refer to this figure to answer problems **21** and **22**.

21. How many centimeters long is each side of
(8)   the square (1 meter = 100 centimeters)?
     50 centimeters

22. a. What is the diameter of the circle?   50 centimeters
(47)
  ▶ **b.** What is the circumference of the circle? (Use 3.14 for π.)
       157 centimeters

23. If the sales-tax rate is 6%, what is the tax on a $12.80 purchase?   77¢
(41)

24. What time is two-and-one-half hours after 10:40 a.m.?   1:10 p.m.
(32)

25. Use a ruler to find the length of this line segment to the nearest
(17)   sixteenth of an inch. $2\frac{10}{16}$ in. = $2\frac{5}{8}$ in.

_____

26. *Connect* What is the area of a quadrilateral with the vertices (0, 0),
(Inv. 7)   (4, 0), (6, 3), and (2, 3)?   12 sq. units

27. What is the name of the geometric solid
(Inv. 6)   at right?   cone

▶ **28.** If the area of a square is one square foot, what is the perimeter?   4 feet
(38)

▶* **29.** Simplify:
(81)
    a. 2 yd + 3 ft   3 yd   **b.** 5 m $\times$ 3 m   15 m^2
    (Write the sum in yards.)

    c. $\frac{36 \text{ ft}^2}{6 \text{ ft}}$ 6 ft   **d.** $\frac{400 \text{ miles}}{20 \text{ gallons}}$ 20 $\frac{\text{miles}}{\text{gallon}}$

* **30.** *Model* Draw a pair of parallel segments that are not the same
(64)   length. Form a quadrilateral by drawing two segments between the
    endpoints of the parallel segments. What is the name of this type
    of quadrilateral?   Sample: ⬜ ; trapezoid

▶ See Math Conversations in the sidebar.

Math Conversations
Discussion opportunities are provided below.

Problem 22b [Analyze]
Extend the Problem
"Suppose that the square is moved and it is to be placed inside the circle. Will the perimeter of the square need to be changed? Explain why or why not." Yes; the perimeter must decrease because the length of any side of the square will be less than the length of the diameter of the circle.

Errors and Misconceptions
Problem 28
Encourage students who have difficulty visualizing the square to draw a picture.

Problem 29
Some students may not recognize that division causes the units to change. To help students understand the need for change, write the equation shown below on the board or overhead.

$$\frac{36 \text{ ft}^2}{6 \text{ ft}} = \frac{6 \cdot 6 \cdot \text{ft} \cdot \text{ft}}{6 \text{ ft}}$$

Invite a student to cancel the terms of the second fraction that can be canceled. $\frac{6}{6}$ and $\frac{\text{ft}}{\text{ft}}$

Then have students note that 'ft' in the numerator is the only unit that remains.

Looking Forward

Performing operations of arithmetic with units of measure prepares students for:

- **Lesson 90,** using direction and the number of degrees in turns to solve problems about measuring turns.

- **Lesson 95,** reducing units of measure before multiplying to solve problems.

- **Lesson 102,** performing operations with units of mass and weight.

- **Investigation 11,** using scale drawings and models to find actual and scale dimensions and to find the scale and the scale factor.

- **Lesson 114,** using unit multipliers to convert from one unit of measure to another.

• Volume of a Rectangular Prism

Objectives
- Find the area of the base of a rectangular prism.
- Find the volume of a rectangular prism.

Lesson Preparation

Materials
- **Power Up L** (in *Instructional Masters*)
- **Investigation Activity 15** (in *Instructional Masters*) or **graph paper**
- **Manipulative kit: wooden color cubes**

Math Language

New	Maintain	English Learners (ESL)
volume	base	layer

Technology Resources

Student eBook Complete student textbook in electronic format.

Resources and Planner CD Blackline masters, plus a pacing calendar with standards.

Test and Practice Generator CD Create additional practice sheets and custom-made tests.

www.SaxonPublishers.com Visit for more student activities and planning materials.

Inclusion

Adaptations CD Adapted lessons, investigations, practice and assessments.

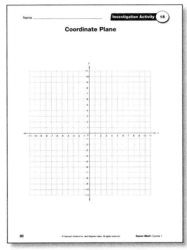

Power Up L   Investigation Activity 15

Meeting Standards

National Council of Teachers of Mathematics (NCTM)

Algebra

AL.1a Represent, analyze, and generalize a variety of patterns with tables, graphs, words, and, when possible, symbolic rules

Geometry

GM.1b Understand relationships among the angles, side lengths, perimeters, areas, and volumes of similar objects

GM.4e Recognize and apply geometric ideas and relationships in areas outside the mathematics classroom, such as art, science, and everyday life

Measurement

ME.1c Understand, select, and use units of appropriate size and type to measure angles, perimeter, area, surface area, and volume

ME.2d Develop strategies to determine the surface area and volume of selected prisms, pyramids, and cylinders

Representation

RE.5a Create and use representations to organize, record, and communicate mathematical ideas

Problem-Solving Strategy: Draw a Diagram

One-fifth of Ronnie's number is $\frac{1}{3}$. What is $\frac{3}{5}$ of Ronnie's number?

(Understand) **Understand the problem.**

"What information are we given?"

One-fifth of Ronnie's number is $\frac{1}{3}$.

"What are we asked to do?"

Determine what $\frac{3}{5}$ of his number is.

(Plan) **Make a plan.**

"What problem-solving strategy will we use?"

We will *draw a diagram* of the "number" divided into its five fractional parts.

(Solve) **Carry out the plan.**

"How do we begin?"

We draw a diagram to help visualize what the question is saying.

Draw a diagram that depicts fifths, and then label one of the fifths $\frac{1}{3}$:

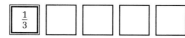

Label each of the fifths as $\frac{1}{3}$:

| $\frac{1}{3}$ | $\frac{1}{3}$ | $\frac{1}{3}$ | $\frac{1}{3}$ | $\frac{1}{3}$ |

"What is $\frac{3}{5}$ of the number depicted?"

$\frac{1}{3} + \frac{1}{3} + \frac{1}{3} = 1$, or $3\left(\frac{1}{3}\right) = 1$

(Check) **Look back.**

"Did we find the answer to the question that was asked?"

Yes. We found that $\frac{3}{5}$ of the number is 1.

Teacher Note: Ask students, what is the number if $\frac{1}{5}$ of the number is $\frac{1}{3}$? They can use the same diagram and add $\frac{1}{3} + \frac{1}{3} + \frac{1}{3} + \frac{1}{3} + \frac{1}{3} = \frac{5}{3} = 1\frac{2}{3}$. To check the answer they can find $\frac{3}{5}$ of $\frac{5}{3}$ or $\frac{3}{5} \times \frac{5}{3} = 1$.

Facts

Distribute **Power Up L** to students. See answers below.

Mental Math

Before students begin the Mental Math exercise, do this counting exercise as a class.

Count by 25s from 25 to 400.

Encourage students to share different ways to mentally compute these exercises. Strategies for exercises **a**, **d**, and **f** are listed below.

a. Multiply 2 × 2, then Add Two Zeros
$2 \times 2 = 4$, so $20 \times 20 = 400$
Use a Multiplication Pattern
$2 \times 2 = 4$; $2 \times 20 = 40$; $20 \times 20 = 400$

d. Break Apart $7.50
$(\$6.00 \div 3) + (\$1.50 \div 3) =$
$\$2 + 50¢ = \$2.50$
Find $\frac{1}{3}$ of 75
$\frac{1}{3}$ of 75 is 25, so $\frac{1}{3}$ of $7.50 is $2.50.

f. Delete a Zero, then Divide
$\frac{80\cancel{0}}{4\cancel{0}} = \frac{80}{4} = 20$

Problem Solving

Refer to **Power-Up Discussion**, p. 426B.

---

2 New Concepts

Instruction

The discussion below will help students compare and contrast perimeter, area, and volume.

"We have measured and calculated the distance around a shape. What term describes the distance around a shape?" perimeter

"We have also measured the amount of surface that is enclosed by the sides of a shape. When we measure the inside of a flat shape, what are we measuring?" its area

"What are we measuring when we measure the volume of a shape?" the amount of space that the shape takes up or occupies

"Perimeter is measured in linear units. Area is measured in square units. How is volume measured?" in cubic units

(continued)

---

facts	Power Up L
mental math	**a. Probability:** What is the probability of rolling an even number on a number cube? $\frac{1}{2}$
	b. Number Sense: $284 - 150$ 134
	c. Calculation: $1.99 + $2.99 $4.98
	d. Fractional Parts: $\frac{1}{3}$ of $7.50 $2.50
	e. Decimals: 2.5×10 25
	f. Number Sense: $\frac{800}{40}$ 20
	g. Measurement: How many ounces are in a cup? 8 oz
	h. Calculation: 10×10, $- 1$, $\div 3$, $- 1$, $\div 4$, $+ 1$, $\div 3$ 3

37 ps

problem solving	One-fifth of Ronnie's number is $\frac{1}{3}$. What is $\frac{3}{5}$ of Ronnie's number? 1

The **volume** of a shape is the amount of space that the shape occupies. We measure volume by using units that take up space, called cubic units. The number of cubic units of space that the shape occupies is the volume measurement of that shape. We select units of appropriate size to describe a volume. For small volumes we can use cubic centimeters or cubic inches. For larger volumes we can use cubic feet and cubic meters.

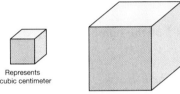

Represents
1 cubic centimeter

Represents
1 cubic inch

Math Language
The **base of a rectangular prism** is one of two parallel and congruent rectangular faces.

To calculate the volume of a rectangular prism, we can begin by finding the area of the base of the prism. Then we imagine building layers of cubes on the base up to the height of the prism.

Facts

Write the abbreviation.	Complete each equivalence.	Complete each conversion.
Metric Units:	Metric Units:	14. 2 liters $= \underline{2000}$ milliliters
1. liter __L__	7. 1 liter $= \underline{1000}$ milliliters	15. 2 liters $\approx \underline{2}$ quarts
2. milliliter __mL__	U.S. Customary Units:	16. 3.78 liters $= \underline{3780}$ milliliters
U.S. Customary Units:	8. 1 cup $= \underline{8}$ ounces	17. 0.5 liter $= \underline{500}$ milliliters
3. ounces __oz__	9. 1 pint $= \underline{16}$ ounces	18. $\frac{1}{2}$ gallon $= \underline{2}$ quarts
4. pint __pt__	10. 1 pint $= \underline{2}$ cups	19. 2 gallons $= \underline{8}$ quarts
5. quart __qt__	11. 1 quart $= \underline{2}$ pints	20. 2 half gallons $= \underline{1}$ gallon
6. gallon __gal__	12. 1 gallon $= \underline{4}$ quarts	21. 8 cups $= \underline{2}$ quarts
	Between Systems:	22–23. A two-liter bottle is a little more than $\underline{2}$ quarts or $\underline{\frac{1}{2}}$ gallon.
	13. 1 liter $\approx \underline{1}$ quart	

Example 1

How many 1-inch cubes are needed to form this rectangular prism? (A 1-inch cube is a cube whose edges are 1 inch long.)

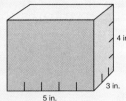

4 in.
3 in.
5 in.

Solution

The area of the base is 5 inches times 3 inches, which equals 15 square inches. Thus 15 cubes are needed to make the bottom layer of the prism.

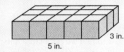

5 in.
3 in.

Reading Math

The formula for the area of the base is $A = l \times w$ or $A = lw$.

The prism is 4 inches high, so we will have 4 layers. The total number of cubes is 4 times 15, which is **60 cubes.**

Notice that in the example above we multiplied the length by the width to find the area of the base. Then we multiplied the area of the base by the height to find the volume.

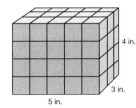

4 in.
3 in.
5 in.

Thinking Skill

Discuss

Does the order in which we multiply the dimensions change the answer? Why or why not?
No, because multiplication is commutative.

We can calculate the volume V of a rectangular prism by multiplying the three perpendicular dimensions of the prism: the length l, the width w, and the height h.

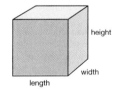

height
width
length

Thus the formula for finding the volume of a rectangular prism is

$$V = lwh$$

---

2 New Concepts (Continued)

Example 1

Instruction

Model this example using the **wooden color cubes** from the Manipulative Kit.

Begin by building the 5 in.-by-3 in. bottom layer, or base, of the prism.

> *"How many cubes are used to form the bottom layer, or the base, of our rectangular prism?"* 15 cubes

Add one layer at a time until the prism is four layers high. After completing each layer, remind students that 15 cubes were used to form the layer.

> *"How many cubes altogether did we use to build this rectangular prism?"* 60 cubes

Help students make the connection that the volume of the rectangular prism can be found by multiplying the length and width of the prism to find the area of the base, then multiplying the area of the base by the prism's height. Then write the formula for finding the volume of a rectangular prism on the board or overhead.

$$V = l \cdot w \cdot h \text{ or } V = lwh$$

(continued)

Math Background

The volume of a prism is different than the surface area of a prism, which students learned about in Investigation 6.

A way for students to think about the surface area of a prism is to think about wrapping a birthday present for a friend. How much wrapping paper would be needed to wrap the present with no overlap?

Besides stacking blocks, other ways for students to think about the volume of a prism is to think about modeling clay or water. How much modeling clay would be needed to form the prism? Or, how much water would be needed to fill it assuming it was hollow?

English Learners

Refer to the cube diagrams on this page. Say,

> *"The diagrams show you layers of cubes that are stacked together to create a rectangular prism. A layer is a single thickness. Layers can be stacked one on top of the other. A good example of layers is a building. Each floor of a building is a layer. "*

Ask students to look around the room for examples of layering. (stacks of books, bricks laid in layers to make a wall, layers of clothes)

2 New Concepts (Continued)

Example 2

Instruction

Explain that the solution (1000 cu. cm) represents 1000 cubic centimeters and could be written as 1000 cm³.

Example 3

Instruction

"When we use the formula V = lwh, can we multiply the numbers for l, w, and h in any order, or must we always multiply the length and the width first, and then multiply that result by the height?" We can multiply the numbers in any order.

"What property of multiplication allows us to multiply the numbers in any order?" the Commutative Property

Example 4

Instruction

Point out that e in the formula $V = e^3$ represents the length of one edge of the cube.

(continued)

Example 2

What is the volume of a cube whose edges are 10 centimeters long?

Solution

Thinking Skill

Generalize

In addition to $V = lwh$, what other formulas could we use to find the volume of a cube?
$V = s \times s \times s$, or $V = s^3$

The area of the base is 10 cm × 10 cm, or 100 sq. cm. Thus we could set 100 one-centimeter cubes on the bottom layer. There will be 10 layers, so it would take a total of 10 × 100, or 1000 cubes, to fill the cube. Thus the volume is **1000 cu. cm.**

10 cm

Example 3

Find the volume of a rectangular prism that is 4 feet long, 3 feet wide, and 2 feet high.

Solution

For *l*, *w*, and *h* we substitute 4 ft, 3 ft, and 2 ft. Then we multiply.

$$V = lwh$$
$$V = (4 \text{ ft})(3 \text{ ft})(2 \text{ ft})$$
$$V = \textbf{24 ft}^3$$

Notice that ft³ means "cubic feet." We read 24 ft³ as "24 cubic feet."

Example 4

Alison put small cubes together to build larger cubes. She made a table to record the number of cubes she used.

Length of Edge (Cubes Along Edge)	2	3	4	5
Volume (Number of Cubes Used)	8	27	64	125

Given this pattern, describe a rule that could be used to find the volume of a cube.

Solution

We can use a pattern to help us find a rule for determining the volume of a cube. In earlier examples we multiplied the length and width and height. For a cube these three measures are equal. We see that 2 × 2 × 2 is 8 and that 3 × 3 × 3 is 27. Thus cubing the edge of a cube gives us the volume, or $V = e^3$.

Practice Set

a. How many 1-cm cubes would be needed to build a cube 4 cm on each edge? 64 cubes

4 cm
4 cm
4 cm

b. What is the volume of a rectangular box that is 5 feet long, 3 feet wide, and 2 feet tall? 30 ft³

▶ **c.** *Analyze* The interior dimensions of a rectangular box are 10 inches by 6 inches by 4 inches. The box is to be filled with 1-inch cubes. How many cubes can fit on the bottom layer? How many cubes can fit in the box? 60 cubes; 240 cubes

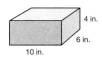

4 in.
6 in.
10 in.

d. Choose the most appropriate unit to measure the volume of a refrigerator. B

   A cubic inches   **B** cubic feet   **C** cubic miles

Written Practice *Strengthening Concepts*

1. Write the number twenty-one and five hundredths. 21.05
(35)

2. Tennis balls are sold in cans containing 3 balls. What would be the total cost of one dozen tennis balls if the price per can was $2.49? $9.96
(15)

▶ **3.** *Analyze* A cubit is about 18 inches. If Ruben was 4 cubits tall, about how many feet tall was he? 6 feet
(15)

* 4. a. Write $\frac{7}{100}$ as a percent. 7%
(75)
    b. Write $\frac{7}{10}$ as a percent. 70%

5. Write 90% as a reduced fraction. Then write the fraction as a decimal number. $\frac{9}{10}$; 0.9
(33, 74)

6. Of the 50 students who went on a trip, 23 wore a hat. What percent of the students wore a hat? 46%
(75)

7. Write $\frac{9}{25}$ as a percent. 36%
(75)

8. *Connect* A box of cereal has the shape of what geometric solid? rectangular prism
(Inv. 6)

Find each unknown number:

9. $w - 3\frac{5}{6} = 2\frac{1}{3}$ $6\frac{1}{6}$
(63)

10. $3\frac{1}{4} - y = 1\frac{5}{8}$ $1\frac{5}{8}$
(63)

11. $6n = 0.12$ 0.02
(45)

12. $0.12m = 6$ 50
(49)

13. $5n = 10^2$ 20
(38)

14. $1\frac{1}{2}w = 6$ 4
(68)

Lesson 82 429

▶ See Math Conversations in the sidebar.

---

2 New Concepts (Continued)

Practice Set
Problem c Error Alert
To determine the number of cubes that can fit inside the box, students must infer that there will be 4 layers of cubes (because the height of the box is 4 inches and the height of each cube or layer is 1 inch).

Problem c Analyze
Extend the Problem
"If we were asked to use the formula V = lwh to solve this problem, we would need to multiply 10 in. by 6 in. by 4 in. What is the product of 10, 6, and 4?" 240

"What is the product when we multiply inches by inches by inches?" cubic inches or in.³

"What is the volume of the rectangular box?" 240 in.³

---

3 Written Practice

Math Conversations
Discussion opportunities are provided below.

Problem 3 Analyze
Extend the Problem
"Write a whole number or a mixed number to represent your approximate height in cubits." Sample: about $3\frac{1}{3}$ cubits (60 inches)

(continued)

Inclusion

Materials: colored cubes

The formula for volume takes on greater meaning when students use manipulatives. Students can use cubes to see how many cubic units are needed to fill a prism and compare that with the results of using the formula.

Have students build the prism shown in Practice Set **a** to demonstrate how the formula works. Tell students to begin with a single layer. Ask,

  "What do you notice about the product l × w and the number of cubic units in a single layer?" They are equal.

Then have students add 3 more layers to the prism. Ask,

  "How can you find the total number of cubic units without counting?" Multiply the product l × w by the height. 4 × 4 × 4 = 64 cubic units

Challenge students to use the cubes to help them solve the following problem:

  "Suppose I have a rectangular prism that has a volume of 20 cubic units. The length and width are both 2 units long. What is the height?" 5 units

Math Conversations

Discussion opportunities are provided below.

Problem 22 [Analyze]

"Which measure of the parallelogram—
20 millimeters or 22 millimeters—represents
its height? Explain why." 20 mm; 20 mm is
a distance that is perpendicular to the base.

After completing the problem, ask

"The height of the parallelogram is shown
inside the parallelogram. Would our
answer change if the height had been
shown outside the parallelogram instead of
inside?" no

Problem 26 [Model]

Extend the Problem

"If you move one vertex of the trapezoid,
you can form a right trapezoid. Which
vertex would you move to form a right
trapezoid? Where would you move the
vertex to?"

Possible answers: move $(-3, 3)$ to $(-2, 3)$;
move $(-2, -1)$ to $(-3, -1)$; move $(1, -1)$ to
$(3, -1)$; move $(3, 3)$ to $(1, 3)$

Errors and Misconceptions

Problem 24

Incorrect prime factorizations can often
be noticed if students take the time that is
needed to check their work.

Remind students of the importance of
checking their work, then point out that
one way to check a prime factorization is to
write the factors in standard form and then
find the product of the factors. If the product
is the same as the given number, the problem
checks.

---

* 15. (75) **a.** What fraction of this group is shaded? $\frac{3}{5}$

b. What percent of this group is
shaded? 60%

16. (53) $0.5 + (0.5 \div 0.5) + (0.5 \times 0.5)$ 1.75

17. (61) $\frac{1}{2} + \frac{1}{5} + \frac{1}{10}$ $\frac{4}{5}$ **18.** (66) $1\frac{4}{5} \times 1\frac{2}{3}$ 3

19. (34) Which digit in 6.3457 has the same place value as the 8 in 128.90? 6

20. (16) Estimate the product of 39 and 41. 1600

21. (23, 58) In a bag there are 12 red marbles and 36 blue marbles.

a. What is the ratio of red marbles to blue marbles? $\frac{1}{3}$

b. [Predict] If one marble is taken from the bag, what is the probability
that the marble will be red? Express the probability ratio as a fraction
and as a decimal. $\frac{1}{4}$; 0.25

⤳ 22. (71) [Analyze] What is the area of this
parallelogram? 500 mm²

23. (71) What is the perimeter of this
parallelogram? 94 mm

▶ 24. (73) Write the prime factorization of 252 using exponents. $2^2 \cdot 3^2 \cdot 7$

25. (60) [Verify] "Some triangles are quadrilaterals." True or false? Why?
False. Quadrilaterals have four sides, but triangles have three sides.

⤳ 26. (64, Inv. 7) [Model] A quadrilateral has vertices with the coordinates $(-2, -1)$,
$(1, -1)$, $(3, 3)$, and $(-3, 3)$. Graph the quadrilateral on a coordinate
plane. The figure is what type of quadrilateral? trapezoid

* 27. (82) This cube is constructed of 1-inch
cubes. What is the volume of the larger
cube? 8 in.³

2 in.
2 in.   2 in.

* 28. (81) Simplify:

a. 3 quarts + 2 pints (Write the sum in quarts.) 4 quarts

b. $\frac{49 \text{ m}^2}{7 \text{ m}}$ 7 m   **c.** $\frac{400 \text{ miles}}{8 \text{ hours}}$ 50 $\frac{\text{miles}}{\text{hour}}$

* 29. (75) Three of the dozen eggs were cracked. What percent of the eggs were
cracked? 25%

* 30. (78) [Estimate] A pint of milk weighs about a pound. About how many
pounds does a gallon of milk weigh? about 8 pounds

26.

y axis graph with points plotted

▶ See Math Conversations in the sidebar.

Looking Forward

Finding the volume of rectangular
prisms prepares students for:

• **Lesson 120,** finding the volume
of cylinders.

• Proportions

Objectives

- Read and write proportions.
- Identify a ratio that forms a proportion with a given ratio.
- Use the scale factor to find a missing term in a proportion.

Lesson Preparation

Materials

- **Power Up I** (in *Instructional Masters*)

Optional

- **Manipulative Kit:** inch rulers
- **Teacher-provided material:** tape, scissors

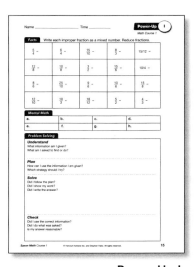

Power Up I

Math Language

New	Maintain	English Learners (ESL)
proportion	ratio	stated

Technology Resources

Student eBook Complete student textbook in electronic format.

Resources and Planner CD Assessment, reteaching, and instructional masters, plus a pacing calendar with standards.

Test and Practice Generator CD Create additional practice sheets and custom-made tests.

www.SaxonPublishers.com Visit for more student activities and planning materials.

Inclusion

Adaptations CD Adapted lessons, investigations, practice and assessments.

Meeting Standards

National Council of Teachers of Mathematics (NCTM)

Numbers and Operations

NO.1d Understand and use ratios and proportions to represent quantitative relationships

NO.3d Develop, analyze, and explain methods for solving problems involving proportions, such as scaling and finding equivalent ratios

Connections

CN.4c Recognize and apply mathematics in contexts outside of mathematics

Problem-Solving Strategy: Use Logical Reasoning/ Make It Simpler

Compare the following two separate quantities:

$$1\frac{7}{8} + 2\frac{5}{6} \bigcirc 3\frac{4}{5} \qquad\qquad 6.142 \times 9.065 \bigcirc 54$$

Describe how you performed the comparisons.

(Understand) **Understand the problem.**

"What information are we given?"

We are shown a sum of mixed numbers being compared to a single mixed number, and a product of decimal fractions being compared to a whole number.

"What are we asked to do?"

We are asked to compare the quantities, and describe how we compared them.

(Plan) **Make a plan.**

"How can we use the information we know to do what we are asked to do?"

We will *use logical reasoning* and number sense about rounding to *make it simpler.*

(Solve) **Carry out the plan.**

"Describe how to approximate $1\frac{7}{8} + 2\frac{5}{6}$?"

Since $1\frac{7}{8}$ is greater than $1\frac{1}{2}$ and since $2\frac{5}{6}$ is greater than $2\frac{1}{2}$, we know that their sum is greater than 4.

"What comparison symbol will we use in the fraction comparison?"

Since $1\frac{7}{8} + 2\frac{5}{6}$ is greater than 4, we know that $1\frac{7}{8} + 2\frac{5}{6} > 3\frac{4}{5}$.

"Is there a way to compare the quantities without multiplying the decimal numbers?"

We can break down 54 into the two factors 6×9. The factors 6 and 9 correspond to the whole-number portions of the factors on the left.

"What comparison symbol will we use? Justify your answer."

$(6.142 \times 9.065) > 54$ because the product of the whole number portions equal 54 and the additional decimal fractions will only increase the product.

(Check) **Look back.**

"Did we complete the task?"

Yes. We compared the quantities and described our solution process.

• **Proportions**

facts | Power Up I

mental math

a. **Probability:** What is the probability of rolling a number less than 3 on a number cube? $\frac{1}{3}$

b. **Number Sense:** 1000 − 125   875

c. **Calculation:** 3 × $3.99 $11.97

d. **Number Sense:** Double $3\frac{1}{2}$.   7

e. **Decimals:** 2.5 ÷ 100   0.025

f. **Number Sense:** 20 × 34   680

g. **Measurement:** How many milliliters are in 4 liters?   4000 mL

h. **Calculation:** 9 × 9, − 1, ÷ 2, + 2, ÷ 6, + 2, ÷ 3   3

problem solving

Compare the following two separate quantities:

$$1\frac{7}{8} + 2\frac{5}{6} \bigcirc 3\frac{4}{5} \qquad 6.142 \times 9.065 \bigcirc 54$$

Describe how you performed the comparisons.   >; >; see script for description

New Concept   *Increasing Knowledge*

If peaches are on sale for 3 pounds for 4 dollars then the ratio $\frac{3}{4}$ expresses the relationship between the quantity and the price of peaches. Since the ratio is constant, we can buy 6 pounds for 8 dollars, 9 pounds for 12 dollars and so on. With two equal ratios we can write a proportion.

> Peaches
> **3 lbs.**
> **for**
> **$4**

Math Language

A **ratio** is a comparison of two numbers by division.

A **proportion** is a true statement that two ratios are equal. Here is an example of a proportion:

$$\frac{3}{4} = \frac{6}{8}$$

We read this proportion as "Three is to four as six is to eight." Two ratios that are not equivalent are not proportional.

---

1   **Power Up**

Facts

Distribute **Power Up I** to students. See answers below.

Mental Math

Before students begin the Mental Math exercise, do this counting exercise as a class.

Count by $\frac{1}{4}$s from $\frac{1}{4}$ to 4.

Encourage students to share different ways to mentally compute these exercises. Strategies for exercises **b** and **f** are listed below.

b. **Subtract 100, then Subtract 25**
   1000 − 100 = 900; 900 − 25 = 875
Subtract 200, then add 75
   1000 − 200 = 800; 800 + 75 = 875

f. **Double 10 × 34**
   2(10 × 34) = 2(340) = 680
Break Apart 34
   20(30 + 4) = 600 + 80 = 680

Problem Solving

Refer to **Power-Up Discussion,** p. 431B.

Facts   Write each improper fraction as a mixed number. Reduce fractions.

$\frac{5}{4} = 1\frac{1}{4}$	$\frac{6}{4} = 1\frac{1}{2}$	$\frac{15}{10} = 1\frac{1}{2}$	$\frac{8}{3} = 2\frac{2}{3}$	$\frac{15}{12} = 1\frac{1}{4}$
$\frac{12}{8} = 1\frac{1}{2}$	$\frac{10}{8} = 1\frac{1}{4}$	$\frac{3}{2} = 1\frac{1}{2}$	$\frac{15}{6} = 2\frac{1}{2}$	$\frac{10}{4} = 2\frac{1}{2}$
$\frac{8}{6} = 1\frac{1}{3}$	$\frac{25}{10} = 2\frac{1}{2}$	$\frac{9}{6} = 1\frac{1}{2}$	$\frac{10}{6} = 1\frac{2}{3}$	$\frac{15}{8} = 1\frac{7}{8}$
$\frac{12}{10} = 1\frac{1}{5}$	$\frac{10}{3} = 3\frac{1}{3}$	$\frac{18}{12} = 1\frac{1}{2}$	$\frac{5}{2} = 2\frac{1}{2}$	$\frac{4}{3} = 1\frac{1}{3}$

Example 1

Instruction

Write the proportion $\frac{2}{3} = \frac{4}{6}$ on the board or overhead. Point out that $\frac{2}{3}$ and $\frac{4}{6}$ are ratios expressed as fractions and that the proportion shows equivalent fractions.

> *"We can demonstrate that the ratios are equal by reducing each fraction in the proportion to lowest terms. Can $\frac{2}{3}$ be reduced?"* no

> *"Can $\frac{4}{6}$ be reduced to $\frac{2}{3}$?"* yes

Explain that since $\frac{2}{3} = \frac{2}{3}$, the ratios are equal.

Example 2

Instruction

Emphasize the idea that proportions must be written in a consistent way, and that the best way for students to be consistent when writing proportions is to write the numbers in the same order as the numbers are given.

Example 3

Instruction

Invite a volunteer to explain how the order of the numbers in the proportion $\frac{2}{6} = \frac{n}{30}$ represent the order of the numbers in the problem.

(continued)

Example 1

Which ratio forms a proportion with $\frac{2}{3}$?

A $\frac{2}{4}$ **B** $\frac{3}{4}$ **C** $\frac{4}{6}$ **D** $\frac{3}{2}$

Solution

Equivalent ratios form a proportion. Equivalent ratios also reduce to the same rate. Notice that $\frac{2}{4}$ reduces to $\frac{1}{2}$; that $\frac{3}{4}$ and $\frac{2}{3}$ are reduced, and that $\frac{4}{6}$ reduces to $\frac{2}{3}$. Thus the ratio equivalent to $\frac{2}{3}$ is **C**.

Verify How can we verify that $\frac{2}{3}$ and $\frac{4}{6}$ form a proportion? Reduce $\frac{4}{6}$ to see if it equals $\frac{2}{3}$. $\frac{4 \div 2}{6 \div 2} = \frac{2}{3}$.

Example 2

Write this proportion with digits: Four is to six as six is to nine.

Solution

We write "four is to six" as one ratio and "six is to nine" as the equivalent ratio. We are careful to write the numbers in the order stated.

$$\frac{4}{6} = \frac{6}{9}$$

We can use proportions to solve a variety of problems. Proportion problems often involve finding an unknown term. The letter a represents an unknown term in this proportion:

$$\frac{3}{5} = \frac{6}{a}$$

Math Language

A **scale factor** is a number that relates corresponding sides of similar figures and corresponding terms in equivalent ratios.

One way to find an unknown term in a proportion is to determine the fractional name for 1 that can be multiplied by one ratio to form the equivalent ratio. The first terms in these ratios are 3 and 6. Since 3 times 2 equals 6, we find that the scale factor is 2. So we multiply $\frac{3}{5}$ by $\frac{2}{2}$ to form the equivalent ratio.

$$\frac{3}{5} \cdot \frac{2}{2} = \frac{6}{10}$$

We find that a represents the number 10.

Example 3

Complete this proportion: Two is to six as what number is to 30?

Solution

We write the terms of the proportion in the stated order, using a letter to represent the unknown number.

$$\frac{2}{6} = \frac{n}{30}$$

English Learners

Refer students to example 2. Write **stated** on the board. Say,

> *"When something is stated, it is said or given. In math, a statement can be made with words or numbers. For example, when you say or write the answer to the problem 3 × 5, you state the answer."*

Ask for volunteers to state ratios and write them in the order stated.

Math Background

Students have previously learned that they can reduce the terms of a fraction by dividing both the numerator and the denominator by a common factor. The idea of reducing the terms of a fraction can also be used to simplify proportion problems. For example, in the proportion $\frac{16}{20} = \frac{n}{50}$, the ratio $\frac{16}{20}$ can be reduced to $\frac{8}{10}$ or to $\frac{4}{5}$. Using either $\frac{8}{10}$ or $\frac{4}{5}$ in place of $\frac{16}{20}$ forms a proportion that can be solved mentally.

$$\frac{8}{10} = \frac{n}{50} \qquad \frac{4}{5} = \frac{n}{50}$$

The value of n in each of the three proportions is 40. By reducing $\frac{16}{20}$ to $\frac{8}{10}$ or $\frac{4}{5}$, the missing term ($n = 40$) is easier to find.

Visit www.
SaxonPublishers.
com/ActivitiesC1
*for a graphing
calculator activity.*

We are not given both first terms, but we are given both second terms, 6 and 30. The scale factor is 5, since 6 times 5 equals 30. We multiply $\frac{2}{6}$ by $\frac{5}{5}$ to complete the proportion.

$$\frac{2}{6} \times \frac{5}{5} = \frac{10}{30}$$

Reduce each ratio to lowest terms. If the ratios are equal, the answer is correct.

The unknown term of the proportion is **10**.

$$\frac{2}{6} = \frac{10}{30}$$

$$\frac{10}{30} \div \frac{10}{10} = \frac{1}{3}$$
$$\frac{2}{6} \div \frac{2}{2} = \frac{1}{3}$$

Evaluate How can we check the answer?

Practice Set

c. $\frac{4}{3} = \frac{12}{w}$; 9; Sample: I copied the proportion the way it was described. I found that $4 \times 3 = 12$, so I multiplied 3 by 3 to complete the proportion.

d. $\frac{6}{9} = \frac{n}{36}$; 24; Sample: Ratios are equal if they reduce to the same fraction. Both $\frac{6}{9}$ and $\frac{24}{36}$ reduce to $\frac{2}{3}$, so they are equal.

a. Which ratio forms a proportion with $\frac{5}{2}$? **C**

  A $\frac{3}{2}$ **B** $\frac{4}{10}$ **C** $\frac{15}{6}$ **D** $\frac{5}{20}$

b. Write this proportion with digits: Six is to eight as nine is to twelve. $\frac{6}{8} = \frac{9}{12}$

c. Write and complete this proportion: Four is to three as twelve is to what number? How did you find your answer?

d. **Explain** Write and complete this proportion: Six is to nine as what number is to thirty-six? How can you check your answer?

Written Practice   *Strengthening Concepts*

1. What is the product when the sum of 0.2 and 0.2 is multiplied by the difference of 0.2 and 0.2? 0
(12, 53)

2. **Analyze** Arabian camels travel about 3 times as fast as Bactrian camels. If Bactrian camels travel at $1\frac{1}{2}$ miles per hour, at how many miles per hour do Arabian camels travel? $4\frac{1}{2}$ miles per hour
(66)

3. **Connect** Mark was paid at a rate of $4 per hour for cleaning up a neighbor's yard. If he worked from 1:45 p.m. to 4:45 p.m., how much was he paid? $12
(32)

4. Write 55% as a reduced fraction. $\frac{11}{20}$
(33)

5. a. Write $\frac{9}{100}$ as a percent. 9%
(75)
   b. Write $\frac{9}{10}$ as a percent. 90%

6. The whole class was present. What percent of the class was present? 100%
(75)

7. **Connect** A century is 100 years. A decade is 10 years.
(29, 75)
   a. What fraction of a century is a decade? $\frac{1}{10}$
   b. What percent of a century is a decade? 10%

8. a. Write 0.48 as a reduced fraction. $\frac{12}{25}$
(73, 75)
   b. Write 0.48 as a percent. 48%

Lesson 83   433

▶ See Math Conversations in the sidebar.

---

2 New Concepts (Continued)

Practice Set

Problem a (Error Alert)

To solve the problem, students must recall that a proportion is made up of two equal ratios. Help students understand that if one ratio is given, they should look for the other ratio that is equal to the given ratio.

Problem c (Error Alert)

An incorrect answer is often caused by writing the ratios in an order that is different from the given order. Explain to students that one way to minimize an error of this nature is to write a proportion, then check the order of the numbers before completing any arithmetic.

Problem d (Explain)

Invite volunteers to demonstrate at the board or overhead different ways to check the answer.

3 Written Practice

Math Conversations

Discussion opportunities are provided below.

Problem 7a (Connect)

Extend the Problem
"What fraction of a century is your age? Give your answer in simplest form."
Sample: 12 years old is $\frac{3}{25}$

Problem 7b (Connect)

Extend the Problem
"What fraction of a decade is your age? Give your answer in simplest form."
Sample: 12 years old is $\frac{6}{5}$

(continued)

Lesson 83   433

Math Conversations

Discussion opportunities are provided below.

Problem 14 `Analyze`

Read the problem aloud. Then invite a volunteer to the board or overhead and ask the volunteer to write a proportion to represent the problem.

Encourage the class to discuss the proportion and decide if the proportion does, or does not, represent the problem, and point out that any decision that is made must be supported in some way (for example, by explanation).

Problem 19 `Analyze`

"When you find the greatest common factor of two numbers, do you find a number that is greater than or equal to the greatest number or less than or equal to the smallest number?" less than or equal to the smallest number

"Is it possible for two numbers to have more than one greatest common factor? If yes, give an example to support your answer." no

"Is it possible for two numbers to have more than one common factor? If yes, give an example to support your answer." Yes; the common factors of 6 and 12, for example, are 1, 2, 3, and 6.

Errors and Misconceptions
Problem 23

To find the area of the shaded triangle, students must recognize that the distance labeled 4 in. represents the height of both triangles.

To help remind students that the height of a triangle will not always be inside the triangle, draw a triangle that has an obtuse angle on the board or overhead.

(continued)

---

9. Write $\frac{7}{8}$ as a decimal number.   0.875
(74)

10. $\left(1\frac{1}{3} + 1\frac{1}{6}\right) - 1\frac{2}{3}$ $\frac{5}{6}$
(48)

11. $1\frac{1}{2} \times 3 \times 1\frac{1}{9}$ 5
(72)

12. $4\frac{2}{3} \div 1\frac{1}{6}$ 4
(68)

13. $0.1 + (1 - 0.01)$ 1.09
(38)

▶*** 14.** `Analyze` Write and complete this proportion: Three is to four as nine is to what number? $\frac{3}{4} = \frac{9}{n}$; 12
(83)

15. `Verify` Which ratio below forms a proportion with $\frac{3}{5}$?   C
(15)

   A $\frac{3}{10}$ **B** $\frac{6}{15}$ **C** $\frac{12}{20}$ **D** $\frac{5}{3}$

16. Write the standard numeral for the following: 80,420
(32)
$$(8 \times 10{,}000) + (4 \times 100) + (2 \times 10)$$

17. **a.** Compare: $2^4 \bigcirc 4^2$ **b.** 1 km $\bigcirc$ 1 mi
(7, 73)

18. Write the prime factorization of both the numerator and the denominator of this fraction. Then reduce the fraction. $\frac{2 \cdot 2 \cdot 2 \cdot 3}{2 \cdot 2 \cdot 2 \cdot 2 \cdot 2} = \frac{3}{4}$
(67)
$$\frac{24}{32}$$

▶*** 19.** **a.** `Analyze` What is the greatest common factor of 24 and 32?   8
(20, 83)
   b. Which two fractions reduce to the same number? $\frac{24}{32}, \frac{9}{12}$

$$\frac{24}{32} \qquad \frac{9}{16} \qquad \frac{9}{12} \qquad \frac{12}{18}$$

20. `Estimate` If the diameter of a ceiling fan is 4 ft, then the tip of one of the blades on the fan moves about how far during one full turn? Choose the closest answer.   C
(47)

   A 8 ft   **B** 12 ft   **C** $12\frac{1}{2}$ ft   **D** 13 ft

21. What is the perimeter of this trapezoid?   56 mm
(8)

* 22. A cube has edges 3.1 cm long. What is a good estimate for the volume of the cube?   27 cm³
(82)

▶*** 23.** **a.** What is the area of this parallelogram?   24 in.²
(71, 79)
   b. What is the area of the shaded triangle?   12 in.²

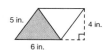

* 24. One fourth of the 120 students took wood shop. How many students did not take wood shop?   90 students
(77)

25. How many millimeters is 2.5 centimeters?   25 millimeters
(7)

▶ See Math Conversations in the sidebar.

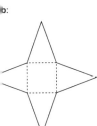

b:

26. **a.** What is the name of this geometric solid?   pyramid
(Inv. 6)

b. Sketch a net of this solid.

27. Simplify:
(81)
   a. 3 quarts + 2 pints (Write the sum in pints.)   8 pints

   b. $\dfrac{64 \text{ cm}^2}{8 \text{ cm}}$ 8 cm

   c. $\dfrac{60 \text{ students}}{3 \text{ teachers}}$ 20 students per teacher

28. DeShawn delivers newspapers to 20 of the 25 houses on North Street.
(75) What percent of the houses on North Street does DeShawn deliver papers to?   80%

29. Sample: ◺

29. **Represent**   Draw a triangle that has two perpendicular sides.
(28, 60)

30. **Analyze**   The ratio of dimes to nickels in Pilar's change box is $\frac{2}{3}$. Pilar
(15, 83) has $0.75 in nickels.

   a. How many nickels does Pilar have?   15 nickels

   b. How many dimes does Pilar have? (*Hint:* Write and complete a proportion using the ratio given above and your answer to **a.**)
   10 dimes
   c. In all, how much money does Pilar have in her change box? $1.75

Early Finishers
Real-World Application

Use a protractor to measure each angle listed. Then classify each angle as acute, right, obtuse, or straight.

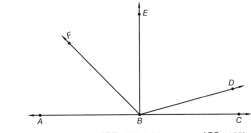

∠ ABF   45°, acute   ∠ ABE   90°, right   ∠ ABD   165°, obtuse
∠ ABC   180°, straight   ∠ FBE   45°, acute   ∠ FBD   120°, obtuse
∠ CBD   15°, acute   ∠ CBE   90°, right   ∠ CBF   135°, obtuse
∠ DBE   75°, acute

Lesson 83   **435**

▶ See Math Conversations in the sidebar.

Errors and Misconceptions
Problem 26

To sketch the net of the pyramid, students will need to recognize that the broken line segments represent an edge of the faces that cannot be seen.

You might choose to have students check their nets by cutting and folding, then using tape to assemble the models.

Looking Forward

Reading, writing, and finding a missing term in a proportion by multiplying by the appropriate scale factor prepares students for:

- **Lesson 85,** using cross products to solve proportions.

- **Lesson 88,** using proportions and ratio boxes to solve ratio problems.

- **Lesson 101,** using proportions and ratio boxes to solve ratio problems involving totals.

- **Lesson 105,** using proportions and ratio boxes to solve percent problems.

• Order of Operations, Part 2

Objectives
• Follow the order of operations when simplifying an expression.

Lesson Preparation

Materials
• **Power Up K** (in *Instructional Masters*)
• **Investigation Activity 15** (in *Instructional Masters*)
• **Teacher-provided material:** calculators

Math Language
English Learners (ESL)
algebraic logic

Technology Resources

Student eBook Complete student textbook in electronic format.

Resources and Planner CD Assessment, reteaching, and instructional masters, plus a pacing calendar with standards.

Test and Practice Generator CD Create additional practice sheets and custom-made tests.

www.SaxonPublishers.com Visit for more student activities and planning materials.

Inclusion

Adaptations CD Adapted lessons, investigations, practice and assessments.

Power Up K   Investigation Activity 15

Meeting Standards

National Council of Teachers of Mathematics (NCTM)

Numbers and Operations

NO.2a Understand the meaning and effects of arithmetic operations with fractions, decimals, and integers

Problem Solving

PS.1b Solve problems that arise in mathematics and in other contexts

Communication

CM.3a Organize and consolidate their mathematical thinking through communication

Problem-Solving Strategy: Work Backwards

Katrina's hourglass and timer runs for exactly three minutes. Jessi's timer runs for exactly four minutes. The two girls want to play a game where they each get one five-minute turn. Explain how the girls can use their timers to mark off exactly five minutes.

(**Understand**) We need to time a 5-minute turn. We have one 3-minute timer and one 4-minute timer.

(**Plan**) We will *work backwards* and *use logical reasoning* to find the answer. We can use the 4-minute timer by itself to mark off four minutes, so we will look for a way to mark off one minute using both timers.

(**Solve**) We see that we can mark off one minute by turning both timers over at the same time. When the 3-minute timer is empty, there is exactly one minute left in the 4-minute timer. At this point the player should begin her turn. When the minute left in the 4-minute timer runs out, we can immediately turn it back over to time the remaining four minutes.

(**Check**) The minute left in Jessi's timer plus the four minutes when it is turned back over totals five minutes.

1 Power Up

Facts

Distribute **Power Up K** to students. See answers below.

Mental Math

Before students begin the Mental Math exercise, do this counting exercise as a class.

Count by 12s from 12 to 144.

Encourage students to share different ways to mentally compute these exercises. Strategies for exercises **c** and **e** are listed below.

c. Add 1¢ and Subtract 1¢
$5.99 + 1¢ = $6 and $2.99 − 1¢ = $2.98;
$6 + $2.98 = $8.98

Round to Dollars, then Subtract 2¢
$6 + $3 = $9; $9 − 2¢ = $8.98

e. Shift the Decimal Point Two Places Right
7.5 × 100 = 750

Break Apart 7.5
$(100 \times 7) + (100 \times \frac{1}{2}) = 700 + 50 = 750$

Problem Solving

Refer to **Power-Up Discussion**, p. 436B.

• Order of Operations, Part 2

Power Up   *Building Power*

facts   Power Up K

mental math

a. **Probability:** What is the probability of rolling a number greater than 2 on a number cube? $\frac{2}{3}$

b. **Calculation:** 980 − 136   844

c. **Calculation:** $5.99 + $2.99 $8.98

d. **Fractional Parts:** $\frac{1}{4}$ of $10.00 $2.50

e. **Decimals:** 7.5 × 100   750

f. **Number Sense:** $\frac{480}{20}$ 24

g. **Measurement:** How many ounces are in a pint?   16 oz

h. **Calculation:** 8 × 8, − 4, ÷ 3, + 4, ÷ 4, + 2, ÷4   2

problem solving

Katrina's hourglass sand timer runs for exactly three minutes. Jessi's timer runs for exactly four minutes. The two girls want to play a game where they each get one five-minute turn. Explain how the girls can use their timers to mark off exactly five minutes.

(Understand) We need to time a 5-minute turn. We have one 3-minute timer and one 4-minute timer.

(Plan) We will *work backwards* and *use logical reasoning* to find the answer. We can use the 4-minute timer by itself to mark off four minutes, so we will look for a way to mark off one minute using both timers.

(Solve) We see that we can mark off one minute by turning both timers over at the same time. When the 3-minute timer is empty, there is exactly one minute left in the 4-minute timer. At this point the player should begin her turn. When the minute left in the 4-minute timer runs out, we can immediately turn it back over to time the remaining four minutes.

(Check) The minute left in Jessi's timer plus the four minutes when it is turned back over totals five minutes.

Facts

Complete each equivalent measure.				Write a unit for each reference.
1. 1 cm	= 10 mm	13. 10 cm	= 100 mm	**Metric Units:**
2. 1 m	= 1000 mm	14. 2 m	= 200 cm	25. The thickness of a dime:
3. 1 m	= 100 cm	15. 5 km	= 5000 m	millimeter
4. 1 km	= 1000 m	16. 2.5 cm	= 25 mm	26. The width of a little finger:
5. 1 in.	= 2.54 cm	17. 1.5 m	= 150 cm	centimeter
6. 1 mi	≈ 1610 m	18. 7.5 km	= 7500 m	27. The length of one big step:
				meter
7. 1 ft	= 12 in.	19. $\frac{1}{2}$ ft	= 6 in.	**U.S. Customary Units:**
8. 1 yd	= 36 in.	20. 2 ft	= 24 in.	28. The width of two fingers:
9. 1 yd	= 3 ft	21. 3 ft	= 36 in.	inch
10. 1 mi	= 5280 ft	22. 2 yd	= 6 ft	29. The length of a man's shoe:
				foot
11. 1 m	≈ 39 in.	23. 10 yd	= 30 ft	30. The length of one big step:
12. 1 km	≈ 0.62 mi	24. 100 yd	= 300 ft	yard

New Concept   *Increasing Knowledge*

Recall that the four operations of arithmetic are addition, subtraction, multiplication, and division. When more than one type of operation occurs in the same expression, we perform the operations in the order described below.

Order of Operations

1. Perform operations within parentheses.
2. Multiply and divide from left to right.
3. Add and subtract from left to right

Example 1

Simplify: 2 · 8 + 2 · 6

Solution

Multiplication and addition occur in this expression. We multiply first.

$$\underset{16}{\underbrace{2 \times 8}} + \underset{12}{\underbrace{2 \times 6}}$$

Then we add.

$$16 + 12 = \mathbf{28}$$

Some calculators are designed to recognize the standard order of operations and some are not. If a variety of calculator models are available in the classroom, you can test their design by using the expression from example 1. Enter these keystrokes:

 [2] [X] [8] [+] [2] [X] [6] [=]

"Algebraic logic" calculators should display the following after the equal sign is pressed:

$$\boxed{28.}$$

Example 2

Simplify: 0.5 + 0.5 ÷ 0.5 − 0.5 × 0.5

Solution

First we multiply and divide from left to right.

$$0.5 + \underset{1}{\underbrace{0.5 \div 0.5}} - \underset{0.25}{\underbrace{0.5 \times 0.5}}$$

Then we add and subtract from left to right.

$$0.5 + 1 - 0.25 = \mathbf{1.25}$$

Manipulative Use

When you discuss the portion of the example 1 solution that involves calculators, distribute calculators throughout the classroom. Ask each student to clear the calculator and then enter the keystrokes exactly as shown in the example solution.

$$2 \cdot 8 + 2 \cdot 6 =$$

Tell students that if 28 is not displayed on the calculator, either the expression was entered incorrectly or the calculator does not have algebraic logic. Explain that a calculator that does not have algebraic logic does not follow the order of operations, but instead performs all operations in the order in which they are entered.

---

2 New Concepts

Instruction

Although students are not expected to simplify expressions with exponents in this lesson, you may want to introduce them to the following mnemonic device, which is discussed in greater detail in Lesson 92, to help them remember the order of operations.

Please	**P**arentheses
Excuse	**E**xponents
My **D**ear	**M**ultiply and **D**ivide from left to right
Aunt **S**ally	**A**dd and **S**ubtract from left to right

Explain that the first letter of each word indicates the operation to be performed, and point out that letter E represents operations with exponents.

Instruction

To give students a problem solving opportunity that involves order of operations, read the problem below or write the problem on the board or overhead.

> *"In Mr. Jackson's store, three shelves display hats for sale. Five of the seven hats on each shelf have been sold. How many hats have not been sold?"*

Write these two equations on the board.

$$(3 \times 7) - (3 \times 5) = n$$
$$3 \times 7 - 5 = n$$

Ask students to discuss and compare the equations and work together to decide which equation represents the information in the problem.

During the discussion, some students may suggest, for example, that parentheses can be placed in the second equation to make it true.

After students have chosen the equation that represents the problem $((3 \times 7) - (3 \times 5) = n)$, lead them to conclude that an equation for this problem cannot be written without including order of operations.

(continued)

Practice Set

Problems a–f Error Alert

After students complete the practice exercises with pencil and paper, have them use a calculator to check their work.

3 Written Practice

Math Conversations

Discussion opportunities are provided below.

Problem 3 Analyze

"How many different operations are present in this expression?" four

"Which of those operations are completed first?" multiply and divide

"Which operation, 6 × 6 or 6 ÷ 6, is completed first? Why?" 6 × 6; multiplication and division are completed from left to right

"After completing the multiplication and the division, which operation is completed next, addition or subtraction? Why?" addition; addition and subtraction are completed from left to right

(continued)

Example 3

Simplify: 2(8 + 6)

Solution

First we perform the operation within the parentheses.

$$2(8 + 6)$$
$$2(14)$$

Then we multiply.

$$2(14) = \mathbf{28}$$

Practice Set ▶ Simplify:

a. $5 + 5 \times 5 - 5 \div 5$ 29 **b.** $32 + 1.8(20)$ 68

c. $5 + 4 \times 3 \div 2 - 1$ 10 **d.** $2(10) + 2(6)$ 32

e. $3 + 3 \times 3 - 3 \div 3$ 11 **f.** $2(10 + 6)$ 32

Written Practice   *Strengthening Concepts*

1. *Classify* What is the ratio of prime numbers to composite numbers in
(23, 65) this list? $\frac{4}{5}$

2, 3, 4, 5, 6, 7, 8, 9, 10

* 2. Bianca poured four cups of milk from a full half-gallon container. How
(78) many cups of milk were left in the container?   4 cups

▶ *** 3.** *Analyze* $6 + 6 \times 6 - 6 \div 6$ 41
(84)

4. Write 30% as a reduced fraction. Then write the fraction as a decimal
(33, 74) number. $\frac{3}{10}$; 0.3

Find the area of each triangle:

* 5.   18 cm^2 *** 6.**   18 cm^2
(79) 6 cm   4 cm   *(79)*   6 cm   9 cm
9 cm   6 cm

* 7. **a.** Write $\frac{1}{20}$ as a decimal number.   0.05
(74, 75) **b.** Write $\frac{1}{20}$ as a percent.   5%

8. *Verify* "Some parallelograms are rectangles." True or false?
(64) Why?   True. Rectangles are special parallelograms that have four right angles.

▶ See Math Conversations in the sidebar.

English Learners

Explain what it means for a calculator to have **algebraic logic**. Say,

"A calculator with algebraic logic will follow the order of operations to solve a problem."

Have students enter the problem in example 1 into their calculators to determine whether their calculator has algebraic logic.

9. What is the area of this parallelogram? 384 cm²
(71)

24 cm 25 cm
16 cm

10. What is the perimeter of this parallelogram? 82 cm
(71)

11. $\left(3\frac{1}{8} + 2\frac{1}{4}\right) - 1\frac{1}{2}$ $3\frac{7}{8}$
(48)

12. $\frac{5}{6} \times 2\frac{2}{3} \times 3$ $6\frac{2}{3}$
(72)

13. $8\frac{1}{3} \div 100$ $\frac{1}{12}$
(68)

14. $(4 - 3.2) \div 10$ 0.08
(53)

15. $0.5 \times 0.5 + 0.5 \div 0.5$ 1.25
(84)

16. $8 \div 0.04$ 200
(49)

17. Which digit is in the hundredths place in 12.345678? 4
(34)

18. The mixed number $5\frac{1}{8}$ is more than 5 but less than 6. Since $\frac{1}{8}$ is less than $\frac{1}{2}$, $5\frac{1}{8}$ is closer to 5 than to 6. Thus, $5\frac{1}{8}$ rounds to 5.

18. **Explain** How do you round $5\frac{1}{8}$ to the nearest whole number?
(51)

▶ **19.** **Analyze** Write the prime factorization of 700 using exponents. $2^2 \cdot 5^2 \cdot 7$
(73)

20. Two ratios form a proportion if the ratios reduce to the same fraction. Which two ratios below form a proportion? $\frac{15}{9}$ and $\frac{35}{21}$
(83)

$$\frac{15}{12} \quad \frac{15}{9} \quad \frac{25}{10} \quad \frac{35}{21}$$

21. **Connect** The perimeter of a square is 1 meter. How many centimeters long is each side? 25 centimeters
(8)

* **22.** Fong scored 9 of the team's 45 points.
(29, 75)
   a. What fraction of the team's points did Fong score? $\frac{1}{5}$

   b. What percent of the team's points did she score? 20%

23. What time is 5 hours 30 minutes after 9:30 p.m.? 3:00 a.m.
(32)

▶* **24.** **Analyze** Write and complete this proportion: Six is to four as what number is to eight? $\frac{6}{4} = \frac{n}{8}$; 12
(83)

25. **Conclude** Figure ABCD is a parallelogram. Its opposite angles (∠A and ∠C, ∠B and ∠D) are congruent. Its adjacent angles (such as ∠A and ∠B) are supplementary. If angle A measures 70°, what are the measures of ∠B, ∠C, and ∠D? m∠B = 110°; m∠C = 70°; m∠D = 110°
(69)

B A
C D

▶* **26.** If each small cube has a volume of 1 cm³, what is the volume of this rectangular prism? 40 cm³
(82)

Simplify:

* **27.** 2 ft + 24 in. (Write the sum in inches.) 48 in.
(81)

Lesson 84 439

▶ See Math Conversations in the sidebar.

Math Conversations

Discussion opportunities are provided below.

Problem 19 Analyze

"In a prime factorization, can a prime factor appear more than once?" yes

"When you write a prime factorization, how do you show that a factor appears more than once?" the factor is written with an exponent

"In a prime factorization, what does an exponent represent?" the number of times a factor appears in the factorization

Problem 24 Analyze

"Explain how to solve this proportion for n." Sample: Look at the relationship of 4 and 8. Since 4 × 2 is 8, the constant factor is 2, so multiply 6 by 2 to learn the value of *n*.

Problem 26 Analyze

Extend the Problem

"How many cubes in the prism are not visible? Explain how you can use the volume of the prism to learn the answer." 12; because each cube has a volume of 1 cm³, subtract the number of visible cubes from 40.

Errors and Misconceptions

Problem 19

Watch for students who list 5^2 as the last factor in the factorization because 5^2 represents 25 and 25 is greater than 2^2 and greater than 7, the other numbers in the factorization.

Work with these students to record the prime factorization correctly, then have them describe to you the correct way to record a prime factorization.

(continued)

Math Conversations

Discussion opportunities are provided below.

Problem 29 Model

Extend the Problem

"What would you estimate the area of the triangle to be?"
Sample: about 8 square units

"What is the computed area of the triangle?" 8 square units

"Compare your estimate with the computed area. How do the answers compare?"
Sample: My estimate was reasonable.

* **28.** **a.** $\dfrac{100\ cm^2}{10\ cm}$ 10 cm
(81)

   b. $\dfrac{180\ pages}{4\ days}$ 45 pages per day

▶ **29.** **Model** A triangle has vertices at the coordinates (4, 4) and (4, 0) and
(Inv. 7) at the origin. Draw the triangle on graph paper. Notice that inside the
triangle are some full squares and some half squares.

   a. How many full squares are in the triangle? 6 full squares

   b. How many half squares are in the triangle? 4 half squares

30. **Analyze** This year Moises has read 24 books. Sixteen of the books
(23) were non-fiction and the rest were fiction. What is the ratio of fiction to
non-fiction books Moises has read this year? $\frac{1}{2}$

Early Finishers
Real-World Application

Alejandra owns a triangular plot of land. She hopes to buy another triangular section adjacent to the one she owns. Use the figure below to find the area of the land Alejandra owns and the area of the land she hopes to buy.

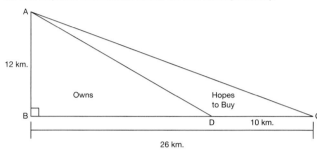

$A = \frac{1}{2}b \times h$; Area of land Alejandra owns: $\frac{1}{2} \times 16 \times 12 = 96\ km^2$.

Area of land Alejandra hopes to buy: $\frac{1}{2} \times 10 \times 12 = 60\ km^2$.

29.

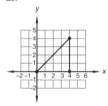

▶ See Math Conversations in the sidebar.

Looking Forward

Using the order of operations to simplify expressions with more than one arithmetic operation prepares students for:

• **Lesson 92,** reviewing the use of the order of operations in simplifying expressions with exponents.

Using Cross Products to Solve Proportions

Objectives

- Use cross products to determine whether two fractions are equal or whether two ratios form a proportion.
- Use cross products to find a missing term in a proportion.

Lesson Preparation

Materials

- **Power Up L** (in *Instructional Masters*)

Optional

- **Investigation Activity 15** (in *Instructional Masters*) or **graph paper**

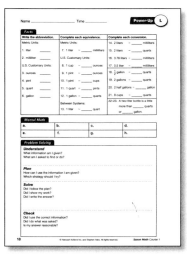

Power Up L

Math Language

New	English Learners (ESL)
cross product	educated guess

Technology Resources

Student eBook Complete student textbook in electronic format.

Resources and Planner CD Assessment, reteaching, and instructional masters, plus a pacing calendar with standards.

Test and Practice Generator CD Create additional practice sheets and custom-made tests.

www.SaxonPublishers.com Visit for more student activities and planning materials.

Inclusion

Adaptations CD Adapted lessons, investigations, practice and assessments.

Meeting Standards

National Council of Teachers of Mathematics (NCTM)

Numbers and Operations

NO.1d Understand and use ratios and proportions to represent quantitative relationships

NO.3c Develop and use strategies to estimate the results of rational-number computations and judge the reasonableness of the results

NO.3d Develop, analyze, and explain methods for solving problems involving proportions, such as scaling and finding equivalent ratios

Problem Solving

PS.1c Apply and adapt a variety of appropriate strategies to solve problems

Problem-Solving Strategy: Use Logical Reasoning/ Guess and Check

Copy this problem and fill in the missing digits. No two digits in the problem may be alike.

$$
\begin{array}{r}
- \ - \ - \\
\times \quad \ 7 \\
\hline
9 \ \_ \ \_
\end{array}
$$

Understand *Understand the problem.*

"What information are we given?"

We are shown a multiplication problem with several missing digits. None of the digits can be repeated.

"What are we asked to do?"

Fill in the missing digits.

Plan *Make a plan.*

"What problem-solving strategy will we use?"

We will *use logical reasoning* and number sense to fill in the missing digits. As necessary, we will *guess and check*.

Solve *Carry out the plan.*

"How can we determine the hundreds digit of the top factor?"

We know that the first digit must be 1, because the number multiplied by 7 must be greater than 100 but less than 200 since the product is in the 900s. We also know that a 2 is carried to the hundreds column for the sum to be 9.

"What choices do we have for the tens digit of the top factor?"

To carry 2 to the tens digit must be 3 or 4. We try 4.

$$
\begin{array}{r}
2 \\
1 \ \_ \ \_ \\
\times \quad \ 7 \\
\hline
9 \ \_ \ \_
\end{array}
\qquad
\begin{array}{r}
2 \\
1 \ 4 \ \_ \\
\times \quad \ 7 \\
\hline
9 \ \_ \ \_
\end{array}
\qquad
\begin{array}{r}
2 \\
1 \ 4 \ 1 \\
\times \quad \ 7 \\
\hline
9 \ 8 \ 7
\end{array}
\qquad
\begin{array}{r}
2 \ 1 \\
1 \ 4 \ 2 \\
\times \quad \ 7 \\
\hline
9 \ 9 \ 4
\end{array}
$$

The tens digit cannot be 4 because the only options of 1 or 2 for the ones position would result in duplicate digits in the product. Therefore, the tens digit must be 3.

"Which digit is in the ones place?"

$$
\begin{array}{r}
2 \\
1 \ 3 \ \_ \\
\times \quad \ 7 \\
\hline
9 \ \_ \ \_
\end{array}
\qquad
\begin{array}{r}
2 \ 1 \\
1 \ 3 \ 2 \\
\times \quad \ 7 \\
\hline
9 \ 2 \ 4
\end{array}
\qquad
\begin{array}{r}
2 \ 2 \\
1 \ 3 \ 4 \\
\times \quad \ 7 \\
\hline
9 \ 3 \ 8
\end{array}
\qquad
\begin{array}{r}
2 \ 3 \\
1 \ 3 \ 5 \\
\times \quad \ 7 \\
\hline
9 \ 4 \ 5
\end{array}
\qquad
\begin{array}{r}
2 \ 4 \\
1 \ 3 \ 6 \\
\times \quad \ 7 \\
\hline
9 \ 5 \ 2
\end{array}
$$

The digits **2, 3, 4,** and **5** in the ones place each result in duplicate digits in the product. Therefore, the digit in the ones place must be **6.**

$$
\begin{array}{r}
1 \ 3 \ 6 \\
\times \quad \ 7 \\
\hline
9 \ 5 \ 2
\end{array}
$$

Check *Look back.*

"Did we complete the task?"

Yes. We filled in the missing digits. No two digits are alike.

• **Using Cross Products to Solve Proportions**

36p3
611
613
633

Power Up · *Building Power*

facts | Power Up L

mental math

a. **Number Sense:** 50 × 50   2500

b. **Number Sense:** 1000 − 625   375

c. **Calculation:** 4 × $3.99 $15.96

d. **Number Sense:** Double $1.25. $2.50

e. **Decimals:** 7.5 ÷ 10   0.75

f. **Number Sense:** 20 × 35   700

g. **Measurement:** How many liters are in 3000 milliliters?   3 L

h. **Calculation:** 7 × 7, + 1, ÷ 2, − 1, ÷ 2, × 5, ÷ 2   30

problem solving

Copy this problem and fill in the missing digits. No two digits in the problem may be alike.

$$\begin{array}{r} - - - \\ \times\ \ \ 7 \\ \hline 9\_\_ \end{array} \qquad \begin{array}{r} 136 \\ \times\ \ \ 7 \\ \hline 952 \end{array}$$

New Concept · *Increasing Knowledge*

We have compared fractions by writing the fractions with common denominators. A variation of this method is to determine whether two fractions have equal **cross products.** If the cross products are equal, then the fractions are equal. The cross products of two fractions are found by cross multiplication, as we show below.

$$8 \times 3 = 24 \qquad \qquad 4 \times 6 = 24$$

Both cross products are 24. Since the cross products are equal, we can conclude that the fractions are equal.

> **Equal fractions have equal cross products.**

Example 1

Use cross products to determine whether $\frac{3}{5}$ and $\frac{4}{7}$ are equal.

$\frac{3}{5}$ $\frac{4}{7}$

Lesson 85   441

Facts

Write the abbreviation.	Complete each equivalence.	Complete each conversion.
Metric Units:	Metric Units:	14. 2 liters = __2000__ milliliters
1. liter __L__	7. 1 liter = __1000__ milliliters	15. 2 liters ≈ __2__ quarts
2. milliliter __mL__	U.S. Customary Units:	16. 3.78 liters = __3780__ milliliters
U.S. Customary Units:	8. 1 cup = __8__ ounces	17. 0.5 liter = __500__ milliliters
3. ounces __oz__	9. 1 pint = __16__ ounces	18. $\frac{1}{2}$ gallon = __2__ quarts
4. pint __pt__	10. 1 pint = __2__ cups	19. 2 gallons = __8__ quarts
5. quart __qt__	11. 1 quart = __2__ pints	20. 2 half gallons = __1__ gallon
6. gallon __gal__	12. 1 gallon = __4__ quarts	21. 8 cups = __2__ quarts
	Between Systems:	22–23. A two-liter bottle is a little more than __2__ quarts or $\frac{1}{2}$ gallon.
	13. 1 liter ≈ __1__ quart	

---

1 Power Up

Facts
Distribute **Power Up L** to students. See answers below.

Mental Math
Before students begin the Mental Math exercise, do this counting exercise as a class.

Count up and down by 5s between −25 and 25.

Encourage students to share different ways to mentally compute these exercises. Strategies for exercises **a** and **f** are listed below.

a. **Multiply 5 × 5, then Add Two Zeros**
   5 × 5 = 25; 50 × 50 = 2500
   Use a Pattern of Products
   5 × 5 = 25; 50 × 5 = 250;
   50 × 50 = 2500

f. **Double 10 × 35**
   10 × 35 = 350; 350 × 2 = 700
   Break Apart 35
   20(30 + 5) = 600 + 100 = 700

Problem Solving
Refer to **Power-Up Discussion**, p. 441B.

2 New Concepts

Instruction
"Look at the arrows through the fractions. What letter of the alphabet is formed by the arrows?" the letter X

Tell students that remembering the letter X can help them remember which numbers to cross multiply.

Example 1

Instruction
"What numbers represent the factors in the cross products of these fractions?"
5 and 4, 7 and 3

(continued)

Instruction

Make sure students understand that when they find cross products, they are simply renaming the fractions with a common denominator. Explain that the cross products are the numerators of these renamed fractions.

To demonstrate this concept, write the fractions $\frac{2}{3}$ and $\frac{3}{5}$ on the board or on an overhead projector.

"What are the cross products of these two fractions?" $2 \times 5 = 10$ and $3 \times 3 = 9$

To confirm that 10 and 9 are the numerators of the two fractions renamed with common denominators, have students rename $\frac{2}{3}$ and $\frac{3}{5}$ with a common denominator of 15. $\frac{10}{15}$ and $\frac{9}{15}$

Then ask students to compare the cross products and the numerators.

"Are the fractions equal?" no

Example 2

Instruction

"What numbers represent the factors in the cross products of these fractions?" 12 and 12, 18 and 8

"To find a cross product, does the order in which you multiply the two factors matter? Why or why not?" No; multiplication is commutative

(continued)

To find the cross products, we multiply the numerator of each fraction by the denominator of the other fraction. We write the cross product above the numerator that is multiplied.

$$21 \nwarrow \quad \frac{3}{5} \times \frac{4}{7} \quad \nearrow 20$$

The cross products are not equal, so **the fractions are not equal.** The greater cross product is above the greater fraction. So $\frac{3}{5}$ is greater than $\frac{4}{7}$.

When we find the cross products of two fractions, we are simply renaming the fractions with common denominators. The common denominator is the product of the two denominators and is usually not written. Look again at the two fractions we compared:

$$\frac{3}{5} \qquad \frac{4}{7}$$

The denominators are 5 and 7.

If we multiply $\frac{3}{5}$ by $\frac{7}{7}$ and multiply $\frac{4}{7}$ by $\frac{5}{5}$, we form two fractions that have common denominators.

$$\frac{3}{5} \times \frac{7}{7} = \frac{21}{35} \qquad \frac{4}{7} \times \frac{5}{5} = \frac{20}{35}$$

The numerators of the renamed fractions are 21 and 20, which are the cross products of the fractions. So when we compare cross products, we are actually comparing the numerators of the renamed fractions.

Example 2

Math Language
A **proportion** is a statement that shows two ratios are equal.

Do these two ratios form a proportion?

$$\frac{8}{12}, \frac{12}{18}$$

Solution

If the cross products of two ratios are equal, then the ratios are equal and therefore form a proportion. To find the cross products of the ratios above, we multiply 8 by 18 and 12 by 12.

$$144 \nwarrow \quad \frac{8}{12} \times \frac{12}{18} \quad \nearrow 144$$

The cross products are 144 and 144, so **the ratios form a proportion.**

$$\frac{8}{12} = \frac{12}{18}$$

Since equivalent ratios have equal cross products, we can use cross products to find an unknown term in a proportion. By cross multiplying, we form an equation. Then we solve the equation to find the unknown term of the proportion.

Math Background

The statement $\frac{1}{2} = \frac{3}{6}$ is an example of a proportion. Because the ratios in a proportion are equal fractions, and equal fractions have equal reciprocals, the statement $\frac{2}{1} = \frac{6}{3}$ is also an example of a proportion.

Example 3

Use cross products to complete this proportion: $\frac{6}{9} = \frac{10}{m}$

Solution

The cross products of a proportion are equal. So 6 times m equals 9 times 10, which is 90.

$$\frac{6}{9} = \frac{10}{m}$$

$$6m = 9 \cdot 10$$

We solve this equation:

$$6m = 90$$

$$m = 15$$

The unknown term is 15. We complete the proportion.

$$\frac{6}{9} = \frac{10}{15}$$

Example 4

Use cross products to find the unknown term in this proportion: Fifteen is to twenty-one as what number is to seventy?

Solution

We write the ratios in the order stated.

$$\frac{15}{21} = \frac{w}{70}$$

The cross products of a proportion are equal.

$$15 \cdot 70 = 21w$$

To find the unknown term, we divide $15 \cdot 70$ by 21. Notice that we can reduce as follows:

$$\frac{\overset{5}{\cancel{15}} \cdot \overset{10}{\cancel{70}}}{\underset{1}{\cancel{21}}} = w$$

The unknown term is **50.**

Practice Set ▸ Use cross products to determine whether each pair of ratios forms a proportion:

a. $\frac{6}{9}, \frac{7}{11}$ no

b. $\frac{6}{8}, \frac{9}{12}$ yes

Use cross products to complete each proportion:

c. $\frac{6}{10} = \frac{9}{x}$ 15

d. $\frac{12}{16} = \frac{y}{20}$ 15

e. Use cross products to find the unknown term in this proportion: 10 is to 15 as 30 is to what number? 45

▸ See Math Conversations in the sidebar.

Example 3
Instruction

A proportion is a true statement that shows two ratios are equal, and when two ratios are equal, the cross products of those ratios are also equal. Explain that this concept is used to solve for a missing term in a proportion.

Example 4
Instruction

Remind students that they now know two different ways to find a missing term in a proportion—using cross products or multiplying by the constant factor—and encourage them to become skilled at using both methods.

Practice Set
Problems a–e [Error Alert]

Before solving each problem, ask students to name the numbers that represent the factors in each pair of cross products.

Teacher Tip

After you complete example 4, engage students in a discussion about **proportions in the real world.** Begin the discussion by offering examples of how proportions are used, such as a cook adjusting measurements in a recipe that makes four servings in order to make ten servings, or an architect making scale drawings of a building. Then encourage students to name or describe other examples.

Math Conversations

Discussion opportunities are provided below.

Problem 5 Conclude

"What is an acute angle?" an angle that has a measure that is less than 90°

"Which angles in triangle ABC are acute angles?" $\angle A$ and $\angle B$

"What does it mean if two angles are complementary?" the sum of the measures of the angles is 90°

"Explain how you can find the measure of $\angle A$, then name its measure. Since $\angle A$ and $\angle B$ are complementary, and the measure of $\angle B$ is 55°, subtract 55° from 90° to find the measure of $\angle A$; 35°.

"What is the sum of all of the angles of the triangle?" 180°

Problem 10 Explain

"What numbers represent the factors in the cross products of this proportion?" 6 and 10, 4 and w

"How are cross products used to find the value of w?" Set the cross products equal to each other and solve the equation for w; divide 60 by 4.

Errors and Misconceptions

Problem 5

Students should not use a protractor to find the measure of the missing angle. Instead, remind students that since the two acute angles are complementary, their measures have a sum of 90°.

(continued)

---

* 1. Twenty-one of the 25 books Aretha has are about crafts. What percent of the books are about crafts?   84%
(75)

2. By the time the blizzard was over, the temperature had dropped from 17°F to − 6°F. This was a drop of how many degrees?   23°F
(14)

3. The cost to place a collect call was $1.50 for the first minute plus $1.00 for each additional minute. What was the cost of a 5-minute phone call? $5.50
(12)

* 4. The ratio of runners to walkers at the 10K fund-raiser was 5 to 7. If there were 350 runners, how many walkers were there?   490 walkers
(80)

▶ *** 5.** **Conclude** The two acute angles in △ABC are complementary. If the measure of $\angle B$ is 55°, what is the measure of $\angle A$?   35°
(69)

6. Athletic shoes are on sale for 20% off. Toni wants to buy a pair of running shoes that are regularly priced at $55.
(41)
   a. How much money will be subtracted from the regular price if she buys the shoes on sale? $11

   b. What will be the sale price of the shoes? $44

7. Freddy bought a pair of shoes for a sale price of $39.60. The sales-tax rate was 8%.
(41)
   a. What was the sales tax on the purchase? $3.17

   b. What was the total price including tax? $42.77

* 8. **a.** Write $\frac{1}{25}$ as a decimal number.   0.04
(74, 75)
   b. Write $\frac{1}{25}$ as a percent.   4%

* 9. Use cross products to determine whether this pair of ratios forms a proportion: not a proportion
(85)
$$\frac{5}{11}, \frac{6}{13}$$

10.
$\frac{4}{6} = \frac{10}{w}$; $w = 15$;
Sample: I set up the proportion, using w for the unknown term. I then cross multiplied 4 times w and 10 times 6 to get the equation $4w = 10 \times 6$. I then solved for w by dividing 60 by 4 to get 15.

▶ *** 10.** **Explain** Use cross products to find the unknown term in this proportion: 4 is to 6 as 10 is to what number? Describe how you found your answer.
(85)

11. $10 \div 2\frac{1}{2}$ 4
(68)

12. $6.5 − (4 − 0.32)$ 2.82
(38)

13. $(6.25)(1.6)$ 10
(39)

14. $0.06 \div 12$ 0.005
(45)

▶ See Math Conversations in the sidebar.

Find each unknown number:

15. $2\frac{1}{2} + x = 3\frac{1}{4}$ $\frac{3}{4}$
(59)

16. $4\frac{1}{8} - y = 1\frac{1}{2}$ $2\frac{5}{8}$
(48)

* 17. $\frac{9}{12} = \frac{n}{20}$ 15
(85)

* 18. Arrange in order from least to greatest: 30%, 0.4, $\frac{1}{2}$
(76)

$$\frac{1}{2}, 0.4, 30\%$$

19. In a school with 300 students and 15 teachers, what is the student-teacher ratio? $\frac{20}{1}$
(23)

20. If a number cube is rolled once, what is the probability that it will stop with a composite number on top?   The probability of rolling a 4 or a 6 is $\frac{1}{3}$.
(58, 65)

21. One fourth of 32 students have pets. How many students do not have pets?   24 students
(77)

22. **Connect** What is the area of a parallelogram that has vertices with the coordinates (0, 0), (4, 0), (5, 3), and (1, 3)?   12 sq. units
(Inv. 7, 71)

* 23. $2 + 2 \times 2 - 2 \div 2$ 5
(84)

24. Alejandro started the 10-kilometer race at 8:22 a.m. He finished the race at 9:09 a.m. How long did it take him to run the race?   47 min
(32)

Reading Math
The symbol ≈ means "is approximately equal to."

25. **Estimate** Refer to the table below to answer this question: Ten kilometers is about how many miles? Round the answer to the nearest mile.   6 miles
(15)

> 1 meter ≈ 1.093 yards
> 1 kilometer ≈ 0.621 mile

* 26. **Analyze** Lindsey packed boxes that were 1 foot long, 1 foot wide, and 1 foot tall into a larger box that was 5 feet long, 4 feet wide, and 3 feet tall.
(82)

3 ft
4 ft   5 ft

a. How many boxes could be packed on the bottom layer of the larger box?   20 boxes

b. Altogether, how many small boxes could be packed in the larger box?   60 boxes

* 27. Simplify:
(81)

a. 2 ft + 24 in. (Write the sum in feet.)   4 ft

b. 3 yd · 3 yd   9 yd²

28. **Connect** A quart is what percent of a gallon?   25%
(75, 78)

> See Math Conversations in the sidebar.

---

3 **Written Practice** (Continued)

Math Conversations
Discussion opportunities are provided below.

Problem 24 Analyze
Extend the Problem
"What proportion could be used to find Alejandro's average speed in kilometers per hour?"
Sample: $\frac{10}{47} = \frac{n}{60}$

"Solve the proportion and round your answer to the nearest kilometer. What was Alejandro's average speed in kilometers per hour?" $\frac{13 \text{ km}}{\text{h}}$

Problem 26 Analyze
Extend the Problem
"Suppose the boxes Lindsey packed measured 2 feet by 2 feet by 2 feet instead of 1 foot by 1 foot by 1 foot. How many whole boxes could Lindsey fit into the 3 ft by 4 ft by 5 ft box? Explain your answer." Four; encourage students to share their explanations.

(continued)

Math Conversations

Discussion opportunities are provided below.

Problem 29 Analyze

Extend the Problem

"Which is greater, the circumference of the circle, or the perimeter of the larger square? Use mental math and use 3 for pi." the perimeter of the larger square

---

Analyze This figure shows a square inside a circle, which is itself inside a larger square. Refer to this figure to answer problems **29** and **30**.

▶ **29.** The area of the smaller square is half the area
(31) of the larger square.

    a. What is the area of the larger square?
      100 cm²
    b. What is the area of the smaller square? 50 cm²

30. **Predict** Based on your answers to the questions in problem 29,
(31) make an educated guess as to the area of the circle. Explain your reasoning. A guess might be about 75 cm². Students will learn to calculate the area of a circle in Lesson 86.

Early Finishers
Real-World Application

One day Mr. Holmes brought home a $50\frac{1}{4}$ ounce tin of maple syrup. Mrs. Holmes knew they could never finish that much maple syrup. Mr. Holmes explained to her that he was going to share the maple syrup with two neighbors. Mr. Holmes brought back $26\frac{1}{4}$ ounces of maple syrup after sharing with both neighbors. How much maple syrup did each of Mr. Holmes' neighbors receive if they received equal amounts of syrup?
$50\frac{1}{4} - 26\frac{1}{4} = 24 \div 2 = 12$ ounces

▶ See Math Conversations in the sidebar.

Looking Forward

Using cross products to identify and solve proportions prepares students for:

- **Lesson 87,** finding missing factors in problems.

- **Lesson 101,** using proportions and ratio boxes to solve ratio problems involving totals.

- **Lesson 105,** using proportions and ratio boxes to solve percent problems.

English Learners

Refer students to problem 30. Explain the meaning of **educated guess.** Say,

"To make an educated guess, you use the information you already know to predict an answer."

Ask for volunteers to tell about a time when they made an educated guess about something. (guessing a students age when you know their grade level, guessing the height of the ceiling based on your own height)

Assessment 30–40 minutes

For use after Lesson 85

Distribute **Cumulative Test 16** to each student. Two versions of the test are available in *Saxon Math Course 1 Course Assessments Book*. Have students complete the **Power-Up Test** first. Allow 10 minutes. Then have students work the 20 numbered items on the **Cumulative Test.** Students may use copies of the answer sheet to record their work. Track individual and class progress with the **Test Analysis** forms.

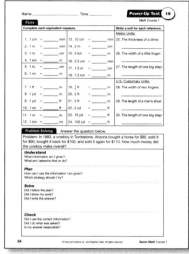

Power-Up Test 16

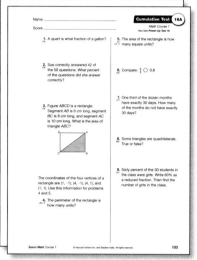

Cumulative Test 16A

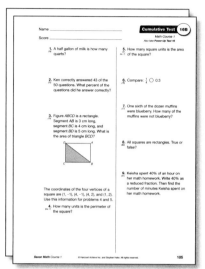

Alternative Cumulative Test 16B

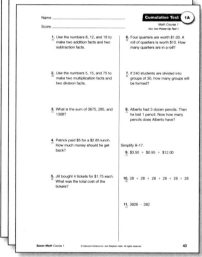

Optional Answer Forms

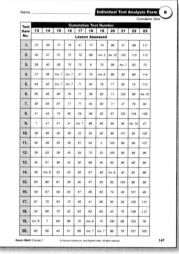

Individual Test Analysis Form

Class Test Analysis Form

Reteaching

Students who score below 80% on the assessment may be in need of reteaching. Look for the causes of student mistakes. If errors are conceptual, refer to the *Reteaching Masters* for reteaching.

Order of Operations
Assign after Lesson 85 and Test 16

Objectives
- Insert parentheses in equations to make them true.
- Write an equation to solve a problem and explain how to use order of operations to solve it.
- Communicate ideas through writing.

Materials
Performance Activity 16

Preparation
Make copies of **Performance Activity 16.** (One each per student.)

Time Requirement
15–30 minutes; Begin in class and complete at home.

Activity
Explain to students that for this activity they will be inserting parentheses in equations to make them true. They will also be writing equations for given situations and explaining if they need to apply the rules of order of operations to solve the equation. Explain that all of the information students need is on **Performance Activity 16.**

Criteria for Evidence of Learning
- Inserts parentheses in equations accurately to make them true.
- Writes an appropriate equation for a problem situation and explains correctly if order of operations should be applied to solve the equation.
- Communicates ideas clearly through writing.

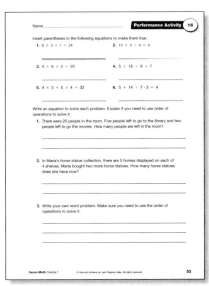

Performance Activity 16

National Council of Teachers of Mathematics (NCTM)

Numbers and Operations
NO.2a Understand the meaning and effects of arithmetic operations with fractions, decimals, and integers

Algebra
AL.2c Use symbolic algebra to represent situations and to solve problems, especially those that involve linear relationships

Problem Solving
PS.1d Monitor and reflect on the process of mathematical problem solving

Communication
CM.3d Use the language of mathematics to express mathematical ideas precisely

• Area of a Circle

Objectives

- Estimate the area of a circle drawn on a grid.
- Use the formula $A = \pi r^2$ to determine the area of a circle.

Lesson Preparation

Materials

- **Power Up G** (in *Instructional Masters*)
- **Investigation Activity 15** (in *Instructional Masters*) or **graph paper**
- **Geometric Formulas poster**
- **Lesson Activity 18 Transparency** (in *Instructional Masters*)

Math Language

English Learners (ESL)
enclosed

Technology Resources

Student eBook Complete student textbook in electronic format.

Resources and Planner CD Assessment, reteaching, and instructional masters, plus a pacing calendar with standards.

Test and Practice Generator CD Create additional practice sheets and custom-made tests.

www.SaxonPublishers.com Visit for more student activities and planning materials.

Inclusion

Adaptations CD Adapted lessons, investigations, practice and assessments.

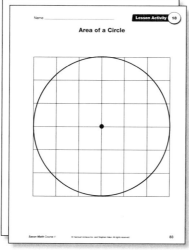

Power Up G

Lesson Activity 18
Investigation Activity 15

Meeting Standards

National Council of Teachers of Mathematics (NCTM)

Measurement

ME.2a Use common benchmarks to select appropriate methods for estimating measurements

ME.2b Select and apply techniques and tools to accurately find length, area, volume, and angle measures to appropriate levels of precision

ME.2c Develop and use formulas to determine the circumference of circles and the area of triangles, parallelograms, trapezoids, and circles and develop strategies to find the area of more-complex shapes

Problem Solving

PS.1b Solve problems that arise in mathematics and in other contexts

Problem-Solving Strategy: Make an Organized List

Thomasita was thinking of a number less than 90 that she says when counting by sixes and when counting by fives, but not when counting by fours. Of what number was she thinking?

(Understand) **Understand the problem.**

"What information are we given?"

Thomasita was thinking of a number that is (1) less than 90, (2) a multiple of 5 and 6, but (3) not a multiple of 4.

"What are we asked to do?"

Determine the number Thomasita was thinking of.

(Plan) **Make a plan.**

"What problem-solving strategy will we use?"

We will *make an organized list* of the multiples of 6 through 90. Thomasita's number is also a multiple of 5, so we will eliminate any numbers that are not multiples of 5. Then we will test the numbers that remain to see whether they are multiples of 4.

(Solve) **Carry out the plan.**

"What are the multiples of 6 that are less than 90?"

6, 12, 18, 24, 30, 36, 42, 48, 54, 60, 66, 72, 78, 84

"Which numbers in our list are also multiples of 5?"

Only 30 and 60

"Of 30 and 60, which is NOT a number Thomasita says when counting by fours?" .

Sixty is a multiple of 4 ($15 \times 4 = 60$), so Thomasita's number must be 30.

(Check) **Look back.**

"Did we complete the task?"

Yes. We found the number less than 90 that is a multiple of 5 and 6 but not of 4. Thomasita was thinking of the number 30.

• **Area of a Circle**

34p3 *611 613 633 625*

Power Up *Building Power*

facts	Power Up G
mental math	**a. Number Sense:** $60 \cdot 60$ 3600
	b. Number Sense: $850 - 170$ 680
	c. Calculation: $\$8.99 + \$4.99$ $13.98
	d. Fractional Parts: $\frac{1}{5}$ of $2.50 $0.50
	e. Decimals: 0.08×100 8
	f. Number Sense: $\frac{360}{120}$ 3
	g. Measurement: How many cups are in a pint? 2 cups
	h. Calculation: $6 \times 6, -6, \div 2, -1, \div 2, \times 8, -1, \div 5$ 11

problem solving
Thomasita was thinking of a number less than 90 that she says when counting by sixes and when counting by fives, but not when counting by fours. Of what number was she thinking? 30

New Concept *Increasing Knowledge*

We can estimate the area of a circle drawn on a grid by counting the number of square units enclosed by the figure.

Example 1

This circle is drawn on a grid.

a. How many units is the radius of the circle?

b. Estimate the area of the circle.

Solution

a. To find the radius of the circle, we may either find the diameter of the circle and divide by 2, or we may locate the center of the circle and count units to the circle. We find that the radius is **3 units.**

Facts
Distribute **Power Up G** to students. See answers below.

Mental Math
Before students begin the Mental Math exercise, do this counting exercise as a class.

Count up and down by 2s between -10 and 10.

Encourage students to share different ways to mentally compute these exercises. Strategies for exercises **b** and **d** are listed below.

b. Add 50 to Each Number
$900 - 220 = 680$
Subtract 50 from Each Number
$800 - 120 = 680$
d. Break Apart $2.50
$(\$2 \div 5) + (50¢ \div 5) = 40¢ + 10¢ = 50¢$
Use a Multiplication Fact
$25 \div 5 = 5; \$2.50 \div 5 = 50¢$

Problem Solving
Refer to **Power-Up Discussion,** p. 447B.

Instruction
Display the **Geometric Formulas** concept poster as you discuss this topic with students.

(continued)

Facts Reduce each fraction to lowest terms.

$\frac{2}{8} = \frac{1}{4}$	$\frac{4}{6} = \frac{2}{3}$	$\frac{6}{10} = \frac{3}{5}$	$\frac{2}{4} = \frac{1}{2}$	$\frac{5}{100} = \frac{1}{20}$	$\frac{9}{12} = \frac{3}{4}$
$\frac{4}{10} = \frac{2}{5}$	$\frac{4}{12} = \frac{1}{3}$	$\frac{2}{10} = \frac{1}{5}$	$\frac{3}{6} = \frac{1}{2}$	$\frac{25}{100} = \frac{1}{4}$	$\frac{3}{12} = \frac{1}{4}$
$\frac{4}{16} = \frac{1}{4}$	$\frac{3}{9} = \frac{1}{3}$	$\frac{6}{9} = \frac{2}{3}$	$\frac{4}{8} = \frac{1}{2}$	$\frac{2}{12} = \frac{1}{6}$	$\frac{6}{12} = \frac{1}{2}$
$\frac{8}{16} = \frac{1}{2}$	$\frac{2}{6} = \frac{1}{3}$	$\frac{8}{12} = \frac{2}{3}$	$\frac{6}{8} = \frac{3}{4}$	$\frac{5}{10} = \frac{1}{2}$	$\frac{75}{100} = \frac{3}{4}$

Example 1
Instruction
Use the transparency of **Investigation Activity 14** Coordinate Plane and an erasable marker to demonstrate how to estimate the area of the circle by counting units.

Draw a circle with a radius of 3 units. Then, mark each square that has about half its area within the circle with a dot so those squares can be counted as half squares. Before you place a dot in a half square, ask the class to confirm that a dot is appropriate. Once you have placed all of the dots, number the whole (or mostly whole) squares 1–24. Then write the following on the board:

$$24 + 8 \left(\tfrac{1}{2}\right) =$$
$$24 + 4 =$$
$$28 \text{ square units}$$

Example 2
Instruction
To reinforce the fact that the estimate found by counting squares is close to the area found by using a formula, point out that the radius of the first circle in example 1, and the radius of the circle in example 2, both have a numerical value of 3. Then point out that the numerical value of the area of the circle in example 2 (28.26) is close to the numerical estimate of the area of the circle in example 1 (28).

(continued)

Thinking Skill
Discuss

What is another way we could count the squares and find the area of the circle? Count the squares outside the circle and subtract them from the area of the square. $36 - 8 = 28$

b. To estimate the area of the circle, we count the square units enclosed by the circle. We show the circle again, this time shading the squares that lie completely or mostly within the circle. We have also marked with dots the squares that have about half their area inside the circle.

We count 24 squares that lie completely or mostly within the circle. We count 8 "half squares." Since $\tfrac{1}{2}$ of 8 is 4, we add 4 square units to 24 square units to get an estimate of **28 square units** for the area of the circle.

Finding the exact area of a circle involves the number π. To find the area of a circle, we first find the area of a square built on the radius of the circle. The circle below has a radius of 10 mm, so the area of the square is 100 mm². Notice that four of these squares would cover more than the area of the circle. However, the area of three of these squares is less than the area of the circle.

The area of the circle is exactly equal to π times the area of one of these squares. To find the area of this circle, we multiply the area of the square by π. We will continue to use 3.14 for the approximation of π.

$$3.14 \times 100 \text{ mm}^2 = 314 \text{ mm}^2$$

The area of the circle is approximately 314 mm².

Example 2

The radius of a circle is 3 cm. What is the area of the circle? (Use 3.14 for π. Round the answer to the nearest square centimeter.)

Solution

We will find the area of a square whose sides equal the radius. Then we multiply that area by 3.14.

Area of square: 3 cm $\times$ 3 cm = 9 cm²

Area of circle: (3.14)(9 cm²) = 28.26 cm²

We round 28.26 cm² to the nearest whole number of square centimeters and find that the area of the circle is approximately **28 cm²**.

English Learners

Write **enclosed** on the board. Refer to solution **b** in example 1 and say,

"When something is enclosed, it is within something or surrounded by something. In example 1, some square units are enclosed by or within the circle."

Ask for students to think of real life situations where someone or something is enclosed.

The area of any circle is π times the area of a square built on a radius of the circle. The following formula uses A for the area of a circle and r for the radius of the circle to relate the area of a circle to its radius:

$$A = \pi r^2$$

Practice Set

a. The radius of this circle is 4 units. Estimate the area of the circle by counting the squares within the circle.   about 50 sq. units

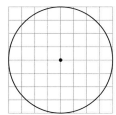

▶ In problems **b–e**, use 3.14 for π.

b. Calculate the area of a circle with a radius of 4 cm.   50.24 cm²

c. Calculate the area of a circle with a radius of 2 feet.   12.56 ft²

d. Calculate the area of a circle with a diameter of 2 feet.   3.14 ft²

e. Calculate the area of a circle with a diameter of 10 inches.   78.5 in.²

Written Practice   *Strengthening Concepts*

1. What is the quotient when the decimal number ten and six tenths is
(49) divided by four hundredths?   265

2. The time in Los Angeles is 3 hours earlier than the time in New York. If it
(32) is 1:15 p.m. in New York, what time is it in Los Angeles?   10:15 a.m.

3. Geraldine paid with a $10 bill for 1 dozen keychains that cost 75¢ each.
(12) How much should she get back in change? $1

▶ * **4.** *Analyze* $32 + 1.8(50)$ 122
(84)

▶ * **5.** *Analyze* If each block has a volume of
(82) one cubic inch, what is the volume of this
tower?   16 in.³

6. *Predict* The ratio of hardbacks to paperbacks in the school library was
(80) 5 to 2. If there were 600 hardbacks, how many paperbacks were there?
240 paperbacks

7. Nate missed three of the 20 questions on the test. What percent of the
(75) questions did he miss?   15%

▶ See Math Conversations in the sidebar.

Instruction

To help students understand the formula for finding the area of a circle, copy the equations and the drawing shown below on the board or overhead.

Area $= \pi \times$ radius squared
$A = \pi r^2$

Practice Set
Problems b–e [Error Alert]

Students should recognize that their answers are approximations, not exact answers, because when π is replaced with 3.14 in the formula $A = \pi r^2$, the value for A is only approximately equal to the area of the circle.

3 Written Practice

Math Conversations

Discussion opportunities are provided below.

Problem 4 *Analyze*

"**What operation is represented by the quantity 1.8 and the quantity 50 in parentheses?**" multiplication

Problem 5 *Analyze*

"**What shape is the tower?**"
rectangular prism

"**What formula is used to find the volume of a rectangular prism?**" $V = lwh$

"**What dimensions represent the length, width, and height of the prism?**"
2 in. by 2 in. by 4 in.

(continued)

Math Conversations

Discussion opportunities are provided below.

Problem 22 Analyze

"What formula is used to find the area of a parallelogram?" $A = bh$

"What formula is used to find the area of a triangle?" $A = \frac{bh}{2}$ or $A = \frac{1}{2}bh$

Problem 25 Connect

An important concept for students to understand is that the cross products of a proportion are equal.

"When two ratios form a proportion, how do the cross products of the proportion compare?" The cross products of a proportion are equal.

Problem 26 Infer

Extend the Problem

"Explain how you could use mental math to estimate the number of complete turns the wheel will make in 1 mile. Then complete your estimate by naming that number of turns." Sample estimates: round 5280 feet to 5000 feet and round 12 feet to 10 feet; round 5280 feet to 4800 feet because 12 is a factor of 48. A reasonable estimate is from 400 to 500 turns.

Errors and Misconceptions

Problem 9a

Remind students who name or record 0.80 as the answer that although the answer is not incorrect, it is customary when working to the right of the decimal point to delete the zero (or zeros) that are to the right of the last significant digit.

Problem 16

The idea that there is only one way to solve a problem of this nature is a misconception. Explain to students (or demonstrate) that multiplying 5 by 30 and dividing the product by 6 produces the same answer as finding $\frac{1}{6}$ of $30 ($30 ÷ 6) and multiplying the quotient by 5. Encourage students to apply this idea as a way to find, then check, a computation.

(continued)

---

8. **Analyze** The credit card company charges 1.5% (0.015) interest on
(41) the unpaid balance each month. If Mr. Jones has an unpaid balance of
$2000, how much interest does he need to pay this month? $30

9. ▸a. Write $\frac{4}{5}$ as a decimal number. 0.8
(74, 75)

 b. Write $\frac{4}{5}$ as a percent. 80%

10. Serena is stuck on a multiple-choice question that has four choices. She
(58) has no idea what the correct answer is, so she just guesses. What is the
probability that her guess is correct? $\frac{1}{4}$

11. $5\frac{1}{2} + 3\frac{7}{8}$ $9\frac{3}{8}$ **12.** $3\frac{1}{4} - \frac{5}{8}$ $2\frac{5}{8}$ **13.** $\left(4\frac{1}{2}\right)\left(\frac{2}{3}\right)$ 3
(59)   (63)   (66)

14. $12\frac{1}{2} \div 100$ $\frac{1}{8}$ **15.** $5 \div 1\frac{1}{2}$ $3\frac{1}{3}$ ▸ **16.** $\frac{5}{6}$ of $30 $25
(68)   (68)   (29)

Find each unknown number:

17. $4.72 + 12 + n = 50.4$ 33.68   **18.** $10 - m = 9.87 $0.13
(43)   (3)

19. $3n = 0.48$ 0.16   **20.** $\frac{w}{8} = \frac{25}{20}$ 10
(45)   (85)

21. **Predict** What are the next three terms in this sequence of perfect
(38) squares?

 1, 4, 9, 16, 25, 36, 49, 64, 81, 100, __121__, __144__, __169__, ...

▸* **22.** **Analyze** This parallelogram is divided into
(71, 79) two congruent triangles.
 a. What is the area of the parallelogram?
 150 cm²
 b. What is the area of each triangle? 75 cm²

10 cm · · · · 12 cm
15 cm

$a = 3.14 r^2$

* **23.** Sydney drew a circle with a radius of 10 cm.
(86) What was the approximate area of the circle?
(Use 3.14 for π.) 314 cm²

10 cm

24. Choose the appropriate unit for the area of a garage. B
(31) **A** square inches   **B** square feet   **C** square miles

25. $\frac{8}{14}$ and $\frac{12}{21}$;
Both ratios reduce to the same fraction, or the cross products are equal.

▸ **25.** **Connect** Which two ratios form a proportion? How do you know?
(83, 85)
 $\frac{9}{12}$ $\frac{8}{14}$ $\frac{12}{21}$ $\frac{20}{36}$

▸ **26.** The wheel of the covered wagon turned around once in about 12 feet.
(86) The diameter of the wheel was about **B**
 A 6 feet   **B** 4 feet   **C** 3 feet   **D** 24 feet

27. Anabel drove her car 348 miles in 6 hours. Divide the distance by the
(81) time to find the average speed of the car. 58 miles/hour

▸ See Math Conversations in the sidebar.

28. *Conclude* The opposite angles of a parallelogram are congruent. The adjacent angles are supplementary. If ∠X measures 110°, then what are the measures of ∠Y and ∠Z?   m∠Y = 70°; m∠Z = 110°
(69, 71)

29. *Estimate* The diameter of each wheel on the lawn mower is 10 inches. How far must the lawn mower be pushed in order for each wheel to complete one full turn? Round the answer to the nearest inch. (Use 3.14 for π.)   31 inches
(47)

➤ **30.** *Connect* The coordinates of three vertices of a parallelogram are (−3, 3), (2, 3), and (4, −1). What are the coordinates of the fourth vertex?   (−1, −1) or (−5, 7) or (9, −1)
(Inv. 7)

Early Finishers
Math and Science

The Great Frigates are large birds with long, slender wings. Frigates are great flyers and have one of the greatest wingspans to weight ratios of all birds. If a 3-pound Great Frigate bird has a wingspan of 6 feet, what would be the approximate wingspan of a 4-pound Great Frigate bird? Assume that the ratio of wingspan to weight is fairly constant.   A 4-pound Great Frigate would have a wingspan of 8 feet.

Lesson 86   451

▶ See Math Conversations in the sidebar.

3 **Written Practice** *(Continued)*

Math Conversations
Discussion opportunities are provided below.

Problem 30 *Connect*
Students will need graph paper to complete this problem.

Explain that there are three possible locations for the fourth vertex. Then challenge students to name all three locations.

Looking Forward

Estimating and calculating the area of circles prepares students for:

- **Lesson 91,** using geometric formulas to calculate area and perimeter.

- **Lesson 118,** estimating the area of shapes.

- **Lesson 120,** finding the volume of cylinders.

• Finding Unknown Factors

Objectives

• Solve a missing factor problem in which the unknown factor is a mixed number.
• Solve a missing factor problem in which the unknown factor is a decimal number.

Lesson Preparation

Materials

• **Power Up D** (in *Instructional Masters*)

Optional

• **Investigation Activity 15** (in *Instructional Masters*) or **graph paper**

Power Up D

Technology Resources

Student eBook Complete student textbook in electronic format.

Resources and Planner CD Assessment, reteaching, and instructional masters, plus a pacing calendar with standards.

Test and Practice Generator CD Create additional practice sheets and custom-made tests.

www.SaxonPublishers.com Visit for more student activities and planning materials.

Inclusion

Adaptations CD Adapted lessons, investigations, practice and assessments.

Meeting Standards

National Council of Teachers of Mathematics (NCTM)

Algebra

AL.2a Develop an initial conceptual understanding of different uses of variables

AL.2c Use symbolic algebra to represent situations and to solve problems, especially those that involve linear relationships

Problem Solving

PS.1c Apply and adapt a variety of appropriate strategies to solve problems

Problem-Solving Strategy: Use Logical Reasoning/ Write an Equation

In his 1859 autobiography, Abraham Lincoln wrote, "Of course when I came of age I did not know much. Still somehow, I could read, write, and cipher to the Rule of Three." Lincoln's words, "to cipher to the rule of three," are what we today call setting up a proportion: "3 is to 12 as 5 is to __." In this book, we use equations to solve proportions like this one: $\frac{3}{12} = \frac{5}{x}$. We find the answer is 20 using both methods.

Cipher to the rule of three the numbers 2, 6, and 7.

(Understand) **Understand the problem.**

"What information are we given?"

To cipher to the rule of three means to find a missing term in a proportion in the form, "A is to B as C is to D," where D is not known.

"What are we asked to do?"

Cipher to the rule of three 2, 6, and 7.

(Plan) **Make a plan.**

"What problem-solving strategy will we use?"

We will *use logical reasoning* and *write an equation*.

(Solve) **Carry out the plan.**

"What is the equation that we need to solve?"

Using 2, 6, and 7, we get $\frac{2}{6} = \frac{7}{x}$.

"What is the relationship of 2 to 6?"

Two is one-third of six (or, when 2 is multiplied by 3 the result is 6).

"What number does 7 have a similar relationship to?"

Seven is one-third of 21.

"What is the missing term of the proportion?" 21

(Check) **Look back.**

"Did we find the answer to the question that was asked?"

Yes. We found that 21 is the result of 2, 6, and 7 ciphered to the rule of three.

"If we write the proportion, does 21 make the proportion a true statement?"

Yes. $\frac{2}{6} = \frac{7}{21}$

• Finding Unknown Factors

1 Power Up

Facts
Distribute **Power Up D** to students. See answers below.

Mental Math
Before students begin the Mental Math exercise, do this counting exercise as a class.

Count up and down by $\frac{1}{8}$s between $\frac{1}{8}$ and 2.

Encourage students to share different ways to mentally compute these exercises. Strategies for exercises **a** and **f** are listed below.

a. Use a Pattern of Products
   $7 \times 7 = 49$; $7 \times 70 = 490$;
   $70 \times 70 = 4900$
   Multiply 7×7, then Add Two Zeros
   $7 \times 7 = 49$; $70 \times 70 = 4900$
f. Double 10×45
   $10 \times 45 = 450$; $450 \times 2 = 900$
   Break Apart 45
   $20(40 + 5) = 800 + 100 = 900$

Problem Solving
Refer to **Power-Up Discussion**, p. 452B.

2 New Concepts

Instruction
To recognize how to solve for an unknown, it may help students to use the generalization that an inverse operation is used to solve for an unknown.

For example, solving for an unknown factor involves division because a factor represents multiplication, and division is the inverse of multiplication.

Example 1
Instruction
"Compare the equation to the division. What part of the equation is equal to the dividend?" the product of the known factor and the unknown factor

"What part of the equation represents the divisor?" the known factor

(continued)

---

facts | Power Up D

mental math
   a. Number Sense: $70 \cdot 70$ 4900
   b. Number Sense: $1000 - 375$ 625
   c. Calculation: $5 \times \$4.99$ $24.95
   d. Number Sense: Double $0.85. $1.70
   e. Decimals: $62.5 \div 100$ 0.625
   f. Number Sense: 20×45 900
   g. Algebra: If $n = 2$, what does $2n$ equal?   4
   h. Calculation: $5 \times 5, -5, \times 5, \div 2, -1, \div 7, \times 3, -1, \div 2$ 10

problem solving
In his 1859 autobiography, Abraham Lincoln wrote, "Of course when I came of age I did not know much. Still somehow, I could read, write, and cipher to the Rule of Three." When Lincoln wrote these words, to "cipher to the rule of three" was what students called setting up a proportion: "3 is to 12 as 5 is to __." In this book we use equations to solve proportions like this one: $\frac{3}{12} = \frac{5}{x}$. We find that the answer is 20 using both methods.
Cipher to the rule of three the numbers 2, 6, and 7.   21

New Concept *Increasing Knowledge*

Since Lesson 4 we have practiced solving unknown factor problems. In this lesson we will solve problems in which the unknown factor is a mixed number or a decimal number. Remember that we can find an unknown factor by dividing the product by the known factor.

Example 1

Solve: $5n = 21$

Solution

Thinking Skill
Verify
Why can we divide the product by the known factor? Multiplication and division are inverse operations.

To find an unknown factor, we divide the product by the known factor.

$$5\overline{)21} \quad \begin{array}{r} 4\frac{1}{5} \\ \hline \end{array}$$
$$\frac{20}{1}$$

$$n = 4\frac{1}{5}$$

Facts | Multiply.

7	4	8	2	0	6	8	5	6	10
$\times 7$	$\times 6$	$\times 1$	$\times 2$	$\times 5$	$\times 3$	$\times 9$	$\times 8$	$\times 2$	$\times 10$
49	24	8	4	0	18	72	40	12	100
9	2	9	7	5	7	6	3	9	5
$\times 4$	$\times 5$	$\times 6$	$\times 3$	$\times 5$	$\times 2$	$\times 8$	$\times 5$	$\times 9$	$\times 4$
36	10	54	21	25	14	48	15	81	20
3	6	8	4	6	8	2	7	5	3
$\times 4$	$\times 5$	$\times 2$	$\times 4$	$\times 7$	$\times 8$	$\times 3$	$\times 4$	$\times 9$	$\times 8$
12	30	16	16	42	64	6	28	45	24
3	7	2	5	3	9	4	0	9	6
$\times 9$	$\times 8$	$\times 4$	$\times 7$	$\times 3$	$\times 7$	$\times 8$	$\times 0$	$\times 2$	$\times 6$
27	56	8	35	9	63	32	0	18	36

Note: We will write the answer as a mixed number unless there are decimal numbers in the problem.

Example 2

Solve: $0.6m = 0.048$

Solution

Thinking Skill

Justify

Write the steps needed to solve example 2.
1. Determine the known factor and the unknown factor.
2. Set up the division and move the decimal one place to the right.
3. Divide and write the answer as a decimal.
4. Multiply to check the answer.

Again, we find the unknown factor by dividing the product by the known factor. Since there are decimal numbers in the problem, we write our answer as a decimal number.

$$06.\overline{)00.48} \quad \begin{array}{r} 0.08 \\ \underline{48} \\ 0 \end{array}$$

$$m = \mathbf{0.08}$$

Example 3

Solve: $45 = 4x$

Solution

This problem might seem "backward" because the multiplication is on the right-hand side. However, an equal sign is not directional. It simply states that the quantities on either side of the sign are equal. In this case, the product is 45 and the known factor is 4. We divide 45 by 4 to find the unknown factor.

$$4\overline{)45} \quad \begin{array}{r} 11\frac{1}{4} \\ \underline{4} \\ 05 \\ \underline{4} \\ 1 \end{array}$$

$$x = \mathbf{11\frac{1}{4}}$$

Practice Set

Solve:

   a. $6w = 21$ $3\frac{1}{2}$ ▸   **b.** $50 = 3f$ $16\frac{2}{3}$ **c.** $5n = 36$ $7\frac{1}{5}$

▸   **d.** $0.3t = 0.24$ 0.8   **e.** $8m = 3.2$ 0.4   ▸   **f.** $0.8 = 0.5x$ 1.6

Written Practice   *Strengthening Concepts*

1. If the divisor is 12 and the quotient is 24, what is the dividend?   288
(4)

2. The brachiosaurus, one of the largest dinosaurs, weighed only $\frac{1}{4}$ as much as a blue whale. A blue whale can weigh 140 tons. How much could a brachiosaurus have weighed?   35 tons
(29)

3. *Analyze* Fourteen of the 32 students in the class are boys. What is the ratio of boys to girls in the class? $\frac{7}{9}$
(23)

Find each unknown number:

  * 4. $0.3m = 0.27$ 0.9   *** 5.** $31 = 5n$ $6\frac{1}{5}$
    (87)   (87)

▸ *** 6.** *Analyze* $3n = 6^2$ 12   *** 7.** $4n = 0.35$ 0.0875
    (38)   (87)

▸ See Math Conversations in the sidebar.

Math Background

In this lesson, students learn that an unknown factor, or a variable, can appear on either side of an equation.

In their future work with equations, students will learn to solve for a variable that appears on both sides of an equation. For example, students will solve an equation such as $3 + b = 2b - 9$ for b.

To solve the equation, students will subtract b from both sides of the equation and add 9 to both sides of the equation. The solution $b = 12$ will be the result of applying the inverse operations of subtract b and add 9.

---

2   New Concepts (Continued)

Example 2
Instruction

"What operation does the term 0.6m represent? Explain why."
Multiplication; 0.6 and m are factors

"To solve for an unknown factor, we divide the product by the known factor. In this equation, which number represents the product?" 0.048

"Which number in the equation represents the known factor?" 0.6

Remind students to always place a decimal point in the quotient of a decimal dividend.

Example 3
Instruction

Students should recognize that an unknown may appear on either side of an equation, and conclude that the steps to follow for finding the value of the unknown do not change.

Practice Set
Problem b   Error Alert

Students will have difficulty writing the quotient as a decimal number because the division produces a repeating decimal. Remind students that decimal quotients are only written when the dividend is a decimal number.

Problems d and f   Error Alert

Watch for students who do not change each divisor to a whole number.

---

3   Written Practice

Math Conversations
Discussion opportunities are provided below.

Problem 6   Analyze
"How must we simplify this equation before we can solve for n?" rewrite 6^2 as 36

(continued)

Math Conversations

Discussion opportunities are provided below.

Problem 18 [Analyze]

Extend the Problem

"How does the total surface area of the visible faces compare to the total surface area of the faces that are not visible? Explain your answer." The areas are equal; the opposite faces of a rectangular prism are congruent.

Errors and Misconceptions

Problem 19

An answer of 210 represents rewriting $2a$ as 215 after substituting 15 for a.

To help students recognize that $2a$ represents two factors, rewrite the expression $2a - 15$ on the board or overhead as shown below.

$$(2)(a) - 5$$

Invite a student to the board or overhead to make the substitution $a = 15$, and then complete the arithmetic.

$$(2)(15) - 5 = 30 - 5 = 25$$

(continued)

---

8. Write 0.25 as a fraction and add it to $3\frac{1}{4}$. What is the sum? $3\frac{1}{2}$
(73)

9. Write $\frac{3}{5}$ as a decimal and add it to 6.5. What is the sum?   7.1
(74)

10. Write $\frac{1}{50}$ as a decimal number and as a percent.   0.02; 2%
(74, 75)

11. $12\frac{1}{5} - 3\frac{4}{5}$ $8\frac{2}{5}$ **12.** $6\frac{2}{3} \times 1\frac{1}{5}$ 8   **13.** $11\frac{1}{9} \div 100$ $\frac{1}{9}$
(63)   (66)   (68)

14. $4.75 + 12.6 + 10$ 27.35   *** 15.** $35 - (0.35 \times 100)$ 0
(38)   (84)

* 16. $4 + 4 \times 4 - 4 \div 4$ 19
(85)

17. Write the decimal numeral twelve and five hundredths.   12.05
(35)

▶*** 18.** Find the volume of this rectangular
(82)   prism.   250 in.³

5 in.
5 in.
10 in.

▶ **19.** [Evaluate] If a equals 15, then what number does $2a - 5$ equal?   25
(47)

20. What is the area of this parallelogram?
(71)   450 mm²

18 mm   20 mm
25 mm

21. What is the perimeter of this parallelogram?   90 mm
(8)

22. [Verify] "All rectangles are parallelograms." True or false?   true
(64)

* 23. Charles spent $\frac{1}{10}$ of his 100 shillings. How many shillings does he still
(77)   have?   90 shillings

24. The temperature rose from $-18°F$ to $19°F$. How many degrees did the
(14)   temperature increase?   37°F

25. How many **centimeters** long is the line below?   4 cm
(7)

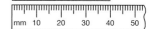
mm 10   20   30   40   50

26. Johann poured 500 mL of water from a full 2-liter container. How many
(78)   milliliters of water were left in the container?   1500 mL

27. Name this geometric solid.   triangular prism
(Inv. 8)

* 28. Simplify:
(81)
   a. 2 meters + 100 centimeters (Write the answer in meters.)   3 meters

   b. $2\,m \cdot 4\,m$ 8 m²

▶ See Math Conversations in the sidebar.

▶* **29.** *Analyze* Solve this proportion: $\frac{12}{m} = \frac{18}{9}$ 6
(84)

30. *Connect* What is the perimeter of a rectangle with vertices at $(-4, -4)$,
(Inv. 7) $(-4, 4)$, $(4, 4)$, and $(4, -4)$?   32 units

Early Finishers
Real-World Application

Frida and her family went on a summer vacation to Chicago, Illinois from Boston, Massachusetts. Her family drove 986 miles in 17 hours.

  a. How many miles per hour did Frida's family average on their drive to Chicago? $986 \div 17 = 58$ miles per hour

  b. If the family's car averages 29 miles per gallon, how many gallons of gas did they use on their trip? $986 \div 29 = 34$ gallons

Lesson 87   455

▶ See Math Conversations in the sidebar.

3 **Written Practice** (Continued)

Math Conversations

Discussion opportunities are provided below.

Problem 29 *Analyze*

"Name the factors of the cross products in this proportion." 12 and 9, 18 and m

"What relationship do the cross products of any proportion share?" the cross products are equal

"What equation may we solve to learn the value of m?" $18m = 108$ or $m = \frac{108}{18}$

Looking Forward

Finding missing factors prepares students for:

• **Lesson 106,** solving two-step equations.

Using Proportions to Solve Ratio Word Problems

Objectives
• Use proportions to solve ratio problems.

Lesson Preparation

Materials
• **Power Up L** (in *Instructional Masters*)
• **Investigation Activity 15** (in *Instructional Masters*) or **graph paper**
• **Manipulative kit: inch rulers**

Math Language

English Learners (ESL)
accumulation

Technology Resources

Student eBook Complete student textbook in electronic format.

Resources and Planner CD Assessment, reteaching, and instructional masters, plus a pacing calendar with standards.

Test and Practice Generator CD Create additional practice sheets and custom-made tests.

www.SaxonPublishers.com Visit for more student activities and planning materials.

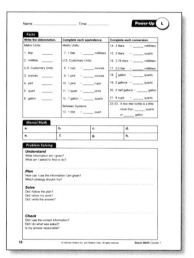

Power Up L

Investigation Activity 15

Inclusion

Adaptations CD Adapted lessons, investigations, practice and assessments.

Meeting Standards

National Council of Teachers of Mathematics (NCTM)

Numbers and Operations

NO.1d Understand and use ratios and proportions to represent quantitative relationships

NO.3d Develop, analyze, and explain methods for solving problems involving proportions, such as scaling and finding equivalent ratios

Problem Solving

PS.1b Solve problems that arise in mathematics and in other contexts

Communication

CM.3b Communicate their mathematical thinking coherently and clearly to peers, teachers, and others

CM.3d Use the language of mathematics to express mathematical ideas precisely

Problem-Solving Strategy: Make It Simpler/ Use Logical Reasoning

Kim hit a target like the one shown 6 times, earning a total score of 20. Find two sets of scores Kim could have earned.

(Understand) **Understand the problem.**

"What information are we given?"

Kim hit the shown target 6 times. She earned a total score of 20.

"What are we asked to do?"

Find two sets of scores Kim could have earned.

(Plan) **Make a plan.**

"What problem-solving strategy will we use?"

We can *make a simpler, but similar problem* by *using logical reasoning* to reduce the search.

(Solve) **Carry out the plan.**

"Can Kim earn a score of 20 in six hits without hitting 7?"

No, because 6 × 3 is only 18.

"If two of Kim's hits are 7, then what do the other four hits total? What combinations equal this total?"

Two 7s is 14, so the other four hits total 6. The only combination of four that total 6 is 3 + 1 + 1 + 1.

"If one of Kim's hits is 7, then what do the other five hits total? What combinations equal this total?"

Five hits total 13. The only combination is 3 + 3 + 3 + 3 + 1.

"What two combinations of six hits total 20?"

7 + 7 + 3 + 1 + 1 + 1 and 7 + 3 + 3 + 3 + 3 + 1

(Check) **Look back.**

"Did we answer the question that was asked?"

Yes. We found that we can form 20 in 6 hits in two different ways.
7 + 7 + 3 + 1 + 1 + 1 = 20 and 7 + 3 + 3 + 3 + 3 + 1 = 20.

Power Up

Facts

Distribute **Power Up L** to students. See answers below.

Mental Math

Before students begin the Mental Math exercise, do this counting exercise as a class.

Count up and down by 25s between −150 and 150.

Encourage students to share different ways to mentally compute these exercises. Strategies for exercises **d** and **f** are listed below.

d. Shift the Decimal Point
$5.00 ÷ 10 = $0.500 = $0.50

Divide $1 by 10, then Multiply by 5
$5(\$1 ÷ 10) = 5(10¢) = 50¢$

f. Cancel Zeros
$$\frac{750}{250} = \frac{75\cancel{0}}{25\cancel{0}} = \frac{75}{25} = 3$$

Use a Multiplication Fact
$75 ÷ 25 = 3$, so $750 ÷ 250 = 3$

Problem Solving

Refer to **Power-Up Discussion**, p. 456B.

2 New Concepts

Instruction

Before discussing the example, remind students that order is a very important part of reading and writing ratios and proportions.

Example 1
Instruction

As you discuss the ratio box, ask students to describe how the order of the numbers in the ratio box represents the order of the numbers in the problem.

(continued)

LESSON 88

• Using Proportions to Solve Ratio Word Problems

facts	Power Up L
mental math	**a. Number Sense:** 80 · 80 6400
	b. Number Sense: 720 − 150 570
	c. Calculation: $1.98 + $1.98 $3.96
	d. Fractional Parts: $\frac{1}{10}$ of $5.00 $0.50
	e. Decimals: 0.15 × 100 15
	f. Number Sense: $\frac{750}{250}$ 3
	g. Measurement: How many milliliters are in 5 liters? 5000 mL
	h. Calculation: 4 × 4, − 1, × 2, + 3, ÷ 3, − 1, × 10, − 1, ÷ 9 11

problem solving	Kim hit a target like the one shown 6 times, earning a total score of 20. Find two sets of scores Kim could have earned. 1, 3, 3, 3, 3, and 7; or 1, 1, 1, 3, 7, 7

New Concept   *Increasing Knowledge*

Proportions can be used to solve many types of word problems. In this lesson we will use proportions to solve ratio word problems such as those in the following examples.

Example 1

The ratio of salamanders to frogs was 5 to 7. If there were 20 salamanders, how many frogs were there?

Solution

In this problem there are two kinds of numbers: ratio numbers and actual-count numbers. The ratio numbers are 5 and 7. The number 20 is an actual count of the salamanders. We will arrange these numbers in two columns and two rows to form a ratio box.

	Ratio	Actual Count
Salamanders	5	20
Frogs	7	f

Facts

Write the abbreviation.	Complete each equivalence.	Complete each conversion.
Metric Units:	Metric Units:	14. 2 liters = __2000__ milliliters
1. liter __L__	7. 1 liter = __1000__ milliliters	15. 2 liters ≈ __2__ quarts
2. milliliter __mL__	U.S. Customary Units:	16. 3.78 liters = __3780__ milliliters
U.S. Customary Units:	8. 1 cup = __8__ ounces	17. 0.5 liter = __500__ milliliters
3. ounces __oz__	9. 1 pint = __16__ ounces	18. $\frac{1}{2}$ gallon = __2__ quarts
4. pint __pt__	10. 1 pint = __2__ cups	19. 2 gallons = __8__ quarts
5. quart __qt__	11. 1 quart = __2__ pints	20. 2 half gallons = __1__ gallon
6. gallon __gal__	12. 1 gallon = __4__ quarts	21. 8 cups = __2__ quarts
	Between Systems:	22–23. A two-liter bottle is a little more than __2__ quarts
	13. 1 liter ≈ __1__ quart	or __$\frac{1}{2}$__ gallon.

We were not given the actual count of frogs, so we use the letter f to stand for the actual number of frogs.

Instead of using scale factors in this lesson, we will practice using proportions. We use the positions of numbers in the ratio box to write a proportion. By solving the proportion, we find the actual number of frogs.

	Ratio	Actual Count
Salamanders	5	20
Frogs	7	f

$\longrightarrow \dfrac{5}{7} = \dfrac{20}{f}$

We can solve the proportion in two ways. We can multiply $\frac{5}{7}$ by $\frac{4}{4}$, or we can use cross products. Here we show the solution using cross products:

$$\frac{5}{7} = \frac{20}{f}$$

$$5f = 7 \cdot 20$$

$$5f = \frac{7 \cdot 20}{5}$$

$$f = 28$$

We find that there were **28 frogs.**

Thinking Skill

Justify

What steps do we follow to find the value of f? Use cross products to form an equation. Then divide both sides of the equation by 5.

Example 2

If 3 sacks of concrete will make 12 square feet of sidewalk, predict how many sacks of concrete are needed to make 40 square feet of sidewalk?

Solution

Thinking Skill

Discuss

Two methods for solving proportions are using cross products and using a constant factor. Under what circumstance is one method preferable to the other? See student work.

We are given the ratio 3 sacks to 12 square feet and the actual count of square feet of sidewalk needed.

	Ratio	Actual Count
Sacks	3	n
Sq. ft	12	40

$\longrightarrow \dfrac{3}{12} = \dfrac{n}{40}$

The constant factor from the first ratio to the second is not obvious, so we use cross products.

$$\frac{3}{12} = \frac{n}{40}$$

$$12 \cdot n = 3 \cdot 40$$

$$n = \frac{3 \cdot 40}{12}$$

$$n = 10$$

We find that **10 sacks** of concrete are needed.

2 New Concepts (Continued)

Example 1

Instruction

"One way to solve for f is to multiply $\frac{5}{7}$ by $\frac{4}{4}$. Why is $\frac{5}{7}$ multiplied by $\frac{4}{4}$?" Multiplying by $\frac{4}{4}$ forms a fraction that is equivalent to $\frac{5}{7}$ and has a numerator of 20.

"5f and 7 · 20 are the cross products of the proportion. What relationship do the cross products of any proportion share?" the cross products are equal

Example 2

Instruction

Have students recall that one way to solve a proportion problem is to use a constant factor. For example, write $\frac{1}{2} = \frac{n}{10}$ on the board or overhead and ask students to name the constant factor. 5

Point out that for some problems, the constant factor is not obvious. In example 2, have students note that the constant factor is not easy to name. However if the ratio $\frac{3}{12}$ is reduced to $\frac{1}{4}$, then the constant factor is evident.

(continued)

2 New Concepts (Continued)

Practice Set

Problems a and b [Error Alert]

Students have learned two ways (using a constant factor and using a ratio box) to solve proportion problems. For problems **a** and **b**, ask students to solve the problems using a ratio box and check their work using a constant factor.

3 Written Practice

Math Conversations

Discussion opportunities are provided below.

Problem 2 Analyze

Extend the Problem

"It is sometimes said that 1 inch of rain is equivalent to 10 inches of snow. If that's true, what is the equivalent rainfall for 4 inches of snow?" 0.4 in. or $\frac{4}{10}$ in.

Problem 4 Analyze

"Which measure of the triangle represents its height? Explain why." 8 mm; Sample explanation: The height of a triangle must be perpendicular to its base.

Problem 5 Model

"Explain how the idea of 'order' is important in this problem." Sample: The order of the numbers in the ratio box must be the same as the order of the numbers in the problem.

(continued)

Practice Set [Model] For each problem, draw a ratio box. Then solve the problem using proportions.

a.

	Ratio	A.C.
DVDs	5	d
CDs	4	60

▶ **a.** The ratio of DVDs to CDs was 5 to 4. If there were 60 CDs, how many DVDs were there?   75 DVDs

b.

	Ratio	A.C.
Home	5	30
Away	3	a

▶ **b.** [Explain] At the softball game, the ratio of fans for the home team to the fans for the away team is 5 to 3. If there are 30 fans for the home team, how many fans for the away team are there? How can you check your answer?   18 fans; by multiplying $\frac{5}{3}$ by $\frac{6}{6}$

Written Practice   *Strengthening Concepts*

1. Mavis scored 12 of the team's 20 points. What percent of the team's points did Mavis score?   60%
(75)

▶ **2.** One fourth of an inch of snow fell every hour during the storm. How many hours did the storm last if the total accumulation of snow was 4 inches?   16 hours
(50)

* **3.** Eamon wants to buy a new baseball glove that costs $50. He has $14 and he earns $6 per hour cleaning yards. How many hours must he work to have enough money to buy the glove?   6 hours
(87)

▶ * **4.** Analyze Find the area of this triangle.   64 mm²
(79)

5.

	Ratio	A.C.
Adults	3	a
Students	5	15

$\frac{3}{5} = \frac{a}{15}$

▶ * **5.** [Model] Draw a ratio box for this problem. Then solve the problem using a proportion.
(88)

The ratio of adults to students on the field trip is 3 to 5. If there are 15 students on the field trip, how many adults are there?   9 adults

* **6.** What is the volume of this rectangular prism?   480 in.³
(82)

Find each unknown factor:

* **7.** $10w = 25$ $2\frac{1}{2}$
(87)

* **8.** $20 = 9m$ $2\frac{2}{9}$
(87)

* **9.** **a.** What is the perimeter of this triangle?   24 in.
(8, 79)
b. What is the area of this triangle?   24 in.²

10. Write 5% as a
(33, 75)
a. decimal number.   0.05   **b.** fraction. $\frac{1}{20}$

11. Write $\frac{2}{5}$ as a decimal, and multiply it by 2.5. What is the product?   1
(74)

▶ See Math Conversations in the sidebar.

English Learners

Refer students to problem 2. Explain the meaning of **accumulation**. Say,

"An accumulation of snow is a large amount of snow."

Ask volunteers to give examples of things they might accumulate. (money, knowledge, friends)

12. Compare: $\frac{2}{3} + \frac{3}{2}$ $\frac{2}{3} \cdot \frac{3}{2}$
(29, 56)

13. $\frac{1}{3} \times \frac{100}{1}$ $33\frac{1}{3}$
(70)

14. $6 \div 1\frac{1}{2}$ 4
(68)

15. $12 \div 0.25$ 48
(49)

16. 0.025×100 2.5
(46)

17. If the tax rate is 7%, what is the tax on a $24.90 purchase? $1.74
(41)

18. The prime factorization of what number is $2^2 \cdot 3^2 \cdot 5^2$?   900
(73)

▶ **19.** (Classify) Which of these is a composite number?   C
(65)

    A 61   **B** 71   **C** 81   **D** 101

20. Round the decimal number one and twenty-three hundredths to the
(51) nearest tenth.   1.2

21. Albert baked 5 dozen muffins and gave away $\frac{7}{12}$ of them. How many
(77) muffins were left?   25 muffins

✗ **22.** $6 \times 3 - 6 \div 3$ 16
(84)

▶ **23.** How many milliliters is 4 liters?   4000 milliliters
(78)

24. (Model) Draw a line segment $2\frac{1}{4}$ inches long. Label the endpoints A and
(69) C. Then make a dot at the midpoint of $\overline{AC}$ (the point halfway between points A and C), and label the dot B. What are the lengths of $\overline{AB}$ and $\overline{BC}$?   See student work. $AB = BC = 1\frac{1}{8}$ in.

25. On a coordinate plane draw a rectangle with vertices at $(-2, -2)$, $(4, -2)$,
(Inv. 7) $(4, 2)$, and $(-2, 2)$. What is the area of the rectangle?   24 sq. units

26. What is the ratio of the length to the width of the rectangle in
(23) problem 25? $\frac{3}{2}$

* **27.** (Explain) How do you calculate the area of a triangle?   Sample: Multiply
(79) the base by the height of the triangle and then divide the product by 2.

28. In the figure at right, angles ADB and BDC
(69) are supplementary.

    a. What is m$\angle ADB$?   135°

    b. What is the ratio of m$\angle BDC$ to m$\angle ADB$? Write the answer as a reduced fraction. $\frac{1}{3}$

✗ **29.** (Analyze) Nathan drew a circle with a radius
(86) of 10 cm. Then he drew a square around the circle.

    a. What was the area of the square?   400 cm²

    b. What was the area of the circle? (Use 3.14 for π.)   314 cm²

* **30.** (Formulate) Write a word problem that can be solved using the proportion
(85) $\frac{6}{8} = \frac{w}{100}$. Solve the problem.   See student work; 75

Lesson 88   459

▶ See Math Conversations in the sidebar.

---

3 Written Practice (Continued)

Math Conversations

Discussion opportunities are provided below.

Problem 19   Classify

"How is a composite number different than a prime number?" Sample: A prime number has exactly two factors; a composite number has three or more factors.

"What characteristic do both prime numbers and composite numbers share?" Sample: Both are whole numbers or counting numbers that are greater than 1.

Problem 29   Analyze

"Use mental math to estimate the area of the square that is outside the circle." A reasonable estimate is 400 cm² − 314 cm² or about 86 cm².

Errors and Misconceptions

Problem 22

Watch for students who do not apply the Order of Operations in this way:

Step 1: 6×3
Step 2: $6 \div 3$
Step 3: $18 - 2$

Problem 23

When changing from one measurement unit to another, students sometimes multiply when they should divide and divide when they should multiply.

Encourage students to become familiar with the following generalizations, and record them for future reference.

- To change from a smaller unit to a larger unit, divide.
- To change from a larger unit to a smaller unit, multiply.

Looking Forward

Solving ratio problems using ratio boxes and proportions prepares students for:

- **Lesson 101,** using proportions and ratio boxes to solve ratio problems involving totals.

- **Lesson 105,** using proportions and ratio boxes to solve percent problems.

- **Lesson 106,** solving two-step equations.

• Estimating Square Roots

Objectives

- Find the square root of a perfect square greater than 100.
- Use guess and check to estimate the square roots of numbers that are not perfect squares.
- Use a calculator to approximate the square root of a number.

Lesson Preparation

Materials

- **Power Up K** (in *Instructional Masters*)
- **Teacher-provided material:** calculators

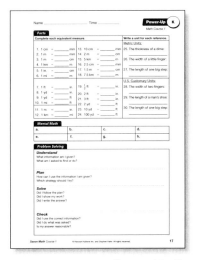

Power Up K

Math Language

New	English Learners (ESL)
irrational numbers	hint

Technology Resources

Student eBook Complete student textbook in electronic format.

Resources and Planner CD Assessment, reteaching, and instructional masters, plus a pacing calendar with standards.

Test and Practice Generator CD Create additional practice sheets and custom-made tests.

www.SaxonPublishers.com Visit for more student activities and planning materials.

Inclusion

Adaptations CD Adapted lessons, investigations, practice and assessments.

Meeting Standards

National Council of Teachers of Mathematics (NCTM)

Numbers and Operations

NO.2c Understand and use the inverse relationships of addition and subtraction, multiplication and division, and squaring and finding square roots to simplify computations and solve problems

NO.3a Select appropriate methods and tools for computing with fractions and decimals from among mental computation, estimation, calculators or computers, and paper and pencil, depending on the situation, and apply the selected methods

NO.3c Develop and use strategies to estimate the results of rational-number computations and judge the reasonableness of the results

Problem-Solving Strategy: Draw a Diagram/
Use Logical Reasoning

A loop of string was arranged to form a square with sides 9 inches long. If the same loop of string is arranged to form an equilateral triangle, how long will each side be? If a regular hexagon is formed, how long will each side be?

(Understand) **Understand the problem.**

"What important information are we given?"

A square formed by a loop of string has sides that are 9 inches long.

"What are we asked to do?"

We are asked to figure out how long each side of an equilateral triangle and a regular hexagon would be if the same loop of string is arranged to form these shapes.

(Plan) **Make a plan.**

"What problem-solving strategy will we use?"

We will *use logical reasoning* and if needed, we will *draw a diagram.*

(Solve) **Carry out the plan.**

"What do we know about the square?"

We know that the sides are each 9 inches.

"What does that tell us about the length of the string forming the loop?"

We can figure out that the perimeter of the square is 36 inches and that means that the length of the string must be 36 inches.

"How can we use that information to figure out the lengths of the sides of an equilateral triangle with the same perimeter?"

The equilateral triangle has 3 equal sides and the perimeter is 36 inches. Therefore, each side must be $36 \div 3$ or 12 inches in length.

"What is the length of each side of a regular hexagon?"

A regular hexagon has 6 sides of equal length. If the perimeter is 36 inches, we know that each side must be $36 \div 6$ or 6 inches.

(Check) **Look back.**

"Did we answer the question that was asked?"

Yes. We found the length of each side of an equilateral triangle and a regular hexagon made from the same loop of string used to form a square with 9-inch sides. Since all of them have perimeters of 36, we know that we have solved it correctly.

Facts
Distribute **Power Up K** to students. See answers below.

Mental Math
Before students begin the Mental Math exercise, do this counting exercise as a class.

Count up and down by 3s between −15 and 15.

Encourage students to share different ways to mentally compute these exercises. Strategies for exercises **b** and **d** are listed below.

b. Subtract 400, then Subtract 5
$1000 − 400 = 600; 600 − 5 = 595$

Count Back by 100's, then by 5
Start with 1000. Count: 900, 800, 700, 600
Start with 600. Count: 595

d. Double $25 and Double $2
$(\$25 \times 2) + (\$2 \times 2) = \$50 + \$4 = \$54$

Double Place Values
$(\$20 \times 2) + (\$7 \times 2) = \$40 + \$14 = \$54$

Problem Solving
Refer to **Power-Up Discussion**, p. 460B.

2 New Concepts

Instruction
Review finding square roots of perfect squares from 1 to 100 with students. Remind them that the square root of a perfect square is found by finding the positive number that, when multiplied by itself, equals the perfect square. Write $\sqrt{1}$, $\sqrt{4}$, $\sqrt{9}$, $\sqrt{16}$, $\sqrt{25}$, $\sqrt{36}$, $\sqrt{49}$, $\sqrt{64}$, $\sqrt{81}$, and $\sqrt{100}$ on the board and have volunteers name each square root. 1, 2, 3, 4, 5, 6, 7, 8, 9, and 10

Example 1
Instruction
Remind students that the product 20×20 can be found by adding two zeros to the product 2×2.

(continued)

LESSON
89
• Estimating Square Roots

Power Up   *Building Power*

facts | Power Up K

mental math

a. **Number Sense:** $90 \cdot 90$ 8100
b. **Number Sense:** $1000 − 405$ 595
c. **Calculation:** $6 \times \$7.99$ $47.94
d. **Number Sense:** Double $27.00 $54.00
e. **Decimals:** $87.5 \div 100$ 0.875
f. **Number Sense:** 20×36 720
g. **Geometry:** A rectangular solid is 5 in. $\times$ 3 in. $\times$ 3 in. What is the volume of the solid?   45 cubic inches
h. **Calculation:** $3 \times 3, + 2, \times 5, − 5, \times 2, \div 10, + 5, \div 5$ 3

problem solving | A loop of string was arranged to form a square with sides 9 inches long. If the same loop of string is arranged to form an equilateral triangle, how long will each side be? If a regular hexagon is formed, how long will each side be?   12 in.; 6 in.

New Concept   *Increasing Knowledge*

We have practiced finding square roots of perfect squares from 1 to 100. In this lesson we will find the square roots of perfect squares greater than 100. We will also use a guess-and-check method to estimate the square roots of numbers that are not perfect squares. As we practice, our guesses will improve and we will begin to see clues to help us estimate.

Example 1
Simplify: $\sqrt{400}$

Solution
We need to find a number that, when multiplied by itself, has a product of 400.

$$\square \times \square = 400$$

We know that $\sqrt{400}$ is more than 10, because 10×10 equals 100. We also know that $\sqrt{400}$ is much less than 100, because 100×100 equals 10,000. Since $\sqrt{4}$ equals 2, the 4 in $\sqrt{400}$ hints that we should try 20.

$$20 \times 20 = 400$$

We find that $\sqrt{400}$ equals **20**.

Facts

Complete each equivalent measure.					Write a unit for each reference.
					Metric Units:
1. 1 cm	= 10 mm	13. 10 cm	= 100 mm		25. The thickness of a dime: millimeter
2. 1 m	= 1000 mm	14. 2 m	= 200 cm		
3. 1 m	= 100 cm	15. 5 km	= 5000 m		26. The width of a little finger: centimeter
4. 1 km	= 1000 m	16. 2.5 cm	= 25 mm		
5. 1 in.	= 2.54 cm	17. 1.5 m	= 150 cm		27. The length of one big step: meter
6. 1 mi	≈ 1610 m	18. 7.5 km	= 7500 m		
					U.S. Customary Units:
7. 1 ft	= 12 in.	19. $\frac{1}{2}$ ft	= 6 in.		28. The width of two fingers: inch
8. 1 yd	= 36 in.	20. 2 ft	= 24 in.		
9. 1 yd	= 3 ft	21. 3 ft	= 36 in.		29. The length of a man's shoe: foot
10. 1 mi	= 5280 ft	22. 2 yd	= 6 ft		
11. 1 m	≈ 39 in.	23. 10 yd	= 30 ft		30. The length of one big step: yard
12. 1 km	≈ 0.62 mi	24. 100 yd	= 300 ft		

Example 2

Simplify: $\sqrt{625}$

Solution

In example 1 we found that $\sqrt{400}$ equals 20. Since $\sqrt{625}$ is greater than $\sqrt{400}$, we know that $\sqrt{625}$ is greater than 20. We find that $\sqrt{625}$ is less than 30, because 30×30 equals 900. Since the last digit is 5, perhaps $\sqrt{625}$ is 25. We multiply to find out.

$$
\begin{array}{r}
25 \\
\times\ 25 \\
\hline
125 \\
50 \\
\hline
625 \\
\end{array}
$$

We find that $\sqrt{625}$ equals **25.**

We have practiced finding the square roots of numbers that are perfect squares. Now we will practice estimating the square root of numbers that are not perfect squares.

Example 3

Math Language
Consecutive whole numbers are two numbers we count in sequence, such as 4 and 5, or 15 and 16.

Between which two consecutive whole numbers is $\sqrt{20}$?

Solution

Notice that we are not asked to find the square root of 20. To find the whole numbers on either side of $\sqrt{20}$, we can first think of the perfect squares that are on either side of 20. Here we show the first few perfect squares, starting with 1.

$$1, 4, 9, 16, 25, 36, 49$$

We see that 20 is between the perfect squares 16 and 25. So $\sqrt{20}$ is between $\sqrt{16}$, and $\sqrt{25}$.

$$\sqrt{16}, \sqrt{20}, \sqrt{25}$$

Since $\sqrt{16}$ is 4 and $\sqrt{25}$ is 5, we see that $\sqrt{20}$ is between **4** and **5.**

$$
\begin{array}{ccc}
\sqrt{16} & \sqrt{20} & \sqrt{25} \\
\vert & & \vert \\
4 & & 5
\end{array}
$$

Using the reasoning in example 3, we know there must be some number between 4 and 5 that is the square root of 20. We try 4.5.

$$4.5 \times 4.5 = 20.25$$

We see that 4.5 is too large, so we try 4.4.

$$4.4 \times 4.4 = 19.36$$

We see that 4.4 is too small. So $\sqrt{20}$ is greater than 4.4 but less than 4.5. (It is closer to 4.5.) If we continued this process, we would never find a decimal number or fraction that exactly equals $\sqrt{20}$. This is because $\sqrt{20}$ belongs to a number family called the **irrational numbers.**

2 New Concepts (Continued)

Example 2
Instruction
To provide additional practice, you might choose to write these square roots on the board or overhead.

$$
\begin{array}{ll}
\sqrt{144} & 12 \\
\sqrt{441} & 21 \\
\sqrt{196} & 14 \\
\sqrt{324} & 18 \\
\end{array}
$$

Example 3
Instruction
Point out that the square root of 20.25 is 4.5 ($\sqrt{20.25} = 4.5$), and the square root of 19.36 is 4.4 ($\sqrt{19.36} = 4.4$).

(continued)

Math Background

Irrational numbers are numbers that cannot be expressed as a ratio of two integers. A number that contains an infinite number of decimal places with nonrepeating digits, such as pi (π), is an irrational number. Square roots of whole numbers that are not perfect squares, such as $\sqrt{21}$ and $\sqrt{150}$ are also irrational numbers.

Square roots of decimal numbers may or may not be irrational. For example, $\sqrt{2.25}$ is not irrational because it can be expressed as 1.5, a decimal that ends ($1.5 \times 1.5 = 2.25$). The square root of 22.5, however, cannot be expressed as a decimal that ends or repeats. So, $\sqrt{22.5}$ is an irrational number.

English Learners

Refer students to example 1. Write the word **hint** on the board. Ask the students if they know the meaning of the word. Say,

"To hint at something means to give a clue or suggestion that includes additional information to help solve a problem."

Ask students to think of clues that help them solve problems in today's lesson.

Practice Set

Problems a–c [Error Alert]

Ask students to explain the reasoning they used to find each square root.

Problems j–l [Error Alert]

To round to two decimal places, or the hundredths place, students must consider the digit in the place to the right of the hundredths place, the thousandths place.

Ask students to describe how the digit in the hundredths place changes if the digit in the thousandths place is 4 or less, or if the digit is 5 or more. 4 or less: the digit in the hundredths place does not change; 5 or more: the digit in the hundredths place is increased by 1.

To write a number rounded to two decimal places, remind students to write only two digits to the right of the decimal point.

3 **Written Practice**

Math Conversations

Discussion opportunities are provided below.

Problem 3 [Analyze]

Extend the Problem

"Doubling a fraction and finding $\frac{1}{2}$ of a fraction both involve multiplication, but doubling a fraction produces a different answer than finding $\frac{1}{2}$ of a fraction. Explain why." Sample: Doubling a fraction is the same as multiplying the numerator of a fraction by 2. Finding $\frac{1}{2}$ of a fraction is the same as multiplying the denominator of the fraction by 2.

Problem 4 [Model]

"Explain how we can use a constant factor to check our answer." Compare 9 and 18 to learn that the constant factor is 2. Then find the product of 2 and 2 and compare the product to the answer found using a ratio box.

(continued)

Reading Math

Recall that the wavy equal sign means "is approximately equal to."

Irrational numbers cannot be expressed exactly as a ratio (that is, as a fraction or decimal). We can only use fractions or decimals to express the *approximate* value of an irrational number.

$$\sqrt{20} \approx 4.5$$

The square root of 20 is approximately equal to 4.5.

Example 4

Use a calculator to approximate the value of $\sqrt{20}$ to two decimal places.

Solution

We clear the calculator and then enter ⌐√⌐ ⌐2⌐ ⌐0⌐ (or ⌐2⌐ ⌐0⌐ ⌐√⌐).[1] The display will show 4.472135955. The actual value of $\sqrt{20}$ contains an infinite number of decimal places. The display approximates $\sqrt{20}$ to nine or so decimal places (depending on the model). We are asked to show two decimal places, so we round the displayed number to **4.47**.

Practice Set ▶ Find each square root:

   a. $\sqrt{169}$ 13   **b.** $\sqrt{484}$ 22   **c.** $\sqrt{961}$ 31

Each of these square roots is between which two consecutive whole numbers? Find the answer without using a calculator.

   d. $\sqrt{2}$ 1 and 2   **e.** $\sqrt{15}$ 3 and 4   **f.** $\sqrt{40}$ 6 and 7

   g. $\sqrt{60}$ 7 and 8   **h.** $\sqrt{70}$ 8 and 9   **i.** $\sqrt{80}$ 8 and 9

▶ [Estimate] Use a calculator to approximate each square root to two decimal places:

   j. $\sqrt{3}$ 1.73   **k.** $\sqrt{10}$ 3.16   **l.** $\sqrt{50}$ 7.07

Written Practice   *Strengthening Concepts*

1. What is the difference when the product of $\frac{1}{2}$ and $\frac{1}{2}$ is subtracted from
(12, 72) the sum of $\frac{1}{4}$ and $\frac{1}{4}$? $\frac{1}{4}$

2. A dairy cow can give 4 gallons of milk per day. How many cups of milk
(78) is that (1 gallon = 4 quarts; 1 quart = 4 cups)?   64 cups

▶ **3.** The recipe called for $\frac{3}{4}$ cup of sugar. If the recipe is doubled, how much
(29) sugar should be used? $1\frac{1}{2}$ cups

4.

	Ratio	A. C.
Sugar	2	s
Flour	9	18

$$\frac{2}{9} = \frac{s}{18}$$

▶ *** 4.** [Model] Draw a ratio box for this problem. Then solve the problem
(88) using a proportion.   4 pounds

The recipe called for sugar and flour in the ratio of 2 to 9. If the chef used 18 pounds of flour, how many pounds of sugar were needed?

---

[1] The order of keystrokes depends on the model of calculator. See the instructions for your calculator if the keystroke sequences described in this lesson do not work for you.

▶ See Math Conversations in the sidebar.

Manipulative Use

To complete example 4, distribute calculators throughout the classroom and have students follow the steps of the solution to find an approximate value for $\sqrt{20}$.

The steps shown in the example may need to be modified for the type of calculator students are using.

▶ * **5.** **Classify** Which of these numbers is greater than 6 but less than 7?   C
(89)
   A $\sqrt{6.5}$ **B** $\sqrt{67}$ **C** $\sqrt{45}$ **D** $\sqrt{76}$

* **6.** Express the unknown factor as a mixed number: $4\frac{2}{7}$
(87)
$$7n = 30$$

7. Amanda used a compass to draw a circle
(47) with a radius of 4 inches.

   a. What is the diameter of the circle?   8 in.

   b. What is the circumference of the
   circle?   25.12 in.

4 in.

Use 3.14 for π.

* **8.** In problem **7** what is the area of the circle Amanda drew?   50.24 in.²
(86)

* **9.** What is the area of the triangle at
(79) right?   20 in.²

6 in.   5 in.
8 in.

10. **a.** What is the area of this
(71) parallelogram?   40 in.²

   b. What is the perimeter of this
   parallelogram?   28 in.

6 in.   5 in.
8 in.

11. Write 0.5 as a fraction and subtract it from $3\frac{1}{4}$. What is the
(63, 73) difference? $2\frac{3}{4}$

12. Write $\frac{3}{4}$ as a decimal, and multiply it by 0.6. What is the product?   0.45
(74)

▶* **13.** **Analyze** $2 \times 15 + 2 \times 12$ 54
(84)

▶* **14.** **Analyze** $\sqrt{900}$ 30
(89)

15. $6 \div 8$ $0.75   **16.** $1\frac{3}{5} \times 10 \times \frac{1}{4}$ 4
(2)   (66)

17. $37\frac{1}{2} \div 100$ $\frac{3}{8}$ **18.** $3 \div 7\frac{1}{2}$ $\frac{2}{5}$
(68)   (68)

19. What is the place value of the 7 in 987,654.321?   thousands
(34)

20. Write the decimal number five hundred ten and five hundredths.   510.05
(35)

21. $30 + 60 + m = 180$ 90
(3)

22. **Analyze** Half of the students are girls. Half of the girls have brown hair.
(72) Half of the brown-haired girls wear their hair long. Of the 32 students,
how many are girls with long, brown hair?   4 students

Lesson 89   463

▶ See Math Conversations in the sidebar.

Math Conversations

Discussion opportunities are provided below.

Problem 5   Classify

*"How can we use the square of 6 and
the square of 7 to find the answer using
mental math?"* Sample: $6^2 = 36$ and $7^2 =$
49, so if a square root is greater than 6 and
less than 7, it is greater than $\sqrt{36}$ and less
than $\sqrt{49}$.

Problem 13   Analyze

*"Which operation in this expression is
completed last? Why?"* Addition; the Order
of Operations states that multiplication is
completed before addition.

Problem 14   Analyze

Challenge students to use mental math to find
the answer. Then discuss how to answer the
problem mentally.

(continued)

3 Written Practice (Continued)

Math Conversations
Discussion opportunities are provided below.

Problem 26 `Analyze`
"Why is it difficult to use a constant factor to solve this proportion?" Sample: By comparing 12 and 21 you learn that the constant factor is not a whole number.

Problem 30 `Analyze`
Extend the Problem
"How many of the small blocks that make up this cube are not visible?" 27

Errors and Misconceptions
Problem 29b
When multiplying units of measure, students need to recognize that the units must change.

Write the repeated multiplications shown below on the board or overhead, then ask students who labeled their answers as inches to represent each expression using an exponent.

$$1 \cdot 1 = 1^2$$
$$8 \cdot 8 = 8^2$$
$$cm \cdot cm = cm^2$$
$$in. \cdot in. = in.^2$$

Refer to the pictograph below to answer problems 23–25.

Books Read This Year

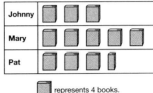

represents 4 books.

23. How many books has Johnny read?   12 books
(Inv. 5)

24. Mary has read how many more books than Pat?   6 more books
(Inv. 5)

25. `Formulate`   Write a question that relates to this graph and answer the question.   See student work.
(Inv. 5)

▶* **26.** `Analyze` Solve this proportion: $\frac{12}{8} = \frac{21}{m}$ 14
(85)

27. The face of this spinner is divided into 12 congruent regions. If the spinner is spun once, what is the probability that it will stop on a 3? Express the probability ratio as a fraction and as a decimal number rounded to the nearest hundredth. $\frac{1}{6}$; 0.17
(58, 74)

28. `Conclude` If two angles are complementary, and if one angle is acute, then the other angle is what kind of angle?   A
(28, 69)

  A acute   **B** right   **C** obtuse

* **29.** Simplify:
(81)
  a. 100 cm + 100 cm (Write the answer in meters.)   2 m

  ▶ **b.** $\frac{(5 \text{ in.})(8 \text{ in.})}{2}$ 20 in.^{2}

▶ **30.** If each small block has a volume of 1 cubic inch, then what is the volume of this cube?   64 in.^{3}
(82)

▶ See Math Conversations in the sidebar.

• Measuring Turns

Objectives

- Identify and describe turns measured in degrees.
- Solve problems involving turns.

Lesson Preparation

Materials

- **Power Up J** (in *Instructional Masters*)
- **Investigation Activity 15** (in *Instructional Masters*) or **graph paper**
- **Teacher-provided material: construction paper**

Optional

- **Teacher-provided material: spinner** marked North, South, East, and West

Math Language

Maintain	English Learners (ESL)
clockwise	lap
counterclockwise	

Technology Resources

Student eBook Complete student textbook in electronic format.

Resources and Planner CD Blackline masters, plus a pacing calendar with standards.

Test and Practice Generator CD Create additional practice sheets and custom-made tests.

www.SaxonPublishers.com Visit for more student activities and planning materials.

Inclusion

 Adaptations CD Adapted lessons, investigations, practice and assessments.

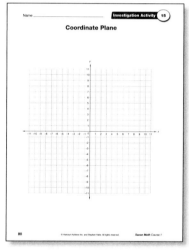

Power Up J   Investigation Activity 15

Meeting Standards

National Council of Teachers of Mathematics (NCTM)

Geometry

GM.4c Use visual tools such as networks to represent and solve problems

GM.4e Recognize and apply geometric ideas and relationships in areas outside the mathematics classroom, such as art, science, and everyday life

Problem Solving

PS.1b Solve problems that arise in mathematics and in other contexts

Problem-Solving Strategy: Use Logical Reasoning/ Make It Simpler

One state used a license plate that included one letter followed by five digits. How many different license plates could be made that started with the letter A?

Understand **Understand the problem.**

"What information are we given?"

License plates consist of one letter followed by five digits.

"What are we asked to do?"

Find how many license plates are possible that start with the letter A.

Plan **Make a plan.**

"What problem-solving strategy will we use?"

We will *use logical reasoning* and *make it simpler* by looking at possible license plates of fewer letters and numbers.

Solve **Carry out the plan.**

"If license plates consisted of two digits, how many different plates would be possible?"

There would be 100 different license plates: 01 through 99, plus 00.

"If license plates consisted of three digits, how many different plates would be possible?"

There would be 1000 different license plates: 001 through 999, plus 000.

"If license plates consisted of four digits, how many different plates would be possible?"

There would be 10,000 different license plates: 00001 through 9999, plus 0000.

"What combinations can be formed with the five digits following the letter? How many combinations is that?"

We can form the combinations 00001 through 99999, plus the combination 00000. That is a total of 100,000 different combinations.

Check **Look back.**

"Did we complete the task?"

Yes. We found that there are 100,000 different license plates that can begin with the letter A and be followed by five digits.

• Measuring Turns

facts	Power Up J
mental math	**a. Power/Roots:** $\sqrt{100}$ 10
	b. Calculation: $781 - 35$ 746
	c. Calculation: $\$1.98 + \$2.98$ $4.96
	d. Fractional Parts: $\frac{1}{3}$ of $24.00 $8.00
	e. Decimals: 0.375×100 37.5
	f. Number Sense: $\frac{1200}{300}$ 4
	g. Geometry: A cube has a height of 4 cm. What is the volume of the cube? 64 cubic centimeters
	h. Calculation: $2 \times 2, \times 2, \times 2, - 1, \times 2, + 2, \div 4, \div 4$ 2

problem solving	One state used a license plate that included one letter followed by five digits. How many different license plates could be made that started with the letter A? 100,000 license plates

New Concept *Increasing Knowledge*

Math Language
Clockwise means "moving in the direction of the hands of a clock." *Counterclockwise* means "moving in the opposite direction of the hands of a clock."

Every hour the minute hand of a clock completes one full turn in a clockwise direction. How many degrees does the minute hand turn in an hour? 360°

Turns can be measured in degrees. A full turn is a 360° turn. So the minute hand turns 360° in one hour.

If you turn 360°, you will end up facing the same direction you were facing before you turned. A half turn is half of 360°, which is 180°. If you turn 180°, you will end up facing opposite the direction you were facing before you turned.

If you are facing north and turn 90°, you will end up facing either east or west, depending on the direction in which you turned. To avoid confusion, we often specify the direction of a turn as well as the measure of the turn. Sometimes the direction is described as being to the right or to the left. Other times it is described as clockwise or counterclockwise.

Example 1

Leila was traveling north. At the light she turned 90° to the left and traveled one block to the next intersection. At the intersection she turned 90° to the left. What direction was Leila then traveling?

Lesson 90   465

Facts   Write each mixed number as an improper fraction.

$2\frac{1}{2} = \frac{5}{2}$	$2\frac{2}{5} = \frac{12}{5}$	$1\frac{3}{4} = \frac{7}{4}$	$2\frac{3}{4} = \frac{11}{4}$	$2\frac{1}{8} = \frac{17}{8}$
$1\frac{2}{3} = \frac{5}{3}$	$3\frac{1}{2} = \frac{7}{2}$	$1\frac{5}{6} = \frac{11}{6}$	$2\frac{1}{4} = \frac{9}{4}$	$1\frac{1}{8} = \frac{9}{8}$
$5\frac{1}{2} = \frac{11}{2}$	$1\frac{3}{8} = \frac{11}{8}$	$5\frac{1}{3} = \frac{16}{3}$	$3\frac{1}{4} = \frac{13}{4}$	$4\frac{1}{2} = \frac{9}{2}$
$1\frac{7}{8} = \frac{15}{8}$	$2\frac{2}{3} = \frac{8}{3}$	$1\frac{5}{8} = \frac{13}{8}$	$3\frac{3}{4} = \frac{15}{4}$	$7\frac{1}{2} = \frac{15}{2}$

---

1 Power Up

Facts
Distribute **Power Up J** to students. See answer below.

Mental Math
Before students begin the Mental Math exercise, do this counting exercise as a class.

Count up and down by $\frac{1}{2}$s between -3 and 3.

Encourage students to share different ways to mentally compute these exercises. Strategies for exercises **c** and **d** are listed below.

c. Round to Dollars, then Subtract 4¢
$\$2 + \$3 = \$5$; $\$5 - 4¢ = \$4.96$
Add 2¢ and Subtract 2¢
$\$1.98 + \$0.02 = \$2$ and $\$2.98 - \$0.02 = \$2.96$
$\$2 + \$2.96 = \$4.96$

d. Use a Division Fact
$24 \div 3 = 8$, so $\$24 \div 3 = \$8$
Use Repeated Addition
$8 + 8 + 8 = 24$, so $\$24 \div 3 = \$8$

Problem Solving
Refer to **Power-Up Discussion**, p. 465B.

2 New Concepts

Instruction
Invite the class to stand and act out different turns.
- Ask students to turn 360° clockwise, then turn 180° counterclockwise.

On a sheet of construction paper, draw the directions north, south, east, and west, and post the paper on a north wall of the classroom.

- Ask students to face north, then turn 90° clockwise.

"What direction are you now facing?" east

- Ask students to face north, then turn 90° counterclockwise.

"What direction are you now facing?" west

(continued)

2 New Concepts (Continued)

Example 1
Instruction

Tell students that the dashes in the diagram indicate the direction in which Leila would have continued had she not turned. Each curved arrow indicates the direction and measure of the turn.

Make sure students notice that turns are measured by the exterior angle and not by the interior angle.

Example 2
Instruction

Remind students that 360° represents the degree measure of a circle, and a circle represents a full turn.

For the solution, point out that there is a third way to solve this problem. Explain that after drawing the two turns, we can see that Andy's turn and Barney's turn together form a whole circle. Therefore, the measure of the two turns combined is 360°. Tell students that since we know that Andy's turn is 90°, Barney's turn is 360° − 90°, or 270°.

(continued)

Solution

A picture may help us answer the question. Leila was traveling north when she turned 90° to the left. After that first turn Leila was traveling west. When she turned 90° to the left a second time, she began traveling to the **south**. Notice that the two turns in the same direction (left) total 180°. So we would expect that after the two turns Leila was heading in the direction opposite to her starting direction.

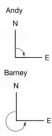

Example 2

Andy and Barney were both facing north. Andy made a quarter turn (90°) clockwise to face east, while Barney turned counterclockwise until he faced east. How many degrees did Barney turn?

Solution

We will draw the two turns. Andy made a quarter turn clockwise. We see that Barney made a three-quarter turn counterclockwise. We can calculate the number of degrees in three quarters of a turn by finding $\frac{3}{4}$ of 360°.

Andy
N

E

Barney
N

E

$$\frac{3}{4} \times 360° = 270°$$

Another way to find the number of degrees is to recognize that each quarter turn is 90°. So three quarters is three times 90°.

$$3 \times 90° = 270°$$

Barney turned **270°** counterclockwise.

Example 3

As Elizabeth ran each lap around the park, she made six turns to the left (and no turns to the right). What was the average number of degrees of each turn?

Math Background

In Geometry, a turn is also called a rotation, which is the movement of a figure about a point, called the point of rotation.

During a rotation, the size and the shape of a figure do not change.

English Learners

Refer students to example 3. Explain the meaning of **lap**. Say,

"A lap around the park is one complete trip around the park. You end at the same place you start."

Ask students to give examples of situations where you complete laps. (running on a track, driving on a go-kart track, swimming)

Solution

Thinking Skill

Discuss

Does the number of laps Elizabeth ran affect the answer? Why or why not?   No. The number of laps she ran does not affect the degrees in one full lap or the number of turns in each lap.

We are not given the measure of any of the turns, but we do know that Elizabeth made six turns to the left to get completely around the park. That is, after six turns she once again faced the same direction she faced before the first turn. So after six turns she had turned a total of 360°. We find the average number of degrees in each turn by dividing 360° by 6.

$$360° \div 6 = 60°$$

Each of Elizabeth's turns averaged **60°**.

Practice Set ▶

a. *Analyze* Jose was heading south on his bike. When he reached Sycamore, he turned 90° to the right. Then at Highland he turned 90° to the right, and at Elkins he turned 90° to the right again. Assuming each street was straight, in which direction was Jose heading on Elkins?   east

▶ b. Kiara made one full turn counterclockwise. Mary made two full turns clockwise. How many degrees did Mary turn? $2 \times 360° = 720°$

▶ c. *Model* David ran three laps around the park. On each lap he made five turns to the left and no turns to the right. What was the average number of degrees in each of David's turns? Draw a picture of the problem.

c.

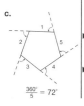

$\frac{360°}{5} = 72°$

Written Practice   *Strengthening Concepts*

1. What is the mean of 4.2, 4.8, and 5.1?   4.7
   (Inv. 5)

2. The movie is 120 minutes long. If it begins at 7:15 p.m., when will it be over?   9:15 p.m.
   (32)

3. Fifteen of the 25 students in Room 20 are boys. What percent of the students in Room 20 are boys?   60%
   (75)

4. This triangular prism has how many more edges than vertices?   3 more edges
   (Inv. 6)

▶ * 5. The teacher cut a 12-inch diameter circle from a sheet of construction paper.
   (86)
   a. What was the radius of the circle?   6 inches

   b. What was the area of the circle? (Use 3.14 for π.)
      113.04 square inches

6. *Explain* Write a description of a trapezoid.
   (64)

6. Sample: A trapezoid is a polygon with four sides. Two of the sides are parallel. The other two sides are not parallel.

7. Arrange these numbers in order from least to greatest: $-4, -2, 0, \frac{1}{2}, 1$
   (14, 17)

   $$1, -2, 0, -4, \frac{1}{2}$$

▶ See Math Conversations in the sidebar.

Inclusion

Material: spinner marked to show north, south, east, and west

Some students may have difficulty visualizing the direction of a turn and the outcome of multiple turns. Review the meaning of *clockwise* and *counterclockwise*, referring to the classroom clock as needed. Remind students that a full turn in either direction is 360°. Ask,

"How many degrees is a half turn?"   180°

"How many degrees is a quarter turn?"   90°

Remind students that a 90° angle forms a corner, and demonstrate a 90° turn by moving the spinner first from north to west and then from north to east. Next, use the spinner to model example 2. Have students count the number of quarter turns as multiples of 90°.

Before showing students how to model example 3, explain that a lap around the park is the same as making a complete circle.

Example 3
Instruction
Once again, point out that the dashes in the diagram indicate the direction Elizabeth would have taken had she not turned, and each curved arrow indicates the direction and measure of the turn.

Also remind students once again that turns are measured by the exterior angle and not by the interior angle.

Practice Set
Problem a   *Analyze*
Encourage students to draw a diagram to help solve this problem.

Problem b   *Error Alert*
This problem contains too much information. Have students identify the unnecessary information before solving the problem. Kiara made one full turn counterclockwise.

Problem c   *Model*
Because all three laps David ran are identical, students need only consider the information related to one lap to answer the question.

---

3 Written Practice

Math Conversations
Discussion opportunities are provided below.

Problem 5   *Analyze*
Extend the Problem
Write "$8\frac{1}{2}$ in. by 11 in." and "11 in. by 14 in." on the board or overhead.

"Many sheets of construction paper measure $8\frac{1}{2}$ in. by 11 in. or 11 in. by 14 in. Could the teacher in this problem have cut out a 12-inch diameter circle from either size sheet? Explain your answer."
No; Sample explanation: A circle cut from the smaller sheet could have a maximum diameter of $8\frac{1}{2}$ in; a circle cut from the larger sheet could have a maximum diameter of 11 in.

(continued)

Math Conversations

Discussion opportunities are provided below.

Problem 8 Analyze

Ask students to write a related equation that can be used to solve the problem, then choose an equation and solve the problem. Sample: $n = \frac{70}{25}$.

Problem 13 Analyze

Tell students which direction in the classroom is north, then encourage them to stand and act out the problem.

Problem 15 Analyze

Challenge students to name the constant factor of the proportion. $2\frac{1}{2}$ or 2.5

Errors and Misconceptions

Problem 21

Students must read carefully to learn that the correct answer represents $\frac{2}{3}$ of the knights, not the $\frac{1}{3}$ of the knights described in the problem.

Problem 22

Because one side of the scale is 12 ounces heavier than the other side, some students may mistakenly move 12 ounces to balance the scale.

Ask these students to find the total weight on each side of the scale after moving 12 ounces from the left to the right. They should conclude that moving 12 ounces simply transposed the total weights, and did not balance the scale.

(continued)

▶ *** 8.** (87) **Analyze** Express the unknown factor as a mixed number: $2\frac{4}{5}$
$$25n = 70$$

Refer to the triangle to answer questions **9–11**.

* 9. (79) What is the area of this triangle? 150 mm^2

10. (8) What is the perimeter of this triangle? 60 mm

25 mm   15 mm   20 mm

* 11. (23, 74) What is the ratio of the length of the shortest side to the length of the longest side? Express the ratio as a fraction and as a decimal. $\frac{3}{5}$, 0.6

12. (63, 73) **Connect** Write 6.25 as a mixed number. Then subtract $\frac{5}{8}$ from the mixed number. What is the difference? $5\frac{5}{8}$

▶*** 13.** (90) **Analyze** Ali was facing north. Then he turned to his left 180°. What direction was he facing after he turned? south

14. (41) Write 28% as a reduced fraction. $\frac{7}{25}$

▶*** 15.** (85) **Analyze** $\frac{n}{12} = \frac{20}{30}$ 8   **16.** (52) $0.625 \div 10$ 0.0625

17. (49) $\frac{25}{0.8}$ 31.25   **18.** (59) $3\frac{3}{8} + 3\frac{3}{4}$ $7\frac{1}{8}$

19. (48) $5\frac{1}{8} - 1\frac{7}{8}$ $3\frac{1}{4}$ **20.** (72) $6\frac{2}{3} \times \frac{3}{10} \times 4$ 8

▶ **21.** (77) One third of the two dozen knights were on horseback. How many knights were not on horseback? 16 knights

▶*** 22.** (18) **Evaluate** Weights totaling 38 ounces were placed on the left side of this scale, while weights totaling 26 ounces were placed on the right side of the scale. How many ounces of weights should be moved from the left side to the right side to balance the scale? (*Hint:* Find the average of the weights on the two sides of the scale.) 6 ounces

23. (82) The cube at right is made up of smaller cubes that each have a volume of 1 cubic centimeter. What is the volume of the larger cube? 27 cubic centimeters

24. (51) Round forty-eight hundredths to the nearest tenth. 0.5

* 25. (89) $\sqrt{144} - \sqrt{121}$ 1

▶ See Math Conversations in the sidebar.

28. 1 pint per day; Sample: They drink about $\frac{1}{2}$ gallon in 1 day. $\frac{1}{2}$ gal = 2 qt, 2 qt = 4 pt, 4 pt ÷ 4 people = 1 pt per person per day

26.
(23)
The ratio of dogs to cats in the neighborhood is 6 to 5. What is the ratio of cats to dogs? $\frac{5}{6}$

27.
(84)
$10 + 10 \times 10 - 10 \div 10$ 109

▶ **28.**
(78)
Analyze The Thompsons drink a gallon of milk every two days. There are four people in the Thompson family. Each person drinks an average of how many pints of milk per day? Explain your thinking.

* **29.**
(81)
Simplify:

  a. 10 cm + 100 mm (Write the answer in millimeters.)   200 mm

  b. 300 books ÷ 30 students   10 books per student

30.
(Inv. 7)
Model On a coordinate plane draw a segment from point A (−3, −1) to point B (5, −1). What are the coordinates of the point that is halfway between points A and B?   (1, −1)

Early Finishers
Real-World Application

The students in Mrs. Fitzgerald's cooking class will make buttermilk biscuits using the recipe below. If 56 students each work with a partner to make one batch of biscuits, how much of each ingredient will Mrs. Fitzgerald need to buy? Hint: Keep each item in the unit measure given.

$1\frac{3}{4}$ cups of all-purpose flour

1 teaspoon of baking soda

1 stick of butter

$1\frac{1}{4}$ cups of milk

56 students ÷ 2 = She needs to buy ingredients for 28 pairs. $1\frac{3}{4} \times 28 = \frac{7}{4} \times \frac{28}{1}$ = 49 cups of all-purpose flour, 28 teaspoons of baking soda, 28 sticks of butter and $1\frac{1}{4} \times 28 = \frac{5}{4} \times \frac{28}{1} = 35$ cups of milk.

Lesson 90   469

▶ See Math Conversations in the sidebar.

3 **Written Practice** *(Continued)*

Math Conversations

Discussion opportunities are provided below.

Problem 28   Analyze
Extend the Problem

"In problem 2 of Lesson 89, we were told that a dairy cow can give 4 gallons of milk per day. At that rate, what percent of the cow's annual output of milk do the Thompson's drink? Use a calculator and round your answer to the nearest percent." 13% (based on a 365-day year)

Looking Forward

Measuring turns prepares students for:

• **Lesson 108,** identifying rotations, translations, and reflections.

• **Lesson 109,** using rotations, translations, and reflections to identify corresponding parts of congruent or similar triangles.

Assessment | 30–40 minutes | For use after Lesson 90

Distribute **Cumulative Test 17** to each student. Two versions of the test are available in *Saxon Math Course 1 Course Assessments Book*. Have students complete the **Power-Up Test** first. Allow 10 minutes. Then have students work the 20 numbered items on the **Cumulative Test.** Students may use copies of the answer sheet to record their work. Track individual and class progress with the **Test Analysis** forms.

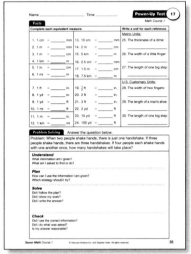

Power-Up Test 17

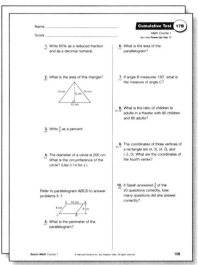

Cumulative Test 17A

Alternative Cumulative Test 17B

Optional Answer Forms

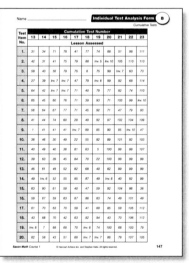

Individual Test Analysis Form

Class Test Analysis Form

Reteaching

Students who score below 80% on the assessment may be in need of reteaching. Look for the causes of student mistakes. If errors are conceptual, refer to the *Reteaching Masters* for reteaching.

You can develop customized benchmark tests using the Test Generator located on the *Test & Practice Generator CD.*

This chart shows the lesson, the standard, and the test item question that can be found on the *Test & Practice Generator CD.*

LESSON	NEW CONCEPTS	LOCAL STANDARD	TEST ITEM ON CD
81	• Arithmetic with Units of Measure		9.81.1
82	• Volume of a Rectangular Prism		9.82.1
83	• Proportions		9.83.1
84	• Order of Operations, Part 2		9.84.1
85	• Using Cross Products to Solve Proportions		9.85.1
86	• Area of a Circle		9.86.1
87	• Finding Unknown Factors		9.87.1
88	• Using Proportions to Solve Ratio Word Problems		9.88.1
89	• Estimating Square Roots		9.89.1
90	• Measuring Turns		9.90.1

Using the Test Generator CD
• Develop tests in both English and Spanish.
• Choose from multiple-choice and free-response test items.
• Clone test items to create multiple versions of the same test.
• View and edit test items to make and save your own questions.
• Administer assessments through paper tests or over a school LAN.
• Monitor student progress through a variety of individual and class reports
  —for both diagnosing and assessing standards mastery.

Comparing Shapes with Different Bases

Assign after Lesson 90 and Test 17

Objectives
- Describe how the appearance of prisms and pyramids changes as the shapes of the bases change.
- Communicate ideas through writing.

Materials
Performance Tasks 17A and **17B**

Preparation
Make copies of **Performance Tasks 17A** and **17B**. (One each per student.)

Time Requirement
30–60 minutes; Begin in class and complete at home.

Task
Explain to students that for this task they will sketch a rectangular prism and then describe how its appearance will change as the shape of the base changes. They will do the same for a pyramid. They will draw conclusions about the faces of prisms and pyramids. Point out that all of the information students need is on **Performance Tasks 17A** and **17B**.

Criteria for Evidence of Learning
- Describes accurately how the appearance of a rectangular prism and a pyramid changes as the shape of the base changes.
- Draws accurate conclusions about the faces and bases of prisms and pyramids.
- Communicates ideas clearly through writing.

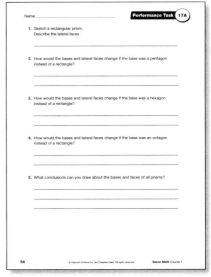

Performance Task 17A

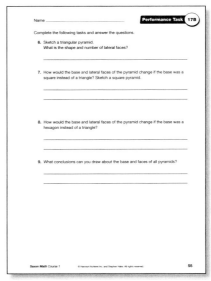

Performance Task 17B

National Council of Teachers of Mathematics (NCTM)

Geometry

GM.1a Precisely describe, classify, and understand relationships among types of two- and three-dimensional objects using their defining properties

GM.4a Draw geometric objects with specified properties, such as side lengths or angle measures

GM.4c Use visual tools such as networks to represent and solve problems

Communication

CM.3d Use the language of mathematics to express mathematical ideas precisely

Connections

CN.4b Understand how mathematical ideas interconnect and build on one another to produce a coherent whole

Focus on
● **Experimental Probability**

Objectives

- Estimate the probability of an event from data gathered by performing a probability experiment.
- Present data in a relative frequency table.
- Conduct probability experiments.

Lesson Preparation

Materials

- **Manipulative kit: number cubes,** two per student
- **Teacher-provided material: 7 marbles or any identical different-colored objects** such as colored paper clips, colored plastic chips, etc., 4 of one color and 3 of a different color distributed per each group of two or three students; **small opaque bag, pencil and paper**

Math Language

New	English Learners (ESL)
experimental probability	opaque
theoretical probability	

Technology Resources

Student eBook Complete student textbook in electronic format.

Resources and Planner CD Assessment, reteaching, and instructional masters, plus a pacing calendar with standards.

Test and Practice Generator CD Create additional practice sheets and custom-made tests.

www.SaxonPublishers.com Visit for more student activities and planning materials.

Inclusion

Adaptations CD Adapted lessons, investigations, practice and assessments.

Meeting Standards

National Council of Teachers of Mathematics (NCTM)

Data Analysis and Probability

DP.4b Use proportionality and a basic understanding of probability to make and test conjectures about the results of experiments and simulations

DP.4c Compute probabilities for simple compound events, using such methods as organized lists, tree diagrams, and area models

Reasoning and Proof

RP.2b Make and investigate mathematical conjectures

RP.2c Develop and evaluate mathematical arguments and proofs

Representation

RE.5a Create and use representations to organize, record, and communicate mathematical ideas

INVESTIGATION 9

In this investigation, students will discover how estimates of probability can be derived from survey data and from frequency tables. Students will also conduct a probability experiment and determine experimental and theoretical probabilities of outcomes.

Instruction

Review the probability experiments in Lesson 58 with students.

Another way for students to think about theoretical and experimental probability is that theoretical probability is what is expected to happen in a great number of trials, and experimental probability is what actually happens in any number of trials.

For the pizza survey point out that in order to survey representative customers, the pizza company needs to survey people who eat the company's pizza at a football game.

Challenge students to explain how mental math can be used to confirm that the sum of the decimal relative frequencies is 1. Sample: Add tenths, then add hundredths; three tenths plus four tenths plus two tenths equals nine tenths, and five hundredths plus five hundredths equals ten hundredths or one tenth, and the sum of nine tenths and one tenth is ten tenths or 1.

(continued)

INVESTIGATION 9

Focus on
• Experimental Probability

In Lesson 58 we determined probabilities for the outcomes of experiments without actually performing the experiments. For example, in the case of rolling a number cube, the sample space of the experiment is {1, 2, 3, 4, 5, 6} and all six outcomes are equally likely. Each outcome therefore has a probability of $\frac{1}{6}$. In the spinner example we assume that the likelihood of the spinner landing in a particular sector is proportional to the area of the sector. Thus, if the area of sector A is twice the area of sector B, the probability of the spinner landing in sector A is twice the probability of the spinner landing in sector B.

Probability that is calculated by performing "mental experiments" (as we have been doing since Lesson 58) is called **theoretical probability.** Probabilities associated with many real-world situations, though, cannot be determined by theory. Instead, we must perform the experiment repeatedly or collect data from a sample experiment. Probability determined in this way is called **experimental probability.**

A survey is one type of probability experiment. Suppose a pizza company is going to sell individual pizzas at a football game. Three types of pizzas will be offered: cheese, tomato, and mushroom. The company wants to know how many of each type of pizza to prepare, so it surveys a representative sample of 500 customers.

The company finds that 175 of these customers would order cheese pizzas, 225 would order tomato pizzas, and 100 would order mushroom pizzas. To estimate the probability that a particular pizza will be ordered, the company uses **relative frequency.** This means they divide the frequency (the number in each category) by the total (in this case, 500).

	Frequency	Relative Frequency
Cheese	175	$\frac{175}{500} = 0.35$
Tomato	225	$\frac{225}{500} = 0.45$
Mushroom	100	$\frac{100}{500} = 0.20$

Notice that the sum of the three relative frequencies is 1. This means that the entire sample is represented. We can change the relative frequencies from decimals to percents.

$$0.35 \longrightarrow 35\% \qquad 0.45 \longrightarrow 45\% \qquad 0.20 \longrightarrow 20\%$$

Math Background

The sample space of a probability experiment is the set of all possible outcomes.

For example, the sample space for an experiment of rolling a 1–6 number cube and tossing a coin at the same time contains 12 outcomes.

{(1, heads), (1, tails), (2, heads), (2, tails), (3, heads), (3, tails), (4, heads), (4, tails), (5, heads), (5, tails), (6, heads), (6, tails)}

Because there are 12 possible outcomes that are equally likely, the theoretical probability of any outcome in the sample set is $\frac{1}{12}$.

Recall from Lesson 58 that we use the term *chance* to describe a probability expressed as a percent. So the company makes the following estimates about any given sale. The chance that a cheese pizza will be ordered is **35%.** The chance that a tomato pizza will be ordered is **45%.** The chance that a mushroom pizza will be ordered is **20%.** The company plans to make 3000 pizzas for the football game, so about 20% of the 3000 pizzas should be mushroom. How many pizzas will be mushroom?   about 600 pizzas

Now we will apply these ideas to another survey. Suppose a small town has only four markets: Bob's Market, The Corner Grocery, Express Grocery, and Fine Foods. A representative sample of 80 adults was surveyed. Each person chose his or her favorite market: 30 chose Bob's Market, 12 chose Corner Grocery, 14 chose Express Grocery, and 24 chose Fine Foods.

1.

	Freq.	Relative Frequency
Bob's Market	30	$\frac{30}{80} = 0.375$
Corner Grocery	12	$\frac{12}{80} = 0.15$
Express Grocery	14	$\frac{14}{80} = 0.175$
Fine Foods	24	$\frac{24}{80} = 0.30$

1. **Represent** Present the data in a relative frequency table similar to the one for pizza.

2. Estimate the probability that in this town an adult's favorite market is Express Grocery. Write your answer as a decimal.   0.175

3. Estimate the probability that in this town an adult's favorite market is Bob's Market. Write your answer as a fraction in reduced form. $\frac{3}{8}$

4. Estimate the chance that in this town an adult's favorite market is Fine Foods. Write your answer as a percent.   30%

5. Suppose the town has 4000 adult residents. The Corner Grocery is the favorite market of about how many adults in the town?
   about 600 adults

Thinking Skill

Discuss

How can the frequency table you made in problem 1 help us find the answer to problem 5?
We can take the relative frequency with which people chose the Corner Grocery and multiply by 4000; 0.15 × 4000 = about 600 adults.

A survey is just one way of conducting a probability experiment. In the following activity we will perform an experiment that involves drawing two marbles out of a bag. By performing the experiment repeatedly and recording the results, we gather information that helps us determine the probability of various outcomes.

Activity

Probability Experiment

Materials needed:

- 6 marbles (4 green and 2 white)
- Small, opaque bag from which to draw the marbles
- Pencil and paper

The purpose of this experiment is to determine the probability that two marbles drawn from the bag at the same time will be green. We will create a relative frequency table to answer the question.

To estimate the probability, put 4 green marbles and 2 white marbles in a bag. Pair up with another student, and work through problems **6–8** together.

"How many cheese pizzas should the company make?" 1050

"Describe two ways to determine the number of tomato pizzas the company should make." Find 45% of 3000 (1350); subtract the sum of 600 and 1050 from 3000 (1350).

For problem **2**, remind students that they can estimate the probability of an event by finding its relative frequency. Have them refer to the relative frequency table they created for problem **1**.

Give students who have difficulty solving problem **5** the following hint.

"Looking at our relative frequency table, we know that 15% of the adults surveyed prefer the Corner Grocery."

Activity

Instruction
The Teacher Tip feature at the bottom of the page contains a list of alternate materials.

(continued)

English Learners

To demonstrate the meaning of the word **opaque**, hold up a small opaque bag, such as a brown paper bag. Say,

"We cannot see through this bag; it is opaque."

Then hold up a clear plastic bag and say,

"This bag is not opaque."

Ask students why the plastic bag is not opaque. We can see through it.

Teachers Tip

If marbles are not available for the **Probability Experiment Activity**, use counters, plastic chips, colored craft sticks, or slips of paper. Note that it is important that differences in the objects cannot be determined by touch and that the objects are identical in size.

Activity (Continued)

For problem **6,** remind students that the marbles are to be drawn without looking, and replaced after the outcome has been recorded.

For problem **7,** students should recognize that the sum of the tallies in each row is divided by 25 because there were 25 draws altogether.

When students have completed the activity, suggest that to increase the size of the sample, the groups can combine their results. Display the combined results in a relative frequency table on the board or overhead.

Students should generalize that the greater the number of trials, the greater the likelihood that the experimental probability of an experiment will approach the theoretical probability.

Extensions

a. *Represent* As a class activity, tally the results and create relative frequency calculations for the responses.

b. *Analyze* Students may remain in their original groups to complete this extension. After students have discussed their individual findings, draw a table on the board or overhead that is similar to the table shown on the next page. Combine the results from the individual groups, record them in the table, and then calculate the relative frequencies. Discuss the findings as a class.

(continued)

Thinking Skill

Predict

Which outcome do you think will occur most often?
Answers will vary. Sample: both green

6. Choose one student to draw from the bag and the other to record results. Shake the bag; then remove two objects at the same time. Record the result by marking a tally in a table like the one below. Replace the marbles and repeat this process until you have performed the experiment exactly 25 times.

Outcome	Tally
Both green	
Both white	
One of each	

7. Use your tally table to make a relative frequency table. (Divide each row's tally by 25 and express the quotient as a decimal.) See student work.

8. Estimate the probability that both marbles drawn will be green. Write your answer as a reduced fraction and as a decimal. See student work; theoretical probability is $\frac{2}{5}$, which equals 0.4.

If, for example, you drew two green marbles 11 times out of 25 draws, your best estimate of the probability of drawing two green marbles would be

$$\frac{11}{25} = \frac{44}{100} = 0.44$$

But this is only an estimate. The more times you draw, the more likely it is that the estimate will be close to the theoretical probability. It is better to repeat the experiment 500 times than 25 times. Thus, combining your results with other students' results is likely to produce a better estimate. To combine results, add everyone's tallies together; then calculate the new frequency.

---

extensions

▶ **a.** *Represent* Ask 10 other students the following question: "What is your favorite sport: baseball, football, soccer, or basketball?" Record each response. Create a relative frequency table of your results. Share the results of the survey with your class.

▶ **b.** *Analyze* In groups, conduct an experiment by drawing two counters out of a bag containing 3 green counters and 3 white counters. Each group should perform the experiment 30 times. Record each group's tallies in a frequency table like the one shown on the next page.

▶ See Math Conversations in the sidebar.

	Both Green		Both White		One of Each	
	Tally	Rel. Freq.	Tally	Rel. Freq.	Tally	Rel. Freq.
Group 1						
Group 2						
Group 3						
Group 4						
Group 5						
Group 6						
Whole Class						

Calculate the relative frequency for each group by dividing the tallies by 30 (the number of times each group performed the experiment). Then combine the results from all the groups. To combine the results, add the tallies in each column and write the totals in the last row of the table. Then divide each of these totals by the *total* number of times the experiment was performed (equal to the number of groups times 30). The resulting quotients are the whole-class relative frequencies for each event. Discuss your findings.

On the basis of their own data, which groups would guess that the probabilities were less than the "Whole class" data indicate? Which groups would guess that the probabilities were greater than the whole class's data indicate?

▶ **c.** Choose a partner and roll two number cubes 100 times. Each time, observe the sum of the upturned faces, and fill out a relative frequency table like the one below. The sample space of this experiment has 11 outcomes.

> *Predict* Are the outcomes equally likely? If not, which outcomes are more likely and which are less likely?

Sum	2	3	4	5	6	7	8	9	10	11	12
Frequency											
Relative Frequency											

After the experiment and calculation, estimate the probability that the sum of a roll will be 8. Estimate the probability that the sum will be at least 10. Estimate the probability that the sum will be odd.

c. No. Sample: Sums such as 3 and 12 can be rolled in only one way: 2 + 1 and 6 + 6. Other sums, such as 7, can be rolled in more than one way. For example, 6 + 1, 5 + 2, and 4 + 3 all equal 7.

▶ See Math Conversations in the sidebar.

c. *Predict* After the activity has been completed, challenge students to explain why some outcomes are more likely than others, and give an example to support their explanation. Sample: There are six different ways to make a sum of 7, but only one way to make a sum of 12.
7: (1, 6), (2, 5), (3, 4), (4, 3), (5, 2), (6, 1)
12: (6, 6)

Looking Forward

Finding experimental probability by collecting data from surveys, presenting data in relative frequency tables, and performing experiments prepare students for:

• **Investigation 10,** performing compound experiments and creating tree diagrams and tables to display results.

Lesson Planner

LESSON	NEW CONCEPTS	MATERIALS	RESOURCES
91	• Geometric Formulas	Index cards	**Power Up H** **Investigation Activity 15** **Geometric Formulas poster**
92	• Expanded Notation with Exponents • Order of Operations with Exponents • Powers of Fractions	Manipulative Kit: inch rulers Index cards	**Power Up L**
93	• Classifying Triangles	Manipulative Kit: Relational GeoSolids, triangular prism Set of triangular cutouts	**Power Up I** **Investigation Activity 15**
94	• Writing Fractions and Decimals as Percents, Part 2		**Power Up K** **Investigation Activity 15**
95	• Reducing Rates Before Multiplying		**Power Up G**
96	• Functions • Graphing Functions	Manipulative Kit: inch rulers	**Power Up D** **Investigation Activity 15** **Lesson Activity 19 Transparency**
97	• Transversals	Construction paper, index cards, markers, city maps, calculators	**Power Up L**
98	• Sum of the Angle Measures of Triangles and Quadrilaterals	Manipulative Kit: inch rulers, protractors Scissors; geometric drawing software	**Power Up J**
99	• Fraction-Decimal-Percent Equivalents	Manipulative Kit: inch rulers, compasses	**Power Up K**
100	• Algebraic Addition of Integers	Manipulative Kit: metric rulers, tiles or counters	**Power Up I**
Inv. 10	• Compound Experiments	Green and white chalk	

Problem Solving

Strategies

- **Make It Simpler** Lesson 98
- **Find a Pattern** Lessons 94, 98
- **Make a Table** Lesson 100
- **Use Logical Reasoning** Lessons 92, 93, 95, 99, 100
- **Draw a Diagram** Lesson 98
- **Work Backwards** Lesson 96
- **Write an Equation** Lessons 91, 97
- **Make an Organized List** Lesson 95

Real-World Applications

pp. 474, 476–483, 485–487, 491–495, 501, 502, 505–507, 510–512, 513–515, 522–523

4-Step Process

Teacher Edition Lessons 91–100 (Power-Up Discussions)

Communications

Discuss

pp. 488, 498

Explain

pp. 481, 487, 515, 522

Formulate a Problem

p. 507

Connections

Math and Other Subjects

Math and Science pp. 491, 492, 505, 506

Math and Architecture p. 512

Math and Language Arts p. 502

Math and Sports pp. 477–479, 507

Math and Geography p. 483

Math to Math

Measurement and Problem Solving Lessons 91, 92, 93, 95, 99

Algebra and Problem Solving Lessons 92, 96, 100

Fractions, Percents, Decimals and Problem Solving Lessons 91, 92, 93, 94, 95, 96, 97, 98, 99, 100

Fractions and Measurement Lessons 92, 95, 96, 97, 98, 99

Measurement and Geometry Lessons 91, 92, 93, 94, 95, 96, 97, 98, 99, 100

Algebra, Measurement and Geometry Lessons 92, 93, 96

Proportional Relationships and Geometry Lesson 93

Probability and Statistics Lessons 91, 92, 93, 94, 95, 96, 97, 98, 99, 100

Representation

Manipulatives/Hands On

pp. 483, 492, 500, 501, 505, 509, 516, 518, 523

Model

pp. 476, 478, 485, 492, 501–502, 510, 516, 521

Represent

pp. 486, 487

Lessons 91–100, Investigation 10

Technology

Student Resources

- eBook
- Online Resources at www.SaxonPublishers.com/ActivitiesC1
  Graphing Calculator Activity Lesson 92
  Online Activities
  Math Enrichment Problems
  Math Stumpers

Teacher Resources

- Resources and Planner CD
- Adaptations CD Lessons 91–100
- Test & Practice Generator CD
- eGradebook
- Answer Key CD

The transition from arithmetic to algebra proceeds in this set of lessons.

Algebraic Thinking

Students connect equations, functions, and the coordinate plane.

Students apply the order of operations to calculations involving exponents in Lesson 92. Students find and apply rules for functions in Lesson 96. Students also create tables of ordered pairs and graph functions. In Lesson 100 students learn to subtract negative numbers through the process of algebraic addition—adding the opposite of the subtrahend.

Equivalence

Representing fraction, decimals, and percents in equivalent forms is emphasized in these lessons.

Lessons 94 provides instruction on writing a fraction, decimal, or mixed number as a percent. In Lesson 99, given one form of a rational number, students find fraction, decimal, or percent equivalents.

Geometry and Measurement

Students use perimeter and area formulas.

Geometry concepts are extended in Lesson 91 where students write formulas for polygons. Calculations with measurements involve dealing with units of measure, including reducing units of measure, the topic of Lesson 95.

Spatial Thinking

Students determine the sum of the angle measures of triangles and quadrilaterals.

After classifying quadrilaterals in Lesson 64, students classify triangles in Lesson 93. In Lesson 97 they classify and find angles formed by parallel lines cut by a transversal. In Lesson 98 students determine the sum of the angle measures of a quadrilateral by applying the relationship between interior and exterior angles.

Probability and Experiments

Students learn the difference between simple and compound experiments.

Investigation 10 continues the study of probability as students calculate the possible outcomes of compound experiments.

Assessment

A variety of weekly assessment tools are provided.

After Lesson 95:
- Power-Up Test 18
- Cumulative Test 18
- Performance Activity 18

After Lesson 100:
- Power-Up Test 19
- Cumulative Test 19
- Customized Benchmark Test
- Performance Task 19

LESSON	NEW CONCEPTS	PRACTICED	ASSESSED
91	• Geometric Formulas	Lessons 91, 92, 93, 95, 112, 113	Tests 19, 20, 21, 22, 23
92	• Expanded Notation with Exponents	Lessons 93, 94, 98, 102, 103, 106, 107, 109, 111, 112, 115, 119, 120	Test 23
	• Order of Operations with Exponents	Lessons 92, 93, 94, 95, 96, 97, 98, 99, 100, 101, 102, 103, 104, 106, 107, 108, 109, 110, 112, 113, 114, 117	Tests 19, 20, 21, 22
	• Powers of Fractions	Lessons 98, 101, 104, 109, 112, 118	Test 19
93	• Classifying Triangles	Lessons 93, 94, 98, 99, 100, 107, 109, 110, 116, 117	Tests 19, 23
94	• Writing Fractions and Decimals as Percents, Part 2	Lessons 94, 95, 96, 97, 98, 99, 100, 101, 102, 103, 104, 106, 111, 117	Test 19
95	• Reducing Rates Before Multiplying	Lessons 95, 96, 98, 101, 104, 105, 106, 107, 108, 109, 111, 112, 114, 115, 116, 117	Tests 21, 23
96	• Functions	Lessons 96, 997, 99, 102, 105, 109, 114, 118, 119	Test & Practice Generator
	• Graphing Functions	Lesson 109	Test & Practice Generator
97	• Transversals	Lessons 97, 98, 102, 114	Test 20
98	• Sum of the Angle Measures of Triangles and Quadrilaterals	Lessons 98, 99, 100, 101, 103, 105, 107, 109, 111, 116, 119	Test 19
99	• Fraction-Decimal-Percent Equivalents	Lessons 99, 100, 101, 102, 103, 104, 105, 106, 107, 108, 109, 110, 111, 112, 113, 114, 115, 116	Tests 20, 21, 22, 23
100	• Algebraic Addition of Integers	Lessons 100, 101, 103, 105, 106, 107, 109, 111, 112, 113, 114, 115, 117, 120	Test 20
Inv. 10	• Compound Experiments	Investigation 10, Lessons 101, 102, 104, 105, 108, 109, 110, 115, 117, 119, 120	Tests 20, 22, 23

• Geometric Formulas

Objectives

• Use formulas to calculate the perimeter and area of squares, rectangles, parallelograms, and triangles.

Lesson Preparation

Materials

• **Power Up H** (in *Instructional Masters*)
• **Investigation Activity 15** (in *Instructional Masters*) or graph paper
• **Teacher-provided material:**
  index cards for formula flashcards

Optional

• **Geometric Formulas poster**

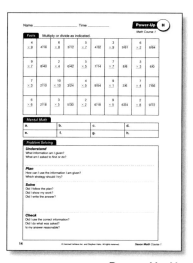

Power Up H

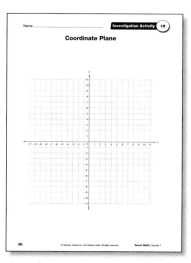

Investigation Activity 15

Technology Resources

Student eBook Complete student textbook in electronic format.

Resources and Planner CD Assessment, reteaching, and instructional masters, plus a pacing calendar with standards.

Test and Practice Generator CD Create additional practice sheets and custom-made tests.

www.SaxonPublishers.com Visit for more student activities and planning materials.

Inclusion

Adaptations CD Adapted lessons, investigations, practice and assessments.

Meeting Standards

National Council of Teachers of Mathematics (NCTM)

Geometry

GM.4d Use geometric models to represent and explain numerical and algebraic relationships

Measurement

ME.2b Select and apply techniques and tools to accurately find length, area, volume, and angle measures to appropriate levels of precision

ME.2c Develop and use formulas to determine the circumference of circles and the area of triangles, parallelograms, trapezoids, and circles and develop strategies to find the area of more-complex shapes

Problem-Solving Strategy: Write an Equation

If Sam can read 20 pages in 30 minutes, how long will it take Sam to read 200 pages?

(Understand) **Understand the problem.**

"What information are we given?"

We know that Sam can read 20 pages in 30 minutes.

"What are we asked to do?"

Find how long it will take Sam to read 200 pages.

(Plan) **Make a plan.**

"What problem-solving strategy will we use?"

We will *write an equation* to solve the problem.

(Solve) **Carry out the plan.**

"What proportion can we write to solve this problem?"

$$\frac{20 \text{ pages}}{30 \text{ min}} = \frac{200 \text{ pages}}{x \text{ min}}$$

"What is our next step?"

Cross-multiply or divide 200 by 20 to find the scale factor.

"How long will it take Sam to read 200 pages?"

300 minutes

"How can we change 300 minutes to hours?"

We can divide by 60 minutes since there are 60 minutes in one hour.
$300 \div 60 = 5$ Sam read 200 pages in 5 hours.

(Check) **Look back.**

"Did we complete the task?"

Yes. We found it would take Sam 300 minutes (5 hours) to read 200 pages.

Facts

Distribute **Power Up H** to students. See answers below.

Mental Math

Before students begin the Mental Math exercise, do this counting exercise as a class.

Count by $\frac{1}{3}$s from $\frac{1}{3}$ to 4.

Encourage students to share different ways to mentally compute these exercises. Strategies for exercises **b** and **f** are listed below.

b. Subtract 800, then Subtract 75
  $1000 - 800 = 200; 200 - 75 = 125$
Subtract 900, then Add 25
  $1000 - 900 = 100; 100 + 25 = 125$
f. Break Apart 42
  $(20 \times 40) + (20 \times 2) = 800 + 40 = 840$
Double 10 × 42
  $10 \times 42 = 420; 420 \times 2 = 840$

Problem Solving

Refer to **Power-Up Discussion**, p. 474F.

2 New Concepts

Instruction

Before students begin the lesson, sketch a square on the board and label one side of the square s.

"The letter s represents the length of each side of this square. We can use the letter P to represent its perimeter. Write a rule that can be used to find the perimeter of a square if we know the length of a side."
$P = s + s + s + s$ or $P = 4s$

"Using the letter A to represent area, write a rule that can be used to find the area of a square if we know the length of a side."
$A = s \cdot s$ or $A = s^2$

Next, draw a rectangle that is longer in one dimension than the other, and label the length l and the width w. Ask students to write a rule for finding the area (A) of the rectangle if the length (l) and width (w) are known. $A = lw$

Ask students to write a rule for finding the perimeter (P) of a rectangle if the length (l) and width (w) are known. $P = l + w + l + w$ or $P = 2l + 2w$ or $P = 2(l + w)$

Then direct students to study the formula table in the lesson and invite volunteers to explain the meaning of the remaining four formulas.

(continued)

• Geometric Formulas

Power Up · Building Power

facts | Power Up H

mental math
  a. **Power/Roots:** $5^2 + \sqrt{100}$ 35
  b. **Number Sense:** $1000 - 875$ 125
  c. **Calculation:** $\$6.99 \times 5$ $34.95
  d. **Number Sense:** Double $125.00. $250.00
  e. **Decimals:** $12.5 \div 100$ 0.125
  f. **Number Sense:** 20×42 840
  g. **Measurement:** How many pints are in a quart?   2 pints
  h. **Calculation:** $3 \times 4, \div 2, \times 3, + 2, \times 2, + 2, \div 2, \div 3$ 7

problem solving | If Sam can read 20 pages in 30 minutes, how long will it take Sam to read 200 pages?   5 hours

New Concept · Increasing Knowledge

We have found the area of a rectangle by multiplying the length of the rectangle by its width. This procedure can be described with the following formula:

$$A = lw$$

The letter A stands for the area of the rectangle. The letters l and w stand for the length and width of the rectangle. Written side by side, lw means that we multiply the length by the width. The table below lists formulas for the perimeter and area of squares, rectangles, parallelograms, and triangles.

Figure	Perimeter	Area
Square	$P = 4s$	$A = s^2$
Rectangle	$P = 2l + 2w$	$A = lw$
Parallelogram	$P = 2b + 2s$	$A = bh$
Triangle	$P = s_1 + s_2 + s_3$	$A = \frac{1}{2}bh$

Facts — Multiply or divide as indicated.

$\begin{array}{r} 4 \\ \times 9 \\ \hline 36 \end{array}$	$4\overline{)16}$	$\begin{array}{r} 6 \\ \times 8 \\ \hline 48 \end{array}$	$3\overline{)12}$	$\begin{array}{r} 5 \\ \times 7 \\ \hline 35 \end{array}$	$4\overline{)32}$	$\begin{array}{r} 3 \\ \times 9 \\ \hline 27 \end{array}$	$9\overline{)81}$	$\begin{array}{r} 6 \\ \times 2 \\ \hline 12 \end{array}$	$8\overline{)64}$
$\begin{array}{r} 9 \\ \times 7 \\ \hline 63 \end{array}$	$8\overline{)40}$	$\begin{array}{r} 2 \\ \times 4 \\ \hline 8 \end{array}$	$6\overline{)42}$	$\begin{array}{r} 5 \\ \times 5 \\ \hline 25 \end{array}$	$7\overline{)14}$	$\begin{array}{r} 7 \\ \times 7 \\ \hline 49 \end{array}$	$8\overline{)8}$	$\begin{array}{r} 3 \\ \times 3 \\ \hline 9 \end{array}$	$6\overline{)0}$
$\begin{array}{r} 7 \\ \times 3 \\ \hline 21 \end{array}$	$2\overline{)10}$	$\begin{array}{r} 10 \\ \times 10 \\ \hline 100 \end{array}$	$3\overline{)24}$	$\begin{array}{r} 4 \\ \times 5 \\ \hline 20 \end{array}$	$9\overline{)54}$	$\begin{array}{r} 9 \\ \times 1 \\ \hline 9 \end{array}$	$3\overline{)6}$	$\begin{array}{r} 7 \\ \times 4 \\ \hline 28 \end{array}$	$7\overline{)56}$
$\begin{array}{r} 6 \\ \times 6 \\ \hline 36 \end{array}$	$2\overline{)18}$	$\begin{array}{r} 3 \\ \times 5 \\ \hline 15 \end{array}$	$5\overline{)30}$	$\begin{array}{r} 2 \\ \times 2 \\ \hline 4 \end{array}$	$6\overline{)18}$	$\begin{array}{r} 9 \\ \times 5 \\ \hline 45 \end{array}$	$6\overline{)24}$	$\begin{array}{r} 2 \\ \times 8 \\ \hline 16 \end{array}$	$9\overline{)72}$

The letters *P* and *A* are abbreviations for *perimeter* and *area.* Other abbreviations are illustrated below:

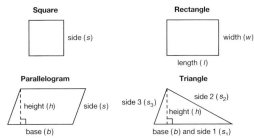

Square

side (*s*)

Rectangle

width (*w*)

length (*l*)

Parallelogram

height (*h*)   side (*s*)

base (*b*)

Triangle

side 3 (s_3)   side 2 (s_2)

height (*h*)

base (*b*) and side 1 (s_1)

Since squares and rectangles are also parallelograms, the formulas for the perimeter and area of parallelograms may also be used for squares and rectangles.

To use a formula, we substitute each known measure in place of the appropriate letter in the formula. When substituting a number in place of a letter, it is a good practice to write the number in parentheses.

Example

Write the formula for the perimeter of a rectangle. Then substitute 8 cm for the length and 5 cm for the width. Solve the equation to find *P.*

Solution

The formula for the perimeter of a rectangle is

$$P = 2l + 2w$$

We rewrite the equation, substituting 8 cm for *l* and 5 cm for *w.* We write these measurements in parentheses.

$$P = 2(8 \text{ cm}) + 2(5 \text{ cm})$$

We multiply 2 by 8 cm and 2 by 5 cm.

$$P = 16 \text{ cm} + 10 \text{ cm}$$

Now we add 16 cm and 10 cm.

$$P = 26 \text{ cm}$$

The perimeter of the rectangle is **26 cm.**

We summarize the steps below to show how your work should look.

$$P = 2l + 2w$$
$$P = 2(8 \text{ cm}) + 2(5 \text{ cm})$$
$$P = 16 \text{ cm} + 10 \text{ cm}$$
$$P = 26 \text{ cm}$$

Instruction

You may wish to display the **Geometric Formulas** concept poster as you discuss this topic with students.

Make sure students understand that although the formulas for the perimeter and the area of parallelograms may be used for squares and for rectangles, the formulas for the perimeter and the area of rectangles and squares cannot be used for parallelograms, because not all parallelograms are rectangles or squares.

Example

Instruction

Write the formulas $P = 2l + 2w$ and $P = l + l + w + w$ on the board or overhead. Explain that the formula for the perimeter of a rectangle, $P = 2l + 2w$, is a shortened way of showing how we add all the sides of a rectangle to find its perimeter, $P = l + l + w + w$.

(continued)

Inclusion

To help students develop confidence in using geometric formulas, have them practice working with perimeter and area without being given any visuals. Refer students to *Geometric Formulas* in the *Student Reference Guide* for help remembering the formulas. Give students the following problems. Ask them to draw and label each figure based on the description in the problem. Then discuss how to use the appropriate formula.

"The distance around a square is 8 feet. How long is each side?" 2 feet

"A rectangle 3 feet long is 7 feet wide. What is the area?" 35 square feet

"A triangle 6 centimeters high has a base 4 centimeters long. How many square centimeters does the triangle cover?" 12 square centimeters

"A parallelogram has a height of 4 feet and a base of 6 feet. An equilateral triangle has a base of 5 feet. Which figure has the greater perimeter?" the parallelogram

2 New Concepts (Continued)

Practice Set

Problem a [Error Alert]

Remind students who do not label their answers as cm² that the product 8 × 5 is 40 and the product cm × cm is cm².

Problem c [Estimate]

Invite students to exchange word problems, then solve the problems and compare answers.

3 Written Practice

Math Conversations

Discussion opportunities are provided below.

Errors and Misconceptions

Problem 6

If students have difficulty understanding how to find the answer, sketch two analog clock faces on the board, with one showing 12:00 and the other showing 12:45.

Explain that when the minute hand completes one full turn around the circular clock face in 60 minutes, it makes a 360° turn. Moving from 12:00 to 12:45, the minute hand makes a three-quarter turn around the clock face, so we multiply $\frac{3}{4}$ by 360°.

Ask students to complete the computation, then compute the number of degrees a minute hand turns in 20 minutes.
$\frac{3}{4} \times 360° = 270°$; $\frac{1}{3} \times 360° = 120°$

Problem 8

Encourage students to use formulas to solve for the perimeter, and for the area, of the parallelogram.

(continued)

Practice Set ▶ **a.** Write the formula for the area of a rectangle. Then substitute 8 cm for the length and 5 cm for the width. Solve the equation to find the area of the rectangle. $A = lw$; $A = (8 \text{ cm})(5 \text{ cm})$; $A = 40 \text{ cm}^2$

b. Write the formula for the perimeter of a parallelogram. Then substitute 10 cm for the base and 6 cm for the side. Solve the equation to find the perimeter of the parallelogram. $P = 2b + 2s$; $P = 2(10 \text{ cm}) + 2(6 \text{ cm})$; $P = 32 \text{ cm}$

▶ **c.** **Estimate** Look around the room for a rectangular or triangular shape. Estimate its dimensions and write a word problem about its perimeter or area. Then solve the problem. *See student work.*

Written Practice   *Strengthening Concepts*

1. What is the ratio of prime numbers to composite numbers in this list? $\frac{1}{2}$
(23, 65)

10, 11, 12, 13, 14, 15, 16, 17, 18, 19, 20, 21

2. Sunrise was at 6:15 a.m. and sunset was at 5:45 p.m. How many hours
(32) and minutes were there from sunrise to sunset? 11 hr 30 min

3.
Leapers | Ratio | A. C. |
Smilers
$\frac{3}{2} = \frac{12}{s}$

	Ratio	A. C.
Leapers	3	12
Smilers	2	s

* 3. **Model** Draw a ratio box for this problem. Then solve the problem using
(88) a proportion. 8 just smiled

When the good news was announced many leaped for joy and others just smiled. The ratio of leapers to smilers was 3 to 2. If 12 leaped for joy, how many just smiled?

4. A rectangular prism has how many more faces than a triangular
(Inv. 6) prism? 1 more face

* 5. Write the formula for the area of a parallelogram as given in this
(91) lesson. Then substitute 15 cm for the base and 4 cm for the height. Solve the equation to find the area of the parallelogram. $A = bh$; $A = (15 \text{ cm})(4 \text{ cm})$; $A = 60 \text{ cm}^2$

▶ *** 6.** **Connect** How many degrees does the minute hand of a clock turn in
(90) 45 minutes? 270°

7. A pyramid with a triangular base is shown at right.
(Inv. 6) **a.** How many faces does it have? 4 faces

b. How many edges does it have? 6 edges

c. How many vertices does it have? 4 vertices

▶ **8. a.** What is the perimeter of this
(71) parallelogram? 44 in.

b. What is the area of this parallelogram? 108 in.²

9 in.   10 in.

12 in.

▶ See Math Conversations in the sidebar.

Teacher Tip

One way to practice formulas is to create and use **formula flashcards.** A formula can be written on one side of a card and the measurement it describes can be written on the other side. For example, "perimeter of a parallelogram" and "$P = 2b + 2s$."

Pairs of students can use the cards as a way to help remember perimeter and area formulas.

9. **a.** Write $\frac{7}{20}$ as a decimal number. 0.35
(74, 75)
　　　b. Write $\frac{7}{20}$ as a percent. 35%

* 10. **Connect** The distance between bases in a softball diamond is
(91) 60 feet. What is the shortest distance a player could run to score a
home run? 240 feet

11. $6\frac{2}{3} + 1\frac{3}{4}$ $8\frac{5}{12}$　**12.** $5 - 1\frac{2}{5}$ $3\frac{3}{5}$　**13.** $4\frac{1}{4} - 3\frac{5}{8}$ $\frac{5}{8}$
(59)　　　　　　　　　(63)　　　　　　　　(63)

14. $3 \times \frac{3}{4} \times 2\frac{2}{3}$ 6　**15.** $6\frac{2}{3} \div 100$ $\frac{1}{15}$　**16.** $2\frac{1}{2} \div 3\frac{3}{4}$ $\frac{2}{3}$
(72)　　　　　　　　　(68)　　　　　　　　(68)

17. Compare: $\frac{9}{20}$ 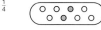 50%
(75)

18. **a.** What fraction of this group is shaded? $\frac{1}{4}$
(75)
　　　b. What percent of this group is
　　　　shaded? 25%

19. If $\frac{5}{6}$ of the 300 seeds sprouted, how many seeds did not sprout?
(77) 50 seeds

▶ **20.** $6y = 10$ $1\frac{2}{3}$　　　　▶* **21.** $\frac{w}{20} = \frac{12}{15}$ 16
(87)　　　　　　　　　　　　(85)

22. What is the area of this triangle? 12 ft²
(79)

5 ft ⟋⟍ 5 ft
|4 ft
6 ft

▶ **23.** The illustration below shows a cube with edges 1 foot long. (Thus, the
(82) edges are also 12 inches long.) What is the volume of the cube in cubic
inches? 1728 in.³

1 ft　1 ft
　　　　12 in.
1 ft
　　　　12 in.
12 in.

24. Write the prime factorization of 225 using exponents. $3^2 \cdot 5^2$
(73)

25. **Connect** The length of segment AC is 56 mm. The length of segment
(69) BC is 26 mm. How long is segment AB? 30 mm

A　　　　　B　　　　C

▶* **26.** **Estimate** On a number line, $\sqrt{60}$ is between which two consecutive
(89) whole numbers? 7 and 8

* **27.** Which whole number equals $\sqrt{225}$? 15
(89)

Lesson 91　477

▶ See Math Conversations in the sidebar.

3 **Written Practice** (Continued)

Math Conversations
Discussion opportunities are provided below.

Problem 20 **Analyze**
"Explain how to find the value of y." divide
10 by 6

*"Why should the value of y be written as
a mixed number and not as a decimal
number?"* Sample: A decimal quotient
should only be given when the dividend is a
decimal dividend.

Point out that the division $10 \div 6$ produces a
quotient that is a repeating decimal.

Problem 21 **Analyze**
To solve a proportion, we can cross multiply
and solve the resulting equation or we can
multiply by a constant factor. With either
method we may use an equivalent form of the
known ration.

*"Which method would you use to solve
this proportion? Why?"* Sample: I would
reduce $\frac{12}{15}$ to $\frac{4}{5}$ and then multiply by the
constant ratio so that I can solve the
proportion mentally.

Problem 23 **Analyze**
Extend the Problem
*"What fraction of a cubic yard is the volume
of the cube?"* $\frac{1}{27}$

Problem 26 **Estimate**
*"How can we use the squares of counting
numbers to solve this problem?"* Sample:
Find the greatest perfect square that is less
than 60 and the least perfect square that is
greater than 60. Since $7^2 = 49$ and $8^2 = 64$,
$\sqrt{60}$ is between 7 and 8.

(continued)

Math Conversations

Discussion opportunities are provided below.

Problem 29 Evaluate

Extend the Problem

Encourage students to compare their area estimates and work cooperatively to explain any unreasonable discrepancies.

Problem 30 Analyze

With students, create a table showing all of the possible outcomes for a coin being tossed three times. The completed table should show these eight possible outcomes:

1st Toss	2nd Toss	3rd Toss
H	H	H
H	H	T
H	T	H
H	T	T
T	H	H
T	H	T
T	T	H
T	T	T

After creating the table, point out that the probability (P) of heads for each toss is $\frac{1}{2}$.

Toss	1st	2nd	3rd
P (heads)	$\frac{1}{2}$	$\frac{1}{2}$	$\frac{1}{2}$

The probability of heads for all three tosses is the product of these probabilities, which is $\frac{1}{8}$.

28.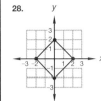

28. **Model** A square has vertices at the coordinates (2, 0), (0, −2), (−2, 0), and (0, 2). Graph the points on graph paper, and draw segments from point to point in the order given. To complete the square, draw a fourth segment from (0, 2) to (2, 0).
(Inv. 7)

▶* **29.** **Evaluate** The square in problem 28 encloses some whole squares and some half squares on the graph paper.
(Inv. 7)

   a. How many whole squares are enclosed by the square?
   4 whole squares
   b. How many half squares are enclosed by the square?   8 half squares

   c. Counting two half squares as a whole square, calculate the area of the entire square.   8 square units

▶* **30.** **Analyze** John will toss a coin three times. What is the probability that the coin will land heads up all three times? Express the probability ratio as a fraction and as a decimal. $\frac{1}{8}$; 0.125
(Inv. 9)

Early Finishers
Real-World
Application

The square practice field where Raul plays baseball has an area of 820 square yards. Before practice, Raul runs once around the bases to warm up.

   a. Estimate the distance Raul runs to warm up. Explain how you made your estimate.

   b. Next week, Raul has to run around the bases twice to warm up for practice. If he practices 3 days next week, estimate the total distance he will run to warm up.
   a. Sample: $A = s^2$, so $820 = s^2$ and $s = \sqrt{820}$. Since $\sqrt{784}$ is 28, and $\sqrt{841}$ is 29, the $\sqrt{820}$ is between 28 and 29. 28 yd × 4 = 112 yd, and 29 yd × 4 = 116 yd. Thus the distance Raul runs to warm up is between 112 yards and 116 yards.
   b. between 672 yards and 696 yards

▶ See Math Conversations in the sidebar.

Looking Forward

Using geometric formulas to calculate area and perimeter prepares students for:

- **Lesson 93,** classifying triangles by their sides and by their angles.

- **Lesson 103,** finding the perimeter of complex shapes.

- **Lesson 107,** finding the area of complex shapes.

Expanded Notation with Exponents
Order of Operations with Exponents
Powers of Fractions

Objectives
- Write the powers of 10 with exponents when writing numbers in expanded notation.
- Simplify expressions with exponents and roots.
- Use exponents with fractions and decimals.

Lesson Preparation

Materials
- **Power Up L** (in *Instructional Masters*)
- **Manipulative kit: inch rulers**

Optional
- **Teacher-provided material: index cards**

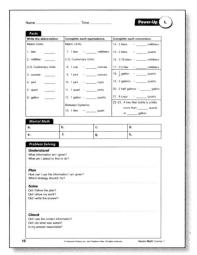

Power Up L

Math Language
Maintain	English Learners (ESL)
expanded notation	nearest
order of operation	

Technology Resources
Student eBook Complete student textbook in electronic format.

Resources and Planner CD Assessment, reteaching, and instructional masters, plus a pacing calendar with standards.

Test and Practice Generator CD Create additional practice sheets and custom-made tests.

www.SaxonPublishers.com Visit for more student activities and planning materials.

Inclusion

Adaptations CD Adapted lessons, investigations, practice and assessments.

Meeting Standards

National Council of Teachers of Mathematics (NCTM)

Numbers and Operations

NO.1a Work flexibly with fractions, decimals, and percents to solve problems

NO.1e Develop an understanding of large numbers and recognize and appropriately use exponential, scientific, and calculator notation

NO.2a Understand the meaning and effects of arithmetic operations with fractions, decimals, and integers

Connections

CN.4b Understand how mathematical ideas interconnect and build on one another to produce a coherent whole

Problem-Solving Strategy: Use Logical Reasoning

The basketball team's points-per-game average is 88 after its first four games. How many points does the team need to score during its fifth game to have a points-per-game average of 90?

(Understand) **Understand the problem.**

"What information are we given?"

The basketball team's points-per-game average is 88 for the first four games.

"What are we asked to do?"

Determine the number of points the team needs to score in game five to have an average of 90.

(Plan) **Make a plan.**

"What problem-solving strategy will we use?"

We will *use logical reasoning* to determine how many points above the desired average the team needs to score in the fifth game.

(Solve) **Carry out the plan.**

"According to the average, how far below the desired average is the team thus far?"

Each of the four average game scores is 2 points below the five-game average score the team is motivated to earn. The team's four-game average is a combined 8 points below the desired average.

"What must the team do in the fifth game to overcome the first four scores?"

They need to score 8 points above the desired average to offset the lower scores. Ninety plus eight is 98.

(Check) **Look back.**

"Did we complete the task?"

Yes. We found the score the team needs (98) to get a five-game average of 90. We can check by finding the average. To find the average we add the five scores: 88 + 88 + 88 + 88 + 98 = 450 and then divide: 450 ÷ 5 = 90.

- **Expanded Notation with Exponents**
- **Order of Operations with Exponents**
- **Powers of Fractions**

Power Up *Building Power*

facts | Power Up L

mental math |
a. **Number Sense:** 30 · 50   1500
b. **Number Sense:** 486 + 50   536
c. **Percent:** 50% of 24   12
d. **Calculation:** $20.00 − $14.75 $5.25
e. **Decimals:** 100 × 1.25   125
f. **Number Sense:** $\frac{600}{30}$ 20
g. **Algebra:** If $n = 3$, what does $5n$ equal?   15
h. **Calculation:** $\sqrt{36}$, + 4, × 3, + 2, ÷ 4, + 1, $\sqrt{}$ [1]   3

problem solving | The basketball team's points-per-game average is 88 after its first four games. How many points does the team need to score during its fifth game to have a points-per-game average of 90?   98

New Concepts *Increasing Knowledge*

expanded notation with exponents |
In Lesson 32 we began writing whole numbers in **expanded notation**. Here we show 365 in expanded notation:

$$365 = (3 \times 100) + (6 \times 10) + (5 \times 1)$$

When writing numbers in expanded notation, we may write the powers of 10 with exponents.

$$365 = (3 \times 10^2) + (6 \times 10^1) + (5 \times 10^0)$$

Notice that 10^0 equals 1. The table below shows whole-number place values using powers of 10:

Trillions			Billions			Millions			Thousands			Ones		
hundreds	tens	ones	hundreds	tens	ones	hundreds	tens	ones	hundreds	tens	ones	hundreds	tens	ones
10^{14}	10^{13}	10^{12}	10^{11}	10^{10}	10^9	10^8	10^7	10^6	10^5	10^4	10^3	10^2	10^1	10^0

---

[1] Read $\sqrt{}$ as "find the square root."

Lesson 92   479

---

1 Power Up

Facts
Distribute **Power Up L** to students. See answers below.

Mental Math
Before students begin the Mental Math exercise, do this counting exercise as a class.

Count up and down by 25s between −150 and 150.

Encourage students to share different ways to mentally compute these exercises. Strategies for exercises **c** and **d** are listed below.

c. **Use a Division Pattern**
$\frac{1}{2}$ of 20 is 10; $\frac{1}{2}$ of 22 is 11; $\frac{1}{2}$ of 24 is 12
Break Apart 24
$(\frac{1}{2}$ of 20) + $(\frac{1}{2}$ of 4) = 10 + 2 = 12

d. **Subtract $14, then Subtract 75¢**
$20 − $14 = $6; $6 − 75¢ = $5.25
Subtract $15, then Add 25¢
$20 − $15 = $5; $5 + 25¢ = $5.25

Problem Solving
Refer to **Power-Up Discussion,** p. 479B.

2 New Concepts

Instruction
Write $10^0 = 1$ on the board or overhead and remind students that any number (except 0) raised to the zero power equals 1.

As students study the table, encourage them to become familiar with the benchmark powers of ten, which include 10^3 (thousands), 10^6 (millions), 10^9 (billions), and 10^{12} (trillions).

(continued)

Facts

Write the abbreviation.	Complete each equivalence.	Complete each conversion.
Metric Units:	Metric Units:	14. 2 liters = __2000__ milliliters
1. liter __L__	7. 1 liter = __1000__ milliliters	15. 2 liters ≈ __2__ quarts
2. milliliter __mL__	U.S. Customary Units:	16. 3.78 liters = __3780__ milliliters
U.S. Customary Units:	8. 1 cup = __8__ ounces	17. 0.5 liter = __500__ milliliters
3. ounces __oz__	9. 1 pint = __16__ ounces	18. $\frac{1}{2}$ gallon = __2__ quarts
4. pint __pt__	10. 1 pint = __2__ cups	19. 2 gallons = __8__ quarts
5. quart __qt__	11. 1 quart = __2__ pints	20. 2 half gallons = __1__ gallon
6. gallon __gal__	12. 1 gallon = __4__ quarts	21. 8 cups = __2__ quarts
	Between Systems:	22–23. A two-liter bottle is a little more than __2__ quarts
	13. 1 liter ≈ __1__ quart	or $\frac{1}{2}$ gallon.

Example 1

Instruction

Have students note that the zeros in the hundreds, tens, and ones places of 186,000 are not included in the expanded notation of the number.

Instruction

You might choose to have students record the Order of Operations on an index card for reference throughout this lesson and for future reference.

Example 2

Instruction

For multiplication and division, it is important for students to understand that the operations of multiplication *and* division in an expression are performed in the order they appear, from left to right. A common error students sometimes make is to begin on the left and perform all of the multiplications in an expression, then begin on the left again and perform all of the divisions.

Students must understand that the same is true for addition and subtraction—the operations of addition *and* subtraction in an expression are performed in the order they appear, from left to right.

(continued)

Example 1

The speed of light is about 186,000 miles per second. Write 186,000 in expanded notation using exponents.

Solution

We write each nonzero digit (1, 8, and 6) multiplied by its place value.

$$186,000 = (1 \times 10^5) + (8 \times 10^4) + (6 \times 10^3)$$

order of operations with exponents

In the order of operations, we simplify expressions with exponents or roots before we multiply or divide.

Order of Operations

1. Simplify within parentheses.
2. Simplify powers and roots.
3. Multiply and divide from left to right.
4. Add and subtract from left to right.

Some students remember the order of operations by using this memory aid:

Please

Excuse

My **D**ear

Aunt **S**ally

The first letter of each word is meant to remind us of the order of operations.

Parentheses

Exponents

Multiplication **D**ivision

Addition **S**ubtraction

Visit www.SaxonPublishers.com/ActivitiesC1 for a graphing calculator activity.

Example 2

Simplify: $5 - (8 + 8) \div \sqrt{16} + 3^2 \times 2$

Solution

We follow the order of operations.

$5 - (8 + 8) \div \sqrt{16} + 3^2 \times 2$	original problem
$5 - 16 \div \sqrt{16} + 3^2 \times 2$	simplified in parentheses
$5 - 16 \div 4 + 9 \times 2$	simplified powers and roots
$5 - 4 + 18$	multiplied and divided
19	added and subtracted

powers of fractions

We may use exponents with fractions and with decimals. With fractions, parentheses help clarify that an exponent applies to the whole fraction, not just its numerator.

$$\left(\frac{1}{2}\right)^3 \text{ means } \frac{1}{2} \cdot \frac{1}{2} \cdot \frac{1}{2}$$

$$(0.1)^2 \text{ means } 0.1 \times 0.1$$

Example 3

Simplify: $\left(\frac{2}{3}\right)^2$

Solution

We write $\frac{2}{3}$ as a factor twice and then multiply.

$$\frac{2}{3} \cdot \frac{2}{3} = \frac{4}{9}$$

Practice Set

a. Write 2,500,000 in expanded notation using exponents.
$(2 \times 10^6) + (5 \times 10^5)$

b. Write this number in standard notation: 5,200,000,000
$$(5 \times 10^9) + (2 \times 10^8)$$

Simplify:

c. $10 + 2^3 \times 3 - (7 + 2) \div \sqrt{9}$ 31

d. $\left(\frac{1}{2}\right)^3$ $\frac{1}{8}$ **e.** $(0.1)^2$ 0.01   ▶ **f.** $\left(1\frac{1}{2}\right)^2$ $2\frac{1}{4}$

g. $(2 + 3)^2 - (2^2 + 3^2)$ 12

Written Practice   *Strengthening Concepts*

1. It is more likely not to rain. If the chance of rain is 40%, then the chance that it will not rain is 60%. So the chance that it will not rain is greater than the chance that it will rain.

1. **Explain** The weather forecast stated that the chance of rain for
(58) Wednesday is 40%. Does this forecast mean that it is more likely to rain or not to rain? Why?

▶ **2.** A set of 36 shape cards contains an equal number of cards with
(58, 74) hexagons, squares, circles, and triangles. What is the probability of drawing a square from this set of cards? Express the probability ratio as a fraction and as a decimal. $\frac{1}{4}$; 0.25

3. **Connect** If the sum of three numbers is 144, what is the average of the
(18) three numbers?   48

4. **Verify** "All quadrilaterals are polygons." True or false?   true
(60)

* **5.** $\sqrt{441}$ 21   ▶ * **6.** $2 \cdot 3^2 - \sqrt{9} + (3 - 1)^3$ 23
(89)   (92)

* **7.** Write the formula for the perimeter of a rectangle. Then substitute 12 in.
(91) for the length and 6 in. for the width. Solve the equation to find the perimeter of the rectangle.
$P = 2l + 2w$; $P = 2(12 \text{ in.}) + 2(6 \text{ in.})$; $P = 36 \text{ in.}$

▶ See Math Conversations in the sidebar.

Math Background

When fractions are raised to a power, they are placed in parentheses to show that the exponent applies to the entire fraction, not just to the numerator. The following examples demonstrate the importance of this distinction.

1. $\left(\frac{2}{5}\right)^2 = \frac{2}{5} \cdot \frac{2}{5} = \frac{4}{25}$

2. $\frac{2^2}{5} = \frac{2 \cdot 2}{5} = \frac{4}{5}$

---

2 New Concepts (Continued)

Example 3
Instruction

"Recall what we learned about a base and an exponent. What is the base in this expression, and what is the exponent?" $\frac{2}{3}$; 2

"What does an exponent tells us about a base?" The exponent tells the number of times the base is used as a factor.

Practice Set
Problem f [Error Alert]

Refer students who have difficulty understanding how to find the answer to look again at example 3, in which a fraction was raised to a power. Students should infer that to find the square of $1\frac{1}{2}$, they should first rewrite the mixed number as an improper fraction.

---

3 Written Practice

Math Conversations
Discussion opportunities are provided below.

Problem 6 [Analyze]

Write the expression on the board or overhead. Invite one volunteer to complete the first step of the Order of Operations (parentheses) and explain why that step is being completed while students complete the operation at their desks.

Invite another volunteer to complete the second step of the Order of Operations (powers and exponents from left to right) and explain why that step is being completed while students complete the operations at their desks.

Continue until the expression has been simplified to 23. Remind students often of the importance of following the Order of Operations.

Errors and Misconceptions
Problem 2

An answer of $\frac{9}{36}$ is not in lowest terms. Remind students that whenever they work with probabilities written as fractions, and in a more general sense, to always express their answer in lowest terms.

(continued)

Math Conversations

Discussion opportunities are provided below.

Problem 17 [Estimate]

"Suppose we did not have to round our answer to the nearest square inch. Our answer still would be an estimate, and not an exact answer. Why?" Pi is used as an approximation; whenever an approximation is used in a computation, the computation will not produce an exact answer.

Problem 19 [Analyze]

Extend the Problem

"To the nearest whole percent, what percent of the letters in your full name are vowels?"

"To the nearest whole percent, what percent of the letters in your full name are consonants?"

Encourage students to use division to make both computations, and then find the sum of the percents. If the sum is not 100%, ask students to explain why. The percents are rounded and not exact.

Problem 20 [Connect]

Tell students which direction in the classroom represents North, then encourage them to stand and act out the problem if they wish. An alternative is to sketch a diagram.

Problem 22 [Analyze]

Challenge students to name the constant factor of the proportion using only mental math. $2\frac{1}{2}$

(continued)

---

8. Arrange these numbers in order from least to greatest: $-1, 0, 0.1, 1$
(44)
$1, 0, 0.1, -1$

9. If $\frac{5}{6}$ of the 30 members were present, how many members were absent?
(77) 5 members

10. Reduce before multiplying or dividing: $\dfrac{(24)(36)}{48}$ 18
(70)

* 11. $\dfrac{\sqrt{100}}{\sqrt{25}}$ 2
(92)

12. $12\frac{5}{6} + 15\frac{1}{3}$ $28\frac{1}{6}$
(59)

13. $100 - 9.9$ 90.1
(38)

14. $\frac{4}{7} \times 100$ $57\frac{1}{7}$
(29)

15. $\frac{5}{8} = \frac{w}{48}$ 30
(42)

16. $0.25 \times \$4.60$ $1.15
(39)

▶*** 17.** [Estimate]   The diameter of a circular saucepan is 6 inches. What is the area of the circular base of the pan? Round the answer to the nearest square inch. (Use 3.14 for π.)   28 square inches
(86)

18. Write $3\frac{3}{4}$ as a decimal number and subtract that number from 7.4.   3.65
(74)

▶ **19.** What percent of the first ten letters of the alphabet are vowels?   30%
(75)

▶*** 20.** [Connect]   Bobby rode his bike north. At Grand Avenue he turned left 90°. When he reached Arden Road, he turned left 90°. In what direction was Bobby riding on Arden Road?   south
(90)

21. [Estimate]   Find the product of 6.95 and 12.1 to the nearest whole number.   84
(51)

▶*** 22.** [Analyze]   Write and solve a proportion for this statement: 16 is to 10 as what number is to 25? $\frac{16}{10} = \frac{w}{25}$; $w = 40$
(85)

23. What is the area of the triangle below?   24 cm²
(79)

11 cm   6 cm

8 cm

24. This figure is a rectangular prism.
(Inv. 6)
   a. How many faces does it have?   6 faces

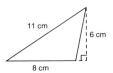

   b. How many edges does it have?
   12 edges

25. [Predict]   Each term in this sequence is $\frac{1}{16}$ more than the previous term. What are the next four terms in the sequence?
(17)

$$\frac{1}{16}, \frac{1}{8}, \frac{3}{16}, \frac{1}{4}, \underline{\frac{5}{16}}, \underline{\frac{3}{8}}, \underline{\frac{7}{16}}, \underline{\frac{1}{2}}, \dots$$

▶ See Math Conversations in the sidebar.

English Learners

In problem 21 explain the term **nearest.** Say,

"When you measure something, you don't always need an exact measurement. You may want to round your answer to the nearest, or closest, whole number."

Have students round different numbers with decimals to the nearest whole number (1.2 to 1, 3.8 to 4, 10.25 to 10).

Use a ruler to find the length and width of this rectangle to the nearest quarter of an inch. Then refer to the rectangle to answer problems **26** and **27**.

$\frac{1}{2}$ in.

$\frac{3}{4}$ in.

➤ **26.** What is the perimeter of the rectangle? $2\frac{1}{2}$ in.
   (91)

➤ **27.** What is the area of the rectangle? $\frac{3}{8}$ in.^{2}
   (91)

28. **Connect** The coordinates of the vertices of a parallelogram are (4, 3),
   (Inv. 7) (−2, 3), (0, −2), and (−6, −2). What is the area of the parallelogram?
   30 sq. units

* **29.** Simplify:
   (81)
   a. (12 cm)(8 cm)   96 cm^2 **b.** $\frac{36 \text{ ft}^2}{4 \text{ ft}}$ 9 ft

30. Fernando poured water from one-pint bottles into a three-gallon bucket.
   (78) How many pints of water could the bucket hold?   24 pints

Early Finishers
Math and Geography

There are close to 4 million people living on the island of Puerto Rico, making it one of the most densely populated islands in the world. If the population density is approximately 1,000 people per square mile, how many people live in a 3.5 square mile area? Write and solve a proportion to answer this question. $\frac{1000 \text{ people}}{1 \text{ sq. mile}} = \frac{x \text{ people}}{3.5 \text{ sq. mile}}$; $x = 1000 \times 3.5 = 3{,}500$; There are about 3,500 people living in a 3.5 square mile area.

▶ See Math Conversations in the sidebar.

Errors and Misconceptions
Problems 26 and 27

Because the length and the width of the rectangle are to be measured to the nearest quarter inch, students must recognize that the eighth-inch marks of their rulers are used to decide which quarter-inch mark to round each of the measures to.

Ask students to identify the marks on their rulers that represent eighth-inch marks.

Looking Forward

Writing the powers of 10 with exponents when writing whole numbers in expanded notation prepares students for:

• **Lesson 113,** multiplying by powers of 10 to write numbers in standard form.

• Classifying Triangles

Objectives

- Classify triangles by the lengths of their sides.
- Classify triangles by the measures of their angles.

Materials

- **Power Up I** (in *Instructional Masters*)

Optional

- **Investigation Activity 15** (in *Instructional Masters*) or graph paper
- **Manipulative Kit: Relational GeoSolids, triangular prism**
- **Teacher-provided material: sets of triangular cutouts**

Math Language

New		English Learners (ESL)
acute triangle	obtuse triangle	constructed
equilateral triangle	right triangle	
isosceles triangle	scalene triangle	

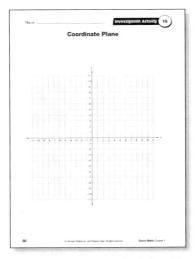

Power Up I   Investigation Activity 15

Technology Resources

Student eBook Complete student textbook in electronic format.

Resources and Planner CD Assessment, reteaching, and instructional masters, plus a pacing calendar with standards.

Test and Practice Generator CD Create additional practice sheets and custom-made tests.

www.SaxonPublishers.com Visit for more student activities and planning materials.

Inclusion

Adaptations CD Adapted lessons, investigations, practice and assessments.

National Council of Teachers of Mathematics (NCTM)

Geometry

GM.1a Precisely describe, classify, and understand relationships among types of two- and three-dimensional objects using their defining properties

GM.4e Recognize and apply geometric ideas and relationships in areas outside the mathematics classroom, such as art, science, and everyday life

Communication

CM.3a Organize and consolidate their mathematical thinking through communication

CM.3c Analyze and evaluate the mathematical thinking and strategies of others

CM.3d Use the language of mathematics to express mathematical ideas precisely

Problem-Solving Strategy: Use Logical Reasoning

Benjamin put 2 purple marbles, 7 red marbles, and 1 brown marble in a bag and shook the bag. If he reaches in and chooses a marble without looking, what is the probability that he chooses a red marble? A purple or brown marble? What is the probability of *not* choosing a red marble? If Benjamin does choose a red marble, but gives it away, what is the probability he will choose *another* red marble?

(Understand) **Understand the problem.**

"What information are we given?"

2 purple marbles, 7 red marbles, and 1 brown marble are mixed in a bag.

"What are we asked to do?"

Determine what the probability is (1) of choosing a red marble, (2) of choosing a purple or brown marble, (3) of not choosing a red marble, and (4) of choosing a red marble after one red marble is removed.

(Plan) **Make a plan.**

"What problem-solving strategy will we use?"

We will *use logical reasoning.*

(Solve) **Carry out the plan.**

"What is the total number of marbles that Benjamin put in the bag?"

10

"What is the probability of choosing a red marble?"

Seven of the ten marbles are red, so the probability is $\frac{7}{10}$.

"What is the probability of choosing a purple or brown marble?"

$\frac{(2 + 1)}{10} = \frac{3}{10}$

"What is the probability of not choosing a red marble?"

Three of the ten marbles are not red, so the probability is $\frac{3}{10}$.

"If Benjamin chooses a red marble and gives it away, how many marbles are left in his bag and how many are red?"

There are nine marbles in the bag and six are red.

"What is the probability of choosing a red marble after a red marble is removed?"

There are 6 red marbles remaining in the bag of 9 marbles, so the probability is $\frac{6}{9} = \frac{2}{3}$.

(Check) **Look back.**

"Did we find the answers to the questions that were asked?"

Yes. We found each of the four probabilities.

Facts
Distribute **Power Up I** to students. See answers below.

Mental Math
Before students begin the Mental Math exercise, do this counting exercise as a class.

Count up and down by $\frac{1}{8}$s between $\frac{1}{8}$ and 3.

Encourage students to share different ways to mentally compute these exercises. Strategies for exercises **b, c,** and **f** are listed below.

b. Change 234 to 200 + 34
  $200 - 50 = 150; 150 + 34 = 184$
  Count Back by Tens
  Start with 234. Count: 224, 214, 204, 194, 184
c. Multiply by $\frac{1}{4}$
  $\frac{1}{4} \times 24 = 6$
f. Find 10 × 25, then Multiply by 3
  $10 \times 25 = 250; 250 \times 3 = 750$
  Multiply Tens, then Ones
  $(30 \times 20) + (30 \times 5) = 600 + 150 = 750$

Problem Solving
Refer to **Power-Up Discussion,** p. 484B.

2 **New Concepts**

Instruction
Point out that a triangle is a polygon, and have students recall that a polygon is a closed, flat shape made up of line segments.

Students should recognize from the table that a scalene triangle and an equilateral triangle have an exact number of equal sides (a scalene triangle has none; an equilateral triangle has three). Students should infer from the table, however, that since an isosceles triangle has *at least* two sides that are equal in length, an equilateral triangle is also an isosceles triangle.

(continued)

Power Up   *Building Power*

facts	Power Up I
mental math	**a. Number Sense:** 40 · 60 2400
	b. Number Sense: 234 − 50 184
	c. Percent: 25% of 24 6
	d. Calculation: $5.99 + $2.47 $8.46
	e. Decimals: 1.2 ÷ 100 0.012
	f. Number Sense: 30 × 25 750
	g. Algebra: If $x = 5$, what does $5x$ equal? 25
	h. Calculation: $8 \times 9, + 3, \div 3, \sqrt{\ }, \times 6, + 3, \div 3, - 10$ 1

problem solving	Benjamin put 2 purple marbles, 7 red marbles, and 1 brown marble in a bag and shook the bag. If he reaches in and chooses a marble without looking, what is the probability that he chooses a red marble? A purple or brown marble? What is the probability of *not* choosing a red marble? If Benjamin does choose a red marble, but gives it away, what is the probability he will choose another red marble? $\frac{7}{10}; \frac{3}{10}; \frac{3}{10}; \frac{2}{3}$

New Concept   *Increasing Knowledge*

Thinking Skill

Generalize

Explain in your own words how the number of equal sides of a triangle compares to the number of equal angles it has.   They are the same.

All three-sided polygons are triangles, but not all triangles are alike. We distinguish between different types of triangles by using the lengths of their sides and the measures of their angles. We will first classify triangles based on the lengths of their sides.

Triangles Classified by Their Sides

Name	Example	Description
Equilateral triangle	△	All three sides are equal in length.
Isosceles triangle	△	At least two of the three sides are equal in length.
Scalene triangle	◿	All three sides have different lengths.

An **equilateral triangle** has three equal sides and three equal angles.

An **isosceles triangle** has at least two equal sides and two equal angles.

A **scalene triangle** has three unequal sides and three unequal angles.

Facts   Write each improper fraction as a mixed number. Reduce fractions.

$\frac{5}{4} = 1\frac{1}{4}$	$\frac{6}{4} = 1\frac{1}{2}$	$\frac{15}{10} = 1\frac{1}{2}$	$\frac{8}{3} = 2\frac{2}{3}$	$\frac{15}{12} = 1\frac{1}{4}$
$\frac{12}{8} = 1\frac{1}{2}$	$\frac{10}{8} = 1\frac{1}{4}$	$\frac{3}{2} = 1\frac{1}{2}$	$\frac{15}{6} = 2\frac{1}{2}$	$\frac{10}{4} = 2\frac{1}{2}$
$\frac{8}{6} = 1\frac{1}{3}$	$\frac{25}{10} = 2\frac{1}{2}$	$\frac{9}{6} = 1\frac{1}{2}$	$\frac{10}{6} = 1\frac{2}{3}$	$\frac{15}{8} = 1\frac{7}{8}$
$\frac{12}{10} = 1\frac{1}{5}$	$\frac{10}{3} = 3\frac{1}{3}$	$\frac{18}{12} = 1\frac{1}{2}$	$\frac{5}{2} = 2\frac{1}{2}$	$\frac{4}{3} = 1\frac{1}{3}$

Thinking Skill

Justify

Is an equilateral triangle also an isosceles triangle? Why or why not? Yes; Sample: An isosceles triangle has 2 or 3 equal sides. An equilateral triangle has 3 equal sides, so it is also an isosceles triangle.

Next, we consider triangles classified by their angles. In Lesson 28 we learned the names of three different kinds of angles: **acute, right,** and **obtuse.** We can also use these words to describe triangles.

Triangles Classified by Their Angles

Name	Example	Description
Acute triangle		All three angles are acute.
Right triangle		One angle is a right angle.
Obtuse triangle		One angle is an obtuse angle.

Each angle of an equilateral triangle measures 60°, so an equilateral triangle is also an acute triangle. An isosceles triangle may be an acute triangle, a right triangle, or an obtuse triangle. A scalene triangle may also be an acute triangle, a right triangle, or an obtuse triangle.

Practice Set

▶ **a.** One side of an equilateral triangle measures 15 cm. What is the perimeter of the triangle?   45 cm

▶ **b.** **Verify** "An equilateral triangle is also an acute triangle." True or false?   true

▶ **c.** **Verify** "All acute triangles are equilateral triangles." True or false?   false

▶ **d.** Two sides of a triangle measure 3 inches and 4 inches. If the perimeter is 10 inches, what type of triangle is it?   isosceles (also acute) triangle

▶ **e.** **Verify** "Every right triangle is a scalene triangle." True or false?   false

Written Practice   *Strengthening Concepts*

1.

	Ratio	A. C.
Length	5	*l*
Width	2	60

$$\frac{5}{2} = \frac{l}{60}$$

▶ *** 1.** **Model** Draw a ratio box for this problem. Then solve the problem using
(88)   a proportion.   150 ft

The ratio of the length to the width of the rectangular lot was 5 to 2. If the lot was 60 ft wide, how long was the lot?

* 2. Mitch does not know the correct answer to two multiple-choice
(Inv. 9)   questions. The choices are A, B, C, and D. If Mitch just guesses, what is the probability that Mitch will guess both answers correctly? $\frac{1}{16}$

3. If the sum of four numbers is 144, what is the average of the four
(18)   numbers?   36

Lesson 93   485

▶ See Math Conversations in the sidebar.

Instruction

One way to help students better understand how triangles are classified is to use construction paper and scissors (or have students use the materials) to create triangle cutouts for an isosceles, an equilateral, and a right triangle. Any triangles that are constructed can be displayed on the overhead.

An alternative to construction is to ask students to sketch each triangle.

Using the cutouts or sketches, students can practice classifying each triangle first by its sides, and then by its angles (for example, equilateral and acute or isosceles and obtuse).

Practice Set

Problems a and d [Error Alert]

If students solve these problems using mental math, encourage them to write and solve an equation to check each problem.

Problems b, c, and e [Verify]

Ask students to use an example to prove, or a non-example to disprove, each statement, then share their examples and non-examples with their classmates.

Math Conversations

Discussion opportunities are provided below.

Problem 1 [Model]

"One way to check our answer is to use a constant factor. What is the constant factor of this proportion?" 30

"How can the constant factor be used to check our answer?" multiply 5 by 30, and compare to 150

(continued)

Math Background

It is possible to classify a triangle solely by its sides. Even if the lengths of the sides of the triangle are not known. For example:

- If a triangle has a 90° angle, a 60° angle, and a 30° angle, the triangle is a scalene triangle because only scalene triangles have three unequal angles.

- If a triangle has two equal angles, it is an isosceles triangle because the sides opposite the equal angles are equal in length.

- If a triangle has three 60° angles, it is an equilateral triangle.

Math Conversations

Discussion opportunities are provided below.

Problem 15 `Conclude`

Extend the Problem

"In what type of triangle are all of the sides a different length?" scalene

"In what type of triangle is one angle measure greater than 90°?" obtuse

"In what type of triangle are all of the angle measures less than 90°?" acute; equilateral

"In what type of triangle are at least two of the sides the same length?" isosceles; equilateral

Problem 17 `Analyze`

"Explain the order in which the operations in this expression must be performed." First: the square (6^2) and square root $\sqrt{9}$; second: division ($36 \div 3$) and multiplication (3×3); third: addition ($10 + 12$) and subtraction ($22 - 9$); the expression simplifies to 13.

Problem 20 `Represent`

With student's help, list on the board or overhead all of the different factor pairs that could be used to begin the factor tree. 2×400; 4×200; 5×160; 8×100; 10×80; 16×50; 20×40; 25×32

As a way of checking their work, encourage individual students to each choose a different factor pair, then compare the completed prime factorizations.

Errors and Misconceptions

Problem 22 `Analyze`

Students must remember to change the divisor to a whole number by shifting the decimal point in the divisor *and* in the dividend at least two places to the right.

It is a good idea for students to place a decimal point in the quotient immediately after shifting the decimal point in the dividend. Although the decimal point may not be included in the final quotient, it will be there if needed and can be easily forgotten if it is placed at a later time.

(continued)

---

4. The rectangular prism shown below is constructed of 1-cubic-centimeter blocks. What is the volume of the prism? 64 cm³
(82)

5. Write $\frac{9}{25}$ as a decimal number and as a percent. 0.30, 30%
(74, 75)

6. Write $3\frac{1}{5}$ as a decimal number and add it to 3.5. What is the sum? 6.7
(74)

7. What number is 45% of 80? 36
(41)

8. $(0.3)^3$ 0.027   **9.** $\left(2\frac{1}{2}\right)^2$ $6\frac{1}{4}$ *** 10.** $\sqrt{9} \cdot \sqrt{100}$ 30
(73)   (73)   (92)

11. Twenty of the two dozen members voted yes. What fraction of the members voted yes? $\frac{5}{6}$
(77)

12. `Analyze` If the rest of the members in problem 11 voted no, then what was the ratio of "no" votes to "yes" votes? $\frac{1}{5}$
(23)

Find each unknown number:

13. $w + 4\frac{3}{4} = 9\frac{1}{3}$ $4\frac{7}{12}$ *** 14.** $\frac{6}{5} = \frac{m}{30}$ 36
(63)   (85)

▶*** 15.** `Conclude` In what type of triangle are all three sides the same length? equilateral triangle
(93)

16. What mixed number is $\frac{3}{8}$ of 100? $37\frac{1}{2}$
(42)

▶*** 17.** `Analyze` $10 + 6^2 \div 3 - \sqrt{9} \times 3$ 13
(92)

18. A triangular prism has how many faces? 5 faces
(Inv. 6)

19. How many quarts of milk is $2\frac{1}{2}$ gallons of milk? 10 quarts
(78)

▶ **20.** `Represent` Use a factor tree to find the prime factors of 800. Then write the prime factorization of 800 using exponents. $2^5 \cdot 5^2$
(65, 73)

21. Round the decimal number one hundred twenty-five thousandths to the nearest tenth. 0.1
(51)

▶*** 22.** $0.08n = \$1.20$ \$15.00
(87)

23. The diagonal segment through this rectangle divides the rectangle into two congruent right triangles. What is the area of one of the triangles? 234 mm²
(79)

18 mm

26 mm

24. Write $\frac{17}{20}$ as a percent. 85%
(75)

20.
one possibility:

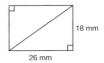

```
        800
       /    \
     10      80
    /  \    /  \
   2   5   8   10
          / \  / \
         2  4 2  5
           / \
          2  2
```

▶ See Math Conversations in the sidebar.

English Learners

In problem **4,** refer to the rectangular prism to explain the term **constructed.** Say,

"When something is constructed, it has been built or put together. This prism has been built with 1-cubic-centimeter blocks."

Have students build different shapes using color cubes, and have them name the shape, starting with: "I constructed (a pyramid)."

▸* 25. *Estimate* On this number line the arrow could be pointing to which of
the following? **B**
(89)

    A $\sqrt{1}$ **B** $\sqrt{2}$ **C** $\sqrt{3}$ **D** $\sqrt{4}$

* 26. Write this number in standard notation: 7,250,000,000
(92)

$$(7 \times 10^9) + (2 \times 10^8) + (5 \times 10^7)$$

27. c. Sample:
The event is
rolling 6 and its
complement
is not rolling 6.
The relationship
between the two
probabilities is
that their sum is 1:
$\frac{1}{6} + \frac{5}{6} = 1$.

27. a. What is the probability of rolling a 6 with a single roll of a number
(58)   cube? $\frac{1}{6}$

    b. What is the probability of rolling a number less than 6 with a single
     roll of a number cube? $\frac{5}{6}$

    c. Name the event and its complement. Then describe the relationship
     between the two probabilities.

28. *Represent* The coordinates of the four vertices of a quadrilateral are
(64,
Inv. 7) $(-3, -2)$, $(0, 2)$, $(3, 2)$, and $(5, -2)$. What is the name for this type of
quadrilateral?   trapezoid

29. 150 cm^2;
Sample: $A = \frac{bh}{2}$,
$A = \frac{(20\ cm)(15\ cm)}{2}$
$= \frac{300\ cm^2}{2}$
$= 150\ cm^2$

▸* 29. *Explain* The formula for the area of a triangle is
(91)

$$A = \frac{bh}{2}$$

If the base measures 20 cm and the height measures 15 cm, then what
is the area of the triangle? Explain your thinking.

30. *Generalize* Write the rule for this sequence. Then write the next
(10, 17) four numbers.

$$\frac{1}{16}, \frac{1}{8}, \frac{3}{16}, \frac{1}{4}, \frac{5}{16}, \frac{3}{8}, \underline{\quad\frac{7}{16}\quad}, \underline{\quad\frac{1}{2}\quad}, \underline{\quad\frac{9}{16}\quad}, \underline{\quad\frac{5}{8}\quad}, \ldots$$

Sample: The rule is add $\frac{1}{16}$ to the preceding number.

Early Finishers
Real-World Application

A teacher emptied a 1.5 oz snack-sized box of raisins into a dish. The
teacher then asked for volunteers to estimate the number of raisins in the
dish. Twelve volunteers gave the following estimates.

     84   100   50   75   66   75   70   90   85   77   91   80

a. stem-and-leaf
plot; Sample: A
stem-and-leaf
plot is the most
appropriate
display because
a circle graph is
used to display
parts of a whole.
See student
graphs.

    a. Which type of display—a circle graph or a stem-and-leaf plot—is the
     most appropriate way to display this data? Draw your display and justify
     your choice.

    b. The dish contained exactly 85 raisins. How many volunteers made a
     reasonable estimate? Give a reason to support your answer. (Hint: You
     might think of how far off an estimate is in terms of a percent of 85.)
     Accept any answer supported by sensible reasoning. Sample based on
     hint; Any answer that is 20% more or less than 85 seems reasonable.
     Since 20% of 85 = 17, and 85 − 17 = 68 and 85 + 17 = 102, any answer
     between 68 and 102 is reasonable. Using plus or minus 20%, all answers
     except two—50 and 66—were reasonable guesses.

Lesson 93   487

▸ See Math Conversations in the sidebar.

3 **Written Practice** *(Continued)*

Math Conversations
Discussion opportunities are provided below.

Problem 25   *Estimate*
*"What do the tick marks on the number line
represent? Explain how you know."* Since
four tick marks create five equal lengths
between consecutive numbers, each tick
mark represents $\frac{1}{5}$. As a decimal number,
each tick mark represents 0.2 because 0.2 is
the quotient of 1 divided by 5.

Problem 29   *Explain*
Extend the Problem
If students struggle solving the following
problem, encourage them to first solve a
simpler problem.

*"How would you find the height of a
triangle given only its area and the
measure of its base?"* $\frac{2A}{b}$.

Teacher Tip

Encourage students to sketch the
figure for problem 28 without graph
paper. However, some students
may need a copy of **Investigation
Activity 15** Coordinate Plane or
graph paper to graph the points
given in this problem.

Looking Forward

Classifying triangles by the lengths
of their sides and by the measures
of their angles prepares students
for:

• **Lesson 110,** determining lines of
symmetry in triangles and other
shapes.

• Writing Fractions and Decimals as Percents, Part 2

Objectives

• Change a fraction, a decimal, or a mixed number to a percent by multiplying by 100%.

Lesson Preparation

Materials

• **Power Up K** (in *Instructional Masters*)
• **Investigation Activity 15** (in *Instructional Masters*) or **graph paper**

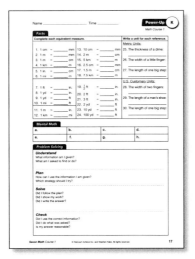

Power Up K

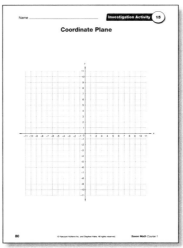

Investigation Activity 15

Technology Resources

Student eBook Complete student textbook in electronic format.

Resources and Planner CD Assessment, reteaching, and instructional masters, plus a pacing calendar with standards.

Test and Practice Generator CD Create additional practice sheets and custom-made tests.

www.SaxonPublishers.com Visit for more student activities and planning materials.

Inclusion

Adaptations CD Adapted lessons, investigations, practice and assessments.

Meeting Standards

National Council of Teachers of Mathematics (NCTM)

Numbers and Operations

NO.1a Work flexibly with fractions, decimals, and percents to solve problems

NO.1c Develop meaning for percents greater than 100 and less than 1

Communication

CM.3a Organize and consolidate their mathematical thinking through communication

Representation

RE.5b Select, apply, and translate among mathematical representations to solve problems

Problem-Solving Strategy: Find a Pattern

What are the next four numbers in this sequence: $\frac{1}{12}, \frac{1}{6}, \frac{1}{4}, \frac{1}{3} \ldots$

Understand *Understand the problem.*

"What information are we given?"

The first four terms of a sequence are $\frac{1}{12}, \frac{1}{6}, \frac{1}{4}$, and $\frac{1}{3}$.

"What are we asked to do"?

Extend the sequence for four more terms.

Plan *Make a plan.*

"What problem-solving strategies could we use?"

We need to *find the pattern* to extend this sequence.

Solve *Carry out the plan.*

"How do we begin?"

We will write the fractions with common denominators (12) and look for
a pattern.

$$\frac{1}{12} \quad \frac{1}{6} \quad \frac{1}{4} \quad \frac{1}{3} \quad \ldots$$
$$\downarrow \quad \downarrow \quad \downarrow \quad \downarrow$$
$$\frac{1}{12} \quad \frac{2}{12} \quad \frac{3}{12} \quad \frac{4}{12}$$

"How do we proceed?"

We can see that the sequence increases by $\frac{1}{12}$th in each term. We will extend the
sequence by adding four more terms and simplify the fractions when possible.

$$\frac{1}{12} \quad \frac{2}{12} \quad \frac{3}{12} \quad \frac{4}{12} \quad \frac{5}{12} \quad \frac{6}{12} \quad \frac{7}{12} \quad \frac{8}{12}$$
$$\downarrow \quad \downarrow \quad \downarrow \quad \downarrow \quad \downarrow \quad \downarrow \quad \downarrow \quad \downarrow$$
$$\frac{1}{12} \quad \frac{1}{6} \quad \frac{1}{4} \quad \frac{1}{3} \quad \frac{5}{12} \quad \frac{1}{2} \quad \frac{7}{12} \quad \frac{2}{3} \quad \ldots$$

Check *Look back.*

"Did we complete the task?"

Yes. We found the next four numbers in the sequence $(\frac{5}{12}, \frac{1}{2}, \frac{7}{12}, \frac{2}{3})$.

• Writing Fractions and Decimals as Percents, Part 2

1 Power Up

Facts
Distribute **Power Up K** to students. See answers below.

Mental Math
Before students begin the Mental Math exercise, do this counting exercise as a class.

Count up and down by 12s between 12 and 144.

Encourage students to share different ways to mentally compute these exercises. Strategies for exercises **b** and **f** are listed below.

b. Add 200, then Subtract 50
$572 + 200 = 772; 772 - 50 = 722$

Add 100, then Count On by Tens
$572 + 100 = 672$; Count: 682, 692, 702, 712, 722

f. Cancel Zeros
$\frac{640}{20} = \frac{64\cancel{0}}{2\cancel{0}} = \frac{64}{2} = 32$

Shift the Decimal Points One Place
$\frac{640}{20} = \frac{64.0}{2.0} = \frac{64}{2} = 32$

Problem Solving
Refer to **Power-Up Discussion**, p. 488B.

2 New Concepts

Instruction
Give students an opportunity to recall the Identity Property of Multiplication and connect the property to writing fractions and decimals as percents.

"Describe the Identity Property of Multiplication." The property states that the product of any number and 1 is equal to that number.

"In this example, why can we multiply $\frac{3}{5}$ by 100%?" Multiplying a number by 100% is the same as multiplying the number by 1, which does not change the value of the number.

(continued)

Power Up · *Building Power*

facts   Power Up K

mental math
a. **Number Sense:** $50 \cdot 70$ 3500
b. **Number Sense:** $572 + 150$ 722
c. **Percent:** 50% of 80   40
d. **Calculation:** $10.00 - $6.36 $3.64
e. **Decimals:** 100×0.02 2
f. **Number Sense:** $\frac{640}{20}$ 32
g. **Algebra:** If $r = 6$, what does $9r$ equal?   54
h. **Calculation:** $4 \times 5, + 1, \div 3, \times 8, - 1, \div 5, \times 4, - 2, \div 2$ 21

problem solving   What are the next four numbers in this sequence: $\frac{1}{12}, \frac{1}{6}, \frac{1}{4}, \frac{1}{3}, \cdots$ $\frac{5}{12}, \frac{1}{2}, \frac{7}{12}, \frac{2}{3}$

New Concept · *Increasing Knowledge*

Move the decimal point two places to the right and write a percent sign.

Thinking Skill

Discuss

How can you use mental math to change a decimal to a percent?

Since Lesson 75 we have practiced changing a fraction or decimal to a percent by writing an equivalent fraction with a denominator of 100.

$$\frac{3}{5} = \frac{60}{100} = 60\%$$

$$0.4 = 0.40 = \frac{40}{100} = 40\%$$

In this lesson we will practice another method of changing a fraction to a percent. Since 100% equals 1, we can multiply a fraction by 100% to form an equivalent number. Here we multiply $\frac{3}{5}$ by 100%:

$$\frac{3}{5} \times \frac{100\%}{1} = \frac{300\%}{5}$$

Then we simplify and find that $\frac{3}{5}$ equals 60%.

$$\frac{300\%}{5} = 60\%$$

We can use the same procedure to change decimals to percents. Here we multiply 0.375 by 100%.

$$0.375 \times 100\% = 37.5\%$$

> **To change a number to a percent, multiply the number by 100%.**

488   *Saxon Math Course 1*

Facts

Complete each equivalent measure.						Write a unit for each reference.
						Metric Units:
1. 1 cm	= 10 mm	13. 10 cm	= 100 mm			25. The thickness of a dime:
2. 1 m	= 1000 mm	14. 2 m	= 200 cm			millimeter
3. 1 m	= 100 cm	15. 5 km	= 5000 m			26. The width of a little finger:
4. 1 km	= 1000 m	16. 2.5 cm	= 25 mm			centimeter
5. 1 in.	= 2.54 cm	17. 1.5 m	= 150 cm			27. The length of one big step:
6. 1 mi	≈ 1610 m	18. 7.5 km	= 7500 m			meter
						U.S. Customary Units:
7. 1 ft	= 12 in.	19. $\frac{1}{2}$ ft	= 6 in.			28. The width of two fingers:
8. 1 yd	= 36 in.	20. 2 ft	= 24 in.			inch
9. 1 yd	= 3 ft	21. 3 ft	= 36 in.			29. The length of a man's shoe:
10. 1 mi	= 5280 ft	22. 2 yd	= 6 ft			foot
11. 1 m	≈ 39 in.	23. 10 yd	= 30 ft			30. The length of one big step:
12. 1 km	≈ 0.62 mi	24. 100 yd	= 300 ft			yard

Example 1

Change $\frac{1}{3}$ to a percent.

Solution

We multiply $\frac{1}{3}$ by 100%.

$$\frac{1}{3} \times \frac{100\%}{1} = \frac{100\%}{3}$$

To simplify, we divide 100% by 3 and write the quotient as a mixed number.

$$\begin{array}{r} 33\frac{1}{3}\% \\ 3\overline{)100\%} \\ \underline{9} \\ 10 \\ \underline{9} \\ 1 \end{array}$$

Example 2

Write 1.2 as a percent.

Solution

We multiply 1.2 by 100%.

$$1.2 \times 100\% = \mathbf{120\%}$$

In some applications a percent may be greater than 100%. If the number we are changing to a percent is greater than 1, then the percent is greater than 100%.

Example 3

Write $2\frac{1}{4}$ as a percent.

Solution

We show two methods below.

Method 1: We split the whole number and fraction. The mixed number $2\frac{1}{4}$ means "$2 + \frac{1}{4}$." We change each part to a percent and then add.

$$2 + \frac{1}{4}$$

$$200\% + 25\% = \mathbf{225\%}$$

Method 2: We change the mixed number to an improper fraction. The mixed number $2\frac{1}{4}$ equals the improper fraction $\frac{9}{4}$. We then change $\frac{9}{4}$ to a percent.

$$\frac{9}{\cancel{4}_{1}} \times \frac{\overset{25}{\cancel{100}}\%}{1} = \mathbf{225\%}$$

Example 1
Instruction

Point out that some fractions convert to whole percents, such as $\frac{1}{4} = 25\%$, while other fractions, such as $\frac{1}{3}$, convert to percents with a fractional component. Fractional percents may be expressed with fractions like $33\frac{1}{3}\%$ or with decimals, such as 12.5%. To avoid repeating decimals, we usually express fractional percents with fractions in this book.

Example 2
Instruction

Tell students that it is helpful to remember that numbers greater than 1 are equivalent to percents greater than 100%. With this knowledge, they can quickly check their answers by making sure that numbers greater than 1 are written as percents greater than 100% and numbers between 0 and 1 are written as percents between 0% and 100%.

Example 3
Instruction

If necessary, demonstrate each step of the method 1 solution (shown below) on the board or overhead.

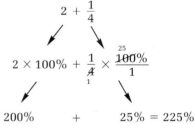

Point out that the terms of the multiplication were reduced by dividing 100 and 4 by the greatest common factor of 100 and 4.

"What is the greatest common factor of 100 and 4?" 4

(continued)

English Learners

In example 3, explain the term **split.** Say,

"When we split something, we divide it or separate it into parts. What happens when you split a sandwich?" You divide it into two or more parts. *"So how do you split the mixed number $3\frac{1}{5}$?"* You separate it into two parts: 3 and $\frac{1}{5}$.

When we split a mixed number, we separate it into two parts, which are, a whole number and a fraction. Ask students to split the following mixed numbers into whole number and fractional parts: $3\frac{2}{3}$, $5\frac{1}{8}$, $11\frac{4}{5}$.

2 New Concepts (Continued)

Example 4

Instruction

"Suppose that we would try to write this quotient as a decimal number instead of as a mixed number. What would we discover?" The quotient would be a repeating decimal; the quotient never ends.

Example 5

Instruction

"Does multiplying $\frac{20}{30}$ or $\frac{2}{3}$ by 100% change the value of either fraction? Explain why or why not." No; 100% is equivalent to 1, and multiplying a number by 1 does not change the value of the number.

Practice Set

Problems a–o [Error Alert]

Remind students that numbers greater than 1 are equivalent to percents greater than 100% and that numbers between 0 and 1 are equivalent to percents between 0% and 100%.

Problems a–i [Error Alert]

Encourage students to check their work by shifting each decimal point two places to the right, and then comparing answers.

Practice Set

Problems j, k, and o [Error Alert]

If the quotients are expressed as decimal numbers, the quotients will be repeating decimals. Remind students to write the quotient of a whole number or mixed number dividend as a whole number or a mixed number.

(continued)

Example 4

Write $2\frac{1}{6}$ as a percent.

Solution

Method 1 shown in example 3 is quick, if we can recall the percent equivalent of a fraction. Method 2 is easier if the percent equivalent does not readily come to mind. We will use method 2 in this example. We write the mixed number $2\frac{1}{6}$ as the improper fraction $\frac{13}{6}$ and multiply by 100%.

$$\frac{13}{6} \times \frac{100\%}{1} = \frac{1300\%}{6}$$

Now we divide 1300% by 6 and write the quotient as a mixed number.

$$\frac{1300\%}{6} = 216\frac{2}{3}\%$$

Example 5

Twenty of the thirty students on the bus were girls. What percent of the students on the bus were girls?

Solution

We first find the fraction of the students that were girls. Then we convert the fraction to a percent.

Girls were $\frac{20}{30}$ $\left(\text{or } \frac{2}{3}\right)$ of the students on the bus. Now we multiply the fraction by 100%, which is the percent name for 1. We can use either $\frac{20}{30}$ or $\frac{2}{3}$, as we show below.

$$\frac{20}{\underset{3}{30}} \times \overset{10}{100}\% = \frac{200\%}{3} = 66\frac{2}{3}\%$$

or

$$\frac{2}{3} \times 100\% = \frac{200\%}{3} = 66\frac{2}{3}\%$$

We find that **$66\frac{2}{3}\%$** of the students on the bus were girls.

Practice Set ▸ Change each decimal number to a percent by multiplying by 100%:

a. 0.5 50%	**b.** 0.06 6%	**c.** 0.125 12.5%
d. 0.45 45%	**e.** 1.3 130%	**f.** 0.025 2.5%
g. 0.09 9%	**h.** 1.25 125%	**i.** 0.625 62.5%

▸ Change each fraction or mixed number to a percent by multiplying by 100%:

j. $\frac{2}{3}$ $66\frac{2}{3}\%$	**k.** $\frac{1}{6}$ $16\frac{2}{3}\%$	**l.** $\frac{1}{8}$ $12\frac{1}{2}\%$
m. $1\frac{1}{4}$ 125%	**n.** $2\frac{4}{5}$ 280%	**o.** $1\frac{1}{3}$ $133\frac{1}{3}\%$

p. What percent of this rectangle is shaded? $83\frac{1}{3}\%$

q. [Connect] What percent of a yard is a foot? $33\frac{1}{3}\%$

▸ See Math Conversations in the sidebar.

▶ *** 1.** *(94)* **Analyze** Ten of the thirty students on the bus were boys. What percent of the students on the bus were boys? $33\frac{1}{3}\%$

2. *(18)* **Connect** On the Celsius scale water freezes at 0°C and boils at 100°C. What temperature is halfway between the freezing and boiling temperatures of water?   50°C

3. *(69)* **Connect** If the length of segment *AB* is $\frac{1}{3}$ the length of segment *AC*, and if segment *AC* is 12 cm long, then how long is segment *BC*?   8 cm

▶ **4.** *(94)* What percent of this group is shaded?   40%

* 5. *(94)* Change $1\frac{2}{3}$ to a percent by multiplying $1\frac{2}{3}$ by 100%. $166\frac{2}{3}\%$

* 6. *(94)* Change 1.5 to a percent by multiplying 1.5 by 100%.   150%

7. *(74)* $6.4 - 6\frac{1}{4}$ (Begin by writing $6\frac{1}{4}$ as a decimal number.)   0.15

▶ *** 8.** *(92)* $10^4 - 10^3$ 9000

9. *(70)* How much is $\frac{3}{4}$ of 360?   270

Tommy placed a cylindrical can of spaghetti sauce on the counter. He measured the diameter of the can and found that it was about 8 cm. Use this information to answer problems **10** and **11**.

Use 3.14 for π.

10. *(47)* The label wraps around the circumference of the can. How long does the label need to be?   25.12 cm

▶*** 11.** *(86)* **Analyze** How many square centimeters of countertop does the can occupy?   50.24 cm²

12. *(61)* $3\frac{1}{2} + 1\frac{3}{4} + 4\frac{5}{8}$ $9\frac{7}{8}$

13. *(72)* $\frac{9}{10} \cdot \frac{5}{6} \cdot \frac{8}{9}$ $\frac{2}{3}$

* 14. *(92)* Write 250,000 in expanded notation using exponents. $(2 \times 10^5) + (5 \times 10^4)$

15. *(1)* $\$8.47 + 95¢ + \$12$ $21.42

16. *(51)* $37.5 \div 100$ 0.375

17. *(85)* $\frac{3}{7} = \frac{21}{x}$ 49

18. *(68)* $33\frac{1}{3} \div 100$ $\frac{1}{3}$

19. *(41)* If ninety percent of the answers were correct, then what percent were incorrect?   10%

20. *(35)* Write the decimal number one hundred twenty and three hundredths.   120.03

21. *(76)* Arrange these numbers in order from least to greatest: $-5.2, -2.5, \frac{2}{5}, \frac{5}{2}$

$$-2.5, \frac{2}{5}, \frac{5}{2}, -5.2$$

Lesson 94   **491**

▶ See Math Conversations in the sidebar.

Math Conversations

Discussion opportunities are provided below.

Problem 1 Analyze

"What is the fraction $\frac{10}{30}$ in lowest terms?" $\frac{1}{3}$

"What is the percent equivalent for $\frac{1}{3}$? Use mental math if you can." $33\frac{1}{3}\%$

After completing the problem, encourage students to become familiar with some of the common percent equivalents so that they can name the equivalents using mental math. Some common equivalents are shown below. Challenge students to name the equivalent for each fraction.

$\frac{1}{2} = 50\%; \frac{1}{3} = 33\frac{1}{3}\%; \frac{2}{3} = 66\frac{2}{3}\%; \frac{1}{4} = 25\%;$

$\frac{3}{4} = 75\%; \frac{1}{5} = 20\%; \frac{2}{5} = 40\%; \frac{3}{5} = 60\%;$

$\frac{4}{5} = 80\%; \frac{1}{10} = 10\%; \frac{3}{10} = 30\%; \frac{7}{10} = 70\%;$

$\frac{9}{10} = 90\%$

Problem 11 Analyze

"The base of the can is in contact with the countertop. What measure of the can do we use to find the area of its base?" radius

"What length represents the radius of the can?" 4 cm

Errors and Misconceptions

Problem 4

If students write the ratio of shaded circles to unshaded circles ($\frac{2}{3}$) and change that ratio to a percent ($66\frac{2}{3}\%$), remind them that the fraction of the group that is shaded is the number of shaded circles divided by the total number of circles.

Problem 8

A common error is to subtract the exponents.

$$10^4 - 10^3 = 10^{4-3} = 10^1 = 10$$

Errors of this nature are not likely to be noticed by students unless they take the time that is needed to check their work. Remind students frequently of the importance of checking work.

$$10^4 - 10^3 = 10,000 - 1000 = 9000$$

Problem 11

Watch for students who incorporate the circumference computation from problem **10** and try to use it to determine the total surface area of the cylinder. These students will be searching for the height of the cylinder, or they will make an assumption with respect to its height.

(continued)

Math Conversations

Discussion opportunities are provided below.

Problem 26 Model

Extend the Problem

Challenge students to solve the following problem using only mental math.

"One leg of a right triangle has endpoints at (0, 0) and (0, 2). The other leg has endpoints at (0, 0) and (2, 0). What is the area of the triangle? Explain how you know." Each leg is 2 units long and forms a right angle, so one leg is the base of the triangle and the other leg is its height; $(2 \times 2) \div 2 = 2$ square units.

---

22. **Conclude** A pyramid with a square base has how many edges?
(Inv. 6)
8 edges

23. What is the area of this parallelogram?
(71)   80 in.^{2}

8 in.
10 in.

* 24. **Classify** The parallelogram in problem **23** is divided into two
(93) congruent triangles. Both triangles may be described as which of the following? C

   A acute   **B** right   **C** obtuse

25. During the year, the temperature ranged from $-37°F$ in winter to 103°F
(14) in summer. How many degrees was the range of temperature for the year? 140°F

▶ **26.** **Model** The coordinates of the three vertices of a triangle are (0, 0),
(Inv. 7, (0, −4), and (−4, 0). Graph the triangle and find its area. 8 sq. units
79)

27. Margie's first nine test scores are shown below.
(Inv. 5)

        21, 25, 22, 19, 22, 24, 20, 22, 24

   a. What is the mode of these scores? 22

   b. What is the median of these scores? 22

* 28. $2^3 + \sqrt{25} \times 3 - 4^2 \div \sqrt{4}$ 15
(92)

29. Sandra filled the aquarium with 24 quarts of water. How many gallons of
(78) water did Sandra pour into the aquarium? 6 gallons

30. A bag contains lettered tiles, two for each letter of the alphabet. What is
(58, 74) the probability of drawing a tile with the letter A? Express the probability ratio as a fraction and as a decimal rounded to the nearest hundredth.
$\frac{1}{26}$; 0.04

26.

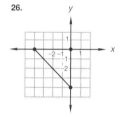

▶ See Math Conversations in the sidebar.

Looking Forward

Changing fractions, decimals, and mixed numbers to percents by multiplying by 100% prepares students for:

• **Lesson 99,** completing tables to show fraction-decimal-percent equivalents.

• **Lesson 115,** converting percents to fractions.

• Reducing Rates Before Multiplying

Objectives

• Cancel units of measure before multiplying.

Lesson Preparation

Materials

• **Power Up G** (in *Instructional Masters*)

Power Up G

Technology Resources

Student eBook Complete student textbook in electronic format.

Resources and Planner CD Assessment, reteaching, and instructional masters, plus a pacing calendar with standards.

Test and Practice Generator CD Create additional practice sheets and custom-made tests.

www.SaxonPublishers.com Visit for more student activities and planning materials.

Inclusion

Adaptations CD Adapted lessons, investigations, practice and assessments.

Meeting Standards

National Council of Teachers of Mathematics (NCTM)

Numbers and Operations

NO.1d Understand and use ratios and proportions to represent quantitative relationships

Measurement

ME.1b Understand relationships among units and convert from one unit to another within the same system

ME.2f Solve simple problems involving rates and derived measurements for such attributes as velocity and density

Problem Solving

PS.1c Apply and adapt a variety of appropriate strategies to solve problems

Problem-Solving Strategy: Make an Organized List/ Use Logical Reasoning

Between the prime number 2 and its double, 4, there is a prime number.

2   ③   4

Is there at least one prime number between every prime number and its double?

Understand   *Understand the problem.*

"What information are we given?"

The prime number 3 is between 2 and its double, 4.

"What are we asked to do?"

Determine if there is a prime number between every prime number and its double.

Plan   *Make a plan.*

"What problem-solving strategy will we use?"

We will *make an organized list.* We will also *use logical reasoning.*

Solve   *Carry out the plan.*

"How do we begin?"

We will begin by listing prime numbers and their doubles and record any prime numbers between them.

2 **3** 4   3 **5** 6   5 **7** 10
7 **11 13** 14
11 **13 17 19** 22   13 **17 19 23** 26

"As the numbers and their doubles grow larger, what do we notice about the number of primes?"

There are more prime numbers between the number and its double.

"Is there at least one prime between a prime number and its double?"

We can predict that there is because as the starting number gets larger, its double gets further away thus leaving more chance that there are prime numbers between them.

"Have we proved it?"

No

Check   *Look back.*

"What is our conclusion?"

Although we have not proved it, we predict that between every prime number and its double, there is at least one prime number.

"Is our conclusion reasonable?"

Yes. The larger the number is that is being doubled, the larger the range of numbers between the number and its double.

Teacher Note: Have students choose a large two-digit prime number and its double and then search for the prime numbers that are between them.

• Reducing Rates
Before Multiplying

625
613
633

---

facts | Power Up G

mental math

a. Number Sense: 60 · 80   4800

b. Number Sense: 437 − 150   287

c. Percent: 25% of 80   20

d. Calculation: $3.99 + $4.28 $8.27

e. Decimals: 17.5 ÷ 100   0.175

f. Number Sense: 30 × 55   1650

g. Algebra: If $w = 10$, what does $7w$ equal?   70

h. Calculation: 6×8, + 1, $\sqrt{}$, × 5, + 1, $\sqrt{}$, × 3, ÷ 2, $\sqrt{}$ 3

problem solving

Between the prime number 2 and its double, 4, there is a prime number

2 ③ 4

Is there at least one prime number between every prime number and its double?   Yes

---

New Concept — Increasing Knowledge

Since Lesson 70 we have practiced reducing fractions before multiplying. This is sometimes called *canceling*.

$$\frac{\overset{1}{\cancel{3}}}{\underset{2}{\cancel{4}}} \cdot \frac{\overset{1}{\cancel{2}}}{\underset{1}{\cancel{3}}} \cdot \frac{\overset{1}{\cancel{5}}}{\underset{2}{\cancel{6}}} = \frac{1}{4}$$

We can cancel **units** before multiplying just as we cancel numbers.

$$\frac{4 \text{ miles}}{1 \text{ hour}} \times \frac{2 \cancel{\text{ hours}}}{1} = \frac{8 \text{ miles}}{1} = 8 \text{ miles}$$

Since rates are ratios of two measures, multiplying and dividing rates involves multiplying and dividing units.

Example 1

Multiply 55 miles per hour by six hours.

---

1 **Power Up**

Facts
Distribute **Power Up G** to students. See answers below.

Mental Math
Before students begin the Mental Math exercise, do this counting exercise as a class.

Count up and down by 20s between −100 and 100.

Encourage students to share different ways to mentally compute these exercises. Strategies for exercises **a** and **c** are listed below.

a. **Use a Multiplication Pattern**
   $6 \times 8 = 48$; $6 \times 80 = 480$; $60 \times 80 = 4800$
   Multiply Tens
   6 tens × 8 tens = (6 × 8) + (tens × tens) = 48 hundreds
c. **Divide 80 by 4**
   $80 \div 4 = 20$
   Use a Multiplication Fact
   Since $4 \times 20 = 80$, $\frac{1}{4}$ of 80 = 20

Problem Solving
Refer to **Power Up Discussion**, p. 493B.

---

2 **New Concepts**

Instruction
Ask students to identify the factor pairs that were canceled and explain why those pairs were canceled. $\frac{3}{6} = \frac{1}{2}$ because the GCF of 3 and 6 is 3; $\frac{2}{4} = \frac{1}{2}$ because the GCF of 2 and 4 is 2; $\frac{5}{5} = \frac{1}{1}$ because the GCF of 5 and 5 is 5.

Remind students that a ratio is a comparison of two quantities by division.

(continued)

Facts   Reduce each fraction to lowest terms.

$\frac{2}{8} = \frac{1}{4}$	$\frac{4}{6} = \frac{2}{3}$	$\frac{6}{10} = \frac{3}{5}$	$\frac{2}{4} = \frac{1}{2}$	$\frac{5}{100} = \frac{1}{20}$	$\frac{9}{12} = \frac{3}{4}$
$\frac{4}{10} = \frac{2}{5}$	$\frac{4}{12} = \frac{1}{3}$	$\frac{2}{10} = \frac{1}{5}$	$\frac{3}{6} = \frac{1}{2}$	$\frac{25}{100} = \frac{1}{4}$	$\frac{3}{12} = \frac{1}{4}$
$\frac{4}{16} = \frac{1}{4}$	$\frac{3}{9} = \frac{1}{3}$	$\frac{6}{9} = \frac{2}{3}$	$\frac{4}{8} = \frac{1}{2}$	$\frac{2}{12} = \frac{1}{6}$	$\frac{6}{12} = \frac{1}{2}$
$\frac{8}{16} = \frac{1}{2}$	$\frac{2}{6} = \frac{1}{3}$	$\frac{8}{12} = \frac{2}{3}$	$\frac{6}{8} = \frac{3}{4}$	$\frac{5}{10} = \frac{1}{2}$	$\frac{75}{100} = \frac{3}{4}$

Example 1

Instruction

Have students write word problems for example 1. Invite volunteers to share their word problems with the class. Sample: "I rode in a car for 6 hours that was traveling at an average speed of 55 miles per hour. During that time, how far did I travel?"

Example 2

Instruction

Point out that feet and foot represent the same unit. The terms are different only in that feet indicates a distance of more than 1 foot.

Practice Set

Problems a–d Error Alert

Before completing the arithmetic for each problem, ask students if there are any number pairs that can be canceled, in addition to the units.

Remind students that canceling number pairs helps increase the likelihood that the product of the factors will be in simplest form.

Solution

Math Language
Recall that a ratio is a comparison of two numbers by division.

We write the rate 55 miles per hour as the ratio 55 miles over 1 hour, because "per" indicates division. We write six hours as the ratio 6 hours over 1.

$$\frac{55 \text{ miles}}{1 \text{ hour}} \times \frac{6 \text{ hours}}{1}$$

The unit "hour" appears above and below the division line, so we can cancel hours.

$$\frac{55 \text{ miles}}{1 \text{ hour}} \times \frac{6 \text{ hours}}{1} = \textbf{330 miles}$$

Connect   Can you think of a word problem to fit this equation?   See student work.

Example 2

Multiply 5 feet by 12 inches per foot.

Solution

We write ratios of 5 feet over 1 and 12 inches over 1 foot. We then cancel units and multiply.

$$\frac{5 \text{ feet}}{1} \cdot \frac{12 \text{ inches}}{1 \text{ foot}} = \textbf{60 inches}$$

Practice Set

When possible, cancel numbers and units before multiplying:

▸ **a.** $\frac{3 \text{ dollars}}{1 \text{ hour}} \times \frac{8 \text{ hours}}{1}$ 24 dollars

▸ **b.** $\frac{6 \text{ baskets}}{10 \text{ shots}} \times \frac{100 \text{ shots}}{1}$ 60 baskets

Reading Math
The abbreviation "kwh" stands for *kilowatt hours,* a rate used to measure energy.

▸ **c.** $\frac{10 \text{ cents}}{1 \text{ kwh}} \times \frac{26.3 \text{ kwh}}{1}$ 263 cents

▸ **d.** $\frac{160 \text{ km}}{2 \text{ hours}} \cdot \frac{10 \text{ hours}}{1}$ 800 km

e. Multiply 18 teachers by 29 students per teacher.   522 students

f. Multiply 2.3 meters by 100 centimeters per meter.   230 cm

g. Solve this problem by multiplying two ratios: How far will the train travel in 6 hours at 45 miles per hour? $\frac{6 \text{ hours}}{1} \cdot \frac{45 \text{ miles}}{1 \text{ hour}} = 270$ miles

Written Practice   *Strengthening Concepts*

1. What is the total price of a $45.79 item when 7% sales tax is added to
(41) the price? $49.00

* 2. Jeff is 1.67 meters tall. How many centimeters tall is Jeff ? (Multiply
(95) 1.67 meters by 100 centimeters per meter.)   167 centimeters

3.   *Analyze*   If $\frac{5}{8}$ of the 40 seeds sprouted, how many seeds did not
(77) sprout?   15 seeds

▸ See Math Conversations in the sidebar.

Math Background

Reducing fraction terms before multiplying simplifies the factors, but does not change the product.

The same concept is true for reducing fraction units before multiplying. Canceling a unit in a numerator and canceling the same unit in a denominator simplifies the factors, but does not change the product.

4. Write this number in standard notation: 560.73
(46)

$$(5 \times 100) + (6 \times 10) + \left(7 \times \frac{1}{10}\right) + \left(3 \times \frac{1}{100}\right)$$

* 5. Change $\frac{1}{6}$ to its percent equivalent by multiplying $\frac{1}{6}$ by 100%. $16\frac{2}{3}\%$
(94)

▶ *** 6.** _Analyze_   What is the percent equivalent of 2.5?   250%
(94)

7. How much money is 30% of $12.00? $3.60
(41)

▶ *** 8.** _Connect_   The minute hand of a clock turns 180° in how many minutes?
(90)   30 minutes

9. _Evaluate_   The circumference of the front tire on Elizabeth's bike is
(27)   6 feet. How many complete turns does the front wheel make as
Elizabeth rides down her 30-foot driveway?   5 turns

10. Chad built this stack of one-cubic-foot
(82)   boxes. What is the volume of the stack?
36 ft^3

11. $\frac{3}{4} + \frac{3}{5}$ $1\frac{7}{20}$
(57)

12. $18\frac{1}{8} - 12\frac{1}{2}$ $5\frac{5}{8}$
(3)

13. $3\frac{3}{4} \times 2\frac{2}{3} \times 1\frac{1}{10}$ 11
(72)

14. $\frac{2^5}{2^3}$ 4
(92)

15. How many fourths are in $2\frac{1}{2}$?   10
(68)

16. $12 + 8.75 + 6.8$ 27.55
(38)

17. $(1.5)^2$ 2.25
(38, 39)

18. $6\frac{2}{5} \div 0.8$ (decimal answer)   8
(74)

19. _Estimate_   Find the sum of $6\frac{1}{4}$, 4.95, and 8.21 by rounding each number
(51)   to the nearest whole number before adding. Explain how you arrived at
your answer.   19; Round $6\frac{1}{4}$ to 6, round 4.95 to 5, and round 8.21 to 8.
Then add 6, 5, and 8.

▶ *** 20.** _Analyze_   The diameter of a round tabletop is 60 inches.
(86)
a. What is the radius of the tabletop?   30 inches

b. What is the area of the tabletop? (Use 3.14 for π.)   2826 square inches

▶ **21.** Arrange these numbers in order from least to greatest: 4%, $\frac{1}{4}$, 0.4
(75)
$$\frac{1}{4}, 4\%, 0.4$$

Find each unknown number.

22. $y + 3.4 = 5$ 1.6
(43)

23. $\frac{4}{8} = \frac{x}{12}$ 6
(85)

24. A cube has edges that are 6 cm long.
(Inv. 6,
82)   **a.** What is the area of each face of the cube?   36 cm^2

b. What is the volume of the cube?   216 cm^3

c. What is the surface area of the cube?   216 cm^2

Lesson 95   495

▶ See Math Conversations in the sidebar.

---

3 **Written Practice**

Math Conversations

Discussion opportunities are provided below.

Problem 6 _Analyze_

"To change a decimal number to a percent, what number is the decimal multiplied by?" 100%

"Multiplying a number by 100 is the same as shifting the decimal point in that number how many places? In which direction?" two places to the right

Remind students that percents can often be greater than 100.

Problem 8 _Connect_

"How many minutes will elapse if the minute hand of a clock goes completely around once?" 60 minutes

"What shape does the end of the minute hand trace as it goes around once?" a circle

"What is the degree measure of a circle?" 360

Problem 20 _Analyze_

"What shape is the tabletop?" a circle

"Is the radius of a circle a line segment that is halfway across a circle, or all the way across?" halfway

"Which factors will you multiply to find the area of the tabletop?" 900 and 3.14

Remind students that they must multiply pi by the square of the radius because the area of a circle equals πr^2.

Errors and Misconceptions

Problem 21

Watch for students who do not change the numbers to the same form before comparing.

Make sure students understand that they can change to fractions, to percents, or to decimals. However, students should generalize that because comparing fractions requires common denominators, they should instead choose to change the fraction to a decimal or to a percent.

(continued)

Math Conversations

Discussion opportunities are provided below.

Problem 25 Connect

"What equation can be used to represent and solve the problem?" Sample: 42 mm − 24 mm = n

"What related equation can be used to represent and solve the problem?" Sample: 24 mm + n = 42 mm

Errors and Misconceptions
Problem 28

When multiplying decimal factors, students must place the same number of decimal places in the product as the sum of the number of decimal places in the factors.

Ask students who do not place two decimal places in the product to count the total number of decimal places in the factors.

▶ **25.** Connect $\overline{AB}$ is 24 mm long. $\overline{AC}$ is 42 mm long. How long is $\overline{BC}$?
(69) 18 mm

$\begin{matrix} A & & B & C \\ \bullet & & \bullet & \bullet \end{matrix}$

* 26. $6^2 \div \sqrt{9} + 2 \times 2^3 - \sqrt{400}$ 8
(89, 92)

27. What is the ratio of a pint of water to a quart of water? $\frac{1}{2}$
(78)

28. 1.08 m²;
Sample: 1.2 m rounds to 1 m and 0.9 m rounds to 1 m. A ≈ (1 m)(1 m) ≈ 1 m². 1.08 m² is close to 1 so I know my answer is reasonable.

▶*** 28.** The formula for the area of a parallelogram is $A = bh$. If the base of a parallelogram is 1.2 m and the height is 0.9 m, what is the area of the parallelogram? How can estimation help you check your answer?
(91)

* 29. Multiply 2.5 liters by 1000 milliliters per liter. 2500 milliliters
(95)

$$\frac{2.5 \text{ liters}}{1} \times \frac{1000 \text{ milliliters}}{1 \text{ liter}}$$

30. If this spinner is spun once, what is the probability that the arrow will end up pointing to an even number? Express the probability ratio as a fraction and as a decimal. $\frac{1}{2}$; 0.5
(58, 74)

Early Finishers
Real-World Application

The local university football stadium seats 60,000 fans, and average attendance at home games is 48,500. It has been determined that an average fan consumes 2.25 beverages per game.

a. If each beverage is served in a cup, about how many cups are used during an average game? Express your answer in scientific notation. 1.09125×10^5 cups

b. Next week is the homecoming game, which is always sold out. A box of cups contains 1×10^3 cups. How many boxes of cups will be needed for the game? 135 boxes

▶ See Math Conversations in the sidebar.

Looking Forward

Reducing, or canceling, units of measure before multiplying to solve a problem prepares students for:

• **Lesson 114,** multiplying by unit multipliers to convert from one unit of measure to another.

Assessment
30–40 minutes

Distribute **Cumulative Test 18** to each student. Two versions of the test are available in *Saxon Math Course 1 Course Assessments Book*. Have students complete the **Power-Up Test** first. Allow 10 minutes. Then have students work the 20 numbered items on the **Cumulative Test.** Students may use copies of the answer sheet to record their work. Track individual and class progress with the **Test Analysis** forms.

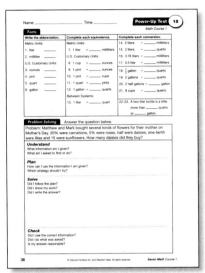

Power-Up Test 18

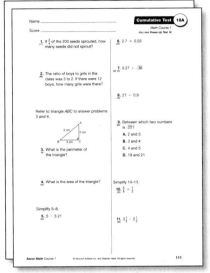

Cumulative Test 18A

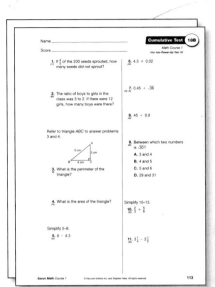

Alternative Cumulative Test 18B

Optional Answer Forms

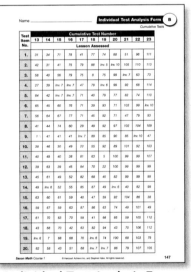

Individual Test Analysis Form

Class Test Analysis Form

Reteaching

Students who score below 80% on the assessment may be in need of reteaching. Look for the causes of student mistakes. If errors are conceptual, refer to the *Reteaching Masters* for reteaching.

Formulas from Tables
Assign after Lesson 95 and Test 18

Objectives
- Write a formula that represents the data in a table.
- Identify a geometrical situation where a formula could be used.
- Communicate ideas through writing.

Materials
Performance Activity 18

Preparation
Make copies of **Performance Activity 18.** (One each per student.)

Time Requirement
15–30 minutes; Begin in class and complete at home.

Activity
Explain to students that for this activity they will write formulas to represent the data in tables. They will identify how these formulas could be used. They will be required to explain their understanding of what a table represents. Explain that all of the information students need is on **Performance Activity 18.**

Criteria for Evidence of Learning
- Writes formulas that accurately represent the data in a table.
- Identifies correctly how a formula could be used.
- Communicates ideas clearly through writing.

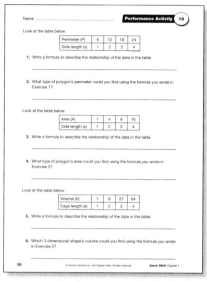

Performance Activity 18

National Council of Teachers of Mathematics (NCTM)

Algebra
AL.1a Represent, analyze, and generalize a variety of patterns with tables, graphs, words, and, when possible, symbolic rules

AL.3a Model and solve contextualized problems using various representations, such as graphs, tables, and equations

Measurement
ME.2c Develop and use formulas to determine the circumference of circles and the area of triangles, parallelograms, trapezoids, and circles and develop strategies to find the area of more-complex shapes

Communication
CM.3d Use the language of mathematics to express mathematical ideas precisely

Connections
CN.4b Understand how mathematical ideas interconnect and build on one another to produce a coherent whole

Representation
RE.5a Create and use representations to organize, record, and communicate mathematical ideas

• Functions
• Graphing Functions

Objectives
- Find the rule for a function.
- Find a missing number in a function table.
- Make a table for a function.
- Graph a function on a coordinate plane.

Lesson Preparation

Materials
- **Power Up D** (in *Instructional Masters*)
- **Investigation Activity 15** (in *Instructional Masters*) or **graph paper**
- **Manipulative Kit: inch rulers**
- **Lesson Activity 19 Transparency** (in *Instructional Masters*)

Math Language

New	English Learners (ESL)
function	weigh(ed)

Technology Resources

Student eBook Complete student textbook in electronic format.

Resources and Planner CD Assessment, reteaching, and instructional masters, plus a pacing calendar with standards.

Test and Practice Generator CD Create additional practice sheets and custom-made tests.

www.SaxonPublishers.com Visit for more student activities and planning materials.

Inclusion

Adaptations CD Adapted lessons, investigations, practice and assessments.

Power Up D

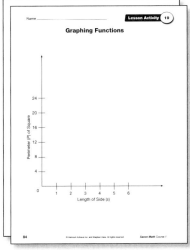

Lesson Activity 19
Investigation Activity 15

Meeting Standards

National Council of Teachers of Mathematics (NCTM)

Algebra

AL.1a Represent, analyze, and generalize a variety of patterns with tables, graphs, words, and, when possible, symbolic rules

AL.3a Model and solve contextualized problems using various representations, such as graphs, tables, and equations

Representation

RE.5a Create and use representations to organize, record, and communicate mathematical ideas

Problem-Solving Strategy: Work Backwards

Copy this factor tree and fill in the missing numbers:

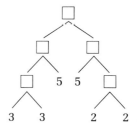

Understand **Understand the problem.**

"What information are we given?"

We are shown a factor tree with some missing numbers.

"What are we asked to do?"

We are asked to fill in the missing numbers in the factor tree.

Plan **Make a plan.**

"How can we use the information we know to do what we are asked to do?"

We will *work backwards* and use number sense to fill in the missing numbers. We will start at the bottom of the tree and work our way up.

Solve **Carry out the plan.**

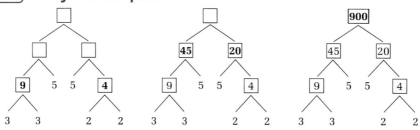

Check **Look back.**

"Did we complete the task?"

Yes. We completed the factor tree by filling in the blanks.

- **Functions**
- **Graphing Functions**

32 pts

613
633
622
631

Power Up | *Building Power*

facts | Power Up D

mental math
- **a. Number Sense:** $70 \cdot 90$ 6300
- **b. Number Sense:** $364 + 250$ 614
- **c. Percent:** 50% of 60   30
- **d. Calculation:** $\$5.00 - \$0.89$ \$4.11
- **e. Decimals:** 100×0.015 1.5
- **f. Number Sense:** $\frac{750}{30}$ 25
- **g. Measurement:** How many pints are in 2 quarts?   4 pints
- **h. Calculation:** $6 \times 6, -1, \div 5, \times 8, -1, \div 11, \times 8, \times 2, +1, \sqrt{\ }$ 9

problem solving | Copy this factor tree and fill in the missing numbers:

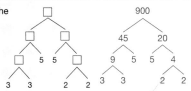

New Concepts | *Increasing Knowledge*

functions | We know that the surface area of a rectangular prism is the sum of the areas of its sides. A cube is a special rectangular prism with six square faces. If we know the area of one side of a cube, then we can find the surface area of that cube. We can make a table to show the surface areas of cubes based on the area of one side of the cube.

Area of Each Side of a Cube (cm²)	Surface Area of the Cube (cm²)
4	24
9	54
16	96
25	150

Lesson 96   497

Facts | Multiply.

7 ×7 = 49	4 ×6 = 24	8 ×1 = 8	2 ×2 = 4	0 ×5 = 0	6 ×3 = 18	8 ×9 = 72	5 ×8 = 40	6 ×2 = 12	10 ×10 = 100
9 ×4 = 36	2 ×5 = 10	9 ×6 = 54	7 ×3 = 21	5 ×5 = 25	7 ×2 = 14	6 ×8 = 48	3 ×5 = 15	9 ×9 = 81	5 ×4 = 20
3 ×4 = 12	6 ×5 = 30	8 ×2 = 16	4 ×4 = 16	6 ×7 = 42	8 ×8 = 64	2 ×3 = 6	7 ×4 = 28	5 ×9 = 45	3 ×8 = 24
3 ×9 = 27	7 ×8 = 56	2 ×4 = 8	5 ×7 = 35	3 ×3 = 9	9 ×7 = 63	4 ×8 = 32	0 ×0 = 0	9 ×2 = 18	6 ×6 = 36

1 Power Up

Facts
Distribute **Power Up D** to students. See answers below.

Mental Math
Before students begin the Mental Math exercise, do this counting exercise as a class.

Count by $\frac{1}{16}$s from $\frac{1}{16}$ to 1.

Encourage students to share different ways to mentally compute these exercises. Strategies for exercises **b** and **d** are listed below.

b. Break Apart 364
$350 + 250 + 14 = 600 + 14 = 614$
Add Hundreds, Tens, and Ones
$500 + 110 + 4 = 610 + 4 = 614$

d. Subtract \$1, then Add 11¢
$\$5 - \$1 = \$4; \$4 + 11¢ = \$4.11$
Subtract 90¢, then Add 1¢
$\$5 - 90¢ = \$4.10; \$4.10 + 1¢ = \$4.11$

Problem Solving
Refer to **Power-Up Discussion**, p. 497B.

---

2 New Concepts

Instruction
To help students understand how the numbers in the first column of the table are generated, explain that the square root of each number in the column will produce the length of each edge of the cube.

For example, if the area of each side of a cube is 4 cm², the length of each edge of the cube is $\sqrt{4}$ cm² or 2 cm. If the area of each side of a cube is 9 cm², the length of any edge of the cube is $\sqrt{9}$ cm² or 3 cm. And so on.

(continued)

Instruction

Emphasize that a rule for a function must be true for every number pair in a function table. If a rule is not true for one (or more than one) number pair, then it is not a correct rule for the function.

Example 1

Instruction

Give students opportunities to find other values for the function in example 1 by asking questions such as

"**If l is 6, what is the value of m?**" 21

"**If l is 30, what is the value of m?**" 45

For enrichment, you may want to review the math background. Neither of the sets of points should be connected to form a straight line.

The graph on the left shows the total number of eggs (e) is a function of the number of cartons (c) of eggs.

The graph on the right shows the fee (f) for parking in a parking lot is a function of time (t).

(continued)

Discuss Use the data in the table to help you create a formula for the surface area of a cube. Let A be the area of each side of the cube and S be the surface area of the cube.

$$(S = 6A)$$

Your formula is an example of a **function**. A function is a rule for using one number (an input) to calculate another number (an output). In this function, side area is the input and surface area is the output. Because the surface area of a cube depends on the area of each side, we say that the surface area of a cube is a function of the area of a side. If we know the area of one side of a cube, we can apply the function's rule (formula) to find the surface area of the cube.

Example 1

Find the rule for this function. Then use the rule to find the value of m when l is 7.

l	m
5	20
7	
10	25
15	30

Solution

We study the table to discover the function rule. We see that when l is 5, m is 20. We might guess that the rule is to multiply l by 4. However, when l is 10, m is 25. Since 10×4 does not equal 25, we know that this guess is incorrect. So we look for another rule.

We notice that 20 is 15 more than 5 and that 25 is 15 more than 10. Perhaps the rule is to add 15 to l. We see that the values in the bottom row of the table ($l = 15$ and $m = 30$) fit this rule. So the rule is, **to find m, add 15 to l.** To find m when l is 7, we add 15 to 7.

$$7 + 15 = 22$$

The missing number in the table is **22.**

Instead of using the letter m at the top of the table, we could have written the rule. In the table at right, $l + 15$ has replaced m. This means we add 15 to the value of l. We show this type of table in the next example.

l	l + 15
5	20
7	
10	25
15	30

Inclusion

When graphing functions, students may need to remember which column of a function table associates with each axis. Say,

"**Remember you have to crawl before you can climb. For each number pair of the function, the first column gives the value along the horizontal axis and the second column gives the value along the vertical axis.**"

Use the graph of the function on the next page to demonstrate. Say,

"**To graph the first number pair from the function's table, you have to crawl 1 before you climb 4. For the second, you have to crawl 2 before you climb 8.**"

Have student volunteers come up and show how to find the next 2 number pairs in the function table.

Example 2

Find the missing number in this function table:

x	2	3	4
3x − 2	4	7	

Solution

This table is arranged horizontally. The rule of the function is stated in the table: multiply the value of *x* by 3, then subtract 2. To find the missing number in the table, we apply the rule of the function when *x* is 4.

$$3x - 2$$
$$3(4) - 2 = 10$$

We find that the missing number is **10**.

graphing functions

Many functions can be graphed on a coordinate plane. Here we show a function table that relates the perimeter of a square to the length of one of its sides. On the coordinate plane we have graphed the number pairs that appear in the table. The coordinate plane's horizontal axis shows the length of a side, and its vertical axis shows the perimeter.

s	P
1	4
2	8
3	12
4	16

We have used different scales on the two axes so that the graph is not too steep. The graphed points show the side length and perimeter of four squares with side lengths of 1, 2, 3, and 4 units. Notice that the graphed points are aligned. Of course, we could graph many more points and represent squares with side lengths of 100 units or more. We could also graph points for squares with side lengths of 0.01 or less. In fact, we can graph points for any side length whatsoever! Such a graph would look like a ray, as shown on the next page.

Example 2

Instruction

"The expression 3x − 2 includes multiplication and subtraction. After substituting a value for x, which operation do you perform first to simplify the expression? Explain why." Multiplication; the Order of Operations states that multiplication is to be performed before subtraction.

Instruction

Place the transparency of **Lesson Activity 19** Graphing Functions on the overhead. First, demonstrate how to graph each number pair from the function table.

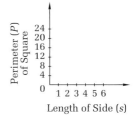

Then ask students to name the rule for this function. $P = s + s + s + s$ or $P = 4s$

Finally, draw a ray to connect the points that have been graphed on the transparency of **Lesson Activity 19** Graphing Functions.

(continued)

Math Background

The points on a graph of a function cannot always be connected to create a straight line.

The graph of some functions is a series of points.

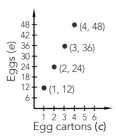

The graph of some functions is a series of segments.

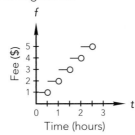

Example 3

Instruction

"The number pairs in a function table are often called ordered pairs because each pair represents a point on a graph. Look at the ordered pairs in the table. Describe an addition rule that is true for all of the ordered pairs." $P = s + s + s$

"Describe a multiplication rule that is true for all of the ordered pairs." $P = 3s$

Copy the function table on the board or overhead to complete the example and write $s + s + s$ or $3s$ in place of P.

(continued)

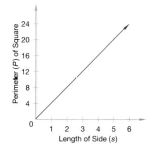

Example 3

The perimeter of an equilateral triangle is a function of the length of its sides. Make a table for this function using side lengths of 1, 2, 3, and 4 units. Then graph the ordered pairs on a coordinate plane. Extend a ray through the points to represent the function for all equilateral triangles.

Solution

Thinking Skill

Generalize

What is the rule for this table?
To find the perimeter P, multiply the side length s by 3.

We create a table of ordered pairs. The letter s stands for the length of a side, and P stands for the perimeter.

s	P
1	3
2	6
3	9
4	12

Now we graph these points on a coordinate plane with one axis for perimeter and the other axis for side length. Then we draw a ray from the origin through these points.

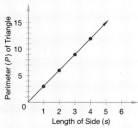

Every point along the ray represents the side length and perimeter of an equilateral triangle.

Practice Set

e.

Q	P
1	2
2	4
3	6
4	8

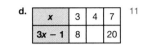

Pounds
8
6
4
2
0
1 2 3 4
Quarts

It is appropriate to use a ray, because any portion of a quart may be weighed.

Generalize Find the missing number in each function table:

▶ **a.** 8

x	y
3	1
5	3
6	4
10	

▶ **b.** 10

a	b
3	8
5	10
7	12
	15

c. 25

x	3	6	8
3x + 1	10	19	

d. 11

x	3	4	7
3x − 1	8		20

▶ **e.** *Model* The chemist mixed a solution that weighed 2 pounds per quart. Create a table of ordered pairs for this function for 1, 2, 3, and 4 quarts. Then graph the points on a coordinate plane, using the horizontal axis for quarts and the vertical axis for pounds. Would it be appropriate to draw a ray through the points? Why or why not?

Written Practice | *Strengthening Concepts*

1. When the sum of 2.0 and 2.0 is subtracted from the product of 2.0 and 2.0, what is the difference?   0
(12, 53)

2. A 4.2-kilogram object weighs the same as how many objects that each weigh 0.42 kilogram?   10 objects
(49)

3. If the average of 8 numbers is 12, what is the sum of the 8 numbers?   96
(18)

4. *Conclude* What is the name of a quadrilateral that has one pair of sides that are parallel and one pair of sides that are not parallel?   trapezoid
(64)

* **5.** **a.** Write 0.15 as a percent.   15%
(94)

  b. Write 1.5 as a percent.   150%

* **6.** Write $\frac{5}{6}$ as a percent. $83\frac{1}{3}\%$
(94)

7. *Classify* Three of the numbers below are equivalent. Which one is not equivalent to the others?   C
(41, 76)

   A 1   **B** 100%   **C** 0.1   **D** $\frac{100}{100}$

8. 11^3 1331   **9.** How much is $\frac{5}{6}$ of 360?   300
(73)   (70)

▶* **10.** *Estimate* Between which two consecutive whole numbers is $\sqrt{89}$?
(89)   9 and 10

▶ See Math Conversations in the sidebar.

---

2 New Concepts (Continued)

Practice Set

Problems a and b [Error Alert]

To help students check if they have written the correct missing number, ask them to name or describe the rule for each function, then check to be sure all of the number pairs in the table fit the rule. a. $x − 2$ (to find y, subtract 2 from x); b. $a + 5$ (to find b, add 5 to a)

Problem e [Model]

Challenge students to write a formula that represents the weight of any number of quarts. Sample: $w = 2q$ where w represents the weight in pounds and q represents the number of quarts.

---

3 Written Practice

Math Conversations

Discussion opportunities are provided below.

Problem 10 [Estimate]

"What is a perfect square?" The product of a whole number and itself.

"How can the idea of a perfect square be used to solve this problem?" Find the greatest perfect square that is less than 89 and find the least perfect square that is greater than 89.

(continued)

English Learners

In problem e, explain the term **weigh**. Say:

"When you want to know how heavy something is, you weigh it. What can you use to weigh an object?" A scale.

"Name a unit of measure used to describe weight." Pound, ounce, kilogram, gram.

Ask students to describe objects they have weighed, the type of scale they used, and how much the object weighed.

Teacher Tip

For Practice Set problem e, students will need graph paper or a copy of **Investigation Activity 15** Coordinate Plane to graph the points.

Math Conversations

Discussion opportunities are provided below.

Problem 12 Generalize

"What operations does the expression 2x − 1 represent?" multiplication and subtraction

"Why is the expression 2x − 1 equal to 7 when x is 4?" Sample: multiply first, then subtract

Problem 29 Analyze

"To simplify this expression, name the order in which the operations must be completed." powers and roots from left to right; multiplication and division from left to right; addition and subtraction from left to right

Errors and Misconceptions

Problem 11

To help students understand that Silvester completes one full turn in one lap of the field, have volunteers walk around three desks or chairs. Students should observe that when volunteers complete one lap, they are facing in the same direction as when they began. In other words, they have turned 360°.

Problem 24

Make sure students can recognize the various divisions of their rulers and generalize that one tick mark divides each inch into halves, three tick marks divide each inch into fourths, seven tick marks divide each inch into eighths, and fifteen tick marks divide each inch into sixteenths.

▶* **11.** *Analyze* Silvester ran around the field, turning at each of the three backstops. What was the average number of degrees he turned at each of the three corners? $\frac{360°}{3} = 120°$
(90)

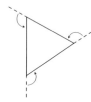

▶* **12.** *Generalize* Find the missing number in this function table.   25
(96)

x	4	7	13	15
2x − 1	7	13		29

13. Factor and reduce: $\frac{(45)(54)}{81}$ 30
(67)

14. $\frac{30}{0.08}$ 375
(49)

15. $16\frac{2}{3} \div 100$ $\frac{1}{6}$
(68)

16. $2\frac{1}{2} + 3\frac{1}{3} + 4\frac{1}{6}$ 10
(61)

17. $6 \times 5\frac{1}{3} \times \frac{3}{8}$ 12
(72)

18. $\frac{2}{5}$ of $12.00 $4.80
(22)

19. $0.12 \times 6.50 $0.78
(39)

20. $5.3 - 3\frac{3}{4}$ (decimal answer)   1.55
(74)

21. What is the ratio of the number of cents in a dime to the number of cents in a quarter? $\frac{2}{5}$
(23)

Find each unknown number:

* **22.** $4n = 6 \cdot 14$ 21
(87)

* **23.** $0.3n = 12$ 40
(87)

▶ **24.** *Model* Draw a segment $1\frac{3}{4}$ inches long. Label the endpoints R and T. Then find and mark the midpoint of $\overline{RT}$. Label the midpoint S. What are the lengths of $\overline{RS}$ and $\overline{ST}$?   See student work. $RS = ST = \frac{7}{8}$ inch
(7)

* **25.** Solve this proportion: $\frac{6}{9} = \frac{36}{w}$ 54
(85)

* **26.** Multiply 4 hours by 6 dollars per hour: 24 dollars
(95)
$$\frac{4 \text{ hours}}{1} \times \frac{6 \text{ dollars}}{1 \text{ hours}}$$

27. *Connect* The coordinates of the vertices of a parallelogram are (0, 0), (6, 0), (4, 4), and (−2, 4). What is the area of the parallelogram?   24 units²
(Inv. 7, 71)

28. *Estimate* The saying "A pint's a pound the world around" refers to the fact that a pint of water weighs about one pound. About how many pounds does a gallon of water weigh?   about 8 pounds
(78)

▶* **29.** *Analyze* $3^2 + 2^3 - \sqrt{4} \times 5 + 6^2 \div \sqrt{16}$ 16
(92)

30. What is the probability of rolling a prime number with one roll of a number cube? Express the ratio as a fraction and as a decimal. $\frac{1}{2}$, 0.5
(58, 74)

▶ See Math Conversations in the sidebar.

• Transversals

Objectives

- Identify transversals, interior angles, alternate interior angles, exterior angles, alternate exterior angles, and corresponding angles.
- Find the measures of the angles formed by a transversal intersecting two parallel lines when the measure of one angle is known.

Lesson Preparation

Materials

- **Power Up L** (in *Instructional Masters*)

Optional

- **Teacher-provided material:** construction paper, index cards, markers, city maps, calculators

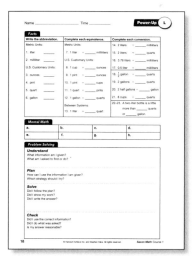

Power Up L

Math Language

New	Maintain	English Learners (ESL)
alternate exterior angles	parallel lines	relative positions
alternate interior angles	supplementary	
corresponding angles		
transversal		

Technology Resources

Student eBook Complete student textbook in electronic format.

Resources and Planner CD Assessment, reteaching, and instructional masters, plus a pacing calendar with standards.

Test and Practice Generator CD Create additional practice sheets and custom-made tests.

www.SaxonPublishers.com Visit for more student activities and planning materials.

Inclusion

Adaptations CD Adapted lessons, investigations, practice and assessments.

Meeting Standards

National Council of Teachers of Mathematics (NCTM)

Geometry

GM.1c Create and critique inductive and deductive arguments concerning geometric ideas and relationships, such as congruence, similarity, and the Pythagorean relationship

GM.4e Recognize and apply geometric ideas and relationships in areas outside the mathematics classroom, such as art, science, and everyday life

Connections

CN.4c Recognize and apply mathematics in contexts outside of mathematics

Problem-Solving Strategy: Write an Equation

Chad and his friends played three games that are scored from 1–100. His lowest score was 70 and his highest score was 100. What is Chad's lowest possible three-game average? What is his highest possible three-game average?

(Understand) **Understand the problem.**

"What information are we given?"

Chad played three games. His lowest score is 70. His highest score is 100.

"What are we asked to do?"

We are asked to find Chad's lowest and highest possible three-game averages.

(Plan) **Make a plan.**

"What problem-solving strategy will we use?"

We will *write equations* to compute each of the two averages.

(Solve) **Carry out the plan.**

"What are possible scores that Chad could have on the third game?"

Since we were told that his lowest score was a 70 and his highest score was 100, the scores for the third game must be between 70 and 100.

"What is Chad's lowest possible average for the three games?"

If Chad scored a 70 on the third game, then the average for all three games would be:
$$(70 + 70 + 100) \div 3 = 80$$

"What is Chad's highest possible average for the three games?"

If Chad made a 100 on the third game, then the average for all three games would be:
$$(70 + 100 + 100) \div 3 = 90$$

(Check) **Look back.**

"Did we find the answers to the questions that were asked?"

Yes. We determined Chad's lowest (80) and highest (90) possible three-game averages.

• **Transversals**

Power Up | *Building Power*

facts | Power Up L

mental math

a. **Number Sense:** 20 · 50   1000

b. **Number Sense:** 517 − 250   267

c. **Percent:** 25% of 60   15

d. **Calculation:** $7.99 + $7.58 $15.57

e. **Decimals:** 0.1 ÷ 100   0.001

f. **Number Sense:** 20 × 75   1500

g. **Measurement:** How many liters are in 1000 milliliters?   1 liter

h. **Calculation:** $5 \times 9, -1, \div 2, -1, \div 3, \times 10, +2, \div 9, -2, \div 2$ 3

problem solving | Chad and his friends played three games that are scored from 1–100. His lowest score was 70 and his highest score is 100. What is Chad's lowest possible three-game average? What is his highest possible three-game average?   80; 90

New Concept | *Increasing Knowledge*

A line that intersects two or more other lines is a **transversal**. In this drawing, line *r* is a transversal of lines *s* and *t*.

Math Language
Parallel lines are lines in the same plane that do not intersect and are always the same distance apart.

In the drawing, lines *s* and *t* are not parallel. However, in this lesson we will focus on the effects of a transversal intersecting parallel lines.

Below we show parallel lines *m* and *n* intersected by transversal *p*. Notice that eight angles are formed. In this figure there are four obtuse angles (numbered 1, 3, 5, and 7) and four acute angles (numbered 2, 4, 6, and 8).

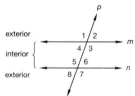

Lesson 97 **503**

Facts

Write the abbreviation.	Complete each equivalence.	Complete each conversion.
Metric Units:	Metric Units:	14. 2 liters = __2000__ milliliters
1. liter ___L___	7. 1 liter = __1000__ milliliters	15. 2 liters ≈ __2__ quarts
2. milliliter __mL__	U.S. Customary Units:	16. 3.78 liters = __3780__ milliliters
U.S. Customary Units:	8. 1 cup = __8__ ounces	17. 0.5 liter = __500__ milliliters
3. ounces __oz__	9. 1 pint = __16__ ounces	18. $\frac{1}{2}$ gallon = __2__ quarts
4. pint __pt__	10. 1 pint = __2__ cups	19. 2 gallons = __8__ quarts
5. quart __qt__	11. 1 quart = __2__ pints	20. 2 half gallons = __1__ gallon
6. gallon __gal__	12. 1 gallon = __4__ quarts	21. 8 cups = __2__ quarts
	Between Systems:	22–23. A two-liter bottle is a little more than __2__ quarts
	13. 1 liter ≈ __1__ quart	or __$\frac{1}{2}$__ gallon.

---

1 Power Up

Facts
Distribute **Power Up L** to students. See answers below.

Mental Math
Before students begin the Mental Math exercise, do this counting exercise as a class.

Count up and down by $\frac{1}{2}$s between −3 and 3.

Encourage students to share different ways to mentally compute these exercises. Strategies for exercises **c** and **f** are listed below.

c. Find $\frac{1}{2}$ of $\frac{1}{2}$ of 60
   $\frac{1}{2}$ of 60 = 30; $\frac{1}{2}$ of 30 = 15
   Divide 60 by 4
   60 ÷ 4 = 15
f. Double 10 × 75
   10 × 75 = 750; 750 × 2 = 1500
   Break Apart 75
   (20 × 70) + (20 × 5) = 1400 + 100 = 1500

Problem Solving
Refer to **Power Up Discussion,** p. 503B.

2 New Concepts

Instruction
Have students note that a transversal can intersect two or more other lines at any angle. For example, the two lines may be parallel and the transversal may intersect at right angles to those lines, the lines may not be parallel (such as lines *s* and *t* in the text), or the traversal may be perpendicular to only one of the lines it intersects.

Of particular interest in this lesson are the relationships between angles formed by a transversal intersecting parallel lines.

(continued)

2 New Concepts (Continued)

Instruction

On the board, draw the figure of parallel lines *m* and *n* and transversal *p* shown on the student page. As the class works through the concepts presented, ask students to identify angles in the figure. For example, after discussing supplementary angles, write the column head "Supplementary Angles" on the board. Then ask volunteers to point to two angles that are supplementary and tell why they think the angles are supplementary. If the class agrees, list the pair under the column head "Supplementary Angles."

Use this method to practice identifying corresponding angles, alternate interior angles, and alternate exterior angles. Encourage students to describe different ways to remember the names of the angle pairs and their relationship.

To complete the lesson, erase the angle numbers and all lists of angle pairs written on the board. Then indicate two corresponding angles as shown below.

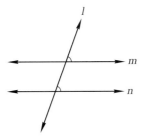

Say,

> **"These two angles are corresponding angles."**

Then invite volunteers to mark and describe different angle pairs.

For students who would benefit for the use of a manipulative, see the Manipulative Use feature on the following page.

For more practice with transversals, post or project a map of your town or city. (A local phone book is sometimes a source of such maps.) Point out examples of transversals intersecting parallel lines, corresponding angles, alternate interior angles, and alternate exterior angles. Then ask volunteers to find other examples on the map.

(continued)

Notice that obtuse angle 1, and acute angle 2, together form a straight line. These angles are **supplementary,** which means their measures total 180°. So if ∠1 measures 110°, then ∠2 measures 70°. Also notice that ∠2 and ∠3 are supplementary. If ∠2 measures 70°, then ∠3 measures 110°. Likewise, ∠3 and ∠4 are supplementary, so ∠4 would measure 70°.

There are names to describe some of the angle pairs. For example, we say that ∠1 and ∠5 are **corresponding angles** because they are in the same relative positions. Notice that ∠1 is the "upper left angle" from line *m*, while ∠5 is the "upper left angle" from line *n*.

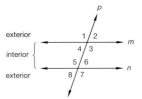

Which angle corresponds to ∠2? Angle 6 corresponds to ∠2.

Which angle corresponds to ∠7? Angle 3 corresponds to ∠7.

Since lines *m* and *n* are parallel, line *p* intersects line *m* at the same angle as it intersects line *n*. So the corresponding angles are congruent. Thus, if we know that ∠1 measures 110°, we can conclude that ∠5 also measures 110°.

The angles between the parallel lines (numbered 3, 4, 5, and 6 in the figure on previous page) are **interior angles.** Angle 3 and ∠5 are on opposite sides of the transversal and are called **alternate interior angles.**

Name another pair of alternate interior angles. angle 4 and ∠6

Alternate interior angles are congruent if the lines intersected by the transversal are parallel. So if ∠5 measures 110°, then ∠3 also measures 110°.

Angles not between the parallel lines are **exterior angles.** Angle 1 and ∠7, which are on opposite sides of the transversal, are **alternate exterior angles.**

Angle 2 and ∠8 are also alternate exterior angles.

Name another pair of alternate exterior angles.

Alternate exterior angles formed by a transversal intersecting parallel lines are congruent. So if the measure of ∠1 is 110°, then the measure of ∠7 is also 110°.

While we practice the terms for describing angle pairs, it is useful to remember the following.

> When a transversal intersects parallel lines, all acute angles formed are equal in measure, and all obtuse angles formed are equal in measure.

Thus any acute angle formed will be supplementary to any obtuse angle formed.

English Learners

In the 2nd paragraph explain the term **relative position.** Say,

> **"Angles have the same relative positions when they are located in similar places. Such angles have equal measures. Name other angles that are equal because of their relative positions."** Angles 2 and 6, 4 and 8, 3 and 7. **"Can you find other angle pairs?"**

When we talk about angles in relative positions, we are referring to equal angles.

Example

Transversal *w* intersects parallel lines *x* and *y*.

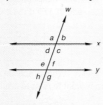

a. Name the pairs of corresponding angles.

b. Name the pairs of alternate interior angles.

c. Name the pairs of alternate exterior angles.

d. If the measure of ∠*a* is 115°, then what are the measures of ∠*e* and ∠*f*?

Solution

a. ∠*a* and ∠*e*, ∠*b* and ∠*f*, ∠*c* and ∠*g*, ∠*d* and ∠*h*

b. ∠*d* and ∠*f*, ∠*c* and ∠*e*

c. ∠*a* and ∠*g*, ∠*b* and ∠*h*

d. If ∠*a* measures 115°, then ∠*e* also measures **115°** and ∠*f* measures **65°**.

Practice Set

Line *f* and *g* are parallel.

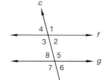

a. Which line in the figure at right is a transversal?   line *c*

b. Which angle is an alternate interior angle to ∠3?   ∠5

c. Which angle corresponds to ∠8?   ∠4

d. Which angle is an alternate exterior angle to ∠7?   ∠1

e. **Conclude** If the measure of ∠1 is 105°, what is the measure of each of the other angles in the figure?

e. Angle 3, ∠5, and ∠7 each measure 105°. Angle 2, ∠4, ∠6, and ∠8 each measure 75°.

Written Practice *Strengthening Concepts*

1. How many quarter-pound hamburgers can be made from 100 pounds of ground beef?   400 hamburgers
   (49)

2. **Connect** On the Fahrenheit scale water freezes at 32°F and boils at 212°F. What temperature is halfway between the freezing and boiling temperatures of water?   122°F
   (18)

Lesson 97   505

▸ See Math Conversations in the sidebar.

---

2 New Concepts (Continued)

Example

Instruction

After completing the solution, copy the diagram from the example on the board or on an overhead transparency for easy reference. Ask individual students to explain how to find the measures of ∠*b*, ∠*c*, ∠*d*, ∠*g*, and ∠*h*. Since ∠*a* measures 115°, then ∠*c* and ∠*g* measure 115° because all obtuse angles formed when a transversal intersects two parallel lines have the same measure. Similarly, since ∠*f* measures 65°, ∠*b*, ∠*d*, and ∠*h* measure 65° because all acute angles formed when a transversal intersects two parallel lines have the same measure.

Practice Set

Problem e [Error Alert]

If students need extra help, ask them to begin by identifying the type of angle (acute, obtuse, or right) that angle 1 represents (obtuse), then look for other obtuse angles in the figure.

Repeat the same steps to identify and locate the acute angles.

Manipulative Use

You can **model** identifying the angles formed by two lines and a transversal by creating a transversal intersecting two parallel lines using strips of paper, markers, and index cards.

Use strips of paper to model transversal *p* intersecting lines *m* and *n* shown on the first lesson page. Write the numerals 1–8 on the index cards and attach each card to the appropriate place on the model.

Refer to this model as you explain corresponding angles, interior angles, and exterior angles. For example, you may ask a volunteer to remove two numbers that are alternate interior angles.

3 Written Practice

Math Conversations
Discussion opportunities are provided below.

Problem 3 Analyze
Extend the Problem
Point out that the given formula typically involves a paper and pencil or calculator computation.

An equivalent formula for converting degrees Celsius to Fahrenheit is to double the Celsius number, subtract 10%, and then add 32. Have students practice this method by mentally converting 10°C, 15°C, and 20°C. 50°F, 59°F, and 68°F

Some students might prefer a simpler, but less exact procedure. Challenge students to write a formula that can be used *mentally* to estimate the Fahrenheit temperature when the Celsius temperature is known. Sample: $F = 2C + 30$ where F represents degrees Fahrenheit and C represents degrees Celsius.

Then provide a variety of Celsius temperatures and invite students to use mental math to change the temperatures to degrees Fahrenheit and compare results.

Problem 11 Analyze
"What is the sum of the angle measures of a parallelogram? Give an example to support your answer." 360°; Sample: A rectangle has four 90° angles, and the sum of those angle measures is 360°. Since a rectangle is a parallelogram, the sum of the angle measures of a parallelogram is 360°.

Problem 21 Predict
Before completing the problem, ask students to discuss the pattern and identify its rule. To find the next term in the sequence, multiply the previous term by $\frac{1}{10}$, or divide the previous term by 10.

Errors and Misconceptions
Problem 11
Some students might be confused by the number of turns. Regardless of the number of turns, one complete "trip" around a convex polygon totals 360°. That is, the sum of the exterior angles is 360°.

(continued)

▶ *** 3.** This function table shows the relationship between temperatures measured in degrees Celsius and degrees Fahrenheit. (To find the Fahrenheit temperature, multiply the temperature in Celsius by 1.8, then add 32.) Find the missing number in the table.
(96)

C	0	10	20	30
1.8C + 32	32	50	68	86

Predict What is special about the result when C = 100? (*Hint:* You may want to refer to problem **2.**) The boiling point of water is 100°C and 212°F.

4. Compare: $\frac{5}{8}$ ⊘ 0.675
(76)

* 5. Write $2\frac{1}{4}$ as a percent.   *** 6.** Write $1\frac{2}{5}$ as a percent.   140%
(94) 225%   (94)

* 7. Write 0.7 as a percent.   *** 8.** Write $\frac{7}{8}$ as a percent. $87\frac{1}{2}$%
(94) 70%   (94)

9. Use division by primes to find the prime factors of 320. Then write the prime factorization of 320 using exponents. $2^6 \cdot 5$
(73)

```
9.        1
       5)5
      2)10
      2)20
      2)40
      2)80
     2)160
     2)320
```

* 10. In one minute the second hand of a clock turns 360°. How many degrees does the minute hand of a clock turn in one minute? $\frac{360°}{60} = 6°$
(90)

▶*** 11.** *Analyze* Jason likes to ride his skateboard around Parallelogram Park. If he made four turns on each trip around the park, what was the average number of degrees in each turn? $\frac{360°}{4} = 90°$
(90)

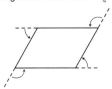

12. $6\frac{3}{4} + 5\frac{7}{8}$ $12\frac{5}{8}$ **13.** $6\frac{1}{3} - 2\frac{1}{2}$ $3\frac{5}{6}$ **14.** $2\frac{1}{2} \div 100$ $\frac{1}{40}$
(59)   (63)   (68)

15. 6.93 + 8.429 + 12   27.359   **16.** (1 − 0.1)(1 ÷ 0.1)   9
(38)   (53)

17. $4.2 + \frac{7}{8}$ (decimal answer)   5.075
(74)

18. Jovita bought $3\frac{1}{3}$ cubic yards of mulch for the garden. She will need 2.5 cubic yards for the flowerbeds. How much mulch is left for Jovita to use for her vegetable garden? Write your answer as a fraction. $\frac{5}{6}$ cubic yards
(73)

19. *Analyze* If 80% of the 30 students passed the test, how many students did not pass?   6 students
(41)

20. Compare: $\frac{1}{2} \div \frac{1}{3}$ ⊘ $\frac{1}{3} \div \frac{1}{2}$
(50)

▶ **21.** *Predict* What is the next number in this sequence?   0.1 (or $\frac{1}{10}$)
(10)
$$\ldots, 1000, 100, 10, 1, \ldots$$

▶ See Math Conversations in the sidebar.

Find each unknown number:

22. $a + 60 + 70 = 180$ 50
(3)

23. $\frac{7}{4} = \frac{w}{44}$ 77
(85)

▶ **24.** The perimeter of this square is 48 in. What is
(79)   the area of one of the triangles?   72 in.²

Refer to the table below to answer problems **25–27.**

Mark's Personal Running Records

Distance	Time (minutes:seconds)
$\frac{1}{4}$ mile	0:58
$\frac{1}{2}$ mile	2:12
1 mile	5:00

25. If Mark set his 1-mile record by keeping a steady pace, then what was
(32)   his $\frac{1}{2}$-mile time during the 1-mile run?   2:30

26. *Conclude* What is a reasonable expectation for the time it would take
(32)   Mark to run 2 miles?   **B**

   A 9:30   **B** 11:00   **C** 15:00

27. *Formulate* Write a question that relates to this table and answer the
(32)   question.   See student work.

* **28.** Transversal *t* intersects parallel lines *r* and *s*. Angle 2 measures 78°.
(97)

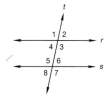

▶ **a.** *Analyze* Which angle corresponds to ∠2?   ∠6

   b. Find the measures of ∠5 and ∠8.   m∠5 = 102°; m∠8 = 78°

* **29.** $10^2 - \sqrt{49} - (10 + 8) \div 3^2$ 91
(92)

30. What is the probability of rolling a composite number with one roll of a
(58)   number cube? $\frac{1}{3}$

Lesson 97   507

▶ See Math Conversations in the sidebar.

---

3 **Written Practice** *(Continued)*

Math Conversations

Discussion opportunities are provided below.

Problem 28a   Analyze

"What does it mean when two angles are corresponding?" Angles are corresponding when they are on the same side of a transversal that intersects two or more parallel lines, and have the same measure.

"To answer the question, why is it important that lines r and s are parallel?" None of the angles will correspond to ∠2 if the lines are not parallel.

Errors and Misconceptions
Problem 24

To find the area of a triangle, students must first find the lengths of the sides of the square. Help them find the length by asking:

"How are the lengths of the sides of a square related?" the sides are the same length

"How many sides does a square have?" 4

"If you know the perimeter, or the distance around a square, how can you find the length of one of its sides?" divide the perimeter or distance around by 4

Looking Forward

Identifying angles formed by transversals (corresponding, alternate interior, and alternate exterior) prepares students for:

- **Lesson 109,** identifying corresponding parts (angles and sides) of congruent and similar figures.

• Sum of the Angle Measures of Triangles and Quadrilaterals

Objectives

- Identify the interior and exterior angles of a polygon.
- Find the sums of the interior angles of a triangle and of a quadrilateral.
- Find the measure of one interior angle in a triangle or quadrilateral when the measures of the other interior angles are known.

Lesson Preparation

Materials

- **Power Up J** (in *Instructional Masters*)
- **Manipulative kit: inch rulers**
Optional
- **Teacher-provided material: protractors, scissors; geometric drawing software**

Power Up J

Math Language

New	English Learners (ESL)
exterior angle	sketch
interior angle	

Technology Resources

Student eBook Complete student textbook in electronic format.

Resources and Planner CD Assessment, reteaching, and instructional masters, plus a pacing calendar with standards.

Test and Practice Generator CD Create additional practice sheets and custom-made tests.

www.SaxonPublishers.com Visit for more student activities and planning materials.

Inclusion

Adaptations CD Adapted lessons, investigations, practice and assessments.

Meeting Standards

National Council of Teachers of Mathematics (NCTM)

Geometry

GM.1a Precisely describe, classify, and understand relationships among types of two- and three-dimensional objects using their defining properties

GM.1c Create and critique inductive and deductive arguments concerning geometric ideas and relationships, such as congruence, similarity, and the Pythagorean relationship

GM.4d Use geometric models to represent and explain numerical and algebraic relationships

Connections

CN.4a Recognize and use connections among mathematical ideas

Problem-Solving Strategy: Draw a Diagram/Find a Pattern/Make It Simpler

If two people shake hands, there is one handshake. If three people shake hands, there are three handshakes. If four people shake hands with one another, we can picture the number of handshakes by drawing four dots (for people) and connecting the dots with segments (for handshakes). Then we count the segments (six). Use this method to count the number of handshakes that will take place between Bill, Phil, Jill, Lil, and Will.

(Understand) **Understand the problem.**

"What information are we given?"

Five people shake hands with one another.

"What are we asked to do?"

Determine how many handshakes occur between the five people.

(Plan) **Make a plan.**

"What problem-solving strategy will we use?"

We will *draw a diagram* and *find a pattern.* By *making simpler,* but similar diagrams of smaller groups, we will more easily find a pattern.

(Solve) **Carry out the plan.**

"How do we begin?"

We will make diagrams for a group of 1, a group of 2, a group of 3, and a group of 4.

1 person	**2 people**	**3 people**	**4 people**
0 handshakes	**1 handshake**		
		3 handshakes	**6 handshakes**

"How can we describe the emerging pattern?"

We see that with the new person shakes the hands of everyone that is already in the group.

"How many handshakes will there be among Bill, Phil, Jill, Lil, and Will?"

When Will joins the group, he will shake hands with the four people in the group. That means there will be four more handshakes in addition to the number of handshakes that occurred with the four people before Will came along. For four people there were 6 handshakes. With Will joining the group, there will be 6 plus 4 handshakes, for a total of 10 handshakes.

(Check) **Look back.**

"Did we answer the question that was asked?"

Yes. We found that with five people there will be a total of 10 handshakes.

"Can we draw a diagram to help us count the handshakes?"

Yes. The ten segments represent ten handshakes.

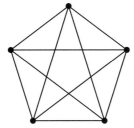

Teacher Note: Challenge students to predict and verify the number of handshakes for 6 people.

• Sum of the Angle Measures of Triangles and Quadrilaterals

Power Up | Building Power

facts | Power Up J

mental math

a. **Number Sense:** $40 \cdot 50$ 2000

b. **Number Sense:** $293 + 450$ 743

c. **Percent:** 50% of 48   24

d. **Calculation:** $20.00 − $18.72 $1.28

e. **Decimals:** 12.5×100 1250

f. **Number Sense:** $\frac{360}{40}$ 9

g. **Measurement:** How many cups are in 2 pints?   4 cups

h. **Calculation:** $8 \times 8, - 1, \div 9, \times 4, + 2, \div 2, + 1, \sqrt{\ }, \sqrt{\ }$ 2

problem solving

If two people shake hands, there is one handshake. If three people shake hands, there are three handshakes. If four people shake hands with one another, we can picture the number of handshakes by drawing four dots (for people) and connecting the dots with segments (for handshakes). Then we count the segments (six). Use this method to count the number of handshakes that will take place between Bill, Phil, Jill, Lil, and Wil.
10 handshakes

New Concept | Increasing Knowledge

If we extend a side of a polygon, we form an **exterior angle.** In this figure $\angle 1$ is an exterior angle, and $\angle 2$ is an **interior angle.** Notice that these angles are supplementary. That is, the sum of their measures is 180°.

Thinking Skill

Verify

Act out the turns Elizabeth made to verify the number of degrees.

Recall from Lesson 90 that a full turn measures 360°. So if Elizabeth makes three turns to get around a park, she has turned a total of 360°. Likewise, if she makes four turns to get around a park, she has also turned 360°.

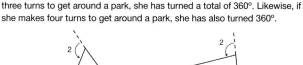

The sum of the measures of angles 1, 2, and 3 is 360°.

The sum of the measures of angles 1, 2, 3, and 4 is 360°.

Facts | Write each mixed number as an improper fraction.

$2\frac{1}{2} = \frac{5}{2}$	$2\frac{2}{5} = \frac{12}{5}$	$1\frac{3}{4} = \frac{7}{4}$	$2\frac{3}{4} = \frac{11}{4}$	$2\frac{1}{8} = \frac{17}{8}$
$1\frac{2}{3} = \frac{5}{3}$	$3\frac{1}{2} = \frac{7}{2}$	$1\frac{5}{6} = \frac{11}{6}$	$2\frac{1}{4} = \frac{9}{4}$	$1\frac{1}{8} = \frac{9}{8}$
$5\frac{1}{2} = \frac{11}{2}$	$1\frac{3}{8} = \frac{11}{8}$	$5\frac{1}{3} = \frac{16}{3}$	$3\frac{1}{4} = \frac{13}{4}$	$4\frac{1}{2} = \frac{9}{2}$
$1\frac{7}{8} = \frac{15}{8}$	$2\frac{2}{3} = \frac{8}{3}$	$1\frac{5}{8} = \frac{13}{8}$	$3\frac{3}{4} = \frac{15}{4}$	$7\frac{1}{2} = \frac{15}{2}$

If Elizabeth makes three turns to get around the park, then each turn averages 120°.

$$\frac{360°}{3 \text{ turns}} = 120° \text{ per turn}$$

If she makes four turns to get around the park, then each turn averages 90°.

$$\frac{360°}{4 \text{ turns}} = 90° \text{ per turn}$$

Recall that these turns correspond to exterior angles of the polygons and that the exterior and interior angles at a turn are supplementary. Since the exterior angles of a triangle average 120°, the interior angles must average 60°. A triangle has three interior angles, so the sum of the interior angles is 180° (3 × 60° = 180°).

> **The sum of the interior angles of a triangle is 180°.**

The sum of angles
1, 2, and 3 is 180°.

Since the exterior angles of a quadrilateral average 90°, the interior angles must average 90°. So the sum of the four interior angles of a quadrilateral is 360° (4 × 90° = 360°).

> **The sum of the interior angles of a quadrilateral is 360°.**

The sum of angles
1, 2, 3, and 4 is 360°.

Example 1

What is m∠A in △ABC?

Solution

The measures of the interior angles of a triangle total 180°.

$$m\angle A + 60° + 70° = 180°$$

Since the measures of ∠B and ∠C total 130°, m∠A is **50°**.

(continued)

2 New Concepts (Continued)

Instruction
A way for students to verify the statement is to draw any triangle, label its angles 1, 2, and 3, then tear off the angles and fit the vertices together so that the angles combine to form a straight angle. Remind students at that time that the measure of a straight angle (or a straight line) is 180°.

Instruction
If students are not convinced that the sum of the measures of the interior angles of any quadrilateral is 360°, have them use a ruler to draw several quadrilaterals, then ask them to use a protractor to measure the angles. Students should then compare the sums of those angle measures to 360°.

An alternative to drawing the figures is to have students use geometric drawing software to draw a variety of polygons and investigate the sums of their angle measures.

Math Background

The shape of a triangle does not change the sum of its angle measures. The sum of the angle measures of *any* triangle is 180°.

Similarly, the shape of a quadrilateral does not change the sum of its angle measures. The sum of the angle measures of *any* quadrilateral is 360°.

2 New Concepts (Continued)

Example 2
Instruction

Students should recognize that the degree measure of the unknown angle is the sum of the known angle measures subtracted from 360°.

Practice Set

Problem e [Error Alert]

If necessary, have students review Lesson 60 to recall characteristics of regular polygons.

Problem f [Error Alert]

Point out that the five turns represent one lap of the park.

3 Written Practice

Math Conversations

Discussion opportunities are provided below.

Problem 2 [Analyze]

"We must change feet to inches. One foot is equal to what number of inches?" 12

"How could we use multiplication and the fact that 1 foot equals 12 inches to solve this problem?" multiply $5\frac{1}{2}$ (or 5.5) by 12

"How many inches tall is Jenny?" 66 inches

"How could we use mental math to check our answer?" Sample: Count on by 12 five times, then add 6.

(continued)

Example 2

What is m∠T in quadrilateral QRST?

Solution

The measures of the interior angles of a quadrilateral total 360°.

$$m\angle T + 80° + 80° + 110° = 360°$$

The measures of ∠Q, ∠R, and ∠S total 270°. So m∠T is **90°**.

Practice Set

Quadrilateral *ABCD* is divided into two triangles by segment *AC*. Use for problems **a–c**.

a. What is the sum of m∠1, m∠2, and m∠3?   180°

b. What is the sum of m∠4, m∠5, and m∠6?   180°

c. [Generalize] What is the sum of the measures of the four interior angles of the quadrilateral?   360°

d. What is m∠P in △PQR?   75°

▶ **e.** What is the measure of each interior angle of a regular quadrilateral?   90°

f.

▶ **f.** [Model] Elizabeth made five left turns as she ran around the park. Draw a sketch that shows the turns in her run around the park. Then find the average number of degrees in each turn.

$\frac{360°}{5} = 72°$

Written Practice   *Strengthening Concepts*

1. When the sum of $\frac{1}{2}$ and $\frac{1}{4}$ is divided by the product of $\frac{1}{2}$ and $\frac{1}{4}$, what is the quotient?   6
(12, 72)

▶ * **2.** [Analyze] Jenny is $5\frac{1}{2}$ feet tall. She is how many inches tall?   66 inches
(95)

3. If $\frac{4}{5}$ of the 200 runners finished the race, how many runners did not finish the race?   40 runners
(77)

▶ See Math Conversations in the sidebar.

English Learners

In problem **f,** explain the term **sketch.** Say,

"When you draw something quickly, without measuring, you do a sketch. Sketch a circle without using a compass." Have students quickly draw a circle by hand without using a compass.

When you sketch you only estimate the measurements, you don't actually measure them. Ask students to sketch a rectangle.

* 4. Lines *p* and *q* are parallel.
(97)

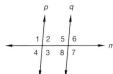

a. Which angle is an alternate interior angle to ∠2?   ∠8

b. If ∠2 measures 85°, what are the measures of ∠6 and ∠7?
m∠6 = 85°; m∠7 = 95°

▶ *** 5.** **Analyze** The circumference of the earth is about 25,000 miles. Write that
(92) distance in expanded notation using exponents.
$(2 \times 10^4) + (5 \times 10^3)$ miles

6. $\frac{15}{16}$ inch;
Sample: Divide
by 2 to find the
radius; multiply
by π to find the
circumference.

6. **Estimate** Use a ruler to measure the
(17, 27) diameter of a quarter to the nearest sixteenth
of an inch. How can you use that information
to find the radius and the circumference of
the quarter?

7. **Connect** Which of these bicycle wheel parts is the best model of the
(27) circumference of the wheel?   **C**

   A spoke   **B** axle   **C** tire

▶ **8.** **Predict** As this sequence continues, each term equals the sum of the
(10) two previous terms. What is the next term in this sequence?   21

                 1, 1, 2, 3, 5, 8, 13, …

9. If there is a 20% chance of rain, what is the probability that it will not
(58) rain?   0.8 or $\frac{4}{5}$

* 10. Write $1\frac{1}{3}$ as a percent. $133\frac{1}{3}$%
(94)

▶*** 11.** **Analyze** 0.08*w* = $0.60 $7.50
(87)

12. $\frac{1 - 0.001}{0.03}$ 33.3
(49)

13. $\frac{3\frac{1}{3}}{100}$ $\frac{1}{30}$
(68)

14. If the volume of each small block is one
(82) cubic inch, what is the volume of this
rectangular prism?   30 cubic inches

15. $6\frac{1}{2}$ + 4.95 (decimal)   11.45
(74)

16. $2\frac{1}{6}$ − 1.5 (fraction) $\frac{2}{3}$
(73)

17. $20.98;
Sample: Round
$19.79 to $20
and 6% to 10%.
10% of $20 is
$2. $20 + $2 =
$22. Since both
numbers were
rounded up, the
actual answer
should be a little
less.

17. If a shirt costs $19.79 and the sales-tax rate is 6%, what is the total
(41) price including tax? Explain how you can check your answer using
estimation.

* 18. What fraction of a foot is 3 inches? $\frac{1}{4}$
(95)

19. What percent of a meter is 3 centimeters?   3%
(75)

▶ See Math Conversations in the sidebar.

Math Conversations

Discussion opportunities are provided below.

Problem 5   Analyze

"In the number 25,000, what place is the digit 2 in?" the ten thousands place

"When we write a number in ten thousands, what power of 10 is used to represent ten thousands?" 10^4

"What place is the digit 5 in?" the thousands place

"What power of 10 is used to represent thousands?" 10^3

Problem 8   Predict

Extend the Problem

Students may be interested to learn that these terms are the beginning terms of the Fibonacci sequence. The Fibonacci sequence is a sequence in which each term is the sum of the two terms that precede it.

Given this information, ask students to predict the tenth term in the sequence. 55

Problem 11   Analyze

"Name a related equation that we can use to solve the problem."
Sample: *w* = $0.60 ÷ 0.08

"What must we remember whenever we divide and the divisor is a decimal number?" Sample: First shift the decimal point in the divisor. Next, shift the decimal point in the dividend the same number of places and in the same direction. Then place a decimal point in the quotient, and divide.

(continued)

3 Written Practice (Continued)

Math Conversations
Discussion opportunities are provided below.

Problem 23 [Conclude]
"What does it mean if two figures are congruent?" Sample: The figures are exactly the same size and shape; the figures are identical in every way.

Problem 24a [Analyze]
"What is the sum of the interior angle measures of any triangle?" 180°

"Explain how to find the measure of interior angle A." Subtract the sum of the two known angle measures from 180°, or 180° − (40° + 110°)

"What is the measure of angle A?" 30°

Problem 24b [Analyze]
"What kind of angle is formed by the 110° angle and angle x?" a straight angle

"What is the measure of a straight angle?" 180°

"Explain how to find the measure of angle x." Subtract 110° from 180°

"What is the measure of angle x?" 70°

Problem 30
Extend the Problem
"Suppose the triangle is a right isosceles triangle. What would the measure of the two congruent angles of the triangle be?" 45°

Errors and Misconceptions
Problem 28
Students must remember to cancel units before multiplying, and to write the unit that was not canceled (ft) in the answer.

---

20. The ratio of children to adults in the theater was 5 to 3. If there were 45 children, how many adults were there?   27 adults
(88)

21. Arrange these numbers in order from least to greatest: $-1, -\frac{1}{2}, 0, \frac{1}{2}, 1$
(14, 17)

$$1, -1, 0, \frac{1}{2}, -\frac{1}{2}$$

22. [Classify] These two triangles together form a quadrilateral with only one pair of parallel sides. What type of quadrilateral is formed?   trapezoid
(64)

▶ **23.** [Conclude] Do the triangles in this quadrilateral appear to be congruent or not congruent?   not congruent
(60)

▶ **24.**   **a.** [Analyze] What is the measure of $\angle A$ in $\triangle ABC$?   30°
(98)

   b. [Analyze] What is the measure of the exterior angle marked x?   70°

25. Write 40% as a
(33, 74)
   a. simplified fraction. $\frac{2}{5}$

   b. simplified decimal number.   0.4

26. The diameter of this circle is 20 mm. What is the area of the circle? (Use 3.14 for π.)   314 mm²
(86)

20 mm

★ **27.** $2^3 + \sqrt{81} \div 3^2 + \left(\frac{1}{2}\right)^2$ $9\frac{1}{4}$
(92)

▶ **28.** Multiply 120 inches by 1 foot per 12 inches.   10 ft
(95)

$$\frac{120 \text{ in.}}{1} \times \frac{1 \text{ ft}}{12 \text{ in.}}$$

29. A bag contains 20 red marbles and 15 blue marbles.
(23, 58)
   a. What is the ratio of red marbles to blue marbles? $\frac{4}{3}$

   b. If one marble is drawn from the bag, what is the probability that the marble will be blue? $\frac{3}{7}$

▶ **30.** [Conclude] An architect drew a set of plans for a house. In the plans, the roof is supported by a triangular framework. When the house is built, two sides of the framework will be 19 feet long and the base will be 33 feet long. Classified by side length, what type of triangle will be formed?   isosceles triangle
(93)

▶ See Math Conversations in the sidebar.

• Fraction-Decimal-Percent Equivalents

Objectives

• Complete a table that shows equivalent fractions, decimals, and percents.

Lesson Preparation

Materials

• **Power Up K** (in *Instructional Masters*)
• **Manipulative kit: inch rulers**
Optional
• **Manipulative kit: compasses**

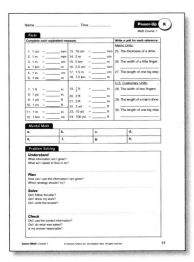

Power Up K

Technology Resources

Student eBook Complete student textbook in electronic format.

Resources and Planner CD Assessment, reteaching, and instructional masters, plus a pacing calendar with standards.

Test and Practice Generator CD Create additional practice sheets and custom-made tests.

www.SaxonPublishers.com Visit for more student activities and planning materials.

Inclusion

Adaptations CD Adapted lessons, investigations, practice and assessments.

Meeting Standards

National Council of Teachers of Mathematics (NCTM)

Numbers and Operations

NO.1a Work flexibly with fractions, decimals, and percents to solve problems

NO.2a Understand the meaning and effects of arithmetic operations with fractions, decimals, and integers

Connections

CN.4a Recognize and use connections among mathematical ideas

Problem-Solving Strategy: Use Logical Reasoning

If the last page of a section of a large newspaper is page 36, what is the fewest number of sheets of paper that could be in that section?

(Understand) **Understand the problem.**

"What information are we given?"

We are told that the last page of a section of a newspaper is page 36.

"What are we asked to do?"

Determine the fewest number of sheets of paper that could be in that section.

(Plan) **Make a plan.**

"What problem-solving strategy will we use?"

We will *use logical reasoning* to determine the minimum number of sheets of paper.

(Solve) **Carry out the plan.**

"How many pages are created with one folded sheet of paper?"

If we fold one sheet of paper and number the pages, we find that there are 4 pages.

"If each folded sheet of paper makes four pages, how many sheets would be needed to make 36 pages?"

We would need 9 sheets of paper, because $36 \div 4 = 9$.

(Check) **Look back.**

"Did we answer the question that was asked?"

Yes. We found the smallest number of sheets of paper that would be needed to make a 36-page section of a newspaper.

"How many sheets of paper are in a section with 30 pages?"

Seven full sheets and one half sheet.

"Can a section of newspaper have an odd number of pages?"

No, if every page of a newspaper is printed and numbered, then the back page of every section is even.

Teacher Note: Ask students what the folios (page numbers) would be on the outside sheet of paper of the 36-page newspaper. (1, 2, 35, 36) Ask what the folios would be for the next sheet. (3, 4, 33, 34) Finally challenge them to tell the folios for the inner most sheet of paper (the ninth one). (17, 18, 19, 20)

• Fraction-Decimal-Percent
Equivalents

39 pb   *611*
613
633

facts   Power Up K

mental math

a. **Number Sense:** 60 · 50   3000

b. **Number Sense:** 741 − 450   291

c. **Percent:** 25% of 48   12

d. **Calculation:** $12.99 + $4.75 $17.74

e. **Decimals:** 37.5 ÷ 100   0.375

f. **Number Sense:** 30 × 15   450

g. **Measurement:** Which is greater 1 liter or 1000 milliliters?   equal

h. **Calculation:** $7 \times 7, + 1, \div 2, \sqrt{\ }, \times 4, - 2, \div 3, \times 5, + 3, \div 3$ 11

problem solving   If the last page of a section of large newspaper is page 36, what is the fewest number of sheets of paper that could be in that section?   9 sheets

New Concept   *Increasing Knowledge*

Fractions, decimals, and percents are three ways to express parts of a whole. An important skill is being able to change from one form to another. This lesson asks you to complete tables that show equivalent fractions, decimals, and percents.

Example

Complete the table.

Fraction	Decimal	Percent
$\frac{1}{2}$	a.	b.
c.	0.3	d.
e.	f.	40%

Solution

The numbers in each row should be equivalent. For $\frac{1}{2}$ we write a decimal and a percent. For 0.3 we write a fraction and a percent. For 40% we write a fraction and a decimal.

a. $\frac{1}{2} = 2)\overline{1.0}$ (0.5)

b. $\frac{1}{2} \times \frac{100\%}{1} = \mathbf{50\%}$

Lesson 99   513

---

1 Power Up

Facts
Distribute **Power Up K** to students. See answers below.

Mental Math
Before students begin the Mental Math exercise, do this counting exercise as a class.

Count by $\frac{1}{3}$s from $\frac{1}{3}$ to 4.

Encourage students to share different ways to mentally compute these exercises. Strategies for exercises **b** and **f** are listed below.

b. **Add 9 to 741, then Subtract 9**
750 − 450 = 300; 300 − 9 = 291
Subtract 500, then Add 50
741 − 500 = 241; 241 + 50 = 291

f. **Find 10 × 15 × 3**
10 × 15 = 150; 150 × 3 = 450
Break Apart 15
(30 × 10) + (30 × 5) = 300 + 150 = 450

Problem Solving
Refer to **Power-Up Discussion**, p. 513B.

2 New Concepts

Example
Instruction
Before completing the table, ask students to recall and describe different methods that can be used to name equivalent fractions, decimals, and percents.

(continued)

Facts

Complete each equivalent measure.

					Write a unit for each reference.
1. 1 cm = __10__ mm	13. 10 cm = __100__ mm	**Metric Units:**
2. 1 m = __1000__ mm	14. 2 m = __200__ cm	25. The thickness of a dime: __millimeter__
3. 1 m = __100__ cm	15. 5 km = __5000__ m	26. The width of a little finger: __centimeter__
4. 1 km = __1000__ m	16. 2.5 cm = __25__ mm	
5. 1 in. = __2.54__ cm	17. 1.5 m = __150__ cm	27. The length of one big step: __meter__
6. 1 mi ≈ __1610__ m	18. 7.5 km = __7500__ m	
		U.S. Customary Units:
7. 1 ft = __12__ in.	19. $\frac{1}{2}$ ft = __6__ in.	28. The width of two fingers: __inch__
8. 1 yd = __36__ in.	20. 2 ft = __24__ in.	
9. 1 yd = __3__ ft	21. 3 ft = __36__ in.	29. The length of a man's shoe: __foot__
10. 1 mi = __5280__ ft	22. 2 yd = __6__ ft	
11. 1 m ≈ __39__ in.	23. 10 yd = __30__ ft	30. The length of one big step: __yard__
12. 1 km ≈ __0.62__ mi	24. 100 yd = __300__ ft	

Instruction

Give students an opportunity to ask any questions they may have about the calculations used to complete the table.

After the table has been completed, remind students that each row of the table shows different names for the same number or amount.

Practice Set
Problems a–l Connect

Invite twelve volunteers to each choose a different problem and then demonstrate on the board how to solve the problem.

---

3 Written Practice

Math Conversations

Discussion opportunities are provided below.

Problem 3 Analyze

"Three-eighths of the votes were 'yes' and three-eighths of the votes were 'no.' What whole number represents all of the votes?" 1

"How is 1 used to find the answer?"
Subtract the sum of the yes votes and the no votes from 1; $1 - \left(\frac{3}{8} + \frac{3}{8}\right)$

Challenge volunteers to explain how mental math can be used to solve the problem. Sample: The sum of $\frac{3}{8}$ and $\frac{3}{8}$ is $\frac{6}{8}$, which is the same as $\frac{3}{4}$. Since 1 is the same as $\frac{4}{4}$, taking $\frac{3}{4}$ away from $\frac{4}{4}$ leaves $\frac{1}{4}$.

Problem 6 Analyze

Point out which direction in the classroom represents east, then invite students to stand and act out the problem.

Errors and Misconceptions
Problem 1

If students have difficulty recognizing that division is used to solve the problem, ask them to first solve a simpler problem using only mental math. For example,

"A ribbon that is 12 inches long can be cut into how many pieces that are each 6 inches long?" 2

"Explain how we can find the number of $1\frac{1}{2}$ inch pieces of ribbon that can be cut from a 12-inch length of ribbon." $12 \div 1\frac{1}{2}$

(continued)

---

c. $0.3 = \frac{3}{10}$ d. $0.3 \times 100\% =$ **30%**

e. $40\% = \frac{40}{100} = \frac{2}{5}$ f. $40\% = 0.40 =$ **0.4**

Practice Set ▶ Connect Complete the table.

Fraction	Decimal	Percent
$\frac{3}{5}$	**a.** 0.6	**b.** 60%
c. $\frac{4}{5}$	0.8	**d.** 80%
e. $\frac{1}{5}$	**f.** 0.2	20%
$\frac{3}{4}$	**g.** 0.75	**h.** 75%
i. $\frac{3}{25}$	0.12	**j.** 12%
k. $\frac{1}{20}$	0.05	5%

Written Practice *Strengthening Concepts*

▶ **1.** Analyze A foot-long ribbon can be cut into how many $1\frac{1}{2}$-inch lengths?   8 lengths
(68)

2. A can of beans is the shape of what geometric solid?   cylinder
(Inv. 6)

▶ **3.** Analyze If $\frac{3}{8}$ of the group voted yes and $\frac{3}{8}$ voted no, then what fraction of the group did not vote? $\frac{1}{4}$
(77)

4. Connect Nine months is
(29, 75)
a. what fraction of a year? $\frac{3}{4}$

b. what percent of a year?   75%

5. One-cubic-foot boxes were stacked as shown. What was the volume of the stack of boxes?   48 ft³
(82)

▶ ***6.** Analyze Tom was facing east. Then he turned counterclockwise 270°. After the turn, what direction was Tom facing?   south
(90)

7. If $\frac{1}{5}$ of the pie was eaten, what percent of the pie was left?   80%
(75)

*8. Write the percent form of $\frac{1}{7}$. $14\frac{2}{7}\%$
(94)

9. $6\frac{3}{4} - 6.2$ (decimal answer)   0.55
(74)

10. $5 \cdot 4 \cdot 3 \cdot 2 \cdot 1 \cdot 0$ 0
(5)

11. $\frac{4.5}{0.18}$ 25   ***12.** $\sqrt{1600}$ 40
(49)   (89)

▶ See Math Conversations in the sidebar.

13. $\sqrt{64} + 5^2 - \sqrt{25} \times (2 + 3)$ 8
(92)

▶ **14.** *Analyze* Solve this proportion: $\frac{15}{20} = \frac{24}{n}$ 32
(85)

15. $12\frac{1}{2} \times 1\frac{3}{5} \times 5$ 100   **16.** $(4.2 \times 0.05) \div 7$ 0.03
(72)   (53)

17. If the sales-tax rate is 7%, what is the tax on a $111.11 purchase?
(41) $7.78

18. *Analyze* The table shows the percent of the population aged 25–64
(Inv. 5)   with some senior high school education. The figures are for the year
2001. Use the table to answer **a–c.**

Country	Percent
Peru	44%
Iceland	57%
Poland	46%
Italy	43%
Greece	51%
Chile	46%
Luxembourg	53%

a. Find the mode of the data.   46%

b. If the data were arranged from least to greatest, which country or
countries would have the middle score?   Poland and Chile

c. What is the term used for the answer to problem **b?** Will this quantity
always be the same as the mode in every set of data? Explain.

19. Write the prime factorization of 900 using exponents. $2^2 \cdot 3^2 \cdot 5^2$
(73)

20. Think of two different prime numbers, and write them on your paper.
(20)   Then write the greatest common factor (GCF) of the two prime
numbers.   The GCF is 1.

21. *Explain* The perimeter of a square is 2 meters. How many centimeters
(7, 8)   long is each side? Explain your thinking.   50 centimeters; $P = 4s$,
2 meters = 200 cm, 200 cm = 4s, 200 ÷ 4 = s, s = 50 cm

* 22. **a.** What is the area of this triangle?   20 cm²
(79, 93)

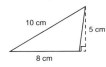

▶ **b.** *Classify* Is this an acute, right, or obtuse triangle?   obtuse triangle

18. **c.** the median;
Sample: The
mode is the
number that
appears most
often. The median
is the number
in the middle.
The median may
be same as the
mode, but it will
not always be the
same.

▶ See Math Conversations in the sidebar.

---

3 **Written Practice (Continued)**

Math Conversations

Discussion opportunities are provided below.

Problem 14 *Analyze*

"When can a fraction be reduced?"
A fraction can be reduced when a common
factor of the numerator and the denominator
is greater than 1.

"Is it possible to reduce $\frac{15}{20}$?" yes

"What is $\frac{15}{20}$ in lowest terms?" $\frac{3}{4}$

Write the proportion $\frac{3}{4} = \frac{24}{n}$ on the board.

**"Explain how we can use cross products to
solve for n."** Sample: Set the cross products
equal to each other and solve for n; $3n = 96$
and $n = 32$.

**"Explain how we can use a constant factor
to solve for n."** Sample: Compare 3 and 24
to learn that the constant factor is 8, then
multiply 4 by 8; $4 \times 8 = 32$

Problem 22b *Classify*

**"How are acute, right, and obtuse triangles
different?"** Sample: All of the angles of an
acute triangle have measures that are less
than 90°; a right triangle has one angle that
measures exactly 90°; an obtuse triangle has
one angle that measures more than 90° but
less than 180°.

(continued)

Math Conversations

Discussion opportunities are provided below.

Problem 27 *Model*

Using a compass, invite students to check their work by bisecting line segment *AC*.

Students may wish to review **Investigation 8:** Geometric Construction of Bisectors, before beginning the construction.

Problem 30 *Generalize*

Extend the Problem

"The table shows the relationship between the radius and a diameter of a circle. Make a table to show the relationship between circumference and diameter using the given diameters. You may use 3, 3.14, or $\frac{22}{7}$ for pi. After your table is complete, write a formula to show the relationship between the circumference and diameter of a circle." Sample: $C \approx 3d$ or $\frac{C}{3} \approx d$

d	C
2.4	7.2
1.4	4.2
5	15
30	90

---

* 23. (98)
   a. What is the measure of $\angle B$ in quadrilateral *ABCD*? 85°

   b. What is the measure of the exterior angle at *D*? 70°

Complete the table to answer problems **24–26.**

	Fraction	Decimal	Percent
* 24. (99)	**a.** $\frac{3}{5}$	0.6	**b.** 60%
* 25. (99)	**a.** $\frac{3}{20}$	**b.** 0.15	15%
* 26. (99)	$\frac{3}{10}$	**a.** 0.3	**b.** 30%

▶ **27.** (17) *Model* Draw $\overline{AC}$ $1\frac{1}{4}$ inches long. Find and mark the midpoint of $\overline{AC}$, and label the midpoint *B*. What are the lengths of $\overline{AB}$ and $\overline{BC}$? See student work. $AB = BC = \frac{5}{8}$ inch

28. (58) There are 32 cards in a bag. Eight of the cards have letters written on them. What is the chance of drawing a card with a letter written on it? 25%

29. (78) Compare: 1 gallon ⊘ 4 liters

▶*** 30.** (27, 96) *Generalize* This function table shows the relationship between the radius (*r*) and diameter (*d*) of a circle. The radius is the input and the diameter is the output. Describe the rule and find the missing number. To find *d* multiply *r* by 2 (*d* = 2*r*); 2.5

r	d
1.2	2.4
0.7	1.4
	5
15	30

Early Finishers
Real-World Application

Jesse displays trophies on 4 shelves in the family room. Two of the 6 trophies on each shelf are for soccer. How many trophies are NOT for soccer?

Write one equation and use it to solve the problem. Sample: 4 × (6 − 2) = 16

▶ See Math Conversations in the sidebar.

Looking Forward

Completing a table that shows fraction-decimal-percent equivalents prepares students for:

• **Lesson 105,** using proportions to solve percent problems.

• **Lesson 113,** expressing fractional numbers in standard notation by multiplying by powers of ten.

• **Lesson 115,** converting mixed number percents to fractions.

• **Lesson 116,** finding compound interest.

• **Lesson 119,** finding a whole when a percent is known by changing the percent to a fraction or a decimal.

• Algebraic Addition of Integers

Objectives
- Use a number line to add integers.
- Identify the opposite of an integer.
- Use algebraic addition to subtract integers.

Lesson Preparation

Materials
- **Power Up I** (in *Instructional Masters*)
- **Manipulative kit: metric rulers**
  Optional
- **Manipulative kit: tiles or counters**

Power Up I

Math Language

New	Maintain
algebraic addition	opposites

Technology Resources

Student eBook Complete student textbook in electronic format.

Resources and Planner CD Assessment, reteaching, and instructional masters, plus a pacing calendar with standards.

Test and Practice Generator CD Create additional practice sheets and custom-made tests.

www.SaxonPublishers.com Visit for more student activities and planning materials.

Inclusion

Adaptations CD Adapted lessons, investigations, practice and assessments.

Meeting Standards

National Council of Teachers of Mathematics (NCTM)

Numbers and Operations

NO.1g Develop meaning for integers and represent and compare quantities with them

NO.2a Understand the meaning and effects of arithmetic operations with fractions, decimals, and integers

Representation

RE.5a Create and use representations to organize, record, and communicate mathematical ideas

Problem-Solving Strategy: Use Logical Reasoning/ Make a Table

How many different triangles of any size are in this figure?

(Understand) **Understand the problem.**

"What information are we given?"

We are given a drawing of a triangle with three lines drawn from one vertex to the opposite side.

"What are we asked to do?"

Find how many different triangles of any size are in the figure.

(Plan) **Make a plan.**

"What problem-solving strategy will we use?"

We will *use logical and spatial reasoning* and *make a table* to find the number of triangles within the large triangle.

(Solve) **Carry out the plan.**

"How can we keep track of the types and number of triangles we find?"

Draw a table and record each triangle size and how many of each size there are.

"What size triangle is the largest and how many are there?"

the one large triangle

"What other sizes of triangles do we see?"

We see the smallest triangles, those made of two small triangles, and those made of three small triangles.

"Let's record the types of triangles and the quantity of each type in our table."

Triangle Type	Quantity
Four-part Triangle	1
Three-part Triangle	2
Two-part Triangle	3
One-part Triangle	4

"How many total triangles did we find?"

10 triangles

(Check) **Look back.**

"Did we complete the task that was given?"

Yes. We found all four sizes of triangles and the number of each type. We counted all 10 triangles.

• Algebraic Addition of Integers

Power Up   *Building Power*

facts   Power Up I

mental math
a. **Number Sense:** 50 · 80   4000

b. **Number Sense:** 380 + 550   930

c. **Percent:** 50% of 100   50

d. **Calculation:** $40.00 − $21.89 $18.11

e. **Decimals:** 0.8 × 100   80

f. **Number Sense:** $\frac{750}{25}$ 30

g. **Measurement:** How many pints are in 2 quarts?   4 pints

h. **Calculation:** 5 + 5, × 10, − 1, ÷ 9, + 1, ÷ 3, × 7, + 2, ÷ 2   15

problem solving   How many different triangles of any size are in this figure?   10

New Concept   *Increasing Knowledge*

Math Language
Integers consist of the counting numbers (1, 2, 3, …), the negative counting numbers (−1, −2, −3, …), and 0. All numbers that fall between these numbers are not integers.

Thinking Skill

Analyze

How is a thermometer like a number line? How is it different? Sample: Both can contain positive and negative integers at even intervals. A number line is usually drawn horizontally. Thermometers are usually vertical.

In this lesson we will practice adding integers.

The dots on this number line mark the integers from negative five to positive five (−5 to +5).

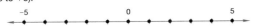

If we consider a rise in temperature of five degrees as a positive five (+5) and a fall in temperature of five degrees as a negative five (−5), we can use the scale on a thermometer to keep track of the addition.

Imagine that the temperature is 0°F. If the temperature falls five degrees (−5) and then falls another five degrees (−5), the resulting temperature is ten degrees below zero (−10°F). When we add two negative numbers, the sum is negative.

$$-5 + -5 = -10$$

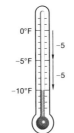

Lesson 100   517

---

1 **Power Up**

Facts
Distribute **Power Up I** to students. See answers below.

Mental Math
Before students begin the Mental Math exercise, do this counting exercise as a class.

Count up and down by 25s between −150 and 150.

Encourage students to share different ways to mentally compute these exercises. Strategies for exercises **a** and **b** are listed below.

  a. **Use a Multiplication Fact**
    Since 5 × 8 = 40, 50 × 80 = 4000
    Find 5 × 800
    5 × 800 = 4000
  b. **Change 380 to 400, then Subtract 20**
    400 + 550 = 950; 950 − 20 = 930
    Add 20 to 380 and Subtract 20 from 550
    400 + 530 = 930

Problem Solving
Refer to **Power-Up Discussion**, p. 517B.

2 **New Concepts**

Instruction
Invite students to name or describe real-world situations that involve integers. Sample:
a temperature of 40° above zero (+40)
a temperature of 8° below zero (−8)
a football gain of 3 yards (+3)
a football loss of 12 yards (−12)
a gain of 50¢ (+50 cents)
a loss of $2 (−2 dollars)

(continued)

Facts   Write each improper fraction as a mixed number. Reduce fractions.

$\frac{5}{4} = 1\frac{1}{4}$	$\frac{6}{4} = 1\frac{1}{2}$	$\frac{15}{10} = 1\frac{1}{2}$	$\frac{8}{3} = 2\frac{2}{3}$	$\frac{15}{12} = 1\frac{1}{4}$
$\frac{12}{8} = 1\frac{1}{2}$	$\frac{10}{8} = 1\frac{1}{4}$	$\frac{3}{2} = 1\frac{1}{2}$	$\frac{15}{6} = 2\frac{1}{2}$	$\frac{10}{4} = 2\frac{1}{2}$
$\frac{8}{6} = 1\frac{1}{3}$	$\frac{25}{10} = 2\frac{1}{2}$	$\frac{9}{6} = 1\frac{1}{2}$	$\frac{10}{6} = 1\frac{2}{3}$	$\frac{15}{8} = 1\frac{7}{8}$
$\frac{12}{10} = 1\frac{1}{5}$	$\frac{10}{3} = 3\frac{1}{3}$	$\frac{18}{12} = 1\frac{1}{2}$	$\frac{5}{2} = 2\frac{1}{2}$	$\frac{4}{3} = 1\frac{1}{3}$

Instruction

Students can use two-color tiles or counters to model integer addition. For example, to model $-5 + -5$, students should choose a color to represent negative, then group 5 tiles of that color and add 5 tiles of the same color to the group. The result (or sum) is 10 tiles of the same color (-10).

Students should generalize from the addition $-5 + -5$ that the sum of two negative numbers is a negative number.

Students should generalize from the sum $-5 + +5$ that sum of two opposite numbers is zero.

Example 1

Instruction

Draw a -9 to $+9$ integer number line on the full width of the board with tick marks as far apart as possible. Choose one student to model the addition in example 1 by standing at 0, moving right 8 spaces $(+8)$ to 8, and then moving back 5 spaces (-5) to end at 3. Keep this number line on the board for students to refer to as you teach this lesson.

(continued)

Imagine a different situation. We will again start with a temperature of 0°F. First the temperature falls five degrees (-5). Then the temperature rises five degrees $(+5)$. This brings the temperature back to 0°F. The numbers -5 and $+5$ are opposites. When we add opposites, the sum is zero.

$$-5 + +5 = 0$$

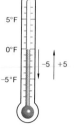

Math Language
Opposites are numbers that can be written with the same digits but with opposite signs. They are the same distance, in opposite directions, from zero on the number line.

Starting from 0°F, if the temperature rises five degrees $(+5)$ and then falls ten degrees (-10), the temperature will fall through zero to -5°F. The sum is less than zero because the temperature fell more than it rose.

$$+5 + -10 = -5$$

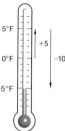

Example 1

Add: $+8 + -5$

Solution

We will illustrate this addition on a number line. We begin at zero and move eight units in the positive direction (to the right). From $+8$ we move five units in the negative direction (to the left) to $+3$.

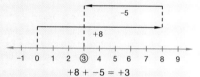

$$+8 + -5 = +3$$

The sum is **+3,** which we write as 3.

Example 2

Add: $-5 + -3$

Math Background

The set of integers consists of the counting numbers, their negatives, and zero.

$$\{\ldots, -3, -2, -1, 0, +1, +2, +3, \ldots\}$$

The set of integers is infinite, and extends without end to the left of 0 and to the right of 0 on the number line.

For positive integers, it is customary to not write the + sign. An integer without a sign is understood to be a positive integer.

Solution

Again using a number line, we start at zero and move in the negative direction, or to the left, five units to −5. From −5 we continue moving left three units to −8.

Thinking Skill

Generalize

When two negative integers are added, is the sum negative or positive?

negative

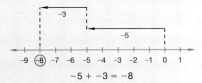

$$-5 + -3 = -8$$

The sum is **−8.**

Example 3

Add: −6 + +6

Solution

We start at zero and move six units to the left. Then we move six units to the right, returning to **zero.**

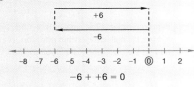

$$-6 + +6 = 0$$

Example 4

Add: (+6) + (−6)

Solution

Sometimes positive and negative numbers are written with parentheses. The parentheses help us see that the positive or negative sign is the sign of the number and not an addition or subtraction operation.

$$(+6) + (-6) = \mathbf{0}$$

Negative 6 and positive 6 are **opposites.** Opposites are numbers that can be written with the same digits but with opposite signs. The opposite of 3 is −3, and the opposite of −5 is 5 (which can be written as +5).

On a number line, we can see that any two opposites lie equal distances from zero. However, they lie on opposite sides of zero from each other.

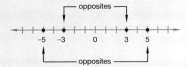

Lesson 100   519

---

2 New Concepts (Continued)

Examples 2 and 3

Instruction

Invite one or more volunteers to use the number line at the board to model the examples.

Example 4

Instruction

Ask several students in the class to name a pair of opposite numbers. Sample: 1 and −1; −237 and 237; 999,999 and −999,999

(continued)

Lesson 100   519

2 New Concepts (Continued)

Example 5

Instruction

Use a number line to help students recognize that every integer has an opposite integer (zero is its own opposite), and the points on the number line corresponding to opposite integers are the same distance from zero (which is also called the origin of the number line).

Instruction

An important concept for students to understand is that instead of subtracting a number, we may add its opposite. And when we add an opposite, it is important for students to recognize that only the number following the subtraction sign is changed to its opposite.

Example 6

Instruction

Have students note in this example that adding an opposite helps simplify the subtraction and makes it easier to find the answer.

(continued)

If opposites are added, the sum is zero.

$$-3 + {}^{+}3 = 0 \qquad -5 + {}^{+}5 = 0$$

Example 5

Find the opposite of each number:

    a. −7   **b. 10**

Solution

The opposite of a number is written with the same digits but with the opposite sign.

    a. The opposite of −7 is **+7,** which is usually written as 7.

    b. The opposite of 10 (which is positive) is **−10.**

Using opposites allows us to change any subtraction problem into an addition problem. Consider this subtraction problem:

$$10 - 6$$

Instead of subtracting 6 from 10, we can add the opposite of 6 to 10. The opposite of 6 is −6.

$$10 + {}^{-}6$$

In both problems the answer is 4. Adding the opposite of a number to subtract is called **algebraic addition.** We change subtraction to addition by adding the opposite of the subtrahend.

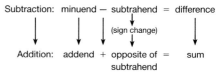

Subtraction: minuend − subtrahend = difference
(sign change)
Addition: addend + opposite of = sum
subtrahend

Example 6

Simplify: −10 − −6

Solution

This problem directs us to subtract a negative six from negative ten. Instead, we may add the opposite of negative six to negative ten.

$$-10 - {}^{-}6$$
$$-10 + {}^{+}6 = -4$$

Example 7

Simplify: (−3) − (+5)

Solution

Instead of subtracting a positive five, we add a negative five.

$$(-3) - (+5)$$
$$\downarrow \quad \downarrow$$
$$(-3) + (-5) = \mathbf{-8}$$

Practice Set

Model Find each sum. Draw a number line to show the addition for problems **a** and **b**. Solve problems **c–h** mentally.

a.

b.

a. $-3 + +4$ +1   **b.** $-3 + -4$ −7

c. $-3 + +3$ 0   **d.** $+4 + -3$ +1

e. $(+3) + (-4)$ −1   **f.** $(+10) + (-5)$ +5

g. $(-10) + (-5)$ −15   **h.** $(-10) + (+5)$ −5

▶ Find the opposite of each number:

i. -8 +8   **j.** 4 −4   **k.** 0 0

▶ Solve each subtraction problem using algebraic addition:

l. $-3 - -4$ +1   **m.** $-4 - +2$ −6

n. $(+3) - (-6)$ +9   **o.** $(-2) - (-4)$ +2

Written Practice   *Strengthening Concepts*

1. If 0.6 is the divisor and 1.2 is the quotient, what is the dividend?   0.72
(39)

2. If a number is twelve less than fifty, then it is how much more than twenty?   18
(12)

▶ **3.** If the sum of four numbers is 14.8, what is the average of the four numbers?   3.7
(18)

▶ *** 4.** *Model* Illustrate this problem on a number line:
(100)
$$-3 + +5$$

* 5. Find each sum mentally:
(100)
a. $-4 + +4$ 0   **b.** $-2 + -3$ −5

c. $-5 + +3$ −2   **d.** $+5 + -10$ −5

* 6. Solve each subtraction problem using algebraic addition:
(100)
a. $-2 - -5$ +3   **b.** $-3 - -3$ 0

c. $+2 - -3$ +5   **d.** $-2 - +3$ −5

▶ *** 7.** *Analyze* What is the measure of each angle of an equilateral triangle?   60°
(93, 98)

Lesson 100   **521**

▶ See Math Conversations in the sidebar.

---

2 New Concepts (Continued)

Example 7
Instruction
Make sure students recognize that only the subtrahend—or the number following the subtraction sign—was changed to its opposite.

Practice Set
Problems i–k (Error Alert)
One way for students to check their work is to find the sum of the number and its opposite. The sum of a number and its opposite is zero.

Problems l–o (Error Alert)
Watch for students who change only the operation, and not the sign of the subtrahend, when adding an opposite.

3 Written Practice

Math Conversations
Discussion opportunities are provided below.

Problem 4 (Model)
"When a number line is used to model an addition or a subtraction, where on the number line does the addition or subtraction begin?" at zero

"If the addition or a subtraction ends to the left of zero, what is the sign of the sum or difference?" negative

"If the addition or a subtraction ends to the right of zero, what is the sign of the sum or difference?" positive

Problem 7 (Analyze)
"Explain how we can use division to find the answer." Since the sum of the angle measures of a triangle is 180°, divide 180° by 3.

Errors and Misconceptions
Problem 3
Watch for students who conclude that the average of the four numbers is 14.8 and write 14.8×4 or 59.2 as the sum of the numbers.

(continued)

Math Conversations

Discussion opportunities are provided below.

Problem 9b Estimate

Extend the Problem

"To play a game using the spinner, suppose each of three players chooses a different number on the spinner. The rule of the game is simple—if the spinner is spun and it points to your number after it stops, you win. Is the game fair or unfair? Explain why." Unfair; Sample: For the game to be fair, the probability of each player winning should be $\frac{1}{3}$.

Problem 12 Analyze

Write the expression on the board or overhead. Ask a volunteer to state the first operation that must be completed to simplify the expression. rewrite 5^2 as 25

Ask a second volunteer to state the next operation that must be completed to simplify the expression. $(25 - 11) = 16$

Continue until the expression is simplified to 75. Then remind students to always follow the Order of Operations whenever they simplify an expression that contains more than one operation.

Errors and Misconceptions

Problem 9a and 9b

If students do not recognize the three congruent sectors as each representing $\frac{1}{6}$ of the circle, suggest that they draw a picture of the spinner but divide the sector labeled "1" into three equal parts.

Ask students to label each new sector "1", and then point out that the spinner is now divided into six equal parts.

(continued)

---

8. Quadrilateral *ABCD* is a parallelogram.
⁽⁷¹⁾ If angle *A* measures 70°, what are the measures of angles *B*, *C*, and *D*?
m∠*B* = 110°; m∠*C* = 70°; m∠*D* = 110°

9. a. $\frac{1}{3}$;
Sample: Two thirds of the top half of the circle is labeled 2.
$\frac{2}{3} \cdot \frac{1}{2} = \frac{1}{3}$

▶ **9. a.** If the spinner is spun once, what is the
⁽⁵⁸⁾ probability that it will stop in a sector with a number 2? How do you know your answer is correct?

b. Estimate If the spinner is spun 30 times, about how many times would it be expected to stop in the sector with the number 3? about 5 times

10. Find the volume of the rectangular prism at
⁽⁸²⁾ right. 210 in.³

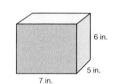

11. Twelve of the 27 students in the class are boys. What is the ratio of girls
⁽²³⁾ to boys in the class? $\frac{5}{4}$

▶* **12.** Analyze $10^2 + (5^2 - 11) \div \sqrt{49} - 3^3$ 75
⁽⁹²⁾

* **13.** The fraction $\frac{2}{3}$ is equal to what percent? $66\frac{2}{3}\%$
⁽⁹⁴⁾

14. If 20% of the students brought their lunch to school, then what fraction
⁽³³⁾ of the students did not bring their lunch to school? $\frac{4}{5}$

* **15.** $\dfrac{4^2}{2^4}$ 1   **16.** $5\frac{7}{8} + 4\frac{3}{4}$ $10\frac{5}{8}$ **17.** $1\frac{1}{2} \div 2\frac{1}{2}$ $\frac{3}{5}$
⁽⁹²⁾   ⁽⁵⁹⁾   ⁽⁶⁸⁾

18. $5 - (3.2 + 0.4)$ 1.4
⁽³⁸⁾

19. Estimate If the diameter of a circular plastic swimming pool is 6 feet,
⁽⁸⁰⁾ then the area of the bottom of the pool is about how many square feet? Round to the nearest square foot. (Use 3.14 for π.) about 28 square feet

20. Sample: Volume is a measure of space. To measure space, we use units that take up space (cubes). We do not use squares to measure volume, because squares do not take up space.

20. Explain We use squares to measure the area of a rectangle. Why do we
⁽⁸²⁾ use cubes instead of squares to measure the volume of a rectangular prism?

21. Solve this proportion: $\dfrac{9}{12} = \dfrac{15}{x}$ 20
⁽⁸⁵⁾

Rectangle *ABCD* is 8 cm long and 6 cm wide. Segment *AC* is 10 cm long. Use this information to answer problems **22** and **23**.

22. What is the area of triangle *ABC*? 24 cm²
⁽⁷⁹⁾

23. What is the perimeter of triangle *ABC*? 24 cm
⁽⁸⁾

▶ See Math Conversations in the sidebar.

24. Measure the diameter of a nickel to the
(27)   nearest millimeter.   21 millimeters

▶* **25.** *Estimate* Calculate the circumference of a
(47)   nickel. Round to the nearest millimeter. (Use
   3.14 for π.)   66 millimeters

26. A bag contains 12 marbles. Eight of the marbles are red and 4 are
(58, 74)   blue. If you draw a marble from the bag without looking, what is the
   probability that the marble will be blue? Express the probability ratio as
   a fraction and as a decimal rounded to the nearest hundredth. $\frac{1}{3}$, 0.33

Connect Complete the table to answer problems 27–29.

	Fraction	Decimal	Percent
▶* **27.** (99)	$\frac{9}{10}$	**a.** 0.9	**b.** 90%
▶* **28.** (99)	**a.** $1\frac{1}{2}$	1.5	**b.** 150%
▶* **29.** (99)	**a.** $\frac{1}{25}$	**b.** 0.04	4%

30. A full one-gallon container of milk was used to fill two one-pint
(78)   containers. How many quarts of milk were left in the one-gallon
   container?   3 quarts

Early Finishers
Choose A Strategy

These three prime factorizations represent numbers that are powers of 10.
Simplify each prime factorization.

   $2^2 \times 5^2$ 100 $2^4 \times 5^4$ 10,000 $2^5 \times 5^5$ 100,000

Use exponents to write the prime factorization of another number that is a
power of 10.   Sample: $1000 = 2^3 \times 5^3$

Lesson 100   523

▶ See Math Conversations in the sidebar.

---

3 **Written Practice** *(Continued)*

Math Conversations
Discussion opportunities are provided below.

Problem 25 *Estimate*
"What formula is used to find the circumference of a circle?" $C = \pi d$

Problem 27 *Connect*
Ask students to decide if they would change
$\frac{9}{10}$ to a decimal first or to a percent first, and
tell why. Then ask them to explain how to
make the change.

Problem 28 *Connect*
Ask students to decide if they would change
1.5 to a fraction first or to a percent first, and
tell why. Then ask them to explain how to
make the change.

Problem 29 *Connect*
Ask students to decide if they would change
4% to a fraction first or to a decimal first, and
tell why. Then ask them to explain how to
make the change.

Early Finishers
You may want to review writing prime
factorizations with exponents using one of the
examples given.

$$100 = 2 \cdot 2 \cdot 5 \cdot 5$$

We group the two 2s and the two 5s. Since
both numbers appear twice, both have an
exponent of 2: $2^2 \times 5^2$.

Looking Forward

Adding and subtracting integers
mentally and with a number line
prepares students for:

- **Lesson 104,** performing an
  algebraic addition activity that
  leads to simplifying expressions
  containing the addition and
  subtraction of several integers.

- **Lesson 112,** multiplying and
  dividing integers.

Assessment · *30–40 minutes* · For use after Lesson 100

Distribute **Cumulative Test 19** to each student. Two versions of the test are available in *Saxon Math Course 1 Course Assessments Book*. Have students complete the **Power-Up Test** first. Allow 10 minutes. Then have students work the 20 numbered items on the **Cumulative Test.** Students may use copies of the answer sheet to record their work. Track individual and class progress with the **Test Analysis** forms.

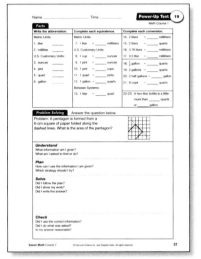

Power-Up Test 19

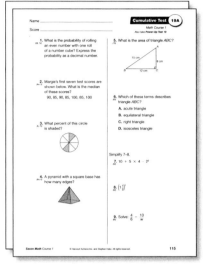

Cumulative Test 19A

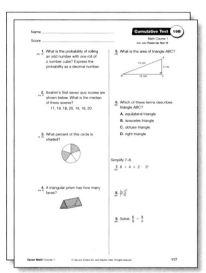

Alternative Cumulative Test 19B

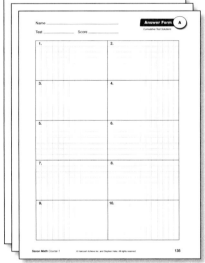

Optional Answer Forms

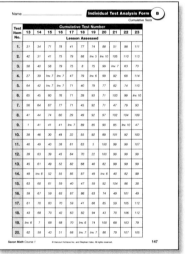

Individual Test Analysis Form

Class Test Analysis Form

Reteaching

Students who score below 80% on the assessment may be in need of reteaching. Look for the causes of student mistakes. If errors are conceptual, refer to the *Reteaching Masters* for reteaching.

You can develop customized benchmark tests using the Test Generator located on the *Test & Practice Generator CD.*

This chart shows the lesson, the standard, and the test item question that can be found on the *Test & Practice Generator CD.*

LESSON	NEW CONCEPTS	LOCAL STANDARD	TEST ITEM ON CD
91	• Geometric Formulas		10.91.1
92	• Expanded Notation with Exponents		10.92.1
	• Order of Operations with Exponents		10.92.2
	• Powers of Fractions		10.92.3
93	• Classifying Triangles		10.93.1
94	• Writing Fractions and Decimals as Percents, Part 2		10.94.1
95	• Reducing Rates Before Multiplying		10.95.1
96	• Functions		10.96.1
	• Graphing Functions		10.96.2
97	• Transversals		10.97.1
98	• Sum of the Angle Measures of Triangles and Quadrilaterals		10.98.1
99	• Fraction-Decimal-Percent Equivalents		10.99.1
100	• Algebraic Addition of Integers		10.100.1

Using the Test Generator CD

• Develop tests in both English and Spanish.

• Choose from multiple-choice and free-response test items.

• Clone test items to create multiple versions of the same test.

• View and edit test items to make and save your own questions.

• Administer assessments through paper tests or over a school LAN.

• Monitor student progress through a variety of individual and class reports —for both diagnosing and assessing standards mastery.

Creating Three-dimensional Figures from Nets
Assign after Lesson 100 and Test 19

Objectives
- Use nets to make three-dimensional figures.
- Find the surface area and volume of three-dimensional figures.
- Communicate ideas through writing.

Materials
Performance Tasks 19A, 19B, and **19C**

Tape

Scissors

Metric Ruler

Preparation
Make copies of **Performance Tasks 19A, 19B,** and **19C.** (One each per student.)

Time Requirement
30–60 minutes; Begin in class and complete at home.

Task
Explain to students that for this task they will use nets to make rectangular prisms, cones, cylinders, and pyramids. They will estimate the surface areas and volumes of these figures. They will also explain why the formula for the surface area of a rectangular prism makes sense. Point out that all of the information students need is on **Performance Tasks 19A, 19B,** and **19C.**

Criteria for Evidence of Learning
- Constructs the three-dimensional figures correctly from the nets.
- Estimates the surface area and volume of each figure.
- Communicates ideas clearly through writing.

Performance Task 19A, 19B,
and 19C

National Council of Teachers of Mathematics (NCTM)

Geometry
GM.4b Use two-dimensional representations of three-dimensional objects to visualize and solve problems such as those involving surface area and volume

GM.4c Use visual tools such as networks to represent and solve problems

Measurement
ME.1c Understand, select, and use units of appropriate size and type to measure angles, perimeter, area, surface area, and volume

ME.2c Develop and use formulas to determine the circumference of circles and the area of triangles, parallelograms, trapezoids, and circles and develop strategies to find the area of more-complex shapes

Communication
CM.3d Use the language of mathematics to express mathematical ideas precisely

Representation
RE.5b Select, apply, and translate among mathematical representations to solve problems

Focus on
● Compound Experiments

Objectives

- Create a tree diagram that shows all possible outcomes of a compound experiment.
- Determine the probabilities of the possible outcomes of a compound experiment.

Lesson Preparation

Materials

Optional
- Teacher-provided material: colored chalk (green and white)

Math Language

New	English Learners (ESL)
compound experiments	replaced
compound outcomes	
tree diagram	

Technology Resources

Student eBook Complete student textbook in electronic format.

Resources and Planner CD Assessment, reteaching, and instructional masters, plus a pacing calendar with standards.

Test and Practice Generator CD Create additional practice sheets and custom-made tests.

www.SaxonPublishers.com Visit for more student activities and planning materials.

Inclusion

Adaptations CD Adapted lessons, investigations, practice and assessments.

Meeting Standards

National Council of Teachers of Mathematics (NCTM)

Data Analysis and Probability

DP.4a Understand and use appropriate terminology to describe complementary and mutually exclusive events

DP.4b Use proportionality and a basic understanding of probability to make and test conjectures about the results of experiments and simulations

DP.4c Compute probabilities for simple compound events, using such methods as organized lists, tree diagrams, and area models

Connections

CN.4b Understand how mathematical ideas interconnect and build on one another to produce a coherent whole

INVESTIGATION 10

In this investigation, students will explore compound probability experiments that consist of two parts, performed in a given order.

After the probability of each part of an experiment has been determined, students will use multiplication to find the probability of compound outcomes.

Instruction

On the board, sketch the spinner shown on the following page.

Next to the drawing of the spinner, use colored chalk to draw four blue marbles and two white marbles.

Then sketch the tree diagram shown on this page, and explain how the spinner outcomes and marble outcomes combine to create the compound outcomes of the experiment.

Point to the drawing of the spinner on the board.

"There are three possible outcomes for the first part of the experiment—the spinner can land on A, B, or C."

Point to the marbles.

"There are two possible outcomes for the second part of the experiment—the marble drawn can be green or white."

"We multiply the number of possible outcomes in the first part of the experiment by the number of possible outcomes in the second part of the experiment to find the total number of possible outcomes for the compound experiment."

Write $3 \times 2 = 6$ on the board.

(continued)

Focus on
• Compound Experiments

Some experiments whose outcomes are determined by chance contain more than one part. Such experiments are called **compound experiments.** In this investigation we will consider compound experiments that consist of two parts performed in order. Here are three experiments:

1. A spinner with sectors A, B, and C is spun; then a marble is drawn from a bag that contains 4 blue marbles and 2 white marbles.

2. A marble is drawn from a bag with 4 blue marbles and 2 white marbles; then, without the first marble being replaced, a second marble is drawn.

3. A number cube is rolled; then a coin is flipped.

The second experiment is actually a way to look at drawing two marbles from the bag at once. We estimated probabilities for this compound experiment in Investigation 9.

A **tree diagram** can help us visualize the sample space for a compound experiment. Here is a tree diagram for compound experiment 1:

Math Language
Recall that the list of all possible outcomes in an experiment is called a *sample space.* A tree diagram is one way to represent the sample space for an experiment.

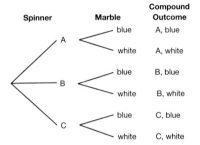

Each *branch* of the tree corresponds to a possible outcome. There are three possible spinner outcomes. For each spinner outcome, there are two possible marble outcomes. To find the total number of **compound outcomes,** we multiply the number of branches in the first part of the experiment by the number of branches in the second part of the experiment. There are $3 \times 2 = 6$ branches, so there are six possible compound outcomes. In the column titled "Compound Outcome," we list the outcome for each branch. "A, blue" means that the spinner stopped on A, then the marble drawn was blue. Although there are six different outcomes, not all the outcomes are equally likely. We need to determine the probability of each part of the experiment in order to find the probability for each compound outcome. To do this, we will use the multiplication principle for compound probability.

Math Background

In a compound probability experiment, events may be independent or not independent.

An example of independent events is spinning a spinner and then tossing a coin. The events are independent because the probability of either coin outcome is not influenced in any way by the spinner outcome.

An example of events that are not independent is choosing one marble, then another marble, from a bag of 5 marbles without replacing the first marble that is chosen. The events are not independent because the probability of selecting one of the remaining marbles in the bag after a marble has been removed is different than selecting one of the marbles in the bag if the first marble was replaced. Since the probabilities of the second event depend upon the outcome of the first event, non-independent events are sometimes called dependent events.

The probability of a compound outcome is the product of the probabilities of each part of the outcome.

We will use this principle to calculate the probability of the first branch of experiment 1, the spinner-marble experiment, which corresponds to the compound outcome "A, blue."

The first part of the outcome is that the spinner stops in sector A. The probability of this outcome is $\frac{1}{2}$, since sector A occupies half the area of the circle.

The second part of the outcome is that a blue marble is drawn from the bag. Since four of the six marbles are blue, the probability of this outcome is $\frac{4}{6}$, which simplifies to $\frac{2}{3}$.

To find the probability of the compound outcome, we multiply the probabilities of each part.

The probability of "A, blue" is $\frac{1}{2} \cdot \frac{2}{3}$, which equals $\frac{1}{3}$.

Notice that although "A, blue" is one of six possible outcomes, the probability of "A, blue" is greater than $\frac{1}{6}$. This is because "A" is the most likely of the three possible spinner outcomes, and "blue" is the more likely of the two possible marble outcomes.

For problems **1–6**, copy the table below and calculate the probability of each possible outcome. For the last row, find the sum of the probabilities of the six possible outcomes.

Thinking Skill

Predict

What do you expect the sum of the probabilities to be? The sum of the probabilities of all possible events is always one.

Outcome	Probability
A, blue	$\frac{1}{2} \cdot \frac{2}{3} = \frac{1}{3}$
A, white	**1.** $\frac{1}{2} \cdot \frac{2}{6} = \frac{1}{6}$
B, blue	**2.** $\frac{1}{4} \cdot \frac{4}{6} = \frac{1}{6}$
B, white	**3.** $\frac{1}{4} \cdot \frac{2}{6} = \frac{1}{12}$
C, blue	**4.** $\frac{1}{4} \cdot \frac{4}{6} = \frac{1}{6}$
C, white	**5.** $\frac{1}{4} \cdot \frac{2}{6} = \frac{1}{12}$
sum of probabilities	▶**6.** $\frac{12}{12} = 1$

▶ See Math Conversations in the sidebar.

Instruction

Make sure students understand that finding the probability of a compound outcome first involves finding probability of each part of the outcome separately.

"To find the probability of the compound outcome 'A, green,' we start in the first part of the experiment and find the probability of the spinner landing on A. Then we will find the probability of drawing a green marble in the second part of the experiment. Once these two probabilities are found, we multiply the two probabilities to find the probability that the compound outcome will occur."

To complete the table, ask students to first write a fraction to represent the probability of each part of the compound outcome. Then before multiplying the fractions, suggest that students cancel, whenever possible, terms of the fractions, and always check to make sure the final product is a fraction in simplest form.

Math Conversations

Discussion opportunities are provided below.

Problem 6 *Analyze*

Point out that problem **6** represents a way for students to check their work. Point out that the sum of the different compound outcomes of the experiment should be 1.

"If the answer to problem 6 is not 1, what do you know?" One or more of the probabilities calculated in 1–5 are incorrect.

(continued)

In step 2 of the experiment on the previous page, explain the concept of replacement. Remove one marble from a bag and then **replace** it. Say,

"I took a marble from the bag and then I replaced it. This means that I put the marble back into the bag."

Now take a marble from the bag, do not replace it, and take a second marble from the bag. Say,

"When I took the second marble from the bag, I did not replace the first marble. If I take a marble without the first marble being replaced, it means that I did NOT put the first marble back in the bag."

With the students, practice both ways of removing marbles—replacing the first marble or "without the first marble being replaced."

Math Conversations

Discussion opportunities are provided below.

Problem 7 [Model]

Remind students that the first marble will not be replaced before the second draw is made.

> **"Suppose a blue marble is drawn first. How many marbles will be in the bag for the second draw, and what colors will those marbles be?"** five marbles; three blue and two white

> **"Suppose a white marble is drawn first. How many marbles will be in the bag for the second draw, and what colors will those marbles be?"** five marbles; four blue and one white

Problem 8 [Represent]

Guide students through both steps for each outcome. For example, explain that the outcome "white, blue" assumes that a white marble is removed on the first draw, leaving four blue marbles and one white marble for the second draw.

> **"Why is there one fewer marble in the bag for the second draw than for the first draw?"** The marble chosen on the first draw is not replaced before the second draw is made.

Problem 9 [Analyze]

After students solve this problem, point out that it would be impossible to draw three white marbles because there are only two white marbles in the bag. Remind students that a probability of 0 means that an outcome is impossible (certain not to happen), and a probability of 1 means that an outcome will occur (certain to happen).

(continued)

For problems **7–9** we will consider compound experiment 2, which involves two draws from a bag of marbles that contains four blue marbles and two white marbles. The first part of the experiment is that one marble is drawn from the bag and is not replaced. The second part is that a second marble is drawn from the marbles remaining in the bag.

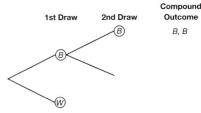

7. **[Model]** Copy and complete this tree diagram showing all possible outcomes of the compound experiment:

$$
\begin{array}{ccc}
\text{1st Draw} & \text{2nd Draw} & \text{Compound Outcome} \\
\end{array}
$$

(tree diagram with 1st Draw B; 2nd Draw B; Compound Outcome B, B; with branch to W)

We will calculate the probability of the outcome blue, blue (B, B). On the first draw four of the six marbles are blue, so the probability of blue is $\frac{4}{6}$, which equals $\frac{2}{3}$.

If the first marble drawn is blue, then three blue marbles and two white marbles remain (see picture at right). So the probability of drawing a blue marble on the second draw is $\frac{3}{5}$. Therefore, the probability of the outcome blue, blue is $\frac{2}{3} \cdot \frac{3}{5} = \frac{2}{5}$.

▶ 8. **[Represent]** Copy and complete this table to show the probability of each remaining possible outcome and the sum of the probabilities of all outcomes. Remember that the first draw changes the collection of marbles in the bag for the second draw.

Outcome	Probability
blue, blue	$\frac{4}{6} \cdot \frac{3}{5} = \frac{2}{5}$
blue, white	$\frac{4}{6} \cdot \frac{2}{5} = \frac{4}{15}$
white, blue	$\frac{2}{6} \cdot \frac{4}{5} = \frac{4}{15}$
white, white	$\frac{2}{6} \cdot \frac{1}{5} = \frac{1}{15}$
sum of probabilities	$\frac{15}{15} = 1$

9. $\frac{2}{6} \cdot \frac{1}{5} \cdot \frac{0}{4} = 0$

  $\frac{4}{6} \cdot \frac{3}{5} \cdot \frac{2}{4} = \frac{1}{5}$

▶ 9. Suppose we draw three marbles from the bag, one at a time and without replacement. What is the probability of drawing three white marbles? What is the probability of drawing three blue marbles?

▶ See Math Conversations in the sidebar.

For problems **10–14**, consider a compound experiment in which a nickel is flipped and then a quarter is flipped.

10.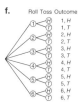

   N   Q Outcome

       H, H
       H, T
       T, H
       T, T

10. *Represent* Create a tree diagram that shows all of the possible outcomes of the compound experiment.

▶ **11.** *Represent* Make a table that shows the probability of each possible outcome.

11.

Outcome	Probability
H, H	$\frac{1}{2} \cdot \frac{1}{2} = \frac{1}{4}$
H, T	$\frac{1}{2} \cdot \frac{1}{2} = \frac{1}{4}$
T, H	$\frac{1}{2} \cdot \frac{1}{2} = \frac{1}{4}$
T, T	$\frac{1}{2} \cdot \frac{1}{2} = \frac{1}{4}$

Use the table you made in problem **11** to answer problems **12–14**.

12. What is the probability that one of the coins shows "heads" and the other coin shows "tails"? $\frac{1}{4} + \frac{1}{4} = \frac{1}{2}$

▶ **13.** What is the probability that at least one of the coins shows "heads"? $\frac{1}{4} + \frac{1}{4} + \frac{1}{4} = \frac{3}{4}$

14. What is the probability that the nickel shows "heads" and the quarter shows "tails"? $\frac{1}{4}$

extensions

Analyze For extensions **a** and **b**, consider experiment 2 in which a bag contains 4 blue marbles and 2 white marbles. One marble is drawn from the bag and not replaced, and then a second marble is drawn.

▶ **a.** Find the probability that the two marbles drawn from the bag are different colors. $\frac{4}{15} + \frac{4}{15} = \frac{8}{15}$

▶ **b.** Find the probability that the two marbles drawn from the bag are the same color. $\frac{2}{5} + \frac{1}{15} = \frac{7}{15}$

Analyze For extensions **c** and **d**, consider experiment 1 involving spinning the spinner and then drawing a marble.

▶ **c.** The complement of "A, blue" is "not A, blue". Find the probability that the compound outcome will *not* be "A, blue." $1 - \frac{1}{3} = \frac{2}{3}$

▶ **d.** Find the probability that the compound outcome will *not* include "A" and will *not* include "blue." $\frac{1}{12} + \frac{1}{12} = \frac{1}{6}$

▶ **e.** The probabilities in exercises **c** and **d** are different. Explain why.

e. The outcomes in **c** can include A and can include blue, just not both. The outcomes in **d** cannot include either A or blue, so there are fewer possibilities.

For extensions **f** and **g**, consider the compound experiment consisting of rolling a number cube and then flipping a quarter.

▶ **f.** *Represent* Draw a tree diagram to show the sample space for the experiment.

f.

Roll Toss Outcome

  1, H
  1, T
  2, H
  2, T
  3, H
  3, T
  4, H
  4, T
  5, H
  5, T
  6, H
  6, T

▶ **g.** Find the probability of each compound outcome. The probability of each compound outcome is $\frac{1}{12}$.

▶ See Math Conversations in the sidebar.

Math Conversations
Discussion opportunities are provided below.

Problem 11 *Represent*
"The experiment is a compound experiment because it consists of two parts. Does the probability of the second part depend on what happens in the first part? Explain your answer." No; explanations will vary.

Problem 13 *Analyze*
Extend the Problem
Invite volunteers who found the correct answer to explain to the class how they solved the problem.

Extensions
a.–b. *Analyze* Because the experiment is a compound experiment, remind students to find the probability of each part of the experiment, then multiply the probabilities.

c.–e. *Analyze* In Extensions **c** and **d**, students must recognize that the word "not" indicates the complement of the given event. Remind students that the sum of the probability of an event, and the probability of the complement of that event, is 1.

f.–g. *Represent* Students must recall that a sample space is the set of all possible outcomes of a probability experiment.

Lesson Planner

LESSON	NEW CONCEPTS	MATERIALS	RESOURCES
101	• Ratio Problems Involving Totals	Manipulative Kit: red and yellow color tiles Shaded and unshaded circles	Power Up H Investigation Activity 15
102	• Mass and Weight	Balls of various sizes Paper clips	Power Up M Investigation Activity 15
103	• Perimeter of Complex Shapes		Power Up M Investigation Activity 15
104	• Algebraic Addition Activity	Manipulative Kit: color tiles	Investigation Activity 15
105	• Using Proportions to Solve Percent Problems	Manipulative Kit: inch or metric rulers	Power Up M
106	• Two-Step Equations		Power Up K
107	• Area of Complex Shapes	Manipulative Kit: inch or metric rulers, compasses Grid paper	Power Up M
108	• Transformations	Scissors, paper or a 3 × 5 index card	Power Up M Investigation Activity 15
109	• Corresponding Parts • Similar Figures	Large cutout triangles *ABC* and *XYZ* from Lesson 108	Power Up N
110	• Symmetry	Manipulative Kit: inch rulers, compasses Grid paper, rectangular-shaped paper, scissors	Power Up M Investigation Activity 15 Lesson Activity 20
Inv. 11	• Scale Factor: Scale Drawings and Models	Manipulative Kit: inch rulers Scissors, plastic straws, glue State map	Investigation Activities 21 and 22

Problem Solving

Strategies

- **Find a Pattern** Lessons 101, 102, 104, 108, 109
- **Make a Chart** Lesson 104
- **Make a Table** Lessons 105, 108
- **Make It Simpler** Lesson 109
- **Use Logical Reasoning** Lessons 103, 105, 107, 110
- **Draw a Diagram** Lesson 106
- **Write an Equation** Lessons 106, 107, 109
- **Guess and Check** Lesson 110

Real-World Applications

pp. 530–532, 535–537, 540–541, 543, 545, 546, 548–552, 555, 556, 558, 560, 563, 564, 566, 569, 570–572, 575–577

4-Step Process

Teacher Edition Lessons 101–110 (Power-Up Discussions)

Communication

Discuss

pp. 543, 553

Explain

pp. 530, 547, 552, 576

Formulate a Problem

pp. 550, 556

Connections

Math and Other Subjects

Math and History pp. 560, 575, 577

Math and Science p. 531

Math and Sports pp. 535, 537, 545, 563

Math to Math

Measurement and Problem Solving Lessons 101, 102, 103, 104, 105, 106, 107, 108, 109, 110

Algebra and Problem Solving Lessons 101, 107, 109

Fractions, Percents, Decimals and Problem Solving Lessons 101, 102, 103, 104, 105, 106, 107, 108, 109, 110

Fractions and Measurement Lessons 101, 105, 106, 107, 109, 110

Measurement and Geometry Lessons 101, 102, 103, 104, 105, 106, 107, 108, 109, 110

Proportional Relationships and Geometry Lessons 109, 110

Probability and Statistics Lessons 101, 102, 103, 104, 105, 106, 108, 109, 110

Representation

Manipulatives/Hands On

pp. 530, 543, 544, 558, 560, 562, 563, 575, 577

Model

pp. 528, 530, 537, 550, 558, 560, 565, 576, 577

Represent

pp. 530, 560, 570

Student Resources

- **eBook**
- **Online Resources** at
  www.SaxonPublishers.com/ActivitiesC1
  Real-World Investigation 6 after Lesson 101
  Online Activities
  Math Enrichment Problems
  Math Stumpers

Teacher Resources

- **Resources and Planner CD**
- **Adaptations CD** Lessons 101–110
- **Test & Practice Generator CD**
- **eGradebook**
- **Answer Key CD**

This section of lessons extends several algebraic ideas involving proportional relationships, integers, and transformational geometry.

Proportional Thinking

Students continue to use a "ratio box" to write and set up proportions for both ratio and percent problems.

Proportional relationships between parts of a whole or parts of a group may generate problems that involve the total in the calculation. Students learn an effective strategy for solving these problems in Lesson 101. Students apply this strategy in Lesson 105 to solve percent problems relating to parts of a whole.

Proportional relationships and similar figures find practical application in scale drawings and models. In Investigation 11 students solve problems related to architectural drawings, maps, and three-dimensional models of objects.

Algebraic Thinking

These lessons extend the concepts of integers and equations.

In Lesson 104 students explore a second model for adding and subtracting positive and negative numbers. In an activity cast as a game, students apply the electric charge model to quickly simplify a string of addition and subtraction operations with integers. In Lesson 106 students learn to solve two-step equations.

Equivalent Measurements

Students convert measurements within the same measurement system.

In Lesson 102 students convert units of weight within the U.S. Customary system and units of mass within the metric system.

Perimeter and Area

Students solve problems involving complex shapes.

In Lesson 103 students find the perimeters of complex shapes, and in Lesson 107 students calculate the areas of these figures.

Spatial Thinking

Students describe relationships involving similarity and congruence.

Students perform geometric transformations in Lesson 108, and in Lesson 109 students identify corresponding parts of congruent or similar figures whose orientations differ. Students identify figures with reflective and rotational symmetry in Lesson 110.

Assessment

A variety of weekly assessment tools are provided.

After Lesson 105:	After Lesson 110:
• Power-Up Test 20	• Power-Up Test 21
• Cumulative Test 20	• Cumulative Test 21
• Performance Activity 20	• Customized Benchmark Test
	• Performance Task 21

LESSON	NEW CONCEPTS	PRACTICED	ASSESSED
101	• Ratio Problems Involving Totals	Lessons 101, 103, 104, 105, 112, 113, 117, 119	Tests 21, 22
102	• Mass and Weight	Lessons 102, 103, 104, 105, 106, 107, 115, 116, 119	Test 21
103	• Perimeter of Complex Shapes	Lessons 103, 104, 105, 106, 107, 108, 110, 112, 114, 115, 118	Tests 21, 22, 23
104	• Algebraic Addition Activity	Lessons 104, 105, 106, 107, 108, 110, 111, 115, 116, 117, 118, 119, 120	Tests 21, 22
105	• Using Proportions to Solve Percent Problems	Lessons 105, 108, 110, 111, 112, 114, 115, 119, 120	Tests 21, 23
106	• Two-Step Equations	Lessons 106, 107, 108, 109, 111, 112, 114, 115, 116, 117, 119	Test 22
107	• Area of Complex Shapes	Lessons 107, 108, 109, 110, 111, 112, 113, 114, 115, 116, 117	Tests 22, 23
108	• Transformations	Lessons 108, 109, 110, 111, 117	Test & Practice Generator
109	• Corresponding Parts	Lessons 109, 110, 111	Test 23
	• Similar Figures	Lesson 109	Test & Practice Generator
110	• Symmetry	Lessons 110, 111, 112, 113, 116, 117, 118, 119	Test 22
Inv. 11	• Scale Factor: Scale Drawings and Models	Investigation 11, Lessons 111, 112, 119	Test & Practice Generator

• Ratio Problems Involving Totals

Objectives

• Use ratio boxes to solve ratio problems that involve totals.

Lesson Preparation

Materials

• **Power Up H** (in *Instructional Masters*)
• **Manipulative kit:** red and yellow counters
• **Teacher-provided material:** buttons, or shaded and unshaded circles

Optional

• **Investigation Activity 15** (in *Instructional Masters*) or **graph paper**

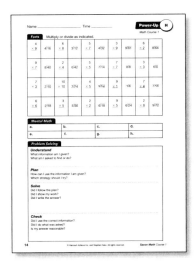

Power Up H

Math Language

Maintain

proportion

Technology Resources

Student eBook Complete student textbook in electronic format.

Resources and Planner CD Assessment, reteaching, and instructional masters, plus a pacing calendar with standards.

Test and Practice Generator CD Create additional practice sheets and custom-made tests.

www.SaxonPublishers.com Visit for more student activities and planning materials.

Inclusion

 Adaptations CD Adapted lessons, investigations, practice and assessments.

Meeting Standards

National Council of Teachers of Mathematics (NCTM)

Numbers and Operations

NO.1d Understand and use ratios and proportions to represent quantitative relationships

NO.3d Develop, analyze, and explain methods for solving problems involving proportions, such as scaling and finding equivalent ratios

Problem Solving

PS.1b Solve problems that arise in mathematics and in other contexts

Problem-Solving Strategy: Find a Pattern

The numbers in these boxes form number patterns. What one number should be placed in both empty boxes to complete the patterns?

1	2	3
2	4	
3		9

Understand *Understand the problem.*

"What information are we given?"

We are shown a square with nine boxes and told that the numbers in those boxes form patterns.

"What are we asked to do?"

We are asked to find one number that fills the empty boxes and completes the patterns.

Plan *Make a plan.*

"How can we use the information to do what we are asked to do?"

We will *find the patterns* in the boxes and find the number that completes the patterns.

Solve *Carry out the plan.*

"What patterns do you see in the horizontal rows?"

Horizontally from left to right, the first row counts up by 1s. It appears that the second row counts up by 2s and that the third row counts up by 3s.

"What patterns do you see in the vertical columns?"

The first column contains multiples of 1, the second column contains multiples of 2, and the third column contains multiples of 3.

"What one number completes the patterns?" 6

Check *Look back.*

"Did we complete the task?"

Yes. We determined the number that should be placed in the empty boxes (6).

"Are there other patterns that give us confidence that our answer is correct?"

Yes, the pattern is also consistent vertically.

"Enlarge the pattern from 3 boxes by 3 boxes to 5 boxes by 5 boxes."

1	2	3	4	5
2	4	6	8	10
3	6	9	12	15
4	8	12	16	20
5	10	15	20	25

"If the pattern were extended to 10 boxes by 10 boxes, what might we call the pattern?"

We would call it a multiplication table.

Facts

Distribute **Power Up H** to students. See answers below.

Mental Math

Before students begin the Mental Math exercise, do this counting exercise as a class.

Count by $\frac{1}{16}$s from $\frac{1}{16}$ to 1.

Encourage students to share different ways to mentally compute these exercises. Strategies for exercises **c** and **d** are listed below.

c. Use a Multiplication Fact
   $4 \times 25 = 100$, so $100 \div 4 = 25$
   Find $\frac{1}{2}$ of $\frac{1}{2}$
   $\frac{1}{2}$ of $100 = 50$; $\frac{1}{2}$ of $50 = 25$

d. Change $18.99 to $19, then Subtract 1¢
   $19 + 5.30 = 24.30$; $24.30 - 1¢$
   $= 24.29$
   Add Dollars and Add Cents
   $18 + 5 + 99¢ + 30¢ = 23 + 129¢$
   $= 24.29$

Problem Solving

Refer to **Power-Up Discussion**, p. 528F.

2 **New Concepts**

Instruction

Remind students that a ratio is a comparison of two quantities by division.

Ratio boxes were first introduced to students in Lesson 80. In Lesson 88, students learned how ratio boxes can be used to find an unknown number in a proportion. You might choose to review those lessons with students before you begin today's lesson.

(continued)

LESSON

101

● Ratio Problems Involving Totals

42 pts

facts | Power Up H

mental math
   a. **Number Sense:** $20 \cdot 300$ 6000
   b. **Number Sense:** $920 - 550$ 370
   c. **Percent:** 25% of 100   25
   d. **Calculation:** $18.99 + 5.30$ $24.29
   e. **Decimals:** $3.75 \div 100$ 0.0375
   f. **Number Sense:** 40×25 1000
   g. **Measurement:** Which is greater: 1 liter or 500 milliliters?   1 liter
   h. **Calculation:** Find half of 100, $- 1$, $\sqrt{}$, $\times 5$, $+ 1$, $\sqrt{}$, $\times 3$, $+ 2$, $\div 2$ 10

problem solving | The numbers in these boxes form number patterns. What one number should be placed in both empty boxes to complete the patterns?   6

1	2	3
2	4	
3		9

New Concept   *Increasing Knowledge*

In some ratio problems a total is used as part of the calculation. Consider this problem:

Thinking Skill

Model

Use red and yellow counters or buttons to model the problem.

> *The ratio of boys to girls in a class was 5 to 4. If there were 27 students in the class, how many girls were there?*

We begin by drawing a ratio box. In addition to the categories of boys and girls, we make a third row for the total number of students. We will use the letters b and g to represent the actual counts of boys and girls.

	Ratio	Actual Count
Boys	5	b
Girls	4	g
Total	9	27

Facts   Multiply or divide as indicated.

$\begin{array}{r} 4 \\ \times 9 \\ \hline 36 \end{array}$	$4\overline{)16}$	$\begin{array}{r} 6 \\ \times 8 \\ \hline 48 \end{array}$	$3\overline{)12}$	$\begin{array}{r} 5 \\ \times 7 \\ \hline 35 \end{array}$	$4\overline{)32}$	$\begin{array}{r} 3 \\ \times 9 \\ \hline 27 \end{array}$	$9\overline{)81}$	$\begin{array}{r} 6 \\ \times 2 \\ \hline 12 \end{array}$	$8\overline{)64}$
$\begin{array}{r} 9 \\ \times 7 \\ \hline 63 \end{array}$	$8\overline{)40}$	$\begin{array}{r} 2 \\ \times 4 \\ \hline 8 \end{array}$	$6\overline{)42}$	$\begin{array}{r} 5 \\ \times 5 \\ \hline 25 \end{array}$	$7\overline{)14}$	$\begin{array}{r} 7 \\ \times 7 \\ \hline 49 \end{array}$	$8\overline{)8}$	$\begin{array}{r} 3 \\ \times 3 \\ \hline 9 \end{array}$	$6\overline{)0}$
$\begin{array}{r} 7 \\ \times 3 \\ \hline 21 \end{array}$	$2\overline{)10}$	$\begin{array}{r} 10 \\ \times 10 \\ \hline 100 \end{array}$	$3\overline{)24}$	$\begin{array}{r} 4 \\ \times 5 \\ \hline 20 \end{array}$	$9\overline{)54}$	$\begin{array}{r} 9 \\ \times 1 \\ \hline 9 \end{array}$	$3\overline{)6}$	$\begin{array}{r} 7 \\ \times 4 \\ \hline 28 \end{array}$	$7\overline{)56}$
$\begin{array}{r} 6 \\ \times 6 \\ \hline 36 \end{array}$	$2\overline{)18}$	$\begin{array}{r} 3 \\ \times 5 \\ \hline 15 \end{array}$	$5\overline{)30}$	$\begin{array}{r} 2 \\ \times 2 \\ \hline 4 \end{array}$	$6\overline{)18}$	$\begin{array}{r} 9 \\ \times 5 \\ \hline 45 \end{array}$	$6\overline{)24}$	$\begin{array}{r} 2 \\ \times 8 \\ \hline 16 \end{array}$	$9\overline{)72}$

In the ratio column we add the ratio numbers for boys and girls and get the ratio number 9 for the total. We were given 27 as the actual count of students. We will use two of the three rows from the ratio box to write a proportion. **We use the row we want to complete and the row that is already complete.** Since we are asked to find the actual number of girls, we will use the "girls" row. And since we know both "total" numbers, we will also use the "total" row. We solve the proportion below.

	Ratio	Actual Count
Boys	5	b
Girls	4	g
Total	9	27

$$\frac{4}{9} = \frac{g}{27}$$
$$9g = 4 \cdot 27$$
$$g = 12$$

We find that there were 12 girls in the class. If we had wanted to find the number of boys, we would have used the "boys" row along with the "total" row to write a proportion.

Example

The ratio of football players to band members on the football field was 2 to 5. Altogether, there were 175 football players and band members on the football field. How many football players were on the field?

Solution

We use the information in the problem to make a table. We include a row for the total. The ratio number for the total is 7.

	Ratio	Actual Count
Football Players	2	f
Band Members	5	b
Total	7	175

Next we write a proportion using two rows of the table. We are asked to find the number of football players, so we use the "football players" row. We know both totals, so we also use the "total" row. Then we solve the proportion.

	Ratio	Actual Count
Football Players	2	f
Band Members	5	b
Total	7	175

$$\frac{2}{7} = \frac{f}{175}$$
$$7f = 2 \cdot 175$$
$$f = 50$$

We find that there were **50 football players** on the field.

---

2 New Concepts (Continued)

Instruction
Emphasize that the order of the terms in the proportion is important. Tell students to make sure they align the numbers in their proportion in the same way the numbers are aligned in the ratio box.

Invite a volunteer to explain how to use a proportion to find the number of *boys* in the class. Using the explanation as a guide, write the proportion and complete the arithmetic that is required to solve the proportion on the board or overhead. $\frac{5}{9} = \frac{b}{27}$; $9b = 5 \cdot 27$; $b = 15$

Example
Instruction
Have students note that 7, the sum of the numbers in the ratio column, is not given in the problem.

Instruction
Ask students to write and solve a proportion to find the number of band members on the football field. $\frac{5}{7} = \frac{b}{175}$; $7b = 5 \cdot 175$; $b = 125$

(continued)

Practice Set
Problems a–b [Error Alert]

Remind students that the order of the terms in each proportion is important, and they should make sure to align the numbers in each proportion the same way as the numbers are aligned in each ratio box.

Math Conversations
Discussion opportunities are provided below.

Problem 1 [Represent]

Extend the Problem
Students are likely to use the ratio box shown below to solve the problem because the terms in the ratio box are in the same order as the terms in the problem.

	Ratio	Actual Count
Boys	3	b
Girls	2	g
Total	5	30

$\dfrac{2}{5} = \dfrac{g}{30}$

If students write the terms in a different order than the order of the terms in the problem, the ratio box can still be used to solve the problem if the terms of the proportion are written in the same order as the terms in the ratio box. For example:

	Ratio	Actual Count
Girls	2	g
Boys	3	b
Total	5	30

$\dfrac{2}{5} = \dfrac{g}{30}$

To reinforce the concept that order is important when writing proportions, have students check their work by rearranging the terms in their ratio boxes and using the new order to write and solve a proportion.

Errors and Misconceptions
Problem 6
If students find $\frac{1}{4}$ of 12 cm and answer 3 cm, they have found the length of $\overline{AB}$. Reread the problem and help students notice that the question asks for the length of $\overline{BC}$.

Problem 8
Remind students that integers are subtracted by adding the opposite of the number being subtracted.

(continued)

Practice Set

a.
Ratio	A. C.
S	5	s
C	3	c
T	8	72

b.
Ratio	A. C.
R	2	r
N	3	n
T	5	60

Represent Use ratio boxes to solve problems **a** and **b**.

▶ **a.** Sparrows and crows perched on the wire in the ratio of 5 to 3. If the total number of sparrows and crows on the wire was 72, how many were crows?   27 crows

▶ **b.** Raisins and nuts were mixed by weight in a ratio of 2 to 3. If 60 ounces of mix were prepared, how many ounces of raisins were used?   24 ounces

c. *Model* Using 20 red and 20 yellow color tiles (or 20 shaded and unshaded circles) create a ratio of 3 to 2. How many of each color (or shading) do you have?   See student work; 12 and 8

Written Practice   *Strengthening Concepts*

1.
Ratio	A. C.
Boys	3	b
Girls	2	g
Total	5	30

▶ *** 1.** *Represent* Draw a ratio box for this problem. Then solve the problem
(101)   using a proportion.   12 girls

The ratio of boys to girls in the class was 3 to 2. If there were 30 students in the class, how many girls were there?

2. *Connect* A shoe box is the shape of what geometric solid?
(Inv. 6)   rectangular prism

3. *Analyze* If the average of six numbers is 12, what is the sum of the six
(18)   numbers?   72

4. If the diameter of a circle is $1\frac{1}{2}$ inches, what is the radius of the
(27, 68)   circle? $\frac{3}{4}$ inch

* 5. What is the cost of 2.6 pounds of meat priced at $1.65 per pound?
(95) $4.29

▶ **6.** Suppose $\overline{AC}$ is 12 cm long. If $\overline{AB}$ is $\frac{1}{4}$ the length of $\overline{AC}$, then how long is
(69) $\overline{BC}$?   9 cm

* 7. Find each sum mentally:
(100)
  a. $-3 + -4$ -7 **b.** $+5 + -5$ 0

  c. $-6 + +3$ -3 **d.** $+6 + -3$ $+3$

▶ *** 8.** Solve each subtraction problem using algebraic addition:
(100)
  a. $-3 - -4$ $+1$ **b.** $+5 - -5$ $+10$

  c. $-6 - +3$ -9 **d.** $-6 - -6$ 0

  e. *Generalize* Describe how to change a subtraction problem into an addition problem.   Sample: Change the sign of the subtrahend and add.

* 9. *Explain* Two coins are tossed.
(Inv. 10)
  a. What is the probability that both coins will land heads up? $\frac{1}{4}$

  b. What is the probability that one of the coins will be heads and the other tails? $\frac{1}{2}$

9. There are four equally likely outcomes.

| HH |
| HT |
| TH |
| TT |

a. One of the four outcomes is *HH*, so the probability is $\frac{1}{4}$.

b. Two of the four outcomes are *HT* and *TH*, so the probability is $\frac{1}{2}$.

▶ See Math Conversations in the sidebar.

Complete the table to answer problems **10–12**.

	Fraction	Decimal	Percent
* 10. (99)	$\frac{3}{4}$	**a.** 0.75	**b.** 75%
* 11. (99)	**a.** $1\frac{3}{5}$	1.6	**b.** 160%
* 12. (99)	**a.** $\frac{1}{20}$	**b.** 0.05	5%

13. $1\frac{1}{2} \times 4$ 6
(66)

14. $6 \div 1\frac{1}{2}$ 4
(68)

15. $(0.4)^2 \div 2^3$ 0.02
(92)

Find each unknown number:

16. $x + 2\frac{1}{2} = 5$ $2\frac{1}{2}$
(43)

17. $\frac{8}{5} = \frac{40}{x}$ 25
(42)

18. $0.06n = \$0.15$ $\$2.50$
(49)

19. $6n = 21 \cdot 4$ 14
(87)

20. **Connect** Nia's garage is 20 feet long, 20 feet wide, and 8 feet high.
(82)

    a. How many 1-by-1-by-1-foot boxes can she fit on the floor (bottom layer) of her garage? 400 boxes

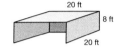

    b. Altogether, how many boxes can Nia fit in her garage if she stacks the boxes 8 feet high? 3200 boxes

21. **Estimate** If a roll of tape has a diameter of $2\frac{1}{2}$ inches, then removing
(47) one full turn of tape yields about how many inches? Choose the closest answer. **C**

    A $2\frac{1}{2}$ in.   **B** 5 in.   **C** $7\frac{3}{4}$ in.   **D** $9\frac{1}{4}$ in.

22. $9^2 - \sqrt{9} \times 10 - 2^4 \times 2$ 19
(92)

Use the figure to answer problems **23** and **24**.

23. Together, these three triangles form what kind of polygon? pentagon
(60)

▶* 24. **Generalize** What is the sum of the measures
(98) of the angles of each triangle? 180°

* 25. At 6 a.m. the temperature was $-8°F$. By noon the temperature was 15°F.
(14, 100) The temperature had risen how many degrees? 23°F

▶ 26. **Connect** To what decimal number is the arrow pointing on the number
(50) line below? 8.8

27. What is the probability of rolling a perfect square with one roll of a
(38, 58) number cube? The probability of rolling 1 or 4 is $\frac{1}{3}$.

▶ See Math Conversations in the sidebar.

Math Conversations

Discussion opportunities are provided below.

Problem 24   Generalize

Extend the Problem

"The figure is a regular pentagon. What is the sum of all of the measures of the interior angles of a regular pentagon? Explain how you know." 540°; Sample: All of the angles of the triangles create the interior angles of the pentagon, and all of the angles of the triangles have a total measure of 180° $\times$ 3 or 540°.

"What is the degree measure of each interior angle of a regular pentagon? Explain how you know." 108°; 540° $\div$ 5

Errors and Misconceptions
Problem 26

Students may count the number of tick marks after 8 and give an answer of 8.4. Work with students to recognize that the space between each whole number on the number line is divided into five equal parts, and each tick mark represents 1 $\div$ 5 or 0.2. The arrow points to 8 + 0.2 + 0.2 + 0.2 + 0.2 or 8.8.

28. **Connect** What is the area of a triangle with vertices located at (4, 0),
(Inv. 7, 79) (0, −3), and (0, 0)?   6 units^2

* 29. **Explain** How can you convert 18 feet to yards?
(95)

30. If a gallon of milk costs $3.80, what is the cost per quart?
(78) $0.95 per quart

Early Finishers
Math and Science

The surface of the Dead Sea is approximately 408 meters below sea level. Its greatest depth is 330 meters. In contrast, Mt. Everest reaches a height of 8,850 meters. What is the difference in elevation between the summit of Mt. Everest and the bottom of the Dead Sea? Show your work.

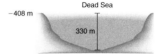
Dead Sea
−408 m
330 m

9588 m; −408 m − 330 m = −738 m; 8850 m − (−738 m) = 9588 m

29. Sample: We set up 18 feet as a fraction and multiply by the number of feet in a yard: $\frac{18 \text{ feet}}{1} \times \frac{1 \text{ yard}}{3 \text{ feet}}$. Then we simplify by canceling: $\frac{18 \text{ feet}}{1} \times \frac{1 \text{ yard}}{3 \text{ feet}} = \frac{18 \text{ yd}}{3} = 6$ yd

Looking Forward

Using ratio boxes and proportions to solve ratio problems involving totals prepares students for:

• **Lesson 105,** solving percent problems using ratio boxes and proportions.

• **Lesson 106,** solving two-step equations and using substitution to check answers.

• **Investigation 11,** solving problems about scale drawings and models using ratio boxes and proportions.

• Mass and Weight

Objectives

- Identify and convert units of mass in the metric system.
- Identify and convert units of weight in the U.S. Customary System.
- Add and subtract measures in pounds and ounces.

Lesson Preparation

Materials

- **Power Up M** (in *Instructional Masters*)

Optional

- **Teacher-provided material:** paper clips, table tennis ball, tennis ball, baseball, football, volleyball, golf ball
- **Investigation Activity 15** (in *Instructional Masters*) or **graph paper**

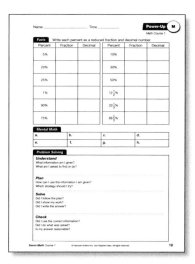

Power Up M

Math Language

New	English Learners (ESL)
mass	midpoint
weight	

Technology Resources

Student eBook Complete student textbook in electronic format.

Resources and Planner CD Assessment, reteaching, and instructional masters, plus a pacing calendar with standards.

Test and Practice Generator CD Create additional practice sheets and custom-made tests.

www.SaxonPublishers.com Visit for more student activities and planning materials.

Inclusion

 Adaptations CD Adapted lessons, investigations, practice and assessments.

Meeting Standards

National Council of Teachers of Mathematics (NCTM)

Measurement

ME.1a Understand both metric and customary systems of measurement

ME.1b Understand relationships among units and convert from one unit to another within the same system

ME.2a Use common benchmarks to select appropriate methods for estimating measurements

Connections

CN.4c Recognize and apply mathematics in contexts outside of mathematics

Problem-Solving Strategy: Find a Pattern

Casting out nines is a technique for checking long multiplication. To cast out nines, we add the digits of each number from left to right and "cast out" (subtract) 9 from the resulting sums. For instance:

6,749	$6 + 7 + 4 + 9 = 26$	$26 - 9 = 17;\ 17 - 9 = $ **8**
$\times\ 85$	$8 + 5 = 13$	$13 - 9 = $ **4**
$\overline{573,665}$	$5 + 7 + 3 + 6 + 6 + 5 = 32$	$32 - 9 = 23;\ 23 - 9 = 14;\ 14 - 9 = $ **5**

To verify the product is correct, we multiply the 8 and the 4 ($8 \times 4 = 32$), add the resulting digits ($3 + 2 = 5$), and compare the result to the product after casting out nines. The number 573,665 results in 5 after casting out nines, so the product is most likely correct. If the numbers had been different, we would know that our original product was incorrect. Matching results after casting out nines does not always guarantee that our product is correct, but the technique catches most random errors.

Check $1234 \times 56 = 69,108$ by casting out nines.

(Understand) **Understand the problem.**

"What information are we given?"

How to cast out nines to check multiplication.

"What are we asked to do?"

Check $1234 \times 56 = 69,106$ by casting out nines.

(Plan) **Make a plan.**

"What problem-solving strategy will we use?"

We will *use the pattern* that has been provided.

(Solve) **Carry out the plan.**

"We will cast nines from the multiplicand, the multiplier, and the product:"

1,234	$1 + 2 + 3 + 4 = 10$	$10 - 9 = $ **1**
$\times\ 56$	$5 + 6 = 11$	$11 - 9 = $ **2**
$\overline{69,108}$	$6 + 9 + 1 + 0 + 8 = 24$	$24 - 9 = 13;\ 13 - 9 = $ **4**

"How do we check our product?"

To check we multiply the 1 and the 2. The resulting digit is 2, which does not equal 4, so our work DOES NOT check. This means the product is incorrect.

(Check) **Look back.**

"Did we do what we were asked?"

Yes, by casting out 9s we determined that the given multiplication is not correct.

"Can we verify our results?"

Yes, by actually doing the multiplication.

LESSON
102
• Mass and Weight

6/3, 6/25, 6/33

facts | Power Up M

mental math
- **a. Number Sense:** 30 · 400   12,000
- **b. Number Sense:** 462 + 150   612
- **c. Percent:** 50% of 40   20
- **d. Calculation:** $100.00 − $47.50 $52.50
- **e. Decimals:** 0.06 × 100   6
- **f. Number Sense:** 50 × 15   750
- **g. Measurement:** How many pints are in 4 quarts?   8 pints
- **h. Calculation:** 12 + 12, + 1, $\sqrt{\ }$, × 3, + 1, $\sqrt{\ }$, × 2, + 2, × 5   50

problem solving

"Casting out nines" is a technique for checking long multiplication. To cast out nines, we sum the digits of each number from left to right and "cast out" (subtract) 9 from the resulting sums. For instance:

$$\begin{array}{r} 6,749 \\ \times \quad 85 \\ \hline 573,665 \end{array}$$

6 + 7 + 4 + 9 = 26   26 − 9 = 17; 17 − 9 = **8**
8 + 5 = 13   13 − 9 = **4**
5 + 7 + 3 + 6 + 6 + 5 = 32   32 − 9 = 23; 23 − 9 = 14; 14 − 9 = **5**

To verify the product is correct, we multiply the 8 and the 4 (8 × 4 = 32), add the resulting digits (3 + 2 = 5), and compare the result to the product after casting out nines. The number 573,665 results in 5 after casting out nines, so the product is most likely correct. If the numbers had been different, we would know that our original product was incorrect. Matching results after casting out nines does not always guarantee that our product is correct, but the technique catches most random errors.

The product is incorrect; See script for explanation.

Check 1234 × 56 = 69,106 by casting out nines.

Physical objects are composed of matter. The amount of matter in an object is its **mass**. In the metric system we measure the mass of objects in milligrams (mg), grams (g), and kilograms (kg).

Math Language
The prefix **kilo-** means *one thousand*. The prefix **milli-** means *one thousandth*. Remembering what the prefixes mean helps us convert units.

Grain of salt
1 milligram

Paper clip
1 gram

Math book
1 kilogram

1000 mg = 1 g   1000 g = 1 kg

Lesson 102   533

Facts   Write each percent as a reduced fraction and decimal number.

Percent	Fraction	Decimal	Percent	Fraction	Decimal
5%	$\frac{1}{20}$	0.05	10%	$\frac{1}{10}$	0.1
20%	$\frac{1}{5}$	0.2	30%	$\frac{3}{10}$	0.3
25%	$\frac{1}{4}$	0.25	50%	$\frac{1}{2}$	0.5
1%	$\frac{1}{100}$	0.01	$12\frac{1}{2}$%	$\frac{1}{8}$	0.125
90%	$\frac{9}{10}$	0.9	$33\frac{1}{3}$%	$\frac{1}{3}$	Rounds to 0.333
75%	$\frac{3}{4}$	0.75	$66\frac{2}{3}$%	$\frac{2}{3}$	Rounds to 0.667

---

1 Power Up

Facts
Distribute **Power Up M** to students. See answers below.

Mental Math
Before students begin the Mental Math exercise, do this counting exercise as a class.

Count up and down by 12s between 12 and 144.

Encourage students to share different ways to mentally compute these exercises. Strategies for exercises **d** and **f** are listed below.

d. Subtract $50, then Add $2.50
$100 − $50 = $50; $50 + $2.50 = $52.50
Subtract $40, then Subtract $7.50
$100 − $40 = $60; $60 − $7.50 = $52.50

f. Break Apart 15
(50 × 10) + (50 × 5) = 500 + 250 = 750
Multiply 50 × 5 × 3
50 × 5 = 250; 250 × 3 = 750

Problem Solving
Refer to **Power-Up Discussion**, p. 533B.

2 New Concepts

Instruction
Remind students that the following generalizations are used when converting from one unit to another, such as from kilometers to meters or from inches to feet.
- To change from a larger unit to a smaller unit, multiply.
- To change from a smaller unit to a larger unit, divide.

For example, to change from kilometers (a larger unit) to meters (a smaller unit), multiply the number of kilometers by 1000. To change from inches (a smaller unit) to feet (a larger unit), divide the number of inches by 12.

(continued)

Instruction

Encourage students to name different objects that can be found in school and weigh about one ounce, about one pound, and about one ton. Sample: ounce: a marker; pound: a workbook; ton: a large lawn tractor used to mow the school lawn

Example 1

Instruction

Have students recall that multiplication is used to change a larger unit to a smaller unit, and division is used to change a smaller unit to a larger unit.

Example 2

Instruction

Remind students to add ounces first so they can regroup before adding pounds.

Demonstrate how an initial sum of 9 lb 18 oz is changed to 10 lb 2 oz, and point out that any sum that is 16 ounces or greater can be rewritten as pounds or pounds and ounces.

(continued)

A particular object has the same mass on Earth as it has on the moon, in orbit, or anywhere else in the universe. In other words, the mass of an object does not change with changes in the force of gravity. However, the **weight** of an object does change with changes in the force of gravity. For example, astronauts who are in orbit feel no gravitational force, so they experience weightlessness. An astronaut who weighs 154 pounds on Earth weighs zero pounds in weightless conditions. Although the weight of the astronaut has changed, his or her mass has not changed.

In the U.S. Customary System we measure the weight of objects in ounces (oz), pounds (lb), or tons (tn). On Earth an object with a mass of 1 kilogram weighs about 2.2 pounds.

Envelope and letter	Shoe	Small car
1 ounce	1 pound	1 ton

16 ounces = 1 pound   2000 pounds = 1 ton

Example 1

Thinking Skill

Predict

When you convert an amount from a larger unit to a smaller unit, will the result be more units or fewer units?
more units

Two kilograms is how many grams?

Solution

One kilogram is 1000 grams. So 2 kilograms equals **2000 grams**.

Some measures are given using a mix of units. For example, Sam might finish a facts practice test in 2 minutes 34 seconds. His sister may have weighed 7 pounds 12 ounces when she was born. The following example shows how to add and subtract measures in pounds and ounces.

Example 2

a. Add: 7 lb 12 oz
        + 2 lb 6 oz

b. Subtract: 9 lb 10 oz
           − 7 lb 12 oz

Solution

a. The sum of 12 oz and 6 oz is 18 oz, which is 1 lb 2 oz. We record the 2 oz and then add the pound to 7 lb and 2 lb.

$$
\begin{array}{r}
\overset{1}{7}\text{ lb }12\text{ oz} \\
+\ 2\text{ lb }\ 6\text{ oz} \\
\hline
10\text{ lb }\ 2\text{ oz}
\end{array}
$$

b. Before we can subtract ounces, we convert 9 pounds to 8 pounds plus 16 ounces. We combine the 16 ounces and the 10 ounces to get 26 ounces. Then we subtract.

Inclusion

Materials: paper clips, table tennis ball, tennis ball, baseball, basketball, football, volleyball, golf ball

Give students hands-on experience with kilograms and grams. Use classroom objects to establish the difference between the two units. Tell students that a paper clip has a mass of about 1 gram. Then tell students that the mass of a math book is about 1 kilogram.

Use the sports balls to give students additional experience with metric measures. Write each metric measure listed below on the board. Then give students the balls and tell them to match each ball with its approximate mass.

table tennis ball (2.5 g), golf ball (46 g), tennis ball (60 g), baseball (140 g), volleyball (280 g), football (425 g), basketball (1,130 g)

After students have chosen a mass for each ball, ask, **"Which ball has about the same mass as your textbook?"** the basketball

$$\begin{array}{r} \overset{8}{\cancel{9}} \text{ lb } \overset{26}{\cancel{10}} \text{ oz} \\ -\ 7 \text{ lb } 12 \text{ oz} \\ \hline \mathbf{1 \text{ lb } 14 \text{ oz}} \end{array}$$

Practice Set

a. Half of a kilogram is how many grams?   500 grams

b. The mass of a liter of water is 1 kilogram. So the mass of 2 liters of beverage is about how many grams?   2000 grams

c.
$$\begin{array}{r} 5 \text{ lb } 10 \text{ oz} \\ +\ 1 \text{ lb } \ 9 \text{ oz} \\ \hline 7 \text{ lb } \ 3 \text{ oz} \end{array}$$

d.
$$\begin{array}{r} 9 \text{ lb } \ 8 \text{ oz} \\ -\ 6 \text{ lb } 10 \text{ oz} \\ \hline 2 \text{ lb } 14 \text{ oz} \end{array}$$

e. A half-ton pickup truck can haul a half-ton load. Half of a ton is how many pounds?   1000 pounds

---

Written Practice   *Strengthening Concepts*

On his first six tests, Chris had scores of 90%, 92%, 96%, 92%, 84%, and 92%. Use this information to answer problems **1** and **2**.

1. **a.** Which score occurred most frequently? That is, what is the mode of
(Inv. 5)   the scores?   92%

b. The difference between Chris's highest score and his lowest score is how many percentage points? That is, what is the range of the scores?   12%

2. What was Chris's average score for the six tests? That is, what is the
(18)   mean of the scores?   91%

3. 30 two-point
baskets; Sample:
$(18 \times 1) + (6 \times 3)$
$+ (b \times 2) = 96$,
$18 + 18 + 2b =$
96, $36 + 2b = 96$,
$2b = 60$, $b = 30$

* 3. In basketball there are one-point baskets, two-point baskets, and
(87)   three-point baskets. If a team scored 96 points and made 18 one-point baskets and 6 three-point baskets, how many two-point baskets did the team make? Explain how you found your answer.

* 4. **Analyze** Which ratio forms a proportion with $\frac{4}{7}$?   C
(83)
  A $\frac{7}{4}$ **B** $\frac{14}{17}$ **C** $\frac{12}{21}$ **D** $\frac{2}{3}$

* 5. Complete this proportion: Four is to five as what number is to
(85)   twenty?   16

6. Arrange these numbers in order from least to greatest:
(50) $-1, -0.1, 0, 0.1, 1$ $-1, 1, 0.1, -0.1, 0$

7. The product of $10^3 \cdot 10^2$ equals which of the following?   C
(92)
  A 10^9 **B** 10^6 **C** 10^5 **D** 10

▶ See Math Conversations in the sidebar.

Practice Set
Problem c Error Alert
If students forget to regroup ounces as pounds and ounces and give an answer of 6 lb 19 oz, remind them to convert any ounce sums that are 16 or greater to pounds or to pounds and ounces.

---

3 Written Practice

Math Conversations
Discussion opportunities are provided below.

Problem 4 Analyze
"A proportion is made up of two ratios. What relationship do the ratios in every proportion share?" In a proportion, the ratios are equal.

"Which fraction is equivalent to $\frac{4}{7}$? Explain how you know." $\frac{12}{21}$; dividing 12 and 21 by 3 reduces the fraction to $\frac{4}{7}$

Errors and Misconceptions
Problem 7
Some students may multiply the exponents and choose b, 10^6. Tell these students to start by simplifying each expression with exponents ($10^3 \cdot 10^2 = 1000 \cdot 100$). Then have them multiply 1000 by 100 and change the product to an expression that has a base of 10 and an exponent. If necessary, refer students to the powers of 10 table in Lesson 92.

(continued)

Math Conversations

Discussion opportunities are provided below.

Problem 19 [Analyze]

Extend the Problem

"How many times more likely is the spinner to stop in Sector 1 than in Sector 2? Explain your reasoning." Three times more likely; the probability of an outcome of 2 is $\frac{1}{4}$ and the probability of an outcome of 1 is $\frac{3}{4}$, and $\frac{1}{4} \times 3 = \frac{3}{4}$.

Problem 23 [Connect]

Invite two volunteers to each write a different equation on the board or overhead that can be used to solve the problem. Sample: 8 lb 4 oz + n = 10 lb 1 oz and n = 10 lb 1 oz − 8 lb 4 oz

Invite students to choose and solve an equation, then compare answers.

Errors and Misconceptions
Problem 23

When subtracting 8 pounds 4 ounces from 10 pounds 1 ounce, there aren't enough ounces to subtract. Watch for students who do not regroup 1 pound as 16 ounces.

(continued)

---

8. The area of the square in this figure is 100 mm².
(86)

    a. What is the radius of the circle?   10 mm

    b. What is the diameter of the circle?   20 mm

    c. What is the area of the circle?
    (Use 3.14 for π.)   314 mm²

[Connect] Complete the table to answer problems **9–11.**

	Fraction	Decimal	Percent
* 9. (99)	$\frac{4}{25}$	**a.** 0.16	**b.** 16%
* 10. (99)	**a.** $\frac{1}{100}$	0.01	**b.** 1%
* 11. (99)	**a.** $\frac{9}{10}$	**b.** 0.9	90%

12. $1\frac{2}{3} + 3\frac{1}{2} + 4\frac{1}{6}$ $9\frac{1}{3}$
(61)

13. $\frac{5}{6} \times \frac{3}{10} \times 4$ 1
(72)

14. $6\frac{1}{4} \div 100$ $\frac{1}{16}$
(68)

15. $6.437 + 12.8 + 7$ 26.237
(38)

16. *Estimate* Convert $\frac{1}{7}$ to a decimal number by dividing 1 by 7. Stop dividing after three decimal places, and round your answer to two decimal places.   0.14
(74)

17. An octagon has how many more sides than a pentagon? 3 more sides
(60)

18. $4 \times 5^2 - 50 \div \sqrt{4} + (3^2 - 2^3)$ 76
(92)

▶*** 19.** *Analyze* Sector 2 on this spinner is a 90° sector. If the spinner is spun twice, what is the probability that it will stop in sector 2 both times? $\frac{1}{4} \cdot \frac{1}{4} = \frac{1}{16}$
(Inv. 10)

20. If the spinner is spun 100 times, about how many times would it be expected to stop in sector 1?   about 75 times
(58)

21. How many 1 inch cubes would be needed to build this larger cube?   64 cubes
(82)

4 in.

22. The average of four numbers is 5. What is their sum?   20
(18)

▶*** 23.** *Connect* When Andy was born, he weighed 8 pounds 4 ounces. Three weeks later he weighed 10 pounds 1 ounce. How many pounds and ounces had he gained in three weeks?   1 pound 13 ounces
(102)

▶ See Math Conversations in the sidebar.

---

* 24. Lines *s* and *t* are parallel.
(97)

    a. Which angle is an alternate interior angle to ∠5? ∠3

    b. If the measure of ∠5 is 76°, what are the measures of ∠1 and ∠2? m∠1 = 76°; m∠2 = 104°

▶ *** 25.** *Generalize* Find the missing number in this function table: 10
(96)

x	1	2	4	5
3x − 5	−2	1	7	

26. What is the perimeter of this hexagon?
(8) Dimensions are in centimeters.
42 centimeters

27. **a.** What is the area of the parallelogram at
(71, 79)   right? 24 in.²

    b. What is the area of the triangle? 6 in.²

    c. What is the combined area of the parallelogram and triangle? 30 in.²

* 28. How many milligrams is half of a gram? 500 milligrams
(102)

29. *Model* The coordinates of the endpoints of a line segment are (3, −1)
(Inv. 7) and (3, 5). The midpoint of the segment is the point halfway between the endpoints. What are the coordinates of the midpoint? (3, 2)

30. *Estimate* Tania took 10 steps to walk across the tetherball circle and
(47) 31 steps to walk around the tetherball circle. Use this information to find the approximate number of diameters in the circumference of the tetherball circle. about 3.1 diameters

Lesson 102   537

▶ See Math Conversations in the sidebar.

3 **Written Practice** *(Continued)*

Math Conversations

Discussion opportunities are provided below.

Problem 25 Generalize

"Explain how to find the unknown number."

Substitute 5 for *x* in the expression 3*x* − 5, then simplify the expression.

Looking Forward

Identifying and converting units of mass and weight and adding and subtracting units of weight prepares students for:

- **Investigation 11,** determining actual and scale dimensions of scale drawings and models.

- **Lesson 113,** adding and subtracting mixed measures.

- **Lesson 114,** using unit multipliers to convert from one unit of measure to another.

• Perimeter of Complex Shapes

Objectives

- Find the perimeter of a complex shape.

Materials

- **Power Up M** (in *Instructional Masters*)

Optional

- **Investigation Activity 15** (in *Instructional Masters*) or **graph paper**

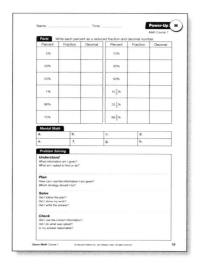

Power Up M

Math Language

English Learners (ESL)

combined

Technology Resources

Student eBook Complete student textbook in electronic format.

Resources and Planner CD Assessment, reteaching, and instructional masters, plus a pacing calendar with standards.

Test and Practice Generator CD Create additional practice sheets and custom-made tests.

www.SaxonPublishers.com Visit for more student activities and planning materials.

Inclusion

Adaptations CD Adapted lessons, investigations, practice and assessments.

Meeting Standards

National Council of Teachers of Mathematics (NCTM)

Measurement

ME.1c Understand, select, and use units of appropriate size and type to measure angles, perimeter, area, surface area, and volume

ME.2b Select and apply techniques and tools to accurately find length, area, volume, and angle measures to appropriate levels of precision

Connections

CN.4b Understand how mathematical ideas interconnect and build on one another to produce a coherent whole

Problem-Solving Strategy: Use Logical Reasoning

Here are the front, top, and side views of an object. Draw a three-dimensional view of the object from the perspective of the upper right front.

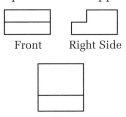

Front   Right Side

Top

(Understand) **Understand the problem.**

"What information are we given?"

We are given pictures of the front, top, and side views of an object.

"What are we asked to do?"

Draw a three-dimensional view of the object from the perspective of the upper right front.

(Plan) **Make a plan.**

"What problem-solving strategy will we use?"

We will *use spatial and logical reasoning* to draw the figure.

(Solve) **Carry out the plan.**

"What does the front view tell us?"

The figure has two layers.

"What does the side view tell us?"

It has a longer rear portion with two layers and a short front portion with one layer. The rear portion looks about twice as long as the front portion.

"What does the top view tell us?"

The front portion is half the length of the rear portion.

"Draw the three-dimensional figure that matches the description."

(Students may instead use unit cubes to construct the figure by stacking 15 cubes to create the three-dimensional figure.)

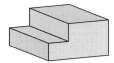

(Check) **Look back.**

"Did we complete the task that was assigned?"

Yes. We created a three-dimensional figure that has the given top, front, and right side views.

1 Power Up

Facts
Distribute **Power Up M** to students. See answers below.

Mental Math
Before students begin the Mental Math exercise, do this counting exercise as a class.

Count by 3s from −30 to 30.

Encourage students to share different ways to mentally compute these exercises. Strategies for exercises **b** and **f** are listed below.

b. Change 543 to 550; then Subtract 7

$550 - 250 = 300;\ 300 - 7 = 293$

Change 543 to 500, then Add 43

$500 - 250 = 250;\ 250 + 43 = 293$

f. Shift the Decimal Points One Place

$\frac{500}{20} = \frac{50.0}{2.0} = \frac{50}{2} = 25$

Cancel Zeros

$\frac{50\not{0}}{2\not{0}} = \frac{50}{2} = 25$

Problem Solving
Refer to **Power-Up Discussion,** p. 538B.

2 New Concepts

Instruction
Explain that an important part of finding the perimeter of a complex shape is finding its missing measures.

The Math Background on the next page contains additional information about solving problems of this nature.

(continued)

LESSON **103**

• Perimeter of Complex Shapes

Power Up *Building Power*

facts Power Up M

mental math

a. **Number Sense:** 50 · 60 3000

b. **Number Sense:** 543 − 250 293

c. **Percent:** 25% of 40 10

d. **Calculation:** \$5.65 + \$3.99 \$9.64

e. **Decimals:** 87.5 ÷ 100 0.875

f. **Number Sense:** $\frac{500}{20}$ 25

g. **Measurement:** How many milliliters are in 10 liters? 10,000 ml

h. **Calculation:** 6 × 6, − 1, ÷ 5, × 6, − 2, ÷ 5, × 4, − 2, × 3 90

problem solving Here are the front, top, and side views of an object. Draw a three-dimensional view of the object from the perspective of the upper right front.

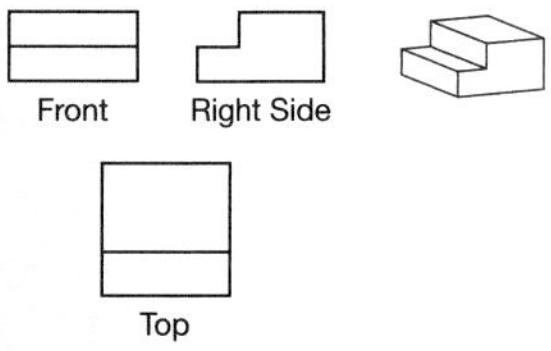

New Concept *Increasing Knowledge*

Thinking Skill
Conclude
Why is the shape described as complex?
Sample: A complex figure is composed of two or more simpler figures.

In this lesson we will practice finding the perimeters of complex shapes. The figure below is an example of a complex shape. Notice that the lengths of two of the sides are not given. We will first find the lengths of these sides; then we will find the perimeter of the shape. (In this book, assume that corners that look square are square.)

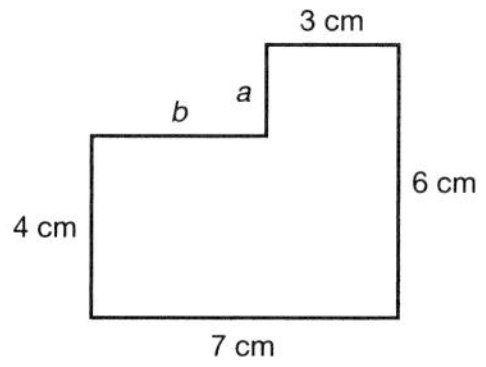

We see that the figure is 7 cm long. The sides marked *b* and 3 cm together equal 7 cm. So *b* must be 4 cm.

$b + 3\text{ cm} = 7\text{ cm}$

$b = 4\text{ cm}$

Facts Write each percent as a reduced fraction and decimal number.

Percent	Fraction	Decimal	Percent	Fraction	Decimal
5%	$\frac{1}{20}$	0.05	10%	$\frac{1}{10}$	0.1
20%	$\frac{1}{5}$	0.2	30%	$\frac{3}{10}$	0.3
25%	$\frac{1}{4}$	0.25	50%	$\frac{1}{2}$	0.5
1%	$\frac{1}{100}$	0.01	$12\frac{1}{2}\%$	$\frac{1}{8}$	0.125
90%	$\frac{9}{10}$	0.9	$33\frac{1}{3}\%$	$\frac{1}{3}$	Rounds to 0.333
75%	$\frac{3}{4}$	0.75	$66\frac{2}{3}\%$	$\frac{2}{3}$	Rounds to 0.667

The width of the figure is 6 cm. The sides marked 4 cm and *a* together equal 6 cm. So *a* must equal 2 cm.

$$4 \text{ cm} + a = 6 \text{ cm}$$
$$a = 2 \text{ cm}$$

We have found that *b* is 4 cm and *a* is 2 cm.

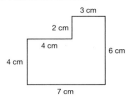

We add the lengths of all the sides and find that the perimeter is 26 cm.

$$6 \text{ cm} + 7 \text{ cm} + 4 \text{ cm} + 4 \text{ cm} + 2 \text{ cm} + 3 \text{ cm} = 26 \text{ cm}$$

Example

Find the perimeter of this figure.

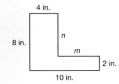

Solution

To find the perimeter, we add the lengths of the six sides. The lengths of two sides are not given in the illustration. We will write two equations to find the lengths of these sides. The length of the figure is 10 inches. The sides parallel to the 10-inch side have lengths of 4 inches and *m* inches. Their combined length is 10 inches, so *m* must equal 6 inches.

$$4 \text{ in.} + m = 10 \text{ in.}$$
$$m = 6 \text{ in.}$$

The width of the figure is 8 inches. The sides parallel to the 8-inch side have lengths of *n* inches and 2 inches. Their combined measures equal 8 inches, so *n* must equal 6 inches.

$$n + 2 \text{ in.} = 8 \text{ in.}$$
$$n = 6 \text{ in.}$$

We add the lengths of the six sides to find the perimeter of the complex shape.

$$10 \text{ in.} + 8 \text{ in.} + 4 \text{ in.} + 6 \text{ in.} + 6 \text{ in.} + 2 \text{ in.} = \mathbf{36 \text{ in.}}$$

Lesson 103   539

---

2 New Concepts (Continued)

Instruction

"Once all of the measures of a figure are known, what operation is used to find its perimeter?" addition

"When we find the perimeter of a figure in centimeters, why is our answer labeled centimeters and not labeled square centimeters?" Sample: Square centimeters involve area and represent multiplying centimeters by centimeters.

Example
Instruction

"Explain how subtraction can be used to find the value of m." subtract 4 from 10

"Explain how subtraction can be used to find the value of n." subtract 2 from 8

"To find the perimeter, we add. How does the number of addends compare to the number of sides of the figure?" The number of addends is the same as the number of sides.

(continued)

Math Background

One strategy for finding missing measures in complex shapes is to draw dashes to extend a figure and label the lengths of its sides.

In the figure at the right, dashes were used to extend the figure and the labels 7 cm and 6 cm were added.

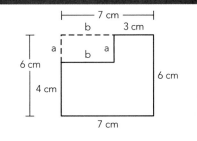

Using dashes to extend figures and labeling known measures can help students more easily recognize the arithmetic that needs to be performed to find unknown measures.

English Learners

In the solution, explain the term **combined.** Say,

"When numbers are combined they are grouped together. To find the length of m in the equation 4 + m = 10, we combine 4 inches with m, because we know that together 4 and m will equal 10 inches."

Ask students to write equations where numbers are combined with a variable.

Practice Set

Problems a and b [Error Alert]

For each shape, students must recognize there are two missing lengths and use the given information to find those lengths. Encourage students who struggle to copy each shape and label the missing lengths with different letters. Then help them write and solve equations to find the missing lengths.

---

3 **Written Practice**

Math Conversations

Discussion opportunities are provided below.

Problem 6 [Analyze]

Invite a volunteer to draw a ratio box on the board or overhead to represent this problem. The third row of the ratio box should display the total number of students. Sample:

	Ratio	Actual Count
Boys	4	b
Girls	7	g
Total	11	33

Ask the class to decide if the ratio box correctly represents the problem, and explain why or why not.

When a correct ratio box has been drawn, have the class refer to it and work together to write a proportion that can be used to solve the problem. Sample: $\frac{7}{11} = \frac{g}{33}$

Ask students to work individually to solve the proportion, then compare answers with their classmates.

Problem 8b [Conclude]

Tell students that the term *literally* means *really* or *actually*.

(continued)

Practice Set ▶ Find the perimeter of each complex shape:

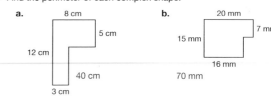

a. 8 cm, 5 cm, 12 cm, 40 cm, 3 cm

b. 20 mm, 7 mm, 15 mm, 16 mm, 70 mm

Written Practice   *Strengthening Concepts*

1. When the sum of $\frac{1}{2}$ and $\frac{1}{3}$ is divided by the product of $\frac{1}{2}$ and $\frac{1}{3}$, what is
(12, 72) the quotient?   5

2. The average age of three men is 24 years.
(18)
    a. What is the sum of their ages?   72 years

    b. If two of the men are 22 years old, how old is the third?   28 years old

3. A string one yard long is formed into the shape of a square.
(38)
    a. How many inches long is each side of the square?   9 in.

    b. How many square inches is the area of the square?   81 in.²

4. Complete this proportion: Five is to three as thirty is to what
(85) number?   18

5. Mr. Cho has 30 books. Fourteen of the books are mysteries. What is the
(23) ratio of mysteries to non-mysteries? $\frac{7}{8}$

▶ *** 6.** [Analyze] In another class of 33 students, the ratio of boys to girls is
(101) 4 to 7. How many girls are in that class?   21 girls

* 7. $100 \div 10^2 + 3 \times (2^3 - \sqrt{16})$ 13
(92)

* 8. Robert complained that he had a "ton" of homework.
(58, 102)
    a. How many pounds is a ton?   2000 pounds

▶   **b.** [Conclude] What is the probability that Robert would literally have a ton of homework?   close to zero

[Connect] Complete the table to answer problems **9–11.**

	Fraction	Decimal	Percent
* 9. *(99)*	$\frac{1}{100}$	**a.** 0.01	**b.** 1%
* 10. *(99)*	**a.** $\frac{2}{5}$	0.4	**b.** 40%
* 11. *(99)*	**a.** $\frac{2}{25}$	**b.** 0.08	8%

▶ See Math Conversations in the sidebar.

12. $10\frac{1}{2} \div 3\frac{1}{2}$ 3
(68)

13. $(6 + 2.4) \div 0.04$ 210
(53)

Find each unknown number:

14. $7\frac{1}{2} + 6\frac{3}{4} + n = 15\frac{3}{8}$ $1\frac{1}{8}$
(61)

15. $x - 1\frac{3}{4} = 7\frac{1}{2}$ $9\frac{1}{4}$
(63)

16. **Verify** Instead of dividing $10\frac{1}{2}$ by $3\frac{1}{2}$, Guadalupe doubled both numbers
(43) before dividing. What was Guadalupe's division problem and its
quotient? $21 \div 7 = 3$

17. **Estimate** Mariabella used a tape measure to find the circumference
(47) and the diameter of a plate. The circumference was about 35 inches,
and the diameter was about 11 inches. Find the approximate number
of diameters in the circumference. Round to the nearest tenth. about
3.2 diameters

▶ **18.** Write twenty million, five hundred thousand in expanded notation using
(92) exponents. $(2 \times 10^7) + (5 \times 10^5)$

19. **List** Name the prime numbers between 40 and 50. 41, 43, 47
(19)

▶* **20.** **Analyze** Calculate mentally:
(100)

    a. $-3 + -8$ -11 **b.** $-3 - -8$ $+5$

    c. $-8 + +3$ -5 **d.** $-8 - +3$ -11

▶* **21.** **Conclude** In $\triangle ABC$ the measure of $\angle A$ is
(98) $40°$. Angles B and C are congruent. What is
the measure of $\angle C$? $70°$

* **22.** **a.** What is the perimeter of this triangle?
(8, 79) 60 mm
    b. What is the area of this triangle? 150 mm²

      c. What is the ratio of the length of the
20 mm side to the length of the longest
side? Express the ratio as a fraction and as a decimal. $\frac{4}{5}$, 0.8

23. **Analyze** The Simpsons rented a trailer that was 8 feet long and 5 feet
(82) wide. If they load the trailer with 1-by-1-by-1-foot boxes to a height of
3 feet, how many boxes can be loaded onto the trailer? 120 boxes

24. What is the probability of drawing the queen of spades from a normal
(58) deck of 52 cards? $\frac{1}{52}$

▶ See Math Conversations in the sidebar.

Math Conversations
Discussion opportunities are provided below.

Problem 20 Analyze
**"For problem a, what is the sign of the sum
when both addends have the same sign?"**
The sign of the sum is the same as the sign
of the addends; because the addends are
negative, the sum is negative.

**"For problems b and d, the operation is
subtraction. Explain how addition can be
used to find the answer."** Subtracting a
number is the same as adding its opposite.

Problem 21 Conclude
**"What is the sum of the angle measures of
any triangle?"** $180°$

After completing the problem, ask,

**"Classify this triangle by its sides. What
kind of triangle is triangle ABC?"** isosceles

Errors and Misconceptions
Problem 18
Suggest to students who struggle that they
first write the number using digits (in other
words, in standard form) before writing the
number in expanded form.

Problem 20
Students may not recognize that the
Commutative Property of Addition allows
them to change the order of the addends. For
example, in problem b, adding an opposite
changes the expression to $-3 + +8$, and
students can add the addends in that order,
or change the order of the addends to $+8 + -3$.

Since the arithmetic is to be performed
mentally, students may find it easier to add
the addends in one order instead of the other.

(continued)

Math Conversations

Discussion opportunities are provided below.

Problem 25a Connect

"Explain how we can identify the number of degrees that each tick mark of this thermometer represents." Sample: Each interval of 10 degrees is divided into 5 equal parts. Since 10 degrees divided by 5 is 2 degrees, each tick mark represents 2 degrees.

Problem 29 Estimate

"A half gallon is the same as what number of quarts?" two

"How many pints are equal to one quart?" two

"How many pints are equal to two quarts?" four

"Since two quarts is the same as a half gallon, how many pints are equal to a half gallon?" four

---

* 25. **a.** Connect What temperature is shown on
(10, 100)   this thermometer?   −8°F

b. If the temperature rises 12°F, what will the temperature be?   4°F

* 26. Find the perimeter of the figure below.   140 mm
(103)

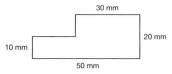

27. **a.** Analyze What is the area of the shaded
(37)   rectangle?   80 mm²

b. What is the area of the unshaded rectangle?   140 mm²

c. What is the combined area of the two rectangles?   220 mm²

28. Connect What are the coordinates of the point halfway between
(Inv. 7)   (−3, −2) and (5, −2)?   (1, −2)

▶* 29. Estimate A pint of milk weighs about 16 ounces. About how many
(78, 102)   pounds does a half gallon of milk weigh?   about 4 pounds

30. Evaluate Ruben walked around a building whose perimeter was shaped
(90)   like a regular pentagon.

a. At each corner of the building, Ruben turned about how many degrees? $\frac{360°}{5} = 72°$

b. What is the measure of each interior angle of the regular pentagon?
$180° − 72° = 108°$

▶ See Math Conversations in the sidebar.

Looking Forward

Finding the perimeter of complex shapes prepares students for:

• **Lesson 107,** finding the area of complex shapes with one or two sides unknown.

• Algebraic Addition Activity

Objectives

• Use the electrical-charge model to add signed numbers.

Lesson Preparation

Materials

Optional
• **Manipulative kit:** color tiles
• **Investigation Activity 15** (in *Instructional Masters*) or **graph paper**

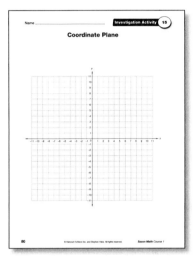

Investigation Activity 15

Math Language

	English Learners (ESL)
	sign

Technology Resources

Student eBook Complete student textbook in electronic format.

Resources and Planner CD Assessment, reteaching, and instructional masters, plus a pacing calendar with standards.

Test and Practice Generator CD Create additional practice sheets and custom-made tests.

www.SaxonPublishers.com Visit for more student activities and planning materials.

Inclusion

Adaptations CD Adapted lessons, investigations, practice and assessments.

Meeting Standards

National Council of Teachers of Mathematics (NCTM)

Numbers and Operations

NO.1g Develop meaning for integers and represent and compare quantities with them

NO.2a Understand the meaning and effects of arithmetic operations with fractions, decimals, and integers

Connections

CN.4a Recognize and use connections among mathematical ideas

Problem-Solving Strategy: Find a Pattern/ Make a Chart

Sonya, Sid, and Sinead met at the gym on Monday. Sonya goes to the gym every two days. The next day she will be at the gym is Wednesday. Sid goes to the gym every three days. The next day Sid will be at the gym is Thursday. Sinead goes to the gym every four days. She will next be at the gym on Friday. What will be the next day that Sonya, Sid, and Sinead are at the gym on the same day?

(Understand) **Understand the problem.**

"What information are we given?"

Sonya, Sid, and Sinead met at the gym on Monday. Sonya goes to the gym every two days, Sid every three days, and Sinead every four days.

"What are we asked to do?"

We are asked to find the next day that the three will be at the gym on the same day.

(Plan) **Make a plan.**

"What problem-solving strategy will we use?"

We will *use the patterns* that have been provided, and *make a chart* of the days each girl is at the gym.

(Solve) **Carry out the plan.**

"What information will we build our chart with?"

We will write abbreviations for days of the week, and we mark the days that each of the three girls is at the gym:

	M	T	W	T	F	S	S	M	T	W	T	F	S	S	M	T	W	T	F	S	S
Sonya	X		X		X		X		X		X		X		X		X		X		X
Sid	X			X			X			X			X			X			X		
Sinead	X				X				X				X				X				X

"What is the next day that Sonya, Sid, and Sinead will all be at the gym?"

All three will next be at the gym on the Saturday 12 days after they met on Monday.

(Check) **Look back.**

"Did we complete the task?"

Yes. We found that the next time Sonya, Sid, and Sinead will be at the gym on the same day will be the Saturday 12 days after they met on Monday.

Teacher Note: Ask students to find the lowest common multiple of 2, 3, and 4. They should find that 12 is the lowest common multiple. Relate this to the problem. The girls met 12 days after Monday. Ask when they will meet again. (12 days after Saturday). Challenge students to solve this problem without drawing the chart.

• Algebraic Addition Activity

611
613
633

Power Up
Building Power

Note: Because the New Concept in this lesson takes about half of a class period, today's Power Up has been omitted.

problem solving

Sonya, Sid, and Sinead met at the gym on Monday. Sonya goes to the gym every two days. The next day she will be at the gym is Wednesday. Sid goes to the gym every three days. The next day Sid will be at the gym is Thursday. Sinead goes to the gym every four days. She will next be at the gym on Friday. What will be the next day that Sonya, Sidney, and Sinead are at the gym on the same day? Saturday

New Concept *Increasing Knowledge*

Thinking Skill

Discuss

What addition equation shows that a positive charge and a negative charge neutralize each other?

$+1 + -1 = 0$

One model for the addition of signed numbers is the number line. Another model for the addition of signed numbers is the electrical-charge model, which is used in the Sign Game. In this model, signed numbers are represented by positive and negative charges that can neutralize each other when they are added. The game is played with sketches, as shown here. The first two levels may be played with two color counters.

Activity

Sign Game

In the Sign Game pairs of positive and negative charges become neutral. After determining the neutral pairs we count the signs that remain and then write our answer. There are four skill levels to the game. Be sure you are successful at one level before moving to the next level.

level 1

Positive and negative signs are placed randomly on a "screen." When the game begins positive and negative pairs are neutralized so we cross out the signs as shown. (Appropriate sound effects strengthen the experience!) (If using counters, remove all pairs of counters that have different colors.)

Before

After

Two positives remain.

---

1 **Power Up**

Today's **Power Up** has been omitted.

Problem Solving
Refer to **Power-Up Discussion**, p. 548B.

2 **New Concepts**

Instruction
First present the game on the board or overhead by drawing various "before" screens. For each screen ask, "How many of which sign will remain?"

Activity

Level 1
Instruction
To complete level 1 of the activity, explain that one negative charge cancels out, or neutralizes, one positive charge. Mark out canceled signs. If students use two-color counters, pairs of opposite colored counters are removed from the game.

(continued)

English Learners

Before the activity, explain the term **signed numbers.** Say,

"Numbers that are signed have a positive or negative symbol or sign (+ or −) in front of them. A number with no sign is a positive number."

Ask a student to draw a number line on the board and label on it three points: one with a + sign, one with a − sign, and one with no sign. (Ex. −3, 5, +7)

Level 2

Instruction

For level 2, draw screens containing various positive and negative integers. For each screen ask, "How many of what sign will remain?" Direct students to first find the total of the positive numbers and the total of the negative numbers. Then they can calculate what remains.

Using counters, have students arrange all of their counters of one color into one stack and all of their counters of the other color into another stack.

The two stacks of counters are then moved close to each other and stacks of equal height and different colors are removed, with one stack of one color remaining.

Level 3

Instruction

As students work through this portion of the lesson, point out that a negative sign implies the opposite of a number. This idea can help students understand dual signs. For example, -3 means "the opposite of 3." Likewise, $-(-3)$ can mean the opposite of negative 3, which is 3. In the same manner, $-(+2)$ is the opposite of positive 2, which is negative 2.

Work through the examples of positives and negatives carefully with students. Help them recognize that every time one negative sign and one positive sign appear together in any order, the result is a negative number, and every time two negative signs appear together or two positive signs appear together, the result is a positive number.

(continued)

After marking positive-negative pairs we count the remaining positives or negatives. In the example shown above, two positives remain. With counters, two counters of one color remain. See whether you can determine what will remain on the three practice screens below:

level 2

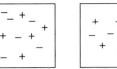

One negative   Zero remain.   All 7 negatives remain.

Positives and negatives are displayed in counted clusters or stacked counters. The suggested strategy is to combine the same signs first. So $+3$ combines with $+1$ to form $+4$, and -5 combines with -2 to form -7. Then determine how many of which charge (sign) remain.

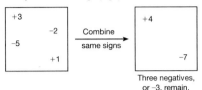

Three negatives, or -3, remain.

There were three more negatives than positives, so -3 remain. With counters, stacks of equal height and different colors are removed. Only one color (or no counters) remains. See whether you can determine how many of which charge will remain for the three practice screens below:

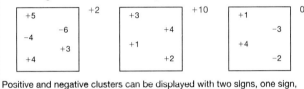

level 3

Positive and negative clusters can be displayed with two signs, one sign, or no sign. Clusters appear "in disguise" by taking on an additional sign or by dropping a sign. The first step is to remove the disguise. A cluster with no sign, with "$-\ -$," or with "$+\ +$" is a positive cluster. A cluster with "$+\ -$" or with "$-\ +$" is a negative cluster. If a cluster has a "shield" (parentheses), look through the shield to see the sign. With counters, for "$-\ -$" invert a negative to a positive, and for "$-\ +$" invert a positive to a negative.

Examples of Positives	Examples of Negatives
$-(-3) = +3$	$-(+2) = -2$
$--2 = +2$	$+(-3) = -3$
$4 = +4$	$+-1 = -1$
$++1 = +1$	$-+4 = -4$

Reading Math

Symbols

A negative sign indicates the opposite of a number. -3 means "the opposite of 3." Likewise, $-(-3)$ means "the opposite of -3," which is 3. $-(+3)$ means "the opposite of $+3$," which is -3.

Teacher Tip

In **level 2 of the activity,** you can provide additional practice **grouping positive and negative numbers** by drawing several level 2 practice screens on the board or overhead and asking individual students to sketch, then solve, each screen. For example, draw a box containing 6, -1, -3, 4, and -2. Then ask students to group the numbers with like signs and determine the remaining number. $+4$

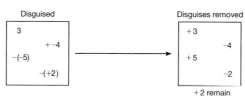

	Disguised		Disguises removed
3			+3
	+−4		−4
−(−5)			+5
	−(+2)		−2
			+2 remain

See whether you can determine how many of which charge remain for the following practice screens:

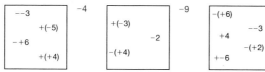

−−3		−4				−9		−(+6)		−7
	+(−5)			+(−3)					−−3	
−+6					−2			+4		
	+(+4)			−(+4)					−(+2)	
								+−6		

level 4 Extend Level 3 to a line of clusters without using a screen.

$$-3 + (-4) - (-5) - (+2) + (+6)$$

Use the following steps to find the answer:

Step 1: Remove the disguises: $-3 - 4 + 5 - 2 + 6$

Step 2: Group forces: $-9 + 11$

Step 3: Find what remains: $+2$

Practice Set

▶ Simplify:

a. $-2 + -3 - -4 + -5$ -6

b. $-3 + (+2) - (+5) - (-6)$ 0

c. $+3 + -4 - +6 + +7 - -1$ $+1$

d. $2 + (-3) - (-9) - (+7) + (+1)$ $+2$

e. $3 - -5 + -4 - +2 + +8$ $+10$

f. $(-10) - (+20) - (-30) + (-40)$ -40

Written Practice   *Strengthening Concepts*

1. *Conclude* A pyramid with a square base has how many more edges
(Inv. 6) than vertices?   3 more edges

* 2. Becki weighed 7 lb 8 oz when she was born and 12 lb 6 oz at 3 months.
(102) How many pounds and ounces did Becki gain in 3 months?   4 lb 14 oz

3. There are 6 fish and 10 snails in the aquarium. What is the ratio of fish
(23) to snails? $\frac{3}{5}$

* 4. A team's win-loss ratio was 3 to 2. If the team had played 20 games
(101) without a tie, how many games had it won?   12 games

Lesson 104   545

▶ See Math Conversations in the sidebar.

Activity *(Continued)*

Level 4
Instruction
The expression below will give students an opportunity to repeat the steps.

$$8 - (+1) + (+5) - (-3) + (-4)$$

Write the expression on the board or overhead. Ask a volunteer to go to the board or overhead and complete step 1—removing the disguises. Then ask a second volunteer to complete step 2—grouping forces. Finally, ask a third volunteer to complete step 3—finding what remains.

As the volunteers complete their work, ask them to describe what they are doing and explain why they are doing it.
Step 1: $8 - 1 + 5 + 3 - 4$;
Step 2: $+16 - 5$ (or $- 5 + 16$);
Step 3: $+11$

---

2 New Concepts *(Continued)*

Practice Set
Problems a–f Error Alert
Before simplifying each expression, ask students to identify the signs that appear together, and explain how they will simplify those signs.

Teacher Tip

In **level 3 of the activity,** you can provide additional practice **identifying positives and negatives and combining integers** by drawing several level 3 practice screens on the board or overhead. For example, draw a box containing $+(-7)$, $+4$, $-(-1)$, and $-(+3)$ and ask a student to determine the remaining number. -5

3 Written Practice

Math Conversations
Discussion opportunities are provided below.

Problem 5 [Analyze]
"This probability experiment has a compound outcome. What operation is used to find the probability of a compound outcome? Explain your answer."
Multiplication; find the probability of each outcome separately, then multiply the probabilities.

Problem 7 [Conclude]
"Think about a square or a rectangle. What is the measure of each angle of a square or rectangle?" 90°

"What is the sum of the angle measures of a square or a rectangle?" 360°

"Are squares and rectangles examples of parallelograms?" yes

"What is the sum of the angle measures of a parallelogram?" 360°

Problem 17 [Analyze]
Explain that students are to write a greater than sign, a less than sign, or an equals sign in the circle. Then point out that the coin tosses represent a probability experiment which contains three parts—the first coin toss, the second coin toss, and the third coin toss.

If students need additional help solving the problem, tell them to find the probability for each toss and then multiply the three probabilities to find the probability of tossing "heads" three times in a row.

Errors and Misconceptions
Problem 6
Watch for students who use the height and not the side length of the parallelogram to determine its perimeter.

(continued)

▶ *** 5.** [Analyze] If Molly tosses a coin and rolls a number cube, what is the probability of the coin landing heads up and the number cube stopping with a 6 on top? $\frac{1}{2} \cdot \frac{1}{6} = \frac{1}{12}$
(Inv. 10)

▶ **6. a.** What is the perimeter of this parallelogram? 30 cm
(71)

    b. What is the area of this parallelogram? 48 cm²

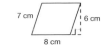

▶ **7.** [Conclude] If each acute angle of a parallelogram measures 59°, then what is the measure of each obtuse angle? 121°
(71)

8. [Estimate] The center of this circle is the origin. The circle passes through (2, 0).
(86)

    a. Estimate the area of the circle in square units by counting squares. Sample: 12 to 14 sq. units.

    b. Calculate the area of the circle by using 3.14 for π. 12.56 sq. units

9. Which ratio forms a proportion with $\frac{2}{3}$? **C**
(83)
  A $\frac{2}{4}$ **B** $\frac{3}{4}$ **C** $\frac{4}{6}$ **D** $\frac{3}{2}$

10. Complete this proportion: $\frac{6}{8} = \frac{a}{12}$ 9
(85)

* 11. What is the perimeter of the hexagon at right? Dimensions are in centimeters. 50 cm
(103)

[Connect] Complete the table to answer problems **12–14.**

	Fraction	Decimal	Percent
* 12. (99)	$\frac{3}{20}$	**a.** 0.15	**b.** 15%
* 13. (99)	**a.** $1\frac{1}{5}$	1.2	**b.** 120%
* 14. (99)	**a.** $\frac{1}{10}$	**b.** 0.1	10%

15. Sharon bought a notebook for 40% off the regular price of $6.95. What was the sale price of the notebook? $4.17
(41)

16. Between which two consecutive whole numbers is $\sqrt{200}$? 14 and 15
(89)

▶ *** 17.** [Analyze] Compare:
(92, Inv. 10)
    $\left(\frac{1}{2}\right)^3 \bigcirc$ the probability of 3 consecutive "heads" coin tosses

18. [Estimate] Divide 0.624 by 0.05 and round the quotient to the nearest whole number. 12
(49)

▶ See Math Conversations in the sidebar.

19. The average of three numbers is 20. What is the sum of the three
(18) numbers? 60

20. Write the prime factorization of 450 using exponents. $2 \cdot 3^2 \cdot 5^2$
(73)

* 21. $-3 + -5 - -4 - +2$ -6
(104)

* 22. $3^4 + 5^2 \times 4 - \sqrt{100} \times 2^3$ 101
(92)

23. How many blocks 1 inch on each edge would it take to fill a shoe box
(82) that is 12 inches long, 6 inches wide, and 5 inches tall? 360 blocks

24. Three fourths of the 60 athletes played in the game. How many athletes
(77) did not play? 15 athletes

* 25. The distance a car travels can be found by multiplying the **speed** of the
(95) car by the amount of **time** the car travels at that speed. How far would
a car travel in 4 hours at 88 kilometers per hour? 352 km

$$\frac{88 \text{ km}}{1 \text{ hr}} \times \frac{4 \text{ hr}}{1}$$

26. *Analyze* Use the figure on the right to
(31) answer **a–c**.

    a. What is the area of the shaded
    rectangle? 60 cm²

    b. What is the area of the unshaded
    rectangle? 48 cm²

    c. What is the combined area of the two
    rectangles? 108 cm²

5 cm
8 cm
12 cm
6 cm

27. *Estimate* Colby measured the circumference and diameter of four
(18, 51) circles. Then he divided the circumference by the diameter of each
circle to find the number of diameters in a circumference. Here are his
answers:

3.12, 3.2, 3.15, 3.1

Find the average of Colby's answers. Round the average to the nearest
hundredth. 3.14

28. *Explain* Hector was thinking of a two-digit counting number, and he
(58) asked Simon to guess the number. Describe how you can find the
probability that Simon will guess correctly on the first try.

29. *Connect* The coordinates of three vertices of a triangle are (3, 5),
(Inv. 7, 79) (−1, 5), and (−1, −3). What is the area of the triangle? 16 sq. units

30. $\frac{2 \text{ gal}}{1} \times \frac{4 \text{ qt}}{1 \text{ gal}} \times \frac{2 \text{ pt}}{1 \text{ qt}}$ 16 pt
(95)

28. There are 90
two-digit counting
numbers. Since
Hector was
thinking of only
one number, the
probability of
correctly guessing
the number in one
try is $\frac{1}{90}$.

▶ See Math Conversations in the sidebar.

Math Conversations
Discussion opportunities are provided below.

Problem 29 Connect
Extend the Problem
*"Use angle measures to classify the triangle
in this problem."* Since one angle of the
triangle is a 90° angle, the triangle is a right
triangle.

*"Consider the vertex (−1, −3) of the
right triangle. What number should the
x-coordinate of that vertex be changed
to so that the triangle would become an
isosceles triangle?"* change −1 to 1

Errors and Misconceptions
Problem 28
Some students may rely on counting to
determine the number of two-digit counting
numbers. Encourage these students to use a
pattern to help find the number, and describe
the pattern shown below to students or write
it on the board or overhead.

From 10 to 19 there are ten counting numbers.
From 20 to 29 there are ten counting numbers.
From 30 to 39 there are ten counting numbers.
And so on.

Help students infer from the pattern that there
are 9 × 10 or 90 two-digit counting numbers.

Using Proportions to Solve Percent Problems

Objectives

- Solve percent problems by creating a ratio box, setting up a proportion, and solving the proportion.

Lesson Preparation

Materials

- **Power Up M** (in *Instructional Masters*)

Optional

- **Manipulative kit:** inch or metric rulers

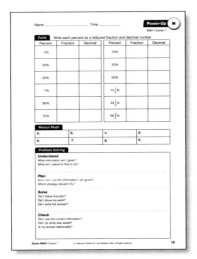

Power Up M

Math Language

Maintain	English Learner (ESL)
percent	dimensions
proportion	

Technology Resources

Student eBook Complete student textbook in electronic format.

Resources and Planner CD Assessment, reteaching, and instructional masters, plus a pacing calendar with standards.

Test and Practice Generator CD Create additional practice sheets and custom-made tests.

www.SaxonPublishers.com Visit for more student activities and planning materials.

Inclusion

Adaptations CD Adapted lessons, investigations, practice and assessments.

Meeting Standards

National Council of Teachers of Mathematics (NCTM)

Numbers and Operations

NO.1a Work flexibly with fractions, decimals, and percents to solve problems

NO.2a Understand the meaning and effects of arithmetic operations with fractions, decimals, and integers

NO.3d Develop, analyze, and explain methods for solving problems involving proportions, such as scaling and finding equivalent ratios

Problem Solving

PS.1b Solve problems that arise in mathematics and in other contexts

Connections

CN.4c Recognize and apply mathematics in contexts outside of mathematics

Problem-Solving Strategy: Make a Table/
Use Logical Reasoning

Copy this problem and fill in the missing digits:

$$\frac{\square}{4} + \frac{\square}{6} = \frac{11}{12}$$

Understand **Understand the problem.**

"What information are we given?"

Two fractions with a sum of $\frac{11}{12}$. The numerator of each addend is missing.

"What are we asked to do?"

Find both of the missing numerators.

Plan **Make a plan.**

"What problem-solving strategy will we use?"

We will *make a table* to find combinations and *use logical reasoning* to choose numerators that fit the problem.

Solve **Carry out the plan.**

"What should we do first?"

We should convert the possible addends into twelfths.

First Addend	Converted to Twelfths	Second Addend	Converted to Twelfths
$\frac{1}{4}$	$\boxed{\frac{3}{12}}$	$\frac{1}{6}$	$\boxed{\frac{2}{12}}$
$\frac{2}{4}$	$\frac{\cancel{6}}{\cancel{12}}$	$\frac{2}{6}$	$\frac{\cancel{4}}{\cancel{12}}$
$\frac{3}{4}$	$\boxed{\frac{9}{12}}$	$\frac{3}{6}$	$\frac{\cancel{6}}{\cancel{12}}$
$\frac{4}{4}$	$\frac{\cancel{12}}{\cancel{12}}$	$\frac{4}{6}$	$\boxed{\frac{8}{12}}$
		$\frac{5}{6}$	$\frac{\cancel{10}}{\cancel{12}}$
		$\frac{6}{6}$	$\frac{\cancel{12}}{\cancel{12}}$

"Now let's find all the possible combinations that add up to $\frac{11}{12}$ by crossing out pairs that don't work and circling those that do."

See above.

"Which combinations work for this particular problem?"

$\frac{3}{4} + \frac{1}{6}$ and $\frac{1}{4} + \frac{4}{6}$

Check **Look back.**

"Did we complete the task that was assigned?"

Yes. We found two solutions that have a sum of $\frac{11}{12}$. We found the missing numerators for each solution.

Facts

Distribute **Power Up M** to students. See answers below.

Mental Math

Before students begin the Mental Math exercise, do this counting exercise as a class.

Count by $\frac{1}{4}$s from -2 to 2.

Encourage students to share different ways to mentally compute these exercises. Strategies for exercises **a** and **c** are listed below.

a. Use a Multiplication Fact
$2 \times 4 = 8$; $200 \times 40 = 8000$
Multiply 2000 by 4
$2000 \times 4 = 8000$

c. Divide 200 by 2
$200 \div 2 = 100$
Double $\frac{1}{2}$ of 100
$\frac{1}{2}$ of $100 = 50$; $50 \times 2 = 100$

Problem Solving

Refer to **Power-Up Discussion**, p. 548B.

Example 1
Instruction

Point out that a good way for students to check their work is to first make an estimate of an answer, and after solving the problem, compare the exact answer to the estimate. After reading the problem, ask,

"Before solving this problem, how could we make an estimate of the answer?" Sample: Thirty percent is about $\frac{1}{3}$. Since about $\frac{1}{3}$ of a number is 12, the number is 3×12 or about 36. An estimate of the answer is 36.

Invite students to share their estimates and explain how they were made.

(continued)

548   *Saxon Math Course 1*

• Using Proportions to Solve Percent Problems

Power Up   *Building Power*

facts	Power Up M
mental math	**a. Number Sense:** $200 \cdot 40$ 8000
	b. Number Sense: $567 - 150$ 417
	c. Percent: 50% of 200 100
	d. Calculation: $17.20 + \$2.99$ \$20.19
	e. Decimals: $7.5 \div 100$ 0.075
	f. Number Sense: $\frac{440}{20}$ 22
	g. Measurement: How many quarts are in 2 gallons? 8 quarts
	h. Calculation: $6 \times 8, + 1, \sqrt{\ }, \times 3, - 1, \div 2, \times 10, - 1, \div 9$ 11

problem solving	Copy this problem and fill in the missing digits: $\dfrac{\square}{4} + \dfrac{\square}{6} = \dfrac{11}{12}$ $\frac{3}{4} + \frac{1}{6}$ and $\frac{1}{4} + \frac{4}{6}$

New Concept   *Increasing Knowledge*

We know that a percent can be expressed as a fraction with a denominator of 100.

$$30\% = \frac{30}{100}$$

A percent can also be regarded as a ratio in which 100 represents the total number in the group, as we show in the following example.

Example 1

Math Language
Percent means per hundred.
30% means 30 out of 100

Thirty percent of the cars in the parade are antique cars. If 12 vehicles are antique cars, how many vehicles are in the parade in all?

Solution

We construct a ratio box. The ratio numbers we are given are 30 and 100. We know from the word *percent* that 100 represents the ratio total. The actual count we are given is 12. Our categories are "Antiques" and "not Antiques."

548   *Saxon Math Course 1*

Facts   Write each percent as a reduced fraction and decimal number.

Percent	Fraction	Decimal	Percent	Fraction	Decimal
5%	$\frac{1}{20}$	0.05	10%	$\frac{1}{10}$	0.1
20%	$\frac{1}{5}$	0.2	30%	$\frac{3}{10}$	0.3
25%	$\frac{1}{4}$	0.25	50%	$\frac{1}{2}$	0.5
1%	$\frac{1}{100}$	0.01	$12\frac{1}{2}\%$	$\frac{1}{8}$	0.125
90%	$\frac{9}{10}$	0.9	$33\frac{1}{3}\%$	$\frac{1}{3}$	Rounds to 0.333
75%	$\frac{3}{4}$	0.75	$66\frac{2}{3}\%$	$\frac{2}{3}$	Rounds to 0.667

	Percent	Actual Count
Antiques	30	12
Not Antiques		
Total	100	

Since the ratio total is 100, we calculate that the ratio number for "not Antiques" is 70. We use n to stand for "not Antiques" and t for "total" in the actual-count column. We use two rows from the table to write a proportion. Since we know both numbers in the "Antiques" row, we use the numbers in the "Antiques" row for the proportion. Since we want to find the total number of students, we also use the numbers from the "total" row. We will then solve the proportion using cross products.

	Percent	Actual Count
Antiques	30	12
Not Antiques	70	n
Total	100	t

$$\frac{30}{100} = \frac{12}{t}$$

$$30t = 12 \cdot 100$$

$$t = \frac{\overset{4}{\cancel{12}} \cdot \overset{10}{\cancel{100}}}{\underset{\underset{1}{3}}{\cancel{30}}}$$

$$t = 40$$

We find that a total of **40 vehicles** were in the parade.

In the above problem we did not need to use the 70% who were "not Antiques." In the next example we will need to use the "not" percent in order to solve the problem.

Example 2

Only 40% of the team members played in the game. If 24 team members did not play, then how many did play?

Solution

We construct a ratio box. The categories are "played," "did not play," and "total." Since 40% played, we calculate that 60% did not play. We are asked for the actual count of those who played. So we use the "played" row and the "did not play" row (because we know both numbers in that row) to write the proportion.

Instruction

If students do not recognize how the ratio number for "not antiques" was found, explain that 100% represents the whole, which is the number of vehicles altogether. The whole has two parts—antiques and not antiques—and one of those parts is given. Help students generalize that to find an unknown part when one part is given, subtract the known part from the whole; $100 - 30 = 70$.

If students made an estimate of the answer prior to completing the problem, ask them at this time to decide the reasonableness of the exact answer by comparing it to their estimate.

Example 2

Instruction

"Did more than half of the team, or less than half of the team, play in the game? Explain your answer." Less than half; $\frac{1}{2}$ is the same as 50%, and 40% is less than 50%.

Help students infer that since the 24 team members who did not play in the game represent more than half of the team, the number of team members who did play is less than 24.

(continued)

Instruction

Emphasize that the order of the terms in the proportion is important. When writing the proportion, tell students to make sure they write the numbers in the order in which they appear in the ratio box.

Demonstrate the multiple steps that are used to reduce the terms of the fraction. Write $p = \frac{40 \cdot 24}{60}$ on the board or overhead. First show students how to reduce 40 and 60 to 4 and 6. Then show students how to reduce 24 and 6 to 4 and 1.

Example 3

Instruction

Before solving the problem, you might choose to ask students to describe different ways to estimate the answer and then state one or more estimates. Then ask them to decide the reasonableness of the estimated answer by comparing it to the exact answer.

Practice Set

Problem c Model

Have students solve the proportion to calculate the number of team members. $t = 30$

Problem e Formulate

Encourage students to exchange percent problems, then solve those problems and compare answers.

	Percent	Actual Count
Played	40	p
Did Not Play	60	24
Total	100	l

$\frac{40}{60} = \frac{p}{24}$

$60p = 40 \cdot 24$

$p = \dfrac{\overset{4}{\cancel{40}} \cdot \overset{4}{24}}{\underset{1}{\underset{8}{\cancel{60}}}}$

$p = 16$

We find that **16 team members** played in the game.

Example 3

Buying the shoes on sale, Nathan paid $45.60, which was 60% of the full price. What was the full price of the shoes?

Solution

Nathan paid 60% instead of 100%, so he saved 40% of the full price. We are given what Nathan paid. We are asked for the full price, which is the 100% price.

	Percent	Actual Count
Paid	60%	$45.60
Saved	40%	s
Full Price	100%	f

$\frac{60}{100} = \frac{45.60}{f}$

$60f = 4560$

$f = 76$

Full price for the shoes was **$76**.

Practice Set

Model Solve these percent problems using proportions. Make a ratio box for each problem.

a.

	%	A.C.
Digital	40	d
Not Digital	60	24
Total	100	t

b.

	%	A.C.
P	70	21
DNP	30	d
T	100	t

a. Forty percent of the cameras in a store are digital cameras. If 24 cameras are not digital, how many cameras are in the store in all? 40 cameras

b. Seventy percent of the team members played in the game. If 21 team members played, how many team members did not play? 9 team members

▶ **c.** **Model** Referring to problem **b**, what proportion would we use to find the number of members on the team? $\frac{70}{100} = \frac{21}{t}$

d. Joan walked 0.6 miles in 10 minutes. How far can she walk in 25 minutes at that rate? Write and solve a proportion to find the answer. $\frac{0.6}{10} = \frac{d}{25}$; 1.5 mi

▶ **e.** **Formulate** Create and solve your own percent problem using the method shown in this lesson. See student work.

▶ See Math Conversations in the sidebar.

* 1. How far would a car travel in $2\frac{1}{2}$ hours at 50 miles per hour?   125 mi
(95)

$$\frac{50 \text{ mi}}{1 \text{ hr}} \times \frac{2\frac{1}{2}\text{ hr}}{1}$$

2. **Connect** A map of Texas is drawn to a scale of 1 inch = 50 miles.
(95) Houston and San Antonio are 4 inches apart on the map. What is the
actual distance between Houston and San Antonio?   200 miles

3. The ratio of humpback whales to orcas was 2 to 1. If there were
(88) 900 humpback whales, how many orcas were there?   450 orcas

4. When Robert measured a half-gallon box of
(82) frozen yogurt, he found it had the dimensions
shown in the illustration. What was the
volume of the box in cubic inches?
122.5 in.³

Frozen Yogurt 5 in.
7 in. 3.5 in.

* 5. Calculate mentally:
(100,
104)   **a.** +10 + −10   0   **b.** −10 − −10   0   **c.** +6 + −5 − −4   +5

▶ * 6. **Estimate** On Earth a 1-kilogram object weighs about 2.2 pounds.
(102) A rock weighs 50 kilograms. About how many pounds does the rock
weigh?   about 110 pounds

* 7. Sonia has only dimes and nickels in her coin jar; they are in a ratio of 3
(101) to 5. If she has 120 coins in the jar, how many are dimes?   45 dimes

▶ * 8. **Analyze** The airline sold 25% of the seats on the plane at a discount.
(105) If 45 seats were sold at a discount, how many seats were on the plane?
How do you know your answer is correct?   180 seats; Sample: $\frac{25}{100} = \frac{45}{s}$,
$25s = 4500$, $s = \frac{4500}{25}$, $s = 180$, $\frac{25}{100} = \frac{45}{180} = \frac{1}{4}$ so 180 is correct.

Connect Complete the table to answer problems **9–11.**

	Fraction	Decimal	Percent
* 9. (99)	$\frac{3}{50}$	**a.** 0.06	**b.** 6%
* 10. (99)	**a.** $\frac{1}{25}$	0.04	**b.** 4%
▶* 11. (99)	**a.** $1\frac{1}{2}$	**b.** 1.5	150%

12. $4\frac{1}{12} + 5\frac{1}{6} + 2\frac{1}{4}$ $11\frac{1}{2}$
(61)

13. $\frac{4}{5} \times 3\frac{1}{3} \times 3$ 8
(72)

14. 0.125×80 10
(39)

15. $(1 + 0.5) \div (1 - 0.5)$ 3
(53)

16. Solve: $\frac{c}{12} = \frac{3}{4}$ 9
(85)

17. What is the total cost of an $8.75 purchase after 8% sales tax
(41) is added? $9.45

▶ See Math Conversations in the sidebar.

Math Conversations
Discussion opportunities are provided below.

Problem 6 **Estimate**
*"Will the rock weigh more than 100 pounds?
Explain why or why not."* Yes; since
1 kilogram weighs more than 2 pounds,
50 kilograms will weigh more than 50 × 2 or
100 pounds.

Problem 8 **Analyze**
*"Before we solve this problem, how can we
make an estimate of what the answer might
be?"* Sample: 25% is the same as $\frac{1}{4}$, and
since we are told that $\frac{1}{4}$ of a number is 45, the
number will be about 4 times greater than 45,
or a little less than 4 × 50, which is 200.

Ask students to make an estimate, and after
solving the problem, use the estimate to
decide the reasonableness of the exact answer.

Problem 11 **Connect**
*"Think about 150%. What general
conclusion can you make that describes
what happens when you change a percent
that is greater than 100 to a decimal
number?"* A percent greater than 100 is
equivalent to a decimal number that is
greater than 1.

(continued)

Math Conversations

Discussion opportunities are provided below.

Problem 19 (Conclude)

"How many angle measures of the quadrilateral are not given? Explain your answer." One, which is $\angle B$; $m\angle A = 115°$, $m\angle C = 90°$, and $m\angle D = 90°$

"What is the sum of the angle measures of a square?" $360°$

"Is a square a quadrilateral?" yes

"What is the sum of the angle measures of a quadrilateral?" $360°$

Problem 28 (Generalize)

"If you think you know what the rule is, what should you do before you write your answer?" Test the rule to make sure it is true for each pair of numbers in the table.

Errors and Misconceptions
Problem 28

When students use data from a table to write a rule to describe a function, they must make sure that the rule is true for each (x, y) pair of numbers in the table. A common error students sometimes make is to look at one pair of numbers and write a rule to describe that pair, without checking to make sure the rule is also true for all of the other number pairs in the table.

---

18. Write the decimal number one hundred five and five hundredths.
(35) 105.05

▶* **19.** (Conclude) The measure of $\angle A$ in quadrilateral $ABCD$ is 115°. What are the measures of $\angle B$ and $\angle C$? $m\angle B = 65°$; $m\angle C = 90°$
(98)

20. Write the prime factorization of 500 using exponents. $2^2 \cdot 5^3$
(73)

21. (Estimate) A quart is a little less than a liter, so a gallon is a little less than how many liters? 4 liters
(78)

22. Diane will spin the spinner twice. What is the probability that it will stop in sector 2 both times? $\frac{1}{16}$
(Inv. 10)

23. The perimeter of this isosceles triangle is 18 cm. What is the length of its longest side? 8 cm
(8)

24. What is the area of the triangle in problem **23**? 12 cm²
(79)

25. The temperature was −5°F at 6:00 a.m. By noon the temperature had risen 12 degrees. What was the noontime temperature? 7°F
(14, 100)

26. The weather report stated that the chance of rain is 30%. Use a decimal number to express the probability that it will not rain. 0.7
(58)

*27. Find the perimeter of this figure. Dimensions are in inches. 48 in.
(103)

Math Language
Recall that a **function** is a rule for using one number to calculate another number.

▶* **28.** (Generalize) Study this function table and describe the rule that helps you find y if you know x. Multiply x by 3 to find y.
(96)

x	$\frac{1}{2}$	1	$1\frac{1}{2}$	2
y	$1\frac{1}{2}$	3	$4\frac{1}{2}$	6

29. A room is 15 feet long and 12 feet wide.
(7, 31)
  a. The room is how many **yards** long and wide?
    5 yards long and 4 yards wide
  b. What is the area of the room in square yards? 20 square yards

*30. (Explain) Ned rolled a die and it turned up 6. If he rolls the die again, what is the probability that it will turn up 6? The probability is $\frac{1}{6}$ because the past outcome does not affect the future outcome.
(58)

▶ See Math Conversations in the sidebar.

Assessment

30–40 minutes

For use after Lesson 105

Distribute **Cumulative Test 20** to each student. Two versions of the test are available in *Saxon Math Course 1 Course Assessments Book*. Have students complete the **Power-Up Test** first. Allow 10 minutes. Then have students work the 20 numbered items on the **Cumulative Test**. Students may use copies of the answer sheet to record their work. Track individual and class progress with the **Test Analysis** forms.

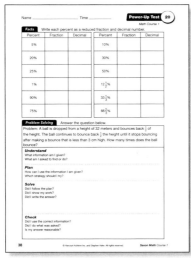

Power-Up Test 20

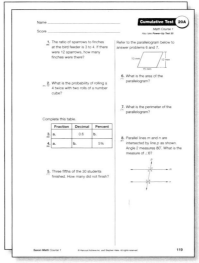

Cumulative Test 20A

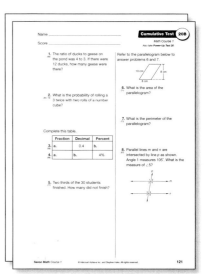

Alternative Cumulative Test 20B

Optional Answer Forms

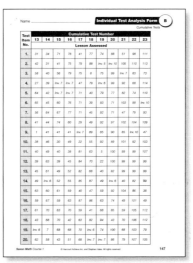

Individual Test Analysis Form

Class Test Analysis Form

Reteaching

Students who score below 80% on the assessment may be in need of reteaching. Look for the causes of student mistakes. If errors are conceptual, refer to the *Reteaching Masters* for reteaching.

Planting a Garden
Assign after Lesson 105 and Test 20

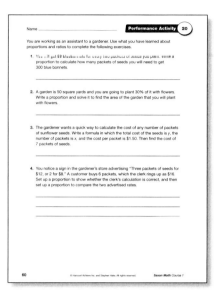

Performance Activity 20

Objectives
- Use ratios to make predictions in proportional situations.
- Use proportions to describe relationships and solve problems.
- Solve equations of the form $y = kx$.
- Communicate ideas through writing.

Materials
Performance Activity 20

Preparation
Make copies of **Performance Activity 20.** (One each per student.)

Time Requirement
15–30 minutes; Begin in class and complete at home.

Activity
Explain to students that for this activity they will be working as an assistant to a gardener. They will solve problems about purchasing and planting seeds. They will be required to look at a solution to a problem and analyze it to see if the solution is correct. Explain that all of the information students need is on **Performance Activity 20.**

Criteria for Evidence of Learning
- Sets up proportions properly and solves them correctly.
- Uses a formula accurately.
- Communicates ideas clearly through writing.

Meeting Standards

National Council of Teachers of Mathematics (NCTM)

Numbers and Operations

NO.1d Understand and use ratios and proportions to represent quantitative relationships

NO.3d Develop, analyze, and explain methods for solving problems involving proportions, such as scaling and finding equivalent ratios

Algebra

AL.2c Use symbolic algebra to represent situations and to solve problems, especially those that involve linear relationships

Problem Solving

PS.1b Solve problems that arise in mathematics and in other contexts

Communication

CM.3d Use the language of mathematics to express mathematical ideas precisely

Connections

CN.4a Recognize and use connections among mathematical ideas

• Two-Step Equations

Objectives

- Solve two-step equations.
- Use substitution to check the answer to a two-step equation.

Materials

- **Power Up K** (in *Instructional Masters*)

Power Up K

Math Language

English Learner (ESL)

maximum

Technology Resources

Student eBook Complete student textbook in electronic format.

Resources and Planner CD Assessment, reteaching, and instructional masters, plus a pacing calendar with standards.

Test and Practice Generator CD Create additional practice sheets and custom-made tests.

www.SaxonPublishers.com Visit for more student activities and planning materials.

Inclusion

Adaptations CD Adapted lessons, investigations, practice and assessments.

Meeting Standards

National Council of Teachers of Mathematics (NCTM)

Numbers and Operations

NO.2c Understand and use the inverse relationships of addition and subtraction, multiplication and division, and squaring and finding square roots to simplify computations and solve problems

Algebra

AL.2a Develop an initial conceptual understanding of different uses of variables

AL.2d Recognize and generate equivalent forms for simple algebraic expressions and solve linear equations

Problem-Solving Strategy: Draw a Diagram/
Write an Equation

Every whole number can be expressed as the sum of, *at most*, four square numbers. In the diagram we see that 12 is made up of one 3 × 3 square and three 1 + 1 squares. The number sentence that represents the diagram is, 12 = 9 + 1 + 1 + 1.

12

Diagram how 15, 18, and 20 are composed of four smaller squares, at most, and then write an equation for each diagram. (Hint: Diagrams do not have to be perfect rectangles.)

(Understand) **Understand the problem.**

"What information are we given?"

We are told that every whole number can be expressed as the sum of, *at most*, four square numbers.

"What are we asked to do?"

(1) Divide the rectangular diagrams for the numbers 15, 18, and 20 into four or fewer squares, and (2) write a number sentence for each diagram. We are permitted to rearrange the small squares.

(Plan) **Make a plan.**

"What problem-solving strategy will we use?"

We have been asked to *draw a diagram* and *write an equation*.

"Can every square number be represented as a square?"

Yes. Every square number is the product of two equal factors, and since the sides of a square are equal, those factors can represent the sides of a square.

(Solve) **Carry out the plan.**

15 = 9 + 4 + 1 + 1   18 = 9 + 9   20 = 16 + 4

(Check) **Look back.**

"Were we able to draw four or fewer squares for each of the numbers?"

Yes, 15 has four squares, 18 has two squares, and 20 has two squares.

"How did drawing diagrams help us show the statement that every whole number can be expressed as the sum of four or fewer square numbers?"

We can *see* that it works for these numbers.

Teacher Note: Have students write the sum of square numbers for numbers 1 to 30. Then ask, why they think that there will always be four or fewer square numbers. Sltudents may realize that if you start with any perfect square such as 36 (1 square), for 37 add one (2 squares), for 38 add one (three squares), for 39 add one (four squares). The next number is the previous perfect square plus 4. Since 4 is a perfect square, there will only be two squares. This pattern will repeat.

• Two-Step Equations

Power Up   *Building Power*

facts	Power Up K
mental math	**a. Number Sense:** 40 · 600 24,000
	b. Number Sense: 429 + 350 779
	c. Percent: 25% of 200 50
	d. Calculation: $60.00 − $59.45 $0.55
	e. Decimals: 1.2 × 100 120
	f. Number Sense: 60 × 12 720
	g. Measurement: Which is greater, 2000 milliliters or 1 liter? 2000 ml
	h. Calculation: Square 5, − 1, ÷ 4, × 5, + 2, ÷ 4, × 3, + 1, √ 5

6 11
6 13
6 31
6 33

problem solving	Every whole number can be expressed as the sum of, *at most,* four square numbers. In the diagram, we see that 12 is made up of one 3 × 3 square and three 1 × 1 squares. The number sentence that represents the diagram is 12 = 9 + 1 + 1 + 1.

1

Diagram how 15, 18, and 20 are composed of four smaller squares, at most, and then write an equation for each diagram. (*Hint:* Diagrams do not have to be perfect rectangles.)   See script for sample diagrams.

Facts

Distribute **Power Up K** to students. See answers below.

Mental Math

Before students begin the Mental Math exercise, do this counting exercise as a class.

Count by 25s from −200 to 200.

Encourage students to share different ways to mentally compute these exercises. Strategies for exercises **b** and **d** are listed below.

b. Add 300, then Add 50
429 + 300 = 729; 729 + 50 = 779
Add Place Values
400 + 300 + 20 + 50 + 9 = 700 + 70 + 9 = 779

d. Subtract $59, then Subtract 45¢
$60 − $59 = $1; $1 − 45¢ = 55¢
Solve an Addition Equation
$59.45 + n = $60.00; n = 55¢

Problem Solving

Refer to **Power-Up Discussion**, p. 553B.

New Concept   *Increasing Knowledge*

Since Lessons 3 and 4 we have solved one-step equations in which we look for an unknown number in addition, subtraction, multiplication, or division. In this lesson we will begin solving two-step equations that involve more than one operation.

Example 1

Solve: $3n − 1 = 20$

Solution

Let us think about what this equation means. When 1 is subtracted from $3n$, the result is 20. So $3n$ equals 21.

$$3n = 21$$

Since $3n$ means "3 times n" and $3n$ equals 21, we know that n equals 7.

$$n = 7$$

Thinking Skill

Discuss

In this two-step equation, what two steps do we use to find the solution?
Multiplying 3 times the value of n and subtracting 1 from the product.

Lesson 106   553

Instruction

Students can think of two-step equations as two operation equations. Although the two operations may be the same, they are often different.

When solving two-step equations, students should generalize that they will need to complete two operations to solve for the unknown.

(continued)

Facts

Complete each equivalent measure.

							Write a unit for each reference.
1. 1 cm	=	10	mm	13. 10 cm	=	100 mm	**Metric Units:**
2. 1 m	=	1000	mm	14. 2 m	=	200 cm	25. The thickness of a dime:
3. 1 m	=	100	cm	15. 5 km	=	5000 m	millimeter
4. 1 km	=	1000	m	16. 2.5 cm	=	25 mm	26. The width of a little finger:
5. 1 in.	=	2.54	cm	17. 1.5 m	=	150 cm	centimeter
6. 1 mi	≈	1610	m	18. 7.5 km	=	7500 m	27. The length of one big step:
							meter
7. 1 ft	=	12	in.	19. $\frac{1}{2}$ ft	=	6 in.	**U.S. Customary Units:**
8. 1 yd	=	36	in.	20. 2 ft	=	24 in.	28. The width of two fingers:
9. 1 yd	=	3	ft	21. 3 ft	=	36 in.	inch
10. 1 mi	=	5280	ft	22. 2 yd	=	6 ft	29. The length of a man's shoe:
11. 1 m	≈	39	in.	23. 10 yd	=	30 ft	foot
12. 1 km	≈	0.62	mi	24. 100 yd	=	300 ft	30. The length of one big step:
							yard

Instruction

Point out that this method of checking is often called checking by substitution. After making a substitution, students must then follow the Order of Operations to simplify each side of the equation.

Example 2

Instruction

To apply inverse operations, students will first need to recognize what operations are present in the equation, then apply the inverse of those operations, one inverse operation at a time.

When working through the steps of the solution, it is important for students to recognize that the inverse operations are always applied to both sides of the equation.

Practice Set

Problems a–f (Error Alert)

Before solving each equation for its unknown, ask these questions.

"What operations are present in this equation?" Sample: addition and multiplication

"What is the inverse of each of those operations?" Sample: The inverse of add 1 is subtract 1 and the inverse of multiply by 3 is divide by 3.

After completing each equation, give students sufficient time to use substitution to check their work.

We show our work this way:

$$3n - 1 = 20$$
$$3n = 21$$
$$n = 7$$

We check our answer this way:

$$3(7) - 1 = 20$$
$$21 - 1 = 20$$
$$20 = 20$$

Example 1 describes one method for solving equations. It is a useful method for solving equations by inspection—by mentally calculating the solution. However, there is an algebraic method that is helpful for solving more complicated equations. The method uses inverse operations to isolate the variable—to get the variable by itself on one side of the equal sign. We show this method in example 2.

Example 2

Solve $3n - 1 = 20$ using inverse operations.

Solution

We focus our attention on the side of the equation with the variable. We see that n is multiplied by 3 and 1 is subtracted from that product. We will undo the subtraction by adding, and we will undo the multiplication by dividing in order to isolate the variable.

Step:	Justification:
$3n - 1 = 20$	Given equation
$3n - 1 + 1 = 20 + 1$	Added 1 to both sides of the equation
$3n = 21$	Simplified both sides
$\dfrac{3n}{3} = \dfrac{21}{3}$	Divided both sides by 3
$n = 7$	Simplified both sides

We performed two operations (addition and division) to the left side of the equation to isolate the variable. Notice that we also performed the same two operations on the right side to keep the equation balanced at each step.

Practice Set

▶ Solve each equation showing the steps of the solution. Then check your answer.

a. $3n + 1 = 16$ **b.** $2x - 1 = 9$

c. $3y - 2 = 22$ **d.** $5m + 3 = 33$

e. $4w - 1 = 35$ **f.** $7a + 4 = 25$

a. $3n + 1 = 16$
$3n = 15$
$n = 5$

b. $2x - 1 = 9$
$2x = 10$
$x = 5$

c. $3y - 2 = 22$
$3y = 24$
$y = 8$

d. $5m + 3 = 33$
$5m = 30$
$m = 6$

e. $4w - 1 = 35$
$4w = 36$
$w = 9$

f. $7a + 4 = 25$
$7a = 21$
$a = 3$

▶ See Math Conversations in the sidebar.

Math Background

In example 1, the explanation for how to solve $3n - 1 = 20$ for n is a way of describing how inverse operations are used to solve for n.

For example, rewriting $3n - 1 = 20$ as $3n = 21$ is the same as adding 1 to both sides of the equation

$$3n - 1 + 1 = 20 + 1$$
$$3n = 21$$

Deciding that $n = 7$ when $3n = 21$ is the same as dividing both sides of the equation by 3.

$$\frac{3n}{3} = \frac{21}{3}$$
$$n = 7$$

This two-step equation was solved using two inverse operations.

1. (Evaluate) The average of three numbers is 20. If the greatest is 28 and the least is 15, what is the third number?   17
(18)

* 2. A map is drawn to the scale of 1 inch = 10 miles. How many miles apart are two points that are $2\frac{1}{2}$ inches apart on the map?   25 mi
(95)

$$\frac{2\frac{1}{2} \text{ in.}}{1} \times \frac{10 \text{ mi}}{1 \text{ in.}}$$

3. What number is one fourth of 360?   90
(29)

4. (Connect) What percent of a quarter is a nickel?   20%
(75)

5. (Analyze) Anita places a set of number cards 1 through 30 in a bag. She draws out a card. What is the probability that the number will have the digit 1 in it? Express the probability as a fraction and as a decimal. $\frac{2}{5}$, 0.4
(58, 74)

Solve and check:

* 6. $8x + 1 = 25$ 3
(106)

* 7. $3w - 5 = 25$ 10
(106)

* 8. Calculate mentally:
(100, 104)

   a. $-15 + +20$ $+5$

   b. $-15 - +20$ -35

   c. $(-3) + (-2) - (-1)$ -4

* 9. A sign in the elevator says that the maximum load is 4000 pounds. How many tons is 4000 pounds?   2 tons
(102)

10. (Connect) One gallon minus one quart equals how many pints?   6 pints
(78)

11. The ratio of kangaroos to koalas was 9 to 5. If there were 414 kangaroos, how many koalas were there?   230 koalas
(88)

(Connect) Complete the table to answer problems 12–14.

	Fraction	Decimal	Percent
12. (99)	$\frac{1}{8}$	a. 0.125	b. 12.5%
13. (99)	a. $1\frac{4}{5}$	1.8	b. 180%
14. (99)	a. $\frac{3}{100}$	b. 0.03	3%

15. $8\frac{1}{3} - 3\frac{1}{2}$ $4\frac{5}{6}$
(63)

16. $2\frac{1}{2} \div 100$ $\frac{1}{40}$
(68)

17. $0.014 \div 0.5$ 0.028
(49)

18. Write the standard notation for the following: 60,907
(92)

$$(6 \times 10^4) + (9 \times 10^2) + (7 \times 10^0)$$

▶ See Math Conversations in the sidebar.

English Learners

In example 9, explain the term **maximum.** Write the word on the board and underline the prefix maxi-. Say,

> *"The prefix maxi- refers to the largest or biggest amount of something. In this case, the elevator can hold a maximum weight load of 4,000 pounds, which means that it can hold up to, and no more than 4,000 pounds."*

Ask students what is the maximum weight they can carry or distance they can run.

---

3 Written Practice

Math Conversations
Discussion opportunities are provided below.

Problem 1 (Evaluate)
"Explain how to find the average of a group of numbers." Divide the sum of the numbers by the number of addends.

"If you know the number of addends, and you know the average, how can you find the sum of the addends?"

If students have difficulty understanding that the answer to the question above is to multiply the number of addends by the average, give them an opportunity to solve a simpler problem, then ask the question a second time. For example,

"Suppose the average of two numbers is 5. What is the sum of those numbers?" 10

"If one of those numbers is 7, what is the other number? Explain how you know." 3; If the sum of two numbers is 10, and one number is 7, the other number is $10 - 7$.

Problem 5 (Analyze)
Extend the Problem
Challenge students to express each of the following answers as a fraction in simplest form.

"What is the probability that Anita will chose a number that is a multiple of 5?" $\frac{1}{5}$

"What is the probability that Anita will choose a prime number?" $\frac{1}{3}$

Errors and Misconceptions
Problem 4
Encourage students who have difficulty solving the problem to begin by writing the number of cents in a quarter (25) and the number of cents in a nickel (5). Then have them find the fraction of a quarter that is a nickel ($\frac{5}{25}$), and convert that fraction to a percent.

For additional practice, ask students to find the percent of a half-dollar that a dime represents.   20%

Problem 18
It is a misconception for students to assume that the number of digits in the expanded notation of a number is the same as the number of digits in the standard notation of that number. Although the number of digits in an expanded notation will sometimes be the same as the number of digits in a standard notation, there will often be a greater number of digits in the standard notation because expanded notations do not include zeros.

(continued)

Math Conversations

Discussion opportunities are provided below.

Problem 22 Connect

"What percent of the individual blocks are not visible?" 25%

Problem 25 Analyze

"This figure has 6 sides. How many side measures of this figure are not given?" two

Sketch the figure on the board or overhead. After labeling the given measures of the figure, invite one or two volunteers to the board or overhead to explain and demonstrate how to find the unknown measures.

Problem 30 Formulate

Extend the Problem

Ask students to exchange questions, then answer the questions and compare answers.

---

19. *Evaluate* The prime factorization of one hundred is $2^2 \cdot 5^2$. The prime factorization of one thousand is $2^3 \cdot 5^3$. Write the prime factorization of one million using exponents. $2^6 \cdot 5^6$
(73)

20. A 1-foot ruler broke into two pieces so that one piece was $5\frac{1}{4}$ inches long. How long was the other piece? $6\frac{3}{4}$ inches
(63)

* **21.** $6 + 3^2(5 - \sqrt{4})$ 33
(92)

▶ **22.** *Connect* If each small block has a volume of one cubic centimeter, what is the volume of this rectangular prism? 24 cubic centimeters
(82)

23. Three inches is what percent of a foot? 25%
(75)

24. Use the figure on the right to answer **a–c.**
(31)
  a. What is the area of the shaded rectangle? 6 cm²

  b. What is the area of the unshaded rectangle? 28 cm²

  c. What is the combined area of the two rectangles? 34 cm²

3 cm
2 cm
4 cm
7 cm

▶* **25.** *Analyze* What is the perimeter of the hexagon in problem 24? 26 cm
(103)

26. *Estimate* The diameter of each tire on Jan's bike is two feet. The circumference of each tire is closest to which of the following? (Use 3.14 for π.) **B**
(47)
  A 6 ft   **B** 6 ft 3 in.   **C** 6 ft 8 in.   **D** 7 ft

* **27.** What is the area of this triangle? 14 cm²
(79)

7 cm
4 cm
5 cm

This table shows the number of miles Celina rode her bike each day during the week. Use this information to answer problems **28–30.**

28. If the data were rearranged in order of distance (with 3 miles listed first and 10 miles listed last), then which distance would be in the middle of the list? 6 miles
(Inv. 5)

29. What was the average number of miles Celina rode each day? 6 miles
(18)

▶* **30.** *Formulate* Write a comparison question that relates to the table, and then answer the question. See student work.
(13)

Miles of Bike Riding for the Week

Day	Miles
Sunday	7
Monday	3
Tuesday	6
Wednesday	10
Thursday	5
Friday	4
Saturday	7

▶ See Math Conversations in the sidebar.

Looking Forward

Solving two-step equations and using substitution to check answers prepares students for:

- **Investigation 11,** using ratio boxes and solving proportions to find corresponding parts of scale drawings or models.

- **Lesson 119,** writing and solving equations to find a whole when a percent is known.

• Area of Complex Shapes

Objectives
• Find the area of a complex shape.

Lesson Preparation

Materials
• **Power Up M** (in *Instructional Masters*)
• **Manipulative kit: compasses**
Optional
• **Manipulative kit: inch or metric rulers**
• **Teacher-provided material: grid paper**

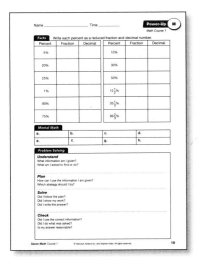

Power Up M

Math Language

	English Learner (ESL)
	extend

Technology Resources

Student eBook Complete student textbook in electronic format.

Resources and Planner CD Assessment, reteaching, and instructional masters, plus a pacing calendar with standards.

Test and Practice Generator CD Create additional practice sheets and custom-made tests.

www.SaxonPublishers.com Visit for more student activities and planning materials.

Inclusion

 Adaptations CD Adapted lessons, investigations, practice and assessments.

Meeting Standards

National Council of Teachers of Mathematics (NCTM)

Geometry

GM.4d Use geometric models to represent and explain numerical and algebraic relationships

Measurement

ME.2c Develop and use formulas to determine the circumference of circles and the area of triangles, parallelograms, trapezoids, and circles and develop strategies to find the area of more-complex shapes

Connections

CN.4b Understand how mathematical ideas interconnect and build on one another to produce a coherent whole

Problem-Solving Strategy: Use Logical Reasoning/
Write an Equation

Laura has nickels, dimes, and quarters in her pocket. She has half as many dimes as nickels and half as many quarters as dimes. If Laura has four dimes, then how much money does she have in her pocket?

(Understand) **Understand the problem.**

"What information are we given?"

Laura has nickels, dimes, and quarters in her pocket. She has half as many dimes as nickels and half as many quarters as dimes.

"What are we asked to do?"

Determine the amount of money Laura has in her pocket, knowing that she has four dimes.

(Plan) **Make a plan.**

"How can we use the information we know to solve the problem?"

We will *use logical reasoning* and number sense to determine the number of quarters and nickels Laura has. Then we *write an equation* for the total value.

(Solve) **Carry out the plan.**

"What is the value of Laura's dimes?"

40¢

"How many quarters does Laura have? What is their value?"

If Laura has half as many quarters as dimes, and Laura has four dimes, then she has two quarters, which is 50¢.

"How many nickels does Laura have? What is their value?"

If Laura has half as many dimes as nickels, and Laura has four dimes, then she has eight nickels, which is 40¢.

"How much money does Laura have in her pocket?"

40¢ + 50¢ + 40¢ = 130¢ or $1.30

(Check) **Look back.**

"Did we answer the question that was asked?"

Yes. We determined how much money Laura has in her pocket ($1.30).

LESSON
107
• Area of Complex Shapes

Power Up   *Building Power*

facts   Power Up M

mental math

a. **Number Sense:** 100 · 100   10,000

b. **Number Sense:** 376 − 150   226

c. **Percent:** 10% of 200   20

d. **Calculation:** $12.89 + $9.99 $22.88

e. **Decimals:** 6.0 ÷ 100   0.06

f. **Number Sense:** $\frac{360}{60}$ 6

g. **Measurement:** How many pints are in a gallon?   8 pints

h. **Calculation:** $10 \times 6, + 4, \sqrt{}, \times 3, + 1, \sqrt{}, \times 7, + 1, \sqrt{}$ 6

problem solving

Laura has nickels, dimes, and quarters in her pocket. She has half as many dimes as nickels and half as many quarters as dimes. If Laura has four dimes, then how much money does she have in her pocket? $1.30

New Concept   *Increasing Knowledge*

In Lesson 103 we found the perimeter of complex shapes. In this lesson we will practice finding the area of complex shapes. One way to find the area of a complex shape is to divide the shape into two or more parts, find the area of each part, and then add the areas. Think of how the shape below could be divided into two rectangles.

Example

Thinking Skill

Classify

Based on the number of sides and their lengths, what is the geometric name of this figure? an irregular hexagon

Find the area of this figure.

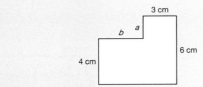

Solution

We will show two ways to divide this shape into two rectangles. We use the skills we learned in Lesson 103 to find that side *a* is 2 cm and side *b* is 4 cm. We extend side *b* with a dashed line segment to divide the figure into two rectangles.

Lesson 107   557

Facts   Write each percent as a reduced fraction and decimal number.

Percent	Fraction	Decimal	Percent	Fraction	Decimal
5%	$\frac{1}{20}$	0.05	10%	$\frac{1}{10}$	0.1
20%	$\frac{1}{5}$	0.2	30%	$\frac{3}{10}$	0.3
25%	$\frac{1}{4}$	0.25	50%	$\frac{1}{2}$	0.5
1%	$\frac{1}{100}$	0.01	$12\frac{1}{2}$%	$\frac{1}{8}$	0.125
90%	$\frac{9}{10}$	0.9	$33\frac{1}{3}$%	$\frac{1}{3}$	Rounds to 0.333
75%	$\frac{3}{4}$	0.75	$66\frac{2}{3}$%	$\frac{2}{3}$	Rounds to 0.667

---

1 Power Up

Facts
Distribute **Power Up M** to students. See answers below.

Mental Math
Encourage students to share different ways to mentally compute these exercises. Strategies for exercises **a** and **c** are listed below.

a. **Add Four Zeros to the Product of 1 × 1**
   $1 \times 1 = 1$; $100 \times 100 = 10,000$
   Multiply Powers of 10
   $100 \cdot 100 = 10^2 \cdot 10^2 = 10^4 = 10,000$

c. **Double 10% of 100**
   10% of 100 = 10; $10 \times 2 = 20$
   Shift the Decimal Point One Place Left
   10% of 200 = 20.0 = 20

Problem Solving
Refer to **Power-Up Discussion**, p. 557B.

2 New Concepts

Instruction
If students find the term *complex shape* intimidating, explain that a complex shape is simply a shape that is made up of two or more smaller shapes.

When working with complex shapes, students should generalize that the area of the entire shape can be found by first finding the area of each of the smaller shapes. Addition is then used to find the sum of the areas.

Example
Instruction

"How many side measures of this figure are given?" four

"How many side measures of this figure must we find?" two

(continued)

② New Concepts (Continued)

Instruction

Sketch the figure on the board or overhead. Invite a volunteer to use the figure to explain how to find the measure of side *a* and how to find the measure of side *b*.

> **"What formula is used to find the area of a rectangle?"** Sample: area equals length times width

Students should conclude from the solution that dividing the figure into smaller parts does not change the shape of the figure, and because the shape of the figure does not change, the area of the figure does not change.

Practice Set

Problem a [Model]

Encourage students who are having difficulty with this problem to label all of the sides of each figure before dividing the figure into rectangles.

Problem b [Error Alert]

After dividing the figure into two parts, make sure students recognize that the base of the triangle has a measure of 4 centimeters and its height has a measure of 6 centimeters.

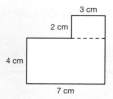

The length and width of the smaller rectangle are 3 cm and 2 cm, so its area is 6 cm². The larger rectangle is 7 cm by 4 cm, so its area is 28 cm². We find the combined area of the two rectangles by adding.

$$6 \text{ cm}^2 + 28 \text{ cm}^2 = \mathbf{34 \text{ cm}^2}$$

A second way to divide the figure into two rectangles is to extend side *a*.

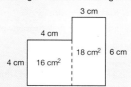

Thinking Skill

Define

What does it mean when we say that the shape of a figure is *complex*? Sample: A complex figure is composed of two or more simpler figures.

Extending side *a* forms a 4-cm by 4-cm rectangle and a 3-cm by 6-cm rectangle. Again we find the combined area of the two rectangles by adding.

$$16 \text{ cm}^2 + 18 \text{ cm}^2 = 34 \text{ cm}^2$$

Either way we divide the figure, we find that its area is 34 cm².

Practice Set
  ▸ **a.** [Model] Draw two ways to divide this figure into two rectangles. Then find the area of the figure each way.

50 square inches

  ▸ **b.** This trapezoid can be divided into a rectangle and a triangle. Find the area of the trapezoid. 72 cm²

Written Practice   *Strengthening Concepts*

1. If the divisor is eight tenths and the dividend is forty-eight hundredths,
(49) what is the quotient? 0.6

2. The plans for the clubhouse were drawn so that 1 inch equals 2 feet. In
(95) the plans the clubhouse was 4 inches tall. The actual clubhouse will be how tall? 8 feet

3. If 600 roses and 800 tulips were sold, what was the ratio of tulips sold
(23) to roses sold? $\frac{4}{3}$

▸ See Math Conversations in the sidebar.

Manipulative Use

Using grid paper and a ruler, invite students to **draw the complex shape** in the example. The grid lines of the paper should be counted so that the drawing is the same shape as the shape in the example. Students can then count grid lines to confirm the missing dimensions, and count grid squares to confirm the area of the shape.

English Learners

In the solution to the example, explain the term **extend**. Draw a square on the board and extend the left side upward and bottom side to the right. Then, connect the endpoints to make a larger square. Say,

> **"To extend something means to make it bigger or to increase its size. When we extend the sides of this square, we can make it larger."**

Ask students to extend the sides of a triangle to form a larger shape.

4. *(8, 60)* **Conclude** What percent of the perimeter of a regular pentagon is the length of one side? 20%

▶ *** 5.** *(102)* **Analyze** The mass of a dollar bill is about one gram. A gram is what fraction of a kilogram? $\frac{1}{1000}$

* 6. *(100, 104)* Calculate mentally:

  a. $+15 + -10$ $+5$

  b. $-15 - -10$ -5

  c. $(+3) + (-5) - (-2) - (+4)$ -4

7. *(92)* $10^3 - (10^2 - \sqrt{100}) - 10^3 \div 100$ 900

▶ *** 8.** *(85, 105)* **Analyze** Complete this proportion: $\frac{6}{u} = \frac{8}{1.2}$ $u = 0.9$

Connect Complete the table to answer problems **9–11.**

	Fraction	Decimal	Percent
9. *(99)*	$1\frac{1}{10}$	**a.** 1.1	**b.** 110%
10. *(99)*	**a.** $\frac{9}{20}$	0.45	**b.** 45%
11. *(99)*	**a.** $\frac{4}{5}$	**b.** 0.8	80%

12. *(61)* $5\frac{3}{8} + 4\frac{1}{4} + 3\frac{1}{2}$ $13\frac{1}{8}$

13. *(72)* $\frac{8}{3} \cdot \frac{5}{12} \cdot \frac{9}{10}$ 1

14. *(38)* $64.8 + 8.42 + 24$ 97.22

▶ **15.** *(93, 98)* **Conclude** If one acute angle of a right triangle measures 55°, then what is the measure of the other acute angle?   35°

16. *(78)* How many ounces is one half of a pint?   8 ounces

* 17. *(106)* Solve and check: $3m + 8 = 44$ $m = 12$

18. *(92)* Write one hundred ten million in expanded notation using exponents. $(1 \times 10^8) + (1 \times 10^7)$

19. *(20)* What is the greatest common factor of 30 and 45?   15

▶ *** 20.** *(29, 31)* A square with sides 1 inch long is divided into $\frac{1}{2}$-by-$\frac{1}{4}$-inch rectangles.

  a. What is the area of each $\frac{1}{2}$-by-$\frac{1}{4}$-in. rectangle? $\frac{1}{8}$ in.^{2}

  b. What fraction of the square is shaded? $\frac{1}{8}$

1 in.

1 in.

$\frac{1}{2}$ in.

$\frac{1}{4}$ in.

21. *(82)* How many blocks that are 1 foot long on each edge would be needed to fill a cubical box with edges 1 yard long?   27 blocks

22. *(49)* $0.3n = \$6.39$ \$21.30

▶ See Math Conversations in the sidebar.

Math Conversations

Discussion opportunities are provided below.

Problem 5   Analyze

To find the fraction of a kilogram that 1 gram represents, students may find it easier to first change 1 gram to kilograms.

> *"Which way does the decimal point shift, and in which direction does it shift, when we change grams to kilograms?"* three places to the left

> *"One gram is the same as what number of kilograms?"* 0.001 kg

Write the decimal number 0.001 on the board or overhead.

> *"What fraction is equivalent to this decimal number?"* $\frac{1}{1000}$

Problem 8   Analyze

Remind students that proportions can be solved by setting the cross products equal to each other and solving for the unknown, or using a constant factor.

For this problem, students are likely to use cross products because the constant factor is not obvious. After students complete the problem, challenge them to name the mixed number that represents the constant factor using only mental math. $\frac{8}{6} = 1\frac{1}{3}$

Errors and Misconceptions
Problem 15

Ask students who conclude there is not enough information present to solve the problem to name the degree measure of a right angle. Then point out that two measures of the triangle angle are given: one measure is 55° and the other measure is 90° because a right triangle contains a right angle.

Problem 20

Some students may assume that the only way to find the area of the shaded part is to find the product of its length and width.

Explain that another way to find the area is to recognize that 1 in. $\times$ 1 in. (or 1 square inch) represents the area of the whole, and the whole is divided into 8 equal parts. Therefore, the area of one part of the whole is simply 1 in.^{2} $\div$ 8 or $\frac{1}{8}$ in.^{2}.

(continued)

Math Conversations

Discussion opportunities are provided below.

Problem 28 [Analyze]

"When we subtract pounds and ounces, in which column do we begin subtracting, the pounds column or the ounces column?" the ounces column

"What must we do to subtract 7 ounces from 3 ounces?" Sample: rename one pound as ounces

"To complete the subtraction, 12 pounds 3 ounces will be renamed as how many pounds and ounces?" 11 pounds 19 ounces

---

* **23.** What is the perimeter of this hexagon?
  (103) 30 cm

* **24.** Divide the hexagon at right into two
  (107) rectangles. What is the combined area of the two rectangles? 41 cm²

* **25.** This trapezoid has been divided into two
  (107) triangles. Find the area of the trapezoid by adding the areas of the two triangles.
  72 cm²

The table shows the age of the first nine American presidents at the time they were inaugurated. Use the information for problems **26–27.**

President	Age in Years at Inauguration
George Washington	57
John Adams	61
Thomas Jefferson	57
James Madison	57
James Monroe	58
John Quincy Adams	57
Andrew Jackson	61
Martin Van Buren	54
William Henry Harrison	68

26. **a.** What age appears most frequently? 57 years
(Inv. 5)

  b. When the ages are arranged in order from least to greatest, what age appears in the middle? 57 years

  c. [Estimate] Find the average age at inauguration of the first nine presidents. Round your answer to the nearest whole year. 59 years

  d. [Connect] Name the mathematical term for the answers to **a, b,** and **c.**
  mode, median, mean

* **27.** [Represent] Choose an appropriate graph and display the data in the
  (Inv. 5) table. See student work.

► * **28.**   12 lb 3 oz
  (102) − 8 lb 7 oz
         3 lb 12 oz

29. See student work.

29. [Model] Use a compass to draw a circle that has a diameter of 10 cm.
(47)

  a. What is the radius of the circle? 5 cm

  b. Calculate the circumference of the circle. (Use 3.14 for π.) 31.4 cm

30. $\dfrac{10\ \text{gallons}}{1} \times \dfrac{31.5\ \text{miles}}{1\ \text{gallon}}$ 315 miles
(95)

► See Math Conversations in the sidebar.

• Transformations

Objectives

- Identify and describe rotations, translations, and reflections.
- Use transformations to change the position of a figure.

Lesson Preparation

Materials

- **Power Up M** (in *Instructional Masters*)
- **Investigation Activity 15** (in *Instructional Masters*) or **graph paper**
- **Teacher-provided material: scissors, paper** or a **3 × 5 card**

Math Language

New	Maintain	English Learners (ESL)
reflect (reflection)	congruent	counter-clockwise
rotate (rotation)		
transformation		
translate		

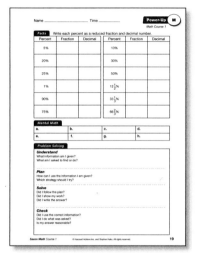

Power Up M

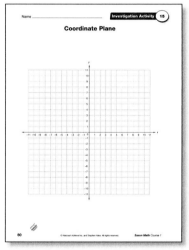

Investigation Activity 15

Technology Resources

Student eBook Complete student textbook in electronic format.

Resources and Planner CD Assessment, reteaching, and instructional masters, plus a pacing calendar with standards.

Test and Practice Generator CD Create additional practice sheets and custom-made tests.

www.SaxonPublishers.com Visit for more student activities and planning materials.

Inclusion

Adaptations CD Adapted lessons, investigations, practice and assessments.

Meeting Standards

National Council of Teachers of Mathematics (NCTM)

Geometry

GM.3a Describe sizes, positions, and orientations of shapes under informal transformations such as flips, turns, slides, and scaling

GM.3b Examine the congruence, similarity, and line or rotational symmetry of objects using transformations

Communication

CM.3d Use the language of mathematics to express mathematical ideas precisely

Problem-Solving Strategy: Use a Table/ Find a Pattern

If two people shake hands, there is one handshake. If three people shake hands, there are three handshakes. From this table can you predict the number of handshakes with 6 people? Draw a diagram or act it out to confirm your prediction.

Number in Group	2	3	4	5	6
Number of Handshakes	1	3	6	10	

(Understand) **Understand the problem.**

"What information are we given?"

We have been given a table that shows the number of handshakes for a specific number of people.

"What are we asked to do?"

Predict the number of handshakes if there are 6 people.

(Plan) **Make a plan.**

"What problem-solving strategy will we use?"

We will *use the table* that has been provided to *find a pattern.*

(Solve) **Carry out the plan.**

"Let's look at the table and see if we can find a pattern. How many handshakes took place with 2 people?" 1

"How many more handshakes happened when we added another person?"

2 more

"Why do you think there were only two more handshakes?"

The new person had to shake hands with the two people that were already there, so there were only two more handshakes.

"How many handshakes took place with 4 people?" 6

"How many more handshakes occurred when we added another person?"

4 more

"Why do you think there were only 4 more handshakes?"

The new person had to shake hands with four people that were already there, so there were only four more handshakes.

"With 5 people we have ten handshakes, can you predict how many handshakes will take place with 6 people?" 15

"How do you know?"

If there are 10 handshakes with 5 people, then adding another person means they will have to shake hands with five people which adds five handshakes.

(Check) **Look back.**

"Did we find the answers to the questions that were asked?"

Yes. We found that fifteen handshakes will occur when there are 6 people.

"Can we draw a diagram to confirm the count?"

Yes, each dot represents a person and each segment between dots represents a handshake.

• Transformations

facts | Power Up M

mental math

a. **Number Sense:** 70 · 70   4900

b. **Number Sense:** 296 − 150   146

c. **Percent:** 25% of $20 $5

d. **Calculation:** $8.23 + $8.99 $17.22

e. **Number Sense:** 75 ÷ 100   0.75

f. **Number Sense:** $\frac{800}{40}$ 20

g. **Measurement:** Which is greater 2 liters or 3000 milliliters?   3000 ml

h. **Calculation:** 8 × 8, − 4, ÷ 2, + 5, ÷ 5, × 8, − 1, ÷ 5, × 2, − 1, ÷ 3   7

problem solving

If two people shake hands, there is one handshake. If three people shake hands, there are three handshakes. From this table can you predict the number of handshakes with 6 people? Draw a diagram or act it out to confirm your prediction.   15 handshakes

Number in Group	Number of Handshakes
2	1
3	3
4	6
5	10
6	

New Concept   *Increasing Knowledge*

Math Language
Two figures are **congruent** if one figure has the same shape and size as the other figure.

One way to determine whether two figures are congruent is to position one figure "on top of" the other. The two triangles below are congruent. As we will see below, triangle *ABC* can be positioned "on top of" triangle *XYZ*, illustrating that it is congruent to triangle *XYZ*.

Lesson 108   561

Facts   Write each percent as a reduced fraction and decimal number.

Percent	Fraction	Decimal	Percent	Fraction	Decimal
5%	$\frac{1}{20}$	0.05	10%	$\frac{1}{10}$	0.1
20%	$\frac{1}{5}$	0.2	30%	$\frac{3}{10}$	0.3
25%	$\frac{1}{4}$	0.25	50%	$\frac{1}{2}$	0.5
1%	$\frac{1}{100}$	0.01	$12\frac{1}{2}$%	$\frac{1}{8}$	0.125
90%	$\frac{9}{10}$	0.9	$33\frac{1}{3}$%	$\frac{1}{3}$	Rounds to 0.333
75%	$\frac{3}{4}$	0.75	$66\frac{2}{3}$%	$\frac{2}{3}$	Rounds to 0.667

Facts
Distribute **Power Up M** to students. See answers below.

Mental Math
Before students begin the Mental Math exercise, do this counting exercise as a class.

Count by $\frac{1}{16}$s from $\frac{1}{16}$ to 1.

Encourage students to share different ways to mentally compute these exercises. Strategies for exercises **b** and **f** are listed below.

b. **Subtract 100, then Subtract 50**
   296 − 100 = 196; 196 − 50 = 146
   Break Apart 296
   250 − 150 + 46 = 100 + 46 = 146

f. **Cancel Zeros**
   $\frac{800}{40} = \frac{80\cancel{0}}{4\cancel{0}} = \frac{80}{4} = 20$
   Shift the Decimal Points One Place
   $\frac{800}{40} = \frac{80.0}{4.0} = \frac{80}{4} = 20$

Problem Solving
Refer to **Power-Up Discussion**, p. 561B.

Instruction
In a general sense, a transformation is a change in a figure's position.

Demonstrate each transformation that is used to position triangle *ABC* on triangle *XYZ*. Prior to this lesson, create large cutouts of triangles *ABC* and *XYZ* from tagboard or construction paper by cutting along the diagonal of a rectangular sheet of paper.

Label the angles of each triangle as shown. Use a marker of one color for the front of each triangle and a marker of another color for the back of each triangle. Rest triangle *XYZ* on the chalk tray or post it on a bulletin board. Demonstrate how to rotate triangle *ABC*, then translate triangle *ABC*, and finally reflect triangle *ABC* in the manner shown on the next pages and until triangle *ABC* is positioned on triangle *XYZ*.

(Note: Keep these cutout triangles for use in Lesson 109.)

(continued)

2 Activity

Instruction

Each transformation is named in blue type and is accompanied by a word in parentheses that describes the transformation in a more general way.

rotate (turn)
translation (slide)
reflect (flip)

As you complete this lesson, include both words each time you talk about a transformation. For example, say "the triangle rotates or turns 90°" instead of saying "the triangle rotates 90°."

Your use of both words will help students better understand the concept of transformations.

Activity

Instruction

Organize students into pairs or small groups and give each pair or group scissors, pencils, and paper.

An alternative to folding and cutting paper is to ask students to form two congruent triangles by cutting a 3 by 5 index card in half along a diagonal.

Have students read the instructions for the activity and give them an opportunity to ask questions before they begin.

During the activity, circulate among the groups and observe students as they perform the transformations, helping individual students as needed.

(continued)

To position triangle *ABC* on triangle *XYZ*, we make three different kinds of moves. First, we **rotate** (turn) triangle *ABC* 90° counterclockwise.

Second, we **translate** (slide) triangle *ABC* to the right so that side *AC* aligns with side *XZ*.

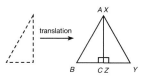

Third, we **reflect** (flip) triangle *ABC* so that angle *B* is positioned on top of angle *Y*.

Thinking Skill

Generalize

If a triangle is rotated, translated, or reflected, will the resulting triangle be congruent to the original triangle? Explain.   Yes. The size and shape of the triangle have not been changed. Only the triangle's position changes.

The three different kinds of moves we made are called **transformations**. We list them in the following table:

Transformations

Name	Movement
Rotation	turning a figure about a certain point
Translation	sliding a figure in one direction without turning the figure
Reflection	reflecting a figure as in a mirror or "flipping" a figure over a certain line

Activity

Transformations

Materials needed:

- scissors
- pencil and paper

Follow these steps to cut out a pair of congruent triangles with a partner or small group.

Step 1: Fold a piece of paper in half.

Step 2: Draw a triangle on the folded paper.

Math Background

A transformation in which the size and the shape of a figure does not change is called an isometry. Rotations, translations, and reflections are all examples of isometries.

Not all transformations are isometries. For example, in a dilation, the shape of a figure does not change, but its size increases. A photograph enlargement is an example of a dilation.

English Learners

Draw a clock face on the board marking 12, 3, 6, and 9. Say:

"When a clock moves in the direction to tell time, we say it is moving clockwise. When something moves in the opposite direction we say it is moving counterclockwise."

Ask a student to draw an arrow inside the clock face moving in the counterclockwise direction. Have students draw different shapes and rotate them in counterclockwise directions.

Step 3: While the paper is folded, cut out the triangle so that two triangles are cut out at the same time.

Have one partner (or group member) place the two triangles on a desk or table so that the triangles are apart and in different orientations. Let the other partner (or group member) move one of the triangles until it is positioned on top of the other triangle. The moves permitted are rotation, translation, and reflection. Take the moves one at a time and describe them as you go. After successfully aligning the triangles, switch roles and repeat the procedure. Allow each student one or two opportunities to perform and describe a transformation.

Practice Set

Sample: The transformations in problems **b, d,** and **e** could each be accomplished by a reflection in a line that does not make up a side of one of the triangles. (That is, the axis of symmetry either lies outside of the triangles or intersects them at only one point.)

▶ **Conclude** For problems **a–e,** what transformation(s) could be used to position triangle I on triangle II? For exercise **f** triangle *ABC* is reflected across the *y*-axis. Write the coordinates of the vertices of △*ABC* and the coordinates of the vertices of its reflection △*A′B′C′* (Read, "*A* prime, *B* prime, *C* prime.") Explain all answers.

a.
reflection

b.
translation

c.
rotation

d.
translation and reflection

e.
rotation and reflection

f.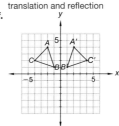

f.
A (−2, 4)	*A′* (2, 4)
B (−1, 1)	*B′* (1, 1)
C (−4, 2)	*C′* (4, 2)

Written Practice   *Strengthening Concepts*

1. What is the sum of the first five positive even numbers?   30
(10)

▶ **2.** **Analyze** The team's win-loss ratio is 4 to 3. If the team has won 12 games, how many games has the team lost?   9 games
(88)

* 3. **Justify** Five students were absent today. The teacher reported that 80% of the students were present. Find the number of students who were present and justify your answer.   20 students; Sample: Five students is 20%, or $\frac{1}{5}$ of the class. So $\frac{4}{5}$ must be 5 × 4, or 20 students.
(105)

Lesson 108   563

▶ See Math Conversations in the sidebar.

Practice Set
Problems a–e Conclude
You might choose to make representative cutouts of each pair of figures and invite volunteers to use the overhead and demonstrate different ways that each transformation can be completed.

Problem f Error Alert
Students must recognize that each vertex of a reflection is the same distance, but an opposite direction, from the axis of reflection.

3 Written Practice

Math Conversations
Discussion opportunities are provided below.

Problem 2 Analyze
"Does the team win more games than it loses, or lose more games than it wins?" The team wins more games than it loses.

"How could we use the fact that the team wins more games than it loses to make an estimate of the exact answer?" Sample: Since the team has won 12 games, and it wins more games than it loses, the exact number of losses will be less than 12.

"Why will the exact number of games the team lost be closer to 12 than to zero?" Sample: The ratio of wins to losses is nearly equal at 4 to 3. So the number of losses will be nearly equal to the number of wins, which is 12.

(continued)

3 Written Practice (Continued)

Math Conversations

Discussion opportunities are provided below.

Problem 7 `Verify`

Students may benefit from tracing the triangles, then cutting them out and varying their arrangement before answering the question.

Problem 9 `Connect`

Ask students to decide if they would change $1\frac{2}{5}$ to a decimal first or to a percent first, and tell why. Then ask them to explain how to make the change.

Problem 10 `Connect`

Ask students to decide if they would change 0.24 to a fraction first or to a percent first, and tell why. Then ask them to explain how to make the change.

Problem 11 `Connect`

Ask students to decide if they would change 35% to a fraction first or to a decimal first, and tell why. Then ask them to explain how to make the change.

Problem 19 `Generalize`

Extend the Problem

"Suppose that the measure of each edge of the cube is changed and the result is that the volume of the cube is now 8 times greater than it was. What measure was each edge of the cube changed to?" 20 cm

Help students generalize that if the edge length of a cube doubles, the volume of the cube becomes 8 times greater. To support the generalization, ask students to find the volume of a cube having an edge measure of 1 cm and compare it to the volume of a cube having an edge length that is double, or 2 cm.

Errors and Misconceptions

Problem 15

Incorrect answers can be caused by simplifying consecutive signs incorrectly. Remind students that consecutive signs that are the same simplify to + and consecutive signs that are different simplify to −.

(continued)

---

4. *(86)* `Estimate` Kaliska joined the band and got a new drum. Its diameter is 12 inches. What is the area of the top of the drum? Round your answer to the nearest square inch. (Use 3.14 for π.) 113 in.²

5. *(77)* Three eighths of the 48 band members played woodwinds. How many woodwind players were in the band? 18 woodwind players

6. *(30)* What is the least common multiple (LCM) of 6, 8, and 12? 24

7. Sample: Rotate triangle I until its orientation matches triangle II's. Then translate triangle I until it is positioned on triangle II.

* 7. *(108)* `Verify` Triangles I and II are congruent. Describe the transformations that would position triangle I on triangle II.

* 8. *(85, 105)* Complete this proportion: $\frac{0.7}{20} = \frac{n}{100}$ 3.5

`Connect` Complete the table to answer problems **9–11.**

	Fraction	Decimal	Percent
9. *(99)*	$1\frac{2}{5}$	**a.** 1.4	**b.** 140%
10. *(99)*	**a.** $\frac{6}{25}$	0.24	**b.** 24%
11. *(99)*	**a.** $\frac{7}{20}$	**b.** 0.35	35%

12. *(63)* $4\frac{3}{4} + \left(2\frac{1}{4} - \frac{7}{8}\right)$ $6\frac{1}{8}$ **13.** *(38)* $1\frac{1}{5} \div \left(2 \div 1\frac{2}{3}\right)$ 1

14. *(38)* $6.2 + (9 - 2.79)$ 12.41   *** 15.** *(104)* $-3 + +7 + -8 - -1$ −3

16. *(41)* `Estimate` Find 6% of $2.89. Round the product to the nearest cent. $0.17

17. *(95)* What fraction of a meter is a millimeter? $\frac{1}{1000}$

18. *(44)* Arrange these numbers in order from least to greatest: 0.3, 0.305, 0.31
0.3, 0.31, 0.305

19. *(82)* If each edge of a cube is 10 centimeters long, then its volume is how many cubic centimeters? 1000 cm³

20. *(92)* $2^5 - 5^2 + \sqrt{25} \times 2$ 17

* 21. *(106)* Solve and check: $8a - 4 = 60$ 8

22. *(28, Inv. 3)* `Conclude` Acute angle *a* is one third of a right angle. What is the measure of angle *a*? 30°

▶ See Math Conversations in the sidebar.

Refer to the figure at right to answer problems **23** and **24**. Dimensions are in millimeters.

* **23.** What is the perimeter of this polygon? 100 mm
(103)

* **24.** What is the area of this polygon? 550 mm²
(107)

25. **Estimate** A pint of water weighs about one pound. About how much
(78) does a two-gallon bucket of water weigh? (Disregard the weight of the
bucket.) about 16 pounds

* **26.** The parallel sides of this trapezoid are
(107) 10 mm apart. The trapezoid is divided
into two triangles. What is the area of the
trapezoid? 160 mm²

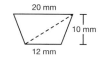

27. The cubic container shown can contain
(78) one liter of water. One liter is how many
milliliters? 1000 milliliters

▸ **28.** **Analyze** A bag contains 6 red marbles and 4 blue marbles. If Delia
(Inv. 10) draws one marble from the bag and then draws another marble
without replacing the first, what is the probability that both marbles will
be red? $\frac{6}{10} \cdot \frac{5}{9} = \frac{1}{3}$

29. One and one half kilometers is how many meters? 1500 meters
(95)

▸ **30.** **Model** On a coordinate plane draw triangle *RST* with these vertices:
(Inv. 7, *R* (−1, 4), *S* (−3, 1), *T* (−1, 1). Then draw its reflection across the *y*-axis.
108) Name the reflection △*R′S′T′*. What are the coordinates of the vertices
of △*R′S′T′*?

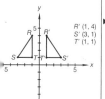

R′ (1, 4)
S′ (3, 1)
T′ (1, 1)

▸ See Math Conversations in the sidebar.

Math Conversations
Discussion opportunities are provided below.

Problem 28 Analyze
*"How many marbles will be in the bag as
Delia is making her second draw?"* nine

Problem 30 Model
Extend the Problem
*"Compare the x- and y-coordinates of the
given vertices to the x- and y-coordinates
of the reflected vertices. Describe what
happened to the x- and y-coordinates in
the reflection."* When reflecting in the
y-axis, the *x*-coordinates become opposites
and the *y*-coordinates are unchanged.

Invite students to predict what will happen to
the corresponding coordinates in a reflection
across the *x*-axis. Sample: When reflecting
across the *x*-axis, the *x*-coordinates are
unchanged and the *y*-coordinates become
opposites.

Invite students to use grid paper to verify their
predictions.

Looking Forward
Identifying, describing, and
performing rotations, translations,
and reflections prepares students
for:

• **Lesson 109,** using rotations,
translations, and reflections to
identify corresponding parts of
congruent or similar triangles.

• Corresponding Parts
• Similar Figures

Objectives

- Identify the corresponding sides and the corresponding angles of two congruent figures.
- Identify similar triangles and their corresponding angles and sides.
- Identify similar rectangles and their corresponding angles and sides.

Lesson Preparation

Materials

- **Power Up N** (in *Instructional Masters*)

Optional

- **Teacher-provided material: large cutout triangles ABC and XYZ** from Lesson 108

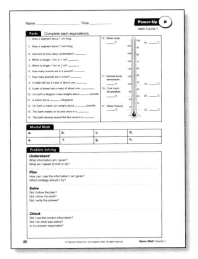

Power Up N

Math Language

New

corresponding parts

similar

Technology Resources

Student eBook Complete student textbook in electronic format.

Resources and Planner CD Assessment, reteaching, and instructional masters, plus a pacing calendar with standards.

Test and Practice Generator CD Create additional practice sheets and custom-made tests.

www.SaxonPublishers.com Visit for more student activities and planning materials.

Inclusion

Adaptations CD Adapted lessons, investigations, practice and assessments.

Meeting Standards

National Council of Teachers of Mathematics (NCTM)

Geometry

GM.1b Understand relationships among the angles, side lengths, perimeters, areas, and volumes of similar objects

GM.1c Create and critique inductive and deductive arguments concerning geometric ideas and relationships, such as congruence, similarity, and the Pythagorean relationship

GM.3a Describe sizes, positions, and orientations of shapes under informal transformations such as flips, turns, slides, and scaling

GM.3b Examine the congruence, similarity, and line or rotational symmetry of objects using transformations

Problem-Solving Strategy: Make It Simpler/Find a Pattern/Write an Equation

One state uses a license plate that contains two letters followed by four digits. How many license plates are possible if all of the letters and numbers are used?

(Understand) ***Understand the problem.***

"What information are we given?"

A state uses license plates that contain two letters followed by four digits.

"What are we asked to do?"

Determine how many license plates are possible if all of the letters and numbers are used.

(Plan) ***Make a plan.***

"What problem-solving strategy will we use?"

We will *make it simpler* by working with the letters and numbers separately, and when we *find a pattern* we will *write an equation* to compute the total number of license plates.

(Solve) ***Carry out the plan.***

"How many different letter combinations are possible?"

Any of the 26 letters of the alphabet could appear in the first position. For each letter A through Z, 26 letters could follow in the second position. Therefore, there are $26 \times 26 = 676$ possible letter combinations.

"How many numerical combinations are possible?"

The digit portion of the license plate can range from 0000 to 9999. For the first position, there are ten possibilities. For the second position, there are ten possibilities. If there are ten possibilities for each position, then there are $10 \times 10 \times 10 \times 10$ or 10,000 different combinations possible.

"How many possible license plates can be made altogether?"

There are 676 letter combinations that can be followed by 10,000 different number combinations. Therefore, there are $676 \times 10,000 = 6,760,000$ possible license plates.

(Check) ***Look back.***

"Did we complete the task?"

Yes. We found how many different license plates are possible if a license plate consists of two letters followed by four digits (6,760,000 license plates).

Teacher Note: You may wish to have students independently check state populations in an atlas or on the Web and list states that could safely use this number/letter system for their license plates without running out of combinations.

1 Power Up

Facts
Distribute **Power Up N** to students. See answers below.

Mental Math
Before students begin the Mental Math exercise, do this counting exercise as a class.

Count down by 25s from 200 to −200.

Encourage students to share different ways to mentally compute these exercises. Strategies for exercises **d** and **e** are listed below.

d. Subtract $7, then Add 13¢
$10 − $7 = $3; $3 + 13¢ = $3.13
Subtract $6, then Subtract 87¢
$10 − $6 = $4; $4 − 87¢ = $3.13

e. Find $\frac{1}{2}$ of 100
$100 \times 0.5 = 100 \times \frac{1}{2} = 100 \div 2 = 50$
Shift the Decimal Points
0.5×100 is the same as 5×10;
$5 \times 10 = 50$

Problem Solving
Refer to **Power-Up Discussion**, p. 566B.

2 New Concepts

Instruction
Students should generalize that when the sides and the angles of similar figures correspond, it means that they occupy the same relative position.

Place the large cutouts of triangles *ABC* and *XYZ* from Lesson 108 on the chalk tray or display them elsewhere in the positions shown on the page. Ask three volunteers to rotate, translate, and reflect triangle *ABC* so that it is positioned on top of triangle *XYZ*. Once triangle *ABC* is correctly positioned, identify the corresponding sides and angles of the two triangles.

(continued)

• Corresponding Parts
• Similar Figures

facts	Power Up N
mental math	**a. Number Sense:** 400 · 30 12,000
	b. Number Sense: 687 + 250 937
	c. Percent: 10% of $20 $2
	d. Calculation: $10.00 − $6.87 $3.13
	e. Decimals: 0.5 × 100 50
	f. Number Sense: 70 × 300 21,000
	g. Measurement: How many cups are in a quart? 4 cups
	h. Calculation: Square 7, + 1, ÷ 2, × 3, − 3, ÷ 8, √ 3

problem solving   One state uses a license plate that contains two letters followed by four digits. How many different license plates are possible if all of the letters and numbers are used?   6,760,000 license plates

New Concepts   Increasing Knowledge

corresponding parts   The two triangles below are congruent. Each triangle has three angles and three sides. The angles and sides of triangle *ABC* **correspond** to the angles and sides of triangle *XYZ*.

By rotating, translating, and reflecting triangle *ABC*, we could position it on top of triangle *XYZ*. Then their **corresponding parts** would be in the same place.

∠*A* corresponds to ∠*X*.
∠*B* corresponds to ∠*Y*.
∠*C* corresponds to ∠*Z*.
$\overline{AB}$ corresponds to $\overline{XY}$.

Facts   Complete each equivalence.

1. Draw a segment about 1 cm long.

2. Draw a segment about 1 inch long.

3. One inch is how many centimeters?   2.54

4. Which is longer, 1 km or 1 mi?   1 mi

5. Which is longer, 1 km or $\frac{1}{2}$ mi?   1 km

6. How many ounces are in a pound?   16

7. How many pounds are in a ton?   2000

8. A dollar bill has a mass of about one   gram.

9. A pair of shoes has a mass of about one   kilogram.

10. On Earth a kilogram mass weighs about   2.2   pounds.

11. A metric ton is   1000   kilograms.

12. On Earth a metric ton weighs about   2200   pounds.

13. The Earth rotates on its axis once in a   day.

14. The Earth revolves around the Sun once in a   year.

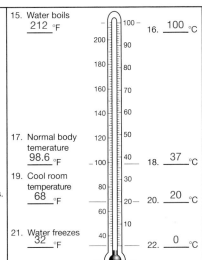

15. Water boils   212   °F
16. 100 °C

17. Normal body temerature   98.6 °F
18. 37 °C

19. Cool room temperature   68 °F
20. 20 °C

21. Water freezes   32 °F
22. 0 °C

$\overline{BC}$ corresponds to $\overline{YZ}$.

$\overline{AC}$ corresponds to $\overline{XZ}$.

If two figures are congruent, their corresponding parts are congruent. So the measures of the corresponding parts are equal.

These triangles are congruent. What is the perimeter of each?

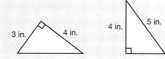

We will rotate the triangle on the left so that the corresponding parts are easier to see.

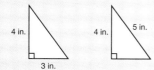

Now we can more easily see that the unmarked side on the left-hand triangle corresponds to the 5-inch side on the right-hand triangle. Since the triangles are congruent, the measures of the corresponding parts are equal. So each triangle has sides that measure 3 inches, 4 inches, and 5 inches. Adding, we find that the perimeter of each triangle is **12 inches.**

3 in. + 4 in. + 5 in. = 12 in.

similar figures | Figures that have the same shape but are not necessarily the same size are **similar.** Three of these four triangles are similar:

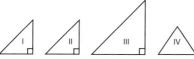

Triangles I and II are similar. They are also congruent. Remember, congruent figures have the same shape *and* size. Triangle III is similar to triangles I and II. It has the same shape but not the same size as triangles I and II. Notice that the corresponding angles of similar figures have the same measure. Triangle IV is not similar to the other triangles.

Analyze Can we reduce or enlarge Triangle IV to make it match the other triangles in the diagram? Explain.   No, it is not similar to the other triangles.

Example 1
Instruction
Remind students that congruent figures are identical in every way.

If students have difficulty visualizing the rotation, ask them to sketch the triangle in its original orientation, then rotate the sketch counterclockwise until its position matches the second triangle (about a 127° rotation).

Instruction
Make sure students understand that congruent figures, such as those in example 1, have the same shape. In other words, congruent figures are similar figures.

Also make sure students understand that when two figures are similar, they will always be the same shape and will often be a different size. In other words, one will be larger than the other. The corresponding angles of the figures will be congruent, and the corresponding sides of the figures will be proportional.

(continued)

Math Background

When two polygons are similar, their corresponding angles are congruent, and the lengths of their corresponding sides exhibit the same ratio.

For example, if two figures are similar, and the lengths of the sides of one figure are three times the lengths of the sides of the other figure, the ratio of lengths of the sides of the larger figure to the lengths of the corresponding sides of the smaller figure is 3 to 1. Such a ratio is sometimes called the ratio of similitude or scale factor.

An additional fact about similar figures is that every figure is similar to itself.

2 New Concepts (Continued)

Example 2

Instruction

To help students visualize the transformation of triangle *ABC*, ask them to sketch and label the triangle on a sheet of paper. Next have them rotate the paper 90° clockwise so that $\overline{AC}$ is vertical. Finally, have them turn the paper over using the edge of the paper parallel to $\overline{AC}$ as the line of reflection. Triangle *ABC* will have the same orientation as the larger triangle.

It is important for students to conclude from the example that the measures of the corresponding angles of similar figures are the same.

Example 3

Instruction

"If two figures are similar, how do the measures of the corresponding angles of those figures compare?" The measures are the same because the angles are congruent.

"If two figures are similar, how do the lengths of the corresponding sides of those figures compare?" Each pair of corresponding lengths are the same ratio.

(continued)

Example 2

The two triangles below are similar. What is the measure of angle A?

Solution

We will rotate and reflect triangle *ABC* so that the corresponding angles are easier to see.

We see that angle *A* in triangle *ABC* corresponds to the 30° angle in the similar triangle. Since corresponding angles of similar triangles have the same measure, the measure of angle *A* is **30°**.

Here are two important facts about similar polygons.

1. The corresponding angles of similar polygons are congruent.
2. The corresponding sides of similar polygons are proportional.

The first fact means that even though the sides of similar polygons might not have matching lengths, the corresponding angles do match. The second fact means that similar figures are related by a scale factor. The scale factor is a number. Multiplying the side length of a polygon by the scale factor gives the side length of the corresponding side of the similar polygon.

Example 3

The two rectangles below are similar. What is the ratio of corresponding sides? By what scale factor is rectangle *ABCD* larger than rectangle *EFGH*?

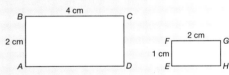

Solution

First, we find the ratios of corresponding sides.

Side *AB*: Side $EF = \frac{2}{1}$

Side BC: Side $FG = \frac{4}{2} = \frac{2}{1}$

In all similar polygons, such as these two rectangles, the ratios of corresponding sides are **equal.**

The sides of rectangle $ABCD$ are 2 times larger than the sides of rectangle $EFGH$. So rectangle $ABCD$ is larger than rectangle $EFGH$ by a scale factor of **2.**

Practice Set

▶ **a.** *Verify* "All squares are similar." True or false?   true

▶ **b.** *Verify* "All similar triangles are congruent." True or false?   false

▶ **c.** *Verify* "If two polygons are similar, then their corresponding angles are equal in measure." True or false?   true

▶ **d.** These two triangles are congruent. Which side of triangle PQR is the same length as $\overline{AB}$?   QR or RQ

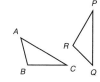

e. *Classify* Which of these two triangles appear to be similar?   I and II

f. These two pentagons are similar. The scale factor for corresponding sides is 3. How long is segment AE? How long is segment IJ?   3 in.; 3 in.

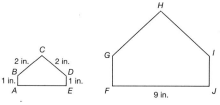

Written Practice   *Strengthening Concepts*

▶ **1.** The first three prime numbers are 2, 3, and 5. Their product is 30. What
(19)   is the product of the next three prime numbers?   1001

2. On the map 2 cm equals 1 km. What is the actual length of a street that
(95)   is 10 cm long on the map?   5 km

3. Between 8 p.m. and 9 p.m. the station broadcasts 8 minutes of
(23)   commercials. What was the ratio of commercial time to noncommercial time during that hour? $\frac{2}{13}$

Lesson 109   569

▶ See Math Conversations in the sidebar.

2 New Concepts (Continued)

Instruction
Students should conclude from the example that a scale factor is a mathematical way to describe the relationship of corresponding sides of similar figures.

Practice Set
Problems a–c Verify
Ask students to make a sketch and use it as an example to prove, or as a non-example to disprove, each statement.

Problem d Analyze
Extend the Problem
To provide additional practice identifying corresponding sides and angles of similar figures have students identify all of the other corresponding sides and angles of triangles PQR and CAB. BC corresponds to $\overline{RP}$; AC corresponds to QP; $\angle B$ corresponds to $\angle R$; $\angle A$ corresponds to $\angle Q$; $\angle C$ corresponds to $\angle P$

3 Written Practice

Math Conversations
Discussion opportunities are provided below.

Errors and Misconceptions
Problem 1
An incorrect product is likely to represent not correctly identifying the next three consecutive prime numbers. Remind students that a prime number is a counting number greater than 1 whose only two factors are 1 and itself.

Work with students to consider the next ten consecutive counting numbers greater than 5. For each number, ask students to name a factor of the number that is not 1 or the number itself. Whenever students cannot name a factor, point out that a factor cannot be named because the number is a prime number.

(continued)

Math Conversations

Discussion opportunities are provided below.

Problem 5 `Conclude`

Remind students that to determine a missing angle measure in a triangle when two angles are given, we must subtract the sum of the given angle measures from 180°.

"In this triangle, the measure of only one angle is given. Explain how we can find the unknown angle measures given only one angle measure of the triangle." Sample: Subtract the known angle measure (90°) from 180° to find the sum of the unknown angle measures. Then divide that sum by 2 because we are told the angles are congruent.

Invite a volunteer to the board or overhead to complete the arithmetic.
$(180° − 90°) ÷ 2 = 45°$

Problem 16 `Represent`

"What equation describes the relationship of y to x?" $y = 2x$

(continued)

16. Sample:

x	2	3	5	10
y	4	6	10	20

---

4. a. `Classify` Which of the following triangles appears to have a right angle as one of its angles?   **C**
(93)

  b. In which triangle do all three sides appear to be the same length?   **A**

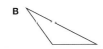

▶ * 5. `Conclude` If the two acute angles of a right triangle are congruent, then what is the measure of each acute angle?   **45°**
(28, 98)

6. Ms. Hernandez is assigning each student in her class one of the fifty U.S. states on which to write a report. What is the probability that Manuela will be assigned one of the 5 states that has coastline on the Pacific Ocean? Express the probability ratio as a fraction and as a decimal. $\frac{1}{10}$, 0.1
(58)

Solve:

* 7. $7w − 3 = 60$ **9**
(106)

* 8. $\frac{8}{n} = \frac{4}{2.5}$ **5**
(85, 105)

`Connect` Complete the table to answer problems **9–11.**

	Fraction	Decimal	Percent
9. (99)	$\frac{5}{8}$	**a.** 0.625	**b.** 62.5%
10. (99)	**a.** $1\frac{1}{4}$	1.25	**b.** 125%
11. (99)	**a.** $\frac{7}{10}$	**b.** 0.7	70%

12. a. If the spinner is spun once, what is the probability that it will stop on a number less than 4? $\frac{3}{4}$
(58)

  b. If the spinner is spun 100 times, how many times would it be expected to stop on a prime number?   50 times

13. Convert 200 centimeters to meters by completing this multiplication: 2 meters
(95)

$$\frac{200 \text{ cm}}{1} \cdot \frac{1 \text{ m}}{100 \text{ cm}}$$

14. $(6.2 + 9) − 2.79$ **12.41**
(38)

15. $10^3 ÷ 10^2 − 10^1$ **0**
(92)

▶* 16. `Represent` Create a function table for *x* and *y*. In your table, record four pairs of numbers that follow this rule:
(96)

$$y \text{ is twice } x$$

17. Write the fraction $\frac{2}{3}$ as a decimal number rounded to the hundredths place.   0.67
(74)

▶ See Math Conversations in the sidebar.

18. The Zamoras rent a storage room that is 10 feet wide, 12 feet long, and
(82) 8 feet high. How many cube-shaped boxes 1 foot on each edge can the
Zamoras store in the room?   960 boxes

▶* **19.** These two rectangles
(109) are similar.

   a. What is the scale factor
   from the smaller rectangle
   to the larger rectangle?   3

   b. What is the scale factor from
   the larger rectangle to the smaller rectangle? $\frac{1}{3}$

20. $0.12m = \$4.20$ $\$35.00$
(49)

* **21.** Calculate mentally:
(100)
   a. $+7 + -8$ -1 **b.** $-7 + +8$ $+1$

   c. $-7 - +8$ -15 **d.** $-7 - -8$ $+1$

Triangles I and II below are congruent. Refer to the triangles to answer
problems **22** and **23**.

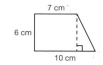

* **22.** What is the area of each triangle?   6 in.^{2}
(109)

▶ **23.** _Conclude_ Name the transformations that would position triangle I on
(108) triangle II.   rotation and translation

* **24.** This trapezoid has been divided into a
(107) rectangle and a triangle. What is the area of
the trapezoid?   51 cm^2

25. _Estimate_ A soup label must be long enough to wrap around a can. If
(47) the diameter of the can is 7 cm, then the label must be at least how
long? Round up to the nearest whole number.   22 cm

▶* **26.** _Analyze_ The triangles below are similar. What is the measure of
(109) angle A?   40°

Math Conversations

Discussion opportunities are provided below.

Problem 19 _Justify_

Extend the Problem

"**Suppose that the side measures of the
larger rectangle are doubled. Do the angle
measures of that rectangle also double?
Give two reasons to justify your answer.**"
No; Sample: The figure is still a rectangle,
and all angle measures of all rectangles
are 90°; all of the corresponding angles of
similar figures are congruent.

Problem 23 _Conclude_

To complete the problem, invite students
to trace each triangle on separate slips of
paper and use the sketches to model the
transformations that are needed to position
one triangle on top of the other. The answer
that is provided is the most likely response.
Ask students who provide other responses to
justify their responses.

Problem 26 _Analyze_

"**If two figures are similar, how do
the measures of the corresponding
angles of those figures compare?**" The
corresponding angles are congruent; they
have the same measure.

(continued)

Math Conversations

Discussion opportunities are provided below.

Problem 28 [Validate]

Extend the Problem

Write 1 in. = 2.54 cm on the board or overhead.

> *"One inch equals 2.54 cm. Is the segment closer to 1 inch or 2 inches long? Explain your answer."* Closer to 1 in.; Sample: Since 1 inch is 2.54 centimeters, 2 inches is about the same as 5 centimeters; the length of the segment is 3.4 cm and 3.4 is closer to 2.54 than to 5.

27. The ratio of almonds to cashews in the mix was 9 to 2. Horace counted
(88) 36 cashews in all. How many almonds were there?   162 almonds

▶ **28.** Write the length of the segment below in
(7, 50) **a.** millimeters.   34 mm

   b. centimeters.   3.4 cm

29. $6\frac{2}{3} \div 100$ $\frac{1}{15}$
(68)

30. Compare: $\left(\frac{1}{10}\right)^2 \bigcirc 0.01$
(92)

Early Finishers
Real-World Application

Issam wants to make a rock garden in his backyard. He bought $\frac{1}{5}$ ton of gravel and $\frac{1}{2}$ ton of rocks. Issam is not sure if the gravel and the rocks will fit on the trailer he rented. If the trailer can carry a maximum load of 1250 pounds, can Issam take all the gravel and rocks in one trip? Note: 1 ton = 2000 pounds. Support your answer.   No; $\frac{1}{5} + \frac{1}{2} = \frac{7}{10}$ ton; $\frac{1 \text{ ton}}{2000 \text{ lbs}} = \frac{0.7 \text{ ton}}{x \text{ lbs}}$, $(0.7)(2000) = x$, $x = 1400$ lbs; Since $1400 > 1250$, Issam will have to make two trips.

▶ See Math Conversations in the sidebar.

• Symmetry

Objectives

- Identify symmetrical figures.
- Draw lines of symmetry in figures and objects.
- Identify figures with rotational symmetry.

Lesson Preparation

Materials

- **Power Up M** (in *Instructional Masters*)
- **Lesson Activity 20** (in *Instructional Masters*)
- **Manipulative kit: inch rulers, compasses**
- *Optional*
- **Investigation Activity 15** (in *Instructional Masters*) or **graph paper**
- **Teacher-provided material: rectangular-shaped paper scissors, grid paper**

Math Language

New	Maintain	English Learners (ESL)
line of symmetry	rotational symmetry	Ferris wheel

Technology Resources

Student eBook Complete student textbook in electronic format.

Resources and Planner CD Assessment, reteaching, and instructional masters, plus a pacing calendar with standards.

Test and Practice Generator CD Assessment, reteaching, and instructional masters, plus a pacing calendar with standards.

www.SaxonPublishers.com Visit for more student activities and planning materials.

Inclusion

Adaptations CD Adapted lessons, investigations, practice and assessments.

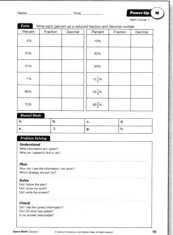

Power Up M

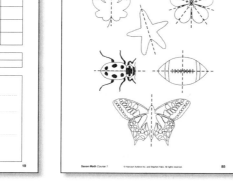

Lesson Activity 20

Meeting Standards

National Council of Teachers of Mathematics (NCTM)

Geometry

GM.3b Examine the congruence, similarity, and line or rotational symmetry of objects using transformations

GM.4e Recognize and apply geometric ideas and relationships in areas outside the mathematics classroom, such as art, science, and everyday life

Communication

CM.3d Use the language of mathematics to express mathematical ideas precisely

Problem-Solving Strategy: Use Logical Reasoning/ Guess and Check

Copy this problem and fill in the missing digits. Use only zeros or ones in the spaces.

$$
\begin{array}{r}
9\_ \\
\_\,\_\,\overline{)\_\,\_\,\_\,\_} \\
99 \\
\_\,\_ \\
\overline{=\,=} \\
\_
\end{array}
$$

[Understand] **Understand the problem.**

"What information are we given?"

We are shown a division problem with digits missing in the dividend, the divisor, and the quotient.

"What are we asked to do?"

Fill in the missing digits using only zeros and ones.

[Plan] **Make a plan.**

"What problem-solving strategy will we use?"

We will *use logical reasoning* and basic number sense to *guess and check*.

[Solve] **Carry out the plan.**

"What is the divisor?"

$9 \times 11 = 99$, so 11 is the divisor.

"What are the possible first three digits of the dividend?"

100, 101, 110, or 111.

"What is the only possibility for the first three digits of the dividend?"

100. (Subtracting 99 from 101 results in 2, not zero or one. The other options result in a two-digit difference.

"What is the only possibility for the last digit of the dividend?"

It must be a 1, and the ones of the quotient is 1. The remainder is 0.

$$
\begin{array}{r}
91 \\
11\overline{)1001} \\
99 \\
\overline{11} \\
11 \\
\overline{0}
\end{array}
$$

[Check] **Look back.**

"Did we complete the task that was assigned?"

Yes. We filled in all the missing digits of the division problem with zeros and ones and the arithmetic is correct.

LESSON
110

• Symmetry

Power Up   *Building Power*

facts   Power Up M

mental math

   a. Number Sense: $90 \cdot 90$ 8100

   b. Number Sense: $726 - 250$ 476

   c. Percent: 50% of $50 $25

   d. Calculation: $7.62 + $3.98 $11.60

   e. Decimals: $8 \div 100$ 0.08

   f. Number Sense: $\frac{350}{50}$ 7

   g. Geometry: A circle has a diameter of 4 yd. What is the circumference of the circle?   12.56 yd

   h. Calculation: Square 10, $- 1$, $\div 9$, $\times 3$, $- 1$, $\div 4$, $\times 7$, $+ 4$, $\div 3$ 20

problem solving

Copy the problem and fill in the missing digits. Use only zeros or ones in the spaces.

```
    9_              91
 _)____      11)1001
              99
   99          11
   --          11
   ==           0
    -
```

New Concept   *Increasing Knowledge*

A figure has line **symmetry** if it can be divided in half so that the halves are mirror images of each other. We can observe symmetry in nature. For example, butterflies, leaves, and most types of fish are symmetrical. In many respects our bodies are also symmetrical. Manufactured items such as lamps, chairs, and kitchen sinks are sometimes designed with symmetry.

Two-dimensional figures can also be symmetrical. A two-dimensional figure is symmetrical if a line can divide the figure into two mirror images. Line *r* divides the triangle below into two mirror images. Thus the triangle is symmetrical, and line *r* is called a **line of symmetry.**

Facts   Write each percent as a reduced fraction and decimal number.

Percent	Fraction	Decimal	Percent	Fraction	Decimal
5%	$\frac{1}{20}$	0.05	10%	$\frac{1}{10}$	0.1
20%	$\frac{1}{5}$	0.2	30%	$\frac{3}{10}$	0.3
25%	$\frac{1}{4}$	0.25	50%	$\frac{1}{2}$	0.5
1%	$\frac{1}{100}$	0.01	$12\frac{1}{2}$%	$\frac{1}{8}$	0.125
90%	$\frac{9}{10}$	0.9	$33\frac{1}{3}$%	$\frac{1}{3}$	Rounds to 0.333
75%	$\frac{3}{4}$	0.75	$66\frac{2}{3}$%	$\frac{2}{3}$	Rounds to 0.667

1 Power Up

Facts
Distribute **Power Up M** to students. See answers below.

Mental Math
Before students begin the Mental Math exercise, do this counting exercise as a class.

Count up and down by $\frac{1}{8}$s between $\frac{1}{8}$ and 2.

Encourage students to share different ways to mentally compute these exercises. Strategies for exercises **a** and **e** are listed below.

   a. Add Two Zeros to the Product 9×9
     $9 \times 9 = 81$; $90 \times 90 = 8100$
   Use a Multiplication Pattern
     $9 \times 9 = 81$; $90 \times 9 = 810$; $90 \times 90 = 8100$
   e. Shift the Decimal Point Two Places Left
     $8 \div 100 = 0.08$
   Write a Fraction, then Write a Decimal
     $8 \div 100 = \frac{8}{100}$; $\frac{8}{100} = 0.08$

Problem Solving
Refer to **Power-Up Discussion,** p. 573B.

2 New Concepts

Instruction
Use the transparency of **Lesson Activity 20** Symmetry to show examples of symmetrical objects in nature, then challenge students to identify classroom objects that are symmetrical.

Point out that a line of symmetry always divides a figure into two congruent figures.

When identifying a line of symmetry, students can think of the line as a fold line in this sense: if the figure is folded in half on that line and the halves of the figure match exactly, the fold line is a line of symmetry. If the halves of the figure do not match exactly, the fold line is not a line of symmetry.

(continued)

② New Concepts (Continued)

Example 1
Instruction
To model the solution, have students fold a sheet of paper that is longer in one dimension than the other and shaped like a rectangle.

Remind students that each sheet of paper is a rectangle, and ask them to fold the paper in half lengthwise, and then unfold it.

"How do the sizes and shapes of the halves compare?" Sample: they are congruent or identical

"You divided the rectangle into two halves that are mirror images of each other. The fold is a line of symmetry."

Now have students fold the paper a different way to show a second line of symmetry.

Example 2
Instruction
If students have difficulty recognizing the lines of symmetry, encourage them to trace the figure and explore different ways to fold the tracing.

(continued)

Example 1

This rectangle has how many lines of symmetry?

Solution

Thinking Skill

Analyze

How can we be sure that there are no more lines of symmetry? Lines of symmetry must pass through the midpoint of the figure to divide the figure in half and form two mirror images. There are no other ways to draw a line through the midpoint that forms mirror images.

There are two ways to divide the rectangle into mirror images:

We see that the rectangle has **2 lines of symmetry**.

Example 2

Which of these triangles does not appear to be symmetrical?

Solution

We check each triangle to see whether we can find a line of symmetry. In choice **A** all three sides of the triangle are the same length. We can find three lines of symmetry in the triangle.

In choice **B** two sides of the triangle are the same length. The triangle in choice **B** has one line of symmetry.

In choice **C** each side of the triangle is a different length. The triangle has no line of symmetry, so the triangle is not symmetrical. The answer is **C**.

Math Background

One misconception that sometimes occurs when identifying the number of lines of symmetry polygons have is to generalize that all polygons of a given classification have the same number of lines of symmetry.

For example, if one dimension of a rectangle is a different measure than the other dimension (such as a rectangle that is longer than it is wide), the rectangle will have two lines of symmetry. Many rectangles have two lines of symmetry.

However, it is incorrect to generalize that all rectangles have two lines of symmetry because a square is a rectangle and a square has four lines of symmetry.

A figure has **rotational symmetry** if the image of the figure re-appears in the same position as it is turned *less than* a full turn. For example the image of a square re-appears in the same position as it is turned 90°, 180°, and 270°.

| original position | 45° turn | 90° turn | 150° turn | 180° turn | 210° turn | 270° turn |

Example 3

Which of these figures have rotational symmetry? Choose all correct answers.

A   B   C   D

Solution

Turning your book might help you see which shapes have rotational symmetry. If the figures in choices A and B are rotated 180°, the images of the figures re-appear, so **choices A and B have rotational symmetry.** The figures in choices C and D re-appear only after a full turn.

Practice Set

a. (**Model**) Draw four squares. Then draw a different line of symmetry for each square.

b. (**Classify**) All but one of these letters can be drawn to have a line of symmetry. Which of these letters does not have a line of symmetry? **F**

    A   **B**   **C**   **D**   **E**   **F**

c. Which two of these letters have rotational symmetry? (*Hint:* Rotating your book might help you find the answer.) **N, O**

    L   **M**   **N**   **O**   **P**   **Q**

Written Practice   *Strengthening Concepts*

1. When the greatest four-digit number is divided by the greatest two-digit number, what is the quotient?   101
(2)

2. The ratio of the length to the width of the Alamo is about 5 to 3. If the width of the Alamo is approximately 63 ft, about how long is the Alamo?   about 105 ft
(88)

3. A box of crackers in the shape of a square prism had a length, width, and height of 4 inches, 4 inches, and 10 inches respectively. How many cubic inches was the volume of the box?   160 in.³
(82)

Crackers   10 in.   4 in.   4 in.

Lesson 110   575

▶ See Math Conversations in the sidebar.

---

2 New Concepts (Continued)

Instruction

It is important for students to understand that if a full turn is required to return a figure to its original position, the figure does not have rotational symmetry

Example 3
Instruction

You might choose to extend the example by encouraging students to draw a variety of shapes and challenge classmates to identify the shapes that have rotational symmetry.

Practice Set
Problem a Model

Drawing the squares on grid or dot paper may help students recognize the different lines of symmetry.

Students should conclude from the problem that a square has four lines of symmetry.

Problem b Classify

Ask volunteers to each choose a different letter (except F) and draw that letter on the board or overhead, and then draw its line of symmetry. A has a vertical line of symmetry; B, C, D, and E each have a horizontal line of symmetry.

Math Conversations

Discussion opportunities are provided below.

Problem 4 | Analyze

Extend the Problem

"What regular polygon has 60° rotational symmetry? Describe a pattern that supports your answer." A regular hexagon. Sample pattern: An equilateral triangle has 3 vertices and 360° ÷ 3 or 120° rotational symmetry; a square has 4 vertices and 360° ÷ 4 or 90° rotational symmetry; a regular pentagon has 5 vertices and 360° ÷ 5 or 72° rotational symmetry; a regular hexagon has 6 vertices and 360° ÷ 6 or 60° rotational symmetry.

Problem 5 | Model

"What must you do to change a triangle by a scale factor of 3?" Sample: Multiply the lengths of the sides of the triangle by 3.

"How do the angle measures of a triangle change when the triangle is made larger by a scale factor of 3?" The angle measures do not change.

Problem 8 | Model

"Are more of the photographs black and white, or color? Explain how you know." Black and white; since 40% of the photographs are color, 100% − 40% or 60% of the photographs are black and white.

"Explain how we could make an estimate of the number of photographs that Ms. Mendez has." Sample: The 12 black and white photographs represent 60% of the total number, so the number of color photographs will be less than 12. The total number of photographs will be less than double 12 or 24.

Errors and Misconceptions

Problem 18

Students should recall that a variety of factor pairs can be used as the first factor pair in the tree.

When writing the prime factorization, students must remember to write the bases, not the exponents, in ascending order. In other words, from least to greatest.

(continued)

▶ **4.** **Analyze** A full turn is 360°. How many degrees is $\frac{1}{6}$ of a turn? 60°
(90)

Refer to these triangles to answer problems 5–7:

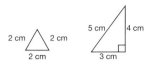

5. Yes, it has both rotational and line symmetry; Sample: I know it has rotational symmetry because it looks the same after it is turned 120° and 240°. I know it has line symmetry because a line can be drawn through the middle of each angle of the triangle so that the two halves are a reflection of each other.

▶ * **5.** **Explain** Does the equilateral triangle have rotational and line symmetry? Use words or diagrams to explain how you know.
(110)

* **6.** Sketch a triangle similar to the equilateral triangle. Make the scale factor from the equilateral triangle to your sketch 3. What is the perimeter of the triangle you sketched? 18 cm
(93, 109)

7. What is the area of the right triangle? 6 cm²
(93)

▶ * **8.** **Model** Draw a ratio box for this problem. Then solve the problem using a proportion. 20 photos
(105)

Ms. Mendez is sorting her photographs. She notes that 12 of the photos are black and white and that 40% of the photos are color. How many photos does she have?

Connect Complete the table to answer problems 9–11.

8.

	%	A.C.
Color	40	c
Black and white	60	12
Total	100	t

	Fraction	Decimal	Percent
9. (99)	$2\frac{3}{4}$	**a.** 2.75	**b.** 275%
10. (99)	**a.** $1\frac{1}{10}$	1.1	**b.** 110%
11. (99)	**a.** $\frac{16}{25}$	**b.** 0.64	64%

12. $24\frac{1}{6} + 23\frac{1}{3} + 22\frac{1}{2}$ 70
(61)

13. $\left(1\frac{1}{5} \div 2\right) \div 1\frac{2}{3}$ $\frac{9}{25}$
(68)

14. $9 - (6.2 + 2.79)$ 0.01
(38)

15. $0.36m = \$63.00$ $175.00
(49)

16. Find 6.5% of $24.89 by multiplying 0.065 by $24.89. Round the product to the nearest cent. $1.62
(51)

17. **Estimate** Round the quotient to the nearest thousandth: 0.016
(51)
$$0.065 \div 4$$

▶ **18.** Write the prime factorization of 1000 using exponents. $2^3 \cdot 5^3$
(73)

19. **Verify** "All squares are similar." True or false? true
(109)

▶ See Math Conversations in the sidebar.

20. $3^3 - 3^2 \div 3 - 3 \times 3$ 15
(92)

* 21. What is the perimeter of this polygon?   44 m
(103)

* 22. What is the area of this polygon?   106 m²
(107)

Triangles I and II are congruent. Refer to these triangles to answer problems **23** and **24.**

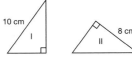

* 23. (*Conclude*) Name the transformations that would position triangle I on
(108) triangle II.   rotation, reflection, and translation

* 24. The perimeter of each triangle is 24 cm. What is the length of the
(8, 109) shortest side of each triangle?   6 cm

25. (*Estimate*) The first Ferris wheel was built in 1893 for the world's fair
(47) in Chicago. The diameter of the Ferris wheel was 250 ft. Find the
circumference of the original Ferris wheel to the nearest hundred
feet.   800 ft

26. Use a ruler to draw $\overline{AB}$ $1\frac{3}{4}$ inches long. Then draw a dot at the midpoint
(7) of $\overline{AB}$, and label the point *M*. How long is $\overline{AM}$?
A⎯⎯⎯⎯⎯⎯M⎯⎯⎯⎯⎯⎯B; $\frac{7}{8}$ inch

27. (*Model*) Use a compass to draw a circle on a coordinate plane. Make
(27, Inv. 7) the center of the circle the origin, and make the radius five units. At
which two points does the circle cross the *x*-axis?   (5, 0) and (−5, 0)

28. What is the area of the circle in problem **27?** (Use 3.14 for π.)
(86) 78.5 sq. units

* 29. $-3 + -4 - -5 - +7$ −9
(104)

* 30. If Freddy tosses a coin four times, what is the probability that the coin
(Inv. 10) will turn up heads, tails, heads, tails in that order? $\frac{1}{16}$

Lesson 110   577

▶ See Math Conversations in the sidebar.

Math Conversations

Discussion opportunities are provided below.

Problem 22 [Infer]

Extend the Problem

Challenge students to demonstrate how a sketch of the polygon can be divided into three different rectangles, and name the measures of those rectangles. Sample: 2 m × 5 m, 5 m × 8 m, 7 m × 8 m

Problem 23 [Conclude]

If students have difficulty visualizing the transformations, ask them to trace or sketch, then cut out, each triangle. After arranging the triangles in the orientation shown in the book, students can explore how different transformations of one triangle can be combined to position it on top of the other triangle.

Errors and Misconceptions

Problem 30

Students must recognize that each toss is an independent event. In other words, the outcome of any toss is not influenced by a previous toss.

Assessment   30–40 minutes   For use after Lesson 110

Distribute **Cumulative Test 21** to each student. Two versions of the test are available in *Saxon Math Course 1 Course Assessments Book*. Have students complete the **Power-Up Test** first. Allow 10 minutes. Then have students work the 20 numbered items on the **Cumulative Test.** Students may use copies of the answer sheet to record their work. Track individual and class progress with the **Test Analysis** forms.

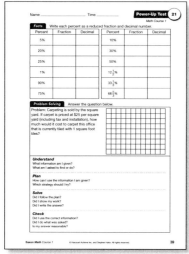

Power-Up Test 21

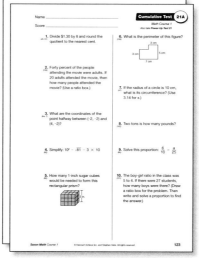

Cumulative Test 21A

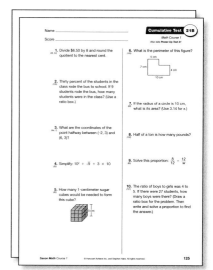

Alternative Cumulative Test 21B

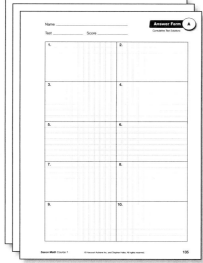

Optional Answer Forms

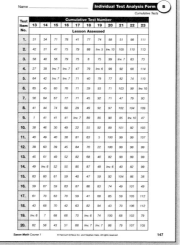

Individual Test Analysis Form

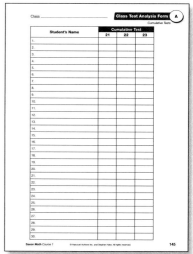

Class Test Analysis Form

Reteaching

Students who score below 80% on the assessment may be in need of reteaching. Look for the causes of student mistakes. If errors are conceptual, refer to the *Reteaching Masters* for reteaching.

Customized Benchmark Assessment

You can develop customized benchmark tests using the Test Generator located on the *Test & Practice Generator CD*.

This chart shows the lesson, the standard, and the test item question that can be found on the *Test & Practice Generator CD*.

LESSON	NEW CONCEPTS	LOCAL STANDARD	TEST ITEM ON CD
101	• Ratios Problems Involving Totals		11.101.1
102	• Mass and Weight		11.102.1
103	• Perimeter of Complex Shapes		11.103.1
104	• Algebraic Addition Activity		11.104.1
105	• Using Proportions to Solve Percent Problems		11.105.1
106	• Two-Step Equations		11.106.1
107	• Area of Complex Shapes		11.107.1
108	• Transformations		11.108.1
109	• Corresponding Parts		11.109.1
109	• Similar Figures		11.109.2
110	• Symmetry		11.110.1

Using the Test Generator CD

- Develop tests in both English and Spanish.
- Choose from multiple-choice and free-response test items.
- Clone test items to create multiple versions of the same test.
- View and edit test items to make and save your own questions.
- Administer assessments through paper tests or over a school LAN.
- Monitor student progress through a variety of individual and class reports —for both diagnosing and assessing standards mastery.

Symmetric Designs

Assign after Lesson 110 and Test 21

Objectives
- Identify the lines of symmetry and the degrees of rotational symmetry in a design.
- Draw a design with a given number of lines of symmetry and degrees of rotational symmetry.
- Communicate ideas through writing.

Materials
Performance Tasks 21A and **21B**

Preparation
Make copies of **Performance Tasks 21A** and **21B.** (One each per student.)

Time Requirement
30–60 minutes; Begin in class and complete at home.

Task
Explain to students that for this task they will be working for a company that makes patios out of tile. They will analyze the symmetry of some of the designs and create symmetric designs. They will be required to explain how a design they created is symmetric. Point out that all of the information students need is on **Performance Tasks 21A** and **21B.**

Criteria for Evidence of Learning
- States accurately the number of lines of symmetry and degrees of rotational symmetry for two designs.
- Draws correctly a design with a given number of lines of symmetry and degrees of rotational symmetry.
- Communicates ideas clearly through writing.

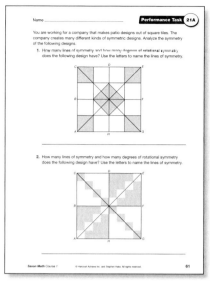

Performance Task 21A

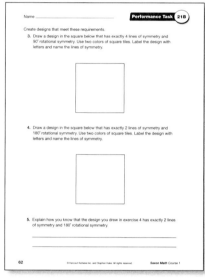

Performance Task 21B

National Council of Teachers of Mathematics (NCTM)

Geometry
GM.3b Examine the congruence, similarity, and line or rotational symmetry of objects using transformations

GM.4c Use visual tools such as networks to represent and solve problems

GM.4e Recognize and apply geometric ideas and relationships in areas outside the mathematics classroom, such as art, science, and everyday life

Communication
CM.3d Use the language of mathematics to express mathematical ideas precisely

Connections
CN.4a Recognize and use connections among mathematical ideas

Focus on
• Scale Factor: Scale Drawings and Models

Objectives

- Use the legend in a scale drawing or model to find the actual measurements of the object being represented.
- Use a proportion to find an unknown measurement in a scale drawing or model problem.
- Determine the scale and scale factor of a rendering.
- Use the scale factor of a model to calculate the dimensions of an actual object.

Lesson Preparation

Materials

- **Investigation Activity 21** (in *Instructional Masters*)
- **Investigation Activity 22** (in *Instructional Masters*)
- **Manipulative kit: rulers**
- **Teacher-provided material:** scissors, plastic straws, glue

Optional
- Inch rulers
- State map

Math Language

New	Maintain	English Learners (ESL)
legend	scale	rendering
scale drawings		
scale factor		
scale model		

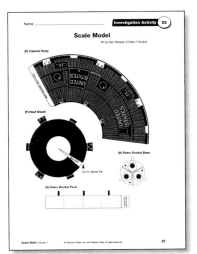

Investigation Activity 21

Investigation Activity 22

Technology Resources

Student eBook Complete student textbook in electronic format.

Resources and Planner CD Assessment, reteaching, and instructional masters, plus a pacing calendar with standards.

Test and Practice Generator CD Create additional practice sheets and custom-made tests.

www.SaxonPublishers.com Visit for more student activities and planning materials.

Inclusion

Adaptations CD Adapted lessons, investigations, practice and assessments.

Meeting Standards

National Council of Teachers of Mathematics (NCTM)

Numbers and Operations

NO.3d Develop, analyze, and explain methods for solving problems involving proportions, such as scaling and finding equivalent ratios

Geometry

GM.4c Use visual tools such as networks to represent and solve problems

GM.4d Use geometric models to represent and explain numerical and algebraic relationships

GM.4e Recognize and apply geometric ideas and relationships in areas outside the mathematics classroom, such as art, science, and everyday life

Measurement

ME.2e Solve problems involving scale factors, using ratio and proportion

In this investigation, students will explore scale drawings and scale models, and use proportions to find the actual dimensions and distances of the two-dimensional and three-dimensional objects the drawings and models represent.

Instruction

For each set of figures shown, have students identify the corresponding sides that are related by each scale factor. Scale factor 3: 3 cm and 9 cm; 4 cm and 12 cm; 5 cm and 15 cm; Scale factor 2: 3 in. and 6 in.; 4 in. and 8 in.

To connect scale drawing to the real world, show students a map of your state.

> *"A map is another example of a scale drawing. This map is a representation of our state."*

Point out the legend on the map. Encourage students to think of other examples of scale drawings and models that they encounter in everyday life. Sample: model cars, trains, or planes; a globe; a floor plan of the school showing the way to the nearest exit

---

Focus on
Scale Factor: Scale Drawings and Models

Recall from Lesson 109 that the dimensions of similar figures are related by a scale factor, as shown below.

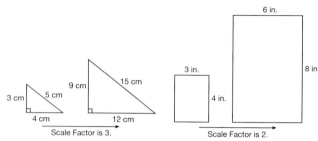

Similar figures are often used by manufacturers to design products and by architects to design buildings. Architects create **scale drawings** to guide the construction of a building. Sometimes, a **scale model** of the building is also constructed to show the appearance of the finished project.

Scale drawings, such as architectural plans, are two-dimensional representations of larger objects. Scale models, such as model cars and action figures, are three-dimensional representations of larger objects. In some cases, however, a scale drawing or model represents an object smaller than the model itself. For example, we might want to construct a large model of a bee in order to more easily portray its anatomy.

In scale drawings and models the **legend** gives the relationship between a unit of length in the drawing and the actual measurement that the unit represents. The drawing below shows the floorplan of Angela's studio apartment. The legend for this scale drawing is $\frac{1}{2}$ inch = 5 feet.

If we measure the scale drawing above, we find that it is 2 inches long and $1\frac{1}{2}$ inches wide. Using these measurements, we can determine the actual dimensions of Angela's apartment. On the next page we show some relationships that are based on the scale drawing's legend.

Math Background

When two figures are similar, they are related by a **scale factor.** The scale factor is a constant ratio, and it describes the increase (such as an enlargement) or the decrease (such as a reduction) in a similarity.

The scale factor is sometimes called the ratio of magnification.

$$\frac{1}{2} \text{ inch } = 5 \text{ feet (given)}$$
$$1 \text{ inch } = 10 \text{ feet}$$
$$1\frac{1}{2} \text{ inches } = 15 \text{ feet}$$
$$2 \text{ inches } = 20 \text{ feet}$$

Since the scale drawing is 2 inches long by $1\frac{1}{2}$ inches wide, we find that Angela's apartment is 20 feet long by 15 feet wide.

▶ 1. **Connect** What are the actual length and width of Angela's kitchen?
   length = 10 feet; width = 5 feet

2. In the scale drawing each doorway measures $\frac{1}{4}$ inch wide. Since $\frac{1}{4}$ inch is half of $\frac{1}{2}$ inch, what is the actual width of each doorway in Angela's apartment? $2\frac{1}{2}$ feet

▶ 3. **Connect** A dollhouse was built as a scale model of an actual house using 1 inch to represent 1.5 feet. What are the dimensions of a room in the actual house if the corresponding dollhouse room measures 8 in. by 10 in.? 12 ft by 15 ft

4. A scale model of an airplane is built using 1 inch to represent 2 feet. The wingspan of the model airplane is 24 inches. What is the wingspan of the actual airplane in feet? 48 feet

The lengths of corresponding parts of scale drawings or models and the objects they represent are proportional. Since the relationships are proportional, we can use a ratio box to organize the numbers and a proportion to find the unknown.

Connect To answer problems 5–8, use a ratio box and write a proportion. Then solve for the unknown measurement either by using cross products or by writing an equivalent ratio. Make one column of the ratio box for the model and the other column for the actual object.

▶ 5. A scale model of a sports car is 7 inches long. The car itself is 14 feet long. If the model is 3 inches wide, how wide is the actual car? $\frac{7}{3} = \frac{14}{w}$; 6 feet

6. $\frac{7}{n} = \frac{14}{4}$; 2 inches; Using the information given I drew a ratio box.

	Model	Actual
Length	7	14
Width	h	4

Then I set up and solved the proportion using cross products. I put 2 into the original equation and found that $\frac{14}{4}$ reduces to $\frac{7}{2}$, so the ratios are equal.

▶ 6. **Explain** For the sports car in problem **5**, suppose the actual height is 4 feet. What is the height of the model? How do you know your answer is correct?

▶ 7. **Analyze** The femur is the large bone that runs from the knee to the hip. In a scale drawing of a human skeleton the length of the femur measures 3 cm, and the full skeleton measures 12 cm. If the drawing represents a 6-ft-tall person, what is the actual length of the person's femur? $\frac{3}{12} = \frac{F}{6}$; $1\frac{1}{2}$ ft

▶ 8. The humerus is the bone that runs from the elbow to the shoulder. Suppose the humerus of a 6-ft-tall person is 1 ft long. How long should the humerus be on the scale drawing of the skeleton in problem **7**? $\frac{h}{12} = \frac{1}{6}$; 2 cm

Investigation 11   **579**

▶ See Math Conversations in the sidebar.

Math Conversations
Discussion opportunities are provided below.

Problem 1 Connect
Students will need a ruler to verify the measure of the length and width of Angela's kitchen in the scale drawing.

"What is the measured length and width of Angela's kitchen?" 1 inch by $\frac{1}{2}$ inch

Problem 3 Connect
"One inch of the scale model represents 1.5 ft of the actual house. How can we use that information to find the distance that 8 inches of the scale model represents?" multiply 1.5 ft by 8

"What distance does 8 inches of the scale model represent?" 12 feet

"What distance does 10 inches of the scale model represent?" 15 feet (1.5 ft × 10)

Problems 5–8 Connect
To complete problems 5–8, students must write the proportions in a consistent or orderly way. To help them write proportions consistently, encourage them to include words in the proportions they write. For example:

$$\frac{\text{model length}}{\text{model width}} = \frac{\text{actual length}}{\text{actual width}}$$

Problem 7 Analyze
More than one method can be used to solve the problem. Encourage volunteers to explain, or demonstrate on the board, the different methods they used to solve the problem.

(continued)

Manipulative Use

Prior to completing problems **5–8**, invite students to work cooperatively to write and solve a proportion that estimates the actual distance between two cities on a map of your state. Invite a volunteer to **measure the distance** between the cities. Then using the legend of the map as a guide, ask the class to write and solve a proportion to estimate the distance. A calculator may be helpful.

Problem 9a `Connect`

"How can we use the idea of corresponding measures to complete the legend for the scale drawing?" Sample: Look for the relationship shared by the given measures which correspond. Those measures are 7 cm and 28 ft, and 4 cm and 16 feet.

"The corresponding measures are 7 cm and 28 cm, and 4 cm and 16 feet. What scale factor do these pairs of numbers represent?" 1 cm = 4 ft

Invite volunteers to explain, or demonstrate on the board, how the scale 1 cm = 4 ft can be derived from the given corresponding measures.

Instruction

After reviewing the scale $\frac{44 \text{ inches}}{264 \text{ inches}}$, have students note that 22 feet was changed to 264 inches before the scale of the rendering was established.

(continued)

---

9. A scale drawing of a room addition that measures 28 ft by 16 ft is shown below. The scale drawing measures 7 cm by 4 cm.

▶ a. `Connect` Complete this legend for the scale drawing:
$$1 \text{ cm} = \underline{\ 4\ } \text{ ft}$$

b. `Estimate` What is the actual length and width of the bathroom, rounded to the nearest foot. length = 8 ft; width = 4 ft

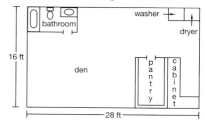

10. A natural history museum contains a 44-inch-long scale model of a *Stegosaurus* dinosaur. The actual length of the *Stegosaurus* was 22 feet. What should be the legend for the scale model of the dinosaur?
$$1 \text{ inch} = \underline{\ 0.5\ } \text{ feet}$$

Maps, blueprints, and models are called *renderings*. If a rendering is smaller than the actual object it represents, then the dimensions of the rendering are a fraction of the dimensions of the actual object. This fraction is called the **scale** of the rendering.

To determine the scale of a rendering, we form a fraction using corresponding dimensions and the same units for both. Then we reduce.

$$\text{scale} = \frac{\text{dimension of rendering}}{\text{dimension of object}}$$

In the case of the *Stegosaurus* in problem **10**, the corresponding lengths are 44 inches and 22 feet. Before reducing the fraction, we will convert 22 feet to 264 inches. Then we write a fraction, using the length of the model as the numerator and the dinosaur's actual length as the denominator.

$$\text{scale} = \frac{44 \text{ inches}}{22 \text{ feet}} = \frac{44 \text{ inches}}{264 \text{ inches}} = \frac{1}{6}$$

So the model is a $\frac{1}{6}$ scale model. The reciprocal of the scale is the **scale factor**. So the scale factor from the model to the actual *Stegosaurus* is 6. This means we can multiply any dimension of the model by 6 to determine the corresponding dimension of the actual object.

11. What is the scale of the model car in problem **5**? What is the scale factor?
$\frac{1}{24}$; 24

12. A scale may be written as a ratio that uses a colon. For example, we can write the scale of the *Stegosaurus* model as 1:6. Suppose that a toy company makes action figures of sports stars using a scale of 1:10. How many inches tall will a figure of a 6-ft-8-in. basketball player be?
8 in.

▶ See Math Conversations in the sidebar.

English Learners

To clarify the meaning of the word **rendering**, say:

"Look at the scale drawing of the bathroom shown on this page. We call this type of drawing a rendering. A rendering is a representation of something by a picture or a model. What is another place in this lesson that shows a rendering?" the scale drawing on the first page of the lesson

13. In a scale drawing of a wall mural, the scale factor is 6. If the scale drawing is 3 feet long by 1.5 feet wide, what are the dimensions of the actual mural?   18 feet by 9 feet

extensions ▶ **a.** *Model*   Make a scale drawing of your bedroom's floor plan, where 1 in. = 3 ft. Include in your drawing the locations of doors and windows as well as major pieces of furniture. What is the scale factor you used?   36

▶ **b.** *Model*   Cut out and assemble the pieces from Activity 21 and 22 to make a scale model of the *Freedom 7* spacecraft. This spacecraft was piloted by Alan B. Shepard, the first American to go into space. With *Freedom 7* sitting atop a rocket, Shepard blasted off from Cape Canaveral, Florida, on May 5, 1961. Because he did not orbit (circle) the earth, the trip lasted only 15 minutes before splashdown in the Atlantic Ocean. Shepard was one of six astronauts to fly a Mercury spacecraft like *Freedom 7*. Each Mercury spacecraft could carry only one astronaut, because the rockets available in the early 1960s were not powerful enough to lift heavier loads.

Your completed *Freedom 7* model will have a scale of 1:24. After you have constructed the model, measure its length. Use this information to determine the length of an actual Mercury spacecraft.

c.

▶ **c.** *Represent*   On a coordinate plane draw a square with vertices at (2, 2), (4, 2), (4, 4), and (2, 4). Then apply a scale factor of 2 to the square so that the dimensions of the square double but the point (3, 3) remains the center of the larger square. Draw the larger square on the same coordinate plane. What are the coordinates of its vertices?   (1, 1), (5, 1), (5, 5), (1, 5)

▶ **d.** *Represent*   Using plastic straws, scissors, and string, make a scale model of a triangle whose sides are 3 ft, 4 ft, and 5 ft. For the model, let $\frac{3}{4}$ in. = 1 foot. What is the scale factor? How long are the sides of the model?   16; $2\frac{1}{4}$ in., 3 in., $3\frac{3}{4}$ in.

e. *Model*   Draw these shapes on grid paper and measure the angles. Write the measure by the angle and then mark each angle as acute, obtuse, or right.

Now use the grid paper to draw each figure increased by a scale factor of 2. Then develop a mathematical argument proving or disproving that the angle classification of the images are the same as the given figures. See student work. Sample: The lengths of the sides of the figures has increased, so their areas are greater. However, the angle measures remain the same. Therefore the classification of the angles remains the same.

Investigation 11   **581**

▶ See Math Conversations in the sidebar.

Instruction

Point out that because the scale factor is the reciprocal of the scale, the values of the numerator and denominator are reversed.

Remind students that the same units must be used for both the model and the actual object when determining the scale and scale factor.

Extensions

a. *Model*   Allow students to make a scale drawing of any room in their home.

b. *Model*   Students will need **Investigation Activities 21** and **22** Scale Model and scissors to complete this extension.

c. *Represent*   After completing this extension, challenge students to compare the coordinates of the original vertices to the corresponding vertices of the larger rectangle and explain the relationship they share.

d. *Represent*   Distribute the materials to each student, or to pairs or small groups of students, to complete this extension.

e. *Model*   If students have difficulty enlarging the figures by a scale factor of 2, have them count squares to double the lengths of the sides of the figures. After using a protractor to measure the angles of the images, students should conclude that while the area increases, the corresponding angle measures do not.

Looking Forward

Using scale models and drawings to determine actual or scale dimensions and finding the scale or scale factor of an object prepares students for:

• **Lesson 114,** converting measures by multiplying by unit multipliers.

Lesson Planner

LESSON	NEW CONCEPTS	MATERIALS	RESOURCES
111	• Applications Using Division	Manipulative Kit: inch and metric rulers, Relational GeoSolids square pyramid	**Power Up N**
112	• Multiplying and Dividing Integers	Paper, scissors	**Power Up M** **Investigation Activity 15**
113	• Adding and Subtracting Mixed Measures • Multiplying by Powers of Ten		**Power Up N** **Investigation Activity 15**
114	• Unit Multipliers		**Power Up M** **Investigation Activity 15**
115	• Writing Percents as Fractions, Part 2		**Power Up N** **Investigation Activity 15**
116	• Compound Interest	Calculators	**Power Up M**
117	• Finding a Whole When a Fraction is Known		**Power Up N** **Investigation Activity 15**
118	• Estimating Area	Overhead marker (for the teacher), grid paper, irregular shapes	**Power Up M** **Lesson Activity 23 Transparency**
119	• Finding a Whole When a Percent Is Known		**Power Up N** **Investigation Activity 15**
120	• Volume of a Cylinder	Real-world examples of cylinders such as a juice can, an oatmeal canister, etc.	**Power Up M** **Investigation Activity 15**
Inv. 12	• Volume of Prisms, Pyramids, Cylinders and Cones • Surface Area of Prisms and Cylinders	Manipulative Kit: Relational GeoSolids square prisms, square pyramids, cylinders and cones Dry rice or salt (enough to fill the Relational GeoSolids cylinder), metric rulers, grid paper	

Problem Solving

Strategies

- **Find a Pattern**   Lesson 113
- **Use Logical Reasoning**   Lessons 111, 114, 117, 120
- **Draw a Diagram**   Lessons 111, 113, 117
- **Work Backwards**   Lesson 112
- **Write an Equation**   Lessons 114, 116, 118, 119
- **Guess and Check**   Lesson 115
- **Make a Chart**   Lesson 113

Real-World Applications

pp. 582–587, 589–594, 596–597, 599–601, 603–605, 607–611, 613–615, 617–621, 624–625, 628–629, 634, 635

4-Step Process

Teacher Edition   Lessons 111–120 (Power-Up Discussions)

Communication

Discuss

pp. 588, 612, 623

Explain

pp. 595, 619, 622, 627

Formulate a Problem

pp. 585, 623

Connections

Math and Other Subjects

Math and Science   p. 596

Math and Art   p. 590

Math and Sports   pp. 599, 601, 624

Math and Music   p. 624

Math to Math

Measurement and Problem Solving   Lessons 111, 112, 113, 114, 115, 116, 117, 118, 119, 120, Inv. 12

Algebra and Problem Solving   Lessons 111, 114, 116, 117, 118, 119

Fractions, Percents, Decimals and Problem Solving   Lessons 111, 112, 113, 114, 115, 116, 117, 118, 119, 120

Fractions and Measurement   Lessons 111, 112, 113, 114, 115, 116, 118, 119

Measurement and Geometry   Lessons 111, 112, 113, 114, 115, 116, 117, 118, 119, 120, Inv. 12

Proportional Relationships and Geometry   Lessons 111, 114, 116

Probability and Statistics   Lessons 113, 114, 115, 116, 117, 118, 119, 120

Math and Logic   Lesson 120, Inv. 12

Representation

Manipulatives/Hands On

pp. 584–585, 596, 600, 605, 608, 614, 616, 618, 625–626

Model

pp. 603, 613, 615, 622, 629

Represent

pp. 610, 615, 624, 635

Formulate an Equation

p. 623

Technology

Student Resources

- eBook
- Calculator   Lesson 116
- Online Resources at www.SaxonPublishers.com/ActivitiesC1
  Graphing Calculator Activity   Lesson 116
  Online Activities
  Math Enrichment Problems
  Math Stumpers

Teacher Resources

- **Resources and Planner CD**
- **Adaptations CD**   Lessons 111–120
- **Test & Practice Generator CD**
- **eGradebook**
- **Answer Key CD**

These lessons close the school year by building on the instruction of rational numbers.

Problem Solving

Word problems involving division are a trouble spot for most students.

Many applications involving division require interpreting the result of the division in the context of the situation. Students solve division problems requiring differing interpretations in Lesson 111.

Algebraic Thinking

Students write equations to solve percent problems.

Students change percents expressed in mixed number form to fractions in Lesson 115, and in Lesson 116 they apply percents to calculate compound interest. In Lessons 117 and 119 they find a whole when a fraction or percent is known. Students multiply and divide integers in Lesson 112.

Measurement Applications

Students solve problems involving mixed measures.

Students solve problems involving addition and subtraction of mixed measures in Lesson 113, and they use unit multipliers to convert measures in Lesson 114.

Spatial Thinking

Students use estimation with geometric figures.

In geometry students apply techniques to estimate the areas of irregular shapes in Lesson 118.

Surface Area and Volume

The connection between surface area and volume is explored.

In Lesson 120 students learn to calculate the volume of a cylinder.

Investigation 12 helps students make the connection between surface area and volume.

Assessment

A variety of weekly assessment tools are provided.

After Lesson 115:
- Power-Up Test 22
- Cumulative Test 22
- Performance Activity 22

After Lesson 120:
- Power-Up Test 23
- Cumulative Test 23
- Customized Benchmark Test
- Performance Task 23

LESSON	NEW CONCEPTS	PRACTICED	ASSESSED
111	• Applications Using Division	Lessons 111, 112, 113, 114, 116, 117, 118	Test 23
112	• Multiplying and Dividing Integers	Lessons 112, 113, 114, 115, 116, 117, 119, 120	Test 23
113	• Adding and Subtracting Mixed Measures	Lessons 113, 114, 115, 116	Test & Practice Generator
113	• Multiplying by Powers of Ten	Lessons 113, 114, 115, 116, 117, 118	Test 23
114	• Unit Multipliers	Lessons 114, 116, 118, 120	Test 23
115	• Writing Percents as Fractions, Part 2	Lessons 115, 116, 118, 119, 120	Test & Practice Generator
116	• Compound Interest	Lessons 117, 118	Test & Practice Generator
117	• Finding a Whole When a Fraction Is Known	Lessons 117, 118, 119, 120	Test & Practice Generator
118	• Estimating Area	Lesson 118	Test & Practice Generator
119	• Finding a Whole When a Percent Is Known	Lesson 119	Test & Practice Generator
120	• Volume of a Cylinder	Lesson 120	Test & Practice Generator
Inv. 12	• Volume of Prisms, Pyramids, Cylinders and Cones	Investigation 12	Test & Practice Generator
Inv. 12	• Surface Area of Prisms and Cylinders	Investigation 12	Test & Practice Generator

• Applications Using Division

Objectives
- Interpret the remainders to division problems that have real-world applications.

Materials
- **Power Up N** (in *Instructional Masters*)
- **Manipulative Kit: inch and metric rulers**

Optional
- **Manipulative Kit: Relational GeoSolids square pyramid**

Power Up N

Technology Resources

Student eBook Complete student textbook in electronic format.

Resources and Planner CD Assessment, reteaching, and instructional masters, plus a pacing calendar with standards.

Test and Practice Generator CD Create additional practice sheets and custom-made tests.

www.SaxonPublishers.com Visit for more student activities and planning materials.

Inclusion

Adaptations CD Adapted lessons, investigations, practice and assessments.

National Council of Teachers of Mathematics (NCTM)

Numbers and Operations

NO.2a Understand the meaning and effects of arithmetic operations with fractions, decimals, and integers

NO.3c Develop and use strategies to estimate the results of rational-number computations and judge the reasonableness of the results

Problem Solving

PS.1b Solve problems that arise in mathematics and in other contexts

Connections

CN.4a Recognize and use connections among mathematical ideas

Problem-Solving Strategy: Draw a Diagram/
Use Logical Reasoning

Twenty students in a homeroom class are signing up for fine arts electives. So far, 5 students have signed up for band, 6 have signed up for drama, and 12 signed up for art. There are 3 students who signed up for both drama and art, 2 students who signed up for both band and art, and 1 student who signed up for all three. How many students have not yet signed up for an elective?

Understand **Understand the problem.**

"What information are we given?"

a. 20 students will be signing up for electives
b. 5 students signed up for band
c. 6 students signed up for drama
d. 12 students signed up for art
e. 3 students signed up for both drama and art
f. 2 students signed up for both band and art
g. 1 student signed up for all three (band, drama, and art).

"What are we asked to do?"

Determine how many students still need to register for their elective(s).

Plan **Make a plan.**

"What problem-solving strategy will we use?"

We will *draw a diagram* and *use logical reasoning*.

Solve **Carry out the plan.**

"How do we begin?"

We will draw and label a Venn diagram, and fill in the correct numbers of students in each section. It is easiest to work backward. We know that there is 1 student in the center section that signed up for all three. We know that 2 students signed up for band and art and 3 students that signed up for drama and art so we can fill in those overlapping sections. Once those numbers are filled in, you can calculate how many students signed up for art only ($12 - 6 = 6$). We can calculate how many students signed up for drama only ($6 - 4 = 2$). Finally, we can calculate the number of students who signed up for band only ($5 - 3 = 2$).

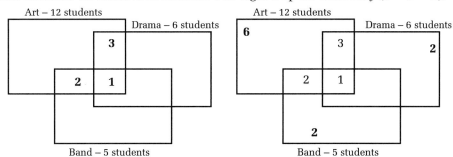

"How many students have signed up for their elective(s)?"

$6 + 2 + 2 + 3 + 2 + 1 = 16$ students.

"How many students still need to sign up?"

$20 - 16 = 4$ students.

Check **Look back.**

"Did we find the answer to the question that was asked?"

Yes. We found that four students still need to register for their elective(s).

1 Power Up

Facts
Distribute **Power Up N** to students. See answers below.

Mental Math
Before students begin the Mental Math exercise, do this counting exercise as a class.

Count up and down by $\frac{1}{2}$s between -3 and 3.

Encourage students to share different ways to mentally compute these exercises. Strategies for exercises **a** and **b** are listed below.

a. Double $\frac{1}{3}$ of 24
$24 \div 3 = 8; 8 \times 2 = 16$
Use Repeated Addition
Since $8 + 8 + 8 = 24$, $\frac{2}{3}$ of $24 = 8 + 8$ or 16.

b. Multiply Tens and Multiply Ones
$7(30 + 5) = 210 + 35 = 245$
Find 7×40, then Subtract 7×5
$7 \times 40 = 280; 7 \times 5 = 35; 280 - 35 = 245$

Problem Solving
Refer to **Power-Up Discussion**, p. 582F.

2 New Concepts

Instruction
The skill of choosing when to round a division quotient up or down is sometimes called interpreting the remainder.

Example 1
Instruction
Explain that the phrase "as balanced as possible" represents dividing the whole into equal groups, if possible. If the whole cannot be divided into equal groups, the groups should be as equal as possible.

(continued)

582 *Saxon* Math Course 1

LESSON 111

• Applications Using Division

Power Up *Building Power*

facts Power Up N

mental math
- **a. Fractional Parts:** $\frac{2}{3}$ of 24   16
- **b. Calculation:** 7×35 245
- **c. Percent:** 50% of $48 $24
- **d. Calculation:** $10.00 − $8.59 $1.41
- **e. Decimals:** 0.5×100 50
- **f. Number Sense:** $\frac{1600}{400}$ 4
- **g. Geometry:** A rectangular solid is 10 ft. $\times$ 6 ft. $\times$ 4 ft. What is the volume of the solid?   240 cubic feet
- **h. Calculation:** $8 \times 8, - 1, \div 9, \times 4, + 2, \div 2, \div 3, \times 5$ 25

problem solving
Twenty students in a homeroom class are signing up for fine arts electives. So far, 5 students have signed up for band, 6 have signed up for drama, and 12 signed up for art. There are 3 students who signed up for both drama and art, 2 students who signed up for both band and art, and 1 student who signed up for all three. How many students have not yet registered for an elective?   4 students

New Concept *Increasing Knowledge*

When a division problem has a remainder, there are several ways to write the answer: with a remainder, as a mixed number, or as a decimal number.

$$4\overline{)15} \quad \begin{array}{r} 3\,R\,3 \end{array} \qquad 4\overline{)15} \quad \begin{array}{r} 3\frac{3}{4} \end{array} \qquad 4\overline{)15.00} \quad \begin{array}{r} 3.75 \end{array}$$

How a division answer should be written depends upon the question to be answered. In real-world applications we sometimes need to round an answer up, and we sometimes need to round an answer down. The quotient of $15 \div 4$ rounds up to 4 and rounds down to 3.

Example 1

One hundred students are to be assigned to 3 classrooms. How many students should be in each class so that the numbers are as balanced as possible?

582   *Saxon Math Course 1*

Facts   Complete each equivalence.

1. Draw a segment about 1 cm long.

2. Draw a segment about 1 inch long.

3. One inch is how many centimeters? __2.54__

4. Which is longer, 1 km or 1 mi? __1 mi__

5. Which is longer, 1 km or $\frac{1}{2}$ mi? __1 km__

6. How many ounces are in a pound? __16__

7. How many pounds are in a ton? __2000__

8. A dollar bill has a mass of about one __gram__.

9. A pair of shoes has a mass of about one __kilogram__.

10. On Earth a kilogram mass weighs about __2.2__ pounds.

11. A metric ton is __1000__ kilograms.

12. On Earth a metric ton weighs about __2200__ pounds.

13. The Earth rotates on its axis once in a __day__.

14. The Earth revolves around the Sun once in a __year__.

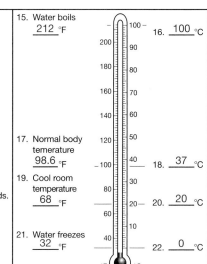

15. Water boils __212__ °F   16. __100__ °C

17. Normal body temerature __98.6__ °F   18. __37__ °C

19. Cool room temperature __68__ °F   20. __20__ °C

21. Water freezes __32__ °F   22. __0__ °C

582   *Saxon* Math Course 1

Solution

Dividing 100 by 3 gives us 33 R 1. Assigning 33 students per class totals 99 students. We add the remaining student to one of the classes, giving that class 34 students. We write the answer **33, 33,** and **34.**

Example 2

Matinee movie tickets cost $8. Jim has $30. How many tickets can he buy?

Solution

We divide 30 dollars by 8 dollars per ticket. The quotient is $3\frac{3}{4}$ tickets.

$$\frac{30 \text{ dollars}}{8 \text{ dollars per ticket}} = 3\frac{3}{4} \text{ tickets}$$

Jim cannot buy $\frac{3}{4}$ of a ticket, so we round down to the nearest whole number. Jim can buy **3 tickets.**

Example 3

Fifteen children need a ride to the fair. Each car can transport 4 children. How many cars are needed to transport 15 children?

Solution

We divide 15 children by 4 children per car. The quotient is $3\frac{3}{4}$ cars.

$$\frac{15 \text{ children}}{4 \text{ children per car}} = 3\frac{3}{4} \text{ cars}$$

Three cars are not enough. Four cars will be needed. One of the cars will be $\frac{3}{4}$ full. We round $3\frac{3}{4}$ cars up to **4 cars.**

Example 4

Dale cut a 10-foot board into four equal lengths. How long was each of the four boards?

Solution

We divide 10 feet by 4.

$$\frac{10 \text{ ft}}{4} = 2\frac{2}{4} \text{ ft} = 2\frac{1}{2} \text{ ft}$$

Each board was $2\frac{1}{2}$ **ft** long.

Example 5

Kimberly is on the school swim team. At practice she swam the 50 m freestyle three times. Her times were 37.53 seconds, 36.90 seconds, and 36.63 seconds. What was the mean of her three times?

Lesson 111   583

Example 2
Instruction
Challenge students to describe different ways to estimate or check the solution using only mental math.

Example 3
Instruction
"How many seats in the cars will not be occupied by a child? Explain how you know." One; Each car can transport 4 children, and 4 cars can transport 4 × 4 or 16 children; 16 − 15 = 1.

Example 4
Instruction
"In this solution, why isn't the quotient rounded up or down?" Sample: The question asks for exact lengths.

(continued)

Example 5

Instruction

Have students note that the quotient is a decimal number because the dividend is a decimal number. Remind students to always place a decimal point in the quotient whenever a dividend is a decimal number.

Practice Set

Problem a [Infer]

Students must infer that only whole numbers can be used to describe each classroom because the quotient represents a number of people.

Problem b [Error Alert]

Encourage students who have difficulty finding the solution to model the problem using coin and bill sets (play money).

Problem c [Infer]

Extend the practice exercises by asking pairs or small groups of students to write and solve two problems, one in which the quotient needs to be rounded down (as shown in example 2 and problem **b**) and one in which the quotient needs to be rounded up (as shown in example 3 and problem **c**). Ask students to present the problems they wrote to the class and compare answers after the problems are solved.

Math Conversations

Discussion opportunities are provided below.

Problem 2 [Analyze]

Extend the Problem

"Suppose the friends decide to leave a 20% tip? What amount of money represents 20% of the bill? Explain how you can use mental math to find the answer." Sample: Finding 10% of a number is the same as shifting the decimal point in that number one place to the left. So 10% of $45 is $4.50, and double that amount is $9.

"What is each friend's share of the bill if they decide to leave a 20% tip?" $13.50

(continued)

Solution

To find the mean we add the three times and divide by 3.

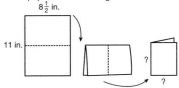

$$\begin{array}{r} 37.53 \\ 36.90 \\ 36.63 \\ \hline 111.06 \end{array} \qquad \begin{array}{r} 37.02 \\ 3\overline{)111.06} \end{array}$$

Kimberly's mean time was **37.02 seconds.**

Practice Set

a. [Infer] Ninety students were assigned to four classrooms as equally as possible. How many students were in each of the four classrooms? 22, 22, 23, 23

b. Movie tickets cost $9.50. Aluna has $30.00. How many movie tickets can she buy? 3 tickets

c. [Infer] Twenty-eight children need a ride to the fair. Each van can carry six children. How many vans are needed? 5 vans

d. Corinne folded an $8\frac{1}{2}$ in. by 11 in. piece of paper in half. Then she folded the paper in half again as shown. After the two folds, what are the dimensions of the rectangle that is formed? How can you check your answer? $5\frac{1}{2}$ in. by $4\frac{1}{4}$ in.; I can check the answer by folding an $8\frac{1}{2}$ in. by 11 in. piece of paper and measuring it.

e. Kevin ordered four books at the book fair for summer reading. The books cost $6.95, $7.95, $6.45, and $8.85. Find the average (mean) price of the books. $7.55

Written Practice   *Strengthening Concepts*

1. Eighty students will be assigned to three classrooms. How many students should be in each class so that the numbers are as balanced as possible? (Write the numbers.) 26, 27, 27
(111)

2. Four friends went out to lunch. Their bill was $45. If the friends divide the bill equally, how much will each friend pay? $11.25
(111)

3. Shauna bought a sheet of 39¢ stamps at the post office for $15.60. How many stamps were in the sheet? 40 stamps
(49)

4. Eight cubes were used to build this 2-by-2-by-2 cube. How many cubes are needed to build a cube that has three cubes along each edge? 27 cubes
(82)

▶ See Math Conversations in the sidebar.

6. 30 cm or 31 cm (Accept either answer. Twelve Inches equals 30.48 cm. which is very near the midpoint of 30 cm and 31 cm.)

5. Write the standard notation for the following: 5043
(92)

$$(5 \times 10^3) + (4 \times 10^1) + (3 \times 10^0)$$

6. *Estimate* Use a centimeter ruler and an inch ruler to answer this
(7) question. Twelve inches is closest to how many centimeters? Round the answer to the nearest centimeter.

* 7. Create a scale drawing of a room at home or of your classroom. Choose
(Inv. 11) a scale that allows the drawings to fit on one sheet of paper. Write the legend on the scale drawing.   See student work.

▶ *** 8.** *Conclude* If two angles of a triangle measure 70° and 80°, then what is
(98) the measure of the third angle?   30°

Connect Complete the table to answer problems **9–11.**

	Fraction	Decimal	Percent
9. (99)	$\frac{11}{20}$	**a.** 0.55	**b.** 55%
10. (99)	**a.** $1\frac{1}{2}$	1.5	**b.** 150%
11. (99)	**a.** $\frac{1}{100}$	**b.** 0.01	1%

▶ *** 12.** *Analyze* Calculate mentally:
(100, 104)
   a. −6 + −12   −18   **b.** −6 − −12   +6

   c. −12 + +6   − 6   **d.** −12 − +6   −18

13. $6\frac{1}{4} \div 100$ $\frac{1}{16}$ **14.** 0.3m = $4.41 $14.70
(68)   (49)

▶ *** 15.** *Analyze* Kim scored 15 points, which was 30% of the team's total.
(105) How many points did the team score in all?   50 points

▶ *** 16.** Andrea received the following scores in a gymnastic event.
(111)

6.7	7.6	6.6	6.7	6.5	6.7	6.8

   The highest score and the lowest score are not counted. What is the average of the remaining scores?   6.7

17. *Formulate* Refer to problem **16** to write a comparison question
(13) about the scores Andrea received from the judges. Then answer the question.   Sample: What was the difference between the highest and lowest scores? 7.6 − 6.5 = 1.1

* 18. What is the area of the quadrilateral below?   40 m²
(107)

19. What is the ratio of vertices to edges on a pyramid with a
(Inv. 6) square base? $\frac{5}{8}$

Lesson 111   585

▶ See Math Conversations in the sidebar.

---

3 **Written Practice** *(Continued)*

Math Conversations

Discussion opportunities are provided below.

Problem 8 Conclude

"What is the sum of the angle measures of any triangle?" 180°

Problem 12 Analyze

Before students calculate each sum or difference, ask them how they will simplify the consecutive signs that are a part of each expression. Problem a: change + − to −; Problem b: change − − to +; Problem c: change + + to +; Problem d: change − + to −

Problem 15 Analyze

Before solving the problem, challenge students to describe a way to estimate the exact answer, then name an estimate of that answer. Sample: Since 30% is less than $\frac{1}{3}$ and greater than $\frac{1}{4}$, the team's total points will range from 15 × 3 or 45 to 15 × 4 or 60 points.

After the problem has been solved, have students check their work by comparing the estimate to the exact answer and making a decision about the reasonableness of that answer.

Errors and Misconceptions
Problem 16

Watch for students who have difficulty naming the quotient because they do not recognize that the divisor of the sum of the addends is 5, not 7.

Remind these students that the highest and lowest scores are not counted, and because there are only 5 addends, the divisor of the sum of the addends is 5.

(continued)

Manipulative Use

Students will need rulers to solve problem **6.** Since it may be difficult for some students to decide if 30 cm or 31 cm represents the correct answer, accept either answer.

Students who are interested in finding a more precise answer can convert 12 inches to centimeters. Tell them that 1 in. equals 2.54 cm. With this information, they should calculate that 12 in. equals 30.48 cm, which is closer to 30 cm than to 31 cm.

For problem **19,** encourage students to examine the square pyramid **Relational GeoSolid** from the Manipulative Kit.

Math Conversations

Discussion opportunities are provided below.

Problem 20 Conclude

Extend the Problem

"Does the triangle have more than two lines of symmetry? If so, how many more?" yes; one more

Problem 27 Connect

Because a variety of answers are possible, ask students to justify their answers. Point out that the best answer involves the least number of transformations.

Problem 30 Evaluate

Extend the Problem

Write "50 miles per hour" and "25,000 miles" on the board or overhead.

"The circumference of the Earth is about 25,000 miles. The average rate in this problem was 50 miles per hour. Using only mental math, estimate the length of time it would take to drive a distance equal to the circumference of the Earth at that average rate." Sample: 25,000 ÷ 50 is the same as 2500 ÷ 5; a reasonable estimate is 500 hours.

"Using only mental math, change the estimate of 500 hours to days." Sample: 24 hours is about the same as 25 hours; a reasonable estimate is 500 ÷ 25 or 20 days.

▶* **20.** **Conclude** Line *r* is called a line of symmetry
(110)   because it divides the equilateral triangle into two mirror images. Which other line is also a line of symmetry?   line *t*

* **21.** Solve and check: $3m + 1 = 100$ 33
(106)

22. Write the prime factorization of 600 using exponents. $2^3 \cdot 3 \cdot 5^2$
(73)

23. **Conclude** You need to make a three-dimensional model of a soup can
(Inv. 6)   using paper and tape. What 3 two-dimensional shapes do you need to cut to make the model?   a rectangle and 2 same-size circles

24. The price of an item is 89¢. The sales-tax rate is 7%. What is the total
(41)   for the item, including tax?   95¢

25. The probability of winning a prize in the drawing is one in a million. What
(58)   is the probability of not winning a prize in the drawing? $\frac{999,999}{1,000,000}$

Conclude Triangles *ABC* and *CDA* are congruent. Refer to this figure to answer problems **26** and **27**.

* **26.** Which angle in triangle *ABC* corresponds to angle *D* in triangle
(109)   *CDA*?   angle *B*

▶* **27.** **Connect** Which transformations would position triangle *CDA* on
(108)   triangle *ABC*?   rotation and possibly translation

28. Malik used a compass to draw a circle with a radius of 5 centimeters.
(47)   What was the circumference of the circle? (Use 3.14 for π.)
31.4 centimeters

29. Solve this proportion: $\frac{10}{16} = \frac{25}{y}$ 40
(85)

▶ **30.** **Evaluate** The formula $d = rt$ shows that the distance traveled (*d*)
(95)   equals the rate (*r*) times the time (*t*) spent traveling at that rate. (Here, *rate* means "speed.") This function table shows the relationship between distance and time when the rate is 50.

t	1	2	3	4
d	50	100	150	200

Find the value of *d* in $d = rt$ when *r* is $\frac{50 \text{ mi}}{1 \text{ hr}}$ and *t* is 5 hr.   250 mi

▶ See Math Conversations in the sidebar.

• Multiplying and Dividing Integers

Objectives

- Calculate the product of two integers.
- Calculate the quotient of two integers.

Materials

- **Power Up M** (in *Instructional Masters*)

Optional

- **Investigation Activity 15** (in *Instructional Masters*) or **graph paper**
- **Teacher-provided material: paper, scissors**

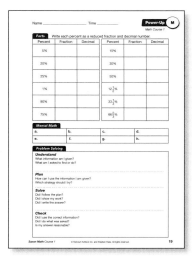

Power Up M

Math Language

	English Learners (ESL)
	wingspan

Technology Resources

Student eBook Complete student textbook in electronic format.

Resources and Planner CD Assessment, reteaching, and instructional masters, plus a pacing calendar with standards.

Test and Practice Generator CD Create additional practice sheets and custom-made tests.

www.SaxonPublishers.com Visit for more student activities and planning materials.

Inclusion

Adaptations CD Adapted lessons, investigations, practice and assessments.

National Council of Teachers of Mathematics (NCTM)

Numbers and Operations

NO.1g Develop meaning for integers and represent and compare quantities with them

NO.2a Understand the meaning and effects of arithmetic operations with fractions, decimals, and integers

NO.2c Understand and use the inverse relationships of addition and subtraction, multiplication and division, and squaring and finding square roots to simplify computations and solve problems

NO.3b Develop and analyze algorithms for computing with fractions, decimals, and integers and develop fluency in their use

Problem-Solving Strategy: Work Backwards

When all the cards from a 52-card deck are dealt to three players, each player receives 17 cards, and there is one extra card. Dean invented a new deck of cards so that any number of players up to 6 can play, and there would be no extra cards. How many cards are in Dean's deck, if the number is less than 100?

(Understand) **Understand the problem.**

"What information are we given?"

When all the cards from a 52-card deck are dealt to three players, each player receives 17 cards, with one card extra.

"What are we asked to do?"

Find how many cards (less than 100) are in a deck that allows up to 6 players, with no extra cards when the cards are all dealt.

(Plan) **Make a plan.**

"What problem-solving strategy will we use?"

We will use number sense and *work backwards*.

"What math knowledge can help us answer the question?"

Multiples of a number have no remainder when divided by the number.

(Solve) **Carry out the plan.**

"What are the multiples of 6 that are less than 100?"

6, 12, 18, 24, 30, 36, 42, 48, 54, 60, 66, 72, 78, 84, 90, 96

"Which multiples of 6 are also multiples of 5?"

30, 60, and 90

"Which of the numbers 30, 60, and 90 is a multiple of 4?"

Only 60.

"Is 60 a multiple of 3 and 2?"

Yes, every multiple of 6 is a multiple of 3 and 2.

"How many cards are in Dean's deck of cards?"

There are 60 cards in his deck.

(Check) **Look back.**

"Did we find the answer to the question that was asked?"

Yes. Dean's deck has 60 cards in it and 60 cards can be dealt equally to 2, 3, 4, 5, or 6 people without having any cards left over.

• Multiplying and Dividing Integers

facts   Power Up M

**mental
math**

a. **Fractional Parts:** $\frac{3}{4}$ of 24   18

b. **Calculation:** 6×48 288

c. **Percent:** 25% of $48 $12

d. **Calculation:** $4.98 + $2.49 $7.47

e. **Decimals:** $0.5 \div 10$ 0.05

f. **Number Sense:** $500 \cdot 30$ 15,000

g. **Geometry:** A cube has a volume of 27 in. What is the length of the sides of the cube?   3 in.

h. **Calculation:** $11 \times 4, + 1, \div 5, \sqrt{}, \times 4, - 2, \times 5, - 1, \sqrt{}$ 7

**problem
solving**   When all the cards from a 52-card deck are dealt to three players, each player receives 17 cards, and there is one extra card. Dean invented a new deck of cards so that any number of players up to 6 can play and there will be no extra cards. How many cards are in Dean's deck if the number is less than 100?   60

New Concept   *Increasing Knowledge*

We know that when we multiply two positive numbers the product is positive.

$$(+3)(+4) = +12$$

positive × positive = positive

Reading Math
$(+3)(+4)$ is the same as 3×4 or $3 \cdot 4$.

Notice that when we write $(+3)(+4)$ there is no $+$ or $-$ sign between the sets of parentheses.

When we multiply a positive number and a negative number, the product is negative. We show an example on this number line by multiplying 3 and -4.

3×-4 means $(-4) + (-4) + (-4)$

Lesson 112   587

Facts   Write each percent as a reduced fraction and decimal number.

Percent	Fraction	Decimal	Percent	Fraction	Decimal
5%	$\frac{1}{20}$	0.05	10%	$\frac{1}{10}$	0.1
20%	$\frac{1}{5}$	0.2	30%	$\frac{3}{10}$	0.3
25%	$\frac{1}{4}$	0.25	50%	$\frac{1}{2}$	0.5
1%	$\frac{1}{100}$	0.01	$12\frac{1}{2}$%	$\frac{1}{8}$	0.125
90%	$\frac{9}{10}$	0.9	$33\frac{1}{3}$%	$\frac{1}{3}$	Rounds to 0.333
75%	$\frac{3}{4}$	0.75	$66\frac{2}{3}$%	$\frac{2}{3}$	Rounds to 0.667

---

1 Power Up

Facts
Distribute **Power Up M** to students. See answers below.

Mental Math
Before students begin the Mental Math exercise, do this counting exercise as a class.

Count up and down by 5s between -25 and 25.

Encourage students to share different ways to mentally compute these exercises. Strategies for exercises **b** and **c** are listed below.

b. **Find 6 × 50, then Subtract 6 × 2**
  $(6 \times 50) - (6 \times 2) = 300 - 12 = 288$
  Multiply Place Values
  $(6 \times 40) + (6 \times 8) = 240 + 48 = 288$

c. **Find 50% of 50% of 48**
  $\frac{1}{2}$ of $48 = $24; $\frac{1}{2}$ of $24 = $12
  Break Apart $48
  $($40 \div 4) + ($8 \div 4) = $10 + $2 = 12

Problem Solving
Refer to **Power-Up Discussion**, p. 587B.

2 New Concepts

Instruction
Remind students that integers involve signs, and it is understood that an integer with no sign is a positive integer.

Explain that multiplication is an efficient way to complete a repeated addition. Have students note that the repeated addition is adding three -4s.

The number line shows that the sum of three -4s is -12, which is the same as the product of 3 and -4.

(continued)

Instruction

Ask students to say a variety of multiplication number sentences that contain a positive integer, a negative integer, and a negative product. Sample: Positive six times negative three is negative eighteen; negative five times positive five is negative twenty-five.

Ask students to say a variety of multiplication number sentences that contain two negative integers and a positive product. Sample: Negative three times negative one is positive three (or three); negative seven times negative two is positive fourteen (or fourteen).

Example
Instruction

Before calculating each product or quotient, ask students to name the sign of the product or quotient.

(continued)

We write the multiplication this way:

$$(+3)(-4) = -12$$

Positive three times *negative* four equals *negative* 12.

positive × negative = negative

When we multiply two negative numbers, the product is positive. Consider this sequence of equations:

1. Three times 4 is 12. $3 \times 4 = 12$
2. "Three times the opposite of 4" is "the opposite of 12." $3 \times -4 = -12$
3. The opposite of "3 times the opposite of 4" is the opposite of "the opposite of 12." $-3 \times -4 = +12$

negative × negative = positive

Recall that we can rearrange the numbers of a multiplication fact to make two division facts.

Thinking Skill

Discuss

How is multiplying integers similar to multiplying whole numbers? How is it different? When multiplying integers, we have to determine the sign of the product as well as its value. Products of whole numbers are always positive.

Multiplication Facts	Division Facts	
$(+3)(+4) = +12$	$\dfrac{+12}{+3} = +4$	$\dfrac{+12}{+4} = +3$
$(+3)(-4) = -12$	$\dfrac{-12}{+3} = -4$	$\dfrac{-12}{-4} = +3$
$(-3)(-4) = +12$	$\dfrac{+12}{-3} = -4$	$\dfrac{+12}{-4} = -3$

Studying these nine facts, we can summarize the results in two rules:

1. If the two numbers in a multiplication or division problem have the **same sign**, the answer is positive.
2. If the two numbers in a multiplication or division problem have **different signs**, the answer is negative.

Example

Calculate mentally:

  a. $(+8)(+4)$ b. $(+8) \div (+4)$

  c. $(+8)(-4)$ d. $(+8) \div (-4)$

  e. $(-8)(+4)$ f. $(-8) \div (+4)$

  g. $(-8)(-4)$ h. $(-8) \div (-4)$

Solution

  a. $+32$ b. $+2$

  c. -32 d. -2

  e. -32 f. -2

  g. $+32$ h. $+2$

Inclusion

Students will develop confidence multiplying and dividing integers if they focus on the two simple rules about signs: If two numbers have the **same sign,** their product and quotient are **positive.** If two numbers have **different signs,** their product and quotient are **negative.**

Reinforce this concept by asking students to name *only* the sign of the answer to several multiplication and division problems that you write on the board. Have students do the same with Lesson Practice *a–h.*

Practice Set ▶ *Predict* First predict which problems will have a positive answer and which will have a negative answer. Then simplify each problem.

a. $(-5)(+4)$ -20 **b.** $(-5)(-4)$ $+20$

c. $(+5)(+4)$ $+20$ **d.** $(+5)(-4)$ -20

e. $\frac{+12}{-2}$ -6 **f.** $\frac{+12}{+2}$ $+6$ **g.** $\frac{-12}{+2}$ -6 **h.** $\frac{-12}{-2}$ $+6$

Written Practice   *Strengthening Concepts*

* 1.
(111) Two hundred students are traveling by bus on a field trip. The maximum number of students allowed on each bus is 84. How many buses are needed for the trip?   3 buses

* 2. *Estimate* The wingspan of a jumbo jet is about 210 feet. The wingspan
(Inv. 11) of a model of a jumbo jet measures 25.2 inches.

▶   **a.** What is the approximate scale of the model? $\frac{1}{100}$

     b. The model is 28 inches long. To the nearest foot, how long is the jumbo jet?   about 233 feet

* 3. Calculate mentally:
(112)
     a. $(-2)(-6)$ $+12$ **b.** $\frac{+6}{-2}$ -3

     c. $\frac{-6}{-6}$ $+1$ **d.** $(-2)(+6)$ -12

* 4. Calculate mentally:
(100)
     a. $-2 + -6$ -8 **b.** $-2 - -6$ $+4$

     c. $+2 + -6$ -4 **d.** $+2 - -6$ $+8$

▶ *** 5.** *Analyze* The chef chopped 27 carrots, which was 90% of the carrots in
(105) the bag. How many carrots remained?   3 carrots

6. Write twenty million, five hundred ten thousand in expanded notation
(92) using exponents. $(2 \times 10^7) + (5 \times 10^5) + (1 \times 10^4)$

7. Find 8% of $3.65 and round the product to the nearest cent. $0.29
(41)

8. $\left(\frac{1}{2}\right)^2 + \frac{1}{8} \div \frac{1}{2}$ $\frac{1}{2}$
(92)

Connect   Complete the table to answer problems **9–11.**

	Fraction	Decimal	Percent
9. (99)	$1\frac{4}{5}$	**a.** 1.8	**b.** 180%
10. (99)	**a.** $\frac{3}{5}$	0.6	**b.** 60%
11. (99)	**a.** $\frac{1}{50}$	**b.** 0.02	2%

Solve:

12. $5\frac{1}{2} - m = 2\frac{5}{6}$ $2\frac{2}{3}$ *** 13.** $\frac{6}{10} = \frac{0.9}{n}$ 1.5
(63)   (85, 105)

Lesson 112   589

▶ See Math Conversations in the sidebar.

---

2 New Concepts *(Continued)*

Practice Set
Problems a–h   [Error Alert]

Before students complete the problems, ask

> *"What is the sign of the product or quotient of two positive integers?"* positive

> *"What is the sign of the product or quotient of a positive integer and a negative integer?"* negative

> *"What is the sign of the product or quotient of two negative integers?"* positive

When multiplying or dividing signed numbers, students should generalize that the product or quotient of two integers with the same sign is positive, and the product or quotient of two integers with different signs is negative.

---

3 Written Practice

Math Conversations

Discussion opportunities are provided below.

Problem 5   [Analyze]

"Before the chef began working, were there more than 27 carrots, or fewer than 27 carrots, in the bag? Explain how you know." More than 27; Sample: 100% represents the total number of carrots in the bag. Since 90% represents 27 carrots, and 90% is less than 100%, 27 carrots represent fewer carrots than the total number of carrots in the bag.

Errors and Misconceptions
Problem 2a

Watch for students who do not recognize that the units for the model and the actual object must be the same before the scale of the model can be calculated.

To help students make the units the same, first point out that the units are feet and inches, and feet must be changed to inches or inches must be changed to feet.

Help students generalize that changing inches to feet will produce numbers for the arithmetic that are less than the numbers that result from changing feet to inches. In other words, smaller numbers are easier to work with than larger numbers.

(continued)

3 Written Practice (Continued)

Math Conversations

Discussion opportunities are provided below.

Problem 17 *Infer*

Extend the Problem

"Suppose the prism is hollow. What is the greatest number of cubes—each measuring 2 cm by 2 cm by 2 cm—that could be placed inside the prism?" eight

Problem 21 *Verify*

One way for students to check their answers is for them to sketch the pattern shown in this problem on a piece of paper, cut it out, and fold it along the dotted lines.

Problem 22 *Classify*

"What word is used to describe a whole number greater than 1 that is not a composite number?" prime

Problem 24 *Conclude*

Extend the Problem

Ask students to draw the two lines of symmetry on their answers.

(continued)

---

* 14. $9x - 7 = 92$ 11
(106)

15. $0.05w = 8$ 160
(49)

16. All eight books in the stack are the same
(15)   weight. Three books weigh a total of six
pounds.

  a. How much does each book weigh?   2 lb

  b. How much do all eight books weigh?
  16 lb

▶ **17.** Find the volume of a rectangular prism using the formula $V = lwh$ when
(91)   the length is 8 cm, the width is 5 cm, and the height is 2 cm.   80 cm³

18. How many millimeters is 1.2 meters (1 m = 1000 mm)?   1200 mm
(95)

* 19. What is the perimeter of the polygon at right?
(103)   (Dimensions are in millimeters.)   54 mm

* 20. What is the area of the polygon in
(107)   problem 19?   110 mm²

▶ **21.** *Verify* If the pattern shown below were cut out and folded on the
(Inv. 6)   dotted lines, would it form a cube, a pyramid, or a cylinder? Explain how
you know.   cube; Sample: A cube has six square faces that are all the
same size.

▶ **22.** *Classify* Which one of these numbers is not a composite number?   D
(65)   **A** 34   **B** 35   **C** 36   **D** 37

23. *Estimate* Debbie wants to decorate a cylindrical wastebasket by
(47)   wrapping it with wallpaper. The diameter of the wastebasket is 12
inches. The length of the wallpaper should be at least how many
inches? Round up to the next inch.   38 inches

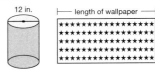

▶* **24. a.** *Conclude* Which one of these letters has two lines of symmetry?   H
(110)

  H   A   V   E

  b. Which letter has rotational symmetry?   H

▶ See Math Conversations in the sidebar.

25. (17) **Connect** Which arrow is pointing to $-\frac{1}{2}$? **B**

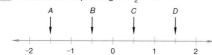

26. (101) The ratio of nonfiction to fiction books on Shawna's bookshelf is 2 to 3. If the total number of books on her shelf is 30, how many nonfiction books are there? **12 nonfiction books**

▶ **27.** (Inv. 7) **Connect** What are the coordinates of the point that is halfway between $(-2, -3)$ and $(6, -3)$? **(2, -3)**

▶ **28.** (Inv. 10) A set of 40 number cards contains one each of the counting numbers from 1 through 40. A multiple of 10 is drawn from the set and is not replaced. A second card is drawn from the remaining 39 cards. What is the probability that the second card will be a multiple of 10? $\frac{3}{39} = \frac{1}{13}$

* **29.** (107) Combine the areas of the two triangles to find the area of this trapezoid. **54 in.²**

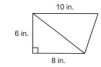

10 in.

6 in.

8 in.

30. (92) $3^2 + 2 \times 5^2 - 50 \div \sqrt{25}$ **49**

Early Finishers
Real-World Application

Hannah's mother gave her $20 for her birthday. Her aunt gave her $25. She spent one-fifth of her birthday money at the bookstore. How much did Hannah spend at the bookstore?

Write one equation and use it to solve the problem.
Sample: ($20 + $25) ÷ 5 = $9

▶ See Math Conversations in the sidebar.

Math Conversations
Discussion opportunities are provided below.

Problem 27 Connect
Continue to encourage students to solve graphing problems by sketching instead of by using graph paper. However, some students may be more comfortable using graph paper or a copy of **Investigation Activity 15** Coordinate Plane to complete the problem.

Problem 28 Analyze
Extend the Problem
"Explain what the complement of a probability event is." The complement is the probability of the event not happening.

"In this problem, the probability that the second card is a multiple of 10 is $\frac{1}{13}$. What is the complement of that event?" $\frac{12}{13}$

• Adding and Subtracting Mixed Measures
• Multiplying by Powers of Ten

Objectives
- Rename units to add and subtract mixed measures.
- Multiply a number by a power of ten to rewrite a number in standard notation.

Lesson Preparation

Materials
- **Power Up N** (in *Instructional Masters*)

Optional
- **Investigation Activity 15** (in *Instructional Masters*) or **graph paper**

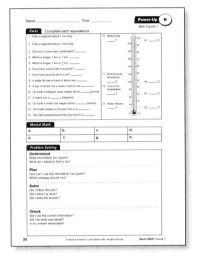

Power Up N

Math Language

Maintain	English Learners (ESL)
powers	instead

Technology Resources

Student eBook Complete student textbook in electronic format.

Resources and Planner CD Assessment, reteaching, and instructional masters, plus a pacing calendar with standards.

Test and Practice Generator CD Create additional practice sheets and custom-made tests.

www.SaxonPublishers.com Visit for more student activities and planning materials.

Inclusion

Adaptations CD Adapted lessons, investigations, practice and assessments.

Meeting Standards

National Council of Teachers of Mathematics (NCTM)

Numbers and Operations

NO.1e Develop an understanding of large numbers and recognize and appropriately use exponential, scientific, and calculator notation

Measurement

ME.1b Understand relationships among units and convert from one unit to another within the same system

Problem Solving

PS.1b Solve problems that arise in mathematics and in other contexts

Problem-Solving Strategy: Make a Chart/
Draw a Diagram/Find a Pattern

A hexagon can be divided into four triangles by three diagonals, drawn from a single vertex. How many triangles can a dodecagon be divided into using diagonals drawn from one vertex?

(Understand) **Understand the problem.**

"What information are we given?"

A hexagon can be divided into four triangles by three diagonals, drawn from the same vertex.

"What are we asked to do?"

Determine how many triangles a dodecagon can be divided into by drawing diagonals from one vertex.

(Plan) **Make a plan.**

"What problem-solving strategy will we use?"

We will *make a chart* and *draw a diagram* to help us *find a pattern*.

(Solve) **Carry out the plan.**

"First, we will draw some polygons and find the number of triangles formed by drawing diagonals from one vertex. Then we will make a table to show the number of triangles that can be formed."

Name of Polygon	Number of Sides	Number of Triangles
Quadrilateral	4	2
Pentagon	5	3
Hexagon	6	4
Octagon	8	6

"What pattern do we see?"

The number of triangles is always 2 fewer than the number of sides.

"How many sides does a dodecagon have?"

12 sides

"Can we use this information to predict the number of triangles that we will get by drawing diagonals from one vertex of a dodecagon?"

Yes. We know that a dodecagon has 12 sides and $12 - 2 = 10$; so there will be 10 triangles formed.

(Check) **Look back.**

"Did we complete the task?"

Yes. We determined that 10 triangles are made from a dodecagon with diagonals from a single vertex.

Teacher Note: Ask students if they can explain why the number of triangles is always 2 fewer than the number of sides. If necessary, ask students which two vertices you can never draw diagonals to. (The two vertices that are right next to the vertex from which you are drawing the diagonals because the line coincides with the side of the polygon. This situation is the same for every polygon making the number of triangles 2 fewer than the number of sides.)

• **Adding and Subtracting Mixed Measures**
• **Multiplying by Powers of Ten**

---

1 Power Up

Facts
Distribute **Power Up N** to students. See answers below.

Mental Math
Before students begin the Mental Math exercise, do this counting exercise as a class.

Count up and down by $\frac{1}{8}$s between $\frac{1}{8}$ and 2.

Encourage students to share different ways to mentally compute these exercises. Strategies for exercises **a** and **f** are listed below.

a. Multiply $\frac{1}{10}$ of 40 by 3
$40 \div 10 = 4$; $4 \times 3 = 12$
Divide 3 × 40 by 10
$(3 \times 40) \div 10 = 120 \div 10 = 12$
f. Shift the Decimal Points Two Places
$\frac{2000}{500} = \frac{20.00}{5.00} = \frac{20}{5} = 4$
Cancel Zeros
$\frac{2000}{500} = \frac{20\cancel{00}}{5\cancel{00}} = \frac{20}{5} = 4$

Problem Solving
Refer to **Power-Up Discussion**, p. 592B.

---

2 New Concepts

Instruction
Ask students to estimate their age in years and months. Point out that the each estimate is an example of a mixed measure.

Example 1
Instruction
"Why is 90 minutes equal to 1 hour 30 minutes?" Sample: There are 60 minutes in 1 hour.

(continued)

---

facts | Power Up N

mental math |
a. **Fractional Parts:** $\frac{3}{10}$ of 40   12
b. **Calculation:** 4×38 152
c. **Percent:** 25% of $200 $50
d. **Calculation:** $100.00 − $9.50 $90.50
e. **Decimals:** $0.12 \div 10$ 0.012
f. **Number Sense:** $\frac{2000}{500}$ 4
g. **Geometry:** A circle has a diameter of 10 mm. What is the circumference of the circle?   31.4 mm
h. **Calculation:** $6 \times 8, + 2, \times 2, − 1, \div 3, − 1, \div 4, + 2, \div 10, − 1$ 0

problem solving | A hexagon can be divided into four triangles by three diagonals drawn from a single vertex. How many triangles can a dodecagon be divided into using diagonals drawn from one vertex?   10 triangles

---

New Concepts — Increasing Knowledge

adding and subtracting mixed measures

Measurements that include more than one unit of measurement are mixed measures. If we say that a movie is an hour and 40 minutes long, we have used a mixed measure that includes hours and minutes. When adding or subtracting mixed measures, we may need to convert from one unit to another unit. In Lesson 102 we added and subtracted mixed measures involving pounds and ounces. In this lesson we will consider other mixed measures.

Example 1

The hike from the trailhead to the waterfall took 1 hr 50 min. The return trip took 1 hr 40 min. Altogether, how many hours and minutes long was the hike?

Solution

We add 50 minutes and 40 minutes to get 90 minutes which equals 1 hour 30 minutes.

Facts   Complete each equivalence.

1. Draw a segment about 1 cm long.

2. Draw a segment about 1 inch long.

3. One inch is how many centimeters? __2.54__

4. Which is longer, 1 km or 1 mi? __1 mi__

5. Which is longer, 1 km or $\frac{1}{2}$ mi? __1 km__

6. How many ounces are in a pound? __16__

7. How many pounds are in a ton? __2000__

8. A dollar bill has a mass of about one __gram__.

9. A pair of shoes has a mass of about one __kilogram__.

10. On Earth a kilogram mass weighs about __2.2__ pounds.

11. A metric ton is __1000__ kilograms.

12. On Earth a metric ton weighs about __2200__ pounds.

13. The Earth rotates on its axis once in a __day__.

14. The Earth revolves around the Sun once in a __year__.

15. Water boils __212__ °F

16. __100__ °C

17. Normal body temperature __98.6__ °F

18. __37__ °C

19. Cool room temperature __68__ °F

20. __20__ °C

21. Water freezes __32__ °F

22. __0__ °C

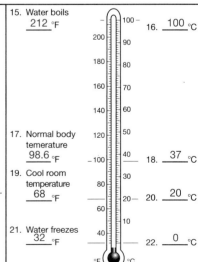

$$1 \text{ hr } 50 \text{ min}$$
$$+ 1 \text{ hr } 40 \text{ min}$$
$$\overline{90 \text{ min}}$$ (which is 1 hr 30 min)

We change 90 minutes to 1 hour 30 minutes. We write "30 minutes" in the minutes column and add the 1 hour to the hours column. Then we add the hours.

$$\overset{1}{1} \text{ hr } 50 \text{ min}$$
$$+ 1 \text{ hr } 40 \text{ min}$$
$$\overline{3 \text{ hr } \overset{90}{\cancel{9}0} \text{ min}}$$
$$\phantom{3 \text{ hr }} 30$$

The hike took **3 hours 30 minutes.**

Example 2

To measure his vertical leap, Tyrone first reaches as high as he can against a wall. He reaches 6 ft 9 in. Then he put chalk on his fingertips, and jumping as high as he can, he slaps the wall. The top of the chalk mark is 8 ft 7 in. How high off the ground did Tyrone leap?

Solution

Thinking Skills

Justify

Why did we need to rename 8 ft before we subtracted? because we can't subtract 9 inches from 7 inches

We find the difference between the two measures. Before we subtract inches, we rename 8 feet 7 inches. The 12 inches combine with the 7 inches to make 19 inches. Then we subtract.

$$\overset{7}{\cancel{8}} \text{ ft } \overset{19}{\cancel{7}} \text{ in.}$$
$$- 6 \text{ ft } 9 \text{ in.}$$
$$\overline{1 \text{ ft } 10 \text{ in.}}$$

Tyrone leaped **1 ft 10 in.**

multiplying by powers of ten

Math Language

In **standard notation** all the digits in a number are shown. When multiplying by powers of ten, only place values containing non-zero digits are shown.

We can multiply by **powers** of ten very easily. Multiplying by powers of ten does not change the digits, only the place value of the digits. We can change the place value by moving the decimal point the number of places shown by the exponent. To write 1.2×10^3 in standard notation, we simply move the decimal point three places to the right and fill the empty places with zeros.

$$1.2 \times 10^3 = 1\underset{\smile}{200} = 1200$$

Example 3

Write 6.2×10^2 in standard notation.

Solution

To multiply by a power of ten, simply move the decimal point the number of places shown by the exponent. In this case, we move the decimal point two places to the right.

$$6.2 \times 10^2 = 6\underset{\smile}{20} = \mathbf{620}$$

---

2 New Concepts (Continued)

Instruction
Make sure students recognize the regrouped 1 that is shown in the hour column.

"What does the regrouped 1 represent?"
60 minutes

Example 2
Instruction
Have students note that the minuend shows a regrouping of feet to inches because 7 inches in the minuend is less than 9 inches in the subtrahend.

Example 3
Instruction
"What is the value of 10^2?" 100

Ask students to check the solution by multiplying 6.2 by 100. 620

"Moving the decimal point to multiply a number by 10^2 is another way of multiplying the number by 100."

Students should generalize from the example that the positive exponent indicates the number of places the decimal point is moved to the right when writing a power of 10 in standard notation.

(continued)

Math Background

Scientific notation is a method of writing a number as the product of a number that is greater than or equal to 1 and less than 10 and a power of 10.

For example, 19,000,000 written in scientific notation is 1.9×10^7 and 8,000,000,000,000 is 8×10^{12}.

Scientists often use scientific notation to express the values of very large numbers, such as the distances between objects in space.

2 New Concepts (Continued)

Example 4
Instruction

Remind students of these generalizations:
- A number in thousands has four places.
- A number in millions has seven places.
- A number in billions has ten places.
- A number in trillions has thirteen places.

Practice Set
Problems a and b [Error Alert]

Students must recognize the need to regroup. In problem a, regroup 1 foot as 12 inches, and regroup 1 hour as 60 minutes in problem b.

Problems e and f [Error Alert]

Students will have difficulty writing the numbers in standard notation unless they first write an equivalent decimal number for $2\frac{1}{2}$ and for $\frac{1}{4}$.

3 Written Practice

Math Conversations

Discussion opportunities are provided below.

Problem 1 [Analyze]

Remind students to place a decimal point in the quotient before beginning the division.

Problem 2 [Estimate]

Some students may benefit from thinking about the length of a bicycle in feet.

"One meter is about the same as what number of feet?" 3

Problem 5 [Analyze]

"How do you know how many places to move the decimal point?" The exponent represents the number of places to move the decimal point to the right.

(continued)

Sometimes powers of ten are named with words instead of numbers. For example, we might read that the population of Hong Kong is about 6.8 million people. The number 6.8 million means $6.8 \times 1,000,000$. We can write this number by shifting the decimal point of 6.8 six places to the right, which gives us 6,800,000.

Example 4

Write $\frac{1}{2}$ billion in standard notation.

Solution

The expression $\frac{1}{2}$ billion means "one half of one billion." First we write $\frac{1}{2}$ as the decimal number 0.5. Then we multiply by one billion, which shifts the decimal point nine places.

$$\frac{1}{2} \text{ billion} = 0.5 \times 1,000,000,000 = \mathbf{500,000,000}$$

Connect How can we write 500,000,000 using powers of ten? 5×10^8

Practice Set ▶ Find each sum or difference:

a.	6 ft 5 in.	b.	3 hr 15 min
	+ 4 ft 8 in.		− 1 hr 40 min
	11 ft 1 in.		1 hr 35 min

Write the standard notation for each of the following numbers. Change fractions and mixed numbers to decimal numbers before multiplying.

c. 1.2×10^4 12,000   d. 1.5 million   1,500,000

▶ e. $2\frac{1}{2}$ billion   2,500,000,000   ▶ f. $\frac{1}{4}$ million   250,000

Written Practice   *Strengthening Concepts*

▶ * **1.** [Analyze] For cleaning the yard, four teenagers were paid a total of
   (111) $75.00. If they divide the money equally, how much money will each teenager receive? $18.75

▶ **2.** [Estimate] Which of the following is the best estimate of the length of
   (7) a bicycle?   **B**

   A 0.5 m   **B** 2 m   **C** 6 m   **D** 36 m

3. If the chance of rain is 80%, what is the probability that it will not rain?
(58) Express the answer as a decimal.   0.2

* **4.** The ratio of students who walk to school to students who ride a bus to
(101) school is 5 to 3. If there are 120 students, how many students walk to school?   75 students

▶ * **5.** [Analyze] Write 4.5×10^6 as a standard numeral.   4,500,000
   (113)

▶ See Math Conversations in the sidebar.

English Learners

In the solution for example 3, explain the term **instead**. Write 10^2 on the board. Explain that this is another way to write 100. Say,

"When there is more than one way to write or express something, we use one form instead of another. Instead means to substitute something. When we write 10^2 instead of 100, we simply substitute one form of the number for another."

Ask a student to write one form of a number, using exponents, and ask another student to use another form of the same number instead.

8. Sample: One method is to convert each fraction to a decimal number, order the decimal numbers, and then place the corresponding fractions in the same order.

17. 34 ft²; Sample: The area of the triangle = $\frac{3 \text{ ft} \times 4 \text{ ft}}{2}$ = 6 ft². The area of the rectangle = 7 ft × 4 ft = 28 ft². Add the two measures to find the area of the trapezoid: 6 ft² + 28 ft² = 34 ft².

* 6. Calculate mentally:
(112)
  a. $(-12)(+3)$ -36 **b.** $(-12)(-3)$ $+36$
  c. $\frac{-12}{+3}$ -4 **d.** $\frac{-12}{-3}$ $+4$

* 7. Calculate mentally:
(100)
  a. $-12 + 3$ 15 **b.** $12 - 3$ -9
  c. $+3 + -12$ -9 **d.** $+3 - -12$ $+15$

8. **Explain** Describe a method for arranging these fractions from least to
(76) greatest:

$$\frac{3}{4}, \frac{3}{5}, \frac{4}{5}$$

Connect Complete the table to answer problems **9–11.**

	Fraction	Decimal	Percent
9. (99)	$\frac{1}{50}$	**a.** 0.02	**b.** 2%
10. (99)	**a.** $1\frac{3}{4}$	1.75	**b.** 175%
11. (99)	**a.** $\frac{1}{4}$	**b.** 0.25	25%

12. $12\frac{1}{4}$ in. $- 3\frac{5}{8}$ in. $8\frac{5}{8}$ in.   **13.** $3\frac{1}{3}$ ft $\times 2\frac{1}{4}$ ft $7\frac{1}{2}$ ft²
(63)   (66)

14. (3 cm)(3 cm)(3 cm)   27 cm³   **15.** 0.6 m × 0.5 m   0.3 m²
(81)   (81)

16. $5^2 + 2^5$ 57
(92)

▶* 17. **Justify** Find the area of this trapezoid. Show and explain your work to justify your answer.
(107)

▶* 18. 2 feet 3 inches − 1 foot 9 inches   6 inches
(113)

* 19. a. **Conclude** Which line in this figure is not a line of symmetry?   line g
(110)

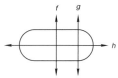

  ▶ **b.** Does the figure have rotational symmetry? (Disregard lines f, g, and h.) Explain your answer.   Yes, the figure will look the same after a 180° turn.

20. How many cubes one centimeter on each edge would be needed to fill this box? 30 cubes
(82)

Lesson 113   595

  ▶ See Math Conversations in the sidebar.

3 **Written Practice** (Continued)

Math Conversations

Discussion opportunities are provided below.

Problem 17   Justify

"*Explain how to find the length of the base of the triangle.*" subtract 7 feet from 10 feet

"*What is the length of the base?*" 3 feet

Problem 19b   Conclude

Extend the Problem

"*Suppose a figure must be turned 360° before it returns to its original position. Does the figure have rotational symmetry?*" no

Challenge students to draw such a figure and share their drawings with their classmates.

Errors and Misconceptions

Problem 18

Students may increase their likelihood of computing the correct difference if they rewrite the problem vertically before beginning the subtraction.

During the subtraction, students must recognize the need for a regrouping and regroup 2 feet 3 inches as 1 foot 15 inches.

Problem 19b

If students immediately dismiss the idea that the figure may have rotational symmetry, check to make sure they are not including lines f, g, and h as part of the figure.

If students are including the lines, explain that they should think about the question a second time and assume the lines and their labels are not present.

(continued)

Math Conversations

Discussion opportunities are provided below.

Problem 22 Analyze

Students should conclude that the prime numbers are factors of 70.

"What are the first seven prime numbers?" 2, 3, 5, 7, 11, 13, and 17

Write 2, 3, 5, 7, 11, 13, and 17 on the board or overhead.

"Which of these prime numbers are factors of 70? Explain how you know." 2, 5, and 7; Sample explanation: When 70 is divided by 2, 5, and 7, the remainder is zero.

Problem 24c Analyze

"Explain how the four angles of a rhombus compare." Opposite angles of a rhombus are congruent (they have the same measure).

"Explain how to find the unknown angle measures." The angle opposite the 61° angle also measures 61°. Subtract the sum 61° + 61° from 360°, then divide the difference by 2 to find the measure of each unknown angle.

"Two angles of the rhombus each measure 61°. What is the measure of each of the other angles of the rhombus?" 119°

Invite a volunteer to demonstrate the arithmetic on the board or overhead.

---

21. Elizabeth worked for three days and earned $240. At that rate, how much would she earn in ten days? $800
(88)

▶ 22. **Analyze** Seventy is the product of which three prime numbers?   2, 5, and 7
(65)

23. Saturn is about 900 million miles from the Sun. Write that distance in standard notation.   900,000,000 miles
(12)

Math Language
A **rhombus** is a parallelogram in which all four sides are equal in length.

* 24. Use the rhombus at the right for problems **a–c**.
(71)
  a. What is the perimeter of this rhombus?   32 in.
  b. What is the area of this rhombus?   56 in.²

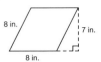
8 in.   7 in.   8 in.

▶ **c.** **Analyze** If an acute angle of this rhombus measures 61°, then what is the measure of each obtuse angle?   119°

25. The ratio of quarters to dimes in Keiko's savings jar is 5 to 8. If there were 120 quarters, how many dimes were there?   192 dimes
(88)

26. **a.** **Connect** The coordinates of the three vertices of a triangle are (0, 0), (0, 4), and (4, 4). What is the area of the triangle?   8 sq. units
(Inv. 7, 79)

  b. If the triangle were reflected across the *y*-axis, what would be the coordinates of the vertices of the reflection?   (0, 0), (0, 4), and (−4, 4)

The following list shows the ages of the children attending a luncheon. Use this information to answer problems **27** and **28**.

8, 9, 8, 8, 7, 9, 12, 12, 11, 16

27. What was the median age of the children attending the luncheon?   9
(Inv. 5)

28. What was the mean age of the children at the luncheon?   10
(Inv. 5)

29. The diameter of a playground ball is 10 inches. What is the circumference of the ball? (Use 3.14 for π.) How can estimation help you determine if your answer is reasonable?   31.4 in.; Sample: I can multiply the diameter by 3 and find that the circumference is a little more than 30.
(47)

├── 10 in. ──┤

30. Find the value of *A* in $A = s^2$ when *s* is 10 m.   100 m²
(91)

▶ See Math Conversations in the sidebar.

Looking Forward

Adding and subtracting mixed measures prepares students for:

• **Lesson 114,** converting measures by multiplying by a unit multiplier.

• Unit Multipliers

Objectives

- Write unit multipliers for equivalent measures.
- Use unit multipliers to convert from one unit to another.

Lesson Preparation

Materials

- **Power Up M** (in *Instructional Masters*)

Optional

- **Investigation Activity 15** (in *Instructional Masters*) or **graph paper**

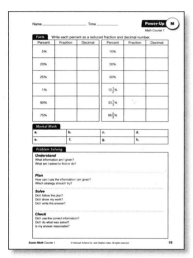

Power Up M

Math Language

New	English Learners (ESL)
unit multiplier	even pace

Technology Resources

Student eBook Complete student textbook in electronic format.

Resources and Planner CD Assessment, reteaching, and instructional masters, plus a pacing calendar with standards.

Test and Practice Generator CD Create additional practice sheets and custom-made tests.

www.SaxonPublishers.com Visit for more student activities and planning materials.

Inclusion

Adaptations CD Adapted lessons, investigations, practice and assessments.

Meeting Standards

National Council of Teachers of Mathematics (NCTM)

Measurement

ME.1b Understand relationships among units and convert from one unit to another within the same system

ME.2f Solve simple problems involving rates and derived measurements for such attributes as velocity and density

Problem Solving

PS.1b Solve problems that arise in mathematics and in other contexts

Problem-Solving Strategy: Write an Equation/
Use Logical Reasoning

On a balanced scale are a 25-gram mass, a 100-gram mass, and five identical blocks marked *x*, which are distributed as shown. What is the mass of each block marked *x*? Write an equation illustrated by this balanced scale.

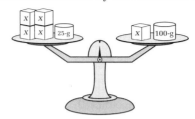

Understand *Understand the problem.*

"What information are we given?"

On one side of a balanced scale, there are 4 blocks of *x* weight and a 25-g mass. On the opposite side of the scale, are 1 block of *x* weight and a 100-g mass.

"What are we asked to do?"

Write the equation that is illustrated by the balanced scale. Find the mass of each block marked *x*.

Plan *Make a plan.*

"What problem-solving strategy will we use?"

We have been asked to *write an equation*, and we will also *use logical reasoning*.

Solve *Carry out the plan.*

"What is the equation illustrated by the balanced scale?"

$4x + 25 = x + 100$

"What equal masses can be removed from both sides of the scale to simplify the equation?"

One *x* block and 25 g can be removed from both sides.

"How could 25 g be removed from both sides of the scale?"

We could remove the 25-g mass from the left side and replace the 100-g mass with a 75-g mass (or three 25-g masses) on the right side.

"What is our simplified equation?"

$3x = 75$

"What is the mass of each block marked x?"

$x = 253$

Check *Look back.*

"How can we verify the solution is correct?"

We will substitute 25 g for *x* into our original equation.

$$4(25) + 25 = (25) + 100$$
$$100 + 25 = 25 + 100$$
$$125 = 125$$

• Unit Multipliers

facts | Power Up M

mental math |
a. **Fractional Parts:** $\frac{7}{10}$ of 40   28

b. **Number Sense:** 6×480 2880

c. **Percent:** 10% of $500 $50

d. **Calculation:** $4.99 + 65¢ $5.64

e. **Decimals:** 0.125×1000 125

f. **Number Sense:** $40 \cdot 900$ 36,000

g. **Geometry:** You need to fill a show box with sand. What do you need to measure to find how much sand you will need?   find the length, width, and height in order to find the volume

h. **Calculation:** $5 \times 7, + 1, \div 4, \sqrt{}, \times 7, - 1, \times 3, - 10, \times 2, \sqrt{}$ 10

problem solving | On a balanced scale are a 25-gram mass, a 100-gram mass, and five identical blocks marked *x*, which are distributed as shown. What is the mass of each block marked *x*? Write an equation illustrated by this balanced scale. 25 g; $4x + 25 = x + 100$

New Concept | Increasing Knowledge

A **unit multiplier** is a fraction that equals 1 and that is written with two different units of measure. Recall that when the numerator and denominator of a fraction are equal (and are not zero), the fraction equals 1. Since 1 foot equals 12 inches, we can form two unit multipliers with the measures 1 foot and 12 inches.

$$\frac{1 \text{ ft}}{12 \text{ in.}} \qquad \frac{12 \text{ in.}}{1 \text{ ft}}$$

Each of these fractions equals 1 because the numerator and denominator of each fraction are equal.

We can use unit multipliers to help us convert from one unit of measure to another. If we want to convert 60 inches to feet, we can multiply 60 inches by the unit multiplier $\frac{1 \text{ ft}}{12 \text{ in.}}$.

$$\frac{\overset{5}{\cancel{60} \text{ in.}}}{1} \times \frac{1 \text{ ft}}{\underset{1}{\cancel{12} \text{ in.}}} = 5 \text{ ft}$$

Lesson 114   597

1 Power Up

Facts
Distribute **Power Up M** to students. See answers below.

Mental Math
Before students begin the Mental Math exercise, do this counting exercise as a class.

Count by $\frac{1}{4}$s from -1 to 1.

Encourage students to share different ways to mentally compute these exercises. Strategies for exercises **a** and **c** are listed below.

a. **Divide 7×40 by 10**
$7 \times 40 = 280; 280 \div 10 = 28$
Multiply $\frac{1}{10}$ of 40 by 7
$\frac{1}{10}$ of $40 = 40 \div 10 = 4; 4 \times 7 = 28$

c. **Shift the Decimal Points**
10% of $500 = 100% of $50; $50
Divide $500 by 10
$\frac{\$500}{10} = \frac{\$50\cancel{0}}{1\cancel{0}} = \frac{\$50}{1} = \$50$

Problem Solving
Refer to **Power-Up Discussion**, p. 597B.

2 New Concepts

Instruction
Remind students that a fraction equal to 1 is also equivalent to 1; equivalent fractions are equal fractions.

One conclusion students should make from the example is that multiplying a number by a unit fraction does not change the value of the number because a unit fraction is equal to 1.

"What does the Identity Property of Multiplication state?" Sample: the product of any number and 1 is that number

(continued)

Facts | Write each percent as a reduced fraction and decimal number.

Percent	Fraction	Decimal	Percent	Fraction	Decimal
5%	$\frac{1}{20}$	0.05	10%	$\frac{1}{10}$	0.1
20%	$\frac{1}{5}$	0.2	30%	$\frac{3}{10}$	0.3
25%	$\frac{1}{4}$	0.25	50%	$\frac{1}{2}$	0.5
1%	$\frac{1}{100}$	0.01	$12\frac{1}{2}$%	$\frac{1}{8}$	0.125
90%	$\frac{9}{10}$	0.9	$33\frac{1}{3}$%	$\frac{1}{3}$	Rounds to 0.333
75%	$\frac{3}{4}$	0.75	$66\frac{2}{3}$%	$\frac{2}{3}$	Rounds to 0.667

Example 1
Instruction

After completing the example, ask students to make a table (using y to represent yards and f to represent feet) showing the relationship of yards and feet. Sample:

Yards (y)	1	2	3	4	5	6
Feet (f)	3	6	9	12	15	18

After the table has been completed, have students write a formula that can be used to change any number of yards to feet, and a formula that can be used to change any number of feet to yards. $y = \frac{f}{3}; f = 3y$

"How many yards are equal to 120 feet? Use a formula you wrote to help decide." 40

"How many feet are equal to 8 yards? Use a formula you wrote to help decide." 24

Practice Set
Problems a–d [Error Alert]

"How can you check that the unit multiplier you wrote is correct?" Sample: Change the unit of the numerator to the unit of the denominator (or vice versa). Then reduce the fraction. If the result is 1, the fraction is a unit multiplier.

(continued)

Example 1

a. Write two unit multipliers using these equivalent measures:

$$3 \text{ ft} = 1 \text{ yd}$$

b. Which unit multiplier would you use to convert 30 yards to feet?

Solution

a. We use the equivalent measures to write two fractions equal to 1.

$$\frac{3 \text{ ft}}{1 \text{ yd}} \qquad \frac{1 \text{ yd}}{3 \text{ ft}}$$

b. We want the units we are changing **from** to appear in the denominator and the units we are changing **to** to appear in the numerator. To convert 30 yards to feet, we use the unit multiplier that has yards in the denominator and feet in the numerator.

$$\frac{30 \text{ yd}}{1} \times \frac{3 \text{ ft}}{1 \text{ yd}}$$

Here we show the work. Notice that the yards "cancel," and the product is expressed in feet.

$$\frac{30 \text{ y\cancel{d}}}{1} \times \frac{3 \text{ ft}}{1 \text{ y\cancel{d}}} = 90 \text{ ft}$$

Example 2

Convert 30 feet to yards using a unit multiplier.

Solution

We can form two unit multipliers.

$$\frac{1 \text{ yd}}{3 \text{ ft}} \text{ and } \frac{3 \text{ ft}}{1 \text{ yd}}$$

We are asked to convert from feet to yards, so we use the unit multiplier that has feet in the denominator and yards in the numerator.

$$\frac{\overset{10}{\cancel{30}} \text{ f\cancel{t}}}{1} \times \frac{1 \text{ yd}}{\cancel{3} \text{ f\cancel{t}}} = 10 \text{ yd}$$

Thirty feet converts to **10 yards.**

Practice Set ▸ a. Write two unit multipliers for these equivalent measures: $\frac{1 \text{ gal}}{4 \text{ qt}}, \frac{4 \text{ qt}}{1 \text{ gal}}$

$$1 \text{ gal} = 4 \text{ qt}$$

▸ b. Which unit multiplier from problem **a** would you use to convert 12 gallons to quarts? $\frac{4 \text{ qt}}{1 \text{ gal}}$

▸ c. Write two unit multipliers for these equivalent measures: $\frac{1 \text{ m}}{100 \text{ cm}}, \frac{100 \text{ cm}}{1 \text{ m}}$

$$1 \text{ m} = 100 \text{ cm}$$

▸ See Math Conversations in the sidebar.

Inclusion

In the inclusion for Lesson 54, students were encouraged to use cancellation before multiplying fractions. As a review, demonstrate how to find the product of $\frac{3}{4}$ and $\frac{8}{9}$.

Then explain that the same process of cancellation makes it easy to convert one unit of measure to another by using a unit multiplier and canceling units. Point out that converting units requires that each measurement in the computation be written with a unit of measure.

Refer students to the **Equivalent Table for Units** in the *Student Reference Guide* and show them how to use the information in the table to write unit multipliers. Emphasize that the unit **being converted** must appear in the **denominator** of the unit multiplier.

Then demonstrate how to use cancellation to convert 64 ounces to pounds:

$$\frac{64 \text{ \cancel{ounces}}}{\cancel{1}} \times \frac{1 \text{ \cancel{pound}}}{16 \text{ \cancel{ounces}}} = 4 \text{ pounds}$$

d. Which unit multiplier from problem **c** would you use to convert 200 centimeters to meters? $\frac{1\,m}{100\,cm}$

e. Use a unit multiplier to convert 12 quarts to gallons.
12 qt $\times \frac{1\,gal}{4\,qt}$ = 3 gal

f. Use a unit multiplier to convert 200 meters to centimeters.
200 m $\times \frac{100\,cm}{1\,m}$ = 20,000 cm

g. Use a unit multiplier to convert 60 feet to yards (1 yd = 3 ft).
60 ft $\times \frac{1\,yd}{3\,ft}$ = 20 yd

1. Tickets to the matinee are $6 each. How many tickets can Maela buy with $20?   3 tickets
(111)

2. *Analyze*   Maria ran four laps of the track at an even pace. If it took 6 minutes to run the first three laps, how long did it take to run all four laps?   8 minutes
(88)

3. Fifteen of the 25 members played in the game. What fraction of the members did not play? $\frac{2}{5}$
(77)

4. Two fifths of the 160 acres were planted with alfalfa. How many acres were not planted with alfalfa?   96 acres
(77)

5. Which digit in 94,763,581 is in the ten-thousands place?   6
(12)

6. a. Write two unit multipliers for these equivalent measures: $\frac{1\,gal}{4\,qt}, \frac{4\,qt}{1\,gal}$
(114)

1 gallon = 4 quarts

b. Which of the two unit multipliers from part **a** would you use to convert 8 gallons to quarts? Why? $\frac{4\,qt}{1\,gal}$; Gallons needs to be in the denominator so that gallons will cancel and the answer will be in quarts.

7. *Estimate*   What is the sum of $36.43, $41.92, and $26.70 to the nearest dollar. $105
(51)

8. $4 + 4^2 \div \sqrt{4} - \frac{4}{4}$ 11
(92)

9. $3\frac{1}{4}$ in. + $2\frac{1}{2}$ in. + $4\frac{5}{8}$ in. $10\frac{3}{8}$ in.
(61)

Connect   Complete the table to answer problems **10–12.**

	Fraction	Decimal	Percent
10. (99)	$\frac{1}{8}$	**a.** 0.125	**b.** 12.5%
11. (99)	**a.** $\frac{9}{10}$	0.9	**b.** 90%
12. (99)	**a.** $\frac{3}{5}$	**b.** 0.6	60%

13. $3.25 \div \frac{2}{3}$ (fraction answer) $4\frac{7}{8}$
(73)

Solve:

14. $3m - 10 = 80$ 30
(106)

15. $\frac{3}{2} = \frac{1.8}{m}$ 1.2
(85, 105)

Lesson 114   **599**

▶ See Math Conversations in the sidebar.

In problem **2**, explain the term **even pace.** Say,

"A pace is a step taken when you run or walk. To keep an even pace is when you take equal steps. So if you run at an even pace, you are running at the same speed, without going slower or faster."

Ask students to give examples of when people or animals could keep an even pace (Samples: a swimmer, a horse trotting, two cars going the same speed.)

Practice Set
Problems e–g [Error Alert]
Remind students to use these generalizations as a way of checking their work. You might choose to write the generalizations on the board or overhead.

- When a larger unit is changed to a smaller unit, the number of units will be more.
- When a smaller unit is changed to a larger unit, the number of units will be fewer.

For example, when 24 inches are changed to feet (a smaller unit is changed to a larger unit), the number of feet will be fewer, or less than 24. 24 in. = 2 ft

When 3 kilometers are changed to meters (a larger unit is changed to a smaller unit), the number of meters will be more, or greater than 3. 3 km = 3000 m

---

Math Conversations
Discussion opportunities are provided below.

Problem 1 [Analyze]
"After the division is completed, what is the remainder?" $2

"What fraction of a ticket has a value of $2?" $\frac{1}{3}$

"What do we do with the remainder in this problem? Explain your answer." Sample: The remainder is not included in the answer because it is not possible to purchase $\frac{1}{3}$ of a ticket.

Errors and Misconceptions
Problems 14 and 15
Because the value of the unknown in many equations is not obvious, it is important for students to check their work by substitution. To check by substitution, students should replace the unknown with the possible answer, then simplify the equation. If the equation simplifies to a true statement (such as 2 = 2), the possible answer should be assumed to be the correct answer.

$$3m - 10 = 80 \qquad\qquad \frac{3}{2} = \frac{1.8}{m}$$
$$3(30) - 10 = 80 \qquad\qquad \frac{3}{2} = \frac{1.8}{1.2}$$
$$90 - 10 = 80 \qquad\qquad (3)(1.2) = (2)(1.8)$$
$$80 = 80 \qquad\qquad 3.6 = 3.6$$

(continued)

Lesson 114   **599**

Math Conversations

Discussion opportunities are provided below.

Problem 18 Analyze

"Explain how we can find the missing side lengths in the polygon." Subtract 9 m from 15 m and subtract 8 m from 10 m

If students have difficulty understanding how the missing measures are found, sketch the polygon on the board or overhead and demonstrate (or invite a volunteer to demonstrate) the relationships that are used to determine the missing measures.

Problem 21 Conclude

"Angle 1 is half the measure of a right angle. What is the measure of angle 1? Explain your answer." The measure of a right angle is 90°; the measure of angle 1 is $\frac{1}{2}$ of 90° or 45°.

Problem 23 Connect

Extend the Problem

Ask students to name the two prime numbers, and the least common multiple, that they wrote. After all of the students have responded, ask

"What do you notice about all of these least common multiples?" Sample: They are each the product of the two prime numbers.

Problem 27 Analyze

Continue to encourage students to solve graphing problems by sketching instead of by using graph paper. However, some students may be more comfortable using graph paper or a copy of **Investigation Activity 15** Coordinate Plane to complete the problem.

(continued)

---

* 16. Calculate mentally:
(112)
  a. $(-5)(-20)$ +100   **b.** $(-5)(+20)$ −100
  c. $\frac{-20}{+5}$ −4   **d.** $\frac{-20}{-5}$ +4

* 17. The distance between San Francisco and Los Angeles is about
(95) 387 miles. If Takara leaves San Francisco and travels 6 hours at an average speed of 55 miles per hour, will she reach Los Angeles? How far will she travel? no; 330 miles

▶* 18. Analyze What is the area of this polygon? 138 m²
(107)

* 19. What is the perimeter of this polygon? 50 m
(103)

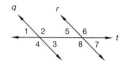

20. Calculate mentally:
(100)
  a. $-5 + -20$ −25   **b.** $-20 - -5$ −15
  c. $-5 - -5$ 0   **d.** $+5 - -20$ +25

▶* 21. Conclude Transversal t intersects parallel lines q and r. Angle 1 is half
(97) the measure of a right angle.

  a. Which angle corresponds to ∠1? ∠5

  b. What is the measure of each obtuse angle? 135°

* 22. Fifty people responded to the survey, a number that represented 5% of
(105) the surveys mailed. How many surveys were mailed? Explain how you found your answer. 1000 surveys; Sample: 5% of the mailed surveys = 50, 0.05m = 50, $\frac{0.05m}{0.05} = \frac{50}{0.05}$, m = 1000

▶ 23. Think of two different prime numbers, and write them on your paper.
(19, 30) Then find the least common multiple (LCM) of the two prime numbers. The LCM will be the product of the prime numbers.

* 24. Write 1.5×10^6 as a standard number. 1,500,000
(113)

25. A classroom that is 30 feet long, 30 feet wide, and 10 feet high has a
(82) volume of how many cubic feet? 9000 ft³

* 26. Convert 8 quarts to gallons using a unit multiplier. $8 \text{ qt} \cdot \frac{1 \text{ gal}}{4 \text{ qt}} = 2$ gal
(114)

▶ 27. Analyze A circle was drawn on a coordinate plane. The coordinates of
(Inv. 7, 86) the center of the circle were (1, 1). One point on the circle was (1, −3).
  a. What was the radius of the circle? 4 units

  b. What was the area of the circle? (Use 3.14 for π.) 50.24 units²

▶ See Math Conversations in the sidebar.

28. During one season, the highest number of points scored in one game
(Inv. 5) by the local college basketball team was 95 points. During that same
season, the range of the team's scores was 35 points. What was the
team's lowest score?   60

* 29. 4 ft 3 in. − 2 ft 9 in.   1 ft 6 in.
(113)

▶ **30.** *Generalize* Study this function table and
(96) describe a rule for finding *A* when *s* is known.
Explain how you know.   Rule: To find *A*,
square *s*; Sample: $1 \times 1 = 1$, $2 \times 2 = 4$,
$3 \times 3 = 9$, $4 \times 4 = 16$, so $s^2 = A$.

s	A
1	1
2	4
3	9
4	16

Early Finishers
*Real-World
Application*

Robin wants to install crown molding in her two upstairs bedrooms. Crown
molding lines the perimeter of a room, covering the joint formed by the
wall and the ceiling. Use the dimensions on the floor plan below to answer
a and **b**.

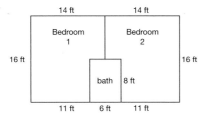

a. How many feet of crown molding will Robin need for both bedrooms?
2(16 ft + 14 ft + 8 ft + 3 ft + 8 ft + 11 ft) = 120 ft

b. If crown molding is sold in 8 ft. sections, how many sections will Robin
need?   120 ÷ 8 = 15 sections

▶ See Math Conversations in the sidebar.

Math Conversations
Discussion opportunities are provided below.

Problem 30 *Generalize*
Extend the Problem
After completing the problem, ask students to
make a table showing the relationship of the
lengths of the sides (*s*) of equilateral triangles
to the perimeters (*P*) of those triangles.
Sample:

Side (*s*)	1	2	3	4	5	6
Perimeter (*P*)	3	6	9	12	15	18

After the table has been completed, have
students write a formula that can be used to
find the perimeter of any equilateral triangle
given a side length, and a formula to find the
side length of an equilateral triangle given its
perimeter. $P = 3s$; $s = \frac{1}{2}$

*"Use a non-example to disprove that the
formula is true for all triangles."*
non-examples will vary

• Writing Percents as Fractions, Part 2

Objectives

• Convert a percent that includes a fraction to a fraction.

Lesson Preparation

Materials

• **Power Up N** (in *Instructional Masters*)

Optional

• **Investigation Activity 15** (in *Instructional Masters*)

Power Up N

Math Language

English Learners (ESL)

container(s)

Technology Resources

Student eBook Complete student textbook in electronic format.

Resources and Planner CD Assessment, reteaching, and instructional masters, plus a pacing calendar with standards.

Test and Practice Generator CD Create additional practice sheets and custom-made tests.

www.SaxonPublishers.com Visit for more student activities and planning materials.

Inclusion

Adaptations CD Adapted lessons, investigations, practice and assessments.

Meeting Standards

National Council of Teachers of Mathematics (NCTM)

Numbers and Operations

NO.1a Work flexibly with fractions, decimals, and percents to solve problems

NO.2a Understand the meaning and effects of arithmetic operations with fractions, decimals, and integers

Communication

CM.3a Organize and consolidate their mathematical thinking through communication

Problem-Solving Strategy: Guess and Check

A famous conjecture states that even numbers greater than two can be written as a sum of two prime numbers $(12 = 5 + 7)$. Another says that any odd number greater than five can be written as the sum of three prime numbers $(11 = 7 + 2 + 2)$. Write the numbers 10, 15, and 20 as the sums of primes. (The same prime number may be used more than once in a sum.)

Understand **Understand the problem.**

"What information are we given?"

Even numbers greater than two can be written as a sum of two prime numbers $(32 = 13 + 19)$. Odd numbers greater than five can be written as the sum of three prime numbers $(33 = 3 + 7 + 23)$.

"What are we asked to do?"

Write the numbers 10, 15, and 20 as the sums of primes.

Plan **Make a plan.**

"What problem-solving strategy will we use?"

We will use an organized *guess and check* method.

Solve **Carry out the plan.**

$$10 = 7 + 3 \text{ or } 5 + 5$$
$$15 = 11 + 2 + 2 \text{ or } 7 + 5 + 3 \text{ or } 5 + 5 + 5$$
$$20 = 17 + 3 \text{ or } 13 + 7$$

Check **Look back.**

"Did we find the answers to the questions that were asked?"

Yes. We found that the even numbers, 10 and 20 could be written as the sum of two prime numbers and the odd number, 15 could be written as the sum of three prime numbers.

1 Power Up

Facts
Distribute **Power Up N** to students. See answers below.

Mental Math
Before students begin the Mental Math exercise, do this counting exercise as a class.

Count up and down by 5s between −25 and 25.

Encourage students to share different ways to mentally compute these exercises. Strategies for exercises **b** and **d** are listed below.

b. Multiply Hundreds, then Ones
$(9 \times 500) + (9 \times 7) = 4500 + 63 = 4563$
Multiply by 10; Subtract 507
$10 \times 507 = 5070$
$5070 - 507 = 4563$

d. Count Up from $9.59
Start with $9.59. Count by 10¢, then by 1¢.
$10¢ + 10¢ + 10¢ + 10¢ + 1¢ = 41¢$
Subtract $9.60, then Add 1¢
$\$10 - \$9.60 = 40¢; 40¢ + 1¢ = 41¢$

Problem Solving
Refer to **Power-Up Discussion**, p. 602B.

2 New Concepts

Instruction
Another way to describe a percent is that a percent is a ratio of a number to 100.

Point out that the first step in the division is to write $33\frac{1}{3}$ as an improper fraction. To complete the division, the dividend is multiplied by the reciprocal of the divisor.

(continued)

• Writing Percents as Fractions, Part 2

Power Up | *Building Power*

facts | Power Up *N*

mental math |
a. **Fractional Parts:** $\frac{3}{4}$ of 16   12
b. **Calculation:** 9×507 4563
c. **Percent:** 10% of $2.50 $0.25
d. **Calculation:** $10.00 − $9.59 $0.41
e. **Decimals:** $0.5 \div 100$ 0.005
f. **Number Sense:** $\frac{2400}{300}$ 8
g. **Probability:** What is the probability of rolling an odd number on a number cube? $\frac{1}{2}$
h. **Calculation:** $10 \times 9, -10, \div 2, +2, \div 6, \times 10, +2, \div 9, -9$ −1

problem solving | A famous conjecture states that any even number greater than two can be written as a sum of two prime numbers $(12 = 5 + 7)$. Another states that any odd number greater than five can be written as the sum of three prime numbers $(11 = 7 + 2 + 2)$. Write the numbers 10, 15, and 20 as the sums of primes. (The same prime number may be used more than once in a sum.) See script for answers.

New Concept | *Increasing Knowledge*

Thinking Skill

Justify

How do we simplify $\frac{50}{100}$ to lowest terms?   Divide 50 and 100 by their GCF, 50.
$\frac{50 \div 50}{100 \div 50} = \frac{1}{2}$

Recall that a percent is a fraction with a denominator of 100. We can write a percent in fraction form by removing the percent sign and writing the denominator 100.

$$50\% = \frac{50}{100}$$

We then simplify the fraction to lowest terms. If the percent includes a fraction, we actually divide by 100 to simplify the fraction.

$$33\frac{1}{3}\% = \frac{33\frac{1}{3}}{100}$$

In this case we divide $33\frac{1}{3}$ by 100. We have performed division problems similar to this in the problem sets.

$$33\frac{1}{3} \div 100 = \frac{\overset{1}{\cancel{100}}}{3} \times \frac{1}{\cancel{100}} = \frac{1}{3}$$

We see that $33\frac{1}{3}\%$ equals $\frac{1}{3}$.

Facts | Complete each equivalence.

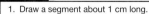

1. Draw a segment about 1 cm long.

2. Draw a segment about 1 inch long.

3. One inch is how many centimeters?   2.54

4. Which is longer, 1 km or 1 mi?   1 mi

5. Which is longer, 1 km or $\frac{1}{2}$ mi?   1 km

6. How many ounces are in a pound?   16

7. How many pounds are in a ton?   2000

8. A dollar bill has a mass of about one   gram.

9. A pair of shoes has a mass of about one   kilogram.

10. On Earth a kilogram mass weighs about   2.2   pounds.

11. A metric ton is   1000   kilograms.

12. On Earth a metric ton weighs about   2200   pounds.

13. The Earth rotates on its axis once in a   day.

14. The Earth revolves around the Sun once in a   year.

15. Water boils   212   °F

16.   100   °C

17. Normal body temerature   98.6   °F

18.   37   °C

19. Cool room temperature   68   °F

20.   20   °C

21. Water freezes   32   °F

22.   0   °C

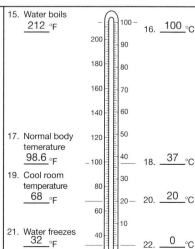

Example

Convert $3\frac{1}{3}\%$ to a fraction.

Solution

We remove the percent sign and write the denominator 100.

$$3\frac{1}{3}\% = \frac{3\frac{1}{3}}{100}$$

We perform the division.

$$3\frac{1}{3} \div 100 = \frac{\overset{1}{\cancel{10}}}{3} \times \frac{1}{\underset{10}{\cancel{100}}} = \frac{1}{30}$$

We find that $3\frac{1}{3}\%$ equals $\frac{1}{30}$.

Practice Set

▶ **a.** Convert $66\frac{2}{3}\%$ to a fraction. $\frac{2}{3}$

▶ **b.** Convert $6\frac{2}{3}\%$ to a fraction. $\frac{1}{15}$

▶ **c.** Convert $12\frac{1}{2}\%$ to a fraction. $\frac{1}{8}$

▶ **d.** Write $14\frac{2}{7}\%$ as a fraction. $\frac{1}{7}$

▶ **e.** Write $83\frac{1}{3}\%$ as a fraction. $\frac{5}{6}$

Written Practice   *Strengthening Concepts*

1. What is the total cost of a $12.60 item plus 7% sales tax? $13.48
(41)

* 2. Convert $16\frac{2}{3}\%$ to a fraction. $\frac{1}{6}$
(115)

3.

	%	A.C.
Correct	90	c
Not Correct	10	3
Total	100	t

▶ *** 3.** **Model** Draw a ratio box for this problem. Then solve the problem using a proportion.   30 questions
(105)

Ines missed three questions on the test but answered 90% of the questions correctly. How many questions were on the test?

4. Sound travels about 331 meters per second in air. How far will it travel in 60 seconds?   19,860 m
(95)

$$\frac{331\ m}{1\ s} \cdot \frac{60\ s}{1}$$

5. Write the standard number for $(5 \times 10^4) + (6 \times 10^2)$.   50,600
(92)

▶ **6.** If the radius of a circle is seventy-five hundredths of a meter, what is the diameter?   1.5 meters
(27, 37)

7. **Estimate** Round the product of $3\frac{2}{3}$ and $2\frac{2}{3}$ to the nearest whole number.   10
(66)

▶ *** 8.** In a bag are three red marbles and three white marbles. If two marbles are taken from the bag at the same time, what is the probability that both marbles will be red? $\frac{3}{6} \cdot \frac{2}{5} = \frac{1}{5}$
(Inv. 10)

Lesson 115   603

▶ See Math Conversations in the sidebar.

Example
Instruction
Make sure students recognize that writing the denominator 100 replaces the percent sign.

"What steps do we follow to complete the division?" Sample: Rewrite $3\frac{1}{3}$ as $\frac{10}{3}$, then multiply $\frac{10}{3}$ by the reciprocal of 100.

Practice Set
Problems a–e   Error Alert
Remind students that percents less than 100% convert to fractions less than 1.

---

3 Written Practice

Math Conversations
Discussion opportunities are provided below.

Problem 3   Model
"What is important to remember when we use the information in a ratio box to write a proportion?" Sample: The order of the terms in the proportion should be the same as the order of the terms in the ratio box.

"After we write a proportion, how do we use the cross products of the proportion to solve for the unknown?" Sample: Set the cross products equal to each other, then use inverse operations to solve for the unknown.

Problem 6   Generalize
Extend the Problem
Challenge students to make a function table to represent the relationship shared by a radius and a diameter of a circle.

Then ask students to write a formula that can be used to find the radius of a circle given a diameter of that circle. Have them also write a formula that can be used to find the diameter of a circle given a radius of that circle.

In each formula they write, have students use d to represent a diameter and r to represent a radius.   Sample:

Radius (r)	1	2	3	4	5
Diameter (d)	2	4	6	8	10

$$r = \frac{d}{2};\ d = 2r$$

(continued)

Math Conversations

Discussion opportunities are provided below.

Problem 13 [Analyze]

"What is the sign of the product or quotient of two negative numbers?" positive

"What is the sign of the product or quotient of two positive numbers?" positive

"What is the sign of the product or quotient of a positive number and a negative number?" negative

Before students simplify each expression, ask them to name the sign of each product or quotient in problems **a–d.** problem **a:** +; problem **b:** −; problem **c:** +; problem **d:** −

Problem 16

Extend the Problem

After students solve this problem, point out that $\frac{22}{7}$ is often used to represent π. Then ask students to use $\frac{22}{7}$ for π and solve the following problem:

"The diameter of a circle is 14 cm. What formula is used to find the circumference of the circle?" $C = \pi d$

Ask students to substitute $\frac{22}{7}$ for π and 14 for d.

"Before multiplying, what terms of the fractions can be reduced? Explain why." 14 and 7; 7 is the greatest common factor of 7 and 14

Have students reduce the terms, then name the answer. 44 cm

(continued)

Connect Complete the table to answer problems **9** and **10**.

	Fraction	Decimal	Percent
9. (99)	$2\frac{2}{5}$	**a.** 2.4	**b.** 240%
10. (99)	**a.** $\frac{17}{20}$	0.85	**b.** 85%

Solve:

* 11. (106) $7x - 3 = 39$ 6

12. (85) $\frac{x}{7} = \frac{35}{5}$ 49

▶*** 13.** (112) Calculate mentally:

    a. $(-3)(-15)$ +45

    b. $\frac{-15}{+3}$ −5

    c. $\frac{-15}{-3}$ +5

    d. $(+3)(-15)$ −45

* 14. (104) $-6 + -7 + +5 - -8$ 0

15. (49) $0.12 \div (12 \div 0.4)$ 0.004

▶ **16.** (74) Write $\frac{22}{7}$ as a decimal rounded to the hundredths place. 3.14

17. (89) What whole number multiplied by itself equals 10,000? 100

* 18. (107) What is the area of this hexagon? 68 cm²

19. (103) What is the perimeter of this hexagon? 36 cm

20. (82) What is the volume of this cube? 27 cm³

21. (Inv. 5) What is the mode of the number of days in the twelve months of the year? 31

22. (88) [Analyze] If seven of the containers can hold a total of 84 ounces, then how many ounces can 10 containers hold? 120 ounces

84 ounces

* 23. (113) Write the standard number for $4\frac{1}{2}$ million. 4,500,000

24. (16) Round 58,697,284 to the nearest million. 59,000,000

25. (50) Connect Which arrow is pointing to 0.4? C

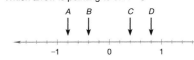

▶ See Math Conversations in the sidebar.

English Learners

In problem **22**, explain the term **container**. Say,

"A container is a thing used to hold or keep something. You can place something inside a container, such as a solid (something hard), a liquid, or even a gas, like oxygen."

Ask students for examples of containers for a solid, a liquid and a gas (Sample: a box, a jar or cup, a balloon).

* 26. When Rosita was born, she weighed 7 pounds 9 ounces. Two months
(102,
113) later she weighed 9 pounds 7 ounces. How much weight did she gain in
two months?   1 lb 14 oz

▶ **27.** **Connect** The coordinates of the vertices of a parallelogram are (0, 0),
(Inv. 7,
71) (5, 0), (6, 3), and (1, 3). What is the area of the parallelogram?
15 sq. units

▶ **28.** Which is the greatest weight?   B
(44)
   A 6.24 lb   **B** 6.4 lb   **C** 6.345 lb

▶* **29.**   2 gal 2 qt 1 pt
(113) + 2 gal 2 qt 1 pt
           5 gal 1 qt

30. **Analyze** Gilbert started the trip with a full tank of gas. He drove
(81) 323.4 miles and then refilled the tank with 14.2 gallons of gas. How can
Gilbert calculate the average number of miles he traveled on each gallon
of gas?   Gilbert can divide 323.4 miles by 14.2 gallons to calculate the
miles per gallon.

Early Finishers
Real-World
Application

A few students from the local high school decide to survey the types of
vehicles in the parking lot. Their results are as follows: 210 cars, 125 trucks,
and 14 motorcycles.

   a. Find the simplified ratios for cars to trucks, cars to motorcycles, and
   trucks to motorcycles.   42 to 25; 15 to 1; 125 to 14

   b. Find the fraction, decimal, and percent for the ratio of cars to the
   total number of vehicles. Round to nearest thousandth and tenth of
   a percent. $\frac{210}{349}$; 0.602; 60.2%

▶ See Math Conversations in the sidebar.

Looking Forward

Changing percents that include
fractions to fractions prepares
students for:

• **Lesson 119,** finding a whole
  when a percent is known by
  writing and solving an equation.

Math Conversations
Discussion opportunities are provided below.

Problem 27   Connect
Extend the Problem
*"You can move one vertex of the
parallelogram and form a trapezoid that
has one pair of congruent sides. To form
such a trapezoid, which vertex would you
move and where?"* Sample: move (1, 3) to
(−1, 3); move (6, 3) to (4, 3); move (5, 0) to
(7, 0); move (0, 0) to (2, 0)

Because a variety of answers are possible,
encourage students to use an overhead grid to
justify their answers.

Problem 28
Students may find it easier to compare the
numbers if they first write zeros so that each
number has the same number of decimal
places.

For example, since 6.345 has three decimal
places, 6.24 can be rewritten as 6.240 and 6.4
can be rewritten as 6.400.

Remind students that comparing begins with
the digits in the greatest place of the numbers,
which for these numbers, is the ones place.

Errors and Misconceptions
Problem 29
Students must recognize that two regroupings
are required: 2 pints must be regrouped as
1 quart and 5 quarts must be regrouped as
1 gallon and 1 quart.

Make sure students understand that by
regrouping, the sum can be written in a
simpler way.

Assessment — 30–40 minutes — For use after Lesson 115

Distribute **Cumulative Test 22** to each student. Two versions of the test are available in *Saxon Math Course 1 Course Assessments Book*. Have students complete the **Power-Up Test** first. Allow 10 minutes. Then have students work the 20 numbered items on the **Cumulative Test.** Students may use copies of the answer sheet to record their work. Track individual and class progress with the **Test Analysis** forms.

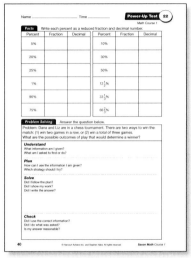

Power-Up Test 22

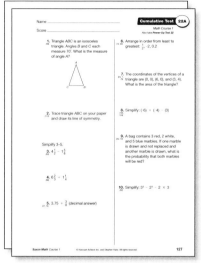

Cumulative Test 22A

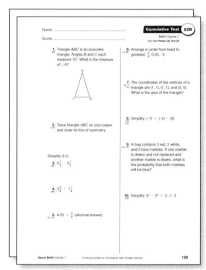

Alternative Cumulative Test 22B

Optional Answer Forms

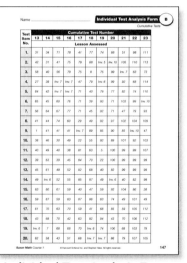

Individual Test Analysis Form

Class Test Analysis Form

Reteaching

Students who score below 80% on the assessment may be in need of reteaching. Look for the causes of student mistakes. If errors are conceptual, refer to the *Reteaching Masters* for reteaching.

Similar Shapes
Assign after Lesson 115 and Test 22

Objectives
- Use proportions to find unknown lengths in similar polygons.
- Communicate ideas through writing.

Materials
Performance Activity 22

Preparation
Make copies of **Performance Activity 22.** (One each per student.)

Time Requirement
15–30 minutes; Begin in class and complete at home.

Activity
Explain to students that for this activity they will be an assistant to an artist who creates rugs with geometric shapes on them. They must use drawings of the shapes on the rugs and their knowledge of similar polygons to find the dimensions of the shapes on the actual rugs. They will also be required to explain whether all squares are similar. Explain that all of the information students need is on **Performance Activity 22.**

Criteria for Evidence of Learning
- Sets up correct proportions and uses them to find unknown lengths in similar polygons.
- Gives a correct explanation of why all squares are similar.
- Communicates ideas clearly through writing.

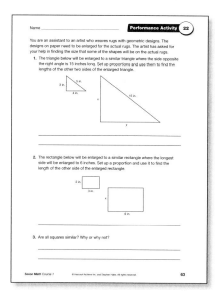

Performance Activity 22

National Council of Teachers of Mathematics (NCTM)

Numbers and Operations

NO.1d Understand and use ratios and proportions to represent quantitative relationships

Geometry

GM.1b Understand relationships among the angles, side lengths, perimeters, areas, and volumes of similar objects

GM.1c Create and critique inductive and deductive arguments concerning geometric ideas and relationships, such as congruence, similarity, and the Pythagorean relationship

GM.4e Recognize and apply geometric ideas and relationships in areas outside the mathematics classroom, such as art, science, and everyday life

Reasoning and Proof

RP.2d Select and use various types of reasoning and methods of proof

Communication

CM.3d Use the language of mathematics to express mathematical ideas precisely

• Compound Interest

Objectives

- Calculate compound interest.
- Use a calculator to compute compound interest.

Lesson Preparation

Materials

- **Power Up M** (in *Instructional Masters*)
- **Teacher-provided material:** calculators

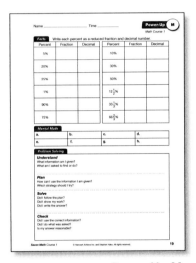

Power Up M

Math Language

New	English Learners (ESL)
compound interest	deposit
interest	
principal	
simple interest	

Technology Resources

Student eBook Complete student textbook in electronic format.

Resources and Planner CD Assessment, reteaching, and instructional masters, plus a pacing calendar with standards.

Test and Practice Generator CD Create additional practice sheets and custom-made tests.

www.SaxonPublishers.com Visit for more student activities and planning materials.

Inclusion

Adaptations CD Adapted lessons, investigations, practice and assessments.

Meeting Standards

National Council of Teachers of Mathematics (NCTM)

Numbers and Operations

NO.1c Develop meaning for percents greater than 100 and less than 1

Algebra

AL.3a Model and solve contextualized problems using various representations, such as graphs, tables, and equations

Problem Solving

PS.1b Solve problems that arise in mathematics and in other contexts

Connections

CN.4c Recognize and apply mathematics in contexts outside of mathematics

Problem-Solving Strategy: Write an Equation

Four identical blocks marked *x*, a 250-gram mass, and a 500-gram mass were balanced on a scale as shown. Write an equation to represent this balanced scale, and find the mass of each block marked *x*.

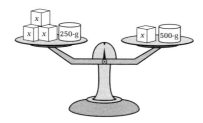

(Understand) **Understand the problem.**

"What information are we given?"

Four identical blocks marked *x*, a 250-g mass, and a 500-g mass are balanced on a scale.

"What are we asked to do?"

Write an equation to represent this balanced scale, and find the mass of each block.

(Plan) **Make a plan.**

"What problem-solving strategy will we use?"

We have been asked to *write an equation* and solve for the mass of each block.

(Solve) **Carry out the plan.**

"What equation can we write to represent the balanced scale?"

$3x + 250 = x + 500$

"What can be removed from both sides of the scale so that it remains balanced?"

One block

"How can we remove 250 g from both sides of the scale?"

Remove the 250-g mass from the left side and replace the 500-g mass with a 250-g mass.

"If we remove a block and 250 g of mass from each side of the scale, what is the simplified equation?"

$2x = 250$

"What is the mass of each of the blocks?"

125 g

(Check) **Look back.**

"How can we verify the solution is correct?"

We will substitute the value for *x* into the original equation:

$$3(125) + 250 = (125) + 500$$
$$375 + 250 = 125 + 500$$
$$625 = 625$$

1 Power Up

Facts

Distribute **Power Up M** to students. See answers below.

Mental Math

Before students begin the Mental Math exercise, do this counting exercise as a class.

Count down by 2s from 10 to −10.

Encourage students to share different ways to mentally compute these exercises. Strategies for exercises **a** and **f** are listed below.

a. **Multiply $\frac{1}{8}$ of 16 by 3**
   $\frac{1}{8}$ of 16 = 16 ÷ 8 = 2; 2 × 3 = 6
   Divide 3 × 16 by 8
   3 × 16 = 48; 48 ÷ 8 = 6

f. **Add Three Zeros to the Product 5 × 4**
   5 × 4 = 20; 50 × 400 = 20,000
   Find 5 · 4000
   50 · 400 = 5 · 4000; 5 · 4000 = 20,000

Problem Solving

Refer to **Power-Up Discussion**, p. 606B.

2 New Concepts

Instruction

Invite students to name real-world situations that involve interest of some kind. Examples: a home mortgage; a student loan for a college or university; an automobile loan; interest earned for a checking account or money market account balance; credit card interest charges

Make sure students recognize that in a simple interest situation, the principal, and the amount of interest earned each year, never changes.

(continued)

LESSON 116 • Compound Interest

facts   Power Up M

mental math
a. **Fractional Parts:** $\frac{3}{8}$ of 16   6
b. **Number Sense:** 4 × 560   2240
c. **Percent:** 50% of $2.50 $1.25
d. **Calculation:** $8.98 + 49¢ $9.47
e. **Decimals:** 0.375 × 100   37.5
f. **Number Sense:** 50 · 400   20,000
g. **Statistics:** Find the mode and range of the set of numbers: 84, 27, 91, 84, 22, 72, 27, 84.   84; 69
h. **Calculation:** 11 × 6, − 2, $\sqrt{\ }$, × 3, + 1, $\sqrt{\ }$, × 10, − 1, $\sqrt{\ }$ 7

problem solving   Four identical blocks marked *x*, a 250-gram mass, and a 500-gram mass were balanced on a scale as shown. Write an equation to represent this balanced scale, and find the mass of each block marked *x*.   125 g; 3x + 250 = x + 500

New Concept   *Increasing Knowledge*

When you deposit money in a bank, the bank uses a portion of that money to make loans and investments that earn money for the bank. To attract deposits, banks offer to pay **interest,** a percentage of the money deposited. The amount deposited is called the **principal.**

There is a difference between **simple interest** and **compound interest.** Simple interest is paid on the principal only and not paid on any accumulated interest. For instance, if you deposited $100 in an account that pays 3% simple interest, you would be paid 3% of $100 ($3) each year your $100 was on deposit. If you take your money out after three years, you would have a total of $109.

Simple Interest

$100.00	principal
$3.00	first-year interest
$3.00	second-year interest
+ $3.00	third-year interest
$109.00	total

Facts   Write each percent as a reduced fraction and decimal number.

Percent	Fraction	Decimal	Percent	Fraction	Decimal
5%	$\frac{1}{20}$	0.05	10%	$\frac{1}{10}$	0.1
20%	$\frac{1}{5}$	0.2	30%	$\frac{3}{10}$	0.3
25%	$\frac{1}{4}$	0.25	50%	$\frac{1}{2}$	0.5
1%	$\frac{1}{100}$	0.01	$12\frac{1}{2}$%	$\frac{1}{8}$	0.125
90%	$\frac{9}{10}$	0.9	$33\frac{1}{3}$%	$\frac{1}{3}$	Rounds to 0.333
75%	$\frac{3}{4}$	0.75	$66\frac{2}{3}$%	$\frac{2}{3}$	Rounds to 0.667

Most interest-bearing accounts, however, are compound-interest accounts. In a compound-interest account, interest is paid on accumulated interest as well as on the principal. If you deposited $100 in an account with 3% annual percentage rate, the amount of interest you would be paid each year increases if the earned interest is left in the account. After three years you would have a total of $109.27.

Visit www. SaxonPublishers. com/ActivitiesC1 *for a graphing calculator activity.*

Compound Interest

$100.00	principal
$3.00	first-year interest (3% of $100.00)
$103.00	total after one year
$3.09	second-year interest (3% of $103.00)
$106.09	total after two years
$3.18	third-year interest (3% of $106.09)
$109.27	total after three years

Example

Mrs. Vasquez opened a $2000 retirement account that has grown at a rate of 10% a year for three years. What is the current value of her account?

Solution

We calculate the total amount of money in the account at the end of each year by adding 10% to the value of the account at the beginning of that year.

First year		Second year		Third year	
Start with	$2000	Start with	$2200	Start with	$2420
Growth rate	× 0.10	Growth rate	× 0.10	Growth rate	× 0.10
Increase	$200.00	Increase	$220.00	Increase	$242.00
=		=		=	
Total	$2200.00	Total	$2420.00	Total	**$2662.00**

Notice that the account grew by a larger number of dollars each year, even though the growth rate stayed the same. This increase occurred because the starting amount increased year by year. The effect of compounding becomes more dramatic as the number of years increases.

In our solution above we multiplied each starting amount by 10% (0.10) to find the amount of increase, then we added the increase to the starting amount. Instead of multiplying by 10% and adding, we can multiply by 110% (1.10) to find the value of the account after each year.

First year		Second year		Third year	
Start with	$2000	Start with	$2200	Start with	$2420
	× 1.10		× 1.10		× 1.10
Total	**$2200.00**	Total	**$2420.00**	Total	**$2662.00**

Lesson 116   607

---

2 New Concepts (Continued)

Instruction

Ask students to compare the totals after three years for the simple interest account and the compound interest account.

"Which account contained more money after three years?" The account earning compound interest.

"Which account would contain more money after ten years? Twenty years? Why?" The compound interest account would contain more money because the amount of interest earned increases each year.

Students should generalize that an amount of money earning compound interest will be significantly greater in the long term than the same amount earning simple interest at the same rate.

Example
Instruction

Point out that multiplying by the sum of 100% and 10% (the interest rate) is a short way to calculate the total amount for each year. Explain that although this method does not give the amount of interest earned each year, the amount could be found by subtracting the starting amount for a year from the total amount.

(continued)

English Learners

Before the example, explain the term **deposit**. Say,

"When we deposit money in the bank, we put money in a bank account to be kept safely and to earn more money. So, money deposited in the bank is money placed into a bank account."

Ask students why people deposit money in the bank and how that can help them.

Instruction

Distribute calculators to students and have them enter the keystrokes shown to find the total amount in the account after one, two, and three years. If the calculator has a "memory recall" key, explain how the key is used.

Practice Set

Problems a–c (Error Alert)

When making a compound interest calculation, it can be difficult for students to look at an answer and decide if that answer is reasonable.

For this reason, encourage students to check their work by using their calculators and performing each calculation a second time.

Problem a Estimate

Remind students that Mrs. Vasquez's retirement account is earning compound interest.

We will use this second method with a calculator to find the amount of money in Mrs. Vasquez's account after one, two, and three years. We use 1.1 for 110% and follow this keystroke sequence:[1]

	Display	
2 0 0 0 × 1 . 1 =	2200	(1st yr)
× 1 . 1 =	2420	(2nd yr)
× 1 . 1 =	2662	(3rd yr)

Math Language

Abbreviations on memory keys may vary from one calculator to another. We will use →M for "enter memory" and MR for "memory recall."

We can use the calculator memory to reduce the number of keystrokes. Instead of entering 1.1 for every year, we enter 1.1 into the memory with these keystrokes:

1 . 1   →M

Now we can use the "memory recall" key instead of 1.1 to perform the calculations. We find the amount of money in Mrs. Vasquez's account after one, two, and three years with this sequence of keystrokes:

	Display	
2 0 0 0 × MR =	2200	(1st yr)
× MR =	2420	(2nd yr)
× MR =	2662	(3rd yr)

Practice Set ▶

a. *Estimate* After the third year, $2662 was in Mrs. Vasquez's account. If the account continues to grow 10% annually, how much money will be in the account **1.** after the tenth year and **2.** after the twentieth year? Round answers to the nearest cent. **1.** $5187.48 **2.** $13,455.00

▶ **b.** *Estimate* Nelson deposited $2000 in an account that pays 4% interest per year. If he does not withdraw any money from the account, how much will be in the account **1.** after three years, **2.** after 10 years, and **3.** after 20 years? (Multiply by 1.04. Round answers to the nearest cent.) **1.** $2249.73 **2.** $2960.49 **3.** $4382.25

See student work. Problems can be collected and then distributed throughout the rest of the year to provide practice on this topic.

▶ **c.** How much more money will be in Mrs. Vasquez's account than in Nelson's account **1.** after three years, **2.** after 10 years, and **3.** after 20 years? **1.** $412.27 **2.** $2226.99 **3.** $9072.75

Connect Find an advertisement that gives a bank's or other saving institution's interest rate for savings accounts. Write a problem based on the advertisement. Be sure to provide the answer to your problem.

Written Practice   Strengthening Concepts

1. John drew a right triangle with sides 6 inches, 8 inches, and 10 inches
(79, 93) long. What was the area of the triangle?   24 in.²

2. If 5 feet of ribbon costs $1.20, then 10 feet of ribbon would cost how
(95) much? $2.40

---

[1] If this keystroke sequence does not produce the indicated result, consult the manual for the calculator for the appropriate keystroke sequence.

▶ See Math Conversations in the sidebar.

3. a. Six is what fraction of 15? $\frac{2}{5}$
(22, 75)
b. Six is what percent of 15? 40%

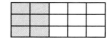

▶ **4.** The multiple-choice question has four choices. Raidon knows that one
(58) of the choices must be correct, but he has no idea which one. If Raidon
simply guesses, what is the chance that he will guess the correct
answer? 25%

5. If $\frac{2}{5}$ of the 30 students in the class buy lunch in the school cafeteria,
(77) what is the ratio of students who buy lunch in the school cafeteria to
students who bring their lunch from home? $\frac{2}{3}$

▶ * **6.** **Connect** Write 1.2×10^9 as a standard number. 1,200,000,000
(113)

▶ **7.** **Evaluate** The cost (c) of apples is related to its price per pound (p) and
(95) its weight (w) by this formula:

$$c = pw$$

Find the cost when p is $\frac{\$1.25}{1 \text{ pound}}$ and w is 5 pounds. $6.25

8. Arrange these numbers in order from least to greatest:
(44) 9.09, 9.9, 9.925, 9.95   9.9, 9.95, 9.925, 9.09

Connect Complete the table to answer problems **9** and **10.**

	Fraction	Decimal	Percent
9. (99)	$3\frac{3}{8}$	**a.** 3.375	**b.** 337.5%
10. (99)	**a.** $\frac{3}{20}$	**b.** 0.15	15%

Solve and check:

* **11.** $9x + 17 = 80$ $x = 7$ * **12.** $\frac{x}{3} = \frac{1.6}{1.2}$ $x = 4$
(106)   (85, 105)

* **13.** $-6 + -4 - +3 - -8$ -5
(104)

14. $6 + 3\frac{3}{4} + 4.6$ (decimal answer)   14.35
(74)

* **15.** The Gateway Arch in St. Louis, Missouri, is approximately 210 yards tall.
(114) How tall is it in feet?   630 feet

16. Use division by primes to find the prime factors of 648. Then write the
(73) prime factorization of 648 using exponents. $2^3 \cdot 3^4$

17. If a 32-ounce box of cereal costs $3.84, what is the cost per
(15) ounce? $0.12 per ounce

16.
```
      1
   3)3
   3)9
  3)27
  3)81
 2)162
 2)324
 2)648
```

▶ See Math Conversations in the sidebar.

---

3 Written Practice

Math Conversations
Discussion opportunities are provided below.

Problem 4 Analyze
Extend the Problem
*"What is the probability, expressed as a
percent, that Raidon will not guess the
correct answer?"* 75%

*"Suppose the question is part of a test that
has twenty questions altogether. If Raidon
guesses each of the 20 answers, how many
answers would you predict that he guesses
correctly? Explain your answer."* Sample:
Five; the probability Raidon will guess one
correct answer is 25%, and 25% of 20 is 5.

Problem 6 Connect
After students solve the problem, invite a
volunteer to say the word name of the answer.
one billion, two hundred million

Problem 7 Infer
Extend the Problem
Challenge volunteers to write a formula that
can be used to find the price per pound (p)
when the weight in pounds (w) and the cost
(c) is known. $p = \frac{c}{w}$

(continued)

Math Conversations

Discussion opportunities are provided below.

Errors and Misconceptions
Problem 23

In some division situations, students must interpret the remainder. This typically involves making one of three choices:

• The whole-number portion of the quotient rounds up.

• The whole-number portion of the quotient stays the same.

• The remainder is the answer.

In problem **1**, the division $306 \div 10$ produces the quotient 30 R6, which represents an average—there are an average of 30 students in each of 10 classrooms with 6 students left over.

Help your students infer that each of these 6 students must be placed in a classroom. Since the maximum number of students in any classroom can be 31, all of the 6 students cannot be placed in the same classroom. Instead, one additional student will be placed in each of six classrooms.

So 4 classrooms each have 30 students. The other six classrooms each have 31 students—the extra students (one in each of six classrooms) represent the remainder of the division $306 \div 10$.

(continued)

---

* 18. Find the area of this trapezoid by combining the area of the rectangle and the area of the triangle.   28 m²
(107)

19. The radius of a circle is 10 cm. Use 3.14 for π to calculate the
(47, 86)
   a. circumference of the circle.   62.8 cm

   b. area of the circle.   314 cm²

20. *Conclude* The volume of the pyramid is $\frac{1}{3}$ the
(82)   volume of the cube. What is the volume of the pyramid?   9 cm³

21. Solve: $0.6y = 54$ 90
(49)

* 22. Calculate mentally:
(112)
   a. $(-8)(-2)$ +16   **b.** $(+8)(-2)$ −16

   c. $\frac{+8}{-2}$ −4   **d.** $\frac{-8}{-2}$ +4

▶ **23.** *Analyze* The 306 students were assigned to ten rooms so that there
(111)   were 30 or 31 students in each room. How many rooms had exactly 30 students?   4 rooms

24. Two angles of a triangle measure 40° and 110°.
(98)
   a. What is the measure of the third angle?   30°

   b. *Represent* Make a rough sketch of the triangle.

25. *Estimate* If Anthony spins the spinner 60 times,
(58)   about how many times should he expect the arrow to stop in sector 3?   **D**

   A 60 times   **B** 40 times

   C 20 times   **D** 10 times

* 26. *Analyze* An equilateral triangle and a
(8, 38)   square share a common side. If the area of the square is 100 mm², then what is the perimeter of the equilateral triangle?   30 mm

* 27. Write $11\frac{1}{9}\%$ as a reduced fraction. $\frac{1}{9}$
(115)

28. The heights of the five starters on the basketball team are listed below.
(Inv. 5)   Find the mean, median, and range of these measures.

   181 cm, 177 cm, 189 cm, 158 cm, 195 cm
   Mean is 180 cm; median is 181 cm; range is 37 cm.

24. b.

▶ See Math Conversations in the sidebar.

* 29. Keisha bought two bunches of bananas. The smaller bunch weighed
_(102, 113) 2 lb 12 oz. The larger bunch weighed 3 lb 8 oz. What was the total
weight of the two bunches of bananas?   6 lb 4 oz

▶* 30. *Classify* Which type of triangle has no lines of symmetry?   C
_(93, 110)
  A equilateral   **B** isosceles   **C** scalene

Early Finishers
*Real-World
Application*

Gerard plays basketball on his high school team. This season he scored 372
of his team's 1488 points.

  a. What percent of the points were scored by Gerard's teammates?   75%

  b. Gerard's team played 12 games. How many points did Gerard average
  per game?   31 points

▶ See Math Conversations in the sidebar.

Lesson 116   **611**

---

3 **Written Practice** *(Continued)*

Math Conversations
Discussion opportunities are provided below.

Problem 30 *Classify*
Encourage students to sketch each triangle
before deciding if the triangle has lines of
symmetry.

● Finding a Whole When a Fraction is Known

Objectives

• Draw a diagram to find a whole in a fractional-parts problem when a fraction is known.

Lesson Preparation

Materials

• **Power Up N** (in *Instructional Masters*)

Optional

• **Investigation Activity 15** (in *Instructional Masters*) or **graph paper**

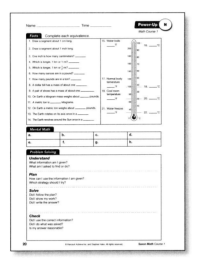

Power Up N

Math Language

English Learners (ESL)

respectively

Technology Resources

Student eBook Complete student textbook in electronic format.

Resources and Planner CD Assessment, reteaching, and instructional masters, plus a pacing calendar with standards.

Test and Practice Generator CD Create additional practice sheets and custom-made tests.

www.SaxonPublishers.com Visit for more student activities and planning materials.

Inclusion

Adaptations CD Adapted lessons, investigations, practice and assessments.

Meeting Standards

National Council of Teachers of Mathematics (NCTM)

Numbers and Operations

NO.1a Work flexibly with fractions, decimals, and percents to solve problems

NO.1d Understand and use ratios and proportions to represent quantitative relationships

NO.2a Understand the meaning and effects of arithmetic operations with fractions, decimals, and integers

Problem Solving

PS.1b Solve problems that arise in mathematics and in other contexts

PS.1c Apply and adapt a variety of appropriate strategies to solve problems

Problem-Solving Strategy: Draw a Diagram/ Use Logical Reasoning

Three numbers add to 180. The second number is twice the first number, and the third number is three times the first number. Create a visual representation of the equation, and then find the three numbers.

(Understand) *Understand the problem.*

"What information are we given?"

There are three numbers with a sum of 180. The second number is twice the first number, and the third number is three times the first number.

"What are we asked to do?"

Create a visual representation of the equation, and then find the three numbers.

(Plan) *Make a plan.*

"What problem-solving strategy will we use?"

Will will *draw a diagram* and *use logical reasoning* to solve for each number.

(Solve) *Carry out the plan.*

"How can we show that the second number is twice the first?"

If we let one block represent the first number, then two blocks would represent the second number. Then the third number can be represented by three blocks since it is three times the first number. Together they add up to 180.

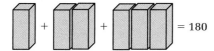

"How do we proceed?"

If six blocks together total 180, then each one has a value of 30. That means the first number is 30, the second is 60 and the third is 90.

(Check) *Look back.*

"How can we verify the solution is correct?"

We can add the three numbers together, $30 + 60 + 90 = 180$ and we check to make sure that the second is twice the first (it is) and the third is three times the first (it is).

1 Power Up

Facts
Distribute **Power Up N** to students. See answers below.

Mental Math
Encourage students to share different ways to mentally compute these exercises. Strategies for exercises **c** and **d** are listed below.

c. Find $\frac{1}{2}$ of $\frac{1}{2}$ of $80

$\frac{1}{2}$ of $80 = $40; $\frac{1}{2}$ of $40 = $20

Divide $80 by 4

25% of $80 = $\frac{1}{4}$ of $80; $80 ÷ 4 = $20

d. Reduce $\frac{5}{20}$

$\frac{5}{20} ÷ \frac{5}{5} = \frac{1}{4}$; $\frac{1}{4}$ is the same as 25%

Multiply $\frac{5}{20}$ by $\frac{5}{5}$

$\frac{5}{20} × \frac{5}{5} = \frac{25}{100}; \frac{25}{100} = 25\%$

Problem Solving
Refer to **Power-Up Discussion,** p. 612B.

2 New Concepts

Instruction
Dividing a rectangle into five parts is a visual way to model the fact that 1 represents all of the students in the class (because 100% = 1), and since $\frac{2}{5}$ of the class are boys, the difference $1 - \frac{2}{5}$ represents the fraction of the class that are girls.

$$1 - \frac{2}{5} = g$$
$$\frac{5}{5} - \frac{2}{5} = g$$
$$\frac{3}{5} = g$$

(continued)

---

facts   Power Up N

mental math

a. Fractional Parts: $\frac{7}{8}$ of 16   14

b. Number Sense: $3 × 760$ 2280

c. Percent: 25% of $80 $20

d. Percent: 5 is what % of 20?   25%

e. Decimals: $0.6 × 40$ 24

f. Number Sense: $60 · 700$ 42,000

g. Statistics: Find the mode and range of the set of numbers: 99, 101, 34, 44, 120, 34, 43.   34; 86

h. Calculation: $8 × 8, -1, ÷ 7, \sqrt{\ }, × 4, ÷ 2, × 3, ÷ 2$ 9

problem solving

Three numbers add to 180. The second number is twice the first number, and the third number is three times the first number. Create a visual representation of the equation, and then find the three numbers.   See script for visual representation; 30, 60, 90

Consider the following fractional-parts problem:

> *Two fifths of the students in the class are boys. If there are ten boys in the class, how many students are in the class?*

Thinking Skill

Discuss

What information in the problem suggests that we divide the rectangle into 5 parts?   Since $\frac{2}{5}$ are boys, we divide the rectangle into five parts.

A diagram can help us understand and solve this problem. We have drawn a rectangle to represent the whole class. The problem states that two fifths are boys, so we divide the rectangle into five parts. Two of the parts are boys, so the remaining three parts must be girls.

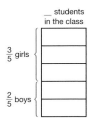

___ students in the class

$\frac{3}{5}$ girls

$\frac{2}{5}$ boys

Facts   Complete each equivalence.

1. Draw a segment about 1 cm long.

2. Draw a segment about 1 inch long.

3. One inch is how many centimeters? __2.54__

4. Which is longer, 1 km or 1 mi? __1 mi__

5. Which is longer, 1 km or $\frac{1}{2}$ mi? __1 km__

6. How many ounces are in a pound? __16__

7. How many pounds are in a ton? __2000__

8. A dollar bill has a mass of about one __gram__.

9. A pair of shoes has a mass of about one __kilogram__

10. On Earth a kilogram mass weighs about __2.2__ pounds.

11. A metric ton is __1000__ kilograms.

12. On Earth a metric ton weighs about __2200__ pounds.

13. The Earth rotates on its axis once in a __day__.

14. The Earth revolves around the Sun once in a __year__.

15. Water boils __212__ °F

16. __100__ °C

17. Normal body temerature __98.6__ °F

18. __37__ °C

19. Cool room temperature __68__ °F

20. __20__ °C

21. Water freezes __32__ °F

22. __0__ °C

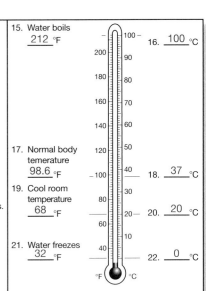

We are also told that there are ten boys in the class. In our diagram ten boys make up two of the parts. Since ten divided by two is five, there are five students in each part. All five parts together represent the total number of students, so there are 25 students in all. We complete the diagram.

25 students in the class	
	5
$\frac{3}{5}$ girls	5
	5
$\frac{2}{5}$ boys	5
	5

Example 1

Three eighths of the townspeople voted. If 120 of the townspeople voted, how many people live in the town?

Solution

We are told that $\frac{3}{8}$ of the town voted, so we divide the whole into eight parts and mark off three of the parts. We are told that these three parts total 120 people. Since the three parts total 120, each part must be 40 (120 ÷ 3 = 40). Each part is 40, so all eight parts must be 8 times 40, which is **320 people.**

___ people live in the town.	
	40
$\frac{3}{8}$ voted.	40
	40
	40
	40
$\frac{5}{8}$ did not vote.	40
	40
	40

Example 2

Six is $\frac{2}{3}$ of what number?

Solution

A larger number has been divided into three parts. Six is the total of two of the three parts. So each part equals three, and all three parts together equal **9.**

The larger number is ___.	
$\frac{2}{3}$ of the number is 6.	3
	3
	3

Practice Set

Model Solve. Draw a diagram for problems **a–c.**

a. 40
| 8 |
| 8 |
| 8 |
| 8 |
| 8 |
$\frac{1}{5}$

▶ **a.** Eight is $\frac{1}{5}$ of what number?   40

b. 20
| 4 |
| 4 |
| 4 |
| 4 |
| 4 |
$\frac{2}{5}$

▶ **b.** Eight is $\frac{2}{5}$ of what number?   20

c. 12
| 3 |
| 3 |
| 3 |
| 3 |
$\frac{3}{4}$

▶ **c.** Nine is $\frac{3}{4}$ of what number?   12

▶ See Math Conversations in the sidebar.

Instruction

Explain that one way to check the answer is to find $\frac{2}{5}$ of 25. The problem states that $\frac{2}{5}$ of the students are boys, and that there are 10 boys in the class. Therefore, $\frac{2}{5}$ of the 25 students should equal 10.

$$\frac{2}{5} \text{ of } 25 = n$$
$$\frac{2}{5} \times \frac{25}{1} = n$$
$$\frac{50}{5} = n$$
$$10 = n$$

Example 2
Instruction

Make sure students recognize that each part is equal to 3 because 6 ÷ 2 = 3.

Practice Set
Problems a–d [Error alert]

Ask students to check their work for each problem by multiplying the fraction that is given by the answer. If the product is equal to the number that is given in the problem, the answer checks. For example, if students find an answer of 40 for problem a, they should check by finding $\frac{1}{5}$ of 40. If the product is equal to the number given in the problem (8), the answer checks.

(continued)

Practice Set

Problem e [Error Alert]

If students struggle solving the problem, offer the following questions.

"If we draw a rectangle to represent the whole class, the rectangle will be divided into five parts. How many of those parts will represent girls? Why?" Three; the problem states that $\frac{3}{5}$ of the class are girls.

"How many girls do the three parts represent?" 18

"To find the number of girls each part represents, we divide the number of girls by the number of parts. What is 18 divided by 3?" 6

"Each part of the rectangle represents 6 students."

---

3 **Written Practice**

Math Conversations

Discussion opportunities are provided below.

Problem 2 [Analyze]

Students must interpret the remainder in this problem. After dividing 130 by 4, ask

"The quotient represents an average of 30 children in each of 4 groups, and the remainder represents two other children who are not in the groups. Why can't we place both of those children in the same group?" The groups will not be as equal as possible.

"How can we include the two children in a group and still make the groups as equal as possible?" Place one child in each of two groups.

(continued)

▶ **d.** Sixty is $\frac{3}{8}$ of what number?   160

▶ **e.** Three fifths of the students in the class were girls. If there were 18 girls in the class, how many students were in the class altogether?   30 students

Written Practice   Strengthening Concepts

d.   160

20
20
20
20
20
20
20
20

$\frac{3}{8}$ {

e.   30 students

$\frac{3}{5}$ were girls. {
6 students
6 students
6 students
6 students
6 students

* 1. Three fifths of the townspeople voted. If 120 of the townspeople voted,
(117) how many people live in the town?   200 people

▶ *** 2.** [Analyze] If 130 children are separated as equally as possible into four
(111) groups, how many will be in each group? (Write four numbers, one for each of the four groups.)   32, 32, 33, 33

3. If the parking lot charges $1.25 per half hour, what is the cost of parking
(32, 95) a car from 11:15 a.m. to 2:45 p.m.? $8.75

4. [Analyze] If the area of the square is 400 m²,
(86) then what is the area of the circle? (Use 3.14 for π.)   1256 m²

5. Only 4 of the 50 states have names that begin with the letter A.
(94) What percent of the states have names that begin with letters other than A?   92%

6. [Connect] The coordinates of the vertices of a triangle are (3, 6),
(Inv. 7, 79) (5, 0), and (0, 0). What is the area of the triangle?   15 sq. units

7. Write one hundred five thousandths as a decimal number.   0.105
(35)

8. [Estimate] Round the quotient of $7.00 ÷ 9 to the nearest cent. $0.78
(51)

9. Arrange in order from least to greatest: $\frac{4}{5}$, 81%, 0.815
(99)
$$81\%, \frac{4}{5}, 0.815$$

Solve and check:

10. $6x - 12 = 60$ $x = 12$ **11.** $\frac{9}{15} = \frac{m}{25}$ $m = 15$
(106)   (85)

12. Six is $\frac{2}{5}$ of what number?   15
(117)

13. $\left(5 - 1\frac{2}{3}\right) - 1\frac{1}{2}$ $1\frac{5}{6}$ **14.** $2\frac{2}{5} \div 1\frac{1}{2}$ $1\frac{3}{5}$
(63)   (68)

15. 0.625×2.4 1.5   **16.** $-5 + -5 + -5$ -15
(39)   (104)

17. The prime factorization of 24 is $2 \cdot 2 \cdot 2 \cdot 3$, which we can write as
(73) $2^3 \cdot 3$. Write the prime factorization of 36 using exponents. $2^2 \cdot 3^2$

▶ See Math Conversations in the sidebar.

18. What is the total price of a \$12.50 item plus 6% sales tax?   \$13.25
(41)

19. What is the area of this pentagon?   80 in.²
(107)

8 in.

5 in.

9 in.

12 in.

20. Write the standard numeral for 6×10^5.   600,000
(113)

21. **Analyze** Calculate mentally:
(112)
a. $\dfrac{-20}{-4}$ +5

b. $\dfrac{-36}{6}$ −6

c. $(-3)(8)$ −24

d. $(-4)(-9)$ +36

22. If each small cube has a volume of one
(82) cubic inch, then what is the volume of this
rectangular solid?   60 in.³

23.
Sample:

23. **Represent** Draw a triangle in which each angle measures less than 90°.
(93) What type of triangle did you draw?   acute triangle

24. **Estimate** The mean, median, and mode of student scores on a test
(Inv. 5) were 89, 87, and 92 respectively. About half of the students scored what
score or higher?   87

25. **Analyze** A bank offers an annual percentage rate (APR) of 6.5%.
(116)
a. By what decimal number do we multiply a deposit to find the total
amount in an account after one year at this rate?   1.065

b. Maria deposited \$1000 into an account at this rate. How much
money was in the account after three years? (Assume that the
account earns compound interest.)   \$1207.95

26. **Analyze** If the spinner is spun twice, what is
(Inv. 10) the probability that the arrow will stop on a
number greater than 1 on both spins? $\frac{9}{16}$

27. **Conclude** By rotation and translation, these
(108) two congruent triangles can be arranged to
form a: **B**

A square   **B** parallelogram   **C** octagon

28. **Model** Draw a ratio box for this problem. Then solve the problem using
(101) a proportion.   See student work; 120 horses

*The ratio of cattle to horses on the ranch was 15 to 2. The combined
number of cattle and horses was 1020. How many horses were on
the ranch?*

Lesson 117   615

▶ See Math Conversations in the sidebar.

---

3 **Written Practice** *(Continued)*

Math Conversations
Discussion opportunities are provided below.

Problem 25 **Analyze**
**"How can we change 6.5% to a decimal
number?"** Sample: Divide by 100%, that is,
shift the decimal point two places to the left
and erase the percent sign.

Problem 26 **Analyze**
**"How many outcomes on the spinner are
greater than 1?"** 6

**"What is the probability of the arrow
pointing to a number greater than 1 if the
spinner is spun once?"** $\frac{6}{8}$ or $\frac{3}{4}$

**"What is the probability of the arrow
pointing to a number greater than 1 if the
spinner is spun a second time?"** $\frac{6}{8}$ or $\frac{3}{4}$

**"What operation is used to find the
probability of a compound event?"**
multiplication

Errors and Misconceptions
Problem 19
Students must recognize that the complex
figure is composed of a rectangle and right
triangle. To find the area of the triangle,
students must find the lengths of the
perpendicular sides of the triangle (both sides
have a length of 4 in.).

Problem 25a
If students name \$207.95 as the answer, point
out that the amount represents the interest
that was earned during the three years. Ask
students to read the problem carefully to
learn that they are being asked to name the
total amount in the account. Students should
conclude that they must include the initial
principal in the total amount.

(continued)

English Learners

In problem **24,** explain the term
respectively. Say:

*"This problem lists three words
and three scores, followed by
the term respectively. This means
that the order of the words
matches one by one to the order
of the listed numbers."*

Have students write a sentence
about four items they want to buy
and have them place each item's
price respectively. Then ask them to
check if the correct price is matched
to the correct item.

Math Conversations

Discussion opportunities are provided below.

Problem 30 Conclude

Encourage students to sketch or trace the figures if they wish, and then look for lines of symmetry by folding the sketches or tracings in a variety of ways.

---

* 29. $\sqrt{100} + 3^2 \times 5 - \sqrt{81} \div 3$ 52
(92)

▶* 30. a. Conclude   Which of these figures has the greatest number of lines
(110)   of symmetry?   **C**

   A △   **B** □   **C** ○

   b. Which of these figures has rotational symmetry?   all

Early Finishers
Real-World
Application

You and your friends want to rent go-karts this Saturday. Go-Kart Track A rents go-karts for a flat fee of $10 per driver plus $7 per hour. Go-Kart Track B rents go-karts for a flat fee of $7 per driver plus $8 per hour.

a. If you and your friends plan to stay for 2 hours, which track has the better deal? Show all your work.   Track B; Sample: Track A:
$C = \$7 \times 2 + \$10$; $C = \$24$, Track B: $C = \$8 \times 2 + \$7 = \$23$
b. Which track is the better value if you stay for four hours?   Track A

▶ See Math Conversations in the sidebar.

Estimating Area

Objectives

- Use a grid to estimate the area of an irregular shape.

Lesson Preparation

Materials

- **Power Up M** (in *Instructional Masters*)
- **Lesson Activity 23 Transparency** (in *Instructional Masters*)
- **Teacher-provided material: overhead marker** (for the teacher), **grid paper**

Optional

- **Teacher-provided material:** grid paper, irregular shapes on pieces of grid paper

Math Language

English Learners (ESL)

acre

Technology Resources

Student eBook Complete student textbook in electronic format.

Resources and Planner CD Assessment, reteaching, and instructional masters, plus a pacing calendar with standards.

Test and Practice Generator CD Create additional practice sheets and custom-made tests.

www.SaxonPublishers.com Visit for more student activities and planning materials.

Inclusion

Adaptations CD Adapted lessons, investigations, practice and assessments.

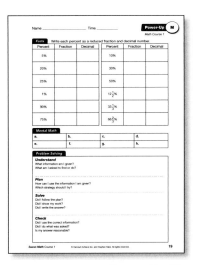

Power Up M

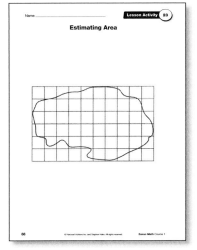

Lesson Activity 23

Meeting Standards

National Council of Teachers of Mathematics (NCTM)

Measurement

ME.1c Understand, select, and use units of appropriate size and type to measure angles, perimeter, area, surface area, and volume

ME.2a Use common benchmarks to select appropriate methods for estimating measurements

Problem Solving

PS.1b Solve problems that arise in mathematics and in other contexts

PS.1c Apply and adapt a variety of appropriate strategies to solve problems

Problem-Solving Strategy: Write an Equation

Carlos reads 5 pages in 4 minutes, and Tom reads 4 pages in 5 minutes. If they both begin reading 200-page books at the same time and do not stop until they are done, how many minutes before Tom finishes will Carlos finish?

(Understand) **Understand the problem.**

"What information are we given?"

Carlos reads 5 pages in 4 minutes and Tom reads 4 pages in 5 minutes.

"What are we asked to do?"

Find how many minutes before Tom finishes, Carlos will finish.

(Plan) **Make a plan.**

"What problem-solving strategy will we use?"

We will *write an equation* for each one and find out how many minutes it will take for each to read 200 pages.

(Solve) **Carry out the plan.**

"How do we proceed?"

We begin by writing a proportion to find how long it will take Carlos to read 200 pages. Then we will write another proportion to find how long it will take Tom.

Carlos's Time

$$\frac{5 \text{ pp}}{4 \text{ min}} = \frac{200 \text{ pp}}{x}$$
$$5x = 800$$
$$x = 160 \text{ min}$$

Tom's Time

$$\frac{4 \text{ pp}}{5 \text{ min}} = \frac{200 \text{ pp}}{x}$$
$$4x = 1000$$
$$x = 250 \text{ min}$$

"What is the difference in Carlos's and Tom's times?"

$250 - 160 = 90$ min. Therefore, Carlos will finish the 200 pages 90 minutes before Tom.

(Check) **Look back.**

"Did we answer the question that was asked?"

Yes. We found that it would take Tom 90 minutes longer to read the 200 pages than Carlos.

• **Estimating Area**

facts | Power Up M

mental math

a. **Fractional Parts:** 6 is $\frac{1}{3}$ of what number?   18

b. **Fractional Parts:** $\frac{2}{3}$ of 15   10

c. **Percent:** 40% of $20 $8

d. **Percent:** 10 is what % of 40?   25%

e. **Decimals:** 0.3 × 20   6

f. **Number Sense:** 300 · 300   90,000

g. **Statistics:** Find the mode and range of the set of numbers: 567, 899, 576, 345, 899, 907.   899; 562

h. **Calculation:** 10 × 10, − 10, ÷ 2, − 1, ÷ 4, × 3, − 1, ÷ 4   8

problem solving | Carlos reads 5 pages in 4 minutes, and Tom reads 4 pages in 5 minutes. If they both begin reading 200-page books at the same time and do not stop until they are done, how many minutes before Tom finishes will Carlos finish?   90 minutes

In Lesson 86 we used a grid to estimate the area of a circle. Recall that we counted squares with most of their area within the circle as whole units. We counted squares with about half of their area in the circle as half units. In the figure at right, we have marked these "half squares" with dots.

We can use a grid to estimate the areas of shapes whose areas would otherwise be difficult to calculate.

Example

A one-acre grid is placed over an aerial photograph of a lake. Estimate the surface area of the lake in acres.

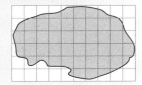

Facts   Write each percent as a reduced fraction and decimal number.

Percent	Fraction	Decimal	Percent	Fraction	Decimal
5%	$\frac{1}{20}$	0.05	10%	$\frac{1}{10}$	0.1
20%	$\frac{1}{5}$	0.2	30%	$\frac{3}{10}$	0.3
25%	$\frac{1}{4}$	0.25	50%	$\frac{1}{2}$	0.5
1%	$\frac{1}{100}$	0.01	$12\frac{1}{2}$%	$\frac{1}{8}$	0.125
90%	$\frac{9}{10}$	0.9	$33\frac{1}{3}$%	$\frac{1}{3}$	Rounds to 0.333
75%	$\frac{3}{4}$	0.75	$66\frac{2}{3}$%	$\frac{2}{3}$	Rounds to 0.667

---

1 Power Up

Facts
Distribute **Power Up M** to students. See answers below.

Mental Math
Encourage students to share different ways to mentally compute these exercises. Strategies for exercises **a** and **d** are listed below.

a. **Use Repeated Addition**
   Since $6 + 6 + 6 = 18$, 6 is $\frac{1}{3}$ of 18.
   Divide 6 by $\frac{1}{3}$
   $6 ÷ \frac{1}{3} = \frac{6}{1} × \frac{3}{1} = \frac{18}{1} = 18$

d. **Reduce $\frac{10}{40}$**
   $\frac{10}{40} = \frac{1}{4}; \frac{1}{4} = 25\%$, so 10 is 25% of 40
   Use Repeated Addition
   $10 + 10 + 10 + 10 = 40$, so 10 is $\frac{1}{4}$ or 25% of 40

Problem Solving
Refer to **Power-Up Discussion**, p. 617B.

2 New Concepts

Example
Instruction
Remind students that one way to check their work is to estimate an answer before solving a problem.

"How many squares are in the grid?"   60

"What does each square of the grid represent?"   1 acre

"How many acres altogether does the grid represent?"   60 acres

Point out that because the entire grid represents 60 acres, the surface area of the lake is less than 60 acres. Then ask students to make an estimate of the surface area of the lake.

(continued)

2 New Concepts (Continued)

Instruction

Place the transparency of **Lesson Activity 23** Estimating Area on the overhead. Use an overhead marker to group whole and nearly whole squares into rectangles for quick counting. Then count half squares and draw a dot on each half square.

On the board, show students how to combine the whole squares and the half squares to estimate the total area of the lake. Write:

37 squares

10 half squares $= 10 \times \frac{1}{2} = 5$ squares

37 squares $+$ 5 squares $= 42$ squares

$= 42$ acres

"We estimate the area to be about 42 acres."

Practice Set

Students should recognize that the grid represents 5×6 or 30 square units, and any estimate of the area of the paw print should be less than 30 square units.

Estimates of the area are likely to vary; accept reasonable estimates.

3 Written Practice

Math Conversations

Discussion opportunities are provided below.

Problem 2 Estimate

Some students may find it helpful to use some sort of benchmark when making an estimate. Point out to these students that the width of a person's little finger nail is about 1 centimeter.

If some students think of the length of a pencil in inches, they will need to convert their estimate of inches to centimeters. Point out that 1 inch is about the same as $2\frac{1}{2}$ centimeters.

(continued)

Solution

Thinking Skill

Explain

Why do you think area in this example is expressed in acres, rather than in square acres? An acre is already a square unit of measure for land area. An acre is 43,650 sq ft.

Each square on the grid represents an area of one acre. The curve is the shoreline of the lake. We count each square that is entirely or mostly within the curve as one acre. We count as half acres those squares that are about halfway within the curve. (Those squares are marked with dots in the figure below.) We ignore bits of squares within the curve because we assume that they balance out the bits of squares we counted that lay outside the curve.

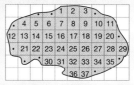

We count 37 entire or nearly entire squares within the shoreline. We also count ten squares with about half of their area within the shoreline. Ten half squares is equivalent to five whole squares. So we estimate the surface area of the lake to be about **42 acres.**

Justify How can we check to see if the answer is reasonable? Multiply 10×6 and subtract the squares outside the lake.

Practice Set Estimate the area of the paw print shown below. Describe the method you used to find your answer. 14 (or 15) square units; See student work.

Written Practice · Strengthening Concepts

1. Tabari is giving out baseball cards. Seven students sit in a circle. If he
(111) goes around the circle giving out 52 of his baseball cards, how many students will get 8 cards? 3 students

▶ **2.** *Estimate* About how long is a new pencil? B
(7)
   A 1.8 cm   **B** 18 cm   **C** 180 cm

3. *Estimate* Texas is the second most populous state in the United States.
(117) About 6 million people under the age of 18 lived in Texas in the year 2000. This number was about $\frac{3}{10}$ of the total population of the state at that time. About how many people lived in Texas in 2000? about 20,000,000

4. *Verify* The symbol $\neq$ means "is not equal to." Which statement is
(76) true? B
   A $\frac{3}{4} \neq \frac{9}{12}$ **B** $\frac{3}{4} \neq \frac{9}{16}$ **C** $\frac{3}{4} \neq 0.75$

618   *Saxon* Math Course 1

▶ See Math Conversations in the sidebar.

Manipulative Use

After completing the example, distribute quarter sheets of grid paper so students can practice estimating the **area of an irregular shape.** Ask each student to draw an irregular shape, then switch papers with a partner and estimate the area of the partner's shape.

English Learners

In the solution, explain the term **acre.** Say:

"An acre is a unit of measure used to describe the area or size of a piece of land. An acre equals about 44 thousand square feet."

Ask students to describe what could happen or be placed inside an acre of land (Samples: growing crops, playing a game; a house, swimming pool or a small lake).

---

5. What is the total price, including 7% tax, of a $14.49 item? $15.50
(41)

6. As Elsa peered out her window she saw 48 trucks, 84 cars, and
(23)   12 motorcycles go by her home. What was the ratio of trucks to
   cars that Elsa saw? $\frac{4}{7}$

7. What is the mean of 17, 24, 27, and 28?   24
(Inv. 3)

8. Arrange in order from least to greatest: $\sqrt{36}, 6.1, 6\frac{1}{4}$
(74)
   $6.1, \sqrt{36}, 6\frac{1}{4}$

▶ *** 9.** **Analyze** Nine cookies were left in the package. That was $\frac{3}{10}$ of the
(117)   original number of cookies. How many were in the package originally?
   30 cookies

10. **Explain** Buz measured the circumference of the trunk of the old oak
(47)   tree. How can Buz calculate the approximate diameter of the tree?   Buz
   can divide the circumference by π (by 3.14) to calculate the diameter.

* 11. Twelve is $\frac{3}{4}$ of what number?   16
(117)

12. $2\frac{2}{3} + \left(5\frac{1}{3} - 2\frac{1}{2}\right)$ $5\frac{1}{2}$ **13.** $6\frac{2}{3} \div 4\frac{1}{6}$ $1\frac{3}{5}$
(72)   (68)

14. $4\frac{1}{4} + 3.2$ (decimal answer)   7.45
(74)

15. $1 - (0.1)^2$ 0.99   **16.** $\sqrt{441}$ 21
(92)   (89)

* 17. On Earth a kilogram is about 2.2 pounds. Use a unit multiplier to convert
(114)   2.2 pounds to ounces. (Round to the nearest ounce.)   35 ounces

18. The quadrilateral at right is a parallelogram.
(71)   **a.** What is the area of the parallelogram?
      24 cm^2
   b. If each obtuse angle measures 127°, then
      what is the measure of each acute angle?
      53°

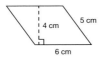

19. What is the perimeter of this hexagon?   14 cm
(103)

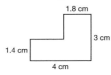

▶ *** 20.** **Conclude** We show two lines of symmetry for
(110)   this square. A square has a total of how many
   lines of symmetry?   4 lines of symmetry

▶ *** 21.** **Estimate** Each edge of a cube measures 4.11 feet. What is a good
(82)   estimate of the cube's volume?   about 64 ft^3

22. Complete the proportion: $\frac{f}{12} = \frac{12}{16}$ 9
(85)

Lesson 118   **619**

▶ See Math Conversations in the sidebar.

---

3 **Written Practice** *(Continued)*

Math Conversations

Discussion opportunities are provided below.

Problem 9   Analyze

"If we draw a rectangle to represent this problem, into how many parts should we divide the rectangle? Why?" 10; the problem describes $\frac{3}{10}$ of the cookies.

"How many parts of the rectangle will represent the number of cookies left in the package?" 3

"What number of cookies will each part of the rectangle represent? Tell why." 3; $9 \div 3 = 3$

"Explain how we can use multiplication to solve the problem." Sample: If each of 10 parts represents 3 cookies, the parts represent 10×3 or 30 cookies altogether.

Problem 20   Conclude

Extend the Problem

Extend this problem by having students copy the square and its two lines of symmetry, and then draw the two additional lines of symmetry.

Problem 21   Estimate

Ask students who give an estimate of a little more than 64 cubic feet to justify their estimates. Sample: Since 4.11 is greater than 4, the estimate will be greater than $4 \times 4 \times 4$ or 64 cubic feet.

(continued)

---

3 Written Practice (Continued)

Math Conversations

Discussion opportunities are provided below.

Problem 26 *Analyze*

Remind students that this problem can be solved two different ways. One way is to multiply the deposit by the interest rate (2.5%) and add the interest amount to the deposit for each year. Another way is to multiply by the sum of 100% and the interest rate (102.5%) to find the total amount for each year.

Errors and Misconceptions

Problem 24

Watch for students who multiply $1.25 \times 10 \times 10 \times 10 \times 10$ to find the answer. Explain to these students that the exponent represents the direction and the number of places the decimal moves; an exponent of +4 or 4 means to move the decimal point 4 places to the right.

You might choose to offer the following problems for additional practice.

$$34.1 \times 10^4 \quad 341,000$$

$$0.0025 \times 10^2 \quad 0.25$$

$$6.97 \times 10^3 \quad 6970$$

Problem 29

You may need to remind students that the white marble was not replaced after it was drawn from the bag, so only 8 marbles (two of which are white) remain in the bag for the second draw.

---

* 23. *(96)* *Generalize* Find the rule for this function. Then use the rule to find the missing number. $y = 5x$; 8

x	y
2	10
3	15
5	25
	40

▶* 24. *(113)* Write the standard number for 1.25×10^4. 12,500

* 25. *(104)* $-5 + +2 - +3 - -4 + -1$ -3

▶* 26. *(116)* *Analyze* Esmerelda deposited $4000 in an account that pays $2\frac{1}{2}\%$ interest compounded annually. How much money was in the account after two years? $4202.50

* 27. *(115)* Convert $7\frac{1}{2}\%$ to a fraction. $\frac{3}{40}$

28. *(14)* At noon the temperature was $-3°$F. By sunset the temperature had dropped another five degrees. What was the temperature at sunset? $-8°$F

▶ 29. *(Inv. 10)* There were three red marbles, three white marbles, and three blue marbles in a bag. Luis drew a white marble out of the bag and held it. If he draws another marble out of the bag, what is the probability that the second marble also will be white? $\frac{2}{8} = \frac{1}{4}$

* 30. *(118)* *Estimate* Humberto is designing a garden. The area of the outer garden, square *ABCD* is 16 units².

a. What is the area of the inner garden square *QRST*? 8 units²

b. Choose the appropriate unit for the area of Humberto's garden. **B**

    A square inches   **B** square feet   **C** square miles

▶ See Math Conversations in the sidebar.

• Finding a Whole When a Percent Is Known

Objectives

• Write and solve an equation to find a whole when a percent is known.

Materials

• **Power Up N** (in *Instructional Masters*)

Optional

• **Investigation Activity 15** (in *Instructional Masters*) or **graph paper**

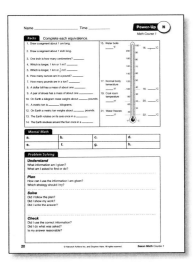

Power Up N

Technology Resources

Student eBook Complete student textbook in electronic format.

Resources and Planner CD Assessment, reteaching, and instructional masters, plus a pacing calendar with standards.

Test and Practice Generator CD Create additional practice sheets and custom-made tests.

www.SaxonPublishers.com Visit for more student activities and planning materials.

Inclusion

Adaptations CD Adapted lessons, investigations, practice and assessments.

Meeting Standards

National Council of Teachers of Mathematics (NCTM)

Numbers and Operations

NO.1a Work flexibly with fractions, decimals, and percents to solve problems

NO.2a Understand the meaning and effects of arithmetic operations with fractions, decimals, and integers

Problem Solving

PS.1c Apply and adapt a variety of appropriate strategies to solve problems

Problem-Solving Strategy: Write an Equation

Michelle's grandfather taught her this math method for converting kilometers to miles: "Divide the kilometers by 8, and then multiply by 5." Michelle's grandmother told her to, "Just multiply the kilometers by 0.6." Use both methods to convert 80 km to miles and compare the results. If one kilometer is closer to 0.62 miles, whose method produces the more accurate answer?

(Understand) **Understand the problem.**

"What information are we given?"

Two methods for converting kilometers to miles: (1) divide the km by 8, then multiply by 5; and (2) multiply the km by 0.6.

"What are we asked to do?"

Use both methods to convert 80 km into miles. Then find out which one is more accurate using the approximation 1 km ≈ 0.62 mi.

(Plan) **Make a plan.**

"What problem-solving strategy will we use?"

We will *write* and solve *an equation* for each method and compare results.

"How would we write each equation?" $(k \div 8) \times 5 = m$ and $k \times 0.6 = m$

(Solve) **Carry out the plan.**

"How many miles is 80 kilometers using Michelle's grandfather's method?"

$(80 \div 8) \times 5 = 50$ miles

"How many miles is 80 kilometers using her grandmother's method?"

$80 \times 0.6 = 48$ miles

"How do the results compare?"

Dividing by 8 and multiplying by 5 results in a number slightly greater than multiply by 0.6.

"Using the approximation 1 km ≈ 0.62 mi, how many miles is 80 km?"

$80 \times 0.62 = 49.6$ mi

"Whose method produced a result closer to 49.6 mi?"

Since 50 is closer to 49.6 than to 48, Michelle's grandfather's method produced a closer result.

(Check) **Look back.**

"Did we find the answers to the questions that were asked?"

Yes. We found the approximate value of 80 km in miles using both methods. We also found that both methods did not produce the same results and we found that Michelle's grandfather's method gave a more accurate approximation.

• Finding a Whole When a Percent Is Known

facts | Power Up N

mental math

a. **Fractional Parts:** $\frac{2}{3}$ of what number is 6?   9

b. **Fractional Parts:** $\frac{7}{10}$ of 60   42

c. **Percent:** 70% of $50 $35

d. **Percent:** 3 is what % of 6?   50%

e. **Decimals:** 0.8×70 56

f. **Number Sense:** $\frac{5000}{25}$ 200

g. **Statistics:** Find the mode and range of the set of numbers: 78, 89, 34, 89, 56, 89, 56.   89; 55

h. **Calculation:** $\frac{1}{2}$ of 50, $\sqrt{\ }$, $\times 6$, $+ 2$, $\div 4$, $\times 3$, $+ 1$, $\times 4$, $\sqrt{\ }$ 10

problem solving | Michelle's grandfather taught her this math method for converting kilometers to miles: "Divide the kilometers by 8, and then multiply by 5." Michelle's grandmother told her to, "Just multiply the kilometers by 0.6." Use both methods to convert 80 km to miles and compare the results. If one kilometer is closer to 0.62 miles, whose method produces the more accurate answer?
grandfather's method: 50 mi; grandmother's method: 48 mi; grandfather

New Concept   *Increasing Knowledge*

We have solved problems like the following using a ratio box. In this lesson we will practice writing equations to help us solve these problems.

> *Thirty percent of the football fans in the stadium are waving team banners. There are 150 football fans waving banners. How many football fans are in the stadium in all?*

The statement above tells us that 30% of the fans are waving banners and that the number is 150. We will write an equation using *t* to stand for the total number of fans.

30% of the fans are waving banners.

$30\% \times \quad t \quad = \quad 150$

Now we change 30% to a fraction or to a decimal. For this problem we choose to write 30% as a decimal.

$$0.3t = 150$$

---

1 Power Up

Facts
Distribute **Power Up N** to students. See answers below.

Mental Math
Encourage students to share different ways to mentally compute these exercises. Strategies for exercises **b** and **d** are listed below.

b. Multiply 7 by $\frac{60}{10}$
$\frac{60}{10} = \frac{6}{1}$ or 6; $7 \times 6 = 42$
Divide 60×7 by 10
$60 \times 7 = 420$; $420 \div 10 = 42$

d. Reduce $\frac{3}{6}$
$\frac{3}{6} = \frac{1}{2}$; $\frac{1}{2} = 0.5$; $0.5 = 50\%$
Use Repeated Addition
Since $3 + 3 = 6$, 3 is $\frac{1}{2}$ or 50% of 6

Problem Solving
Refer to **Power-Up Discussion**, p. 621B.

---

2 New Concepts

Instruction
If a fraction is used to represent 30%, the unknown (*t*) in the equation $\frac{3}{10}t = 150$ is isolated by multiplying both sides of the equation by $\frac{10}{3}$. Since students have not yet learned this technique, ask them to always change each percent to a decimal.

(continued)

---

1. Draw a segment about 1 cm long.

2. Draw a segment about 1 inch long.

3. One inch is how many centimeters? __2.54__

4. Which is longer, 1 km or 1 mi? __1 mi__

5. Which is longer, 1 km or $\frac{1}{2}$ mi? __1 km__

6. How many ounces are in a pound? __16__

7. How many pounds are in a ton? __2000__

8. A dollar bill has a mass of about one __gram__.

9. A pair of shoes has a mass of about one __kilogram__.

10. On Earth a kilogram mass weighs about __2.2__ pounds.

11. A metric ton is __1000__ kilograms.

12. On Earth a metric ton weighs about __2200__ pounds.

13. The Earth rotates on its axis once in a __day__.

14. The Earth revolves around the Sun once in a __year__.

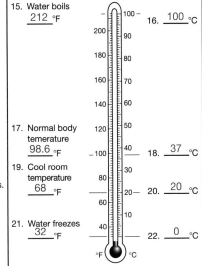

15. Water boils __212__ °F   16. __100__ °C

17. Normal body temperature __98.6__ °F   18. __37__ °C

19. Cool room temperature __68__ °F   20. __20__ °C

21. Water freezes __32__ °F   22. __0__ °C

Example 1

Instruction

Dividing 120 by 0.3 is the same as dividing each side of the equation by 0.3.

Example 2

Instruction

Tell students that example 2 asks the same question as example 1, but in a different way (both questions involve finding a whole when a percent is known).

Explain that both questions could be worded in the same way. Example 2 could be rewritten as "Twenty-five percent of what number is 16?" and example 1 could be rewritten as "One hundred twenty is 30% of what number?"

(continued)

Now we find *t* by dividing 150 by three tenths.

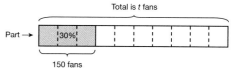

We find that there were 500 fans in all. We can use a model to represent the problem.

Total is *t* fans

Part → | 30% |

150 fans

Example 1

Thirty percent of what number is 120? Find the answer by writing and solving an equation. Model the problem with a sketch.

Solution

To translate the question into an equation, we translate the word *of* into a multiplication sign and the word *is* into an equal sign. For the words *what number* we write the letter *n*.

Thirty percent of what number is 120?

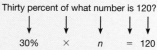

$$30\% \times n = 120$$

Thinking Skill

Explain

How can we check the answer? Sample answer: Substitute 400 for *n* and solve the equation.

We may choose to change 30% to a fraction or a decimal number. We choose the decimal form.

$$0.3n = 120$$

Now we find *n* by dividing 120 by 0.3.

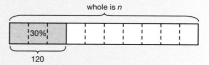

Thirty percent of **400** is 120.

We were given a part (30% is 120) and were asked for the whole. Since 30% is $\frac{3}{10}$ we divide 100% into ten divisions instead of 100.

whole is *n*

| 30% |

120

Example 2

Sixteen is 25% of what number? Solve with an equation and model with a sketch.

We translate the question into an equation, using an equal sign for *is*, a multiplication sign for *of*, and a letter for *what number*.

Sixteen is 25% of what number?

↓   ↓   ↓   ↓   ↓

16   =   25% ×   *n*

Because of the way the question was asked, the numbers are on opposite sides of the equal sign as compared to example 1. We can solve the equation in this form, or we can rearrange the equation. Either form of the equation may be used.

$$16 = 25\% \times n$$

$$25\% \times n = 16$$

Thinking Skill

Discuss

Why did we use a fraction to solve this problem rather than a decimal? It is easier to mentally divide 16 by $\frac{1}{4}$ than by 0.25.

We will use the first form of the equation and change 25% to the fraction $\frac{1}{4}$.

$$16 = 25\% \times n$$

$$16 = \frac{1}{4}n$$

We find *n* by dividing 16 by $\frac{1}{4}$.

$$16 \div \frac{1}{4} = \frac{16}{1} \times \frac{4}{1} = 64$$

Sixteen is 25% of **64**.

We are given a part and asked for the whole. Since 25% is $\frac{1}{4}$ we model 100% with four sections of 25%.

whole is *n*

25% | | |

16

Practice Set

Formulate Translate each question into an equation and solve:

a. Twenty percent of what number is 120? $0.2n = 120$; 600

b. Fifty percent of what number is 30? $\frac{1}{2}n = 30$; 60

c. Twenty-five percent of what number is 12? $\frac{1}{4}n = 12$; 48

d. Twenty is 10% of what number? $20 = 0.10n$; 200

e. Twelve is 100% of what number? $12 = 1n$; 12

f. Fifteen is 15% of what number? $15 = 0.15n$; 100

g. Write and solve a word problem for the equation below.

$$15\% \times n = 12$$

g. Samples: Fifteen percent of what number is 12?; Twelve sixth graders had parts in the school play. If 15% of the sixth graders were in the play, how many sixth graders are there in all?; $n = 80$

2 **New Concepts** *(Continued)*

Example 2 (Continued)
Instruction
Have students note that the division is multiplication by the reciprocal of the divisor.

To find a % of a #.
change the % to a dec.#
and ÷ the # by the dec.

OR

change the % to a ~~reduced~~
fraction and × the # by
the reciprocal of the fraction.

Math Conversations

Discussion opportunities are provided below.

Problem 3 Analyze

Invite volunteers to suggest equations to represent this problem. Then ask the class to discuss the equations and choose one that can be used to solve the problem.

Sample: $10\% \cdot n = 6$

Erase the equations that were not chosen.

> *"To begin solving this equation, let's change 10% to a decimal number. What decimal number represents 10%?"* 0.1

Write $0.1n = 6$ on the board or overhead.

> *"What division can we complete to find the value of n?"* $6 \div 0.1$

Problem 7b Represent

Extend the Problem

Challenge students to classify the triangle two ways—by its sides and by its angles. isosceles; right

Problem 10 Analyze

> *"What equation can we use to represent this problem?"* Sample: $20\% \cdot n = 12$

Write the equation on the board or overhead.

> *"Describe the steps we need to complete to solve for the unknown."* Sample: Divide 12 by 0.2

Errors and Misconceptions

Problem 16

Students who answered 25 kilometers found only the biking portion of the event. Point out the phrase "total distance". Students need to write a proportion for the total distance. $\frac{2}{5} = \frac{10}{x}$

(continued)

---

1. Divide 555 by 12 and write the quotient
(25)
  a. with a remainder. 46 R 3

  b. as a mixed number. $46\frac{1}{4}$

2. The six gymnasts scored 9.75, 9.8, 9.9, 9.4, 9.9, and 9.95. The lowest
(37) score was not counted. What was the sum of the five highest scores? 49.3

▶ *** 3.** **Analyze** Cantara said that the six trumpet players made up 10% of the
(105) band. The band had how many members? 60 members

* 4. Eight is $\frac{2}{3}$ of what number? 12
(117)

5. Write the standard number for the following: 186,000
(92)
$$(1 \times 10^5) + (8 \times 10^4) + (6 \times 10^3)$$

* 6. On Rob's scale drawing, each inch represents 8 feet. One of the rooms
(Inv. 11) in his drawing is $2\frac{1}{2}$ inches long. How long is the actual room? 20 feet

7. Two angles of a triangle each measure 45°.
(98)
  a. **Generalize** What is the measure of the third angle? 90°

▶   **b.** **Represent** Make a rough sketch of the triangle.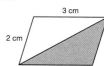

* 8. Convert $8\frac{1}{3}\%$ to a fraction. $\frac{1}{12}$
(115)

9. Nine dollars is what percent of $12? 75%
(75)

▶*** 10.** **Analyze** Twenty percent of what number is 12? 60
(119)

* 11. Three tenths of what number is 9? 30
(117)

12. $(-5) - (+6) + (-7)$ −18   **13.** $(-15)(-6)$ +90
(104)   (112)

14. Reduce: $\frac{60}{84}$ $\frac{5}{7}$ **15.** $2\frac{1}{2} - 1\frac{2}{3}$ $\frac{5}{6}$
(29)   (63)

▶ **16.** **Analyze** Stephen competes in a two-event race made up of biking and
(101) running. The ratio of the length of the distance run to the length of the bike ride is 2 to 5. If the distance run was 10 kilometers, then what was the total length of the two-event race? 35 kilometers

17. The area of the shaded triangle is 2.8 cm². What is the area of the
(79) parallelogram? 5.6 cm²

                                     3 cm

          2 cm

18. The figurine was packed in a box that was 10 in. long, 3 in. wide, and
(82) 4 in. deep. What was the volume of the box? 120 in.³

▶ See Math Conversations in the sidebar.

19. A rectangle that is not a square has a total of
(110) how many lines of symmetry?
2 lines of symmetry

20. *Conclude* If this shape were cut out and
(Inv. 6) folded on the dotted lines, would it form a
cube, a pyramid, or a cone?   pyramid

21. $3m - 5 = 25$ 10
(106)

✎ **22.** *Generalize* Write the rule for this
(96) function as an equation. Then use the
rule to find the missing number.
$y = 4x$; 8

x	y
3	12
4	16
6	24
	32

23. How many pounds is 10 tons?   20,000 pounds
(102)

▶ **24.** *Classify* Which of these polygons is not a quadrilateral?
(64)
  A parallelogram   **B** pentagon   **C** trapezoid
  B

25. Compare: area of the square $\ominus$ area of the circle
(86)

▶ **26.** *Evaluate* The coordinates of three points that are on the same line
(Inv. 7) are $(-3, -2)$, $(0, 0)$, and $(x, 4)$. What number should replace x in the
third set of coordinates?   6

27. Robert flipped a coin. It landed heads up. He flipped the coin a second
(58) time. It landed heads up. If he flips the coin a third time, what is the
probability that it will land heads up? $\frac{1}{2}$

28. James is going to flip a coin three times. What is the probability that the
(Inv. 10) coin will land heads up all three times? $\frac{1}{8}$

29. The diameter of the circle is 10 cm.
(38, 86)
  a. What is the area of the square?   25 cm^2

  b. What is the area of the circle?   78.5 cm^2

10 cm

30. What is the mode and the range of this set of numbers?
(Inv. 5)
          4, 7, 6, 4, 5, 3, 2, 6, 7, 9, 7, 4, 10, 7, 9
Mode is 7; range is 8.

▶ See Math Conversations in the sidebar.

Math Conversations
Discussion opportunities are provided below.

Problem 22 *Generalize*
"Describe the rule using words." Sample:
y is four times *x*; *x* is one-fourth *y*

Before having students write the rule and
the missing number, remind them of the
importance of checking to be sure the rule is
true for all of the *x*, *y* pairs in the table.

After the problem has been completed,
challenge students to use their rule and name
x when *y* is 100.   25

Problem 24 *Classify*
Extend the Problem
Challenge students to name as many different
quadrilaterals as possible.

Problem 26 *Connect*
Continue to encourage students to solve
graphing problems by sketching instead of by
using graph paper. However, some students
may be more comfortable using graph paper or
a copy of **Investigation Activity 15** Coordinate
Plane to complete the problem.

• Volume of a Cylinder

Objectives

- Calculate the volume of a cylinder by multiplying the area of a circular end of the cylinder by the height of the cylinder.

Lesson Preparation

Materials

- **Power Up M** (in *Instructional Masters*)

Optional

- **Investigation Activity 15** (in *Instructional Masters*) or **graph paper**
- **Teacher-provided material: real-world models of cylinders such as a juice can, an oatmeal canister, etc.**

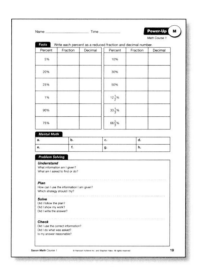

Power Up M

Technology Resources

Student eBook Complete student textbook in electronic format.

Resources and Planner CD Assessment, reteaching, and instructional masters, plus a pacing calendar with standards.

Test and Practice Generator CD Create additional practice sheets and custom-made tests.

www.SaxonPublishers.com Visit for more student activities and planning materials.

Inclusion

Adaptations CD Adapted lessons, investigations, practice and assessments.

Meeting Standards

National Council of Teachers of Mathematics (NCTM)

Geometry

GM.4b Use two-dimensional representations of three-dimensional objects to visualize and solve problems such as those involving surface area and volume

GM.4e Recognize and apply geometric ideas and relationships in areas outside the mathematics classroom, such as art, science, and everyday life

Measurement

ME.1c Understand, select, and use units of appropriate size and type to measure angles, perimeter, area, surface area, and volume

ME.2b Select and apply techniques and tools to accurately find length, area, volume, and angle measures to appropriate levels of precision

ME.2d Develop strategies to determine the surface area and volume of selected prisms, pyramids, and cylinders

Problem-Solving Strategy: Use Logical Reasoning

To remind himself of where he buried his treasure, a pirate made this map. He made two of the statements true and one statement false to confuse his enemies in case they captured the map. How will the pirate know where he buried his treasure?

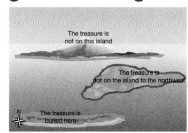

(Understand) **Understand the problem.**

"What information are we given?"

A treasure map has three statements, one of which is false,

"What are we asked to do?"

Determine where the treasure is buried.

(Plan) **Make a plan.**

"What problem-solving strategy will we use?"

We will *use logical reasoning.*

(Solve) **Carry out the plan.**

"How do we begin?"

We will falsify each of the three statements separately, and check for the truth of the remaining two statements when we do so:

| If the top statement is false, then the other two are also false. | If the middle statement is false, then the other two are also false. | If the bottom statement is false, then the other two are TRUE. |

"Where is the treasure?"

The treasure is on the island furthest to the east.

(Check) **Look back.**

"Did we complete the task that was assigned?"

Yes. We determined on which island the treasure was buried.

Facts

Distribute **Power Up M** to students. See answers below.

Mental Math

Encourage students to share different ways to mentally compute these exercises. Strategies for exercises **a** and **f** are listed below.

a. **Double $\frac{1}{3}$ of 27**
   $\frac{1}{3}$ of 27 = 27 ÷ 3 = 9; 2 × 9 = 18
   Use Repeated Addition
   9 + 9 + 9 = 27; $\frac{2}{3}$ of 27 = 9 + 9 = 18

f. **Add Three Zeros to the Product $1 \cdot 2 \cdot 3$**
   $1 \cdot 2 \cdot 3 = 6$; $10 \cdot 20 \cdot 30 = 6000$
   Use the Associative Property
   $10(20 \cdot 30) = 10(600) = 6000$

Problem Solving

Refer to **Power-Up Discussion**, p. 626B.

---

2 New Concepts

Instruction

Show students everyday objects that are in the shape of a cylinder, such as a juice can, an oatmeal canister, a soup can, or a new piece of chalk.

(continued)

LESSON 120

• Volume of a Cylinder

facts   Power Up M

mental math

a. **Fractional Parts:** $\frac{2}{3}$ of 27   18
b. **Percent:** 80% of $60 $48
c. **Fractional Parts:** $\frac{3}{4}$ of what number is 9?   12
d. **Percent:** 5 is what % of 5?   100%
e. **Decimals:** 0.8×400 320
f. **Number Sense:** $10 \cdot 20 \cdot 30$ 6000
g. **Statistics:** Find the mode and range of the set of numbers: 908, 234, 980, 243, 908, 567.   mode: 908; range: 746
h. **Calculation:** $\frac{1}{4}$ of 24, × 5, + 5, ÷ 7, × 8, + 2, ÷ 7, + 1, ÷ 7   1

problem solving

To remind himself of where he buried his treasure, a pirate made this map. He made two of the statements true and one statement false to confuse his enemies in case they captured the map. How will the pirate know where he buried his treasure?
See script for explanation

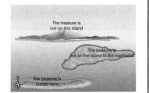

New Concept   *Increasing Knowledge*

Imagine pressing a quarter down into a block of soft clay.

 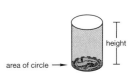

Thinking Skill

What is the formula for the area of a circle? $A = \pi r^2$

As the quarter is pressed into the block, it creates a hole in the clay. The quarter sweeps out a cylinder as it moves through the clay. We can calculate the volume of the cylinder by multiplying the area of the circular face of the quarter by the distance it moved through the clay. The distance the quarter moved is the **height** of the cylinder.

Facts   Write each percent as a reduced fraction and decimal number.

Percent	Fraction	Decimal	Percent	Fraction	Decimal
5%	$\frac{1}{20}$	0.05	10%	$\frac{1}{10}$	0.1
20%	$\frac{1}{5}$	0.2	30%	$\frac{3}{10}$	0.3
25%	$\frac{1}{4}$	0.25	50%	$\frac{1}{2}$	0.5
1%	$\frac{1}{100}$	0.01	$12\frac{1}{2}$%	$\frac{1}{8}$	0.125
90%	$\frac{9}{10}$	0.9	$33\frac{1}{3}$%	$\frac{1}{3}$	Rounds to 0.333
75%	$\frac{3}{4}$	0.75	$66\frac{2}{3}$%	$\frac{2}{3}$	Rounds to 0.667

Example

The diameter of this cylinder is 20 cm. Its height is 10 cm. What is its volume?

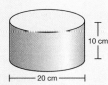

10 cm

20 cm

Solution

Thinking Skill

Explain

Why is the volume of this cylinder an approximation and not a precise number? *because the area of the circular base is found using an estimate for π*

To calculate the volume of a cylinder, we find the area of a circular end of the cylinder and multiply that area by the height of the cylinder—the distance between the circular ends.

Since the diameter of the cylinder is 20 cm, the radius is 10 cm. A square with a side the length of the radius has an area of 100 cm². So the area of the circle is about 3.14 times 100 cm², which is 314 cm².

10 cm   100 cm²

20 cm

Now we multiply the area of the circular end of the cylinder by the height of the cylinder.

$$314 \text{ cm}^2 \times 10 \text{ cm} = 3140 \text{ cm}^3$$

We find that the volume of the cylinder is approximately **3140 cm³**.

Practice Set

▶ A large can of soup has a diameter of about 8 cm and a height of about 12 cm. The volume of the can is about how many cubic centimeters? Round your answer to the nearest hundred cubic centimeters. *600 cm³*

8 cm

SOUP   12 cm

Written Practice *Strengthening Concepts*

1. Write the prime factorization of 750 using exponents. $2 \cdot 3 \cdot 5^3$
(73)

2. **Estimate** About how long is your little finger? **C**
(7)

   A 0.5 mm   **B** 5 mm   **C** 50 mm   **D** 500 mm

Lesson 120   **627**

▶ See Math Conversations in the sidebar.

Instruction

Point out that finding the area of a cylinder involves two attributes of the cylinder—its height and the area of its base.

Example

Instruction

Students may be interested to learn that the cylinder in the example is sometimes called a right cylinder. Invite students to suggest reasons why it is called a "right" cylinder.

Remind students that 3.14 is an approximation of pi (π). Point out that the area of the circle is about pi times 100 cm².

Make sure students understand that units of volume are cubic units, and they notice the cubic centimeters label in this solution.

Practice Set (Error Alert)

Watch for students who use 8 cm as the area of the base of the cylinder.

Math Background

As students will discover in Investigation 12, the formula for the volume of a cylinder is $V = \pi r^2 h$. In the formula, r represents the radius of the base of the cylinder, and h represents the cylinder's height.

③ Written Practice

Math Conversations
Discussion opportunities are provided below.

Problem 10 [Analyze]
"If 24 guests represent $\frac{4}{5}$ of the guests who were invited, were more than 24 guests or fewer than 24 guests invited to the party? Explain how you know." More than 24; Sample: 100% represents all of the invitees, 100% is equivalent to 1, and 1 is equivalent to $\frac{5}{5}$. Since $\frac{5}{5}$ is greater than $\frac{4}{5}$, $\frac{5}{5}$ is greater than 24.

Problem 19 [Infer]
Extend the Problem
Write the formula $A = s^2$ on the board or overhead and remind students that the formula is used to find the area of a square.

Challenge students to explain or demonstrate how the concept of inverse operations can be used to isolate s. $\sqrt{A} = \sqrt{s^2}$

Then point out that the information needed to solve problem 19—the length of the side of a square given its area—is found by taking the square root of the area.

Errors and Misconceptions
Problem 5
To successfully simplify the expression, students must recognize that 10^0 is another name for 1.

To demonstrate that $10^0 = 1$, write the following pattern on the board or overhead.

10^3	10^2	10^1	10^0
1000	100	10	

Ask students to consider the descending pattern 1000, 100, and 10, and help them recognize that the rule of the pattern is divide by 10. So, $10^0 = 1$ because the next term in the pattern is $10 \div 10$ or 1.

Problem 12
Watch for students who simplify $2\frac{2}{3}$ by canceling the 2s. This error will often produce the incorrect answer $\frac{5}{6}$.

(continued)

---

3. *(88)* **Analyze** If 3 parts is 24 grams, how much is 8 parts?   64 grams

4. *(85)* Complete the proportion: $\frac{3}{24} = \frac{8}{w}$ 64

▶ 5. *(92)* Write the standard number for $(7 \times 10^3) + (4 \times 10^0)$.   7004

6. *(12)* Use digits to write two hundred five million, fifty-six thousand.   205,056,000

7. *(Inv. 5)* The mean of four numbers is 25. Three of the numbers are 17, 23, and 25.
   a. What is the fourth number?   35
   b. What is the range of the four numbers?   18

8. *(100, 112)* Calculate mentally:
   a. $-6 - -4$ -2
   b. $-10 + -15$ -25
   c. $(-10)(-10)$ $+100$

* 9. *(115)* Write $16\frac{2}{3}\%$ as a reduced fraction. $\frac{1}{6}$

▶* 10. *(117)* **Analyze** Twenty-four guests came to the party. This was $\frac{4}{5}$ of those who were invited. How many guests were invited?   30 guests

11. *(61)* $1\frac{1}{3} + 3\frac{3}{4} + 1\frac{1}{6}$ $6\frac{1}{4}$ ▶ 12. *(72)* $\frac{5}{6} \times 3 \times 2\frac{2}{3}$ $6\frac{2}{3}$

13. *(38)* $5.62 + 0.8 + 4$ 10.42   14. *(49)* $0.08 \div (1 \div 0.4)$ 0.032

15. *(104)* $(-2) + (-2) + (-2)$ -6 16. *(89)* $\sqrt{2500} + \sqrt{25}$ 55

* 17. *(114)* At $1.12 per pound, what is the price per ounce (1 pound = 16 ounces)? $0.07 per ounce

18. *(47)* The children held hands and stood in a circle. The diameter of the circle was 10 m. What was the circumference of the circle? (Use 3.14 for π.)   31.4 m

▶ 19. *(38)* **Analyze** If the area of a square is 36 cm², what is the perimeter of the square?   24 cm

20. *(82)* If each small cube has a volume of 1 cm³, then what is the volume of this rectangular solid?   24 cm³

21. *(105)* Sixty percent of the votes were cast for Shayla. If Shayla received 18 votes, how many votes were cast in all?   30 votes

22. *(Inv. 10)* **Evaluate** Kareem has a spinner marked A, B, C, D. Each letter fills one fourth of the face of his spinner. If he spins the spinner three times, what is the probability he will spin A three times in a row? $\frac{1}{64}$

23. *(58)* If the spinner from problem 22 is spun twenty times, how many times is the spinner likely to land on C?   5 times

▶ See Math Conversations in the sidebar.

24.
(100)
a. $(-8) - (+7)$ -15 **b.** $(-8) - (-7)$ -1

25.
(104)
$+3 + -5 - -7 - +9 + +11 + -7$ 0

26.
(Inv. 7, 79)
Connect The three vertices of a triangle have the coordinates (0, 0), (−8, 0), and (−8, −8). What is the area of the triangle?   32 sq. units

27.
(Inv. 10)
Kaya tossed a coin and it landed heads up. What is the probability that her next two tosses of the coin will also land heads up? $\frac{1}{4}$

* 28.
(120)
The inside diameter of a mug is 8 cm. The height of the mug is 7 cm. What is the capacity of the mug in cubic centimeters? (Think of the capacity of the mug as the volume of a cylinder with the given dimensions.)   351.68 cm³

├─ 8 cm ─┤

7 cm

Use 3.14 for π.

29.
(78)
Estimate A cubic centimeter of liquid is a milliliter of liquid. The mug in problem 28 will hold how many milliliters of hot chocolate? Round to the nearest ten milliliters.   350 milliliters

30.

	%	AC
Correct	90	c
Incorrect	10	4
Total	100	t

▶* 30.
(105)
Model Draw a ratio box for this problem. Then solve the problem using a proportion.   36 questions

Ricardo correctly answered 90% of the trivia questions. If he incorrectly answered four questions, how many questions did he answer correctly?

Early Finishers
Choose A Strategy

Lisa plans to use 20 tiles for a border around a square picture frame. She wants a two-color symmetrical design that has a 2 to 3 ratio of white tiles to gray tiles. What could her design look like?   Strategy: Make a Model, Act It Out, or Draw a Picture
Accept any answer that meets the criteria. Two possible answers are shown.

▶ See Math Conversations in the sidebar.

Math Conversations
Discussion opportunities are provided below.

Problem 30 Model
Students must complete an additional step beyond solving the proportion.

"If you know the number of incorrect answers, and you know the number of answers altogether, how can you find the number of correct answers?" Subtract the number of incorrect answers from the total number of answers.

Early Finishers
Students may use tiles from the manipulative kit for this activity. However, if tiles are not available, they can use grid paper. Students should discover that 20 tiles can be arranged to form a square border. You may need to remind them that the tiles must be in a 2 to 3 ratio of gray to white tiles (8 gray tiles; 12 white tiles) *and* form a symmetrical design.

Assessment 30–40 minutes   *For use after Lesson 120*

Distribute **Cumulative Test 23** to each student. Two versions of the test are available in *Saxon Math Course 1 Course Assessments Book*. Have students complete the **Power-Up Test** first. Allow 10 minutes. Then have students work the 20 numbered items on the **Cumulative Test**. Students may use copies of the answer sheet to record their work. Track individual and class progress with the **Test Analysis** forms.

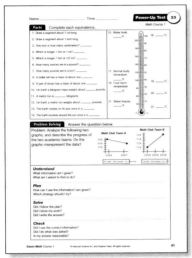

Power-Up Test 23

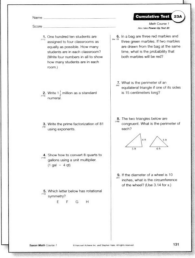

Cumulative Test 23A

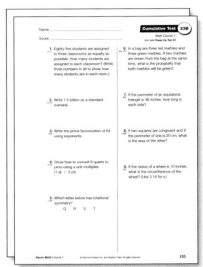

Alternative Cumulative Test 23B

Optional Answer Forms

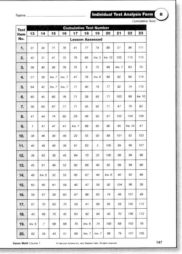

Individual Test Analysis Form

Class Test Analysis Form

Reteaching

Students who score below 80% on the assessment may be in need of reteaching. Look for the causes of student mistakes. If errors are conceptual, refer to the *Reteaching Masters* for reteaching.

You can develop customized benchmark tests using the Test Generator located on the *Test & Practice Generator CD*.

This chart shows the lesson, the standard, and the test item question that can be found on the *Test & Practice Generator CD*.

LESSON	NEW CONCEPTS	LOCAL STANDARD	TEST ITEM ON CD
111	• Applications Using Division		12.111.1
112	• Multiplying and Dividing Integers		12.112.1
113	• Adding and Subtracting Mixed Measures		12.113.1
	• Multiplying by Powers of Ten		12.113.2
114	• Unit Multipliers		12.114.1
115	• Writing Percents as Fractions, Part 2		12.115.1
116	• Compound Interest		12.116.1
117	• Finding a Whole When a Fraction is Known		12.117.1
118	• Estimating Area		12.118.1
119	• Finding a Whole When a Percent Is Known		12.119.1
120	• Volume of a Cylinder		12.120.1

Using the Test Generator CD

• Develop tests in both English and Spanish.

• Choose from multiple-choice and free-response test items.

• Clone test items to create multiple versions of the same test.

• View and edit test items to make and save your own questions.

• Administer assessments through paper tests or over a school LAN.

• Monitor student progress through a variety of individual and class reports —for both diagnosing and assessing standards mastery.

Drawing by Scale

Assign after Lesson 120 and Test 23

Objectives

- Use a scale drawing to make a drawing that is actual size.
- Communicate their ideas through writing.

Materials

Performance Tasks 23A and **23B**

Preparation

Make copies of **Performance Tasks 23A** and **23B.** (One each per student.)

Time Requirement

30–60 minutes; Begin in class and complete at home.

Task

Explain to students that for this task they will be working for a toy company. Their task will be to use a scale drawing of the first floor of a dollhouse to make a drawing that is the actual size. They will also be required to explain how they did this. Point out that all of the information students need is on **Performance Tasks 23A** and **23B.**

Criteria for Evidence of Learning

- Draws the first floor of the dollhouse in actual size.
- States the scale factor correctly.
- Communicates ideas clearly through writing.

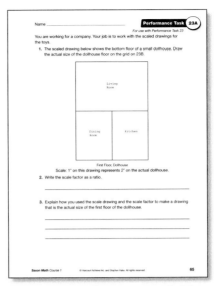

Performance Task 23A

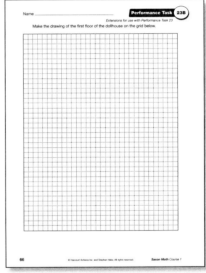

Performance Task 23B

National Council of Teachers of Mathematics (NCTM)

Geometry

GM.4a Draw geometric objects with specified properties, such as side lengths or angle measures

GM.4d Use geometric models to represent and explain numerical and algebraic relationships

GM.4e Recognize and apply geometric ideas and relationships in areas outside the mathematics classroom, such as art, science, and everyday life

Measurement

ME.2e Solve problems involving scale factors, using ratio and proportion

Connections

CN.4c Recognize and apply mathematics in contexts outside of mathematics

Focus on
- ## Volume of Prisms, Pyramids, Cylinders and Cones
- ## Surface Area of Prisms and Cylinders

Objectives

- Derive the formula for the volume of a pyramid using the formula for the volume of a prism.
- Determine the volume of a pyramid using the geometric formula.
- Derive the formula for the volume of a cone using the formula for the volume of a cylinder.
- Determine the volume of a cone using the geometric formula.
- Derive the formula for the surface area of a prism.
- Derive the formula for the surface area of a cylinder.

Lesson Preparation

Materials

- **Manipulative kit: Relational GeoSolids square prisms, square pyramids, cylinders and cones**
- **Teacher-provided material: rice or salt** (enough to fill the Relational GeoSolids cone), **metric rulers, grid paper**

Technology Resources

Student eBook Complete student textbook in electronic format.

Resources and Planner CD Assessment, reteaching, and instructional masters, plus a pacing calendar with standards.

Test and Practice Generator CD Create additional practice sheets and custom-made tests.

www.SaxonPublishers.com Visit for more student activities and planning materials.

Inclusion

Adaptations CD Adapted lessons, investigations, practice and assessments.

Meeting Standards

National Council of Teachers of Mathematics (NCTM)

Geometry

GM.4b Use two-dimensional representations of three-dimensional objects to visualize and solve problems such as those involving surface area and volume

GM.4d Use geometric models to represent and explain numerical and algebraic relationships

GM.4e Recognize and apply geometric ideas and relationships in areas outside the mathematics classroom, such as art, science, and everyday life

Measurement

ME.1c Understand, select, and use units of appropriate size and type to measure angles, perimeter, area, surface area, and volume

ME.2d Develop strategies to determine the surface area and volume of selected prisms, pyramids, and cylinders

In this investigation, students will explore the surface area and volume of three-dimensional objects.

Instruction

Have students note that the triangular faces of the pyramid are congruent because the base of the pyramid is a square and all four sides of a square are congruent.

Have students also note that the height of the pyramid is a line segment that is perpendicular to the base. One endpoint of the height is at the apex of the pyramid and the other endpoint is at the center of the base.

Whenever students work with formulas involving h for height, remind them that the height of a polygon or solid is perpendicular to its base.

INVESTIGATION 12

Focus on

• Volume of Prisms, Pyramids, Cylinders, and Cones

• Surface Area of Prisms and Cylinders

volume of prisms and pyramids

As we learned in Investigation 6, a **prism** is a polyhedron with two congruent, parallel bases. A **pyramid** is a three-dimensional object with a polygon as its base and triangular faces that meet at a vertex.

The height of a prism is the perpendicular distance from the prism's base to its opposite face. The height of a pyramid is the perpendicular distance from the pyramid's base to its vertex.

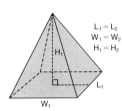 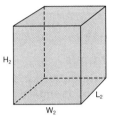

$L_1 = L_2$
$W_1 = W_2$
$H_1 = H_2$

In the figure above, the base of the pyramid is congruent to the bases of the prism, so $L_1 = L_2$ and $W_1 = W_2$. Also, the height of the two solids is the same so $H_1 = H_2$.

Thus, the fundamental difference between the two solids is that the pyramid has a vertex rather than a second base. As a result, its volume is smaller. We can see this clearly when we compare the Relational GeoSolids of the two figures.

We know from Lesson 82 that the formula for finding the volume of a prism is:

$$V = lwh$$

Since lw gives us the area of the base, we can also write the formula as:

$$V = \text{area of } B \times h$$

We can use this formula to derive (develop) the formula for the volume of a pyramid. To find the volume of a pyramid, we first find the volume of a similar prism (cube).

By drawing segments from one vertex of a cube to four other vertices, we can see how a cube can be divided into pyramids. The base of the cube is the base of one pyramid. Its right face is the base of a second pyramid and its back face is the base of the third pyramid.

Math Background

A polyhedron (plural: "polyhedra" or occasionally "polyhedrons") is a three-dimensional solid which is composed of a number of polygons. If the polygons are congruent, the polyhedron is said to be regular because all of its sides and all of its angles are equivalent. A regular polyhedron is sometimes called a regular solid.

Examples of regular polyhedrons include a tetrahedron (4 faces), a cube (6 faces), an octahedron (8 faces), a dodecahedron (12 faces), and an icosahedron (20 faces).

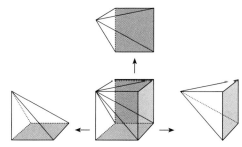

We see that the cube is divided into three congruent pyramids indicating that the volume of each pyramid is $\frac{1}{3}$ the volume of the cube.

To find the volume of one pyramid, we find the volume of $\frac{1}{3}$ of a prism with the same base and height.

$$V \text{ of a pyramid} = \frac{1}{3} \text{ area of } B \times \text{height} = \frac{1}{3}(B \times h)$$

Generalize Use the derived formula to find the volume of each of the following pyramids.

1.   80 ft^3

8 ft
5 ft
6 ft

2.   128 ft^3

12 ft
$5\frac{1}{3}$ ft
6 ft

3.   7.812 m^3

2.8 m
2.7 m
3.1 m

volume of cylinders and cones

A **cylinder** is a solid with two circular bases that are opposite and parallel to each other. Its face is curved. A **cone** is a solid with one circular base and a single vertex. Its face is curved. In the figure below, the base of the cone is congruent to the bases of the cylinder, and the height of the two solids is the same. Thus, the fundamental difference between the two solids is that the cone has a vertex rather than a second base. As a result, its volume is smaller.

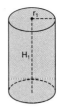

Using your Relational GeoSolids of a cone and a cylinder, demonstrate the difference in volume. First fill the cone with rice or salt. Then empty the cone into the cylinder. Repeat two more times to show that the volume of the cylinder is three times the volume of the cone.

In Lesson 120, we learned that the volume of a cylinder can be found by multiplying the area of the circular end and multiplying the result by the height of the cylinder. We can express this process as a formula:

$$V \text{ of a cylinder} = \pi \cdot r^2 \times h, \text{ or } \pi \cdot r^2 h$$

Look at the figures below. Apply what we learned about the volumes of a prism and a pyramid to make a reasonable statement about the volumes of a cylinder and a cone.

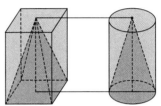

Recall that the volume of a pyramid is $\frac{1}{3}$ the volume of a rectangular prism with the same base and height. The same relationship is true for cones and cylinders. That is, the volume of the cone is $\frac{1}{3}$ the volume of a cylinder with the same height and base area.

$$V \text{ of a cone} = \frac{1}{3} \text{ area of } B \times \text{height} = \frac{1}{3}(B \times h)$$

When we insert the formula for B, the area of the base of the cylinder, we get:

$$V \text{ of a cone} = \frac{1}{3}(\pi r^2 h)$$

Generalize Use the appropriate formulas to find the volume of each of the following:

▶ **4.** Leave π as π.
125π cm^3

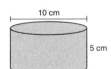

10 cm

5 cm

▶ See Math Conversations in the sidebar.

▶ **5.** Use $\frac{22}{7}$ for π. Estimate to find the answer.
1540 ft³

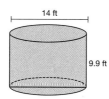

14 ft

9.9 ft

▶ **6.** Leave π as π.
1.2π in.³

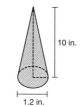

10 in.

1.2 in.

surface area of a prism

The **surface area** of a prism is equal to the sum of the areas of its surfaces. In **Investigation 6,** we found that we could use a net to help us find surface area.

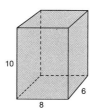

10

6

8

If we compare the rectangular prism in the Relational GeoSolids to the figures on the previous page, we see that we can find the surface area by adding the area of the six sides.

Area of two faces (top and bottom) = $(6 \times 8) + (6 \times 8)$

Area of two faces (sides) = $(6 \times 10) + (6 \times 10)$

Area of two faces (front and back) = $(8 \times 10) + (8 \times 10)$

Thus the total surface area of the prism is 376 in.²

From this, we can develop a formula for the surface area of a prism:

$$SA = 2lw + 2lh + 2wh$$

h

w

l

▶ *Generalize* Find the surface area of the following rectangular prisms.

7. 1014 cm²

13 cm

8. 96 units²

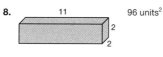

11

2

2

Investigation 12 **633**

▶ See Math Conversations in the sidebar.

Math Conversations

Discussion opportunities are provided below.

Problem 5

When finding the area of the base, remind students to look for opportunities to cancel terms of the fractions.

$$B = \frac{22}{\underset{1}{7}} \cdot \frac{\overset{1}{7}}{1} \cdot \frac{7}{1} = 154 \text{ ft}^2$$

Problem 6

Students should recognize that multiplying the area of the base by the height gives the volume of a cylinder and that the volume of the cone is $\frac{1}{3}$ the volume of that cylinder.

Instruction

Have students recall that a rectangular prism has six surfaces and that the opposite surfaces are congruent.

Invite a volunteer to explain how the formula $SA = 2lw + 2lh + 2wh$ represents the six surfaces of the cube.

Math Conversations

Discussion opportunities are provided below.

Problem 7

"How can multiplying by 6 help us find the surface area of the cube?" Since all six faces of a cube are congruent, multiply the area of one face by 6.

Problem 8

"To find the surface area of this rectangular prism, why do we need to only find the area of three of its surfaces?" Opposite faces of a rectangular prism are congruent.

Instruction

Help students understand that the surface area of a solid is different than the lateral surface area of a solid. Point out that surface area represents the entire surface of a solid while lateral area does not include the area of the base(s).

Math Conversations

Discussion opportunities are provided below.

Problem 9

Make sure students recognize that the cylinder has three surfaces and finding the surface area of the cylinder involves finding the sum of the areas of those three faces.

Remind students to label measures of area as square units and measures of volume as cubic units.

---

surface area of a cylinder

We can think of the surface area of a cylinder as having three parts—the area of the two bases and the area of its face, its **lateral surface area.** A net of the cylinder makes this easy to see.

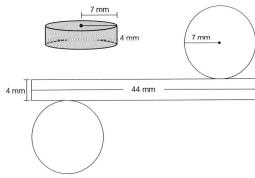

To calculate the area of the circular bases, use the formula for the area of a circle, $A = \pi r^2$. Since there are two bases, multiply the formula by 2.

$$\text{Area} = 2\pi r^2$$

To calculate the lateral surface area, which is a rectangle, use the formula for the area of a rectangle lw. In this case, the length (l) is the circumference of the circle, or $2\pi r$. The width (w) is height of the cylinder. We'll use $\frac{22}{7}$ for π.

We can calculate the surface area of the cylinder above as follows:

$$SA = 2\pi r^2 + 2\pi rh$$
$$SA \approx 2 \cdot \left(\frac{22}{7}\right) \cdot 7^2 + 2 \cdot \left(\frac{22}{7}\right) \cdot 7 \cdot 4$$
$$SA \approx 2 \cdot \left(\frac{22}{7}\right) \cdot 7^2 + 2 \cdot \left(\frac{22}{7}\right) \cdot 7 \cdot 4$$
$$SA \approx 308 + 176$$
$$SA \approx 484 \text{ mm}^2$$

The surface area of the cylinder is about 484 mm².

Applications

▶ 9. Martin is installing a 10-feet-tall cylindrical tank to collect rainwater. He wants to know how much water the tank can hold. If the radius of the tank is 2 feet, what is the approximate volume of the tank? To wrap the *entire* tank with insulation, Martin needs to find the total surface area. Draw a net of the cylinder and estimate the surface area. Leave π as π. 40π ft³; 48π ft²

▶ See Math Conversations in the sidebar.

▶ **10.** *Estimate* Lydia is making coffee for dinner guests and wants to know how much ground coffee her new filter will hold. Estimate the volume of a cone-shaped filter with a diameter of 14 cm and a height of 9 cm. Use $\frac{22}{7}$ for π.   462 cm³

▶ **11.** A cone is inscribed in a right cylinder as shown. What is the volume of the cone? What is the surface area of the cylinder? Leave π as π.   125π in.³; 200π in.²

▶ **12.** Jenna's piano teacher gave her a pyramid-shaped metronome to count time. The metronome's base measures 4 inches by $3\frac{1}{2}$ inches. Calculate the metronome's volume if its height is 9 in.   42 in.³

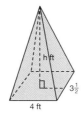

▶ **13.** *Estimate* Geoff and Sasha drew a sketch of a skateboard ramp they plan to build using scrap wood. To determine how much wood they need to build the ramp, which is shaped like a right triangular prism, estimate the total surface area.   Estimate should be close to 293 ft².

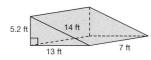

extensions

a. *Represent* Draw a rectangular prism with the same base and height as the pyramid shown. Calculate the volume of the prism. Units are in meters.   117 m³

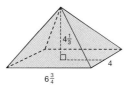

▶ **b.** *Represent* Sketch a cone inside the pyramid shown with the same height. The diameter of the cone's base equals the width of the pyramid's base. Find the volume of the cone. Leave π as π. Discuss which is greater, the volume of the cone or the volume of the pyramid.   See student work. 36π cubic units; the volume of the pyramid is greater.

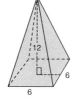

Investigation 12   **635**

▶ See Math Conversations in the sidebar.

Math Conversations
Discussion opportunities are provided below.

Problem 10
Students should infer that the diameter of the cone must be halved because the formula $A = \pi r^2$, the area of its base, uses radius.

When finding the area of the base, remind students to look for opportunities to cancel terms of the fractions.

Problem 11
To find the volume of the cone, students should recall that its volume will be $\frac{1}{3}$ the volume of the cylinder.

Problem 12
Finding the height of the pyramid involves isolating h in the formula $V = \frac{1}{3}(B \times h)$. To isolate h, remind students to apply the reciprocal to both sides of the equation and then apply the inverse operation.

$$h = \frac{3\,V}{B}$$

Problem 13
Help students recognize that only two of the five surfaces of the prism are congruent.

Extensions

a. One way for students to check their work is to decide if the volume of the prism is three times the volume of the pyramid or decide if the volume of the pyramid is $\frac{1}{3}$ the volume of the prism.

b. If students need help comparing the volumes, ask them to consider the base of each solid and lead them to infer that because the area of the square is greater than the area of the circle inscribed in the square, the volume of the pyramid is greater than the volume of the cone.

(continued)

Extensions (continued)

c. Have students recall that the formula $V = s^3$ is used to find the volume of a cube.

One way for students to determine the edge length of the cube is to ask themselves what number cubed is equal to 27 inches. Since $3 \times 3 \times 3 = 27$, the length of each edge of the cube is 3 inches.

d. Students should recognize that because all six surfaces of a cube are congruent, multiplying the area of one surface by 6 will equal the surface area of the cube.

▶ **c.** Find the surface area of a cube that has a volume of 27 in.³   54 in.²

▶ **d.** Find the surface area of a cube with an edge of 4 cm.   96 cm²

e. The heights of a rectangular prism with a square base and a cylinder are equal, and the diameter of the cylinder is equal to one edge of the prism's square base. Develop a mathematical argument to prove that surface areas of the two figures are not equal. (*Hint:* Use what you know about the areas of circles and squares to prove your answer.)
The circumference of the cylinder's circular base is about 3 times its diameter. The perimeter of the square is 4 times the length of one of its side, which is the same as 4 times the diameter. Since the perimeter of the square is greater, its surface area must be greater than the surface area of the cylinder.

▶ See Math Conversations in the sidebar.

MATH GLOSSARY WITH SPANISH VOCABULARY

GLOSSARY

A

acute angle
ángulo agudo
(28)
An angle whose measure is more than 0° and less than 90°.

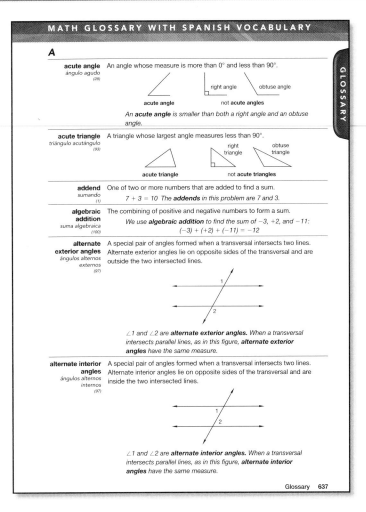

right angle | obtuse angle

acute angle | not acute angles

An acute angle is smaller than both a right angle and an obtuse angle.

acute triangle
triángulo acutángulo
(93)
A triangle whose largest angle measures less than 90°.

right triangle | obtuse triangle

acute triangle | not acute triangles

addend
sumando
(1)
One of two or more numbers that are added to find a sum.

*7 + 3 = 10 The **addends** in this problem are 7 and 3.*

algebraic addition
suma algebraica
(100)
The combining of positive and negative numbers to form a sum.

*We use **algebraic addition** to find the sum of −3, +2, and −11:*
$(−3) + (+2) + (−11) = −12$

alternate exterior angles
ángulos alternos externos
(97)
A special pair of angles formed when a transversal intersects two lines. Alternate exterior angles lie on opposite sides of the transversal and are outside the two intersected lines.

*∠1 and ∠2 are **alternate exterior angles**. When a transversal intersects parallel lines, as in this figure, **alternate exterior angles** have the same measure.*

alternate interior angles
ángulos alternos internos
(97)
A special pair of angles formed when a transversal intersects two lines. Alternate interior angles lie on opposite sides of the transversal and are inside the two intersected lines.

*∠1 and ∠2 are **alternate interior angles**. When a transversal intersects parallel lines, as in this figure, **alternate interior angles** have the same measure.*

Glossary 637

---

a.m.
a.m.
(32)
The period of time from midnight to just before noon.

*I get up at 7 **a.m.** I get up at 7 o'clock in the morning.*

angle(s)
ángulo(s)
(28)
The opening that is formed when two lines, rays, or segments intersect.

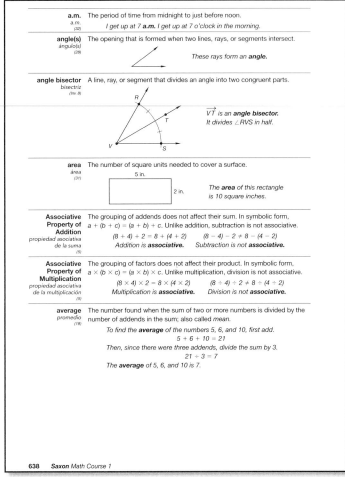

*These rays form an **angle**.*

angle bisector
bisectriz
(Inv. 8)
A line, ray, or segment that divides an angle into two congruent parts.

$\vec{VT}$ *is an **angle bisector**. It divides ∠RVS in half.*

area
área
(31)
The number of square units needed to cover a surface.

5 in. | 2 in.

*The **area** of this rectangle is 10 square inches.*

Associative Property of Addition
propiedad asociativa de la suma
(5)
The grouping of addends does not affect their sum. In symbolic form, $a + (b + c) = (a + b) + c$. Unlike addition, subtraction is not associative.

$(8 + 4) + 2 = 8 + (4 + 2)$ $(8 − 4) − 2 ≠ 8 − (4 − 2)$
*Addition is **associative**.   Subtraction is not **associative**.*

Associative Property of Multiplication
propiedad asociativa de la multiplicación
(5)
The grouping of factors does not affect their product. In symbolic form, $a × (b × c) = (a × b) × c$. Unlike multiplication, division is not associative.

$(8 × 4) × 2 = 8 × (4 × 2)$ $(8 ÷ 4) ÷ 2 ≠ 8 ÷ (4 ÷ 2)$
*Multiplication is **associative**.   Division is not **associative**.*

average
promedio
(18)
The number found when the sum of two or more numbers is divided by the number of addends in the sum; also called *mean*.

*To find the **average** of the numbers 5, 6, and 10, first add.*
$5 + 6 + 10 = 21$
Then, since there were three addends, divide the sum by 3.
$21 ÷ 3 = 7$
*The **average** of 5, 6, and 10 is 7.*

638 *Saxon* Math Course 1

B

bar graph(s)
gráfica(s) de barras
(Inv. 1)
Displays numerical information with shaded rectangles or bars.

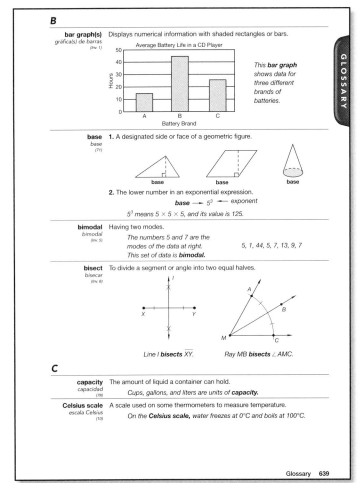

*This **bar graph** shows data for three different brands of batteries.*

base
base
(71)
1. A designated side or face of a geometric figure.

base | base | base

2. The lower number in an exponential expression.

base ⟶ 5^3 ⟵ exponent

5^3 means $5 × 5 × 5$, and its value is 125.

bimodal
bimodal
(Inv. 5)
Having two modes.

*The numbers 5 and 7 are the modes of the data at right. This set of data is **bimodal**.*   5, 1, 44, 5, 7, 13, 9, 7

bisect
bisecar
(Inv. 8)
To divide a segment or angle into two equal halves.

*Line l **bisects** $\overline{XY}$.*   *Ray MB **bisects** ∠AMC.*

C

capacity
capacidad
(78)
The amount of liquid a container can hold.

*Cups, gallons, and liters are units of **capacity**.*

Celsius scale
escala Celsius
(10)
A scale used on some thermometers to measure temperature.

*On the **Celsius scale**, water freezes at 0°C and boils at 100°C.*

Glossary 639

---

chance
posibilidad
(58)
A way of expressing the likelihood of an event; the probability of an event expressed as a percentage.

*The **chance** of snow is 10%. It is not likely to snow.*
*There is an 80% **chance** of rain. It is likely to rain.*

circle
círculo
(27)
A closed, curved shape in which all points on the shape are the same distance from its center.

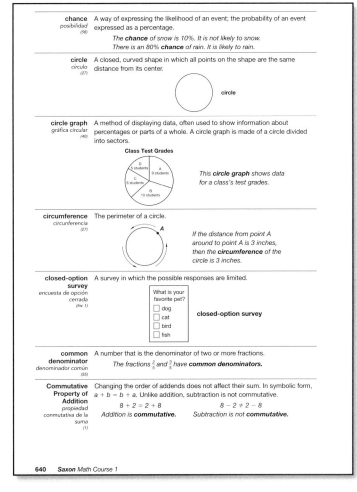

circle

circle graph
gráfica circular
(40)
A method of displaying data, often used to show information about percentages or parts of a whole. A circle graph is made of a circle divided into sectors.

Class Test Grades

D 5 students | A 9 students | C 6 students | B 10 students

*This **circle graph** shows data for a class's test grades.*

circumference
circunferencia
(27)
The perimeter of a circle.

*If the distance from point A around to point A is 3 inches, then the **circumference** of the circle is 3 inches.*

closed-option survey
encuesta de opción cerrada
(Inv. 1)
A survey in which the possible responses are limited.

What is your favorite pet?
☐ dog
☐ cat
☐ bird
☐ fish

closed-option survey

common denominator
denominador común
(55)
A number that is the denominator of two or more fractions.

*The fractions $\frac{2}{5}$ and $\frac{3}{5}$ have **common denominators**.*

Commutative Property of Addition
propiedad conmutativa de la suma
(1)
Changing the order of addends does not affect their sum. In symbolic form, $a + b = b + a$. Unlike addition, subtraction is not commutative.

$8 + 2 = 2 + 8$ $8 − 2 ≠ 2 − 8$
*Addition is **commutative**.   Subtraction is not **commutative**.*

640 *Saxon* Math Course 1

Commutative Property of Multiplication *propiedad conmutativa de la multiplicación* (3)	Changing the order of factors does not affect their product. In symbolic form, $a \times b = b \times a$. Unlike multiplication, division is not commutative. $8 \times 2 = 2 \times 8$ $8 \div 2 \neq 2 \div 8$ *Multiplication is **commutative.** Division is not **commutative.***
compass *compás* (27)	A tool used to draw circles and arcs. 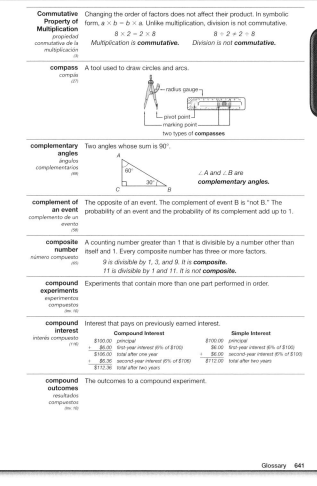two types of **compasses**
complementary angles *ángulos complementarios* (69)	Two angles whose sum is 90°. $\angle A$ and $\angle B$ are **complementary angles.**
complement of an event *complemento de un evento* (58)	The opposite of an event. The complement of event B is "not B." The probability of an event and the probability of its complement add up to 1.
composite number *número compuesto* (65)	A counting number greater than 1 that is divisible by a number other than itself and 1. Every composite number has three or more factors. *9 is divisible by 1, 3, and 9. It is **composite.*** *11 is divisible by 1 and 11. It is not **composite.***
compound experiments *experimentos compuestos* (Inv. 10)	Experiments that contain more than one part performed in order.
compound interest *interés compuesto* (116)	Interest that pays on previously earned interest. **Compound Interest** **Simple Interest** $100.00 *principal* $100.00 *principal* + $6.00 *first-year interest (6% of $100)* $6.00 *first-year interest (6% of $100)* $106.00 *total after one year* + $6.00 *second-year interest (6% of $100)* + $6.36 *second-year interest (6% of $106)* $112.00 *total after two years* $112.36 *total after two years*
compound outcomes *resultados compuestos* (Inv. 10)	The outcomes to a compound experiment.

concentric circles *círculos concéntricos* (27)	Two or more circles with a common center. 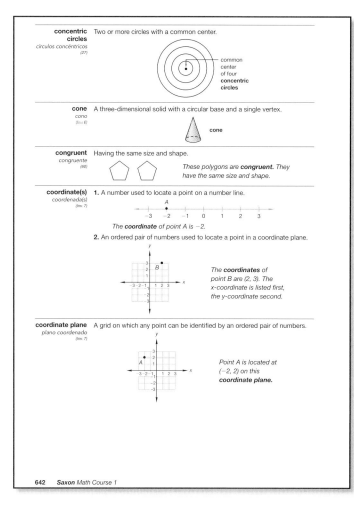common center of four **concentric circles**
cone *cono* (Inv. 6)	A three-dimensional solid with a circular base and a single vertex. cone
congruent *congruente* (60)	Having the same size and shape. *These polygons are **congruent.** They have the same size and shape.*
coordinate(s) *coordenada(s)* (Inv. 7)	**1.** A number used to locate a point on a number line. *The **coordinate** of point A is −2.* **2.** An ordered pair of numbers used to locate a point in a coordinate plane. *The **coordinates** of point B are (2, 3). The x-coordinate is listed first, the y-coordinate second.*
coordinate plane *plano coordenado* (Inv. 7)	A grid on which any point can be identified by an ordered pair of numbers. *Point A is located at (−2, 2) on this **coordinate plane.***

corresponding angles *ángulos correspondientes* (97)	A special pair of angles formed when a transversal intersects two lines. Corresponding angles lie on the same side of the transversal and are in the same position relative to the two intersected lines. 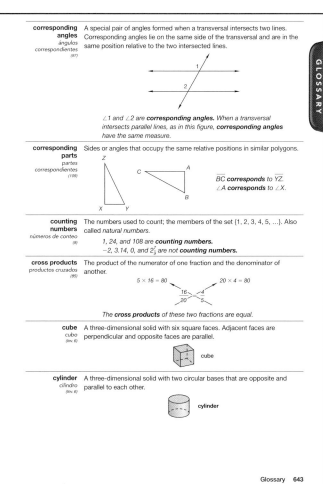$\angle 1$ and $\angle 2$ are **corresponding angles.** When a transversal intersects parallel lines, as in this figure, **corresponding angles** have the same measure.
corresponding parts *partes correspondientes* (109)	Sides or angles that occupy the same relative positions in similar polygons. $\overline{BC}$ **corresponds** to $\overline{YZ}$. $\angle A$ **corresponds** to $\angle X$.
counting numbers *números de conteo* (9)	The numbers used to count; the members of the set {1, 2, 3, 4, 5, …}. Also called *natural numbers*. *1, 24, and 108 are **counting numbers.*** *−2, 3.14, 0, and $2\frac{7}{9}$ are not **counting numbers.***
cross products *productos cruzados* (85)	The product of the numerator of one fraction and the denominator of another. $5 \times 16 = 80$ $20 \times 4 = 80$ *The **cross products** of these two fractions are equal.*
cube *cubo* (Inv. 6)	A three-dimensional solid with six square faces. Adjacent faces are perpendicular and opposite faces are parallel. cube
cylinder *cilindro* (Inv. 6)	A three-dimensional solid with two circular bases that are opposite and parallel to each other. cylinder

D

data *datos* (Inv. 4)	Information that is gathered and organized in a way that conclusions can be drawn from it.
data points *puntos de datos* (Inv. 5)	Individual measurements or numbers in a set of data.
decimal number *número decimal* (34)	A numeral that contains a decimal point. *23.94 is a **decimal number** because it contains a decimal point.*
decimal places *cifras decimales* (34)	Places to the right of a decimal point. *5.47 has two **decimal places.*** *6.3 has one **decimal place.*** *8 has no **decimal places.***
decimal point *punto decimal* (34)	The symbol in a decimal number used as a reference point for place value. 34.15 **decimal point**
degree (°) *grado* (Inv. 3)	**1.** A unit for measuring angles. 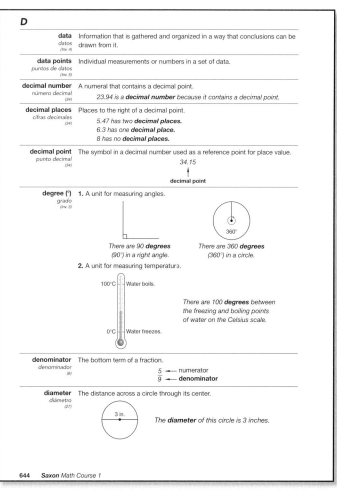*There are 90 **degrees** (90°) in a right angle.* *There are 360 **degrees** (360°) in a circle.* **2.** A unit for measuring temperature. 100°C — Water boils. 0°C — Water freezes. *There are 100 **degrees** between the freezing and boiling points of water on the Celsius scale.*
denominator *denominador* (6)	The bottom term of a fraction. $\dfrac{5}{9}$ ← numerator ← denominator
diameter *diámetro* (27)	The distance across a circle through its center. 3 in. *The **diameter** of this circle is 3 inches.*

difference *diferencia* *(1)*	The result of subtraction. $12 - 8 = 4$ The **difference** in this problem is 4.
digit *dígito* *(2)*	Any of the symbols used to write numbers: 0, 1, 2, 3, 4, 5, 6, 7, 8, 9. The last **digit** in the number 7862 is 2.
dividend *dividendo* *(2)*	A number that is divided. $12 \div 3 = 4 \quad 3\overline{)12}^{\,4} \quad \frac{12}{3} = 4$ The **dividend** is 12 in each of these problems.
divisible *divisible* *(19)*	Able to be divided by a whole number without a remainder. $4\overline{)20}^{\,5}$ The number 20 is **divisible** by 4, since $20 \div 4$ has no remainder. $3\overline{)20}^{\,6\ R\ 2}$ The number 20 is not **divisible** by 3, since $20 \div 3$ has a remainder.
divisor *divisor* *(2)*	**1.** A number by which another number is divided. $12 \div 3 = 4 \quad 3\overline{)12}^{\,4} \quad \frac{12}{3} = 4$ The **divisor** is 3 in each of these problems. **2.** A factor of a number. 2 and 5 are **divisors** of 10.

E

edge *arista* *(Inv. 6)*	A line segment formed where two faces of a polyhedron intersect. 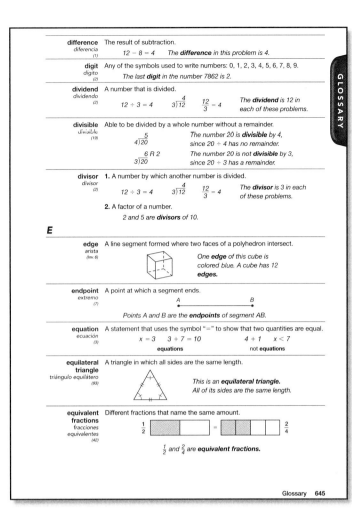 One **edge** of this cube is colored blue. A cube has 12 **edges**.
endpoint *extremo* *(7)*	A point at which a segment ends. A •————————• B Points A and B are the **endpoints** of segment AB.
equation *ecuación* *(3)*	A statement that uses the symbol "=" to show that two quantities are equal. $x = 3 \quad 3 + 7 = 10$ \quad $4 + 1 \quad x < 7$ **equations** \quad not **equations**
equilateral triangle *triángulo equilátero* *(93)*	A triangle in which all sides are the same length. This is an **equilateral triangle**. All of its sides are the same length.
equivalent fractions *fracciones equivalentes* *(42)*	Different fractions that name the same amount. $\frac{1}{2}$ [====] = [== = =] $\frac{2}{4}$ $\frac{1}{2}$ and $\frac{2}{4}$ are **equivalent fractions**.

---

estimate *estimar* *(16)*	To determine an approximate value. We **estimate** that the sum of 199 and 205 is about 400.
evaluate *evaluar* *(73)*	To find the value of an expression. To **evaluate** $a + b$ for $a = 7$ and $b = 13$, we replace a with 7 and b with 13: $7 + 13 = 20$
even numbers *números pares* *(10)*	Numbers that can be divided by 2 without a remainder; the members of the set $\{\ldots, -4, -2, 0, 2, 4, \ldots\}$. **Even numbers** have 0, 2, 4, 6, or 8 in the ones place.
event *evento* *(58)*	Outcome(s) resulting from an experiment or situation. • Events that are certain to occur have a probability of 1. • Events that are certain not to occur have a probability of zero. • Events that are uncertain have probabilities that fall anywhere between zero and one.
expanded notation *notación expandida* *(32)*	A way of writing a number as the sum of the products of the digits and the place values of the digits. In **expanded notation** 6753 is written $(6 \times 1000) + (7 \times 100) + (5 \times 10) + (3 \times 1)$.
experimental probability *probabilidad experimental* *(Inv. 9)*	The probability of an event occurring as determined by experimentation. If we roll a number cube 100 times and get 22 threes, the **experimental probability** of rolling three is $\frac{22}{100}$, or $\frac{11}{50}$.
exponent *exponente* *(38)*	The upper number in an exponential expression; it shows how many times the base is to be used as a factor. base $\longrightarrow 5^3 \longleftarrow$ **exponent** 5^3 means $5 \times 5 \times 5$, and its value is 125.
exponential expression *expresión exponencial* *(73)*	An expression that indicates that the base is to be used as a factor the number of times shown by the exponent. $4^3 = 4 \times 4 \times 4 = 64$ The **exponential expression** 4^3 is evaluated by using 4 as a factor 3 times. Its value is 64.
expression *expresión*	A combination of numbers and/or variables by operations, but not including an equal or inequality sign. $\quad$ equation $\quad$ inequality $3x + 2y\,(x - 1)^2 \quad y = 3x - 1 \quad x < 4$ **expressions** $\quad$ not **expressions**
exterior angle *ángulo externo* *(98)*	In a polygon, the supplementary angle of an interior angle. 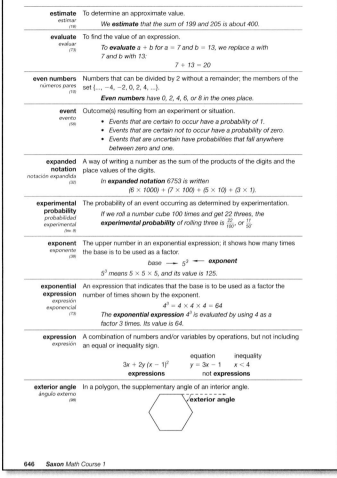 **exterior angle**

F

face *cara* *(Inv. 6)*	A flat surface of a geometric solid. One **face** of the cube is shaded. A cube has six **faces**.
fact family *familia de operaciones* *(1)*	A group of three numbers related by addition and subtraction or by multiplication and division. The numbers 3, 4, and 7 are a **fact family**. They make these four facts: $3 + 4 = 7 \quad 4 + 3 = 7 \quad 7 - 3 = 4 \quad 7 - 4 = 3$
factor *factor* *(2)*	**1.** Noun: One of two or more numbers that are multiplied. $3 \times 5 = 15$ The **factors** in this problem are 3 and 5. **2.** Noun: A whole number that divides another whole number without a remainder. The numbers 3 and 5 are **factors** of 15. **3.** Verb: To write as a product of factors. We can **factor** the number 15 by writing it as 3×5.
factor tree *árbol de factores* *(65)*	A method of finding all the prime factors of a number. 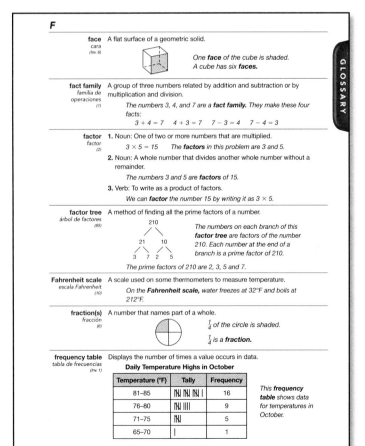 The numbers on each branch of this **factor tree** are factors of the number 210. Each number at the end of a branch is a prime factor of 210. The prime factors of 210 are 2, 3, 5 and 7.
Fahrenheit scale *escala Fahrenheit* *(10)*	A scale used on some thermometers to measure temperature. On the **Fahrenheit scale**, water freezes at 32°F and boils at 212°F.
fraction(s) *fracción* *(6)*	A number that names part of a whole. $\frac{1}{4}$ of the circle is shaded. $\frac{1}{4}$ is a **fraction**.
frequency table *tabla de frecuencias* *(Inv. 1)*	Displays the number of times a value occurs in data.

Daily Temperature Highs in October

Temperature (°F)	Tally	Frequency
81–85	IIII IIII IIII I	16
76–80	IIII IIII	9
71–75	IIII	5
65–70	I	1

This **frequency table** shows data for temperatures in October.

---

function *función* *(96)*	A rule for using one number (an input) to calculate another number (an output). Each input produces only one output. $y = 3x$ | x	y
3	9
5	15
7	21
10	30 | There is exactly one resulting number for every number we multiply by 3. Thus, $y = 3x$ is a **function**.

G

geometric solid *sólido geométrico* *(Inv. 6)*	A three-dimensional geometric figure. 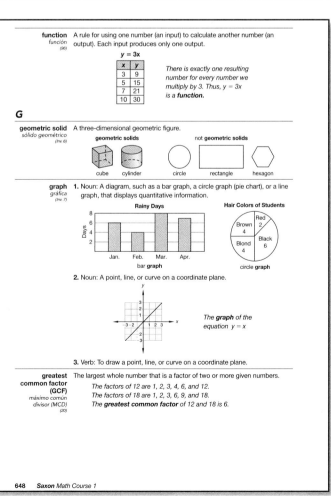 geometric solids $\qquad$ not **geometric solids** cube $\quad$ cylinder $\qquad$ circle $\quad$ rectangle $\quad$ hexagon
graph *gráfica* *(Inv. 7)*	**1.** Noun: A diagram, such as a bar graph, a circle graph (pie chart), or a line graph, that displays quantitative information. **Rainy Days** $\qquad$ **Hair Colors of Students** bar **graph** $\qquad$ circle **graph** **2.** Noun: A point, line, or curve on a coordinate plane. The **graph** of the equation $y = x$ **3.** Verb: To draw a point, line, or curve on a coordinate plane.
greatest common factor (GCF) *máximo común divisor (MCD)* *(20)*	The largest whole number that is a factor of two or more given numbers. The factors of 12 are 1, 2, 3, 4, 6, and 12. The factors of 18 are 1, 2, 3, 6, 9, and 18. The **greatest common factor** of 12 and 18 is 6.

H

height
altura
(71)

The perpendicular distance from the base to the opposite side of a parallelogram or trapezoid; from the base to the opposite face of a prism or cylinder; or from the base to the opposite vertex of a triangle, pyramid, or cone.

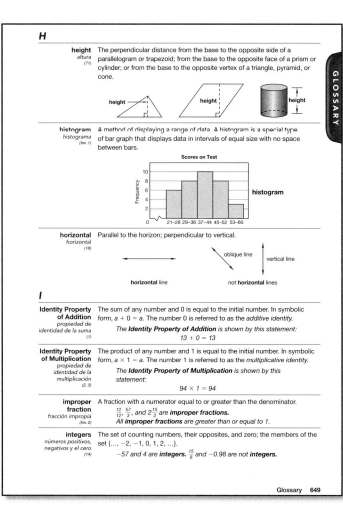

histogram
histograma
(Inv. 1)

A method of displaying a range of data. A histogram is a special type of bar graph that displays data in intervals of equal size with no space between bars.

Scores on Test

histogram

horizontal
horizontal
(18)

Parallel to the horizon; perpendicular to vertical.

oblique line

vertical line

horizontal line

not **horizontal** lines

I

Identity Property of Addition
propiedad de identidad de la suma
(1)

The sum of any number and 0 is equal to the initial number. In symbolic form, $a + 0 = a$. The number 0 is referred to as the *additive identity*.

The **Identity Property of Addition** is shown by this statement:

$$13 + 0 = 13$$

Identity Property of Multiplication
propiedad de identidad de la multiplicación
(2, 3)

The product of any number and 1 is equal to the initial number. In symbolic form, $a \times 1 = a$. The number 1 is referred to as the *multiplicative identity*.

The **Identity Property of Multiplication** is shown by this statement:

$$94 \times 1 = 94$$

improper fraction
fracción impropia
(Inv. 2)

A fraction with a numerator equal to or greater than the denominator.

$\frac{12}{12}$, $\frac{57}{3}$, and $2\frac{15}{2}$ are **improper fractions.**

All **improper fractions** are greater than or equal to 1.

integers
números positivos, negativos y el cero
(14)

The set of counting numbers, their opposites, and zero; the members of the set $\{\ldots, -2, -1, 0, 1, 2, \ldots\}$.

-57 and 4 are **integers.** $\frac{15}{8}$ and -0.98 are not **integers.**

---

interest
interés
(116)

An amount added to a loan, account, or fund, usually based on a percentage of the principal.

If we borrow $500.00 from the bank and repay the bank $575.00 for the loan, the **interest** on the loan is $575.00 − $500.00 = $75.00.

interior angle
ángul interno
(98)

An angle that opens to the inside of a polygon.

interior angle

This hexagon has six **interior angles.**

International System
Sistema internacional
(7)

See **metric system.**

intersect
intersecar
(28)

To share a point or points.

These two lines **intersect.**
They share the point M.

inverse operations
operaciones inversas
(1)

Operations that "undo" one another.

$a + b - b = a$
$a - b + b = a$

Addition and subtraction are **inverse operations.**

$a \times b \div b = a \quad (b \neq 0)$
$a \div b \times b = a \quad (b \neq 0)$

Multiplication and division are **inverse operations.**

$\sqrt{a^2} = a \quad (a \geq 0)$
$(\sqrt{a})^2 = a \quad (a \geq 0)$

Squaring and finding square roots are **inverse operations.**

irrational numbers
números irracionales
(89)

Numbers that cannot be expressed as a ratio of two integers. Their decimal expansions are nonending and nonrepeating.

π and $\sqrt{3}$ are **irrational numbers.**

isosceles triangle
triángulo isósceles
(93)

A triangle with at least two sides of equal length.

Two of the sides of this **isosceles triangle** have equal lengths.

L

least common multiple (LCM)
mínimo común múltiplo (mcm)
(30)

The smallest whole number that is a multiple of two or more given numbers.

Multiples of 6 are 6, 12, 18, 24, 30, 36, ...
Multiples of 8 are 8, 16, 24, 32, 40, 48, ...
The **least common multiple** of 6 and 8 is 24.

---

legend
rótulo
(Inv. 11)

A notation on a map, graph, or diagram that describes the meaning of the symbols and/or the scale used.

kitchen

living/dining

bath

$\frac{1}{4}$ inch = 5 feet

The **legend** of this scale drawing shows that $\frac{1}{4}$ inch represents 5 feet.

line
línea
(7)

A straight collection of points extending in opposite directions without end.

A   B

line AB or **line** BA

line graph
gráfica lineal
(18)

A method of displaying numerical information as points connected by line segments.

Income (in thousands)

Years of Education

This **line graph** has a horizontal axis that shows the number of completed years of education and a vertical axis that shows the average yearly income.

line of symmetry
línea de simetría
(110)

A line that divides a figure into two halves that are mirror images of each other.

lines of symmetry

not **lines of symmetry**

line plot
diagrama de puntos
(Inv. 4)

A method of plotting a set of numbers by placing a mark above a number on a number line each time it occurs in the set.

This is a **line plot** of the numbers 5, 8, 8, 10, 10, 11, 12, 12, 12, 12, 13, 13, 14, 16, 17, 17, 18, and 19.

M

mass
masa
(102)

The amount of matter in an object.

Grams and kilograms are units of **mass.**

mean
media
(18)

See **average.**

median
mediana
(Inv. 5)

The middle number (or the average of the two central numbers) of a list of data when the numbers are arranged in order from the least to the greatest.

In the data at right, 7 is the **median.**

1, 1, 2, 5, 6, 7, 9, 15, 24, 36, 44

---

metric system
sistema métrico
(7)

An international system of measurement based on multiples of ten. Also called *International System.*

Centimeters and kilograms are units in the **metric system.**

minuend
minuendo
(1)

A number from which another number is subtracted.

$12 - 8 = 4$ The **minuend** in this problem is 12.

mixed number(s)
número(s) mixto(s)
(17)

A whole number and a fraction together.

The **mixed number** $2\frac{1}{3}$ means "two and one third."

mode
moda
(Inv. 5)

The number or numbers that appear most often in a list of data.

In the data at right, 5 is the **mode.**

5, 12, 32, 5, 16, 5, 7, 12

multiple(s)
múltiplo(s)
(25)

A product of a counting number and another number.

The **multiples** of 3 include 3, 6, 9, and 12.

N

negative numbers
números negativos
(9)

Numbers less than zero.

-15 and -2.86 are **negative numbers.**
19 and 0.74 are not **negative numbers.**

net
red
(Inv. 12)

A two-dimensional representation of a three-dimensional figure.

top

back   side   front   side

bottom

nonexample
contraejemplo
(Inv. 2)

A nonexample is the opposite of an example. Nonexamples can be used to prove that a fact or a statement in mathematics is incorrect.

The integer 7 is a **nonexample** of an even number, and a circle is a **nonexample** of a polygon.

number line
recta numérica
(9)

A line for representing and graphing numbers. Each point on the line corresponds to a number.

number line

$-2 \quad -1 \quad 0 \quad 1 \quad 2 \quad 3 \quad 4 \quad 5$

numerator
numerador
(6)

The top term of a fraction.

$\dfrac{9}{10}$ ← **numerator**
     ← denominator

O

oblique line(s)
línea(s) oblicua(s)
(28)

1. A line that is neither horizontal nor vertical.

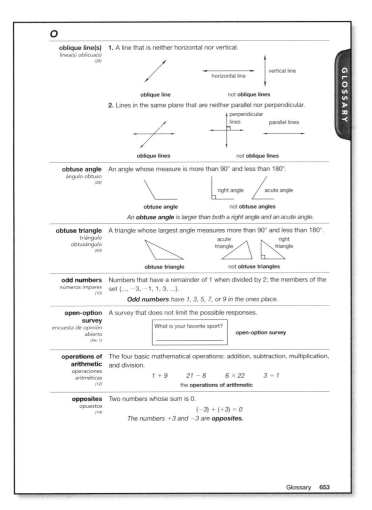

oblique line   not **oblique lines**

2. Lines in the same plane that are neither parallel nor perpendicular.

oblique lines   not **oblique lines**

obtuse angle
ángulo obtuso
(28)

An angle whose measure is more than 90° and less than 180°.

obtuse angle   not **obtuse angles**

*An **obtuse angle** is larger than both a right angle and an acute angle.*

obtuse triangle
triángulo obtusángulo
(93)

A triangle whose largest angle measures more than 90° and less than 180°.

obtuse triangle   not **obtuse triangles**

odd numbers
números impares
(10)

Numbers that have a remainder of 1 when divided by 2; the members of the set {..., −3, −1, 1, 3, ...}.

Odd numbers have 1, 3, 5, 7, or 9 in the ones place.

open-option survey
encuesta de opinión abierta
(Inv. 1)

A survey that does not limit the possible responses.

What is your favorite sport?   **open-option survey**

operations of arithmetic
operaciones aritméticas
(12)

The four basic mathematical operations: addition, subtraction, multiplication, and division.

$1 + 9$ $21 − 8$ $6 × 22$ $3 ÷ 1$

the **operations of arithmetic**

opposites
opuestos
(14)

Two numbers whose sum is 0.

$(−3) + (+3) = 0$

*The numbers +3 and −3 are **opposites**.*

---

order of operations
orden de las operaciones
(5)

The order in which the four fundamental operations occur.

1. Simplify powers and roots.

2. Multiply or divide in order from left to right.

3. Add and subtract in order from left to right.

With parentheses, we simplify within the parentheses, from innermost to outermost, before simplifying outside the parentheses.

ordered pair
par ordenado
(Inv. 7)

A pair of numbers, written in a specific order, that are used to designate the position of a point on a coordinate plane. *See also* **coordinate(s).**

$(0, 1)$ $(2, 3)$ $(3.4, 5.7)$ $\left(\frac{1}{2}, -\frac{1}{2}\right)$

ordered pairs

origin
origen
(Inv. 7)

1. The location of the number 0 on a number line.

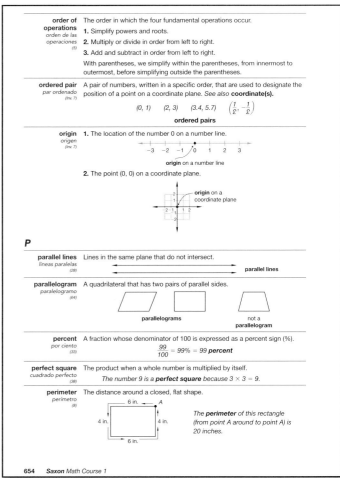

origin on a number line

2. The point (0, 0) on a coordinate plane.

origin on a coordinate plane

P

parallel lines
líneas paralelas
(28)

Lines in the same plane that do not intersect.

parallel lines

parallelogram
paralelogramo
(64)

A quadrilateral that has two pairs of parallel sides.

parallelograms   not a **parallelogram**

percent
por ciento
(33)

A fraction whose denominator of 100 is expressed as a percent sign (%).

$\frac{99}{100} = 99\% = 99$ **percent**

perfect square
cuadrado perfecto
(38)

The product when a whole number is multiplied by itself.

*The number 9 is a **perfect square** because $3 × 3 = 9$.*

perimeter
perímetro
(8)

The distance around a closed, flat shape.

The **perimeter** of this rectangle (from point A around to point A) is 20 inches.

---

perpendicular bisector
mediatriz
(Inv. 8)

A line, ray, or segment that intersects a segment at its midpoint at a right angle, thereby dividing the segment into two congruent parts.

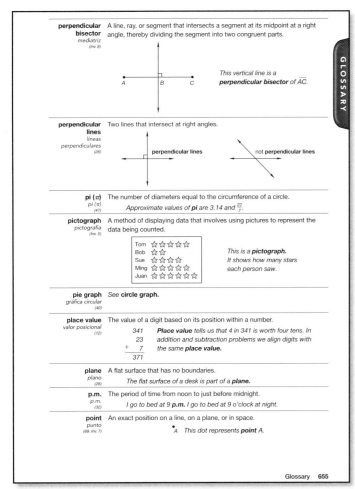

This vertical line is a **perpendicular bisector** of $\overline{AC}$.

perpendicular lines
líneas perpendiculares
(28)

Two lines that intersect at right angles.

perpendicular lines   not **perpendicular lines**

pi (π)
pi (π)
(47)

The number of diameters equal to the circumference of a circle.

*Approximate values of **pi** are 3.14 and $\frac{22}{7}$.*

pictograph
pictografía
(Inv. 5)

A method of displaying data that involves using pictures to represent the data being counted.

Tom   ☆☆☆☆☆
Bob   ☆☆
Sue   ☆☆☆☆
Ming ☆☆☆☆☆
Juan ☆☆☆☆☆

This is a **pictograph.**
It shows how many stars each person saw.

pie graph
gráfica circular
(40)

See **circle graph.**

place value
valor posicional
(12)

The value of a digit based on its position within a number.

341
23
+ 7
───
371

Place value tells us that 4 in 341 is worth four tens. In addition and subtraction problems we align digits with the same **place value.**

plane
plano
(28)

A flat surface that has no boundaries.

*The flat surface of a desk is part of a **plane**.*

p.m.
p.m.
(32)

The period of time from noon to just before midnight.

*I go to bed at 9 **p.m.** I go to bed at 9 o'clock at night.*

point
punto
(69, Inv. 7)

An exact position on a line, on a plane, or in space.

•A   *This dot represents **point** A.*

---

polygon
polígono
(60)

A closed, flat shape with straight sides.

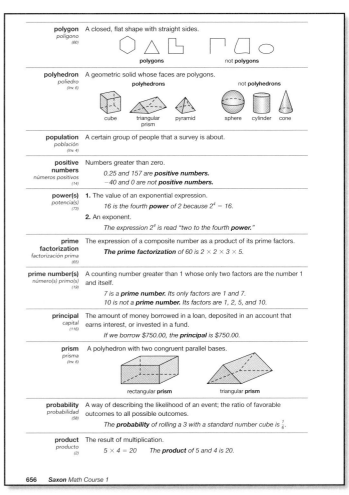

polygons   not **polygons**

polyhedron
poliedro
(Inv. 6)

A geometric solid whose faces are polygons.

polyhedrons   not **polyhedrons**

cube   triangular prism   pyramid   sphere   cylinder   cone

population
población
(Inv. 4)

A certain group of people that a survey is about.

positive numbers
números positivos
(14)

Numbers greater than zero.

*0.25 and 157 are **positive numbers.***
*−40 and 0 are not **positive numbers.***

power(s)
potencia(s)
(73)

1. The value of an exponential expression.

*16 is the fourth **power** of 2 because $2^4 = 16$.*

2. An exponent.

*The expression 2^4 is read "two to the fourth **power**."*

prime factorization
factorización prima
(65)

The expression of a composite number as a product of its prime factors.

The prime factorization of 60 is $2 × 2 × 3 × 5$.

prime number(s)
número(s) primo(s)
(19)

A counting number greater than 1 whose only two factors are the number 1 and itself.

*7 is a **prime number**. Its only factors are 1 and 7.*
*10 is not a **prime number**. Its factors are 1, 2, 5, and 10.*

principal
capital
(116)

The amount of money borrowed in a loan, deposited in an account that earns interest, or invested in a fund.

*If we borrow $750.00, the **principal** is $750.00.*

prism
prisma
(Inv. 6)

A polyhedron with two congruent parallel bases.

rectangular **prism**   triangular **prism**

probability
probabilidad
(58)

A way of describing the likelihood of an event; the ratio of favorable outcomes to all possible outcomes.

*The **probability** of rolling a 3 with a standard number cube is $\frac{1}{6}$.*

product
producto
(2)

The result of multiplication.

$5 × 4 = 20$ *The **product** of 5 and 4 is 20.*

proportion *proporción* (83)	A statement that shows two ratios are equal. $$\frac{6}{10} = \frac{9}{15}$$ These two ratios are equal, so this is a **proportion**.
protractor *transportador* (Inv. 3)	A tool used to measure and draw angles. protractor
pyramid *pirámide* (Inv. 6)	A three-dimensional solid with a polygon as its base and triangular faces that meet at a vertex. pyramid

Q

quadrilateral *cuadrilátero* (60)	Any four-sided polygon. *Each of these polygons has 4 sides. They are all **quadrilaterals**.*
qualitative *cualitativo* (Inv. 4)	Expressed in or relating to categories rather than quantities or numbers. ***Qualitative data** are categorical: Examples include the month in which someone is born and a person's favorite flavor of ice cream.*
quantitative *cuantitativo* (Inv. 4)	Expressed in or relating to quantities or numbers. ***Quantitative data** are numerical: Examples include the population of a city, the number of pairs of shoes someone owns, and the number of hours per week someone watches television.*
quotient *cociente* (2)	The result of division. $12 \div 3 = 4 \quad 3\overline{)12}^{\,4} \quad \frac{12}{3} = 4$ *The **quotient** is 4 in each of these problems.*

R

radius *radio* (27)	(Plural: *radii*) The distance from the center of a circle to a point on the circle. *The **radius** of circle A is 2 inches.*

---

range *intervalo* (Inv. 5)	The difference between the largest number and smallest number in a list. *To calculate the **range** of the data at right, we subtract the smallest number from the largest number. The **range** of this set of data is 29.* 5, 17, 12, 34, 29, 13
rate *tasa* (23)	A ratio of measures.
ratio *razón* (23)	A comparison of two numbers by division. *There are 3 triangles and 6 stars. The **ratio** of triangles to stars is $\frac{3}{6}$ (or $\frac{1}{2}$), which is read as "3 to 6" (or "1 to 2").*
rational numbers *números racionales* (23)	Numbers that can be expressed as a ratio of two integers.
ray *rayo* (7)	A part of a line that begins at a point and continues without end in one direction. A B **ray** *AB*
reciprocals *recíprocos* (30)	Two numbers whose product is 1. $\frac{3}{4} \times \frac{4}{3} = \frac{12}{12} = 1$ *Thus, the fractions $\frac{3}{4}$ and $\frac{4}{3}$ are **reciprocals**.*
rectangle *rectángulo* (64)	A quadrilateral that has four right angles. rectangles not **rectangles**
rectangular prism *prisma rectangular* (Inv. 6)	See **prism**.
reduce *reducir* (26)	To rewrite a fraction in lowest terms. *If we **reduce** the fraction $\frac{9}{12}$, we get $\frac{3}{4}$.*
reflection *reflexión* (108)	Flipping a figure to produce a mirror image. reflection

---

regular polygon *polígono regular* (60)	A polygon in which all sides have equal lengths and all angles have equal measures. **regular polygons** not **regular polygons**
rhombus *rombo* (64)	A parallelogram with all four sides of equal length. **rhombuses** not **rhombuses**
right angle *ángulo recto* (28)	An angle that forms a square corner and measures 90°. It is often marked with a small square. **right angle** obtuse angle acute angle not **right angles**
right triangle *triángulo rectángulo* (93)	A triangle whose largest angle measures 90°. acute triangle obtuse triangle **right triangle** not **right triangles**
rotation *rotación* (108)	To rotate, or turn a figure about a specified point is called the *center of rotation.* rotation
rotational symmetry *simetría rotacional* (110)	A figure has rotational symmetry when it does not require a full rotation for the figure to look as if it re-appears in the same position as when it began the rotation, for example, a square or a triangle. original position 45° turn **90° turn** 150° turn **180° turn** 210° turn **270° turn**
round *redondear* (16)	A way of estimating a number by increasing or decreasing it to a certain place value. Example: 517 **rounds** to 520

S

sales tax *impuesto sobre la venta* (41)	The tax charged on the sale of an item and based upon the item's purchase price. *If the **sales-tax** rate is 7%, the **sales tax** on a $5.00 item will be $5.00 × 7% = $0.35.*

---

sample *muestra* (Inv. 1)	A smaller group of a population that a survey focuses on.
sample space *espacio muestral* (58)	Set of all possible outcomes of a particular event. *The **sample space** of a 1–6 number cube is {1, 2, 3, 4, 5, 6}.*
scale *escala* (10)	A ratio that shows the relationship between a scale drawing or model and the actual object. *If a drawing of the floor plan of a house has the legend 1 inch = 2 feet, the **scale** of the drawing is $\frac{1 \, in.}{2 \, ft} = \frac{1}{24}$.*
scale drawing *dibujo a escala* (Inv. 11)	A two-dimensional representation of a larger or smaller object. *Blueprints and maps are examples of **scale drawings**.*
scale factor *factor de escala* (Inv. 11)	The number that relates corresponding sides of similar geometric figures. 25 mm 10 mm 10 mm 4 mm *The **scale factor** from the smaller rectangle to the larger rectangle is 2.5.*
scale model *modelo a escala* (Inv. 11)	A three-dimensional rendering of a larger or smaller object. *Globes and model airplanes are examples of **scale models**.*
scalene triangle *triángulo escaleno* (93)	A triangle with three sides of different lengths. *All three sides of this **scalene triangle** have different lengths.*
sector *sector* (Inv. 5)	A region bordered by part of a circle and two radii. *This circle is divided into 3 **sectors**.*
segment *segmento* (7)	A part of a line with two distinct endpoints. A B **segment** *AB* or **segment** *BA*
sequence *secuencia* (10)	A list of numbers arranged according to a certain rule. *The numbers 2, 4, 6, 8, ... form a **sequence**. The rule is "count up by twos."*
similar *semejante* (109)	Having the same shape but not necessarily the same size. Corresponding angles of similar figures are congruent. Corresponding sides of similar figures are proportional. *$\triangle ABC$ and $\triangle DEF$ are **similar**. They have the same shape but not the same size.*

---

simple interest *interés simple* (116)	Interest calculated as a percentage of the principal only.

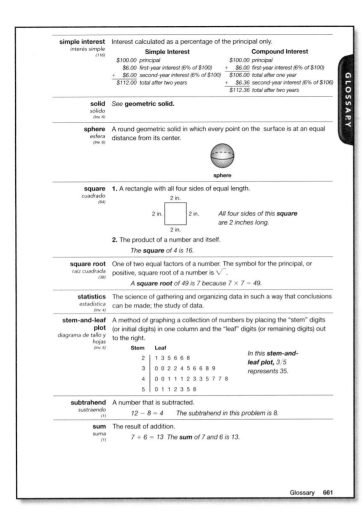

Simple Interest	**Compound Interest**
$100.00 principal	$100.00 principal
$6.00 first-year interest (6% of $100)	+ $6.00 first-year interest (6% of $100)
+ $6.00 second-year interest (6% of $100)	$106.00 total after one year
$112.00 total after two years	+ $6.36 second-year interest (6% of $106)
	$112.36 total after two years

solid *sólido* (Inv. 6)	*See* **geometric solid.**
sphere *esfera* (Inv. 6)	A round geometric solid in which every point on the surface is at an equal distance from its center.

sphere

square *cuadrado* (64)	**1.** A rectangle with all four sides of equal length.

All four sides of this **square** *are 2 inches long.* (2 in. on each side)

2. The product of a number and itself.

The **square** *of 4 is 16.*

square root *raíz cuadrada* (38)	One of two equal factors of a number. The symbol for the principal, or positive, square root of a number is $\sqrt{\ }$. *A* **square root** *of 49 is 7 because* $7 \times 7 = 49$.
statistics *estadística* (Inv. 4)	The science of gathering and organizing data in such a way that conclusions can be made; the study of data.
stem-and-leaf plot *diagrama de tallo y hojas* (Inv. 5)	A method of graphing a collection of numbers by placing the "stem" digits (or initial digits) in one column and the "leaf" digits (or remaining digits) out to the right.

Stem	Leaf
2	1 3 5 6 6 8
3	0 0 2 2 4 5 6 6 8 9
4	0 0 1 1 1 2 3 3 5 7 7 8
5	0 1 1 2 3 5 8

In this **stem-and-leaf plot,** $3/5$ *represents 35.*

subtrahend *sustraendo* (1)	A number that is subtracted. $12 - 8 = 4$ *The subtrahend in this problem is 8.*
sum *suma* (1)	The result of addition. $7 + 6 = 13$ *The* **sum** *of 7 and 6 is 13.*

---

supplementary angles *ángulos suplementarios* (69)	Two angles whose sum is 180°.

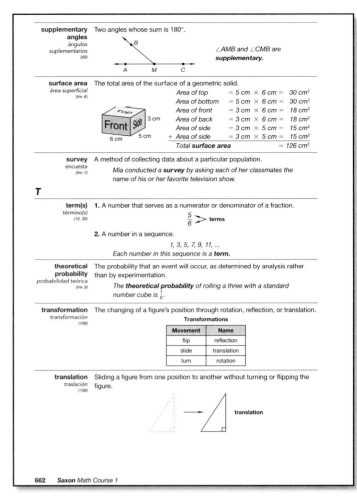

$\angle AMB$ *and* $\angle CMB$ *are* **supplementary.**

surface area *área superficial* (Inv. 6)	The total area of the surface of a geometric solid.

Area of top	$= 5\ cm \times 6\ cm =$ 30 cm²
Area of bottom	$= 5\ cm \times 6\ cm =$ 30 cm²
Area of front	$= 3\ cm \times 6\ cm =$ 18 cm²
Area of back	$= 3\ cm \times 6\ cm =$ 18 cm²
Area of side	$= 3\ cm \times 5\ cm =$ 15 cm²
+ Area of side	$= 3\ cm \times 5\ cm =$ 15 cm²
Total **surface area**	$=$ 126 cm²

survey *encuesta* (Inv. 1)	A method of collecting data about a particular population. *Mia conducted a* **survey** *by asking each of her classmates the name of his or her favorite television show.*

T

term(s) *término(s)* (10, 30)	**1.** A number that serves as a numerator or denominator of a fraction. $\frac{5}{6}$ — terms

2. A number in a sequence.

1, 3, 5, 7, 9, 11, ...
Each number in this sequence is a **term.**

theoretical probability *probabilidad teórica* (Inv. 9)	The probability that an event will occur, as determined by analysis rather than by experimentation. *The* **theoretical probability** *of rolling a three with a standard number cube is* $\frac{1}{6}$.
transformation *transformación* (108)	The changing of a figure's position through rotation, reflection, or translation.

Transformations

Movement	Name
flip	reflection
slide	translation
turn	rotation

translation *traslación* (108)	Sliding a figure from one position to another without turning or flipping the figure.

translation

---

transversal *transversal* (97)	A line that intersects one or more other lines in a plane.

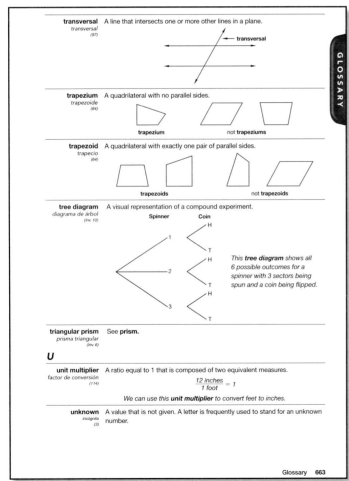

transversal

trapezium *trapezoide* (64)	A quadrilateral with no parallel sides.

trapezium   not **trapeziums**

trapezoid *trapecio* (64)	A quadrilateral with exactly one pair of parallel sides.

trapezoids   not **trapezoids**

tree diagram *diagrama de árbol* (Inv. 10)	A visual representation of a compound experiment.

Spinner   Coin

This **tree diagram** *shows all 6 possible outcomes for a spinner with 3 sectors being spun and a coin being flipped.*

triangular prism *prisma triangular* (Inv. 6)	*See* **prism.**

U

unit multiplier *factor de conversión* (114)	A ratio equal to 1 that is composed of two equivalent measures. $$\frac{12\ inches}{1\ foot} = 1$$ *We can use this* **unit multiplier** *to convert feet to inches.*
unknown *incógnita* (3)	A value that is not given. A letter is frequently used to stand for an unknown number.

U.S. Customary System *Sistema usual de EE.UU.* (7)	A system of measurement used almost exclusively in the United States. *Pounds, quarts, and feet are units in the* **U.S. Customary System.**

V

vertex *vértice* (28)	(Plural: *vertices*) A point of an angle, polygon, or polyhedron where two or more lines, rays, or segments meet.

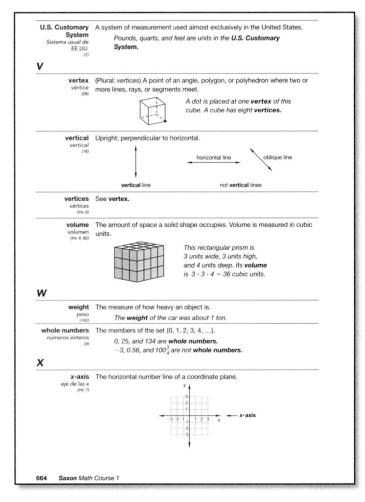

A dot is placed at one **vertex** *of this cube. A cube has eight* **vertices.**

vertical *vertical* (18)	Upright; perpendicular to horizontal.

horizontal line   oblique line

vertical line   not **vertical** lines

vertices *vértices* (Inv. 6)	*See* **vertex.**
volume *volumen* (Inv. 6, 82)	The amount of space a solid shape occupies. Volume is measured in cubic units.

This rectangular prism is 3 units wide, 3 units high, and 4 units deep. Its **volume** *is* $3 \cdot 3 \cdot 4 = 36$ *cubic units.*

W

weight *peso* (102)	The measure of how heavy an object is. *The* **weight** *of the car was about 1 ton.*
whole numbers *números enteros* (9)	The members of the set {0, 1, 2, 3, 4, ...}. *0, 25, and 134 are* **whole numbers.** -3, *0.56, and* $100\frac{3}{4}$ *are not* **whole numbers.**

X

x-axis *eje de las x* (Inv. 7)	The horizontal number line of a coordinate plane.

x-axis

Y

y-axis
eje de las y
(Inv. 7)

The vertical number line of a coordinate plane.

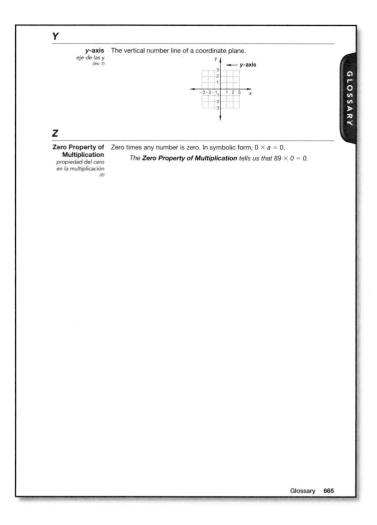

Z

Zero Property of Multiplication
propiedad del cero en la multiplicación
(2)

Zero times any number is zero. In symbolic form, $0 \times a = 0$.

The **Zero Property of Multiplication** tells us that $89 \times 0 = 0$.

References in color indicate content exclusive to the Teacher's Manual.

"are in" as indicator of division, 135
Arithmetic mean. *See* Mean
Arithmetic operations. *See also* Addition;
    Division; Multiplication; Subtraction
    alignment in, 191
    answer terms of, 65
    with money, 7–18, 92, 258, 362, 379, 616
    rules for decimals, 276–277
    SOS memory aid, 295–298, 306–309
    terms tor answers ot, 65
    with units of measure, 421–425
    words that indicate, 250
Assessment. *See* Cumulative assessment;
    Customized benchmark assessment;
    Power-Up tests
Associative property, 30
Average, 93–98. *See also* Mean
Axis, horizontal and vertical, 95, 363

B

Bar graphs, 55, 84, 211, 265
Base(s)
    base ten, 64, 179
    exponents and, 196
Bases of geometric figures
    abbreviations for, 475
    cylinders, 634
    parallelograms, 370
    prisms, 630
    pyramids, 315, 630
    rectangular prism, 426
Base ten place value system, 64, 179
Benchmarks to estimate length, 37
Bimodal distribution, 267
Bias, in surveys, 214
Bisectors
    angle, 418–420
    geometric construction of, 417–420
    perpendicular, 417–418
Body temperature, 51
Boiling point, 51

C

Calculators. *See also* Graphing calculator,
    online activity references
    with algebraic logic, 437
    for checking answers, 608
    for compound interest, 608
    for converting fractions to decimals, 386
    finding square roots with, 462
    memory keys on, 608
    order of operations and, 74, 437
    simplifying with, 231–232
Canceling
    in reducing fractions, 358–362, 376
    in the Sign Game, 543
    unit multipliers and, 597–598
Capacity, 404–407
"Casting out nines," 533
Categories, explaining, 400
Celsius (C), 51, 80
Centimeter (cm), 37, 422
Centimeter cubed (cm³), 318
Centimeter squared (cm²), 164, 197, 409, 422
Chance, 299–305, 471. *See also* Probability
Checking answers. *See also* Inverse
    operations
    in addition problems, 8, 9
    calculators for, 608
    in division problems, 25, 272
    estimating for, 617

guess-and-check method, 28, 460–464
    in mixed number problems, 329–332, 343
    in multiplication problems, 15, 43
    pairing technique, 63
    in subtraction problems, 9, 20, 61, 251
    in unknown-number problems, 19, 20,
        25–26
Cipher to the rule of three, 452
Circle graphs, 205–215, 264–265
Circles
    activity, 142
    area of, 447–451, 626
    circumference of, 141–142, 244–246
    compasses for drawing, 142
    diameter of, 141–142, 190, 246
    fractional parts of, 115
    measures of, 141–144
    perimeter of. *See* Perimeter
    radius of, 141–142, 190
Circular cylinders. *See* Cylinders
Circumference, 141–142, 244–246. *See
    also* pi
Classification
    parallelograms, 334
    of polygons, 311
    of quadrilaterals, 333–337
    of triangles, 311, 484–487
Clock faces, fractional parts of, 111, 115
Clockwise/counterclockwise, 465
Closed curve, 23
Closed-option surveys, 57
Coins, problems using, 7
Coin toss experiments, 302
Combining, in word problems, 58–62
Commas in number systems, 64–65
Common denominators. *See also*
    Denominators
    in addition and subtraction of fractions,
        127–131
        renaming both fractions, 289–294
        renaming one fraction, 285–288
    least common, 286, 320–321
    in multiplication and division of
        fractions, 342
    for subtraction of mixed numbers,
        329–332
Common factors. *See* Factors; Greatest
    Common Factor (GCF)
Common multiples, 156, 157
Common polygons, 311
Communication
    Discuss, 13, 14, 15, 19, 20, 24, 43, 47, 75,
        83, 112, 113, 123, 128, 139, 142, 151,
        159, 218, 250, 256, 300, 307, 346,
        359, 369, 404, 427, 448, 457, 467,
        471, 488, 498, 543, 553, 588, 612,
        623
    Formulate a problem, 26, 35, 57, 61, 62,
        67, 79–80, 86, 97, 98, 140, 252, 261,
        293, 308, 330, 344, 345, 361, 378,
        459, 464, 550, 556, 585, 623
    Writing about mathematics, 11, 16, 17,
        21, 22, 24, 27, 30, 31, 33, 34, 41, 44,
        45, 49, 52, 67, 69, 71, 72, 79, 85, 91,
        92, 97, 104, 107–108, 111, 125, 129,
        143, 144, 148, 219, 223, 224, 246,
        253, 258, 267, 270, 278, 287, 290,
        305, 313, 323, 328, 330, 335, 340,
        346, 356, 363, 373, 381, 384, 391,
        392, 402, 405, 410, 433, 439, 444,
        458, 459, 467, 481, 487, 515, 522,
        530, 547, 552, 576, 595, 619, 622, 627

Commutative property
    of addition, 8, 9, 10
    of multiplication, 13, 246, 427, 428
    subtraction and the, 8, 10
Comparing
    decimals, 231–234
    defined, 173
    exponential expressions, 381
    fractions, 395–398, 441–446
    geometric solids, 315
    integers, 47
    number lines for, 46–49
    ratios and, 494
    symbols, for
        equal to (=), 47, 381
        greater than (>), 47, 110, 381
        less than (<), 47, 381
    word problems about, 68–72
Compasses
    activity, 142
    for bisecting angles, 418–420
    for bisecting segments, 417–418
    drawing with, 142, 418
    investigations, 417–420
    types of, 142
Complementary angles, 353–357
Complementary probability, 301–303, 400,
    524–527
Complex shapes
    area of, 557–560
    defined, 538, 557
    drawing, 484, 538
    perimeter of, 538–542
Composite numbers, 102, 337
Compound interest, 606–611
Compound outcomes, 524–526
Cones, 314, 630–636
Congruence in geometric figures, 311,
    408, 426, 561, 562, 566–567
Consecutive integers, 88
Construction, of bisectors in geometric
    figures, 417–420
Content highlights. *See* Section overviews
Content trace. *See* Section overviews
Conversion. *See also* Equivalent; Mixed
    measures
    of area, 618
    decimals
        fraction equivalents, 381–382,
            385–389, 395–398
        by multiplication, 488–492
        percent equivalents, 216–217,
            390–394, 488–492
        probabilities to, 387
        ratios to, 385–389
    defined, 152
    fractions
        decimal equivalents, 381–382
        decimals equivalents, 385–389,
            395–398
        by division, 385–389
        percent equivalents, 216–217, 390–394,
            488–492, 602–605
    improper fractions
        to mixed numbers, 133, 324–328, 342
        mixed numbers to, 324–328, 342
    of length
        centimeters to millimeters, 38, 39
        feet to yards, 598
        inches to centimeters, 38
        meters to centimeters, 38
    metric system, 404

mixed numbers, 534
    to improper fractions, 324–328, 342
    by multiplication, 488–492
    percents
        decimal equivalents, 216–217, 390–394, 488–492
        fraction equivalents, 216–217, 390–394, 488–492, 602–605
        by multiplication, 488–492
        to probability, 301–302
    prefixes for, 533
    of ratios to decimals, 385–389
    unit multipliers for, 597–598
    units of measure, 323, 357, 404–405, 412, 534, 572
    U.S. Customary System, 404–405
Coordinate plane, 363–367, 499–500, 581
Corresponding angles, 504, 567–569
Corresponding parts, 566–572, 579
Counterclockwise/clockwise, 465
Counting exercises (Power-Up). *Counting exercises are found in the teacher wrap on the first page of every lesson.*
"Counting by twos," 51
Counting numbers
    defined, 46
    integers as, 74, 517
    multiples and, 156
    whole numbers and, 46
Cross products and proportions, 441–446
Cubed numbers, exponent indicating, 380
Cubes (geometric figures). *See also*
    Number cubes
    area of, 497
    attributes of, 314
    drawing, 314
    faces of, 315
    nets, 318, 319
    as rectangular prisms, 497
    as regular polyhedrons, 314
    volume of, 318, 428
Cubic centimeters (cm³), 318
Cubic units, 318, 426
Cumulative assessment, 53A, 81A, 108A, 135A, 160A, 186A, 210A, 238A, 263A, 288A, 313A, 341A, 362A, 394A, 416A, 446A, 469A, 496A, 523A, 552A, 577A, 605A, 629A
Cup (c.), 404–405
Customized benchmark assessment, 53B, 108B, 160B, 210B, 263B, 313B, 362B, 416B, 469B, 523B, 577B, 629B
Cylinders
    area of, 634–635
    attributes of, 314
    bases of, 634
    drawing, 314, 316
    height of, 626
    volume of, 626–629, 631–633

D

Data. *See also* Graphs
    collecting, 211–215
    displaying
        bar graphs, 211, 213, 265
        circle graphs, 264
        histograms, 55
        line graphs, 211, 305
        line plots, 211, 213, 266, 279
        pictographs, 264
        qualitative, 211–213, 264–265

quantitative, 211–213, 266–267
stem-and-leaf plots, 264–267, 384, 487
    interpreting, 211–215
    mean, 95, 266
    median, 266
    mode, 266
    organizing, 211–215
    qualitative, 211–213, 264–265
    quantitative, 211–213, 266–267
    range, 266
Data point, 266
Decimal division, 236, 272–273, 385
Decimal numbers. *See* Decimals
Decimal place values, 8, 9, 178–181, 184, 239
Decimal points
    aligning by, 8, 9, 192
    "and" in reading or writing, 240
    in decimal division, 236, 272–273, 385
    money and, 8, 13, 15
    in multiplication by tens and hundreds, 240
    purpose of, 178, 184, 241
    shifting by division or multiplication, 240, 272–273
    whole numbers and, 195–199
    words that indicate, 240
Decimals
    adding, 8–9, 191–194, 276–277
        to whole numbers, 195–199
    "and" in reading or writing, 184
    arithmetic operations rule, 276–277
    comparing, 231–234
    converting
        by multiplication, 488–492
        probabilities to, 387
        ratios to, 385–389
    dividing
        rules for, 276–277
        by ten and by one hundred, 272–276
        by whole numbers, 235–238
    dividing by, 254–258
    equivalent, 236
    expanded notation, 239–243
    fraction equivalents, 381–382, 385–389, 395–398, 513–516
    mixed, 183
    multiplying, 200–204, 232, 239–243, 276–277
    on number lines, 259–263
    percent equivalents, 216–217, 390–394, 488–492, 513–516
    reading, 182–186
    rounding, 268–271
    simplifying, 231–234
    subtracting, 191–194, 276–277
        from whole numbers, 195–199
    unknown factors in, 452–455
    unknown numbers in, 225–230
    writing
        alignment in, 8
        in expanded notation, 239–243
        fraction equivalents, 182–186, 380–384, 385–389, 513–516
        as percents, 390–394, 488–492, 513–516
        probabilities as, 387
        ratios as, 385–389
        and reading, 182–186
Decimals Chart, 276–279
Degrees, measuring turns by, 465
Denominators. *See also* Common
    denominators; Fractions

decimals as, 182
least common, 286, 320–321
mixed numbers to improper fractions, 325
multiplying, 150–151
as term of a fraction, 32, 127, 343
Diagrams. *See also* Draw a picture or diagram
    graphs. *See* Graphs
    ratio boxes. *See* Ratio boxes
Diameter
    defined, 141, 190
    formula for, 246
    radius and, 141–142
Dice (dot cubes), 68, 174
Difference. *See also* Subtraction
    defined, 8, 11
    greater-lesser, 68
    later-earlier, 69, 170–171
    in operations of arithmetic, 8, 65
Digits
    place value of, 64
    shown in standard notation, 593
    summing for factors, 113
Discuss. *See* Communication
Distance. *See also* Length
    average, 263, 455
    estimating, 478
    measuring, 59, 478
Distribution, bimodal, 267
Dividends
    defined, 14, 103
    function of, 22
    missing, 25
Divisibility, 112–116
Division
    answers as mixed numbers, 132–135
    "are in" as indicator of, 135
    checking answers, 15, 25, 272
    converting fractions to decimals using, 385–389
    by decimals, 254–258
    of decimals
        rules for, 276–277
        by ten and by one hundred, 272–276
        by whole numbers, 235–238
    dividends. *See* Dividends
    divisors. *See* Divisors
    equivalent, 225–230
    even numbers and, 51
    fact families, 8–12
    factors and, 99
    "for each" in, 123, 422
    by fractions, 33
    of fractions, 359
        common denominators and, 152–153, 342
        by fractions, 280–285
    of integers, 587–591
    long versus short method, 15
    mental math, 272–276
    of mixed numbers, 349–352
    of money, 12–18, 362, 379
    multiplication as inverse of, 15, 24, 452
    odd numbers and, 51
    order of operations, 29, 30, 47
    by primes, 337–341
    quotients. *See* Quotients
    remainders in, 15, 582
    short-division method, 15
    of signed numbers, 588
    symbols for, 14, 133, 385
    of units of measure, 421–425

INDEX

F

Faces
  on number cubes, 18
  of rectangular prisms, 315
Fact families
  addition and subtraction, 7–11
  division and multiplication, 8–12
Facts Practice (Power-Up)
  Each lesson Power-Up presents a facts
    practice that builds fluency in basic
    math facts.
Factor pairs, 102
Factors. *See also* Prime factorization
  bases and, 196
  common factors, 105–106, 152, 175
  constant, 413–421
  defined, 12, 99, 105
  divisibility tests for, 112
  division and, 99
  equal to one, 280–285
  in estimation, 30
  of even numbers, 101, 112
  greatest common. *See* Greatest
    Common Factor (GCF)
  multiplying, 12, 99
  of positive integers, 99–100, 105–106,
    114, 280–281, 441–442
  of prime numbers, 101, 106
  products and, 12, 99
  reducing fractions and, 150–155, 175
  strategy for finding, 100
  of ten, 100
  unknown
    in addition and subtraction, 18–22
    on both sides of an equation, 453
    calculating, 24
    decimal numbers, 452–455
    in division and multiplication, 23–27
    method of solving for, 452–453
    mixed numbers, 452–455
    in multiplication, 123
  whole numbers and, 102, 105
Factor trees, 337–341
Fahrenheit (F), 51, 80
Figures. *See* Geometric figures
Find a pattern. *See* Problem-solving
    strategies
Fluid ounces, 405
Foot (ft), 37
"for each"
  in division problems, 423
  in rate problems, 123
Formulas
  for area
    of bases, 427
    of circles, 448–449, 626
    of parallelograms, 369, 370, 371,
      409, 474
    of rectangles, 200, 474
    of squares, 196, 474
    of triangles, 409, 474
  for bases, of prisms, 630
  common rates, 123
  for length
    circumference, 246
    diameter, 246
  for perimeter
    of octagons, 311
    of parallelograms, 474
    of rectangles, 474
    of squares, 474
    of triangles, 474

for volume
    of cubes, 428
    of cylinders, 627
    of prisms, 630
    of pyramids, 630–631
Formulate a problem. *See* Communication
Four-step problem-solving process, 3, 7,
    18, 23, 28, 36, 42, 59, 63, 69, 70, 87, 436
Fractional parts of the whole
    equal groups stories with, 117–121
    naming parts of, 32–35
Fractional-parts statements, 399–403
Fraction bar indicating division (—), 14,
    133, 385
Fraction-decimal-percent equivalents,
    513–516
Fraction-decimal-percent table, 514
Fraction manipulatives, 109–111
Fractions. *See also* Denominators; Mixed
    numbers
  adding
    with common denominators, 127–131,
      342
    with different denominators, 285–294
    SOS memory aid, 295–298, 342
    three or more, 320–323
    three-step process, 295–298
  canceling terms, 358–362, 376
  common, 32
  with common denominators. *See*
    Common denominators
  comparing, 395–398, 441–446
  decimal equivalents, 381–382, 385–389,
    395–398, 513–516
  denominator. *See* Denominators
  dividing
    by fractions, 280–285, 342, 359
    whole numbers by, 33, 259–263
  equal to one, 221–224, 290, 597–598
  equivalent
    cross products for determining,
      441–446
    defined, 137
    equal fractions as, 597
    example of, 152
    fraction-decimal-percent, 513–516
    writing, 391
  exponents and, 479–484
  finding the whole using, 612–616
  improper, 138, 324–328, 342
  lowest terms, defined, 277
  multiplying
    common denominators for, 342
    cross product, 441–446
    process of, 150–155
    reducing before, 358–362
    three or more, 375–379
  on number lines, 87–92
  numerators. *See* Numerators
  percent equivalents, 216–217, 390–394,
    488–492, 513–516, 602–605
  reciprocals. *See* Reciprocals
  reducing. *See* Reducing fractions
  renaming
    multiplying by one, 221–224, 290
    purpose of, 307
    without common denominators,
      285–294
  simplifying, 276–279
  SOS memory aid for solving problems
    with, 295–298, 342, 349
  subtracting

with common denominators, 127–131,
    342
  with different denominators, 285–294
  three-step process, 295–298
  from whole numbers, 187–190
terms of, 157
unknown numbers, 225–230
visualizing on clock faces, 111
writing
    decimal equivalents, 182–186,
      380–384, 385–389, 513–516
    percent equivalents, 174–177,
      513–516, 602–605
    as percents, 390–394, 488–492
    whole numbers as, 151
Fractions chart, 375–379
Freedom 7 spacecraft, 581
Freezing point, 51
Frequency tables, 54–57, 470–473
Functions, 497–502, 552

G

Gallon (gal), 404–405
Gauss, Karl Friedrich, 63
GCF (Greatest common factor). *See*
    Greatest Common Factor (GCF)
Geometric figures
  bases of. *See* Bases of geometric
    figures
  bisectors, 417–420
  circles. *See* Circles
  congruence in, 311, 408, 426, 562,
    566–567
  corresponding parts, 566–572, 579
  cubes. *See* Cubes (geometric figures)
  cylinders. *See* Cylinders
  perimeter of. *See* Perimeter
  polygons. *See* Polygons
  prisms. *See* Prisms
  quadrilaterals. *See* Quadrilaterals
  rectangles. *See* Rectangles
  similarity in, 566–572
  solids. *See* Solids
  squares. *See* Squares
  symmetry in, 573–578
  triangles. *See* Triangles
Geometric formulas, 474–478. *See also*
    Formulas
Graphing calculator, online activity
    references 74, 106, 157, 269, 364, 433,
    480, 607
Graphing functions, 497–502
Graphs
  bar, 55, 84, 265
  circle, 205–215, 264–265
  on the coordinate plane, 363–367,
    499–500, 581
  data on
    bar graphs, 211, 213, 265
    histograms, 55
    line graphs, 211, 305
    line plots, 211, 266, 305
    pictographs, 264
    stem-and-leaf plots, 264–267, 384, 487
  histograms, 55–57
  line, 93–98, 211
  on number lines. *See* Number lines
  pictographs, 264
  reading, 84
  stem-and-leaf plots, 267
Great Britain, 37

Marbles, 302–303, 400, 471–473, 524–526
Mass versus weight, 533–537
Math and other subjects
    and architecture 323, 512
    and art 332, 347, 590
    and geography 57, 75, 77, 84, 130, 131,
        148, 233, 273, 287, 330, 483
    history 52, 53, 63, 69, 70, 81, 85, 91,
        103, 114, 119, 148, 154, 229, 270, 283,
        296, 334, 360, 452, 560, 575, 577
    music 327, 360, 624
    other cultures 30, 37, 433
    science 36, 52, 53, 62, 66, 71–73, 76,
        77, 79, 80, 85, 97, 98, 103, 106, 108,
        125, 130, 134, 154, 159, 223, 242,
        248, 267, 275, 288, 297, 301, 306,
        307, 308, 313, 361, 374, 377, 382,
        401, 402, 403, 414, 444, 453, 491,
        492, 505, 506, 531, 596
    sports 26, 41, 44, 56, 61, 86, 91, 99, 107,
        120, 122, 126, 134, 135, 154, 155,
        216, 229, 236, 243, 252, 280, 283,
        298, 323, 351, 395, 401, 415, 444, 445,
        477–479, 507, 545, 563, 599, 601, 624
Math Background, 1, 9, 10, 15, 19, 24, 29,
    33, 37, 43, 47, 51, 54, 65, 69, 74, 83, 88,
    95, 100, 102, 106, 110, 113, 118, 133,
    137, 142, 146, 151, 157, 162, 170, 176,
    179, 183, 188, 196, 201, 207, 222, 226,
    232, 240, 246, 255, 260, 267, 273, 278,
    281, 290, 300, 307, 311, 314, 326, 327,
    334, 338, 347, 350, 354, 359, 363, 381,
    386, 400, 405, 409, 417, 422, 427, 432,
    442, 453, 461, 466, 470, 481, 485, 494,
    499, 509, 518, 524, 539, 554, 562, 567,
    574, 578, 593, 627, 630
Math language, 21, 22, 64, 65, 74, 84, 88,
    103, 105, 114, 122, 127, 135, 138, 146,
    152, 156, 165, 190, 211, 216, 222, 225,
    260, 262, 277, 286, 302, 308, 311, 319,
    333, 350, 369, 376, 380, 405, 408, 417,
    418, 426, 431, 432, 442, 461, 465, 494,
    503, 529, 533, 548, 552, 561, 593, 596,
    608
Math to math.
    Algebra, Measurement, and Geometry,
        320B
    Algebra and Problem Solving, 7B, 58B,
        112B, 164B, 216B, 268B, 320B,
        368B, 474B, 528B, 582B
    Fractions and Measurement, 7B, 58B,
        112B, 164B, 216B, 320B, 368B,
        474B, 528B, 582B
    Fractions, Percents, Decimals, and
        Problem Solving, 7B, 58B, 164B,
        216B, 268B, 320B, 368B, 474B,
        528B, 582B
    Measurement and Geometry, 7B, 58B,
        112B, 164B, 216B, 268B, 320B, 474B,
        528B, 582B
    Probability and Statistics, 268B, 320B,
        474B, 528B, 582B
    Problem Solving and Measurement, 7B,
        58B, 112B, 164B, 216B, 268B, 320B,
        368B, 474B, 528B, 582B
    Proportional Relationships and
        Geometry, 320B, 528B, 582B
Mean, 95, 266–267, 313. See also Average
Measurement. See also Units of measure
    abbreviations of. See Abbreviations
    of angles, 161–163
    of area. See Area

benchmarks for, 37, 405, 534, 553
of capacity, 404–407
of circles. See Circles
common rates, 123
of height. See Height
of length. See Length
linear. See Length
parallax in, 50
of perimeters. See Perimeter
protractors for, 161–163
ratios of, 123–124
of rectangles. See Rectangles
of surface area. See Area
of temperature, 51, 52
of turns, 465–469
of volume. See Volume
Measures of central tendency. See Mean;
    Median; Mode
Median, 266–267, 313
Memory aids
    calculator keys, 608
    decimal number chart, 277
    Please Excuse My Dear Aunt Sally, 480
    SOS, 295–298, 306–309, 342, 349,
        375–379
Mental Math Power-Up. A variety of mental
    math skills and strategies are developed
    in the lesson Power Ups.
Meter (m), 37
Metric system, 37, 38, 404–405. See also
    Units of measure
Mile (mi), 37
Miles per gallon (mpg), 123
Miles per hour (mph), 123, 422
Milliliter (mL), 404
Millimeter (mm), 37
Minuends, 8, 19
Minus sign. See Negative numbers;
    Signed numbers
Mirror images, 574
Missing numbers. See Unknown numbers
Mixed measures. See also Units of
    measure
    adding and subtracting, 298, 534,
        592–596
Mixed numbers. See also Improper
    fractions
    adding, 136–140, 306–309
    "and" in naming, 184
    converting
        to improper fractions, 324–328, 342
        by multiplication, 488–492
    defined, 88
    dividing, 349–352
    division answers as, 132–135
    factor trees, 339
    multiplying, 326, 342–345
    on number lines, 87–92
    ratios as, 122
    subtracting
        with common denominators, 329–332
        and reducing answers, 136–140
        with regrouping, 188, 250–253
    unknown factors in, 452–455
Mode, 266–267, 313
Models. See also Make a model;
    Representation
    of addition situations, 109, 127, 228,
        285–287, 290, 295, 306–307, 320–
        321
    of subtraction situations, 127–129,
        187–188, 250–251, 290–291, 296

of parallelograms, 369
to scale, 578–581
Money
    arithmetic operations with, 7–18, 92,
        235, 258, 362, 379, 616
    coin problems, 7
    decimal places in, 8, 13, 179
    interest, compound and simple, 606–611
    rate in, 123
    rounding with, 268–270
    subtracting, 7–11
    symbol for, 8, 13
    writing, 79, 195
Multiples. See also Least common
    multiple (LCM)
    calculating, 132–135
    common, 156, 157, 286, 320
Multiplication. See also Exponents
    associative property of, 30
    checking answers, 15, 25, 43
    commutative property of, 13, 246, 427,
        428
    of decimals, 200–204, 232, 239–243,
        276–277
    division as inverse of, 15, 24, 452
    fact families, 8–12
    factors and, 12, 24, 99
    of fractions
        common denominators and, 342
        cross product, 441–446
        process of, 150–155
        three or more, 375–379
    by fractions equal to one, 221–224
    by hundreds, 239–243
    identity property of, 14, 222, 280, 488
    of integers, 587–591
    mental math for, 239–243
    of mixed numbers, 326, 342–345
    of money, 12–18
    "of" as term for, 150
    "of" as term in, 350
    order of operations, 29, 65
    partial products, 13
    by powers of ten, 592–596
    reducing rates before, 493–496
    of signed numbers, 587–589
    symbols for, 12, 13, 31, 422
    by tens, 13, 239–243
    of three numbers, 30
    two-digit numbers, 13
    of units of measure, 421–425
    unknown numbers in, 23–27, 123
    of whole numbers, 12–18, 588
    words that indicate, 150, 350
    zero property of, 14
Multiplication sequences, 50
Multistep problems, 65–66

N

Naming. See also Renaming
    "and" in mixed numbers, 184
    angles, 145–149
    complex shapes, 557
    fractional parts, 32
    lines, 353
    polygons, 311
    powers of ten, 594
    rays, 353
    segments, 353–354
Negative numbers. See also Signed
    numbers

ratios relationship to, 431–432, 442–443, 529
solving
  percent problems with, 548–552
  using a constant factor, 457
  using cross-products, 441–446
tables and, 39, 413–414, 497–501, 513–514, 548–550
unknown numbers in, 432, 442–443
wrlting, 432
Protractors, measuring and drawing angles, 161–163
Pyramids, 314, 315, 630–636

Q

Quadrilaterals
  classifying, 311, 333–337
  defined, 311, 333
  parallelograms as. See Parallelograms
  rectangles. See Rectangles
  squares. See Squares
  sum of angle measures in, 508–512
Qualitative data, 212–213, 264–265
Quantitative data, 212–213, 266–267
Quart (qt.), 404–405
Quotients. See also Division
  calculating, 22
  in decimal division, 235–236, 272–273
  as decimals, 385
  defined, 14
  in equivalent division problems, 225
  missing, 25
  in operations of arithmetic, 65
  of signed numbers, 588

R

Radius (radii), 141–142, 190
Range, 266–267, 300, 308, 313
Rates, 122–126
  reducing before multiplying, 493–496
Ratio boxes, 456–458, 528–529, 548–550
Ratios
  as comparisons, 494
  converting to decimals, 385–389
  defined, 122, 431, 494
  equivalent, 432, 442
    writing, 385–389
  fractional form of, 122–126
  problems involving totals, 528–532
  proportions and, 431–432, 442–443, 529
  reducing, 153
  symbols for (:), 122
  win-loss, 123
  word problems
    using constant factors, 413–421
    using proportions, 456–459
    using ratio boxes, 456–458
  writing decimal equivalents, 385–389
Rays
  defined, 146
  lines and segments, 36–41
  naming, 353
  properties of, 37
  symbol for, 37, 353
Reading
  decimal points, 240
  decimals, 182–186
  exponents, 196, 380–381
  graphs, 84
  large numbers, commas in, 64–65
  powers, 380–381

Reading math, 25, 31, 38, 47, 64, 65, 73, 79, 95, 110, 133, 147, 150, 161, 175, 196, 197, 240, 246, 266, 343, 353, 368, 409, 423, 427, 462, 494, 544, 567
Real-world application problems 9, 11–13, 16, 17, 20–22, 26, 27, 30, 31, 32, 34, 37, 39, 40–44, 46, 48, 51–62, 66, 67, 69–73, 75–77, 79, 80, 81, 83, 84, 86–88, 91–95, 98, 103, 104, 106–108, 114, 116, 117, 119–121, 124–131, 134, 135, 138–140, 143–145, 148–150, 153–155, 159, 160 163, 216, 218–220, 229, 230, 233, 234, 236–238, 242, 243, 247–250, 252–254, 256–264, 267, 268–275, 278, 280, 283, 284, 289, 290, 292–299, 301, 304, 306–309, 312, 313, 316, 317, 322, 323, 327, 330, 332, 334, 335, 336, 340–342, 344, 345, 347, 351, 355, 357, 360–362, 372, 374, 377–378, 382, 383, 387–389, 391–393, 395–397, 399, 401–403, 404, 406–408, 410, 413, 414, 416, 421, 424–425, 428–429, 431, 433–435, 438–440, 444–445, 449–451, 453–454, 456–459, 462, 466–469, 474, 476–483, 485–487, 491–495, 501, 502, 505–507, 510–512, 513–515, 522–523, 530–532, 535–537, 540–541, 543, 545, 546, 548–552, 555, 556, 558, 560, 563, 564, 566, 569, 570–572, 575–577, 582–587, 589–594, 596–597, 599–601, 603–605, 607–611, 613–615, 617–621, 624–625, 628–629, 634, 635
Reciprocals
  calculating, 156–160
  defined, 157, 260, 350
  in division of fractions, 281, 359
  product of, 349
Rectangles
  area of, 164–168, 364–365, 474
    formula for, 200
  characteristics of, 333
  drawing, 319
  lines of symmetry, 574
  as parallelograms, 334, 371
  perimeter of, 364–365, 474
  similar, 568–569
  as squares, 334
  vertices of, 365
Rectangular prisms
  attributes of, 314
  bases of, 426
  cubes as, 497
  drawing, 314, 315
  faces of, 315
  surface area of, 497
  volume of, 426–430
Reducing fractions
  by canceling, 358–362, 376
  common factors in, 150–155, 175
  by grouping factors equal to one, 280–285
  manipulatives for, 136–140
  before multiplying, 493–496
  prime factorization for, 346–348
  rules for, 307
  and units of measure, 423
Reflections (flips) of geometric figures, 562–564
Regrouping in subtraction of mixed numbers, 188, 250–253, 329–332
Regular polygons, 44, 311
Relationships

of corresponding sides, 569
inverse operations. See Inverse operations
ratios and proportions, 431–432, 442–443, 529
remainders-divisors, 15
sides to angles in triangles, 484
sides to vertices in polygons, 311
spatial, in cube faces, 315
Relative frequency, 470
Remainder
  in decimal division, 236
  divisors and, 15
  as mixed numbers, 132–135
  writing, 582
  of zero, 99
Reminders. See Memory aids
Renaming. See also Naming
  fractions
    multiplying by one, 221–224, 290
    purpose of, 307
    SOS memory aid, 295–298
    without common denominators, 285–294
  mixed measures, 593
  mixed numbers, 306–309
Renderings, 580
Representation
  Formulate an equation, 61, 66, 70, 71, 76, 79, 80, 85, 114, 134, 135, 143, 148, 159, 219, 229, 237, 242, 247, 252, 270, 283, 296, 312, 382, 387, 388, 396, 415, 416, 623
  Manipulatives/Hands-On, 8, 13–15, 32, 33, 37, 38, 45, 48–50, 72, 76, 78, 82, 88–91, 94, 98, 104, 107, 109–111, 115, 121, 125–129, 136–138, 140, 142, 143, 148, 149, 151, 162, 163, 221, 230, 231, 245, 248, 251, 257, 265, 282, 286, 289, 291, 301, 302, 305, 315, 352, 364–366, 369–371, 379, 394, 398, 405, 408, 415, 425, 427, 429, 435, 459, 469, 483, 492, 500, 501, 504, 505, 509, 516, 518, 523, 530, 543, 544, 558, 560, 562, 563, 575, 577, 584–585, 596, 600, 605, 608, 614, 616, 618, 625–626
  Model, 38, 42, 45, 94, 97, 98, 100, 104, 109, 110, 115, 119, 120, 121, 125, 126, 129, 135–138, 140, 143, 148, 149, 151, 159, 217, 223, 224, 230, 237, 245, 247, 252, 256, 260, 274, 275, 279, 284, 288, 294, 305, 312, 324, 334, 355, 367, 369, 370, 379, 394, 398, 401, 402, 406, 408, 414, 416, 425, 430, 440, 458–459, 462, 467, 469, 476, 478, 485, 492, 501–502, 510, 516, 521, 528, 530, 537, 550, 558, 560, 565, 576, 577, 603, 613, 615, 622, 629
  Represent, 10, 11, 14, 16, 17, 31, 34, 35, 44, 45, 48, 49, 53, 54, 55, 57, 62, 76, 80–81, 86, 90, 91, 103, 106, 110, 115, 116, 121, 127, 131, 135, 142, 147, 155, 162, 163, 222, 224, 257, 271, 279, 284, 296, 304, 315, 318, 319, 323, 325, 339, 344, 348, 356, 357, 365–367, 370, 373, 388, 396, 415, 416, 435, 486, 487, 530, 560, 570, 610, 615, 624, 635
Representative samples, 214
Rhombus, 333–334, 596

Width, abbreviation for, 475
Win-loss ratio, 123
Work backwards. *See* Problem-solving
    strategies
Write a number sentence or equation. *See*
    Problem-solving strategies
Writing. *Also see* Communication
    decimals. *See* Decimals
    equations, 19, 543
    exponents, 196, 380–381
    fractions. *See* Fractions
    large numbers, 64–65
    money, 79, 195
    numbers. *See* Expanded notation;
        Proportions; Standard notation
    percents. *See* Percents
    proportions, 432
    ratios, 385–389
    remainders, 582
    whole numbers
        with decimal points, 195–199
        as fractions, 151, 342

X

x-axis, 363
x symbol for multiplication, 12, 441

Y

y-axis, 363
Years. *See* Age, calculating; Elapsed-time

Z

Zero
    in division, 14
    in expanded notation, 169
    exponents and, 381
    in multiplication, 14
    opposite of, 74
    as placeholder, 205–215, 277
    as power, 381
    properties of, 51, 73, 74, 101
    remainders of, 99
    in rounding, 82
    sign of, 73, 74
    trailing, 14
    in whole numbers, 46
Zero property of multiplication, 14

	COURSE 1	COURSE 2	COURSE 3
NUMBERS AND OPERATIONS			
Numeration			
digits	●		
read and write whole numbers and decimals	●	●	▲
place value to trillions	●	●	▲
place value to hundred trillions		●	▲
number line (integers, fractions)	●	●	▲
number line (rational and irrational numbers)		●	●
expanded notation	●	●	
comparison symbols (=, <, >)	●	●	▲
comparison symbols (=, <, >, ≤, ≥)		●	▲
compare and order rational numbers	●	●	▲
compare and order real numbers		●	●
scientific notation		●	●
Basic operations			
add, subtract, multiply, and divide integers	●	●	▲
add, subtract, multiply, and divide decimal numbers	●	●	▲
add, subtract, multiply, and divide fractions and mixed numbers	●	●	▲
add, subtract, multiply, and divide algebraic terms		●	●
add and subtract polynomials			●
add, subtract, multiply, and divide radical expressions			●
multiply binomials			●
mental math strategies	●	●	●
regrouping in addition, subtraction, and multiplication	●	●	▲
multiplication notations: $a \times b$, $a \cdot b$, $a(b)$	●	●	▲
division notations: division box, division sign, and division bar	●	●	▲
division with remainders	●	●	▲
Properties of numbers and operations			
even and odd integers	●	●	▲
factors, multiples, and divisibility	●	●	▲
prime and composite numbers	●	●	▲
greatest common factor (GCF)	●	●	▲
least common multiple (LCM)	●	●	▲
divisibility tests (2, 3, 5, 9, 10)	●	▲	▲
divisibility tests (4, 6, 8)		●	▲
prime factorization of whole numbers	●	▲	▲
positive exponents of whole numbers, decimals, fractions	●	●	▲
positive exponents of integers		●	▲
negative exponents of whole numbers		●	▲
negative exponents of rational numbers			●
square roots	●	●	●
cube roots		●	●
order of operations	●	●	▲
inverse operations	●	●	●

● Introduce and Develop
▲ Maintain and Apply

	COURSE 1	COURSE 2	COURSE 3
Estimation			
round whole numbers, decimals, mixed numbers	●	●	▲
estimate sums, differences, products, quotients	●	●	▲
estimate squares and square roots	●	●	●
determine reasonableness of solution	●	●	●
approximate irrational numbers		●	●
ALGEBRA			
Ratio and proportional reasoning			
fractional part of a whole, group, set, or number	●	●	▲
equivalent fractions	●	●	▲
convert between fractions, terminating decimals, and percents	●	●	▲
convert between fractions, repeating decimals, and percents		●	▲
reciprocals of numbers	●	●	▲
complex fractions involving one term in numerator/denominator		●	●
complex fractions involving two terms in numerator/denominator			●
identify/find percent of a whole, group, set, or number	●	●	▲
percents greater than 100%	●	●	▲
percent of change		●	●
solve proportions with unknown in one term	●	●	▲
find unit rates and ratios in proportional relationships	●	●	●
apply proportional relationships such as similarity, scaling, and rates	●	●	●
estimate and solve applications problems involving percent	●	●	●
estimate and solve applications problems involving proportional relationships such as similarity and rate		●	●
compare and contrast proportional and non-proportional linear relationships (direct and inverse variation)			●
Patterns, relations, and functions			
generate a different representation of data given another representation of data		●	●
use, describe, extend arithmetic sequence (with a constant rate of change)	●	●	●
input-output tables	●	●	●
analyze a pattern to verbalize a rule	●	●	▲
analyze a pattern to write an algebraic expression			●
evaluate an algebraic expression to extend a pattern		●	●
compare and contrast linear and nonlinear functions		●	●
Variables, expressions, equations, and inequalities			
solve equations using concrete and pictorial models	●	●	▲
formulate a problem situation for a given equation with one unknown variable		●	●
formulate an equation with one unknown variable given a problem situation	●	●	●
formulate an inequality with one unknown variable given a problem situation			●
solve one-step equations with whole numbers	●	▲	▲
solve one-step equations with fractions and decimals		●	▲
solve two-step equations with whole numbers	●	●	▲
solve two-step equations with fractions and decimals		●	●
solve equations with exponents			●

● Introduce and Develop
▲ Maintain and Apply

	COURSE 1	COURSE 2	COURSE 3
solve systems of equations with two unknowns by graphing			•
graph an inequality on a number line		•	•
graph pairs of inequalities on a number line			•
solve inequalities with one unknown		•	•
validate an equation solution using mathematical properties		•	•
GEOMETRY			
Describe basic terms			
point	•	•	▲
segment	•	•	▲
ray	•	•	▲
line	•	•	▲
angle	•	•	▲
plane	•	•	▲
Describe properties and relationships of lines			
parallel, perpendicular, and intersecting	•	•	•
horizontal, vertical, and oblique	•	•	•
slope		•	•
Describe properties and relationships of angles			
acute, obtuse, right	•	•	•
straight		•	•
complementary and supplementary	•	•	•
angles formed by transversals	•	•	•
angle bisector	•	•	
vertical angles		•	•
adjacent angles		•	•
calculate to find unknown angle measures	•	•	•
Describe properties and relationships of polygons			
regular	•	•	•
interior and exterior angles	•	•	
sum of angle measures	•	•	•
diagonals		•	•
effects of scaling on area		•	•
effects of scaling on volume		•	•
similarity and congruence	•	•	•
classify triangles	•	•	•
classify quadrilaterals	•	•	•
Use Pythagorean theorem to solve problems			
Pythagorean theorem involving whole numbers		•	•
Pythagorean theorem involving radicals			•
trigonometric ratios			•
3-Dimensional figures			
represent in 2-dimensional world using nets	•	•	•
draw 3-dimensional figures	•	•	•
Coordinate geometry			
name and graph ordered pairs	•	•	•
intercepts of a line		•	•
determine slope from the graph of line		•	•
formulate the equation of a line		•	•

● Introduce and Develop
▲ Maintain and Apply

	COURSE 1	COURSE 2	COURSE 3
identify reflections, translations, rotations, and symmetry	●	●	●
graph reflections across the horizontal or vertical axes	●	●	●
graph translations		●	●
graph rotations			●
graph dilations			●
graph linear equations		●	●

MEASUREMENT

Measuring physical attributes

	COURSE 1	COURSE 2	COURSE 3
use customary units of length, area, volume, weight, capacity	●	●	●
use metric units of length, area, volume, weight, capacity	●	●	●
use temperature scales: Fahrenheit, Celsius	●	●	●
use units of time	●	●	●

Systems of measurement

	COURSE 1	COURSE 2	COURSE 3
convert units of measure	●	●	●
convert between systems	●	●	●
unit multipliers	●	●	●

Solving measurement problems

	COURSE 1	COURSE 2	COURSE 3
perimeter of polygons, circles, complex figures	●	●	●
area of triangles, rectangles, and parallelograms	●	●	●
area of trapezoids		●	●
area of circles	●	●	●
area of semicircles and sectors		●	●
area of complex figures	●	●	●
surface area of right prisms and cylinders	●	●	●
surface area of spheres		●	●
surface area of cones and pyramids			●
estimate area	●	●	●
volume of right prisms, cylinders, pyramids, and cones	●	●	●
volume of spheres		●	●
estimate volume	●	●	●

Solving problems of similarity

	COURSE 1	COURSE 2	COURSE 3
scale factor	●	●	●
similar triangles		●	●
indirect measurement		●	●
scale drawings: two-dimensional	●	●	●
scale drawings: three-dimensional			●

Use appropriate measurement instruments

	COURSE 1	COURSE 2	COURSE 3
ruler (U.S. customary and metric)	●	●	▲
compass	●	●	●
protractor	●	●	●
thermometer	●	●	▲

DATA ANALYSIS AND PROBABILITY

Data collection and representation

	COURSE 1	COURSE 2	COURSE 3
collect and display data	●	●	●
tables and charts	●	●	▲

● Introduce and Develop
▲ Maintain and Apply

	COURSE 1	COURSE 2	COURSE 3
frequency tables	●	●	●
pictographs	●	●	
line graphs	●	●	▲
histograms	●	●	▲
bar graphs	●	●	▲
circle graphs	●	●	▲
Venn diagrams		●	●
scatter plots			●
line plots	●	●	▲
stem-and-leaf plots	●	●	▲
box-and-whisker plots		●	●
choose an appropriate graph	●	●	●
identify bias in data collection		●	▲
analyze bias in data collection			●
draw and compare different representations	●	●	●

Data set characteristics

	COURSE 1	COURSE 2	COURSE 3
mean, median, mode, and range	●	●	▲
select the best measure of central tendency for a given situation		●	●
determine trends from data		●	●
predict from graphs		●	●
recognize misuses of graphical or numerical information		●	●
evaluate predictions and conclusions based on data analysis		●	●

Probability

	COURSE 1	COURSE 2	COURSE 3
experimental probability	●	●	●
make predictions based on experiments	●	●	●
accuracy of predictions in experiments	●	●	●
theoretical probability	●	●	●
sample spaces	●	●	▲
simple probability	●	●	▲
probability of compound events	●	●	●
probability of the complement of an event	●	●	●
probability of independent events	●	●	●
probability of dependent events		●	●
select and use different models to simulate an event			●

PROBLEM SOLVING

Connections

	COURSE 1	COURSE 2	COURSE 3
identify and apply mathematics to everyday experiences	●	●	●
identify and apply mathematics to activities in and outside of school	●	●	●
identify and apply mathematics in other disciplines	●	●	●
identify and apply mathematics to other mathematical topics	●	●	●

Problem-solving skills and tools

	COURSE 1	COURSE 2	COURSE 3
use a problem-solving plan	●	●	▲
evaluate for reasonableness	●	●	▲
use a proportion	●	●	▲
use a calculator	●	●	▲
use estimation	●	●	▲
use manipulatives	●	●	▲

● Introduce and Develop
▲ Maintain and Apply

	COURSE 1	COURSE 2	COURSE 3
use mental math	●	●	▲
use number sense	●	●	▲
use formulas	●	●	▲

Problem-solving strategies

	COURSE 1	COURSE 2	COURSE 3
choose a strategy	●	●	▲
draw a picture or diagram	●	●	▲
find a pattern	●	●	▲
guess and check	●	●	▲
act it out	●	●	▲
make a table, chart, or graph	●	●	▲
work a simpler problem	●	●	▲
work backwards	●	●	▲
use logical reasoning	●	●	▲
write a number sentence or equation	●	●	▲

Communication

	COURSE 1	COURSE 2	COURSE 3
relate mathematical language to everyday language	●	●	●
communicate mathematical ideas using efficient tools	●	●	●
communicate mathematical ideas with appropriate units	●	●	●
communicate mathematical ideas using graphical, numerical, physical, or algebraic mathematical models	●	●	●
evaluate the effectiveness of different representations to communicate ideas	●	●	●

Reasoning and proof

	COURSE 1	COURSE 2	COURSE 3
justify answers	●	●	●
make generalizations	●	●	●
make conjectures from patterns	●	●	●
make conjectures from sets of examples and nonexamples	●	●	●
validate conclusions using mathematical properties and relationships	●	●	●

ALGEBRA TOPICS APPENDIX

	COURSE 1	COURSE 2	COURSE 3
graph sequences			●
formulate the equation of a line with given characteristics			●
formulate the equation of a line parallel/perpendicular to a given line			●
solve proportions with an unknown in two terms			●
graph linear inequalities			●
factor quadratics			●
solve quadratic equations			●
solve systems of linear equations using substitution			●
solve systems of linear equations using elimination			●
formulate an equation with two unknown variables given a problem situation			●
solve systems of linear inequalities with two unknowns			●
graph systems of linear inequalities			●

● Introduce and Develop
▲ Maintain and Apply